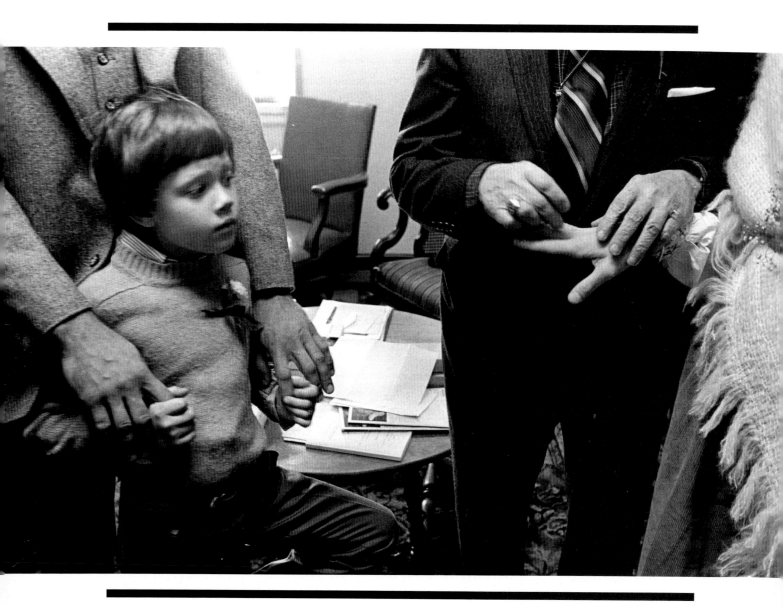

PHOTOGRAPH BY ABIGAIL HEYMAN

THE EVOLVING THERAPIST

THE EVOLVING THERAPIST

TEN YEARS OF THE FAMILY THERAPY NETWORKER

Edited by
Richard Simon
Cindy Barrilleaux
Mary Sykes Wylie
Laura M. Markowitz

THE FAMILY THERAPY NETWORK
Washington, DC

THE GUILFORD PRESS
New York · London

© 1992 THE FAMILY THERAPY NETWORK
7705 13th Street, N.W.
Washington, DC 20012

Copublished with
THE GUILFORD PRESS
A Division of Guilford Publications Inc.
72 Spring Street, New York, NY 10012

Printed in the United States of America

This book is printed on acid-free paper

Last digit is print number: 9 8 7 6 5 4 3 2 1

Library of Congress Cataloging-in-Publication Data

The evolving therapist: ten years of the family therapy networker
    edited by Richard Simon . . . [et al.]
        p.   cm.
    Includes index.
    Contents first appeared in The family therapy networker
    ISBN 0-89862-253-0 (hardcover)—ISBN 0-89862-268-9 (pbk.)
    1. Family psychotherapy. I. Simon, Richard, 1949–
    II. Family therapy networker.
    RC488.5.B495 1992   91-43237
    616.89'156—dc20   CIP

Cover and book design by Jann Alexander
Cover calligraphy by Julian Waters
Typesetting by Wordscape
Copyediting by Karen Craft
Printed by Maple-Vail

PHOTOGRAPH BY ABIGAIL HEYMAN

Contents

SECTION III

Defining Our Task:
Philosophy and Ethics in Psychotherapy

SECTION IV

Gender Riddles:
New Answers To Old Questions?

SECTION V

The Pulse of the Family:
Inside the Experience of Change

Introduction

THE FAMILY THERAPY NETWORKER, WHOSE 10th anniversary this volume celebrates, was born at a time when therapists were looking for a new way to communicate among themselves. More than any other therapeutic approach of the 1970s and early 1980s, family therapy captured the hearts and minds of the newly minted therapists fresh out of graduate school, and won over experienced therapists unsatisfied with traditional models and looking for more effective tools. There was a sense of excitement and expansion and even a messianic aura to what was then known as the Family Therapy Movement. Its gurus, true believers and polemicists kept going around making the case for the family approach and describing their success stories; even if you were skeptical, it was all hard to dismiss. The family field kept growing, like a big, noisy party down the block, and you couldn't help but be curious about what was going on over there.

The field's journals earnestly attempted to chronicle the development of family therapy technique, but their academic format prevented them from conveying the power and the color of the grass-roots movement that was shaking up clinics, training programs, psychiatric hospitals and private practices all around the country. This was a period of clinical experimentation propelled by a sense of the unlimited potential of the new family therapy models, and it seemed to demand a different kind of publication. Increasingly, therapists didn't want to hear from authors who sounded like distant experts perched on their podiums. They wanted to hear colleagues sharing their experiences of frustration, discovery, challenge, confusion and, above all, intellectual adventure that were so much a part of the explosive growth of the family movement.

After several years as a small, regional newsletter published in Washington, D.C.—first dubbed, "The Family Shtick," and later, in a small concession to respectability, "Family Therapy Practice Network Newsletter"—*The Family Therapy Networker* was launched in 1982. It was conceived as a feature magazine covering the unfolding of a new field, serving a community of practitioners who shared a fascination with a new idea whose time had come.

With contributions written by a nucleus of mostly unpublished writers, the *Networker* offered down-to-earth features about the common problems therapists faced in practice every day. A nationwide readership of practitioners embraced us immediately, welcoming a forum that allowed ordinary therapists to describe their ideas and experiences in their own voices, without assuming the lackluster tone of academic writing.

We soon discovered that the family therapy beat took in a lot of territory—case studies, theoretical papers, magazine and newspaper reprints, descriptions of training workshops, book reviews, interviews, history, sociology, anthropology, philosophy, family memoirs, short stories, social commentary. Everywhere we looked we saw topics that could be freshly illuminated by the brave new light of systems thinking.

Families and family therapy have changed in the last 10 years, and this collection attempts to tell part of the story of what happened to both society and the therapy profession during this time. As a field, family therapy has grown up, evolving from a group of true believers and insurgents who had an answer for everything to a less grandiose, much savvier profession with a hard-won knowledge of both our strengths and limitations.

In order to tell the story of how family therapy has come of age over the past decade, we have divided this collection of articles into seven sections, each of which tracks a particular theme that has figured prominently in our pages:

Throughout the '80s, family therapists kept discovering that along with their flesh-and-blood clients, previously unrecognized forces from the larger world haunted the therapy room, often determining the possibility of change. Therapists' fantasies of clinical omnipotence gave way to a far more balanced appreciation of how social, political, economic and cultural factors provide the hidden framework of the therapy experience. Section I of this collection, "Riding the Whirlwind," reports family therapists' encounters with homelessness, the AIDS epidemic, the increasing fragmentation of the American family and other sad legacies of the '80s.

At the same time that they deepened their respect for the power of context and the looming influence of social issues, family therapists also recognized that solving the world's problems was not their area of expertise. The heart and soul of the

Networker was its coverage of clinical innovation and its sensitivity to the dilemmas therapists encounter in everyday practice. Section II, "On the Front Lines," chronicles what the past 10 years have taught family therapists about responding to such common presenting problems as alcoholism, couples conflict and the crisis of divorce.

During the 1980s, as family therapy became increasingly accepted as a treatment method and no longer a rebel movement, the field came under a new ethical and philosophical scrutiny. Section III, "Defining Our Task," conveys this prevailing spirit of self-examination and growing doubts about theories that assume families *need* the problems they bring to treatment, and therapists who believe they know best how clients should lead their lives.

Without question, the most charged debate we covered in the '80s was triggered by the feminist critique of the field. Family therapy's early theories showed little interest in the differences between the experiences of men and women. Section IV, "Gender Riddles," collects some of the many articles the *Networker* has published on feminism and gender issues, including several recent pieces on the efforts of men to plunge into the taboo-laden world of their inner lives.

Although systems theory teaches us the importance of seeing interactions from many different vantage points, the clinical literature is dominated by one perspective—the view from the therapist's chair. But how does the process of change look from where the clients are sitting? Section V, "The Pulse of the Family," reflects our continuing investigation of the experiences of family therapy's consumers, and of the inner, emotional life of families.

As the field emerged from its adolescence and its practitioners aged, we began to understand what it meant to be a family therapist across the full span of a professional career. What happened to clinicians once they moved past their need to prove themselves to their colleagues and clients? How did they handle the challenges of staying creatively alive? Section VI, "Being There," includes some of our most candid articles about the stages therapists pass through in the unending process of coming of age as people and clinicians.

In 1983, family therapist Frank Pittman began writing a regular column for the

Networker that grew out of his love for movies. It offered one therapist's after-hours view of popular culture seen through the lens of his clinical experience. Frank adds a distinctive voice to the *Networker*, and Section VII, "The Screening Room," is a sampling of some of his most memorable columns.

In addition to feature articles, we have included some of the other elements that have made the *Networker* such a lively publication. Clearly, we have been a publication that subscribers wanted to talk back to, and we have included some of the point-and-counterpoint exchanges that enlivened our Letters department. The visual design of the *Networker* has also been a major part of its success and this collection includes a generous sampling of the art and photography that have made ours a publication that doesn't depend solely on the power of the written word for its impact.

It is, of course, impossible to predict what each of you will discover for yourselves as you read this collection. But we can confidently say that you will encounter no permanent truths in any of the articles we have selected, no theories without blind spots, no clinical techniques that work all the time. Family therapy has often been described as a field of awestruck seekers worshipping clinical wizards and trying to find magical solutions to life's problems. The only magic you will encounter in these pages is the effect that curiosity, attentiveness and critical intelligence have in remedying the main occupational hazards of our trade: boredom and burnout.

Many of us began in this field with the idea that the knowledge we needed to acquire was something bounded and finite, that we could eventually know it all, then relax and call ourselves Master Therapists. But it's becoming increasingly plain that in this business, the learning just goes on and on. Of course, to people responsible for turning out a magazine every two months, that's not such terrible news. Whatever else we may doubt, it's a consolation to be certain that there will always be unanswerable questions, puzzling cases that defy any formula, and plenty of material for the next issue of the *Networker*.

RICHARD SIMON
CINDY BARRILLEAUX
MARY SYKES WYLIE
LAURA M. MARKOWITZ

Acknowledgments

SYSTEMS THEORY TEACHES THAT, IN THE final analysis, everything is connected to everything else, but we will have to draw an arbitrary line in acknowledging the people who made this book and *The Family Therapy Networker* possible. The whole idea of starting an informal, professional network enabling family therapists to better communicate with one another was hatched and nurtured by Family Therapy Network founder Chuck Simpkinson. Without his vision and support, there would never have been a *Networker*. A spirit of collaboration has always given the *Networker* its special spark. We have been privileged to be part of a creative team that has made us a productive work family. Although she has moved on to pursue other interests, the *Networker*'s first managing editor, Liane White, brought both her aesthetic sensibility and flair for organization to the production of the magazine. Circulation manager George Woolley has made sure that all the quality and effort that go into each issue are carried over to our subscription services and customer relations. Accountant Anthony Divers and editorial assistant Rose Levine keep the everyday chaos of life in our offices within bounds and make sure that we present an orderly face to the world. Art director Jann Alexander keeps teaching us new ways of adding visual power to the magazine, incorporating the work of some of the nation's best photographers and illustrators. Creative consultant Dick Anderson, who has been with the *Networker* since its earliest days, specializes in crystallizing the often-ponderous ideas of our profession and coming up with headlines and illustration ideas that bring freshness to familiar themes.

But ultimately the core of the *Networker* is its writers. Their commitment to describing their work clearly and compellingly and their willingness to bear the scrutiny of their colleagues are what make the *Networker* come alive.

Riding the Whirlwind

The Family Confronts Social Change

PHOTOGRAPH BY ELLIOTT ERWITT/MAGNUM

*L*ASTING RITES

RITUAL IS ALIVE AND WELL
IN MODERN SOCIETY

By David I. Kertzer

IN HIS CLASSIC LECTURE ON "TABOO," THE RE-nowned British anthropologist Radcliffe-Brown told of an Australian who ran into a Chinese man as the latter was taking a bowl of rice to place on his brother's grave. In a condescending tone, the Australian asked the other man if he supposed that his brother would be able to eat the rice. "No," the Chinese man responded, "but since you ask, I suppose that you in this country place flowers on the graves of your dead in the belief that they will enjoy looking at them and smelling their sweet perfume."

The naivete of the Australian's question is perhaps all too obvious, for surely he fails to recognize the cardinal principle that the value of ritual comes through its symbolic and social meaning, not from the literal format of the rite itself. Yet, some of the doubts underlying his own skeptical question are shared by many observers of contemporary family life: Aren't family rituals today less important than they were in the past? Isn't it true that, like it or not, modern society is moving away from such family rites as those encountered by the Australian, toward a more "rationalistic" basis for behavior? Or does ritual do something for us as members of families that cannot be done as well in any other way?

Before we go any further, let's pause a moment to consider just what is meant by "ritual." The term is used in a multitude of ways, from the restrictive sense of ritual as religious ceremony, to a much broader usage that refers to any standardized set of symbolic actions. From a family therapist's viewpoint, it is significant that Freud himself saw religious ritual as the product of family ritual, rather than the other way around. For Freud, the prototype of all religious ritual was totemism, which originated in the family rite developed by the patricidal brothers to cope with their guilt. According to Freud, the first religious ritual was a family dinner.

We needn't subscribe to Oedipal theory, however, to appreciate how ritual permeates our lives. What makes ritual stand out even more in our intensely pragmatic, results-oriented culture is that it focuses on conventionalized actions that have little instrumental significance. Ritual is about symbolic meanings, and the experience of ritual has a formal quality to it. Ritual imbues certain times and places with special significance; it creates a realm that takes us out of the everyday. The repetition of ritual helps create a much-needed sense of continuity in our lives by linking the past to the present and the present to the future.

THE NOTION THAT RITUAL IS ON THE WAY OUT, that it is a characteristic of primitive, small-scale societies, and that it is being progressively displaced in modern, bureaucratic society, has a long pedigree. It was certainly implicit in the work of many of the 19th-century cultural evolutionists, and influenced such 20th-century anthropologists as Bronislaw Malinowski. Malinowski argued that much of ritual results from people's experience in facing situations whose outcomes are of great importance to them, yet in which the forces at work are beyond rational understanding. In such circumstances, he argued, people feel a need to take some action to give themselves the illusion of control. Here we find rain dances in the southwestern American desert and Melanesian rites guarding canoes against sudden storms.

Having taken a limited perspective on the meaning of ritual, many modern thinkers have concluded that scientific understanding will eventually displace ritual in human society, or at least in those areas of society which are subject to scientific study. Presumably, as modern psychology and sociology provide people with better understanding of family behavior, they will be able to confront their relationships more objectively, tracing the real roots of the difficulties and taking sensible actions to relieve them. The southern Italian widow will no longer have to wear black clothes the rest of her life; she can undergo analysis about her feelings of guilt and loss instead!

Yet not all those who detect a historical decline in the prevalence of ritual view the triumph of rational thought over traditional cultural forms as a healthy development. Nostalgia for the ritualized era of old

remains strong in certain quarters, as was evident in President Reagan's recent farewell address to the nation, in which he specifically called for a "greater emphasis on civic ritual." A variant of this same view can be found among antimodernist intellectuals, critics of the technological mass society. Take, for example, the recent exchange between Joseph Campbell and Bill Moyers in their widely praised—and widely watched—television series on the power of myth:

CAMPBELL: A ritual is an enactment of a myth. By participating in a ritual, you are participating in a myth.

MOYERS: So what happens when a society no longer embraces powerful mythology?

CAMPBELL: What we've got on our hands. As I say, if you want to find what it means . . . to have a society without any rituals, read *The New York Times*.

This exchange was followed by a more specific complaint, that the decline of rituals has undermined the transition to adulthood of the nation's youth, leading to a variety of social problems:

MOYERS: Society has provided them [young people] no rituals by which they become members.

CAMPBELL: None. There's been a reduction . . . of ritual . . . And so much of our ritual is dead.

A LOOK AT AMERICAN SOCIETY TODAY HARDLY reveals the kind of ritual-less society described by Moyers and Campbell. Even in the case of the transition to adulthood, rather than witnessing the demise of rites of transition, we see the continued central role played by such rites. The high school graduation ritual, often protracted over a long period of ceremonies and observances, provides a key reference point for many of the country's youth, publicly signaling their change of status while celebrating a variety of both official and unofficial values.

Where I live, in Brunswick, Maine, it is hard to

pass a week during the school year without running into high school seniors and their parents raising funds for the spring's much-anticipated graduation rites. From intergenerational car washes at banks to bake sales held outside supermarkets—these activities highlight the impending event for families of the graduates at the same time as they call attention to the graduates and their families in the larger community. The latest twist on these occasions—promoting drug-free high school graduations—further ties the rites into the values publicly promulgated by a society increasingly concerned about the role of alcohol and drugs in the problematic transition to adulthood.

High school and college graduations also provide important ritual occasions to express the changing role of the child in the family and to allow the emotional bond between parent and child to be reaffirmed at a time of transition in their relationship. Indeed, it can easily be argued that such rites of transition from childhood dependency to young adult independence are much more prevalent in America today than they were 100 years ago. There are a variety of reasons for this. In the past, the transition to independence was typically more gradual. Taking a full-time job was not generally coincident with leaving home. Often the transition to adulthood took place at marriage; consequently, a much higher proportion of the young people faced this passage without two surviving parents.

R ITUAL IS STILL A VITAL PART OF CONTEMPORARY life. But what exactly does ritual do, and why is it such an important force in family life today?

Our self-image, and the image we have of others, is crafted in part through a process of identification between the individual and larger groups, be they ethnic, religious, political or whatever. These include both social groups that a person enters by birth—such as Muslim or Sikh or Jew—and those that we opt to identify ourselves with at some other point in

life, such as Rotarian or Republican. Family groups identify themselves in a similar fashion. Just what a family consists of is not biologically ordained, and indeed differs from society to society. It is through symbolic means that the boundaries of the family are drawn and the common identity of family members is asserted.

Ritual provides one of the most efficient ways for these identifications to be made. I wear certain clothing, I say an oath, I sing a song, I fast on a certain day, I wear a certain headdress, I address people with a certain term, and by doing so I consider myself and am considered by others to belong to a particular group—be it Boy Scouts or skinheads. Similarly, by participating with others in certain rites—from Thanksgiving dinner to Passover Seder, from weddings to funerals—I objectify and establish my relationship with a particular family group. To eschew such ritual participation—as in the cases of the cousins who never attend each other's family's weddings and funerals—is in fact to redefine oneself outside the family group.

Family rites not only have form, but also substance, and that substance consists of symbols. Family rites not only determine an individual's identity as a group member, but also create an image of the nature and values of the family group. The ritual process does this by using symbols to link family groups to larger social groupings. In America, for example, we can scarcely separate symbols of ethnic affiliation from the rites of family life. To be Italian American is to use certain ritualized patterns of speech in the family to refer to certain relatives (il nonno, zio), to go to church with one's mother and light a candle to a saint, to stroll through the summer festa to the patron saint, pasting the $10 bill your father gave you onto the saint's statue as it is paraded through the street, and to eat pasta at family dinners. In short, the rites that provide family identity are not separate from the rites that provide ethnic and other forms of identity.

We also encounter ritualization in the use of terms of address. I recall witnessing a discussion over a decade ago in Italy at a local Communist Party headquarters. Considerable emotion animated a debate over how to address members of the local Socialist Party, now that the alliance between the two parties at the national level was coming apart. Political solidarity was appropriately shown by the use of less formal terms of address and the accompanying use of less formal verb forms. Now that a change in political relations had occurred, the comrades decided that their socialist neighbors should henceforth be addressed more formally.

How far is this from the role played by ritualized greetings and forms of address between family members in America? Whether a child by a previous marriage addresses her stepfather as "Dad" or as "Bruce" is of no small significance. Lack of distinctive terms for certain kin is a sign of ambiguity in relationships. For example, unlike many other peoples, Americans have no separate terms of address for parents-in-law. We have basically three choices: dad (or father, pop, mom, mother, etc.); title plus last name (Mrs. Smith); or first name (Gertrude). Yet all of these pose potential problems for the new son- or daughter-in-law. The father-in law is not seen as socially equivalent to one's "dad," yet use of the title plus last name seems to show a degree of distance that may be offensive. Use of the first name creates the opposite problem, appearing to claim an intimacy and level of equality that do not, or should not, exist.

WHETHER IN CORONATION CEREMONIES OR presidential inaugurations, in striking up the chords to "Hail to the Chief" or employing ritualized forms of address such as "Mr. President," ritual has the power to legitimize social arrangements. This is because rites serve to link a sacred past to the present. Though times change, the very fact of the fixity of ritual forms makes them a point of security and comfort. Indeed, the seeming fixity of the rite can serve to mask the fact of social change, creating a sense of continuity that would otherwise be difficult to maintain. By celebrating Thanksgiving or Christmas in the same way each year, by singing the National Anthem at sporting events, and saying the Pledge of Allegiance in school, we create the sensation that our family and our country are basically the same now as they were years ago and that our relationship to each is unchanged.

Family rites provide a sense of continuity in the face of major changes. The same passionate insistence on not tampering with ritual forms that can be found among the religiously devout is easily matched when we look at the practice of many family rituals. Take the case of families who insist that everyone come together for Sunday dinner. From the parents' point of view, the fact that some of the children have married and moved away should not alter the rite. They should still be at the table every Sunday. To alter the rite is to threaten the family itself, its identity and its integrity. Likewise, the decision to celebrate Christmas in one's own home after marriage, and not in one's parents' home, may trigger resistance and resentment.

AS SOCIETIES BECOME LARGER, RITUAL BECOMES of greater, not lesser, importance in providing a mechanism that allows people to feel bonds of solidarity with others in the society, even others whom they rarely or never see. In addition, the important role played by ritual in creating solidarity among members of smaller social groupings, such as families, goes on undiminished. The bounds of the family are defined through participation in a well-defined cycle of ritual—baptisms, First Communions, Bar Mitzvoth, graduations, weddings, anniversaries, funerals and so on. These rites form the engine driving the kinship system in the United States. In many small-scale *(continued on page 9)*

New Divorce Rituals

THE TRANSITION FROM A TROUBLED MARRIAGE TO A CIVIL DIVORCE IS NOT A SIMPLE ONE, YET, AS a society, we do little to support it. The caseloads of most therapists are filled with couples who are legally divorced but still emotionally married. Unlike other important life transitions, divorce is distinguished by the utter absence of accepted rituals to acknowledge the emotional impact of this momentous, frequently turbulent shift in people's lives.

As a family therapist, I have been interested in developing positive ways of helping divorcing couples acknowledge that whatever the ties that may still bind them, henceforth the special relationship we call "marriage" is over. I have found rituals an invaluable tool in helping couples take the step of finally severing their emotional bond—whatever the legal status of their relationship. It is only when people take this step that they are free to discover what kind of new life they wish to create for themselves.

Mary and Harv had been divorced for six years, but were still as tangled up with each other as ever. Mary was a tall, regal-looking woman; Harv was slender and nervous. Their only child was eight. Since their divorce, both had found all other relationships to be superficial. Yet, despite sincere attempts to get back together, the same struggles that had ended their marriage in the first place tore them apart again and again. Like many couples, they couldn't be married and they couldn't let go of what their marriage might be, and their ability to ignore the reality of what it had become held them together.

Initially, I had tried to help them reconcile with each other. Finally, I asked if they would agree to an apparently crazy way of resolving their dilemma. They agreed; they no longer had anything to lose. I gave them detailed directions to a small town in Michigan's upper peninsula and told them to take along their old wedding rings.

With an air of dramatic expectancy, they set off for a 14-hour drive. Following instructions, they took fare on a two-hour boat tour up the Lake Superior coastline. They spent the first part of the trip reviewing their life together. Once they were one hour out, they went to the upper deck of the boat. There, while holding hands, they cast their rings into one of the coldest, deepest lakes in the world, a lake whose reputation, I had reminded them, has always been to "never give up her dead."

With some couples, a divorce ritual has led to a renewed commitment and a decision to continue together in a new way. For others, it has provided a way of bringing a difficult, ambivalent relationship to its conclusion. Harv and Mary spoke little on their drive back. Upon their return, each later told me, they were filled with extreme sadness and then an understanding that it was time to let go. From this point, they went their separate ways.

I have had some unhappily married couples melt down their wedding rings and forge them into new ones to symbolize their commitment to a fresh start. I have thought of doing something like that with divorced couples who must now devote themselves to bringing up their children without a marital bond tying them together. These rings could represent the beginning of this new relationship. I have asked other couples, still struggling to end their emotional bondage to each other, to write out the details of their troubled pasts or collect artifacts from their marriages, or gather special photos. They have then disposed of these items in a ritual fashion as a way of letting go of their troubled pasts.

Karen and David kept finding their reasonable attempts to divorce overpowered by their extreme anger that kept them tied to each other. I asked them to write detailed accounts of all the memories that currently fueled their anger and stood in the way of their moving on. It took about a month before they finally agreed that their troubled marriage was encapsulated in these individual written memories. Already they were calmer with each other. Together they burned the pages one by one, mingled the ashes and put them in a jar. I asked them to take the jar of ashes and an envelope containing my instructions and drive north to an old log chapel on a ridge in a virgin white pine forest. At the old chapel, they were to sit quietly for a time and then decide whether or not they were truly ready to let their marriage go. Deciding that they were ready, they picked a spot outside the chapel, took off their wedding rings, dug a hole, and quietly placed the ashes and their rings in an unmarked grave. Both Karen and David drove home with a sense of lightness that they said they hadn't felt since the beginning of their marriage. They went on to complete the divorce and peacefully finalized a visitation agreement for their two children.

OTHER IDEAS ABOUT HOW TO CHANGE THE TENOR OF DIVORCE HAVE COME TO MY MIND. WHY NOT A divorce modeled after a raucous New Orleans funeral? There would be mournful music played on the way to the ceremony, and upbeat, high-stepping jazz afterward. The couple could return their rings, exchanging new vows promising to work together in their children's best interest. Each spouse in turn, when asked whether they wished to continue to be married to the other, could respond, "I don't!" The minister could conclude the ceremony by saying, "I now pronounce you Man and Woman."

This may sound farfetched, but who's to say that divorce can't be an affirmation that life does indeed go on? I can't help but feel that divorcing couples deserve the same amount of loving support in starting a new life that they received when they were first married. □

–Jerome A. Price
JULY 1989

JEROME A. PRICE *is the director of the Michigan Family Institute, Huntington Woods, MI.*

(continued from page 6) societies, extended kin groups have a number of well-defined functions, including the exclusive control of land and other property needed to sustain life. In our own society, ritual is the primary tool for defining and maintaining these nonresidential groupings, groupings that have no legal status at all.

This is why the question of who is invited to a wedding, or the order in which people are informed of a kinsperson's death, and by whom, or who is sent a Christmas card or birthday present can generate such great emotion. In a society lacking other institutions for defining the kin group, such rites not only define who is in and who is out, but are also employed to rank order the importance of each kinsperson with respect to the others. Just as the May Day rites provide the Kremlin leadership with an opportunity to exhibit a public rank ordering of the political powers-that-be, so do family ritual observations call on the family to create a rank ordering of kin. Only the inner circle may be invited to holiday occasions, while progressively wider circles are invited to other rites, such as the Fourth of July picnic or Memorial Day softball game.

Another feature of ritual that makes it so valuable is its ability to generate feelings of social solidarity in the absence of any sharing of beliefs. There is a long Judeo-Christian intellectual tradition—evident in the earlier quote from Campbell—that holds that myth (or belief) is primary and ritual is derivative. In this view, ritual is simply the playing out of that myth. Anthropologists, however, have more commonly held a very different position, drawing on the century-old work of a Scottish historian of ancient religions, Robertson Smith. Based on his studies of the ancient Semites, Smith concluded that what really mattered to these people was that the ritual be properly performed. The explanation that they assigned to the action was of much less importance and, indeed, might vary from person to person.

Rites, despite Campbell's claim, are not simply stylized statements of belief, and the power of the rites does not depend on having everyone interpret them in the same way. The gathering of the family on Christmas, to take but one example, may be interpreted by the mother in religious terms as the celebration of the birth of Jesus, by the father in terms of its financial implications, and by the small children in terms of Santa Claus and the North Pole. Yet, through their joint participation in the rites, the family is drawn together. Moreover, memories of previous performances of the rite themselves become a powerful force in giving meaning to future performances, even though the family's situation may change dramatically in the interim.

Although the power of ritual does not depend on the sharing of belief, it is nonetheless true that rituals provide a potent mechanism for shaping people's beliefs. Anthropologist Clifford Geertz identifies this in his usual elegant way: "It is in some sort of ceremonial form . . . that the moods and motivations which sacred symbols induce in men and the general conceptions of the order of existence which they formulate for men meet and reinforce one another." He continues, "In a ritual, the world as lived and the world as imagined, fused under the agency of a single set of symbolic forms, turn out to be the same world. . . ."

RITUALS, IN SHORT, ENCOURAGE US TO INTERPRET reality in certain ways. Certainly our views of our parents are molded in part by childhood ritual experiences. In the classic American case, the father sits at the head of the dinner table, while the mother serves. In some families, the father may bless his children. In others, the mother may lead songs of thanksgiving at the dinner table. Such rites not only help shape our views of our parents but also, just because of their attachment to the events of daily living, serve to bind these memories and these images to us long after they were enacted; indeed, often until long after our parents have died. What from some viewpoints can be seen as the epitome of the material aspect of daily life—eating—becomes a symbolically laden daily reminder of our family bonds.

Ritual can also provide a potent vehicle for *changing* both people's perceptions and their social relations. A man and woman may live together for years, yet still the eventual wedding has great significance: it changes the status of the couple in the eyes of the community and, in particular, it has a major impact on the way kinspeople view the in-marrying partner, who, through ceremony, becomes kin. Indeed, if ritual is becoming any less important in advanced, industrial societies, it is certainly not evident from our wedding rites, which are among the most elaborate in the world.

FAR FROM DIMINISHING IN IMPORTANCE WITH THE rise of modern, bureaucratic, industrial society, rituals continue to play a crucial role at all levels of society. Those who prophesied their decline are guilty of misunderstanding both what makes ritual so socially significant and the nature of humanity itself. The power of ritual derives both from the importance of emotion to our thinking and from the fact that our thinking must share in the same symbolic language as is found in ritual. The notion that we will somehow "outgrow" ritual is the product of a peculiar intellectualist conceit.

The continued power of ritual is nowhere more clear than in the rites in which American family life is steeped. Not only are new ritual forms arising, but old forms are being reborn. Take, for example, one of the rites of passage most cherished by anthropologists, the couvade, the surprisingly widespread practice in various small-scale societies in which the husband of the pregnant wife must observe a series of ritual customs. In general, these entail behavior by which the husband ritually imitates the condition of the mother-to-be. He takes to bed, observes a strict diet, and demands attention. In short, through ritual, the man becomes part of the birthing event,

identifying himself more closely both with his wife and with the newborn.

How far a leap is it from the exotic rites of the couvade to the recent innovations in birthing practices in the United States? Preparation for childbirth is no longer simply a matter to be dealt with by the woman who is to give birth, but involves her husband as well. Such is the case of the popular Lamaze method. The husband must now go through the same preparatory behavior as his pregnant wife, from attending weekly instructional sessions to spending endless evenings for months in anticipatory joint panting. Indeed, American men have gone one step further than the peoples practicing the classic couvade, for they participate in the birth itself, behavior rarely found among men in societies of the past.

No doubt some of our old rituals will decline in importance, yet others will arise as new social needs provoke a ritual response. This is the phenomenon that literature on family ritual addresses, and this is addressed elsewhere in this issue. The tremendous upsurge in divorce over the past decades, for example, has yet to prompt a satisfactory ritual response. Such a response must be multifaceted, involving not simply a much-needed rite of transition, but also ritual resolution of the ambiguities and wounds to family relations occasioned by the divorce. The recent feeble attempt of greeting card companies to create a "happy divorce" card is not much of a contribution here, though it expresses widespread recognition of a need for a new rite of passage. In the wake of divorce, moreover, old family rituals become not only a means for adjusting to new family circumstances. They may also become a battleground. Where the children go for Thanksgiving dinner and Christmas morning and how they celebrate their birthdays, for example, may become a ritual field on which the war between the parents is waged. The very importance of these rites to the family identity can make such struggle all the more tragic. On the other hand, in some cases these rites bind the noncustodial parent to the children in a way that might not otherwise exist.

Other social changes doubtless presage other areas of family ritual development. One of the most striking family problems that our society confronts today is the high rate of childbearing by young, unwed teenagers in our large cities' slums. The reason most commonly given by sociologists and psychologists for the phenomenon is that childbirth provides them with their only way to be recognized as adults. Many of them will never go through a graduation exercise, nor is marriage an attractive (or even available) option.

We might ask here whether the lack of other rites of passage to adulthood in American society—rites through which the society publicly recognizes the young person as having passed on to a new status—contributes to this problem.

The importance of family observance of religious ritual, highlighted in our discussion of the Jewish immigrants in Los Angeles, raises another kind of question here. Insofar as sectors of American society are moving away from religious ritual, are they unwittingly losing an important part of family life? Of course, this change works both ways, since it is through the association of religion with the fondly remembered family rites of childhood that the individual also becomes bound to the religious group. However, we are left with the question of whether declining family religious practices—a phenomenon that is far from universal in our society—may create the need for new ritual forms in family life.

One final aspect of current changes in family ritual life that merits mention concerns not the lack of ritual, but rather the possibly unfortunate forms that rituals may take. Here it is hard to avoid thinking of the widely lamented commercialism and materialism that have afflicted various family rites, especially those identified with Christmas or Channukah gift-giving. Insofar as parental love becomes measured by the size of gifts—the principle of love requited by loot—contemporary family rites not only reflect, but in fact socialize children into the values of a materialistic society. The issue of changing family rites, then, is not simply a matter of inventing new rites, or resuscitating old ones, but also of altering the symbolism of some of the ones we already have.

The need for further development of family ritual is clear. But we shouldn't conclude from this that ritual has somehow become an endangered species in American society. Joseph Campbell could not have been reading his *New York Times* very carefully, because, far from describing a "society without any rituals," the pages of the *Times* are regularly filled with accounts of the modern rites of state and society. But perhaps Campbell was so enamored of myth that he succumbed to one of the most abiding—yet unsubstantiated—myths of Western intellectuals: that the depersonalizing forces of modern life will entirely loosen the deeply emotional grip ritual that continues to exert on our hearts and minds. ∎

DAVID I. KERTZER *is professor of anthropology at Bowdoin College, Brunswick, ME.*

See references, page 563.

11

PHOTOGRAPH BY SKIP BROWN

THE RESOUNDING SILENCE

TODAY'S ADULTS AND TEENAGERS ARE WORLDS APART

By Patricia Hersch

ON A BEAUTIFUL SPRING EVENING IN SAN FRANcisco, I stood at the intersection of Sutter and Polk streets, a cheerful, crowded jumble of boutiques and bookstores, head shops and bead shops, restaurants and bars. The corner was thronged with students and tourists, straights and gays, and bunches of teenagers leaning against the window of a pizza shop. They wore the uniforms and insignia of their various tribes: leather-clad punks, California surfers, Eastern preppies, suburban gypsies and born-again hippies. Boys and girls laughed and joked together, jostled and pushed one another with the rough physical affection with which kids treat their friends and fellow tribespeople. It was a cheerful, ordinary scene, except that they all faced outward, watching the passersby and especially the cars, with much more than casual interest. This was a typical business night, and they were all shrewdly assessing the crowd for potential customers—the men who would pay for an hour or two of their sexual services.

And men were watching them. They passed on foot, giving them furtive, speculative glances, or cruised slowly by in cars, or sat silently in a local ice cream shop, smoking, drinking coffee, looking at one young person, then another, studying the merchandise, figuring the going rate.

I went into a pizza shop, gave my order, and sat down to watch this evening ritual. A tall, nice-looking boy came in, glanced around in agitation, and then, seeing me—a woman sitting alone in a restaurant virtually empty except for a trio of drunks and a young couple—came over to my table. Very straightforward, very earnest, he held up a bright red sweatshirt and asked me, "Which one do you think I should wear, the one I have on, or this one?" He pulled off the sweatshirt he was wearing—a tourist's souvenir with the Golden Gate Bridge and a sailboat on the front—and replaced it with the red one.

"I like the red one," I said.

"Are you sure?" he asked.

"Definitely," I answered. "It brings out your nice tan."

He smiled, thanked me, and told me he was here from New York, visiting his brother. During the few minutes we talked, he kept glancing nervously at the door. Finally, he got up, asked me one more time if the sweatshirt looked okay, and then went out into the street. I knew he had no brother in San Francisco, no place to go, no money, no belongings, and that I had been calmly telling him what article of clothing would make him a more appealing prostitute. Now, as I looked outside, I saw that all the other kids were gone—I watched the last one step into a car and go off into the night with a stranger.

As everyone who picks up a newspaper or watches television knows, there is nothing at all unusual about this story; the shock has become familiar, almost banal. Yet, in the three years that I have been exploring the new world of adolescents, I am still not prepared for the sight of children living out a latter-day Dickensian nightmare—sleeping on the floors of Grand Central Station or New York's Port Authority Bus Terminal, selling themselves for sex in a parking lot at three in the afternoon, dealing drugs in the morning on Times Square, hustling in San Francisco's tenderloin district, begging for money on the streets of every city in America.

Even more haunting is the realization that these kids are not part of an alien, un-American subgroup, the perverse effluvia of some foreign underclass. These are Everybody's kids. They are the children of doctors, lawyers and other professionals as often as they are the children of the poor and disenfranchised. Because their own homes have failed them, they try now to create some evocation of family life with their friends on the street.

Nor are they really different from those we see in schools, in the malls, at fast-food restaurants, coming out of movie theaters and record shops. These street kids represent one end of a continuum that includes all adolescents; they are only the most extreme product of the systematic neglect, disregard and devaluation with which American society treats a whole generation of young people. The lonely and chaotic lives of the San Francisco adolescent prostitutes are not so far removed from the rootless, hap-

hazard, directionless lives of suburban kids who end up in therapists' offices, if not on the streets.

Most adults don't like adolescents very much. As if looking at them through the eyes of juvenile court officers, we expect the worst, and tough, self-conscious adolescents' belligerence makes us defensive and anxious. Yet there is, even within many of the most incorrigible teenagers, a kind of sweetness, a universal child, open and vulnerable. If you take the time to talk to them, to get to know them, even the toughest little hookers or drug dealers can show themselves to be warm, engaging, kind, cranky, oppositional, profane and exasperating—just like all other kids.

SAY THE MAGIC WORD "ADOLESCENTS" TO MOST adults and you're likely to get a litany of complaints: They spend all of their time in front of the tube or playing video games. They lack ambition and they won't read. They want instant gratification. They have no values, no interests. Having learned the alphabet from Sesame Street when they were only two, by the time they are 15 they decide good grades, or, for that matter, any higher mental functions, are "uncool."

Most parents feel an uneasiness, at times bordering on panic, about their abilities to help their children through this notoriously rocky time of life, sharing the fears of one psychologist who recently told me, "Teenagers are never very far from a wrong turn." This dismay goes beyond the customary parental grumbling about the sorry state of the younger generation. Study after study tells us how troubled kids are today. "Turning Points", the 1989 report of the Carnegie Council on Adolescent Development, for example, warns that "by age 15, substantial numbers of American youth are at risk of reaching adulthood unable to meet adequately the requirements of the workplace, the commitments of relationships in families and with friends, and the responsibilities of participation in a democratic society. These youths are among the estimated seven million young people—one in four adolescents—who are extremely vulnerable to multiple high-risk behaviors and school failure. Another seven million may be at moderate risk. . . ." In other words, half of all adolescents are at some risk for serious problems like substance abuse; early, unprotected sexual intercourse; dangerous, accident-prone life-styles; delinquent behavior; and dropping out of school. The Carnegie report concludes that today's children are susceptible to "a vortex of new risks . . . almost unknown to their parents or grandparents."

Something is troubling about adolescent life today far beyond the old "adjustment problems" of growing up, and family therapists, especially those with long experience in practice, have had a front-row seat for viewing the spectacular changes in adolescent life and mores over the past three decades. Recalling the children of the rebellious '60s, family therapist Don-David Lusterman observes, "The kids then had real old-fashioned angst. Now they have a kind of weakness and a sense that nothing is going anywhere, that there will be no place for them, and that they won't find a healthy, lasting relationship. They are prematurely sexual and don't really enjoy it. Sex is just there—another thing to be done." They don't even really suffer the *sturm und drang* that used to be one of the nice, healthy parts of being an adolescent, according to Lusterman: "The kids of the '60s would complain, 'I am so tortured, I am so angry at my parents and furious that I have to grow up.' There was a sense of some substance to their complaints; they were reading, so they would talk about Hermann Hesse, for example, someone who symbolized these issues—they had a meaningful cultural context." But today, says Lusterman, "The kids I see are just whipped—they are empty in the main. My job, more than anything else, is to find some piece of themselves that they can like. In the '60s even very deprived kids, even kids acting out in antisocial ways, had some crazy kind of

idealism. But now, you feel you've got to begin by breathing life into them; they are so discouraged."

But before we deplore the absence of character and old-fashioned virtues in today's teenagers, we must recognize that young people reflect the world we give them. In fact, what seems dysfunctional in teenagers may actually be functional ways of dealing with the crazy environment they inherited. By now, we are all too familiar with the vast social changes that followed World War II—the decline of the traditional family and rising rates of divorce, dual-career marriages, stepfamilies, increase in runaways, use of drugs and alcohol, confusion about male and female roles, about the meaning of family. But what we have yet to recognize is how these social changes have transformed the experience of growing up.

More American children of this generation have been raised in day care than ever before, and more have spent long hours alone at home while parents worked. More have grown up in neighborhoods where nobody's home. In short, according to David Waters, associate professor in the Department of Family Medicine at the University of Virginia, "The general level of supervision and involvement is way down, at the same time the general level of adult distress and adult distraction is up." One teen described her generation as the children of "in-between parents," adults who parent their children in between all the other things they have to do.

Today's kids, whether from inner cities or the suburbs or rural towns, must navigate a narrow course between drugs, alcohol, crime, and various forms of danger. My 16-year-old son was meeting a cousin he hadn't seen for a long time, over spring break; these two straight, nice kids, seeking ground to relate to each other, spoke about overdoses and killings in their middle-class suburban high schools. Nearly every teenager I have met knows another teenager who committed suicide. They accept a threatening world as normal.

Furthermore, in an era defined by rapid change,

all kids come to accept the impermanence of even the most intimate relationships. Even children from intact families despair of ever finding the same kind of love and commitment for themselves. One girl attacked her parents for having a stable, long-term marriage: "You guys don't understand that you are oddballs. I don't have any friends whose parents still like each other, sleep together, stay married."

"There has been an erosion of the protection adolescents used to have," says C. Gibson Dunn, medical director of the Springwood Psychiatric Institute. "Not only are they exposed to higher levels of stimulation, violence, uncertainty and the anxiety of too many choices," says Dunn, "but they have lost the extended family to turn to when they are confused or unhappy. . . . Presumably, parents are no worse than they've ever been," he says, "but before, if things weren't going well, you could always wander over to an aunt or an uncle or a grandparent or a neighbor who'd been there your whole life, and sort of hang out and get some emotional comfort out of that even if you didn't talk directly about what was bothering you." Dunn believes that sense of community is missing for today's adolescents. "They don't have a place to belong, they don't feel they have a haven, so crises become individual rather than shared, or else they share their troubles with a group of other kids who have banded together because they are all going through similar crises in isolation." Often, Dunn suggests, this camaraderie in crisis magnifies suffering and glorifies suicide and suicide pacts.

THE MOST STUNNING CHANGE FOR ADOLESCENTS today is their aloneness. A common scenario for the working family starts with full-time day care soon after birth, but with each passing year, unless a family is lucky, child care becomes less consistent. Children spend time with many different caretakers, spending more hours with them than with their own parents. By the time the children are eight or nine, often earlier, caretaking arrangements are even more patchwork, and often the child is left alone for an hour or two every day. By age 10, parents are frequently so exhausted by the relentless struggle to find consistent, reliable, affordable care providers that they decide by default that their children can safely be left alone.

When the child is young and home alone, the parents may call frequently, but as the child matures, the calls come less often. This coincides with a subtle shift of parental attitude: until children are 10, parents speak of love, nurturing and quality time. They cherish each stage of development, proudly display pictures and schoolwork on the refrigerator door. But somewhere around age 12, weekly schedules and list of chores replace the artwork on the refrigerator door, and the language takes a harder edge. Parents talk of boundaries, behavioral contracts, family meetings, *consequences*. Working parents now call home more to check up on their adolescents than to affirm a loving connection.

We assume teenagers welcome their hours alone, but one 17-year-old girl confided that she had been left to take care of herself for more than eight years. "It's okay, I guess," she said. "I go home and watch my soaps and MTV, and talk on the phone, but I really wish my mom and I had more time. I guess you could say I miss her." What are such children missing? What conversations? What experiences? What learning? What bonding?

Later, when the kids are older and have more time on their hands, there are no parents at home to see what they are doing. It is natural to fill the time by creating a family of friends who are also alone. It is also much easier to get into a liquor cabinet or take drugs or have sex when parents are out of the house. All parents know is whether their child is sober or not when they get home. Mothers and fathers aren't available to give the on-the-spot support kids often need. Kids cannot use their parents as the age-old excuse to back off from something they might not want to do—"I'm sorry. I can't because my mom's here." Now the kids have all the responsibility for making decisions, often in a void, or with their jerry-built, ersatz family of other lonely kids.

This generation of adolescents has been robbed of the gift of time. We have created the myth of quality time, the idea that we can efficiently fit child-rearing into our busy schedules. "But the fact is that quality time is invariably embedded in quantity time," says David Waters. "You can't suddenly buzz in with your 12-year-old and turn on quality time in the few minutes you have before dinner, or after dinner, or before you have to go out for a meeting— you have to work on it." Says social worker Nancy Wilson, "Parenting isn't an activity you can schedule. A lot of the problems we are seeing are the result of kids not being nourished at the right time or in the right way—somehow they missed it."

Relationships with adolescents take doggedness and tenacity, which too many parents are too weary to pursue. "It takes a lot of push, time and courage to keep going toward the kid, to try to break through, because kids are very good at fending you off," explains Waters, "and they really make you prove yourself if they stop trusting you or stop feeling close to you. They make you earn your way back in, and a lot of parents don't have the time or energy to do it—they make a pass or two at it, but the kid says, 'Screw you,' and the parents back off and say, 'I can't do a thing with them.'" Braulio Montalvo, a family therapist doing a research project on adolescence for the Children's Coalition in Albuquerque, feels that the issue of time is at the core of how adults fail kids today: "The kids haven't changed as much as their support networks. The family has truly become enfeebled—parents have less time with kids. They seem to believe that kids are like trees: you give them a little water and they grow by themselves. It's unbelievable."

The absence of adults in their homes and neigh-borhoods offers limited role models for teens, and encourages them to set their own standards. Elena Nightengale, author, with Lisa Wolverton, of *Adolescent Rolelessness in Modern Society*, is troubled by the fact that segregation by age has increased in each decade so that we see less and less mixing of generations, creating "an alienation and a lack of modeling on the previous generation that sets kids aside. . . . Rather than being included as necessary members of the family, they are allowed to do 'their own thing,' which separates them even more."

We criticize adolescents for being an unmotivated, passive, entertain-me generation, but we created the void in their lives. "If you talk to gym teachers," high school teacher and soccer coach Scott Mack explains, "you find out that it is difficult to get kids to play games just for fun. Why? Because they don't play at home, they don't play pickup games at the vacant lot because there is no vacant lot. They haven't grown up with the natural and easy access to other kids where play evolves, because they are not allowed to leave the house. I know parents who have elementary-age kids who have to come in the house and lock the doors; they are not allowed out of the house until an adult comes home. They play Nintendo or they watch TV." Or maybe a child is at home with a parent, but all the other kids are in day care. The joys of childhood play that we remember from our youth have been circumscribed for this generation.

Barbara Fletcher, guidance counselor and coordinator of peer counseling at a Virginia high school, takes it a step further. "Teenagers have no sense of self in what will really make them happy," says Fletcher. "All they hear from the media is 'Make money, look good, and be cool'; and not only be cool but be shifty—trick people, get away with things, don't work to get something. Nobody tells them, 'It is important for you to know about the world, to be able to do math, to take care of yourself.' It feels good to know these things.' Nobody shows them that. When I ask them, 'What do you like to do?,' they answer, 'Party.' 'What else do you like to do?' 'Oh, I don't know.' They just float."

THE RITUALS THAT STRUCTURE LIFE GET SHORT shrift in the fast-paced lives most families lead, particularly by the time kids are adolescents. It is often a hassle for parents, once they get home, to corral their kids for dinner. Youngsters have been on their own so much that feeding themselves is no big deal. Eating together as a family is becoming a lost institution. The dinner table used to be the place where a family came together and conversed, argued, laughed and shared the events of their day. Family meals were part of the texture of growing up. Members of families knew one another—their likes, their dislikes; it was a place where, over the years, the family stories got passed from one generation to another.

Shared meals are often lost because of the pressures on working parents who must balance their family life and their full-time jobs. "The parent who's just gotten home at 8 p.m.," explains David Marsden, superintendent at the Fairfax County Juvenile Detention Center, asks, 'Do I want to yell and scream to get everybody to sit down at this table, or do we just all go in and watch the damn TV because my priority right now is peace and quiet and not a hassle?'" Kids sense parents' vulnerabilities and quickly take advantage: "I can be out of your hair real quick if I can call for a pizza or rent a video." Almost inevitably, the tired parent caves in, and eventually such exchanges become commonplace, constituting a breakdown of communal family life.

Choices and opportunities in society are a double-edged sword. On the one hand, many kids have grown up comfortable with men and women sharing roles once segregated by sex. But on the other hand, the constant renegotiation of roles by their parents creates a fluid environment that can confuse kids. Even in a healthy home, what are the effects of having parents trying to figure out who does what all the time? What does it mean for a society when you've got a whole generation of parents reinventing who they are? It creates a lack of security if parents do not know from week to week what they are supposed to do, and have no time to figure it out. How much harder is it for their children to grow into secure adults?

Parents tend to tolerate more in their children partly because the lines are blurred. How else can we explain parents allowing an occasional drunk by their 15-year-old, or taking for granted intercourse at that age? These days, behaviors are tolerated in kids that would have been unheard-of 10 years ago, and with the peculiar comfort parents find in thinking "at least they didn't do it at 12."

Fluid family structures often obscure the necessary boundary between generations. Nancy Wilson explains how this confusion angers many adolescents she sees in her practice: "They are always angry at their parents and oftentimes it is at their unpredictability," says Wilson. "They don't know where they are going to be, what they are going to say. Sometimes the parents overdo it; sometimes they underdo it. I think kids want to grow up faster and take care of their own lives because they feel it isn't being done very well by their parents." Or sometimes the kids are so parentified and already take so much responsibility for themselves that they get heady with their own power and accept no adult intervention. Either way, power balances between the generations are skewed. When a kid grows up seeing that dinner is anything, anywhere, anytime, and that daily rules can be changed at will, it is easy to develop the attitude, "If you can get away with it, do it."

ADOLESCENCE IS A TIME FOR YOUNG PEOPLE TO prove their worthiness to themselves and to society. But we live in a culture that denies them meaningful avenues of expression, that tries to ignore them. "Adolescents crave some sort of initiation in a broader, deeper context of life," explains David Oldfield, author of *The Journey: A Creative Approach to the Necessary Crises of Adolescence.* "They want structure, ritual and they want participation in a small, initiated group of people who have power together. . . . But we do whatever we can to disempower our adolescents: we take away their power to work, we put them in huge, anonymous high schools where they can't really form powerful identities. In fact, most of us are threatened when we see a group of adolescents walking together. 'Uh-oh, they must be up to no good.' They need to be empowered and if we don't empower them, they will empower themselves."

Adolescents are denied the kind of meaningful struggles that would provide them with the opportunities they crave to show the adult world their value as they move toward adulthood. "Maybe it is ironic, but some of the more well-adjusted kids you meet have faced adversity," says high school teacher Mack. "Mom's moved away; dad died of cancer; they're living with grandmother; they don't have enough money to go to college; they have to work. And you see this kid who is really dynamic. So many times you see kids whose parents have a lot of money but don't have the time for them, kids who have a car and nice clothes but everything is too easy. They're smart, but school isn't a meaningful challenge. They get depressed; they get bored. It's almost as if they try to make life a challenge by making it more difficult on themselves."

The buzzword of the '60s to describe teenagers' disaffection from the adult world was "the generation gap." Presumably there was a conflict of understanding that separated adolescents from their parents. But according to psychologist James Hillman, in *Puer and Senex*, the conflict of generations these days is "sometimes no longer a conflict of misunderstanding but a silence, for there is a division of communication

systems between age and youth; the latter learns today not through traditional forms and printed words but from altogether other media in our urban collective. Youth forms a social class, self-enclosed and uninitiated by its elders and that is largely without communication outside of itself."

So in the vacuum, adolescents act out, often in self-destructive ways, to declare themselves different, individual, adult. In a society without clearly defined markers for what it means to be an adult woman or an adult man, teenagers invent their own challenges to overcome. We end up with the strange rites of Satanism, stage diving at concerts, inserting a bong (a plastic tube) down one's stomach to hasten drunkenness.

When an adult acts foolishly, when we want to pass judgment, we say he or she is "adolescent." "There is no honor, no respect for adolescents," says Oldfield. Today's adolescents are adrift in a society that gives them neither actual time and attention nor a sense of tradition to sustain them. This is as true for adolescents in suburbia as it is for those living on the streets. The latter may be more damaged and in greater pain, but all adolescents live in a world that fails to embrace them. "It is as if there is no space for adolescents," says Braulio Montalvo.

Therapists are often assigned the job of helping adolescents and their families navigate successfully though this tumultuous passage. But all too often, therapists wind up making a difficult situation worse. Says family therapist Lee Combrinck-Graham, director of Chicago's Institute of Juvenile Research, "Experts have contributed enormously to the problem by acting as if they know something that the teenagers and their parents don't know, offering a level of expertise that generally interferes with any natural resource system that a teenager has. Instead of saying to the family, 'Your kid needs attention,' we often say, 'Your kid needs expert intervention' and mystify the family even further."

Montalvo believes that family therapists need to

get engaged in the larger issues. "To really service adolescents, we need to look in a very comprehensive way at society at large," says Montalvo. "What are we doing for families to help them raise kids? We now have an army of single parents bringing up kids with their left hand, trying to do their best with no support, with shabby-quality day care, dangerous neighborhoods, questionable schools—it is just tough. I don't think that it's a fantasy that raising kids today is harder; I think it's a reality."

T HE SPIRIT OF ADOLESCENCE IS ONE OF ENERGY and hope waiting to be tapped. We have seen its enormous power in the crowds of young people demonstrating in Eastern Europe. We saw its courage and commitment in the bloodied faces of students in China. "When the Berlin Wall was coming down," recounts Montalvo, "my daughter was in Italy. She and two friends decided to do everything to get to the wall." They were drawn like a magnet to see it. The train was jam-packed with other young people on a pilgrimage to be part of what was happening.

Recalls Montalvo, "She described it to me in a call from the train station: 'Dad, we can't get there because of how many kids want to go.' What were they looking for? It was absolutely the power of youth prevailing; of a world that can be changed, a world that doesn't have to be a stinker. I think that is the spirit of adolescence and when that is gone, we are going to be in trouble." ■

PATRICIA HERSCH *is a free-lance writer who lives in Reston, VA.*

Letters to the Editor

I WAS SITTING IN MY DAD'S OFFICE WHEN HE showed me your issue "Alien Nation: Life in Teenage America." He said, "This is about your people. See what you think." So I sat down and read it. The cover started me with a bad feeling about being a teenager, like we are not part of society. After reading the first half of the article by Patricia Hersch, I became depressed. Nothing about it was positive. Everything focused on drugs, drinking and bad attitudes of teens. The second half of the article suggested that parents who work a lot have troubled kids, and that parents should feel crummy along with their teenagers.

I want to say that every teenager is unique, and not all are troubled or lack ambition. People don't give credit to the teenagers who work hard and stay off drugs and alcohol. And every parent is different; you can't assume that parents' love for their children depends on how much they work.

Society pays most attention to the teenagers who get in trouble. As we struggle to grow up, it stings when adults emphasize the worst in teenagers. As adults, your positive feelings will bring out positive attitudes in today's teenagers.

Elizabeth A. Doherty
Roseville, MN
The author of the letter is 14 years old.

THIS SOCIETY SUFFERS FROM A *BAD ATTI-tude* about adolescents, who are typically depicted as bellicose, weird and incomprehensible. Viewing teenagers in this way fosters fear and helplessness among adults, forcing our young people into positions of greater desperation, outlandishness and hopelessness. Generally, I think the "Alien Nation" issue of the *Networker* reinforced this bad atti-tude. In fact, I think it's very possible that sensational coverage, such as that in the *Networker*, is now a part of teenagers' problems, offering a distorted view not only to their parents and mental health professionals, but to teenagers themselves.

Many of us evaluate our own children through the distorted lens of the media, so that it is a surprise and shock to parents when their adolescents are not troublemakers, or worse. It would be a good idea to pay more attention to kids who are doing fine—the athletes, newspaper editors, artists, scholars in our high schools. Why not feature them and their families in a future issue of the *Networker* and call it "The Nation's Future"? In the meantime, each one of us can do something and get a bunch of other people to do something. I call it the "Adolescent Attention Campaign." Start paying attention to adolescents, especially the ones who are not going out of their way to attract attention. Invite your teenagers out for dinner at a fancy restaurant for no particular reason. Ask them to spend a weekend evening with the family, because you really want to spend time together. Ask their opinions on important things, like the budget, the Middle East, world economics. Give them respect.

Then start noticing other kids. Look for the well-behaved or quiet kids in public places. Think of the nice kid who packs your groceries at the supermarket or helps out at the gas station or sells tickets at the movies. Talk to him or her, and think of a compliment or comment that conveys what you've noticed.

Get the media to feature successful, competent adolescents.

Let's stop proliferating this *bad attitude.*
Lee Combrinck-Graham
Evanston, IL

PHOTOGRAPH BY CHARLES HARBUTT/ACTUALITY

After the Anger, What Then?

The ACOA Movement Is Sending Tremors Through the Mental Health Field

By Lily Collet

M Y FATHER'S DRINKING BEGAN IN THE BROWN-stone college town to which he returned in 1944 after a shell exploded above his foxhole in Italy. "There were probably about a dozen of us, all wounded veterans," he wrote to me, four years ago, in his spidery hand, on six sheets of legal paper, documenting a lifetime of heavy drinking but rejecting the label I'd just found for him: *alcoholic.* "We regularly went to a club in the evenings and drank steadily for a couple of hours, perhaps in the evening, perhaps late into poker games that lasted to breakfast time. There was one awful morning that I woke up totally disoriented, not merely as to time or place, but as to who, in fact, I was."

He was responding to a letter from me that recalled our family's unhappiest years and pleaded with him to join Alcoholics Anonymous. "On the whole, I resist the interpretation that things in the family began to go wrong because of booze," he replied. "My memory is that I became insanely ambitious for you and let the love go out of our relationship—prior to, and simultaneous with, beginning to drink more regularly. While it did not

originate the problem, it sure as hell could not have helped. . . I know that booze is not the central issue, and I am going to lick it."

I put down the letter in a fury and stared out the window. For years I lived with a sense that I had failed my father. Now the tables were turned: he was the one on the hot seat. His letter had left out the worst things—the under-the-influence interrogations at the dinner table, the time he visited my mother in the hospital and was so drunk that he pissed in the bedside chair. After years of blind suffering I could not name, I had an explanation and I did not plan to lose it in subtle distinctions.

The year was 1985. I had never before thought of my father as alcoholic. But a new psychological label had become a social movement and stampeded into the national consciousness. It was the skeleton key to my family closet, an Archimedean leverage point from which I planned to move my whole world. My pain was no longer my fault, or even my father's—it was the fault of a "family disease" that had infected and affected us all.

It didn't matter that no therapist had given me

permission to define myself as an Adult Child of an Alcoholic, or that there was no diagnosis in the DSM III. No matter that some theorists were bemoaning the return of "disease" as a metaphor for soul-pain, or that many family therapists would have questioned the centrality of alcohol in our family's unhappiness. After all, I was part of a generation that had been questioning authority since the Vietnam War.

What mattered more was that newspaper articles and a few women therapists with little standing in any psychological establishment—psychoanalyst Alice Miller and alcoholism counselors Claudia Black and Janet Woititz—were speaking truths about my childhood that I'd never heard from "anointed" therapists steeped in Freudian drive theory, Transactional Analysis, Reichian therapy, or Ericksonian hypnosis. I was part of a lay movement and a consumer revolt against the "experts" to whom our parents had given so much power.

W E MEMBERS OF THE BABY BOOM WEREN'T the first generation to grow up with alcoholism, but we were the first to transform a private and shameful history into a huge grass-roots movement and a therapeutic and literary market. We were primed for it in the '50s and early '60s, the era of Old Fashioneds, cocktail parties and the suburban daddy who drank his way home on the train. "The fathers of the baby boomers were members of a 'wet' generation for whom drinking was a symbol of generational rebellion," says Robin Room of the Alcohol Research Group at the University of California at Berkeley, pointing to the influence of the hard-drinking "Lost Generation" of writers, heavy wartime drinking and the prosperity of postwar America.

Nobody talked about "children of alcoholics" then—just as nobody talked about incest, child abuse, domestic violence, or post-traumatic stress disorder. When I was 12, my best friend Janet was a

little adult who cooked her meals out of cans. Her mother once "fell asleep" on the couch with a cigarette, started a fire, and was inexplicably angry when Janet told about it at show-and-tell. At our house, nothing seemed so obviously amiss. Yet my father seemed to fade away, while my mother grew anxious, lonely and larger than life. I never did my homework, my middle brother wet his bed until he went to boarding school, my youngest brother—who is now a heavy drinker—developed asthma, would not eat, and tormented our Siamese cat.

In the early '60s, our worried parents packed the family off to the respected Judge Baker Guidance Center in Boston; my brother played checkers with his therapist and my parents were told not to let us kids crawl into bed with them on Sunday mornings. Nobody even raised the question of my father's quietly increasing drinking. Nobody gave us the tools to think of him as alcoholic, or even to see his private relationship with alcohol as part of our family dynamics.

For years after I left home, my scattered worries about my father's drinking lay jumbled in some emotional back closet. The first light went on in 1977, when my first boyfriend returned to town from his isolated homestead in the tropics. I had always known that his mother was alcoholic, but now I discovered what it had done to him. When we were kids, it seemed his crazy family had simply made him stronger. He had gotten into Harvard while raising three younger siblings and ferrying his suicidal, drunken mother to psychiatric hospitals and emergency rooms. At 30, his hidden wounds were surfacing. He spent weeks playing Pachelbel on my phonograph, going to Alateen meetings for teenage children of alcoholics, and crying.

The second light went on in 1983, at my bridesmaids dinner. I looked at the beautiful faces around me in the candlelight: Susan, an elegant magazine writer sometimes paralyzed with self-doubt; Lisa, a workaholic graphic designer; Adrianne, a technical writer with a young baby, abandoned by a man in AA who was as old as her alcoholic father had been when he died; Sara, involved with a series of emotionally abusive men. We all confessed we had mothers or fathers with drinking problems.

TWO YEARS LATER, I FOUND MYSELF ON MY WAY to the Monday Night Meeting for Adult Children of Alcoholics, sponsored by Al Anon. We met in a Methodist church basement on the seedy fringe of San Francisco's Castro district. It was a day-care center during the day, and when the big chairs were taken, we sat in concentric circles on tiny wooden toddlers' chairs with our knees up. There were usually more than a hundred of us, mostly baby-boom age and mostly white. There were business suits, T-shirts and jeans, and sometimes a fresh-faced young girl with a black-and-white mohawk and a scorpion tattooed on her wrist. There, surrounded by children's drawings and alphabet cards, we read aloud the 12 Steps of Alcoholics Anonymous.

Every week a volunteer spoke for 10 minutes, following a simple format: "what it was like" growing up; what grown-up crisis brought him or her into the program; and "what it's like now," after "working the Steps." Then the meeting would be thrown open to the floor. There was no therapist and no boss. The meeting was free—although most of us put a dollar in the basket. We identified ourselves by our first names only, and didn't mention our jobs or outside status symbols. "Crosstalk"—commenting or giving advice—was forbidden.

We listened to everyone. An ex-junkie, ex-con, ex-hustler told us one night that he'd been conceived in a barn and spent his childhood sleeping in bathtubs in abandoned buildings. Now he worked in an ice cream parlor and went to Narcotics Anonymous and Al Anon meetings. "I'm practicing abstinence from my family," he said.

The details of the stories changed, but not the underlying feelings of denial and shame expressed, often for the first time. One woman used to rip the American Airlines labels off her father's luggage because she was afraid someone might think the AA stood for Alcoholics Anonymous. Her father, a successful businessman, passed out one night in a restaurant with his face in a plate of spaghetti. A huge table full of relatives went on as though nothing had happened. The woman, then 10 years old and afraid her father would suffocate, walked over with a studied casualness, lifted his head, wiped off his face, and leaned him back in his chair. "I learned that if nobody was willing to face up to the fact that a man's head was in the spaghetti, then the truth must be dangerous," she says. "I've since learned that the truth doesn't kill. Silence kills."

The ritual form of the meeting, from the opening welcome to the closing circle where we all held hands, came from Al Anon, the group founded in 1951 by wives of alcoholics. But the content of the people's sharings, I later learned, was quite different. "Regular" Al Anon was more inspirational, more peaceful and less psychological than our Monday Night Meeting. Its members were more likely to share little successes—accounts of relinquishing control to a "higher power," or of "lovingly detaching" from the alcoholics in their lives. In "regular" Al Anon, beginners were subtly encouraged, by example, to stop ventilating rage and grief within two or three months. Instead, they listened to old-timers share, learned to take responsibility for making their own lives happier, and found sponsors (mentors) to help them "work the 12 Steps" in a systematic way.

In our ACOA group, the process of "working the Steps" took much longer, and sometimes never happened at all. Some old-timers spoke of detachment, and hanging up nicely on drunken 3 a.m. calls. But many of us shared memories of the past, not victories of the present. For my first two years, I cried once during almost every meeting. I betrayed the family secrets: I told of being hit so hard that my father left red palm prints on my thighs; I admitted I had been depressed for years.

What little theory we had was a mélange of self-help literature, the 12 Steps and the facts of our own lives. We heard "children of alcoholics learn not to trust, not to think and not to feel." We used Al Anon slogans: "'No' is a complete sentence," and "There are no victims, only volunteers." We heard the "three C's"—"you didn't cause it, you couldn't cure it, and you couldn't control it," and the "three A's"—"awareness, acceptance, *then* action." In telling their life stories, people used concepts borrowed from psychoanalyst Alice Miller and spoke of "re-parenting the inner child," and trying to break out of cycles of isolation and overresponsibility. It was safe to recall almost any victimization of childhood: incest, beating, pulling your unconscious brother in out of the snow. It was safe to admit having done almost anything in adulthood: working in the sex industry, attempting suicide, falling in love with addicts and alcoholics, staying for years in jobs you hated. It was less easy to do what Al Anon pamphlets encouraged—to describe little victories of "experience, strength and hope" and to "keep the focus on ourselves," rather than blaming our alcoholic relatives or trying to figure out why they did what they did.

A S WE PSYCHOLOGICALLY ORIENTED BABY boomers poured into Al Anon in the early 1980s, one or two new meetings for ACOAs were registered at Al Anon headquarters in New York every day. This tidal wave of newcomers, new to the traditions of Al Anon, shook—and continues to shake—the organization. "Al Anon is trying to stay very firm," says an anonymous spokeswoman at the headquarters recently. "All of a sudden, your ground gets shook up, and I'm hoping everybody is patient enough."

The Adult Children are angry—and many are angrier at anxious and angry nonalcoholic mothers than they are with their warm, alcoholic fathers. "When I was first in Al Anon, I was angry, too, and expressing it is important," said the Al Anon spokeswoman, herself both the child and the spouse of alcoholics. "But later I realized that harboring it wasn't any good for me, and things smoothed out."

We ACOAs are like the army of soldiers that sprang up overnight in the old myth. The tremors from this army are being felt in therapists' offices across the country. A spiritually based lay movement is challenging a secular, psychological priesthood. "It's a grass-roots movement that has revolutionized mental health and nobody's adjusted to it," says Stephanie Brown, the founder of the Stanford Alcohol Clinic, and the author of a widely respected academic book on treating adult children of alcoholics. "Patients are diagnosing themselves, and saying they want a treatment designed for them. They're often more informed than the therapists. It's terrorizing both the chemical dependency and the mental health fields, because it reveals big holes in theory and practice in both worlds. The chemical dependency counselors have no theory or practice of long-term development; the rest of the mental health field is splintered and overspecialized and often unaware of the special dynamics of chemical dependency. There's no longer any single theory or treatment that will do the trick."

Like a 900-pound gorilla, the ACOA movement cannot be ignored, and it is forcing the creating of bridges: between individuals and family therapy; between family therapists and chemical dependency counselors; between M.F.C.C.s and L.C.S.W.s; between once antipsychological 12 Steppers and often antispiritual psychologists.

Some principles of family therapy have been brought to a mass audience, and at the same time the ACOA movement's poignant insights have literally struck home for some therapists. "Suddenly I had a language," says a family therapist who had grown up in a home where Daddy (*continued on page 29*)

Recovery: A Modern Initiation Rite

A LEGACY OF DISTRUST STILL EXISTS BETWEEN THE RECOVERY MOVEMENT AND THE MENTAL health community—much to the disservice of millions of addicts who need access to both. Many therapists remain deeply uncomfortable with the spiritual dimensions of the 12-Step programs. The insistence that addicts give themselves up to a "higher power" strikes many as superstitious and as likely to foster emotional dependency as drugs or alcohol. On the other hand, people who believe that their lives have been saved by this movement often resent therapists for giving so much attention to seemingly abstract psychodynamic issues and completely missing the point that the addict's present life is out of control. They particularly value the spiritual component of 12-Step programs that help them face, often for the first time, the painful question for which their addiction had been a kind of anesthetic: Why am I here? What is the meaning of my life?

Therapists might be more hospitable to the 12-Step programs if they could visualize this quest for meaning—also one goal of therapy—as an initiation rite, a structured passage from childhood to adulthood once present in all cultures. The traditional function of the initiation ritual was developmental; it provided a formal, socially sanctioned transition between childhood and adulthood. But it also imbued this shift with cultural grandeur and religious significance. Through initiation rituals, young people in traditional societies could confront and resolve existential anxieties about death and the meaning of life, learn what would be expected of them as adults, and direct their energies and emotional turbulence into socially productive channels. The lack of a formal initiation has left a social vacuum in our society, and is linked to increasing self-destructive behavior, particularly among adolescents and young men and women. Lacking meaningful and evocative ceremonies of transition, many young people turn to alcohol, drugs, aggression, even suicide in a lost, desperate grasp for transcendence.

Indeed, several pioneers in the mental health field believed that addiction was related to unfulfilled spirituality. William James thought alcoholics were "frustrated mystics." Carl Jung speculated that addiction to alcohol might represent an unconscious longing for "spirit." In the mid-1930s, he gave up on a patient, calling his alcoholism "hopeless," and sent him on a search for "vital, spiritual experience." This now-famous search led indirectly to the founding of Alcoholics Anonymous. Gregory Bateson analyzed the success of AA, describing how the alcoholic's surrender—withdrawing from the field and allowing a higher power to take up the struggle—provides a profound cognitive and emotional shift of self to context, much like an initiation rite process.

The initiation process can be divided into three parts. The process begins when the initiate is separated from the family and goes through a period of hardship and anonymity during which the individual's old identity is broken down. It is completed when the initiate experiences a symbolic rebirth and becomes reintegrated into the community, with a new identity based on a deeper appreciation of the mysteries of existence. Most traditional rites include a physical ordeal, like circumcision, starvation, isolation or other rituals meant to simulate a death experience. After surviving, the initiate is instructed in the tribal lore, often including a dramatic reenactment of myths about the origins of society and a ceremonial renewal of the laws and customs presumably given to a people by their creator at the beginning. Initiates are expected to surrender childhood fantasies of being perpetually cherished by solicitous kin. They are made to realize that a transcendent reality, not individual human will, guides the universe, and that they must submit to responsibilities clearly defined within a vast cosmological framework. Often, an initiate is given a new name symbolic of the new status.

The recovery movement bears some striking resemblances to this process. The first of the 12 Steps—acknowledging one's powerlessness and lack of control over one's life—corresponds to the initiate's realization that his or her life, as an individual outside a cultural and religious network, has no meaningful purpose. As anthropologists know well, the uninitiated are not considered real human beings within their society. Addicts must next recognize the insufficiency of their own will; only after realizing their fundamental powerlessness and spiritually surrendering themselves can they remake their own lives. In both initiation and recovery, subjects must break with their past; the addict is told to cleave to the new network and forsake the "people, places and things" associated with the old life of addiction. By attending meetings, the addict learns the history and folklore of the recovery movement. Nameless, shorn of the old identity, not yet reborn, the addict observes others reenact the passage from despair to recovery, reads the literature describing the 12 Steps, and hears the folklore and sayings of the movement. At some point, the addict, like the initiate, may seek a sponsor as a guide on the journey of recovery.

Having spiritually surrendered the old self, the addict is now ready to make reparations to those he or she has harmed and enter the role of the newly reborn self. Neither dependent nor completely independent, the recovering addict experiences a new relation to a higher power and a deeper sense of responsibility to others. Eventually, the addict is ready to face the challenge of the 12th Step: transmitting the legacy of recovery to others, by initiating them into the fellowship.

In a brilliant adaptation of traditional initiation ritual, the recovery movement recasts the addict's dissipation, dissolution and self-destruction not as final in themselves, but as elements of an unexpectedly larger, expanded reality. Within the 12-Step paradigm, "hitting bottom" is transformed from the last step in a fatal process to the first step of recovery. The addict's ruin is no longer the meaningless end of a sorry melodrama, but the crucial prelude to the recognition of personal helplessness, corresponding to the ordeal leading to ritual death in initiation rites.

Unlike initiates in tribal societies, however, who leave the initiation process to blend with the larger community, recovering addicts never abandon their identification with the addiction, and never reach a point when they can say with confidence that their passage is complete. Perhaps in cultures where the sacred permeates every activity, one initiation experience is enough to orient the person for life, but in our culture, where the sacred occupies a tenuous place, the 12-Step fellowships believe that only constant recognition of the individual ego's vulnerability will fortify the addict against the amoral and seductive cultural ethos of instant self-gratification.

Like initiates, recovering addicts have undergone an intense reorientation to their world, a powerful reeducation process, and have been forced—for spiritual, social and even physical survival—to become new people. In a sense, therapy also aims to help clients shed a brittle and outgrown husk and emerge "reborn." Yet, therapy alone cannot provide the rugged fellowship of others who have "been through it" themselves; only through this common struggle can addicts be compelled to see the world as bigger than their own individual need. □

—David Dan
SEPTEMBER 1990

DAVID DAN, M.S.W., *is director of Lower Merion Counseling Services in suburban Philadelphia, PA.*

(continued from page 26) passed out under the Christmas tree. She had never thought of him as alcoholic until she attended a workshop on alcoholic family roles. "In a funny way, learning that I had lived with alcoholism gave me a perspective on myself that allowed me to feel less sick," she says.

Some therapists have responded with caution, hostility, or even envy. Others—of widely ranging competence and experience—have jumped on the bandwagon, advertising themselves as ACOA specialists. And a growing group have found a middle ground: they encourage clients to join 12-Step programs and are fashioning ways for the two forms of healing to support each other.

Jo-Ann Krestan, a family therapist based in Brunswick, Maine, and coauthor, with Claudia Bepko, of *The Responsibility Trap,* believes that 12-Step groups provide a sense of mutual helping that therapy can't. "Shame has to be healed, not in isolation, but in community," she says. "And therapy is not about mutuality. No matter how egalitarian you are, the therapist has the power."

Bepko adds that the emotional work encouraged by the ACOA movement must often be done before Adult Children can take on more cognitive forms of therapy. Bepko, trained as a Bowen-style family therapist, found that Adult Children often do not respond well at first to the Bowen approach's nonemotional coaching to change family patterns of interaction. "When people begin to realize they have been affected by alcoholism, they go through a period of being very angry, feeling a lot of grief and experiencing themselves as victims," she says. "Often it's not possible to do the coaching until they have a chance to sit with those feelings, feel them, and work them through. Then they're ready to move to a more cognitive level and change some of the family patterns and dynamics."

Some family therapists—such as psychiatrist David Berenson of Mill Valley, California—live with a little cognitive dissonance. "The systems theorist part of me doesn't like the labeling, but the clinician within me finds it's very helpful to send people to a program where they can relate to people's stories," says Berenson, who routinely recommends clients to 12-Step programs if they qualify. "The label can be very helpful as a way to begin experiencing emotions—and then later it's necessary to take the label off. And then there's the practical issue," he says with a smile. "I like to combine 12-Step programs and therapy, but the truth is, it cuts down on the number of therapy sessions. Nevertheless, I prefer it, because it also cuts down on transference. People get many of their needs for emotional and social support met, so all of their emotional intensity is not channeled into the therapy session. I can be more of a consultant, and their sponsor does more of the direct helping."

Some therapists who are enthusiastic about older 12-Step groups like AA and Al Anon are nonetheless cautious about the newer groups for ACOAs. Janet Woititz, a chemical dependency counselor and author of the best-selling book *Adult Children of Alcoholics,* recommends that her clients spend a year in AA or "regular" Al Anon before attending groups targeted for ACOAs. "If the ACOA groups spend their time returning to the traumas of childhood and blaming parents, they are counterindicated," she says.

Tarpley Richards Long, an L.C.S.W. in private practice in Washington, D.C., has had clients attend a single ACOA meeting and never go back. "There are some meetings, usually the ones connected with Al Anon, that adhere closely to the 12-Step program and use solid common sense expressed in workable, day-to-day language," she says. "Then there are ACOA splinter groups that are almost like leaderless psychotherapy groups, where people stand up and talk about how they've been harmed by their parents, and give long, wrenching descriptions of incest. The antidote for people who have difficulty with feelings is not to flood them with feelings but to be gradual and very cautious."

AFTER 18 MONTHS IN MY MONDAY NIGHT MEET-
ing, I found myself a sponsor and systemically
worked the 12 Steps. At first, the steps seemed
pious and irrelevant: *I'm trying to work out my pain.
What does making lists of my faults or figuring out who
my "higher power" is have to do with anything?* I did
them only because I was still desperate. In practice,
it boiled down to this: I tried to refrain from the
busybody quality that was hurting my new marriage
and to express what I needed without blame. I
admitted that I couldn't do it alone. I straightened
out my relationships by admitting my faults and paying my debts, and I accepted help from a Higher
Power whom I defined simply as a "force of rhythm
and meaning" in the universe.

Sometimes I still cried at meetings, and yes, once
in a while meetings were a ritual blame-a-thon for us
all. But for me, those years of grief and rage—as I
reinterpreted my family history, putting alcohol back
in the picture—were necessary ones. I had had "a
normal response to an abnormal situation." My
father's cruelty came not because I deserved it, nor
from gratuitous meanness. It was the striking-out of
a man who was often under the influence of alcohol,
hung over, or desperately trying to keep his drinking
under control. This explanation—this new myth, if
you will—allowed me to admit what had happened
to me without giving up my love for him, or his for
me.

In Al Anon I found acceptance, a community of
peers, a priesthood of all believers, help freely given
in a society otherwise dominated by the market
economy. There was someone there to hear me as
long as I needed to grieve. In a culture where we
hardly know how to talk to one another anymore except in the language of television commercials and
bumper stickers, we members of the Monday Night
Group found a way to speak of what holds meaning. In a culture where real community is scarce and
families broken, we were a real community, albeit an
anonymous, instant one, reconstituting each week

and then dissolving into the night. In a culture with
an exaggerated sense of human perfectibility and the
efficacy of human will, we had a metaphor—"disease"—that allowed us to face our problems and get
help from each other without blaming ourselves, or
others, for our limitations.

WE BORROWED THE DISEASE METAPHOR
wholesale from Alcoholics Anonymous,
which describes alcoholism as a progressive,
fatal disease that can never be cured, but only ar-
rested through abstinence. This metaphor is now
widely applied—to compulsive spending, sex, gambling, overeating and "codependence"—and there
are Anonymous groups to match. Participants say
the metaphor works: they stop searching for causes
and get group support to change unwanted behavior. I visited a Debtors Anonymous meeting once,
and I heard more sanity about American compulsive
consumerism than I have ever heard anywhere. But
there are limits to the accuracy of the metaphor.
Abstinence—the solution for alcoholics—obviously
cannot be practiced 100 percent when it comes to
eating, having relationships, or taking care of others.
In the absence of a subtle and well-articulated theory integrating the existing body of psychological
knowledge with the realities of life in alcoholic families, the popular movement has cobbled together
psychological models populated by black and white
stick figures.

"The popular press is at the vanguard of the
movement," says Stephanie Brown. "The media has
defined a clinical mental health population by lifting
denial, but it stopped there. Practitioners and
patients are getting hooked into assuming they can
read self-help books and change a lifetime of development, which is absurd." Brown is particularly
impatient with the buzzword "codependence,"
which was first used to describe partners "addicted"
to rescuing and caretaking alcoholics, and then
extended to ACOAs with similar low self-esteem.

Codependence theorists now call the behavior epidemic. They describe a fairly universal set of human weaknesses, including the compulsive practice of self-denial, dishonesty, and what used to be a virtue—putting another's needs before your own.

"Codependence is a global term describing a reactive, submissive stance to a dominant other—something that is part of all human behavior but is now being perceived as entirely negative," says Brown. "There's such a thing as healthy dependence—being able to rely on someone else to do what they say they'll do, in a partnership, for example. The codependence label is antineedy, antidependent; it's very isolating and it reinforces all the problems Adult Children bring from their childhoods. It encourages rejecting others, being unkind and ungiving, and it's antagonistic to good, healthy altruism. I was walking down the street with a colleague, and when I leaned over to pick up a piece of paper she told me I was being codependent. Multiply that attitude exponentially and you have a ludicrous and inhuman world."

For Jo-Ann Krestan—a strong believer in AA and Al Anon—the lens of codependency can discourage people from negotiating changes in their relationships. "I had a client who was trying to renegotiate the rules of her relationship and get her needs met. Her partner got angry, and punished her by withdrawing," Krestan says. "At their respective meetings of Codependents Anonymous, both were told, 'What do you expect? You can't get water from a dry well!' That's ignoring a systems view of change—of course, the first reaction is negative. You've got to hang in there past that first reaction."

Krestan is also alarmed by what she sees as a tendency of the mass movement and its gurus to offer an implied promise that there is a sanctuary, somewhere, from the pain, limitation and imperfection associated with being human. "I've seen people clutching checklists as if they were Bibles," she says. "I've spoken at conferences where I've been overwhelmed by the pain in the room, and I didn't want

to be one more broken promise," says Krestan, who is frustrated by what she calls a "lunatic fringe" that has overglobalized the insights of addiction theory.

"I've wanted alcoholic-family issues to have a serious hearing within family therapy, and that was beginning to happen," says Krestan. "Now there's a backlash, and why wouldn't there be? I'm worried by simple solutions—that if you do 'recovery' right you can have it all; that the child within will be healed, and the adult will have no pain; that relationships are not work; that parents or partners are to blame and you don't have to take personal responsibility." To Krestan, even the label of the movement is a contradiction in terms. In the long run, Krestan said, "You cannot be an 'Adult *Child*.'"

For some therapists, the label "Adult Children" conjures up images of people living forever under the volcanoes of their childhoods, feeling condemned and defined by their pasts. Says Michael Elkin, a Boston therapist and former heroin addict who wrote *Families Under the Influence*, "If you identify yourself as a survivor of incest or abuse, you are making an existential and self-hypnotic statement that defines you by the most destructive thing that ever happened to you. In the short term, it's important to say it, but you can get stuck there—just as it's important to express your anger, but if you're still doing that six months later, you've got caught. We all want to feel like victims. Self-righteous indignation is the hardest drug to beat."

Such excesses within the ACOA self-help movement may tempt some therapists with limited training in addiction to dismiss it. But the grass-roots movement—with all its limitations—shows that professionals have failed to grapple with the realities of people's lives. "The reason this is a grass-roots movement—just like the movement around sexual abuse and domestic violence—is that as professionals we've been sitting on our hands for years, not being helpful," says Lori Dwinell, a Seattle-based psychiatric social worker specializing in grief, depression and alcoholism. "Some family therapists say 12-Step programs are a cult. But what infuriates them is that it's not *their* cult, not *their* special language being spoken. The issue is control. Self-help movements can do harm as well as good, but they are a reality of the contemporary scene. The people involved are fairly sophisticated shoppers. If you don't speak their language—or more importantly, let them speak it—they'll go somewhere else, to someone less snooty about how they frame their problem."

I RECENTLY CALLED MY OLD SPONSOR ON THE phone. Raised in Morocco, Australia, and all around the world by an alcoholic, pot-smoking father, he joined the Monday Night Meeting at 22, lonely, depressed, and afraid to pursue his ambition to act. He is 27 now and on the brink of qualifying for Artists' Equity; he rarely goes to the Monday Night Meeting anymore. "I got lots of awareness and acceptance, but I wasn't getting any action," he explains. "I'd pray for knowledge of God's will for me, and then I would sit and wait for something to happen. I didn't get that it was up to me." I asked him whether he thought that ACOA meetings were keeping people stuck. "The program works. People will grow up and get out of the victim role if they do the Steps—but not all of them do," he says. "ACOA is like a hospital ward or a recovery room. The point is to get better and go out in the world, not to live in the hospital forever."

When I drop into the Monday Night Meeting these days, I find that many of my old companions have gone on, and in their place are newcomers first coming to terms with their family alcoholism. Sometimes I hear people talking as though their problems were simply choosing "bad" people—addicts, alcoholics, abusers—and that once they "recover" they will find mythical "good" people who will treat them well. But on the whole, what I have seen in myself

and others is healing, something magical that I can't even try to explain.

I see my father now not so much as an alcoholic but as someone who has moved in and out of alcoholic activity all his life. He has never stopped drinking, but he hasn't drunk himself into the grave or the mental hospital in the inexorable progressive way that AA literature describes. (He may, if my mother dies before him, and if he does, I'm sure I'll find myself back in "regular" Al Anon.) In any case, I'm less preoccupied with it, and once in a while, when I hear that familiar slurred and absent tone on the phone, I don't prolong the call. I finally quit a job I'd kept for years because I was afraid my father would disapprove if I left.

I'm happier in my own life, my marriage is happier, and I do more of what I want these days. Two years after I wrote my father those angry, grieving and accusatory letters—two years of Al Anon, some bitter fights, a few family therapy sessions with my parents and individual therapy with someone supportive of 12-Step programs—I was ready to make a week-long visit home.

My father wrote to me—a brief letter, on two sheets of white stationery—shortly after he and my mother dropped me off at the airport limousine. "Imagine my surprise last Monday, the day after taking you to the limo, when I discovered a turning point—that a visit from a truly benign being gave me a week of unalloyed and quite exceptional pleasure," he wrote. "The being was not exactly a stranger, but she was, in some way difficult to describe, new, with a competent and generous interest in what I was doing. . . We ached the afternoon you left, but now we remember simply the joy." ■

"LILY COLLET" *is the pseudonym of a Mill Valley, CA, writer whose work has been published in* The New Yorker, Mother Jones, The Washington Post *and elsewhere.*

PHOTOGRAPH BY STEPHEN SHAMES/MATRIX

RESTORING THE SOUL OF THE FAMILY

GRANDPARENT-HEADED FAMILIES FIGHT THE ODDS AGAINST SURVIVAL

By Bruce Buchanan and Jay Lappin

A THERAPIST IS CONDUCTING A SESSION WITH A 63-year-old black grandmother, Louise, and three of her grandchildren, Janet, 14, Derek, 12, and Krista, two and a half. This is only the family's third session in six weeks; they have canceled or failed to show up for three other appointments. Derek is the identified patient, although everyone in the room could easily carry that honor. A sullen, angry boy, Derek has already been held back once in school and appears to be failing again. His teachers are fed up with his mouthy attitude and clownish horseplay, and his school counselor has already talked with Louise several times. Louise quietly listened to the standard discipline-begins-at-home lecture, not even bothering to voice her real feeling that "when he's in school, he's your problem." Derek's mother, Sheila, is a crack addict, and his father is in jail for drug dealing.

Two years ago, Derek and his sisters were living with Sheila in an increasingly common urban horror story. Sheila had ceased functioning as a mother, letting her children look after themselves, even selling the family's food to support her habit. Janet and Derek were truant from school for most of the year. Janet, starved for any affection and human warmth, had become sexually active and acquired a sexually transmitted disease by her 12th birthday. Graced with a cheerful spirit and strong capacity for survival, Janet learned to bend to her mother's exaggerated mood swings to avoid being beaten. Derek wasn't so lucky. When Sheila craved the pipe, which was most of the time, she became desperate and violent. Merely a sideways glance or barely audible mutter from Derek would earn him another scar from a fist, belt buckle or ironing cord. Eventually, Derek simply ran away from home, and began sleeping in abandoned cars.

During that time, Louise, who didn't realize just how bad things were, tried to help out, though in mostly unhelpful ways. She would yell at the kids to mind their mom, and give Sheila a few extra dollars in return for another iron-clad guarantee that the money would be well spent. Finally, the birth of Sheila's crack-addicted and neurologically impaired baby, Krista, made reality undeniable. Louise, the hospital and Child Protective Services intervened, and Grandmom reluctantly became a full-time mother again.

TODAY THE THERAPIST, EILEEN, A YOUNG WOMAN in her midtwenties, listens to Louise, battle-worn and angry, attack Derek and the therapy team as well. "I've had it. This ain't helping. He's not getting any better—he's getting worse. This kid, you can't crack him. He doesn't do anything I tell him. He just sasses me and gives me that look of his. I'm telling you—he's evil and I've had it. He needs to be put away in a home or something. I'm not dealing with him no more!" Derek turns away and silently looks down at his Nikes. Janet, as if to agree with her grandmother, shakes her head and takes Krista on her lap to stop her crying.

Eileen unconsciously pulls her chair a half-step away from Louise and toward Derek. She takes a deep breath and thinks to herself, "No wonder this kid runs away," and tries to lower the tension in the room while simultaneously coming to Derek's rescue. Eileen turns to Louise and says, "I can tell that you're really upset and I understand your anger, but I don't think that what you are doing is helpful. There's no way that Derek will be able to change if he only hears criticism. As for us not helping—well, Louise, therapy is a slow process, and you have missed a lot of sessions." Louise simply glares at Eileen in disgust and says, "You don't get it. I didn't ask for this—he's the problem. The boy is bad, and I'm not dealing no more—you keep him!"

The intercom buzzes with a message from the supervisor to Eileen, asking her to take a break and consult with the team behind the mirror. Once out of the room, Eileen pours out her frustration to her colleagues and supervisor. Just as Louise has had it with Derek, Eileen would like to be rid of Louise. The training group is demoralized; this is the third time in a week they've heard a custodial grandmother push vigorously for placement of one or more of her grandchildren. This is also the third time in a

week that the therapist has been drawn in by the pain of a child, almost to the point of excluding the adult, who then feels abandoned in the therapeutic relationship.

The team encourages Eileen to vent her distress, but then asks what she thinks Louise's experience must be. Quickly she is able to take a more systemic stance. The decision is made that if the goal is to keep the family together, Eileen must convince Louise that she is in her corner 100 percent. Again, for the third time this week, the team will practice and observe a major sequence of interventions that we have loosely termed "You're stuck with me."

THE DEPTH OF THE CRACK CRISIS REALLY HIT home for us this past year, when we found that among the 60 families seen by the training group we direct and supervise, we repeatedly encountered grandparent-headed families caught in the same struggles as Louise and her family. For therapists working with poor, urban families in which both parents are impaired by drugs, willing grandparents are often the last hope before one or more of the children must be placed in the custody of the Department of Human Services.

As we tried to find ways to help these families, we realized that we had to rewrite the book of structural family therapy. We found that our families were not the same ones Salvador Minuchin talked about in *Families of the Slums* or *Families and Family Therapy*. The grandmother-headed households in today's crack-devastated neighborhoods are making a crazy stew of standard organizational patterns, blending ingredients from step, extended and foster families, liberally sprinkled with gerontologic and addiction issues as well. We no longer had the luxury of simply restoring hierarchies, creating boundaries, and breaking through enmeshment patterns. The families we saw were so dramatically disconnected, so chaotic, that they barely hung together at all; they had been robbed of the very soul of their identities as families.

WHEN EILEEN RECONVENES THE SESSION, Louise has her overcoat on and her purse in her lap, making all too clear her intentions. Derek continues to look down, refusing to let his sadness or anxiety show. Eileen pulls her chair closer to Louise and says, "Louise, I think I owe you an apology. I didn't realize before how much Derek was pushing you to the wall. Even in here he's doing it, muttering under his breath and disrespecting you. I don't think he has any idea of what you've done for him and his sisters. You saved their lives! They could have been dead in another week, but you refused to let it happen. You have sacrificed a period of your life when you should be able to put up your feet and watch the world go by in order to give these kids a family and a future. And this is the thanks you get. You keep giving and giving, and Derek's just taking and taking, and you're not getting anything back. I think it stinks. And I can certainly see that if Derek doesn't begin to change soon, placement may be the only alternative." Louise looks down, her eyes filling up with tears, and says, "I'm just so tired. I just don't know how much more I can take."

Eileen then says, "Louise, I would like to have another member of the team meet with Derek in a separate room to try and find out what's making him tick and how to help him, while you and I meet so that I have more of a chance to understand what Derek is like at home. Would that be all right with you?" Much of Louise's rage has drained away, and now, looking spent and tired, she just nods "Okay." Eileen has accomplished the first goal agreed upon behind the mirror. Louise is able to see that she is no longer quite so isolated, so unsupported. And, perhaps even more important, Eileen has acknowledged Louise's sacrifice for her grandchildren.

At the emotional heart of the grandparent-headed family is the experience of ambivalence, in itself nothing new to therapists, but showing up here with a ferocity that demands far more from the therapist than mere technical expertise. These grandparents—primarily grandmothers—must choose between accepting and struggling through a forced second parenthood under harrowing conditions or salvaging some remnants of their own lives by abandoning their grandchildren. But despite the immensity of this decision, how these women feel at any moment of any day typically rides upon scores of small interactions. If she receives a hug or smile from a grandchild, or a real sign of support from a friend, teacher or neighbor, it may be enough to anchor her in the sense that "this is my family—it's hard, but it's worth it." Alternatively, the turmoil of dealing with an unappreciative, hostile kid who refuses to do his homework, an unexpected visit from an addicted and disruptive daughter, or a delay in a public assistance check can make her give up— "These aren't my kids; I shouldn't have to be doing this for the second time around."

Therapists must be capable of the kind of empathy that allows them to understand both sides of a grandparent's dilemma. In the clinic, we see the ambivalence acted out dramatically during crisis periods. The rapid shift from expressions of complete loyalty to the grandchildren to bitter denunciation of them during a session—often within seconds—can be unsettling to a therapist, who must develop a tolerance for these instantaneous flips and a sensitivity to what triggers them. We must be sounding boards for both sides of the ambivalence and, even more, tenacious advocates for the full and open expression of it. If a grandmother cuts herself off from her own internal dialogue, she is likely to vacillate wildly between guilt-induced overinvolvement with her grandchildren and resentful desires to abandon them.

Often we introduce the grandmother to her own ambivalence by voicing for her the half she is unable to admit. A number of common themes turn up, including her resentment, the feeling that she has been cheated out of a deserved retirement, and the defeated sense that she has failed her first go-round of child rearing. The emergence of these "gypsy truths" often releases a wellspring of emotion that dissipates the anger, blame and punishment the grandmother usually directs at the child.

Though our goal is to keep families intact when possible, we don't try to talk a grandmother out of her conviction that her grandchildren should go into placement. Trying to argue her into family preservation only creates an escalating sequence of attack and defense and leaves her feeling that nobody is listening to her. Instead, we discuss placement as a real option, though not a very desirable one. When we make plain to the grandmother the realities of placement—the paucity of decent facilities for poor children and the loss of control that the family will experience—she usually rethinks her decision to have the child "put away" somewhere. Simply discussing placement as a concrete possibility, however, helps the grandmother regard the therapist as an ally rather than a child saver, and makes her more likely to be open to therapeutic challenges further down the road.

A S EILEEN LISTENS TO LOUISE—CLOSELY, WITHout trying to persuade her of anything—she is able to appreciate the oppressive sense of isolation that dominates her life and her disappointment at Derek's rejection of her attempts to help him. The two discuss placement as a choice, and Louise begins to equivocate. Meanwhile, another therapist meets with Derek. A typical crack kid, robbed of his childhood, he has lived his life taking care of adults. Throughout the meeting, his own ambivalence emerges, toward both his mother and grandmother. He worries about his mom, afraid that she will overdose or get killed. He feels guilty about not being with her, not watching out for her. At the same time, he remembers the beatings but dismisses them, preferring to idealize his mother. He doesn't like living with his grandmother. "All she wants me

to do is rest," he complains. "I can't go outside like a normal kid. I think she thinks I'm a rest machine." But, finally, he admits that as much as he doesn't like living with his grandmother and listening to her yelling, he is also frightened that he might not have a home in the near future—that Grandmom will die because he will give her a nervous breakdown or a heart attack, or that she'll simply kick him out. Derek gives the okay for the therapist to let his grandmother know about his fears.

The stage is set, and Louise, Eileen and Derek's therapist meet together. Louise is now more relaxed; she feels she's been heard and the severity of Derek's behavior is not being dismissed. She can absorb the report that Derek is hurting badly and that his fear of becoming a "hot potato" actually contributes to his bad behavior.

We now present a new challenge to Louise. She must decide up front whether she wants the team to help her deal with Derek in the family or if the goal should be family separation and placement. Either way, Eileen explains, the team is committed to her and Derek, to see them through the entire process, no matter what it takes or however difficult. What won't work, however, is to leave Derek's place in the family continually threatened and contingent upon his good behavior—"If you're good, you can stay. One wrong move, and out you go." We give no guarantees that Derek's behavior will improve if Louise tells him that she's not placing him, only that it cannot improve if he doesn't develop the security that comes with having a home where he belongs. We predict that he may become temporarily even more obnoxious if he hears he's staying with Louise; he will need to put her decision to the test.

Louise hears and understands. Supported by the therapist, within the cooling distance provided by her separate work with Eileen, she can allow herself to be touched by Derek's misery. She wants to keep Derek in the family, as long as she knows she can count on getting help. Again we challenge her. "Are you sure? Let's really think this through. You don't want to promise to contend with his next school suspension or temper tantrum, only to feel you can't stand it and have to change your mind in a week or so. We all know Derek pretty well. As you said, Louise, he's tough to crack"—an intentional modification of Louise's earlier statement that "you can't crack him." Louise insists that she's ready. Derek and the girls are brought back into the room.

Louise talks to Derek, who looks more anxious than before. "Derek, listen to me—I've been talking with Eileen about your behavior. I don't like it, and we're gonna keep coming here so it can get better. And Eileen is going to visit the school with me to discuss with Miss Johnson and Mr. Matthews how to help you there. But there's somethin' else I want you to know—you ain't gonna go in no home or hospital. You're gonna stay with me and Janet and Krista. But you're gonna change. You're stuck with me, you hear?"

Derek looks down and doesn't answer.

Eileen interjects, "Get him to answer you, Louise—you deserve an answer."

Louise sharpens her voice. "Look at me, Derek. Don't look down at your shoes. I asked you a question—you hear me?"

Derek looks up and says, "Yeah."

Louise says, "You better say 'Yeah,' because from now on the buck stops here."

Finally, to seal the matter and to further convince Louise that the team is with her, she is asked to give Derek a consequence for his actions before and during the session.

IN THE DAYS AND WEEKS TO FOLLOW, EILEEN WILL deal with the best and worst of Louise and Derek. Louise will change her mind again, and, as predicted, Derek will give Louise ample reason to reconsider placement. These first weeks are typically a period of maximum therapist involvement, when the time spent on case management often equals the hours in actual family contact. At this point, the therapist visits the home and school and works with other community resources to ease some of the grandmother's burden.

To an outsider, our therapists at this stage can appear overinvested in their clients or hyperresponsible. But we believe that if clinicians dealing with such vast and complex problems take their jobs seriously, they will have to leave the sanctuary of their offices. Just to make use of the available resources, they will have to become as proficient at working different city bureaucracies as old-style ward heelers.

Furthermore, we believe that unless therapists are wholeheartedly committed to keeping families together, they will find themselves quickly swept along by the grandmother's urgency to drop her burdensome grandchild in somebody else's lap. Or the therapists' own disapproval and dislike of the grandmother will undermine their resolution to preserve the family, and they both will be parties to an unspoken agreement in favor of placement.

The therapeutic strategy is to create between clinician and grandmother a kind of model for the relationship between grandmother and grandchild. Just as Louise has been coached to tell Derek that he's stuck with her—she won't let him go—so Eileen shows Louise that she won't be easy to shake off, either; she will hang in even when Louise is at her infuriating worst. Granted, this dogged pursuit of family solidarity requires a certain degree of therapeutic heroism, but a therapist-warrior who won't be easily daunted also gives a grandmother like Louise the courage to continue struggling on behalf of her family. Nonetheless, there is a big difference between heroics and martyrdom, which therapists and grandmothers both need to understand in order to avoid burnout. Eileen, therefore, will not take over for Louise, but she will work aggressively with her to expand her own network of resources in the family, the church, the neighborhood and the social services system.

Once we are sure the family is reasonably stable—once we don't hear at every session demands or heartfelt pleas to remove the child from the home—we can work on increasing the mutual pleasure that is the real glue holding families together. During this time, we assign tasks and rituals designed to further increase the grandparent's effectiveness, promote the health of the family, and counter discouragement and exhaustion. Many of these tasks are designed to help the grandmother to "steal back her grandparenthood"—time-limited tasks that break through the daily drudgery of reparenting. At these times, we assign activities such as having the grandmother share old photo albums and pass on the oral history of the family through stories to the kids, or giving a tour of old neighborhoods and homes where family members have lived. It not only develops a healthier heritage for the family, but it also creates an empowering teacher-student bond between the grandparent and grandkids.

When we assign tasks designed to allow grandmoms time off from parenting, we make sure that another adult is on hand as a parental surrogate to keep the kids in line. The grandmother isn't permitted to discipline during these times—she can only play, indulge, or pass on those parts of family culture that only she can know. Younger kids love it, and while adolescents put up initial resistance to it, their hunger for health usually wins out and they, too, end up sitting in wonder, though with a teenager's veil of cynicism. These tasks create a special atmosphere of mutual appreciation and giving, a time in which the family's memory banks, already overstocked with painful episodes and crises, can be resupplied with pleasant, or at least ordinary, nontraumatic aspects of family history.

This is our *modus operandi*. Would that it were all so simple and neat. Though we have helped most of the grandparents and grandchildren who have come to the clinic stay together as a family, a few kids have been placed. In those cases, we have held true to our original promise of guiding the family through the separation process as smoothly as possible. In a couple of cases, we have pushed for placement against the wishes of the grandmother. Even with our bias toward family preservation, and an eye to the unheralded strengths of the family, we do not minimize severe dysfunction; the safety of the child always comes first.

Sometimes a grandmother simply isn't able to provide the type of home or parental guidance that a child needs, but pride and shame won't allow her to realize it. Such was the case of 14-year-old Charlene. A chronic runaway, when she was not with her grandmother, Charlene hung out in crackhouses, using coke and contracting venereal infections. She was in real danger of acquiring AIDS. Her grandmother, in spite of all our efforts, simply refused to see what was happening to the girl, never confronted her, and fought any notion of placement. Unfortunately, even after an inpatient hospitalization and many attempts to get her placed, some involving the Child Protective Services, Charlene is still on the streets—one of those children who fall between the cracks of an overwhelmed and somewhat callous social services system. At last report, she had been gang-raped, but the only one pressing charges, besides us, was a pimp who was lining her up for his business. Still, the therapist continues to try, and hopefully she'll still be alive when we finally find a place for her.

Fortunately, we see more Louises and Dereks than Charlenes. Otherwise, we would all lose hope. As it is, hope, commitment and faith are what pull us and the grandmothers through. The grandmothers continually speak of the support they get from their religion and the church for getting through the day-to-day struggle. Their most fervent prayers are for their children to stop taking drugs; sometimes, when their prayers are answered, it is because their children have adopted their own spirituality as a first step toward recovery.

Even when their sons and daughters don't get well, the grandmothers still hold on to their faith and find their rewards in seeing their grandchildren become young again.

As Mary, one of the grandmothers, said, "I see him getting there—the street stuff is not getting in the house anymore. I can see a little light. He's alive again." ■

BRUCE BUCHANAN, M.A., M.S., *is director, Post-Masters Certificate Program in Family Therapy, University of Pennsylvania–Philadelphia Child Guidance Clinic and in private practice, Professional Services Group, Philadelphia, PA.*

JAY LAPPIN, M.S.W., A.C.S.W., *is associate director, Post-Masters Certificate Program in Family Therapy, University of Pennsylvania–Philadelphia Child Guidance Clinic. He is also in private practice in W. Collingswood, NJ.*

AN AIDS JOURNAL

CONFRONTING THE SPECTER OF A MODERN PLAGUE

By Gillian Walker

AUGUST 3RD: SOME OF US FROM THE ACKERMAN Institute's AIDS Project have been invited today to give a training session on working with AIDS patients for the nursing staff in the Riker's Island Prison hospital ward. There, in the prison hospital's tiny, stifling cafeteria, we are assaulted by a wave of rage. I am reminded of my husband's story about how the victims of the Bangladesh flood mobbed the reporters there to cover the story, bombarding them with tales of their suffering, not because the reporters could be of help, but simply because the survivors had a compelling need to have someone bear witness to what had happened to them.

The prison hospital staff tell us angrily that serving their 30 inmate patients with AIDS has them totally overwhelmed. They have no formal training in working with chronically ill AIDS patients, no AIDS education, and they are frightened. One person worried, "We've got a bumper crop of mosquitoes on Riker's this year. They say you can't get it from them, but we're scared." Their supplies and equipment are inadequate or inappropriate for their needs: rubber gloves are in short supply and often staff have to buy their own; their hospital gowns are short-sleeved, exposing arms to blood products and bodily wastes during medical or cleaning procedures.

They give us a tour of the prison hospital ward. The concrete floors are bare, there are no screens in the windows, and, on this 90-plus-degree day, no air-conditioning. The AIDS patients are locked behind bars each night in tiny cells so narrow that, when there is a medical emergency, the nurse is hard put to squeeze between bed and wall. In the lavatories are open latrines where prisoners with diarrhea, a common AIDS symptom, must have to stand in their own waste and that of others.

If patients have a severe medical crisis, they are shackled and taken to Kings County Hospital for emergency medical care. Since prisoners are considered the lowest of the low, lower still if drug users, and particularly dangerous if they have AIDS, they are not welcomed. As soon as they can survive without emergency treatment, the patients are returned to the prison, which, bad as it is, many prefer to the hospital.

The nursing staff, many of whom come from the same socioeconomic backgrounds as the prisoners, are people of love, courage and dedication. They are haunted by the prisoners' conditions, as well as frightened for themselves. But when they ask for improvements, they are told that this is a prison, not a hospital.

Talking with the staff about families and family therapy seems irrelevant in the face of the appalling reality of human misery.

MIDNIGHT, AUGUST 10TH: READING. MY LIVING room table is covered with papers, books, journals—an avalanche of information on AIDS. With so much uncertainty about AIDS and its dangers, so much new research going on, it is essential to keep on top of it all. The material enables me to answer the questions my clients are constantly asking.

Today a woman wanted to know the chances that her husband, a health care worker who had stuck himself with a needle that had been used on an AIDS patient, would himself get AIDS. "Most people develop antibodies by six weeks. A very small percentage do not," I told her. "On balance, if he's clean at six weeks, you can consider that he's okay. You'd better know, though, that there's a slight risk. But if you look at statistics, the odds are against his being infected."

So many of the answers to questions about AIDS have to do with statistics and probabilities. There are few certainties.

Being a part of the AIDS Project is like no other experience I've had as a family therapist. The project began three years ago, when a group of externs in the Ackerman Institute Family Therapy Training Program decided they wanted to continue their training. Laurie Kaplan, one of the externs, suggested that the group focus on a population family therapists were not serving—AIDS patients and their families. And so our group formed, with John

Patten and myself serving as codirectors. For the past two years, the team has met every Monday to see AIDS cases. Recently, we have also begun conducting trainings and consultations for health care workers around New York City.

So much has changed in our understanding of AIDS in such a short time. I remember seeing a number of hemophiliacs in the Ackerman Chronic Illness Project just a few years ago and talking with my AIDS researcher friends about the need for a clean blood supply long before an AIDS screening test was developed. Hemophiliacs require Factor 8, a blood product that must be made from the blood of thousands of donors, rendering hemophiliacs especially vulnerable to problems in the blood supply. At that time, the National Hemophilia Association and hemophilia physicians were telling patients to infuse as usual, even though some critics felt they were making a tragic error. Medical thinking at the time was that bleeds to the joint were more dangerous than the possibility of exposure to AIDS. I thought that if I were the mother of a hemophiliac, I would look for a Rasputin or try ice or hypnosis before I'd agree to infuse my child. But in reality, I suppose that I would follow my doctor's advice.

I remember one beautiful 4-year-old boy who was just going on home infusion. His mother had just been devastated by the loss of a brother to cancer. She and her husband started having bitter quarrels. Sensitive to his mother's grief and anger, the 4-year-old made an apparent suicide attempt. The little boy clearly understood his mother's unhappiness and felt with a child's prescience that her grief was also for him. He decided she would be better off were he to die. With careful therapy, the boy was reassured and the parents resolved their differences.

This morning, I was supervising a case in which the patient was a 10-year-old hemophiliac who was HIV positive and might be showing early symptoms of AIDS. The therapist reported that the mother was severely depressed and that the couple was fighting. Suddenly, I realized that the boy was the same child with whom I had worked so many years ago.

AUGUST 12TH: MILTON ERICKSON, THE GREAT hypnotherapist, has been our project's presiding spirit. Erickson once wrote: "Psychotherapists . . . tend to overemphasize the matter of adjustment to illness, handicaps, and death. There is a lot of hogwash going around about assisting families' grieving. I think you ought to bear in mind that the day you were born is the day you started dying. And some are more efficient than others and don't waste a lot of time dying and there are others who wait a long time."

I think often of the story Erickson used to tell about his experience of getting polio when he was 17: "Our country doctor had called in two . . . consultants and they told my mother, 'The boy will be dead by morning.'

"I was infuriated. The idea of telling a mother that her son would be dead by morning! It's outrageous!

"Afterwards, my mother came into the room, bland of face. She thought I was delirious because I insisted she move the large chest into my room, in order for it to be at a different angle beside the bed. She put it beside the bed one way and I kept telling her to move it back and forth, until I was satisfied. That chest was blocking my view through the window—and I was damned if I would die without seeing the sunset. I only saw half of it. I was unconscious for three days."

Erickson, of course, survived, and often it seems to me that much of our work with AIDS patients is about moving the chest so that people can see the sunset.

Both John Patten and I met Erickson in Phoenix many years ago. His was an unforgettable presence—confined to a wheelchair, color-blind, and dressed in the only color he could recognize, outrageous purple. Twice crippled with polio, Erickson

had difficulty speaking, and used every form of communication available to him, mumbling absurd jokes with Zen meanings, using every moment of life to the fullest.

The attitude Erickson's work exemplifies is very similar to that of the grass-roots groups that have worked most closely with AIDS patients, like the People With AIDS (PWA) coalition and the Gay Men's Health Crisis (GMHC). Surviving with AIDS depends in great part on attitude, determination, hopefulness, taking charge of one's medical care, and improving the quality of one's life. PWA and GMHC attempt to counter the despair of being considered "terminally, inevitably, fatally ill" by helping people learn to live with AIDS. They focus not on death but on connecting to the warmth of support systems, on providing opportunities for recreation, friendship, informal gatherings, meals shared together. The PWA Coalition's wonderful book, *Surviving and Thriving With AIDS,* has become a guidebook for us and our patients.

Today in a staff meeting, someone mentioned John Patten's beautiful work with Patrick, who, as an adult, had ritualized the childhood abuse he had received from his mother into sadomasochistic sexual practices. "If I saw my mother again, she would kill me or I would kill her," he said in an early session. When Patrick was diagnosed with AIDS, his S&M practices grew all the more dangerous because of the possibility of his wounds becoming infected and the danger of his blood infecting his partner. John worked with him hypnotically, emphasizing how his masochism protected his partner's needs in the same way that as a child he scrved as the whipping boy for his mother's own deep frustrations. Through his therapy with John, Patrick learned to utilize his newfound sensitivity in counseling other AIDS patients in S&M bars. Toward the end, he was reconciled with his mother before dying suddenly (not wasting any time at all, as Erickson might have noted) after a deeply satisfying last six months of his life.

AUGUST 13TH: I AM AT THE GAY MEN'S HEALTH Crisis today to do intakes. GMHC is the oldest, largest and most respected AIDS social service organization in the city. Our first impressions of GMHC made our team at Ackerman anxious to belong. We were all struck by the love, compassion, humor, and, perhaps most of all, by the open displays of affection so seldom seen in straight clinics and so necessary to people working in this area. Moreover, all this joy and affirmation of life existed in an organization whose staff spent much of its time dealing with death and dying, and not just the death of others—many staff members were themselves infected with the very disease they were treating.

Much to our surprise, our initial reception at GMHC was one of suspicion. Here we were, professionals from a prestigious institute, generously offering our services. The GMHC staff, however, did not take it for granted that we were not homophobic. In fact, they suspected that we were. Before we could join in working with them, we were forced to look at our prejudices and assumptions. A major part of our time in that first year was spent examining our attitudes toward life-styles that, for many of us, were alien.

The very skepticism of the Gay Men's Health Crisis toward our motivation—their suspicion that we were just another bunch of people getting on the AIDS bandwagon, exploiting the gay community, making our careers out of AIDS—was something we had to come to terms with and utilize in an Ericksonian sense. If the GMHC staff was skeptical about us, then we could take one of two positions: we could look at their skepticism and deepen our understanding of ourselves by addressing the issues they raised, or we could defend ourselves. I must say I veered between the two positions. There were days when I felt blind rage that I, who was such a good citizen, should not be accepted by this organization, and other days when I realized that the GMHC staff was more aware of my prejudices than I was.

We began to listen to the statements we made about cases—"Oh, what did that poor hemophiliac do to deserve AIDS?" Initially, this viewpoint seemed so reasonable to us; we did not hear the implicit prejudice and homophobia in it. Later it dawned on us that if the AIDS patient was gay, we were presuming that he had somehow brought this on himself.

Eventually, we began to feel a part of the gay community through our work at GMHC. We shared our sadness about clients, our hopes for a cure, or at least a life-prolonging medication, and our laughter—somehow the latest AIDS jokes always found their way first to the Gay Men's Health Crisis.

To work with AIDS, one must move out of the family therapy office into the community itself. Doing intakes in SRO rooms, the homes of the poor, in hospitals across the city, I began to see the conditions under which people with AIDS must live. It is a shock to see the yellow sign posted on the hospital room door, THIS IS A CONTAGIOUS DISEASE: BEWARE OF BODILY FLUIDS. Often the patient doesn't know or understand that the sign is there for all to see; he will assure you that his mother, sister, or brother do not know his diagnosis, even though they visit him daily.

My client at GMHC today tells me that he was recently diagnosed with AIDS. Because of fatigue, he was unable to work, could no longer afford to live independently, and was forced to move in with his mother. He expects to die soon. Since his diagnosis, he has become celibate, a short step from his sporadic dating pattern, but one that isolates him intolerably and leaves him bereft of human touch. Actually, attempts at celibacy after being diagnosed with AIDS sometimes backfire; in their starvation for intimacy, some people may launch into reckless sexual indulgence.

I sit with my client as he talks about his sense of loss—loss of identity as a working person, as a well person, and his loss of sexuality. He feels doubly stigmatized—by his gayness and by AIDS. The reddish-purple lesions of Karposi's on his skin are particularly hard for him to deal with. It is as if he carries with him the humiliation of a scarlet letter.

As the interview continues, I have two goals. The first is to offer medical information that will allow him to counter the common belief that AIDS is immediately fatal and that life with AIDS is a time of unspeakable misery. Slowly I introduce information about the available drugs that treat AIDS as a chronic condition. I sense the beginning of hope. The message of GMHC and the PWA Coalition is always, "Look, you have a future. You can live. Start to fight. Get involved, connect." Without hope, without support, morbidity and depression set in.

The second goal is to begin to connect him to the large network of people with AIDS. I know that entering this network will mitigate his sense of isolation. Initially he may be hesitant, not wishing to see himself irrevocably stamped as a person with AIDS, condemned to the society of others with AIDS. But once he can accept the richness of human connection that AIDS organizations can give, a social healing can begin.

I refer him to GMHC's telephone outreach, which calls clients regularly to check up on progress and encourages them to use services that will bring them into contact with other people. As I talk, he begins to relax, to look as though there is some hope for his life. I imagine that if he gets connected at GMHC, two months from now, even if his symptoms increase, he will be a different person. The gay community's response to AIDS has created informal support networks that provide many men with the most intimate friendships they have ever known.

AUGUST 21ST: STIGMATIZATION DOMINATES THE experience of AIDS. The disease is associated with behavior and symptoms for which society has the most complex ambivalence and dread—drug usage, sexual deviance, disfigurement and physical

dependency. The experience of stigmatization may be more devastating if the person has not had past experience of being, in Erving Goffman's term, a "discredited person," or if he has hitherto been able to successfully conceal his difference from the normal world.

Many of my clients have had to face this crisis. A gay young man named Joseph successfully achieved an accommodation between his two worlds, concealing his gayness from work associates and family, revealing it only to other gays and trusted straight friends. Now the diagnosis of AIDS has flooded him with the reality of difference. He fears that his friends will see him not as Joseph but as an ill person, ill and infectious. How will Joseph now tell those who were unaware of his secret life? He is now facing the prospect that his fragile structure of accommodation may shatter. Profound feelings of guilt have begun to overwhelm his carefully constructed identity as a gay man.

But the stigmatization of AIDS is not, of course, confined to gays. Today another client of mine, a leukemia patient who has functioned successfully, managing his "respectable" illness with medications and transfusions, describes to me his nightmarish experience of the past few months. Returning to work after going into remission, he readjusted quickly and his coworkers began to forget that he had been ill. Then a diagnosis of HIV infection put everything in jeopardy. He became obsessed with a skin rash, frightened that others could see his disfigurement and guess his condition. He worried over who knew, whom he could safely tell about his illness. He tried to decide whether he should inform his cardiologist, and if he did would the cardiologist still treat him? When the cardiologist seemed abrupt during an appointment, he wondered whether the doctor already knew from some report, or if his own tension had communicated the truth during their conversation. When making love to his wife, he imagined that she saw him as he saw himself, disfigured, poisonous. He became scrupulously careful not to ejaculate inside her, even with a condom. Afterward, he washed obsessively to remove the poison from his body.

Increasingly disoriented as everything familiar crumbled, he made a suicide gesture with an unloaded gun. He remembers being at that moment almost in a trance as he pulled the trigger. But it jammed, catching his finger. The pain and bleeding jarred him awake. Frightened at his loss of control, he allowed himself to be committed to a hospital. In the hospital, the nightmare began again—strange glances, an isolated room, a sensation that people were avoiding him or being too kind. When he was allowed out of his room, he realized that there was a red-and-white HIV infection precaution sign posted on his door.

SEPTEMBER 3RD: THIS MORNING A GAY COUPLE came to see me; one partner has been diagnosed as HIV positive. They are ambivalent about whether the other partner should be tested—"Isn't it better to hold on to a hope that at least one of us will survive?" The presenting problem is odd, in that they are here because they think that they must be having a problem, although neither feels much anxiety. While their relationship is closer, more intimate, and even physically more affectionate than ever before, they have lost all interest in having sex, once an important part of their long and faithful relationship.

As we talk, I learn that it has been a hard year. Several close friends have died this last summer. Their world is one of continual loss and mourning. Do they fear sexual intimacy because it is a painful reminder of potential loss, and of all those lovers, their friends, who have died?

Later in the day, I ask a colleague whether he is seeing many couples who avoid sex after a partner's diagnosis for AIDS. He says yes, it is tremendously prevalent. There is an inextricable connection between disease and contamination. My clients had spoken of their relationship as being more playful and childlike than it was before, as if nongenital play is somehow comforting. It reminds them of being small children, protecting each other against the storm. We talked of a world in which the young are dying, falling like soldiers on the battlefield. The need for comfort is enormous, but it seems to be often separate from sexual need. The odd thing, my clients say, is that they don't even notice the absence of sex. It doesn't seem to matter anymore.

SEPTEMBER 4TH: I AM REVIEWING THE TAPE OF A session with a well-educated gay couple in their twenties who are not observing safer-sex procedures. They are passionately sexual with each other, with all the ardor of the very young. George tests negative, Peter positive. Peter is showing the first signs of the disease: night fevers, diarrhea and weight loss so severe that one can see the outline of his bones beneath his skin. George says that it is he who should die, not Peter; he was the promiscuous one, the one who used drugs while Peter was always faithful and good. They have been together seven years. Neither feels that he could survive the loss of the other. George feels that were he to ask Peter to use a condom, he would be reminding Peter (and himself) of Peter's disease at that moment when the sweetness of lovemaking makes them most vulnerable to feelings of loss. "I am so frightened for him," George says, his young eyes filling with tears. Their dream is that they die together. A version of Romeo and Juliet, an AIDS suicide pact.

SEPTEMBER 7TH: THE 17TH CENTURY'S METAphysical poets, with their fascination with the entanglement of sex and death, wrote in another age when lovers died young. Today their work captures the mood of our times. I read it not only to comfort myself with its beauty, but also to understand the sexual experience of people who are ill, infected, or at risk for infection. The tender intimacy of sex stirs the most profound longings for the eternal union of the lovers, but ecstasy is shrouded with grief. Paradoxically, the sexual act must encompass the knowledge that sex is, literally, the instrument of the beloved's loss.

> *So, so break off this last lamenting kiss*
> *which sucks two soules and vapors both away,*
> *Tame thou ghost that way and let me turn thus*
> *And let ourselves benight our happiest days*
> *Goe, and if that word have not quite killed thee*
> *Ease me with death, by bidding me goe too.*
> —JOHN DONNE
> "THE EXPIRATION"

SEPTEMBER 29TH: WE ARE DOING A STAFF CONsultation for the pediatrics department of a city hospital. This morning, the staff observes while I interview a single mother whose 6-year-old boy, Michael, has AIDS. The boy has been hospitalized here several times before. He has pneumonia now, but the presenting problem is his repeated attempts to pull out his IV, as well as his intense depression and rage. During prior hospital stays, Michael was a model patient. This time, however, he is tremendously upset and the staff blame his mother, who they feel is cold and erratic. Michael was diagnosed with AIDS at the age of one and a half. He had done well medically, although he did not grow normally. At age 6, he weighed only 30 pounds. He was immensely bright, had attended kindergarten, made friends, and his mother planned for him to enter first grade this past September.

Last August he developed chicken pox. Instead of being admitted to our hospital, which Michael regarded as a second home, he was sent to a large city hospital with the facilities for handling highly infectious diseases. The pediatrics staff here were furious at this administrative decision. At the huge, impersonal city hospital, he was put in isolation, a terrible blow to the child and to his mother. After

four days, his mother also developed chicken pox and could no longer visit him. Michael panicked. He tried to pull out his IV, thinking perhaps that if he were not tethered, he could get home to his mother and safety.

When the staff there tried to hold him down, he became terribly angry, lashing out, trying to bite. So he was tied down and caged in a special restraining crib. He had to urinate and defecate in his bed. When he refused to eat, not wanting to capitulate to this terrible place, all his toys were removed from the room.

His mother found him there three weeks later in a bare room, restrained, caged. He melted into her arms and clung to her. He was a good little boy in the hospital after that, but when he went home he was very, very angry with her.

I don't want to imply that the staff of this city hospital was not caring or that they didn't want Michael to get better. But, like most staffs, they, too, were afraid of contamination. They were afraid of being bitten, they were afraid of a needle stick if they had to change his IV or give him an injection and he struggled and kicked too much.

After Michael was released, it was time for school. His mother, in her determination to give him a normal life, took him to his new first grade. Michael found that at this new school, his friends from nursery school began to jeer at him because he was so disfigured by the chicken pox. Not only was he shriveled, a tiny little thing, but he was covered with scars. Other parents told their children not to play with him because they suspected his illness was more serious than chicken pox. They demanded that the school tell them the status of his disease, something that under New York State law the school could not do.

Michael did what was sensible for a 6-year-old: he blocked out his pain and the humiliation by sleeping through the day. Of course, that meant that he was very energetic at three o'clock in the afternoon.

Soon he developed insomnia. By the time he got to the hospital with this new bout of pneumonia, he was not only a very sick little boy indeed, but also angry, depressed, and refusing to talk. He would not respond to the nurses, and he refused to have his IV unless his mother was present. So the nurses insisted on her being there.

Oddly enough, Michael's depression may have been made worse by the good intentions and caring of our hospital staff. When he came back to the hospital, so hideously disfigured with chicken pox scars, so depressed and silent, the staff felt terribly guilty, especially the pediatrician who had taken care of him since he was a baby. The staff, not able to bear the reproach that Michael's misery represented, struck out at the mother for not responding adequately to her son's depression. They wanted her to make up for the comfort they hadn't been able to give Michael when he was sick. But their reproachfulness may have prompted the mother to visit her son a little less. Eventually, this created a cycle in which the staff became even more angry, distressed and helpless at the little boy's refusal to let them comfort him.

Having heard the staff's presentation of the case, I sat with my eyes full of tears. I thought of Michael's mother waiting outside to see me and wondered how I would get through this interview without breaking down. Fortunately, the mother, a slim, 29-year-old black woman, who had been going through this since she was 23, had such strength and courage that she carried me through. "People here think that I don't know that Michael may die," she told me. "I know very well that he may die. But if he dies, right up to the end I want him to know that I, at least, believed that he was a normal boy."

What the staff saw as her coldness was, to her, a refusal to indulge her son, to give in to his manipulations. She was determined he would be "normal."

"He's a clever little boy," she said. "He does what he needs to do to get what he wants, but sometimes it's not good for him, and I won't tolerate that."

At the end of the interview I said, "You know, you're training him to be a little soldier and he needs to be a little soldier in fighting the big war he's facing. I think you've done very well in preparing him for that. But, as you know, every soldier after a long battle needs a little R and R, a time when the women hold him and cuddle him and comfort him. In a war, all men need to be babied a little because they have to do such superhuman things. And babying in that way doesn't turn them into babies, it turns them into brave men. Since your little boy has to be so brave, such a big soldier, I think he needs you to give him some R and R."

This mother was not someone who talked to her son much about his emotions, but in her own way she knew how to comfort him. Because that way was alien to the more middle-class and psychologically minded members of the staff, they didn't understand what she was doing. After the interview, however, they more clearly recognized that underlying her apparent coldness was an enormous determination to have her son live a normal life in a world that was hostile and increasingly stigmatizing to people with his illness.

OCTOBER 14TH: TONIGHT I READ C. S. LEWIS'S *The Silver Chair* to my 9-year-old son, Philip: *But the strange thing was that the funeral music for King Caspian still went on though no one could tell where it came from. They were walking beside the stream and Aslan the lion was before them: and he became so beautiful and the music so despairing that Jill did not know which of them it was that filled her eyes with tears. Then Aslan stopped and the children looked into the stream. And there on the golden gravel on the bed of the stream lay King Caspian dead with the water flowing over him like liquid glass.*

As I read, the unshed tears of the day well up. Philip puts his arms around me. "Don't cry, Mom," he says, and reminds me, "Aslan's with them." Each time Aslan appears, with his promise of gentleness and protection, Philip feels a strange exaltation, imagining a world where pain stops and the dead are risen.

OCTOBER 16TH: PHILIP WORE A GAY MEN'S Health Crisis T-shirt to school today. When I asked him what he would say if people teased him about being gay, he answered, "I'll say I'm too young to know."

I am proud of him; he insisted on going with me to the Gay and Lesbian Rights March on Washington to demonstrate for more AIDS funding. He has a strong sense of commitment to civil rights and gay issues. Wearing the T-shirt could lead to trouble at school, but he is willing to confront the questions.

I think Philip is helping me deal with a subtle homophobia I hadn't expected of myself. He is teaching me to be open to whatever sexual identity he may develop, and that is harder for me than I thought it would be.

OCTOBER 12TH: TODAY ON THE SENATE FLOOR, Jesse Helms said, "We've got to call a spade a spade . . . and a perverted human being a perverted human being" as he distributed GMHC's safer-sex comic book to all senators and representatives. The Helms amendment prohibiting the distribution of federal funds to organizations that "promote or encourage homosexual activity" passed the Senate 98 to 2.

Debates on the moral content of educational materials about AIDS have paralyzed government efforts to provide information about the epidemic to the people who need it. Safer-sex education programs, which have proven immensely effective in the gay community and which have been entirely funded by the private sector, are not offered in the inner city, where they are just as needed, because government funding would be required. This is true in spite of the fact that IV drug users, their sexual partners and their babies account for the largest number of new AIDS cases in New York City. As a result, the death rate from AIDS continues to soar within the inner city.

OCTOBER 31ST: TODAY THE AMERICAN ASSOCIA- tion for Marriage and Family Therapy, the major family therapy professional organization, gave a leadership award to Theresa Crenshaw, a sex therapist who is on the President's Commission on AIDS. Crenshaw represents a dangerous mood in the country right now, one which equates HIV infection with moral disorder. It is a mood Patrick Buchanan once sarcastically expressed in his comment that "the poor homosexuals, they have declared war on nature and now nature is exacting an awful retribution." The equation of HIV infection with moral disorder provides a rationalization for depriving citizens of basic rights.

Crenshaw is on record as saying, "Protecting the civil rights of some, while impinging on the civil rights of others, is resulting in greater numbers of infected people. Our society cannot let the exercise of the rights of someone who is infected cause someone else to become infected." Crenshaw believes that mandatory AIDS testing will not drive people underground, that you can legislate sexual morality, that contact tracing should be mandatory. She also voiced support for California's Proposition 64, which called for mandatory testing and quarantine for individuals deemed to prove a risk to others.

If civil liberties are sacrificed in an attempt to contain AIDS, these measures may have the opposite effect, forcing AIDS carriers underground. If discrimination, loss of basic rights to housing, insurance, education or work follow from a positive AIDS test result, why should people risk testing? As a society, we are facing a choice in how we approach the AIDS epidemic. We can treat people with AIDS as the bad, the *other*, and take away their rights, or we can treat this disease as if it belongs to all of us.

If we recognize that we are all brothers and sisters at risk, our only choice is to extend to the infected the same protections and rights that we would want for ourselves.

NOVEMBER 25TH: TODAY I WAS AT THE HOSPITAL, where I regularly consult on AIDS cases. I saw Michael, the 6-year-old who has been in and out of the pediatric ward so many times. He was sleeping and very beautiful. His thinness reminds me of the haunting children of Ethiopia. Last month, he went home with his mother shortly after our interview, but was recently readmitted because of lung complications. The pediatrician told me that now Michael often sits in his wheelchair at the nursing station with a sheet over his head. When his mother comes, he throws off the sheet and mother and son just hold each other, looking into each other's eyes with longing and love.

Our AIDS project is now more than two years old. When we started, no one was thinking about involving families in the treatment of AIDS patients. But in our work with medical professionals around New York City, we've been able to show how families can be brought in as allies within the medical system. At this time of crisis and burnout for so many health care professionals working with AIDS, our message has been received with interest and enthusiasm. Through our trainings and consultations, we have introduced family therapy in many medical settings, not only in relationship to AIDS treatment, but also to all kinds of medical conditions.

Today I saw a mother who is HIV positive and whose baby is dying of AIDS, while the pediatric staff observed. There is no one-way mirror on the unit; patient, family, therapist, hospital staff all sit together in one room during the interview. These sessions are almost always a powerful, healing experience for all of us, breaking down the barriers among the people involved in a case and creating a palpable sense of community. As we sit side by side in the room, responding to the emotion and intensity of the interview, it becomes immediately apparent that we are all in this together.

The mother had also brought her 7-year-old son to the interview. He seemed so frail, so tiny and so wise. He talked about the way he protects his mother. As she cries, he expresses his fear that she too will die. He had hidden his fears from her because he did not want to upset her, but he needed to ask her questions about her health and their future. He said, with a child's wisdom, "I know she can't really tell me if she'll get sick because she doesn't have the book of the future." But when she told him of her determination to live, he smiled and said he felt much better.

What she said was this, "When I was young I kept putting things off. Now with this virus I have no time. I want to live for my son. I want to live so that he'll say one day, 'I'm tired of you, you old lady.' I want to live for myself. There's a rainbow out there, and I want it. I may not make it, but I am sure going to try for it.'" ∎

GILLIAN WALKER, M.S.W., *is a senior staff member at the Ackerman Institute for Family Therapy and Codirector of its AIDS Project in New York, NY.*

THE SHELTER

EVERY DAY IS A STRUGGLE
TO KEEP THE FAITH

By Lascelles W. Black

MONDAY: THE MORNING LIGHT IS GRAY AND THE wind blowing down the hill is cold, damp, and seems like the breath of the large brick building that dominates the skyline. It is not really the tallest structure in the neighborhood, but it is the most imposing, appearing in the winter half light like a cross between Castle Mordor and Darth Vader's winter home. It was built as an Armory, a warlike building designed to be formidable, constructed to keep people out, not to welcome them like the large church diagonally across from it. Now it is a shelter, a place where more than 600 homeless men seek refuge.

New York City's Human Resources Administration runs the shelter; their staff provides case management and medical and job referrals. The shelter's client-staff ratio is hopelessly inadequate and staff turnover is high, mainly because of burnout. Few people can face the anger and depression of the men for long.

I work for a Community Support Systems (CSS) program placed within the shelter and administered by a nearby hospital. We provide mental health counseling, family therapy, job counseling, referrals to alcohol and drug abuse programs and occasionally assistance with carfare. But one of our most important services is the free phone we provide. It is a major help to people in the shelter who don't have the money for a phone call, and has made the difference in many men getting and keeping a job, renewing severed family ties, and getting themselves placed in needed programs.

Inside, I am greeted by five or six clients waiting for our program to open so they can get a cup of coffee; the shelter does not provide coffee for the residents. I make a phone call to the clinic on the first floor (operated by another nearby hospital) to inform our program's female staff members who prudently wait there that I, a male, have arrived. After coffee, the staff—one psychiatrist, one administrator, two social workers, two case managers and a secretary—begin seeing clients. I am a case manager here and I work primarily with the "first-timers," recent arrivals to the shelter. My job is to help them get out of the shelter before they are "shelterized," absorbed and lost within the shelter system.

Part of my caseload consists of clients who are established in the shelter system and have learned to survive here. One client is an artist, Hispanic, in his midthirties. He speaks as little as possible to the staff or other clients. This man approached me on the main floor about two months ago and asked if we provide art materials in our program. I told him about our art class. Now he comes here daily and docs his paintings of bowls of fruit and landscapes in the Impressionist style. His pictures radiate light and color and tell of memories far from this city.

Then there is the "caretaker," a client who believes he looks after us. He is a 30-year-old white man who has spent, by his estimation, more than 20 years in mental institutions. His experience has made him very good at assessing when other clients are suicidal or losing touch with reality. He likes to make coffee, clean the office, and do errands for staff, but he does not like to be thanked or told he is doing a good job. Another client I call the "sleeper," a black man in his early twenties, who spends most of the morning or the afternoon sleeping on the couch. He has politely declined offers of assistance, but has promised to talk with us soon.

Although we were set up primarily as a mental health program, we are open to all clients, with no appointment necessary. Since the circumstances that lead to homelessness and shelter life itself are very depressing, we see anyone who is depressed; the client does not have to be in crisis. Although the majority of the men in the shelter are from the neighborhood, the shelter does not bring a family perspective to bear on their problems. But our program does, and, when possible, we assist clients to maintain or reestablish family contact.

Today I have a new client. He was a sergeant in the Vietnam War, and is still having trouble adjusting to peacetime and finding a place in our society. Well groomed, well dressed, well spoken and apparently well fed, he does not fit the stereotypical image of a homeless man. But for his age, I think, he

could reenlist. Then he tells me his problem. He has recently been released from prison, after serving eight years, and he is hooked on heroin again. He wants a methadone program. We discuss the ramifications of this: there are some professionals who think that replacing one addiction with another is not really helping the client, and that the side effects of methadone can be quite severe. It might be better to get into a drug-free program. The choice is the client's, however, and he has been in a methadone program before and sees it as his only answer.

I make phone calls to several programs and find two that will see him tomorrow. One says it will take 10 days for him to be accepted and the other says five days. He chooses the quicker acceptance, although I tell him the other is a better program. He wants to get out of the shelter as soon as possible. He tells me about his wife and children, whom he has not seen in more than six years, although he has kept in touch by mail and phone. "She wouldn't divorce me even though I begged her to, because she still loves me." Why hasn't he seen them for so long? He didn't want them to see him in prison and now he doesn't want them to see him hooked. He firmly believes a methadone program will help him take control of his life. I think to myself that methadone didn't work before—why should it work now? Before we conclude, I ask him about combat flashbacks. He says, "I have dreams about the war," but he doesn't consider these flashbacks. We make an appointment for him to attend a Vietnam Veterans group.

During the lunch hour, I meet with John English and his parents. John is a 36-year-old man who came to the shelter after a quarrel with his stepfather. He believes that the police have implanted a radar device in his brain so they can keep track of him. "They did this," he said, "because they think I attacked a woman." But he explained that when he broke the bottle against the wall, he meant her no harm; he was only trying to stop the voices swearing in his head. She was a bystander who was frightened by his behavior and screamed for the police. He spent a month in Rikers Island Prison for this. Now he believes the police can read his thoughts from six blocks away and he can hear them doing this. The voices, which he calls projections, still swear at him.

John decided to prove his independence and sanity by leaving his stepfather's home and finding a place of his own, and to do this he chose the shelter as his base. It is fairly typical for younger men to come directly from home to the shelter, as lack of available housing leaves them no other choice. But John is not typical because of his age and his mental problems.

In the family meeting, Mr. English tries to reason with John and when John feels cornered by his step-father's reasoning, he complains that the smell of the old man's breath is overpowering. Mrs. English, who has had multiple sclerosis since a year after her marriage, criticizes them both for not listening to what she is saying. During a pause in the argument, I ask Mr. English if he really expects John to be logical. He says no. John then tells him, "Just because I can't be logical doesn't mean I can't make sense." Mr. English thinks this over and agrees that John can make sense. They start listening to each other. Mr. English now tries to understand what John is saying instead of trying to convince him to follow instructions. John eventually agrees to let his step-father help him find a safe place to live, and Mr. English agrees to let John stay at the shelter until the new home is found. Mrs. English says, "That's what I was trying to say."

TUESDAY: I RECEIVE A LETTER FROM A POSTMASTER in a small town in Florida. It is about a former client, Mr. Duncan, and the news is good. I recall the case. The old man was traveling from Massachusetts to Florida, and he changed trains in Penn Station. He fell asleep in the station and woke up to find all his belongings and identification gone.

Only his bus ticket receipts remained in his pocket. After the police brought him to the shelter, I made phone calls to various agencies that assist travelers, but to no avail. One social worker yelled over the phone at me, "You must be new. Don't you know all the old bums in the city want to go to Florida for the winter?" Shelter staff and people from other agencies did not believe his story. I chose to persist.

Getting information from Mr. Duncan was a slow process. He had had a stroke, and his memory was impaired. He said he had daughters living in the city, but he hadn't seen them since their early teens, and he was not sure how long ago that was. I tried the telephone directory without success. Then I asked how he supported himself in Florida. By fishing, he said, and trading some of the catch for the things he needed. How does he pay his rent? "Oh," he said, "I'm on social security." A call to the social security office verified this (he remembered his social security number). His next month's check was mailed to the shelter.

This process of seeking aid for him took one month. When he left for Florida, I gave him two self-addressed envelopes, and asked him to write me so I would know he arrived safely. Another month went by and I did not hear from him so I wrote the postmaster in his town. He told me Mr. Duncan picked up his mail at the local post office and was known there. The postmaster's letter said Mr. Duncan arrived safely, he was doing fine and remembered me. The postmaster also advised that I not expect a letter, since, while Mr. Duncan said he would write, he would likely forget again in a few minutes.

Just before lunch, the veteran returns from the methadone program. He is feeling very happy because he is positive he will be accepted there. He says he is determined to stop using heroin, and in fact he has not used it in more than a week. This proves his high motivation, he says. How can I tell him this does not help his chances of being accepted into the methadone program?

After lunch I accompany another case manager who is escorting her client to the hospital. The Emergency Medical Service had to be called because he was decompensating rapidly and having dangerous hallucinations. He is another veteran, a marksman in the army, who has suffered brain damage, most probably from drug use.

Talking with his worker, the client, Carlton, alternately becomes the four or five different people who "live inside" him, including a very seductive woman and a dangerous man who could hurt people. In the ambulance he keeps repeating, "I see Carlton over there. He says, 'I'm the real Carlton.' I say, 'Shit, that's why I'm crazy.' " Then he starts mumbling what sounds like gibberish to me, and I marvel at his worker's ability to understand his speech. Carlton cooperates with the process of hospitalization, but his admission takes the whole afternoon. The hospital keeps him for observation.

Shelter residents like Carlton seldom have friends, as the mentally ill do not usually interact with the rest of the population and the healthy residents tend to ignore them. Often, if they have money, a welfare check or cigarette money from the family, they are robbed and exploited. In fact, robbery and exploitation are quite common in the shelter and that is why the men form groups, not formal organized gangs but a buddy system where friends back each other. The population is too transient to form gangs, and sometimes the man who is a buddy in the morning will steal your bus fare for a fix or a drink at night. There are few close friendships here, but good deeds are done also. Last night an old man came in, lost and confused, with $279 in his pocket. He would not trust the staff to put the money in the safe. A young man, a drug addict, stood by the old man's bed all night to make sure that no one robbed him while he slept. Staff found the old man's family today. The young man said he did it because "he looks like my grandfather."

WEDNESDAY: THIS MORNING WILLIAM HARTLEY is waiting for me when I arrive. There is always that one client who gets to you, the one who can get behind your screen of objectivity and occupy your mind even in your leisure hours. That is how William affects me. He is a 27-year-old man who looks like he is 20 or 21. The hardships of his life do not show on his face. He has served five years in prison for armed robbery, but his manner is gentle and polite. His acts of violence have mostly been directed at himself.

On my second day on the job, our entire staff was called down to the main floor to deal with a crisis. There was a man up in the rafters threatening to jump. That man was William Hartley. The fall, at least 50 feet to the concrete floor, would certainly have killed him. The workers and some clients quickly piled mattresses below him. People were shouting, "Don't do it." One young man yelled "Jump! It'll bring the TV cameras and then people will know what it's like in here." Security guards dragged the troublemaker from the building. Meanwhile, the man in the rafters pulled out a rope made from knotted bed sheets, tied one end to the steel beams and slipped a noose over his head. When his girlfriend and his 2-year-old son were brought to help talk him down, he screamed in agony, "Get my son outta here! Whose crazy idea was that?" Finally, another shelter resident succeeded in talking him down, and police and emergency medical services took him away.

The next morning, William became my first client. He was raised by foster parents and was about 12 years old when he met his biological mother. He was visiting the younger sister of his foster mother, and she casually introduced him to another woman in the apartment, saying, "This is your real mother." William kept in touch with his mother, and after the death of his foster parents, he moved in with her and his half brothers. He was about 19 at the time.

THE SHELTER

William could not believe his mother loved him, and she could never do enough to convince him that he meant as much to her as her other children. She explained the circumstances of his birth, how she was a young girl unable to care for herself and a baby. They were deserted by his father, so she left him with the older, childless couple. I got this information from both William and his mother, with whom I spoke on the phone because she would not meet with me. Ms. Hartley spoke with both of us often on the phone and William visited her home, but she would not let him move in with her again because she was convinced that would cause trouble for the whole family. I supported her in this decision, and William came to understand her point of view. It took weeks of counseling and phone calls to his mother, but he eventually got a job and moved away from the shelter. The last I had heard from him, he was doing well working as a security guard. Now he is back.

William sits at my desk with his chin on his chest and his hands between his knees. When I ask him what brings him back to the shelter, he whispers one word, "Crack." He was living with his cousin's family, but they kicked him out because he stole from them. Could I help him get his things from them? Could I help him get his job back? He says his use of crack has not affected his work because he only used it on his days off and he did not miss a day of work until his cousin threw him out. I tell him that he is deceiving himself if he thinks crack has not affected his job performance; I ask him if he has been late for work after his days off. He says yes, and he has been late other times also. Sometimes he did use the drug when he had to be at work the next day. We talk about the dangers of addiction, the physical, mental and emotional damage crack inflicts on users and their families, but he has heard it all before. I have seen other clients like this who made it out of the shelter but return when trouble strikes and there is no one else to turn to. This is especially true when the trouble involves drugs, and the man's family refuses to take him back because they have already been burned so many times in the past. In those cases, the man either returns to the shelter or sleeps in abandoned buildings. Returning to the shelter can be an indication that someone is sincerely trying to change. I believe this is true of William.

With William's agreement, I set up an appointment for him with a physician I know who works with crack users. Then I call his cousin to discuss the possibility of William's returning to remove his belongings from the apartment. The cousin is adamant; he will not allow William to reenter the apartment, and will put the things out on the street. Valuable things could get stolen that way, I remind him. The cousin does not want that to happen, so he suggests that I come for the things while William waits in the street. I agree.

I call William's job, and his boss says he has been a good and reliable worker. He is only angry that William has been absent without calling. I let William speak to him, and William explains that family troubles have kept him from work. I wonder to myself if I am doing the right thing by passively supporting this half truth. I decide that my role as advocate dictates I should not intervene because that would destroy his second chance with the company. William is told to report to work the next morning.

William waits in the car while I go up to his cousin's apartment. His cousin turns out to be not a blood relative, but a lifelong friend who really cares for him. He is deeply hurt by William's theft and does not want to hear the promise of compensation that I bring. He is touched when I tell him that William wants his little girl to keep the portable TV; nevertheless, he wants William to stay away from him and get his act together. He is sorry William had to return to the shelter (he lived there himself briefly), but he also thinks this is light punishment for what William did. If another man had stolen his stereo, he would have pressed charges. I collect the garbage bags of clothes and tapes and bring them down to the car. I wonder if the things his cousin said are true, that William is just a people user and doesn't give a damn about anyone. If so, why did he give his TV to the child? A portable TV is a precious item in a shelter. We return to the shelter.

I have just finished my lunch when Arthur Brown comes into the office. He is speaking to himself in angry tones. Since there is already a client at my desk, I tell Arthur I will see him next. He makes a nasty comment about drug addicts, meaning my client, then leaves the office. Later, Arthur comes looking for me. He walks past me and goes directly to the center of the room and challenges me to come fight him. I offer to talk over the problem right away, but he doesn't want to talk. He says he wants to "beat the shit" out of me. I ask what he thinks I have done to anger him. He says I prevented him from getting a job. I quickly think back to last week. Arthur, who is mentally handicapped and unable to read, applied for a job well beyond his ability and asked me for a reference. I told him that I could not do that because I would only be setting him up for failure. I suggested another job instead where he would have more supervision. He refused my offer, and I had not seen him since then. Now he is standing in the middle of the room yelling at me.

Again I try to get him to talk to me, but his anger escalates and he rips off his shirt. I warn him that I cannot permit this behavior to continue and advise him that I will have to call security if he does not get control of himself. The threats and verbal abuse continue. I look around the room. There are several clients sitting around but most of them are ignoring us. One staff member tries to calm her clients during this outburst; another remains busy at his desk; only one comes to my aid. He tries to reason with Arthur and places himself between us. Now Arthur has to look over my coworker's shoulder to swear at me.

These incidents have happened before. When staff get in trouble there is a dangerous lack of support, and this is affecting the morale of the program. Finally, my director tells me to go call security. I descend three flights of stairs knowing that if Arthur breaks away and comes after me, I don't stand a chance on these stairs. I report the incident to security, and five guards remove Arthur from the office.

The threat of client-on-client violence is ever present, but client violence toward staff seldom occurs. Clients' resentments toward staff are more likely to be expressed through a slashed tire or a broken car antenna, which is hard to trace, than with a direct assault. Staff members are concerned that there isn't an effective policy for dealing with these incidents, and there is not enough security to offer adequate protection.

THURSDAY: THIS MORNING I DO OUTREACH. I GO down to the ground floor of the shelter and try to engage new clients. I look out onto a sea of beds, more than 300 of them, spaced about three feet apart. The old men and the physically handicapped are placed in a separate corner to minimize their chances of being exploited. Men can be robbed at night when the lights are dimmed and they are sleeping, but the old are easy prey anytime.

The bed linens are all that familiar shade of institutional white, except for the occasional colored or patterned pillowcase someone has brought from wherever used to be home. A few men are lying in bed, some are still getting dressed to go out to whatever their day's activity will be—job search, apartment search, family connection, drug connection. They get dressed standing in full view of everyone. Depersonalized and "shelterized," many appear to have grown accustomed to the lack of privacy, and make little or no attempt to cover themselves even when female staff pass by.

I see a young man carrying a large garbage bag. I approach and greet him. He says he is doing fine. I tell him about our program and invite him to come visit us. He says he is not interested. I ask what's in the bag. "Empty soda cans," he replies. He collects them for the deposits. I tell him he could get four or five Coke bottles a day from our office. He replies, "I don't do bottles, only aluminum cans." As he walks away, I make a note to speak with him again next week.

Another young man I speak to says that the CSS program I work for only has crazy people. That pre-conception is the biggest obstacle to getting people involved in our program. I tell him that I know the staff is a bit off the wall, but most of the clients are quite sane. He says his name is Ivan and he may come to talk to me tomorrow. What's wrong with right now, I ask? He says maybe he'll see me later. We pick up about 20 percent of our clients through outreach, the rest are referred to us by shelter staff and other clients. I wander around talking to more residents before going back to the office.

Ivan has come to see me. I ask him what made him decide to come up and he says, "I don't really have my shit together like I pretend down there. I need help." He is 21 years old. His mother caught him with a couple of friends using cocaine in her home and she kicked him out. She told him not to return until he has a job, an apartment, a bank account, and is drug free. That was two months ago. He had not seen or heard from her since. He is worried because they both have no other family; his father is recently deceased. His mother has a heart condition, and he is concerned that something may happen to her and that he won't be around to help.

I ask if he is drug free now, and he says he is. He broke off with those friends a month ago and came to the shelter. I ask him, "Why not call your mother now and let her know where you are? She might think you are in jail, or worse." It had not occurred to him that she might be worried also. He is afraid to call her and asks me to do it for him.

I call Ivan's mother at work and she is grateful for news that he is alright. If she hadn't heard from him

by the weekend, she was going to report him to the police as a missing person. She says, "Yes, I told him to get out and get a job, but I didn't say he couldn't phone or come visit." I give the phone to Ivan.

I have found that reestablishing family contact is easier if I make two things clear at the start. I am not trying to convince the family members to take the client back into the home, and I am not holding the family responsible for the client's homelessness. Once this is understood people are more open to discussion and helping their homeless relative.

FRIDAY: WILLIAM IS WAITING FOR ME THIS MORNing, dressed in his security guard uniform. He is smiling and standing straight, and he tells me he is going to work at noon. His job means a lot to him because he gets to work with a dog and he guards an apartment building where families with children live. He loves the attention he gets from the children. He hopes to have a family of his own one day. "No," he tells me, there is no chance of his getting back with his son's mother. She won't even let him see the boy. William is angered by her actions, but he says he stays away because he is afraid she will call the police on him again.

He has not kept the appointment I made for him with the physician because he is feeling fine and he wants to work. I remind him that the large quantity of crack he told me he used can cause physical damage and he should have an examination. He takes the physician's number and uses my phone to make an appointment for next week. I ask when he plans to get help with his drug addiction, and he replies that he is not addicted. He insists he has no desire to use drugs and he is going to work, save his money, and get out of the shelter again. "What will happen," I ask him, "when you cash your next paycheck and you have all that money in your hand?" "I won't spend it," he tells me. "I will put it in the shelter safe and only take out enough each day to go to work."

William thanks me again for helping him get his clothes from his cousin's place. He admits again that he destroyed a good friendship because of drugs and says he still intends to pay for the things he stole. He really believes he can do all these things, and he is partially right. He has proved he can save money and get out of the shelter; his problem is that when he is living on his own, he gets involved with the wrong kinds of friends. He makes an appointment to see me next week and he leaves for work.

I haven't seen the artist since Monday, so I ask the clients where he is. They tell me that he left for California on Wednesday. He did not say much about leaving, just that his family agreed to have him live with them again and sent him a ticket, so he left. Now I think I understand the quality of the light in his impressionist paintings. The shimmering light, the wide-open spaces were his memories of the home he had left.

Ivan has come to see me. Again he thanks me for making the phone call to his mother. He had dinner with her last night, and he is spending the weekend with her. I listen while he reviews the events that preceded his departure from his home. He lived with his mother and his father all his life. He is their only child. Last summer he lost his job, and since his father was ill he did not try to find another job; instead he stayed home to look after his dad. When his father died in the fall, Ivan and his mother did not talk much about their loss. They grieved silently and separately. With his father gone, Ivan found himself with time on his hands. He had used drugs occasionally before, and he started hanging out with unemployed friends. Soon they were using Ivan's home as a safe house in which to get high, and it was during one of these parties that his mother came home early and caught him with cocaine.

Ivan tells me that he always was able to talk things over with his mother, but that day she went into a blind rage and would not listen to anything he said. Ivan understands the feeling of betrayal piled upon loss that his mother experienced. He does not expect her to tell him he can move back home after this weekend. He knows he will have to make his own home now, but he also knows he has not lost his mother.

After lunch the veteran comes to see me. He asks me to phone the methadone program to find out if he has been accepted. I make the call and the news is not good. I am told that the client's sample tested negative, no trace of illegal drugs, and I should advise him to return to the methadone program Monday morning and give another sample. I am told he will understand the message. I relay the information to him and tears stream down his face. "Do you know what they are telling me to do, sir?" he asks. "I have no money! Do you know what I will have to do to get ten dollars? I don't want to do that anymore!"

John English and his stepfather have come to see me. Mr. English has found a basement apartment that is acceptable to John, and John is moving there today. It is quite far from his parents' home, but it is near his aunts and cousins, so he will have family contact and Mr. English won't have to respond to every minor crisis personally. The person renting John the apartment has known him for many years and understands his condition. I ask John about getting back on his medication, but he refuses to do that. He reasons that since the medication can't cure him there is no point taking it. I tell him that I understand what he means, but I disagree with him and I ask if he knows the difference. He replies, "Yes! I disagree with Donald Trump building big apartment buildings for the rich when poor people can't find anywhere to live, but I understand that cities like to compete for who has the tallest buildings." He is right: just because he is not logical does not mean he can't make sense. John tells me that if the voices become too much for him, he will go to the hospital. The Englishes thank me for my help, and I thank them for coming to say good-bye.

IT IS SNOWING WHEN I LEAVE WORK TODAY. I LOOK out at the empty lot directly across from the building. It is strewn with garbage and weeds. I wonder if, in the spring, the men would like to clean it up and use it as a recreation area. I wonder if, in the spring, I will still be working here. The burnout rate is very high among the staff. I am aware that my own sense of burnout comes more from the constraints of the larger systems than from the problems of the men. I ask myself why I do this work. I think I do it because I like being with people and helping when I am able to. I am disturbed and distressed every day as I pass the empty apartment buildings that stand decaying near the shelter. These empty buildings could be rehabilitated, but the city responds to plans for more shelters more readily than to plans for affordable housing. I know that almost anyone can become homeless; I have met Ph.D.s, teachers and businessmen living here alongside the untrained, the unskilled and the mentally ill.

The cold wind hits me, and I button my coat against the chill. It is hard to think of spring at this time, but this must be what it is like for the men in the shelter. It is the faith that conditions will change that keeps them going every day, and I share that faith. Of course, I am speaking of the ones that haven't given up. Many have. And what of their families? What conflict rages within Ivan's mother tonight while she wonders if she did the right thing? Is Mr. English wondering, as I am, if John's voices will drive him from the apartment back to a mental hospital? Where is Arthur tonight? I had heard that he was suspended from the shelter Wednesday night for fighting with another client. I have no idea what will happen with any of these men. I only know that I am never bored working at the shelter and being invited each day to enter the lives of so many people. And at those moments when a client and I develop trust in each other, I am at once honored and humbled. ∎

LASCELLES W. BLACK, M.S.W., *is on the staff of Morrisania Neighborhood Family Care Center, Bronx, NY.*

PHOTOGRAPH BY ALON REININGER/CONTACT PRESS IMAGES

HOMOSEXUALITY: ARE WE STILL IN THE DARK?

CONFRONTING HOMOPHOBIA IN THE THERAPY ROOM

By Laura M. Markowitz

THIRTY YEARS AGO, THE AGENDA FOR THERAPISTS working with homosexuals, stated or otherwise, was likely to be "conversion" to heterosexuality. Whether through confrontation, subtle persuasion, exploration of childhood trauma, or even electroshock, the goal was to reclaim the homosexual from the ranks of social misfits. Not surprisingly, gays and lesbians were, at best, reluctant consumers of the therapies of that era.

In 1969, the Stonewall riot, a spontaneous protest triggered by a police raid of a gay and lesbian bar in Greenwich Village, marked the beginning of the fight for gay and lesbian civil rights and the move out of the closet for millions in the United States. By 1973, the American Psychiatric Association (APA) had struck homosexuality from its Diagnostic and Statistical Manual of Psychiatric Disorders (DSM II), ending sanctioned prejudice by mental health professionals and finally conceding there was no more pathology in gays and lesbians than in heterosexuals. But while homosexuality was depathologized, therapists were given no guidance as to how to work with their gay and lesbian clients.

This is still largely the case. Within the field of family therapy, for example, there is little or no discussion of gay and lesbian treatment issues at conferences or in the mainstream literature. Those who do participate in gay/lesbian workshops or read or write about treatment issues are almost always homosexual themselves. Few graduate programs include required reading on same-sex couples or discussion of homosexuality. Today, gay and lesbian issues continue to be ignored by most therapists.

The result is that many heterosexual therapists think that avoiding society's classic fear and loathing of gays and lesbians is all they need to work effectively with this population. "Most family therapists have the correct politics in their heads," says family therapist David Treadway, "but we don't deal with our deeper prejudices and reactivity regarding lesbians and gays. The treatment of homosexuals today is similar to the therapy we did before the feminist critique got us to look at the disempowering messages therapy-as-usual was sending our female clients."

Many gay and lesbian clients believe their straight therapists still harbor the assumption that it is less than normal or less preferable to be homosexual. "Some family therapists think that somewhere in the family system you can find the roots or cause of homosexuality, that it secretly has something to do with family dysfunction," says Marianne Walters, one of the founders of the Women's Project in Family Therapy. "Family therapists haven't yet considered what it means that our theory is based on a heterosexual model. I understand why gays and lesbians would only want to see gay and lesbian therapists."

On the other hand, gays and lesbians are hungry for what family therapists can offer. "This population needs and craves a strong connection with their families of origin, and they are striving to create meaningful family systems for themselves," says David Treadway. But when straight therapists do treat gays and lesbians, they often ignore or underestimate the experiential gulf that separates therapist and client. Without an understanding of the extent to which we all internalize the belief that homosexuality is a perversion, a character defect, or a moral flaw, even the best-intentioned therapist will echo the negative messages gay and lesbian clients have been bombarded with, often making matters worse.

FOR YEARS, JAMES HAD WRESTLED WITH QUEStions about his own sexuality, but the summer of his junior year in college everything came to a head. He had spent his vacation dreaming obsessively about his college roommate, desperately missing him, counting the days until fall semester began. Then, a few weeks before the start of school, the roommate called to say he was taking a year off to be with his girlfriend in California.

"I was more depressed than I had ever been in my life," says James. "I went to see a therapist, who at first seemed pretty cool. He said he didn't care at all whether or not I was gay, but that maybe my feelings for Sam were all part of a fantasy I had gotten lost in. He told me not to write to Sam or see him

for a while, 'until you get over your confusion.' He suggested I buy a copy of *Playboy*, and asked me to describe my idea of a sexy woman.

"I never went back to see him, but it took another six months of depression before I finally came out to myself and found a gay therapist who could help me understand what was happening."

James's therapist probably thought he was helping a confused young man keep his options open. But it is exactly this kind of approach that has convinced many gay and lesbian clients that straight therapists don't understand their struggles and are secretly threatened by their sexuality. "What the therapist in this case did is dismiss James's feelings as having no meaning," says gay family therapist John Patten of the Ackerman Institute of Family Therapy. "When a client like James has a fantasy, the therapist's job is to explore it, not treat it as if it were dangerous. The therapist frightened James away from his feelings, reinforcing the inner voice that was telling him there was something wrong with those feelings."

The themes of shame, secrecy, and fear of disclosure are inevitably part of the freight most gay and lesbian clients bring to therapy. Straight therapists who are not familiar with this emotional constellation and how it changes through the coming-out process can give clients some very bad advice.

Vicky was a 38-year-old divorcee with two teenage children. After two years with a therapist whom she found extremely helpful in guiding her through her divorce, Vicky came out to herself. "But when I told my therapist I had realized I was a lesbian, her first response was that I shouldn't burden my children by telling them," recalls Vicky. She left therapy a year later, and soon after started dating a woman, who then moved in with her. "The kids accepted the arrangement at first, but after a while they caught on that there was something else going on, and started to act up," says Vicky. "I wanted to come out to them, but I had my therapist's voice in my head telling me it would be bad for them. For three years, my home was a war zone, until both kids decided to move in with their father. After they left, my lover and I were too tired from all the fighting and the resentment over losing the kids to save the relationship, and she moved out. I woke up one morning, alone, and close to suicide."

No doubt the therapist in this case thought she was protecting Vicky and her children. "She was apparently concerned that if Vicky raised the issue of her sexuality to her adolescent children, it would be harmful to them," says family therapist Claudia Bepko. "But it's the secrecy itself that is most damaging to families in this situation. If Vicky was comfortable about her own choice, she could have supported her children while they grappled with understanding and accepting her lesbianism. Instead of helping Vicky prepare for the various reactions she might encounter coming out, the therapist amplified Vicky's own fear that there was something destructive in her choice that needed to be hidden."

ANY DISCUSSION OF THE DIFFICULTIES HOMOSEX-uals and heterosexuals experience when they try to bridge the chasm between them, whether in therapy or outside it, brings up the issue of homophobia. As with other words, like "sexism" and "racism," that condemn once socially accepted behavior, "homophobia" can put us off, make us anxious to protect ourselves from perceived accusations of bigotry. But homophobia is not only a conscious attitude or set of beliefs. It is also a visceral experience that emotionally resonates to our core sense of ourselves.

Ignorance, insensitivity, stereotyped thinking, outright prejudice, discrimination and a host of negative attitudes all can be loosely grouped under the umbrella of homophobia At its most blatant, homophobia takes the form of outrage that enables gay-bashers to feel justified in striking out against those they consider traitors to the natural order of human

relationships. Most of us experience a quieter, more subtle type of homophobia when we encounter homosexuality—it is startling to have our unthinking assumptions about our sexual identities jostled. We may not go on the attack when we feel these uncomfortable stirrings, but despite our best intentions, our hostility, fear and fumbling self-consciousness may spew out.

Because of what they represent for straight society, gays and lesbians are in the unenviable position of regularly setting off these anxious rumblings. To protect themselves, they learn to label these overt and covert expressions of disapproval and rejection as homophobia, putting the burden back where they feel it belongs. As a result, some straight therapists describe sessions with lesbian and gay clients as walks through a jungle filled with hidden patches of quicksand. "I wait for the ax to fall, for my lesbian and gay clients to accuse me of being homophobic," says one straight therapist. "And the fact is, usually they're right."

Assumptions about homosexuality are often based on lack of information or outright false notions, and most people, including mental health professionals, aren't sensitized to recognizing these errors. Therapists can clarify their own feelings and attitudes about homosexuality by visualizing a spectrum of attitudes, with most straight clinicians falling somewhere between the two extremes. At one end, a faulty assumption is that, whatever the presenting complaint, homosexuality is the fundamental problem. "I went to therapy after I had been out to myself and in most areas of my life for 15 years," says one 55-year-old man. "We spent the first session arguing about whether homosexuality is biologically or sociologically based. Finally, I told him it didn't really matter—I was gay, and that was a fact. I had come to therapy to deal with my anger toward my alcoholic father, who was ill, close to dying. He asked me if I had come out to him and I said no, our relationship had never been that good, and there were so many other problems between us that I didn't want to add another. The therapist told me that until I came out to my dad, I wouldn't be able to have an equal relationship with him. I was frustrated—he was missing the point. It was like knowing I was gay was a clinical buoy the therapist could cling to, that somehow everything in my life was going to be about my sexuality."

At the other extreme, a therapist might believe that homosexual preference makes absolutely no difference at all, so why make a big deal about it? "I was miserable because it was another Christmas and my family hadn't invited my lover home with me for the holiday," remembers 32-year-old Heidi, a graphic artist. "I had been out to them for a few years, and they were civil to Becky, but they never really acknowledged our relationship. Invitations to family events never included her. I felt angry, and I asked my therapist what to do. She seemed surprised, and said she thought I was used to the arrangement by now, and wondered why I was so upset. When I said I thought my parents were being homophobic, she asked me, 'Don't you think they might want to have just family for the holidays? After all, Christmas is traditionally a family-only holiday.' When I told her that Becky *was* my family, she asked me why I was taking such a belligerent stance."

When straight therapists are confronted with their conflictual feelings about homosexuality, they can either deny them or face them. "The first time I did work with a training program at a gay and lesbian community center, I wore my heterosexuality on my sleeve and came across very macho," says family therapist Michael Elkin. "The gay and lesbian therapists picked it up and accused me of not liking them, having contempt for them, not knowing about them. Of course, I got defensive, but my defensiveness revealed to me that something was going on. I discovered I had an enormous amount of discomfort with whatever homosexual feelings I, myself, might have. But extreme homophobic reac-

tions lost leverage with me when I accepted that homosexuality was a potential in me."

Family therapists, whose training typically deemphasizes countertransference issues, may be more comfortable finding quick solutions to problems than tracking—or even seeing—the dynamics of homophobia in the therapist-client relationship. "It can be frightening when the straight therapist begins to experience feelings of attraction to gay or lesbian clients," says lesbian family therapist Cindy Myers, who conducts workshops helping therapists examine their own sexual attitudes. "Society dumps its anxiety about sexuality onto lesbians and gays. I've spoken to many straight therapists who say they were all too ready to blame their gay or lesbian clients for their own discomfort in therapy or who automatically concluded those clients were being seductive."

While the feelings may be unavoidable, the therapists must decide whether they will allow them to go underground or whether they will use their discomfort to help them do some serious thinking about their own sexuality. "I can't imagine doing family therapy without having done some important thinking about my own family of origin," says family therapist Frederick Brewster. "In the same way, I think we need to examine our own ideas about sexuality and our own stereotypes of homosexuality before we work with gays and lesbians. Which of our own issues are spilling over into the therapy room? How are we reacting emotionally to what the client is saying?"

David Scasta, editor of *The Journal of Gay and Lesbian Psychotherapy*, thinks that doing therapy with gays and lesbians is not for every clinician, but is a specialized field that requires a heightened level of self-awareness, and commitment to becoming educated about gay and lesbian issues. "All of us—gay and straight—absorb the abundance of homophobic messages out there. Gay and lesbian therapists, through their own coming-out processes, have usually been forced to confront their internalized fears and stereotypes. Straight therapists need to do the same kind of self-examination to make sure their homophobia doesn't intrude into their clinical work."

Once therapists have begun to examine their own fears, they are less likely to succumb to homophobia in sessions.

"When I feel anxious," says Michael Elkin, "I will tell the client that I am getting uncomfortable, since the client is probably feeling it too. After I tell them, I help them process it—we talk about what it means about our relationship, how they feel about it. Sometimes, I just own it to myself, and I try to understand what it was that made me feel threatened. My job, when I am doing therapy, is to notice the part of me that is withholding love and putting out judgment, and to keep processing it and getting help with it."

One of the first agendas of therapy with homosexual clients can be acknowledging the differences between therapist and client, and recognizing the very likely possibility that suspicion and misunderstanding will occur. "When I start therapy with a lesbian couple, I tell them that, as a heterosexual man, I may sometimes be off base in my attitudes and ways of thinking about them," says Treadway. "I tell them that I need them to let me know if they pick that up from me, and I admit that I might need information to understand their internal experience."

Further complicating therapy involving a straight therapist and homosexual clients is that the clients may be on their guards to perceived judgments, or may test their straight therapists for latent homophobia. One straight therapist rescued a session in which "a gay client told me about a comment his boss had made that the client considered homophobic. I asked him what he thought was homophobic about it. 'I'm not paying you to educate you about homophobia,' he snapped at me. I was taken aback, and had to explain that I wasn't asking for my own edification, but that I was asking in the same way that I might ask why he thought his mother's forget-ting his birthday every year was rejecting—it was to challenge him to describe exactly what the experience meant to him."

Straight therapists may be on probation while their homosexual clients try to gauge whether they are truly trustworthy. "I remember one gay couple I saw who would explicitly describe their sex life, and it made me extremely uncomfortable," says Elkin. "But I also wondered what was going on—why were they telling me this stuff? It was way more detail than heterosexual couples usually go into with me. I began suspecting they were testing me, so I told them I was having a reaction and asked why they needed to be that explicit. They owned up to the fact that they were testing me, which led to a great discussion of their discomfort about working with a heterosexual therapist."

While therapists who are working with lesbian and gay clients need to stay attuned to their own subjective reactions, resolving the therapist's homophobia should not become the goal of treatment. "If a client feels I have been homophobic, I will talk to them about what they felt when they perceived themselves as under attack, and what they felt it meant about our relationship, but I will keep it on what they heard rather than on what I may or may not have said," says Elkin. "I will do this whether I agree it was homophobic or not, because that isn't the issue. That they feel attacked is the issue, and I have to assume that the feeling excites their shame, and resonates with some attacks they are making on themselves."

"Use the process of self-examination to compensate for the way our culture handicaps us when it comes to understanding sexuality," counsels Cindy Myers. "We have all—gay, lesbian, and straight—been taught to fear our different sexual feelings. By undertaking the task of examining our own attitudes about sexuality, we can really join with gay and lesbian clients, not just pretend we have and endure sweaty palms as we wait to be found out."

T HE CONVENTIONAL WISDOM IN THE THERAPY world has been that every couple—lesbian, gay, or straight—grapples with the same standard issues of communication and intimacy. But it is an oversimplification to say that the same techniques and theories applied to straight couples will fit lesbian and gay couples. "For a long time, I thought the same way many white people used to think—that they weren't supposed to mention racial differences because it might mean they were racist," says David Treadway. "When I first started working with lesbian couples, I thought, 'Relationships are relationships.' I tried not to notice that a couple was lesbian. It turned out not to be a useful way of working. I was ignoring the fact that gays and lesbians live in a hostile world and rejecting society, and that having partners of the same gender creates a unique relationship dynamic."

Unfortunately, many therapists are unfamiliar with same-sex couples and know only old stereotypes of rigid butch and femme roles, which were the primary way of same-sex relating in the days before Stonewall. One partner played the submissive "female" role, and the other the dominant "male" role. This was an attempt by gays and lesbians to mimic the straight society from whom they craved approval. The image of women and men in drag still exists in the minds of most straight people. Treadway remembers when he first worked with lesbian couples, he unconsciously assigned "male" and "female" labels to the partners based on how feminine or masculine they seemed: "It was hard to shift gears and realize they were both women. It was brand new for me, and I didn't know how to think about their relationship in any other terms but male/female."

Therapists who move in too quickly to focus on communication problems in a same-sex couple are likely to miss the larger picture. "The couple or family status is constantly being questioned and challenged by the mainstream society; internalized

homophobia is an ongoing presence in both partners. Whether, when and how to come out is a continuing question, and negotiating roles in a same-sex relationship is a persistent challenge," say lesbian family therapists Julie Mencher and Suzanne Slater in their work in progress on the lesbian family life cycle.

The fact that same-sex couples have to balance stress in so many systems at once—their own families of origin, their relationship, the gay/lesbian community, their ethnic or religious communities, and mainstream society—makes their efforts at forming a family an impressive juggling act. And the complexity of a relationship between people with the same gender socialization can create further confusion and conflict, yet the problem may not be evident to the straight therapist.

Mark and Keith hit a crisis four years into their relationship when Mark decided to go back to work as a waiter. Keith, who had been supporting them both on his physician's salary while Mark kept house, was upset by Mark's decision. But the more he tried to convince Mark to stay at home, the more determined Mark was to work, despite his lover's protests.

They went to a gay therapist in a last effort to save their relationship. The therapist reframed the problem for the men. "He explained that when the couple consists of two men, both of whom have been socialized to be breadwinners and providers, there is a strong need for equality between the partners," says Mark. "He said I may have been feeling less of a man because I was 'kept.' It finally sunk in for Keith why I was insisting on working eight hours a day and putting my paycheck toward household expenses even if I didn't need to. I needed to feel equal to him. After that, Keith respected my decision and we got along better than ever."

In his book *Counseling Same-Sex Couples*, gay family therapist Douglas Carl describes how men have been trained to be sexual (*continued on page 73*)

Beware the Well-Intentioned Therapist

I AM A GAY MAN. UNFORTUNATELY, IT TOOK 45 YEARS, TWO MARRIAGES, TWO DIVORCES, AND 15 years of therapy before I could acknowledge this fact. It isn't too surprising that I repressed my true sexuality for so long, given our society's fear and loathing of homosexuals and my own deeply religious Catholic upbringing. In my case—and I suspect in many others—psychotherapy also supported this repression.

My experience as a therapy client was rich and valuable, and I had the privilege of working with therapists whom I greatly respect. But none of them was prepared to help me wrestle with fundamental questions about my sexuality, and none of them was brave enough to ask me the question that might have saved me—and two ex-wives—a lot of pain: "Do you think you might be gay?"

I had initially begun psychotherapy after two years of impotence and my first divorce. I was miserable at being apart from my 2-year-old son, and was increasingly depressed. Carol, my first therapist, taught me how to recognize and express my anger toward the important women in my life. My work with her freed me from my deep despondency, but failed to help me confront the question of my sexuality. Early on in therapy, I admitted to Carol that I had never had a masturbatory fantasy about women, but that I had been having sexual fantasies about men since age 12. I remember being surprised that she never asked me anything further about these feelings. Instead, she framed my impotence as evidence of my underground anger toward women. It was my way of withholding myself from them, she said.

After three years of therapy, Carol decided that I would benefit from work with a man and referred me to her colleague, Bill. His reaction to my confused tale of my fantasy interest in men and lack of erotic feeling for women was much like Carol's. I soon stopped bringing up the issue of my sexuality with him.

At this time, I met another woman with whom I fell in love, and we were married. My lack of sexual interest was a problem between us from the start, and together we went to couples counseling. Again I was told that I was withholding sex because I had deep anger toward women. I felt lost. I knew I loved this woman deeply, as I had my first wife, but when I confided my secret fears about my sexuality to my therapists they were waved aside. Again I was told to work on my anger toward the women in my life. I was feeling worse and worse about myself, and my marriage was deteriorating.

A year before my second wife and I divorced, I took a final stab at therapy. This time something very basic began to become clear about my lifelong struggle with myself and my effort to be acceptable and to please others. Still, my therapist encouraged me to try to make a go of it with my wife. Shortly after terminating with him, I got a divorce—enduring the painful separation from my infant daughter—and was able to face my sexual desires frankly, and finally come out to myself. Looking back, I can see that I had to leave therapy before coming out because my therapist, who had been helpful in many other ways, had been sending me clear, if unspoken, messages that he was afraid to deal with my questions about my sexual identity.

WHY WERE THESE THERAPISTS SO RELUCTANT TO HELP ME FACE MY OWN SEXUAL IDENTITY QUESTIONS? I repeatedly admitted my lack of sexual interest in women, along with an attraction to men that I had felt since puberty, yet not one of my therapists asked me if I thought I might be gay. It is only now, years later, that I can appreciate the struggles my therapists had that led them to avoid discussing the subject of homosexuality with me. A few years ago, I learned that at the time I was in therapy with Bill, he was himself dealing with his feelings about an older brother who had come out. Further, at the time I was in couples therapy, my therapist was estranged from his gay teenage son. But beyond whatever was happening in their own families, there was a more pervasive issue at work. All of my therapists were heterosexual, and all had operated on the automatic assumption that everyone is or should be straight. Their heterosexism was a major stumbling block for me.

During my own 15-year career as a psychotherapist, I have seen this heterosexism manifested in many ways. In supervision groups, I have watched as therapists discovered that the real reason they terminated a gay client was their own fear of homosexuality, not the implacable resistance of which they had accused the client. In a male therapist support group, I had to confront the incessant "queer" jokes that I found so offensive. And I have found myself unwilling to confront a therapist friend who claimed to have no difficulty accepting that I am gay, as long as we didn't discuss the disgusting aspects of sex between men. Reflecting on this, I realize that it's harder, and no less painful, to deal with "well-intentioned" heterosexism.

Hindsight allows me now to see how inevitable my confusion was during all those difficult years. Of course a gay man not out to himself in a society as homophobic as ours would feel low self-esteem and low self-acceptance. My own fear of being gay was exacerbated by the pressure we all experience to be heterosexual, and compounded by the ignorance and fear of my therapists.

I understand perfectly why most gays and lesbians would only want to see a gay or lesbian therapist. If I ever go into therapy again, I will only go to a gay therapist. Until therapists of all professions genuinely and thoughtfully deal with their homophobia, their offices will not be a safe place for me to try to understand myself and make wise choices in a world that can be so hostile to those who live life outside the sexual mainstream. I am appalled at the thought of a young person— or a person young in his or her self-knowledge of being homosexual—seeking help from a therapist who has no real understanding of his or her own homophobia. However well intentioned they might be, these therapists may be offering fear and confusion, masquerading as healing. □

—George Woolley
MAY/JUNE 1990

GEORGE WOOLLEY *is the circulation manager of the* Networker.

(continued from page 70) predators while women are taught not to be sexual but domestic. "Now, instead of a predator coupling with someone who works to keep the home together emotionally, we have two predators trying to maintain a relationship," writes Douglas Carl. "Now, instead of someone taught to be sexually aggressive coupling with a mate taught to be sexually more passive, we have two sexually passive women in the same relationship who may feel, for example, that there is intrinsically something wrong with sexual aggression or even with sexual instigation."

Shared gender training creates other special problems for same-sex couples. For example, men are taught from youth not to show strong emotions, and jealousy is regarded as unmasculine and shameful. Therapists need to be aware that the partners in a gay couple may really need more assurance from one another than do most heterosexual partners. "It goes beyond jealousy," says John Patten. "There is little outside support to lend stability to the relationship other than what the couple creates for itself, so any excursion outside the couple boundary can seem threatening to a partner. There is also the reality that many, although not all, gay men lean primarily toward monogamy but believe that it is okay to stray from time to time as long as you don't talk about it, and as long as you play it safe."

Straight therapists often make the mistake of pathologizing patterns in same sex couples that actually serve to protect the relationship. In lesbian couples, for example, enmeshment is often viewed as the primary difficulty. In contrast, Suzanne Slater and Julie Mencher view the higher level of fusion in lesbian relationships as a useful compensatory mechanism. "The entire culture is trying to pull a lesbian couple apart—telling them they're not a couple at all, or saying homosexuality is sick and perverted, or it's destroying their families," says Slater. "And under the surface of the couple's thoughts is their own homophobic whisper, 'Lesbian relationships never last. This is doomed from the start.' So couples respond to that pressure by pulling tightly together and blurring their distinctions—a creative and useful way to hold together under that strain."

But fusion isn't just a response to homophobia. "Lesbian partners will describe the level of involvement they have in one another's lives, and their therapist will usually tell them they are too enmeshed," says Mencher. "The literature that automatically calls fusion pathological is based on a male model of development that values distance over affiliation, and heterosexual models that view a large dose of difference and distance as normative. Lesbian relationships are the closest we can get to understanding how women relate outside the patriarchy, and what we are finding is that some fusion is a normative expression of what women want—they enjoy and are nourished by a great deal of closeness and interaction."

One of Slater's clients, Maria, was 26 when her parents confronted her about her relationship with her roommate, Sarah. Maria admitted that she and Sarah were lovers, and her mother told her she would have to choose between her family or Sarah. The thought of being cut off from her close, Italian American family was agonizing, but she did not want to leave Sarah. At first, she agreed to see her family on any terms, which meant Sarah was not invited and she could not talk about her life-style.

Maria and Sarah's response to this pressure was to create their own close-knit family. They got a pet together, which became their child. They bought a house together, bought furniture together, including a double bed. They imbued all their homemaking with ritual significance, each purchase or home improvement affirming their commitment to one another. This intense closeness gave Maria the ability to meet her family's ultimatum from a position of strength. She eventually insisted that whenever she was invited, Sarah had to be welcome as well, and that the family acknowledge her relationship.

Surprised by her insistence, and impressed by her commitment to Sarah, the family agreed.

"Fusion allowed Maria to shift the power dynamic," says Suzanne Slater. "This isn't to say fusion was not also problematic, but it gave Maria the support she needed to take a stand with her family." Slater also works on helping lesbian couples face their differences and deal with conflict. Frequently, she begins by telling partners to stop wearing each other's clothes. "For weeks, one couple came in wearing identical shoes," recalls Slater. "I mentioned it one week, and the next week they came in and pointed out first thing that they were wearing different shoes. But they were horrified to discover they had on identical socks. I told them sometimes it could feel great to have similar socks, and some days you might want your own. It opened them up to considering how they hadn't tolerated much difference in their relationship, and how they could enjoy and borrow from each other's uniqueness."

WE HAVE YET TO FIT THE IMAGE OF TWO GAY dads or two lesbian moms going to a PTA meeting at their child's school among our pictures of accepted forms of family life. For many gay and lesbian clients, this lack of acceptance is at the core of their problem. They come to family therapy in search of what they cannot give themselves: affirmation that, yes, they are a family—that being two people, with or without children, who love each other and are committed to being together, constitutes family.

Traditionally, families have looked to rituals to provide them with their sense of connection to each other and a feeling of their place in the world. Increasingly, gays and lesbians, refusing to remain outcasts on the margins of society, are celebrating their connections to lovers, friends, family, and community. The friends and brothers of one lesbian, whose lover died in a car crash, had a ceremony presenting the grieving woman with a black shawl that

represented her mourning and acknowledged her widowhood. They gathered together a year later to mark the end of the formal period of mourning and presented her with a many colored shawl that represented healing. One gay couple who adopted a baby invited their family and friends to a family-forming ritual. The couple ceremoniously presented their baby to the assembled guests, announcing her name, the names of her new grandparents, aunts, uncles and parents, and officially proclaiming themselves a family. The child was passed from person to person, and each one pronounced her full name. Then individuals read poems, passages and prayers of love and support for the new family.

Twenty years ago, the prospect of gay men raising children, lesbians bearing children by alternative insemination and being open about their arrangement, and same-sex couples fighting for the same benefits as married people was literally unimaginable. Back then, the idea of same-sex couples having weddings and inviting their extended families could only have been a comic's homophobic fantasy.

But times are changing.

It is a perfect, blue-skied Arizona day as Miguel and Tom prepare to formally join their lives together. As the flute and piano begin a gentle Brahms piece, the two men walk between teary-eyed friends, coworkers who don't know what to make of it, and Mexican and Irish relatives from both sides who watch the proceedings with mixed emotions. Miguel's father hasn't come. Neither has Tom's sister-in-law or nephew.

The ceremony is brief. They address each other, describing how they discovered their love for each other eight years ago. Tom looks over the faces of his family—cousins, aunts, uncles, even a great-uncle. He has been to their weddings, to ceremonies for the births of their children and parties marking their anniversaries, and never expected them to share in his life the same way. He is amazed to see how open their faces are now, how much love for him they have, and he remembers how he almost didn't invite them, assuming they wouldn't want to come.

Miguel looks over at his mother and their eyes meet. He sees in his mother's face the love and acceptance he thought he had forsaken when he came out so many years ago. She has stood by him despite his father's refusal to come today. That means everything.

After the ceremony, there are toasts. Tom's mother is standing with her arm around Miguel, and Miguel's mother is pouring champagne for the guests. It is Miguel's mother who taps her glass and gets everyone's attention.

"When I married Miguel's father, I remember wishing that my children would be as happy on their wedding days as I was on mine. Today, that wish has come true. It hasn't been easy for Miguel and Tom. We've given them a hard time," there is some laugh-

ter, "and they've had to overcome more than most people to get to this day. But today they've made a promise to each other to continue to grow in their love, to be a blessing to each other and to us. They have made us proud today. I am lucky to have this gay son." ■

LAURA M. MARKOWITZ *is the assistant editor of the* Networker.

NOTE: Parents and Friends of Lesbians and Gays (PFLAG) is a national organization that provides information for and fights discrimination against homosexuals and offers support to the families of gays and lesbians. Address: PFLAG, National Office, P.O. Box 27605 Washington, DC 20038. (202) 638-4200.

See references, page 563.

75

Letters to the Editor

THOROUGHLY ENJOYED YOUR LAST ISSUE ("Gays and Lesbians Are Out of the Closet"). I had planned not to renew my subscription a few months ago, but finally, at the last minute, I decided to renew because I wanted to see this issue. I was not disappointed! I hope you will continue to include gay family issues in future publications.

Katherina A. Briccetti
Berkeley, CA

PLEASE CANCEL AND REFUND MY SUBSCRIP-tion. Your publication is basically too antiquated. Any organization that can endorse the psychological deviance that history has proven over and over to be detrimental both intra- and interpersonally is not worth my support or time.

Christopher M. Hunt
Atlanta, GA

I WANT TO CONGRATULATE YOU AND YOUR staff on the excellent issue on gay and les-bian concerns. It is so rare to find such un-biased, in-depth coverage of this important issue. We need more brave souls like you to help destroy negative stereotypes and myths about gays and les-bians and to help therapists guide gay clients toward happy, fulfilled gay lives.

As a rabbi, I work with very many people who are struggling with this issue, both parents whose children are coming out and individuals coming out themselves. It is so sad to me that so much suffering takes place over what should be a joyous decision/identity, a choice about love. After all, we are talking about people lov-ing people, not about ax murderers. Gay or lesbian identity simply isn't a tragedy. It is one more decent way to live in this world.

Julie Greenberg
Philadelphia, PA

IN REACTION TO THE NETWORKER'S SPECIAL feature on gay and lesbian families, I was disappointed to find that there was no mention of the difficulties faced by homosexu-al therapists working with heterosexual clients. I read the issue avidly, but was left with all the questions and struggles I face myself as a straight client working with a lesbian thera-pist. Although the issues are not exactly the same when the sexual orientations of client and therapist are reversed, the *Networker* helped me feel validated in my need to raise and discuss this issue as part of my own thera-py. Because I was ashamed to share with my therapist the pieces of homophobia that I have absorbed from this horribly homophobic soci-ety of ours, it took me seven months in thera-py with her to raise the issue, even though I knew before I began working with her that she was lesbian. And so I am still left with questions of how gay and lesbian therapists work with straight clients and specifically how they deal with their own "coming out" issues in their profession, to their clients, and in their communities. It seems to me that there is a larger fundamental question here, which is: Can we be effective therapists to clients who are significantly different from ourselves? From my dual perspective as a client and as a therapist myself, I believe that we can.

Annie Kiermaier
Union, ME

I WAS PLEASED TO FIND THE JANUARY/FEBRU-ary issue featured therapeutic work with gays and lesbians. However, I want to take exception to an opinion asserted by some of the authors: that heterosexuals aren't qualified to help them. In his article, "Beware the Well-Intentioned Therapist," George Woolley con-cludes, "If I ever go into therapy again, I will

Letters to the Editor

only go to a gay therapist."

I have specialized in work with gay men since 1968. I am currently in private practice and 90 percent of my clients are gay men, and have been since I first came to Denver in 1977. If the fact that I am a heterosexual were a liability, I would not have a busy, well-established practice.

I believe that the differences between straight men and gay men are actually not as great as the differences between men and women. Through *gender empathy* I can understand how a gay man thinks and feels quite well. Because I have seen over 1,000 gay men in my career, I have a good basis for confronting the homophobia of men struggling to come out, and it has more weight coming from a straight man who is not perceived as having a vested interest. I think this is particularly true for men who are married, and I also work with their spouses. It is also an advantage in instances where gay men believe they cannot be accepted by the straight men around them if their sexuality was known—particularly their fathers.

I do believe working with the gay community is a specialty, not easily taken on by the generalist. It is important to have specialized knowledge of the subculture, the unique qualities of same-sex partnerships, the medical and psychological ramifications of being HIV positive and many other things mentioned in your January/February issue.

However, to say that the mere fact of being gay makes one a better therapist seems to promote a prejudice which homosexuals decry when applied to themselves: "Don't judge me by my sexuality. Judge me by my individual merits."

Michael E. Holtby
Denver, CO

AS A THERAPIST WHO WORKS WITH GAY and lesbian clients, I applaud your recognition that homosexuality needs to be seen as a sound, valid life-style rather than as an unhealthy anomaly or perversion.

However, having facilitated a support group for bisexual women for three years, I was dismayed when your articles fell into the traditional dichotomous view of labeling persons as either "straight" (presumably heterosexual) or "gay" (homosexual). We need to move from a dualistic notion of sexuality and recognize that sexual attraction to both men and women can exist side by side within the same person. Although some bisexuals may be in a transitory stage (from heterosexuality to homosexuality, or the reverse) in my experience, most bisexuals are persons who have chosen an ongoing life-style of expanding their emotional and sexual relationships to include both sexes.

Unfortunately, society (and *The Family Therapy Networker*) generally seems to recognize only two options—heterosexual or gay/lesbian.

Nancy M. Casey
Rochester, NY

I WAS SURPRISED BY THE NUMBER OF LETTERS in response to your issue about gays and lesbians. Assuming that, at least to some extent, these letters are a proportionate sampling of your readership and that the writers are practicing therapists, the conclusions are troubling, to say the least. I never would have suspected that members of the therapeutic community would be less tolerant than the average "Donahue" audience. I had not realized how widespread and entrenched homophobia is. The radicalization of gays and lesbians as evinced by groups such as Queer

Letters to the Editor

Nation is far more justified than I had thought.

Richard A.B. Gleiner
New York, NY

THE LETTERS IN RESPONSE TO YOUR ISSUE about gay and lesbian concerns were most interesting. Although the number representing positive reactions was somewhat reassuring, the negative responses were surprisingly vituperative. I was under the impression that at least part of the role of the therapist is to be empathic and caring, not only with those the therapist agrees with.

Matt Lowman
San Francisco, CA

PHOTOGRAPH BY STUART FRANKLIN/MAGNUM

SONG WITHOUT WORDS

LISTENING TO JAPANESE FAMILIES

By Linda Bell

WE AMERICANS KNOW HOW TO TALK; THE Japanese, with their emphasis on empathy and intuition, know how to listen. To the Japanese, Westerners' talkativeness makes us seem arrogant and hyperactive. They sometimes wonder if we are afraid of silence. In Japan, the most important communication takes place nonverbally. Restrained and disciplined in public, the Japanese nonetheless have rich inner lives, and perhaps more inner emotional freedom than many in our overtly less inhibited society. During a two-year sabbatical in Japan, while my husband and I were visiting researchers at the Japanese National Institute of Mental Health, I too began to wonder about Americans' emphasis on the intellect and verbal skills. Why do we have to talk so much?

Our stay in Japan, as well as contacts with Japanese families here in the States, have given me the opportunity to spend many hours contemplating the differences between Japanese and American cultures. Nowhere are the differences more apparent than in attitudes toward childrearing. When I first saw my own newborn child, I thought about how helpless and dependent he was: I wanted to help him grow strong and self-sufficient. A Japanese mother by contrast wants to strengthen her child's connectedness with a loving family. Mother-child symbiosis lasts longer and is valued more highly in Japan than in America. Until a child's sixth birthday, the parents focus almost exclusively on nurturing that child, accommodating themselves to childish whims. Even during the later years of childhood and adolescence, the child/student is the center of the family and almost no sacrifice is considered excessive if it will contribute to his or her educational advancement.

Although the Japanese are trying to integrate modern values of individualism and autonomy with traditional patterns of family and social harmony, their cultural priorities are still the reverse of ours. Americans cherish individual expression; Japanese cherish harmony in the group. Japanese parents put family harmony first when raising children; American parents are more likely to emphasize individual self-actualization. I want my children to be independent, to take a stand against the group and fight for their rights, if necessary. I distrust "groups," which might negatively influence my children's lives or potentially lead them into trouble. In Japan, however, the word for "different" is the same as the word for "wrong." For them, the group is more likely to offer a comfortable, familial experience, in which people feel nurtured and protected.

Whereas Americans "launch" their adult children—send them "out into the world"—Japanese children never "break away." The family maintains a strong sense of connectedness throughout the life cycle. While American mothers threaten to punish their children by making them stay at home, Japanese mothers threaten to punish children by putting them out of the house. My 4-year-old learned quickly that ghosts come out after dark in Japan; for safety, he had to come inside the house. In Japan, the mother and baby are one unit. Many American mothers carry babies on their backs in specially designed sling packs, but only in Japan have I seen coats that covered both mother and baby together.

JAPANESE ARE MORE LIKELY THAN AMERICANS TO experience themselves as part of a flowing stream, integrated within a larger whole; a sense of oneness and unity between self and others is highly valued. A Japanese colleague working in the United States once told me that Americans give the impression of not wanting to be intruded on by anybody. The result was that she was left feeling somehow isolated when interacting with Americans.

While harmony is the ideal in Japan, conformity is often the experience. The individual's self-concept is not actively developed in Japan to the extent that it is in the United States. There is no show-and-tell in Japanese schools. Children aren't encouraged to have a personal opinion. One Japanese student listening to American family discussions was amazed that the children speak their feelings and say what they think. A Japanese friend in the United States was perturbed by a questionnaire her third-grade

daughter brought home. On it were a lot of incomplete sentences focusing on personal attitudes: "My favorite animal is . . . ," "I like my family because . . . ." Neither mother nor daughter had ever been asked these particular questions before. What were the right answers? Another Japanese friend told me that it was as an adult, while talking with her English teacher, that she first made the important distinction between "the Japanese answer" and "my own answer." "We are not so conscious of our real desires," says another Japanese living in the United States, "so conformity is not so difficult."

Just as Americans downplay mutual dependency or avoid closeness for fear of threatening individuality, the Japanese downplay individual differences and resist highlighting individuality for fear of damaging harmony. A writer for the *Japan Times* recently reported that a high percentage of young people said they would be true to their own values, something he thought a very *bad* sign, indicating selfishness and egotism. Traditionally in Japan, self-discipline and self-control are highly valued and highly developed. Self-sacrifice is honored, even to the extent of "killing off" one's own feelings out of respect for others. To the Japanese, a strong person is one who sacrifices self in service to others.

A GROUP OF JAPANESE GATHERED TOGETHER IS like a clutch of different-colored foam rubber balls, compressed into a small space; the balls can adapt, accommodate their shape in order to make a fit. Americans are more like wooden cubes. To fit the same number of Americans into the same space might require cutting off a few sharp corners or edges—we seem to require more elbow room or we end up poking each other. In a Japanese group, mutual accommodation is the preferred style, on the theory that if each member feels supported, the goals of the group will be more readily achieved. An individual's needs are met because someone else notices and cares, not because of self-promotion. In any case, the true self is felt as a silent, inward awareness, rather than expressed in a demonstration of public self-assertion.

A JAPANESE THERAPIST WORKING WITH A FAMILY is most likely to notice first the difficulty family members have depending upon one another for emotional support and nurturance, their inability to care for and connect with one another. In contrast, an American therapist is more likely to pick up the intrusions by Japanese family members into one another's private space, the lack of individuality and autonomy. In a country settled by immigrants, most American families have ancestors who had to cut ties with family and culture and begin again, alone, in a new environment. A Japanese person's experience of family goes back several generations, perhaps hundreds of years; the ashes of these family members are entombed together in a family grave.

When I teach, I often ask people to make a symbolic picture of their family. In a kind of picture I saw for the first time in Japan, the colors—each representing a family member—all intermingle, though none lose their individual essence. This view of the Japanese family and relationship carries over into Japanese family therapy. Compared with American therapy, the bond between therapist and patient in Japan is deeper and more permanent. Empathic communication, expressions of mutual acceptance, and forgiveness of human imperfections supply the connective tissue between the therapist and family members. Further, the relationship does not end, once therapy is finished, but, like the family itself, goes on forever. The sense of oneness and mutuality between therapist and patient creates an almost mystical sense of connection, a bond made by fate.

The Japanese pattern of communication depends primarily on intuition and nonverbal cues. Close family members or friends expect almost telepathic mutual understanding. In Japan, I worked with a group of mental health professionals, mostly

women, who had left their families, often including children, behind while they attended 6- to 12-month professional development programs in Tokyo. We talked about how often they contacted their families, either by letter or phone call. I discovered, to my initial surprise, that I wrote many more letters home and made more phone calls than they did. In fact, some of the women told me they almost never wrote or called; doing so would be a sign of something wrong. They felt so deeply connected to their families that they didn't require letters or phone calls. By implication, writing letters or phoning was a sign of being out of (empathic) touch!

AMERICAN CHILDREN LEARN TO EXPRESS THEIR ideas orally; Japanese children learn to pay attention to the face, to read nonverbal cues, and to listen well. In a healthy American family, members share their feelings by talking; in a healthy Japanese family, such verbal sharing is not considered necessary or even desirable. For a Japanese man to say he can take his wife for granted is a compliment—she is like the air, and he can count on her.

When having our son tested for a private school in the United States, his Japanese teacher was asked to fill out an American form with a question about whether the child could "control his feelings." On a corresponding Japanese questionnaire, which the teacher showed us, was a question about whether the child "manages to express his feelings." Several times, Japanese colleagues, in sharing their feelings with me, said, "I can't say that in Japanese," suggesting that the very structure of the language forbade the verbal expression of emotions. The Japanese distrust words and verbal skills: "words are just words." Greater weight is placed on intuition and experience—sensing, touching, doing.

During my first months in Japan, when sitting behind the mirror during therapy sessions, I would often question my Japanese colleagues about the content of the therapy discussion. Sometimes the answer was, "I don't know," and I would wonder how they could listen and not know what people were saying? When I began working in front of the mirror, I was often told, "*That* was very interesting, but we could never do *that*; you could do *that* because you are a foreigner." "That" was my habit of asking for clarification when I did not understand, or pursuing a fuzzy answer to elicit a clearer one. Such behavior was acceptable from foreigners, but a fellow Japanese is expected to know the meaning through empathy. Asking for explicit verbal communication is considered rude and intrusive, and shows that the therapist lacks intuitive understanding.

Western visitors observing Japanese family therapy were sometimes mystified. What were they doing? What was the focus? Often the sessions seemed to us to move slowly, because we Americans did not sense the active, underground bonding. Because we could not read the faces and missed the nonverbal communication, we caught perhaps 20 percent of what was happening, and thus often felt at a loss. A Japanese colleague once critiqued my work by saying, "You seem to think words are important." From her perspective, my overemphasis on words transformed the family's communication into something less substantial, more superficial or shallow, than it would have been had I left things less explicit and depended on my intuition.

In my clinical work, I found most striking the difference between Japanese and American attitudes toward marriage. For me, marriage is the core of the family; being a good parent depends upon a vital, supportive relationship with my husband that meets both our emotional needs. If my relationship with my husband becomes cool, distant, or angry, our children will suffer. If reconciliation is impossible, then it is better for all of us that we divorce.

Most Japanese would consider parents immature who separated simply because they no longer cared for each other. Marital difficulties—dissension, isolation, overbearing in-laws, even physical abuse—are to be endured for the sake of the family's integrity. Traditionally, the Japanese expect from marriage not personal fulfillment, which they might seek in work, in raising children, in a love affair, but certain standards of behavior and responsibility. They expect to find happiness within themselves.

More jarring to the Western consciousness is the accepted supremacy of the parent-child bond, especially that between mother and children. The traditional bond between a mother and a first son is a highly enmeshed relationship that continues throughout the son's adult life. One 35-year-old client, a Japanese businessman living with his own family in Europe, told me he could not read his mother's letters without experiencing such an emotional storm inside that he could think of nothing else for two weeks afterward.

A typical family therapy case in Japan exhibits a distant marriage, a strong bond between father and paternal grandmother, and another between mother and son. The presenting problem may be a young adolescent's refusal to attend school or, sometimes, the physical abuse of the mother, most often by a son. An adolescent son's violence can cause the mother serious injury, but she generally accepts it, feeling that responding in kind simply fuels the fire. The mother submits, hoping that eventually her suffering will evoke her child's empathy. The only time a Japanese adult ever became openly angry at me was when I suggested to a badly bruised mother that she should not have allowed her son to beat her. She vehemently insisted that only *because* her son had seen her bruises and suffering had he stopped the abuse and agreed to return to school.

It often seemed to me that a family's difficulties were exacerbated by their placing an extremely high value on harmony, self-sacrifice, suffering and empathy. Yet, listening to this mother's protest moved me to reconsider; perhaps her behavior was not "crazy." I thought of Gandhi and of my own Quaker background, and wondered why this way of "accepting the child's anger" was such a difficult concept for me.

Several Japanese colleagues told me that the Oedipal myth was not very useful to them. The child in Japan is never shoved from the nest, and the son never loses the Oedipal struggle—there is no struggle; his primacy is accepted from the moment of birth. That this blood bond could ever be secondary to the marital one is almost unimaginable.

ONE SUMMER MY FAMILY SPENT SIX WEEKS AT A cabin on a lake. Twice, we invited Japanese friends to visit. We discussed among ourselves where our guests would sleep, then decided to wait until each family arrived to suggest their own arrangements. We did not imagine the result in spite of having read and heard about it often. In both cases, the parents slept in separate beds—each with one or more children! Sleeping with an adult is thought to provide children with a sense of security.

Historically in Japan, a newly married couple moved in with the husband's parents, creating a three-generation household. New wives were basically apprenticed to their mothers-in-law, expected to nurture children, in-laws, and husband, often to the tune of constant criticism. In recent times, the father typically devotes himself to his work and is rarely home. Mother is entirely responsible for managing home and children, controlling the family's finances, overseeing the children's education, and serving and supporting her husband. She is experienced as both self-sacrificing and powerful, the foundation of the home. Once, behind a mirror observing a marital session with a professional couple, both doctors, I heard the husband complain that his wife did not prepare a sack lunch for their late-adolescent son. I suggested to my colleagues that since the father was concerned, he might prepare the lunch himself. Everyone laughed heartily at what they took to be a joke.

Today, most young Japanese want a personally fulfilling marriage, more on the Western model. Many young women are refusing to move in with their mothers-in-law, and unhappy wives are more likely than before to seek divorce, especially after the children are grown. But the conflicts accompanying these transitions can be wrenching. Parents, for example, may ask their independently minded offspring, "But who will take care of the graves?" If no one chooses to live with the parents, to maintain the family house and property, if children all live in other towns, who will care for the parents, the grandparents and the ancestors? This represents a break with hundreds of years of tradition. To the older generation, it seems unfair that they honored, obeyed and cared for their parents and now are being deserted by their own children. On the other hand, they also are becoming aware of what they missed. An older Japanese colleague once observed wistfully that he and his wife had never held hands.

JAPANESE CULTURE IS ORGANIZED AROUND PRINCIples of wholeness and complementarity, a respect for all elements of being, and a refusal to divide experience into mutually contradictory categories. When we were toilet training our young son, we taught him to pee on a tree in the backyard. Observing this, a Japanese babysitter taught him to first apologize to the tree. She explained that not only did this show respect for the tree, his apology would also inhibit angry spirits.

The awareness of the indivisibility of creation extends to the Japanese acceptance of death as part of the fullness of life. A Japanese painting of a flower bouquet is likely to include all stages of life, from fresh new buds, to wilted and decaying blossoms. The Japanese never see evil in a child; children are gods—or gifts of gods. Basic human nature is thought to be good. They do not share our dualistic tendency to regard human motivation as either good or evil. Japanese are more likely to accept the whole of human nature, defects and graces alike, and thus may have less need for protecting themselves from guilt or for blaming others. In our litigious society, with 15 times as many lawyers per capita as Japan, we put enormous energy into protecting ourselves from blame, assigning blame to others, going to court to discover who is to blame. In Japan, even the criminal is partly right, the victim partly wrong. The Japanese are much more likely to accept blame and to apologize. Apology, they believe, is the gateway to forgiveness, rehabilitation and social acceptance.

Americans tend to polarize experience, isolating individual elements of life into good or bad, right or wrong, truth or falsehood. The Japanese, on the other hand, are more likely to see opposites flowing from or even fulfilling each other. In success is the seed of failure, in sadness the germ of future happiness. Matriarchy and patriarchy are yin and yang, each intrinsic to an indivisible whole. One extreme flows into the other. Working with Japanese clients, I came to believe that Americans cut off their feelings at the neck, in order to repress what they think is unacceptable in themselves. The Japanese cut off their feelings at the face, displaying only the appropriate demeanor for the occasion and context, but unafraid to experience internal feelings and ideas that Americans would find shameful and repugnant. They seem freer to have a rich inner life because they do not censor their own emotions, however strictly they control their behavior.

These two principles—wholeness and complementarity—underlie the social relativism for which the Japanese are famous. Americans are uncomfortable with relativism; they prefer seeing themselves and their families as unified, stable, single entities. When asked to make a symbolic picture of their family, Americans will usually make one picture, whereas the Japanese families will make more than one—"this is us when father is home," "this is the family at dinner time," "this shows the family's emotional relations." A Japanese colleague teased me about my "one true self," because like other Westerners, I believe that if my behavior is inconsistent in different situations I am being somehow false, untrue to myself. The Japanese understand that different roles and contexts allow or even demand different aspects of the self to emerge. External behavior and inner feelings are separate, though coexisting, worlds, and society's requirements do not bind the life of the mind.

What seem like contradictions to us work quite harmoniously in the Japanese temperament. For example, they believe that commitment and effort can achieve anything; they are highly ambitious, and prepared to endure much suffering to achieve their goals. At the same time, they relish the experience of being passively nurtured; the experience of dependency is central to the Japanese personality. The Japanese believe in accommodation to the group, self-sacrifice on behalf of society and family, apology, and humility as a means to peaceful reconciliation. Yet they also admire the strong, determined individual, the independent spirit of the samurai.

Undoubtedly, there are many ways to understand truth. Westerners seek to understand their world through intellect—logic and reason; Japanese, through intuition. Japanese culture is distrustful of language and reveres the nonverbal. Nevertheless, as a Westerner, I have tried to analyze the essence of the Japanese experience and set it down in the medium of words. I am aware that while I have jotted down some of the notes, the music of Japanese culture will always escape description. ∎

LINDA BELL, PH.D., *is an associate professor of behavioral sciences, and former director of training in family therapy at the University of Houston—Clear Lake, Houston, TX.*

See references, page 563.

We are all being forced to see that there are many beliefs, multiple realities . . . a daunting profusion of worldviews. . . . We cannot choose not to make choices.

WALTER TRUETT ANDERSON
MAUREEN O'HARA

PHOTOGRAPH BY EUGENE RICHARDS/MAGNUM

PHOTOGRAPH BY SYLVIA PLACHY

PHOTOGRAPH BY SYLVIA PLACHY

PHOTOGRAPH BY EUGENE RICHARDS/MAGNUM

PHOTOGRAPH BY PAUL FUSCO/MAGNUM

PHOTOGRAPH BY JAMES NACHTWEY/MAGNUM

On the Front Lines

FACING
THE CHALLENGES
OF EVERYDAY
PRACTICE

PHOTOGRAPH BY ABIGAIL HEYMAN

*K*NOW THY SELVES

THE INNER LIVES OF COUPLES THERAPY

By Richard Schwartz

EVERY COUPLES THERAPIST KNOWS THE EXPERI-ence. Just moments ago, as you talked to the wife and then her husband, you were struck by how likable each one seemed. You sensed their warmth, their humor.

But now you've hit on one of *those* issues—perhaps it's a conflict about an in-law, or something about sex, or even the proverbial struggle about the toothpaste tube—and, suddenly, the people whose company you were enjoying earlier appear to have left the room. Faces tighten, bodies grow stiff, nobody's hearing anything anymore. Now two unyielding go-for-the-jugular combatants are sitting in front of you. And they're not the only ones who have undergone a dramatic transformation. Suddenly, you're not quite present in the room, either. As garbled little voices in your head issue their fuzzy instructions, the couple before you begins to fade. You tell yourself you must do *something*. Meanwhile, you note with some distress, a decidedly unprofessional feeling of panic has begun rising within you.

Of course, one doesn't have to sit in a room with warring couples in order to find evidence that we all

regularly experience rather dramatic shifts in our moment-to-moment sense of ourselves. We all know what it's like to experience a seemingly trivial incident as a life-or-death struggle, and then later, looking back over the experience, to find ourselves totally unable to understand what the sense of peril was about. It is as if some other person were feeling the anxiety—a person whose dilemma may even seem quite laughable in retrospect. However hard we may try to maintain a consistent front for the world, we know that our private world can vary wildly from moment to moment. Somewhere deep within us we're aware that our ability to draw on our resources—our stores of confidence, flexibility, experience and worldly wisdom—is not entirely under our control.

MOST FAMILY THERAPY THEORIES ARE BASED ON the idea that when you get to the core of a family's problems, you usually find conflicts between the marital couple. But what do you do then? Systems-based theories get rather vague at this point. When faced with the task of overcoming obstacles to marital intimacy, behaviorally oriented family therapy technique and theory provide few clear guidelines.

Family therapy's great insight was that our behavior was intricately related to our social context. For 25 years we've seen how fruitful it can be to relate individual family members' symptoms—from bedwetting and bulimia to delinquency and depression—to interactional patterns, and to use concepts like triangulation, boundaries, hierarchies, and so forth to make order of a bewildering array of family relationships. It is now becoming increasingly clear, however, that the family therapy paradigm did not go far enough in revising our concept of the individuals who enact these patterns.

One still finds family therapists defining their clients as "needy," "nurturing," "angry," "overinvolved," as if everyone possesses some consistent quality of personhood that is maintained throughout the day. We may have just one body, but do we really have just one personality? Doesn't each of us contain many personalities? Aren't we quite different with different people and in different circumstances?

Of course, once one begins talking about what goes on "inside" people, it becomes difficult to offer proof of anything. In this piece I would like to invite the reader to leave open the empirical question of whether or not we all, to some extent, have multiple personalities. Instead, I would like to show the clinical possibilities that open up once one begins to use the metaphor that we are each a living community of selves.

THROUGH THE DAY WE REGULARLY PASS, OFTEN imperceptibly, from self to self. Because of the speed and fluidity of this process, and the fact that we have such a limited vocabulary for distinguishing among these inner selves, we don't usually attend to the ways this inner community conducts its business. Just as in observing client families, it is far easier to become absorbed in the content and thus ignore the process, so we may notice thoughts running through our heads without recognizing that they emerge from a range of recurrent types of conversations that we carry on with ourselves. Of course, the exact quality of these conversations can be extraordinarily elusive. We are capable of having any number going on at the same time, and what is more, we can converse with ourselves in many "languages," some of which take place in a private, idiosyncratic vocabulary of images or body sensations rather than a language of words.

Over the past five years, as I have tried to apply family systems principles to understanding inner experience, I have been struck by how readily both clients and colleagues take to the idea that they have not one but many selves. With surprising ease, people can identify inner selves that are activated under different circumstances in their lives, selves that are in conflict with each other, selves they like and selves they don't. Once we get beyond our cultural bias for viewing ourselves as consistent, unitary individuals who "know their own minds"—what I call the Myth of the Monolithic Self—the multiplicity paradigm makes a lot of intuitive sense.

Our lives are very complex. We have to do and think many things at once. We need many specialized minds, operating with a certain amount of autonomy and internal communication, to accomplish all of this simultaneous activity. How else are we to understand mental phenomena like the "spontaneous inspiration" involved in creativity, in which the answers to problems come to us "out of the blue" in the middle of the night? Religious conversions, the "out of character" behavior triggered by drug or alcohol intoxications, the experience of suddenly falling in or out of love, or the phenomenon of multiple personality disorder are all examples of people's capacity to undergo a dramatic and sudden personality change.[1] These are not simply a matter of a shifting set of emotions or thought patterns, but instead often represent a change to a completely different worldview, complete with consistent values, interests, beliefs and feelings.

THE MORE I EXPLORE WITH CLIENTS THE NUANCES of their subjective experience of themselves, the more the analogy of a family or community makes sense in understanding this inner world. The partial selves that inhabit this world are both interconnected and autonomous. These subpersonalities, like members of an "external family," vie for control, interact sequentially, organize into alliances and, at times, go to war with each other.

The most important—but not the only—factor shaping the organization of this inner community is our experience in our families of origin. We tend to identify with, rely on and listen to the parts of us that our family valued or that helped us play a particular family role while growing up. At the same time, we tend to distance from or stifle parts that our families disapproved of. Some of our inner selves relate to us in the same way that one or the other of our parents did, while other selves battle those parental replicas. Each of these partial selves is a discrete and autonomous mental system that has an idiosyncratic range of emotion, style of communication, and set of abilities, intentions and functions. Each is organized around a particular premise or set of premises about the world and how to survive or thrive within it.

These premises shape the tone and "personality" of each of our selves. Frequently, these selves view the world from a very limited perspective. People in whom the inner selves are highly isolated or polarized may have either a very constricted or a very impulsive quality to their behavior, unable to follow through on plans that are apparently in their own best interests.

Some of our inner selves maintain the viewpoints we held when we were much younger. So when these parts take over, we may find ourselves reacting

to the world as adults in the same way we did as children, somehow unable to draw upon all the experience, knowledge and personal resources we have acquired in the intervening years. For example, a person who experienced frequent unwelcome surprises growing up might have a voice within him that repeatedly says, "Prepare for the worst" whenever faced with uncertainty in a relationship. The person who identifies with that attitude as a general survival strategy for anticipating disappointment may not even be aware of how it can become a self-fulfilling prophecy.

Each of our partial selves has a different intention for us and, based on that intention, assumes a different role within us. Because each part's "agenda," no matter how well intentioned, is different, inevitably the parts conflict with each other. How those conflicts are handled will often determine whether our inner selves polarize and, in the process, become extreme and/or destructive rather than remain valuable resources to draw upon.

Before trying to comprehend the complex blending of two people's internal families that takes place in a marriage, it is important to understand a little more about these internal systems. While I believe that no two people's internal families are identical, I consistently find a common set of subpersonalities representing some basic intentions in most people. The danger in describing these commonalities is that therapists will impose on clients theoretical preconceptions about their partial selves rather than listening closely to and trusting the client's own description of his or her inner world. With that caveat firmly in mind, I will describe a few of the many subpersonalities I commonly find activated in intimate relationships.

WE ALL FACE THE JOB OF CONTROLLING OUR relationships to ensure that we are not hurt by others and that we have some reliable means of getting our desires met. When we find ourselves in emotionally threatening relationship conflicts, our family experience generally teaches us to access certain parts of ourselves and not others. All marital therapists are familiar with couples who seem to tear into each other at every opportunity. Other couples may be equally extreme in the opposite direction, anxiously avoiding any show of anger or open conflict.

A person's Social Adviser or Asserter may be modeled on a parent or may be shaped more indirectly by family values. People who grew up in families in which differences were tolerated and productively negotiated may have access to a part that is a calm and flexible Adviser that helps them assert themselves when conflict begins to erupt. On the other hand, someone who grew up in a family in which the open expression of differences was frowned upon or resulted in emotional abuse may have an internal image of an inner self aroused by family struggles that is a kind of monster to be kept under wraps at all costs. The result of such polarization in many people is that this Asserter, rather than being flexible, has become extremely angry and if activated in conflict may stubbornly cling to a position of "Stand your ground at any cost," or "Get them before they get you." When two partners adopt this position, we see the kind of rigidly black/white, "I-am-totally-right; you-are-totally-wrong" battles that are the death of negotiation and the bane of the couples therapist.

OUR BEHAVIOR IS ALWAYS IMPLICITLY ORGANIZED by our expectations of others as well as our ideas about what we are capable of doing. When faced with a challenge, most of us have had the experience of hearing voices within us expressing very different views of our chances, from "You can do it" to "You'll never make it" to "It doesn't matter either way." Particularly relevant to couples cases is an internal self that I call the Passive-Pessimist that, like the Asserter, is concerned with

protecting the individual from harm.

The strategy of the Passive-Pessimist is opposite to and often in conflict with that of the Asserter. The Passive Pessimist withdraws rather than asserts itself or attacks. Its main intention is to avoid the risk of possible rejection or failure, in extreme cases devaluing all close relationships and drastically minimizing what can be expected from others. In couples who seem "dead to each other," this particular subpersonality is dominant in both partners, producing a protective, mutually reinforced state of apathy and lowered expectation.

OUR EXPERIENCE OF EMOTIONAL VULNERABILITY is a powerful activator in our inner world. The vulnerable or needy subself is often referred to as the inner child, although that image does not fit all people's experience. Whatever it is called, within each of us there is a part that seeks intimacy, closeness and nurturance. It is the source of our deepest experiences of love and empathy, as well as pain, emptiness and loneliness when it is hurt or neglected. Typically, it communicates less through words than through the language of physical sensation, making itself known to us by how we feel in our hearts and in our guts.

This Intimacy Seeker within us is an aspect of our experience that family therapists have often been accused of overlooking, especially in their work with couples. Nevertheless, it provides the motive force behind our deepest relationships, our desire to love and be loved. Every couples therapist knows that the most touching and memorable sessions occur when this aspect of each partner is able to locate its counterpart in the other. On the other hand, the most explosive sessions—as well as the most lifeless—often result from the couple's fear of activating this inner experience of vulnerability.

Of course, the complement to the vulnerable member of one spouse's internal family is often the nurturer in the other. In this culture men and women are taught very different ways of relating to this inner nurturer. Men are encouraged to distance from it as much as possible, while women, particularly those in traditional patriarchal families, are sometimes given the message that they should always take care of others before themselves. As I will describe later, couples therapy is often most effective when it can get beyond issues of who's taking care of whom and awaken in both partners their ability to nurture themselves as well as each other.

MAINTAINING INTIMACY IN OUR SOCIAL RELAtionships is only part of the challenge we face in daily life. We all need to find ways to feel proud of our competence and achievement in our chosen social roles. In some people, however, the parts of the internal family concerned with personal achievement are at odds with partial selves seeking emotional intimacy. For example, a powerful part of the inner world is what I call the Striver, a self that expresses disdain for emotional relatedness. Its focus is on productivity, success and competitiveness. We live in a culture that highly encourages the elevation of this aspect of the individual. The Striver communicates to the individual through idealized images of personal triumph and devalues activities or other inner selves or people that don't contribute directly to personal advancement. Typically, people highly identified with the Striver in them disdain emotional vulnerability in both themselves and other people because they fear such feelings will interfere with their productivity and blunt their competitive edge.

We all have an Evaluator within us that makes sure our behavior fits with our beliefs about ourselves and with our personal or social values. The Evaluator often takes the role of an observing monitor of our behavior and of people's reactions to it. The likelihood of its becoming a critical perfectionist increases if it believes that an individual is inadequate and needs the help of others to survive. For example, the Evaluator may give the message, "You must look and behave properly or you will be deserted." This inner Evaluator is often a parental voice that may also take aim at one's spouse if he or she is not meeting its standards.

Finally, many marital symptoms are related to the effects of an internal Pleasure Seeker that is especially alive to the possibilities of enjoyment in life. When a person feels emotionally vulnerable, the Pleasure Seeker may take over and direct him or her to indulge in some distracting or anesthetizing activities like a food, alcohol, drug, sex, or work binge. As one might expect, this pleasure-seeking self is often polarized with the Striver and the Evaluator.

I want to emphasize again that this brief list of inner selves is not to be reified as the objective reality of everyone's psyche. These sketches are highly generalized depictions that have emerged from hundreds of interviews with clients regarding their internal lives. Doing therapy always involves a tricky balancing act of trying to avoid imposing a set of rigid, Procrustean categories on clients, while not becoming so afraid of reification that one wanders without a map through the mind field they give us of their own experience.

THE PICTURE I HAVE PAINTED SO FAR OF THE inner world has been incomplete. I have yet to discuss a crucial participant of this internal family—a part I call the Self. The Self resides in the center of the "you" that the parts try to influence. It is the Self that gives us a sense of continuity, our experience of being an "I" rather than a fragmented accumulation of competing subselves.

When their Self is elevated within the internal family, people are able to achieve a "meta-perspective" that is broader than the limited viewpoint of any one part of the internal system. From the Self springs empathy and compassion for the predicaments of partial selves as well as other people. When one's Self is differentiated from one's parts and elevated within the internal hierarchy, one experiences a state that has been referred to as being "centered," a state of feeling calm, secure, lighthearted and "in the present."

Being in this state of the Self is comparable to what people perceive while in meditation, an experience of remaining outside the flux of moment-to-moment identification with a particular part of themselves. However, the Self is capable of going beyond being a passive witness and can and should be highly active in our internal politics, assuming a leadership role in orchestrating our various subpersonalities and in dealing with the "external" world. I have never treated a case in which the Self, once it was clearly identified and differentiated from the parts, was not capable of assuming a central role in guiding experience. Nor have I ever found anyone who didn't have a Self. As Milton Erickson noted so often, people truly do have all the resources they need once they know how to access them.

Once the Self is accessed, the therapist and client can collaborate immediately on the process of differentiating and elevating it to the position of leadership. In that position the Self can, for example, comfort and soothe frightened children within, or calm down rageful defenders, or redirect overzealous Strivers. The Self can act as a therapist to the internal family by getting polarized inner antagonists to deal with each other and by helping the whole inner community to depolarize and restructure. While this may sound like a difficult process, I find that in most clients the various members of their inner family welcome this kind of leadership once they are convinced that the Self can be trusted. And remember, the mind has many languages. It's not that all this takes place in lengthy dialogues. It can happen quickly through symbolic communication, dreams, changes in body awareness, etc.

M Y GOAL IN MARITAL THERAPY IS TO PROMOTE the Self-leadership of each spouse so that the two Selves can work together to help their

two internal families become a more harmonious "blended family," one in which as many partial selves as possible are satisfied. This usually involves a rhythmic shifting between two phases of therapy, one of which involves one spouse watching as the other works on his or her internal family through imagery or "open-chair" techniques, and the other phase in which the spouses negotiate issues between them while trying to maintain Self-leadership. The following case shows how viewing people as having multiple selves can be put to use with couples, especially when more traditional family therapy approaches have led to a dead end.

John and Mary are an attractive, articulate, professional couple in their early forties. Childless by choice, and without regret, they have been married 18 years. They tell Bill, their therapist, that while things have never been perfectly smooth, they have been fighting constantly the past eight months, ever since John became the manager of a department full of women. John says that he can no longer stand Mary's jealousy and incessant grilling as to who he was with all day. Bill teaches them to make "I" statements rather than blaming each other, and to listen carefully to each other and feed back what was heard to ensure that "the message sent is the message received." They agree to set aside more time to spend together and the session ends on an upbeat and hopeful note.

The next week, however, it is immediately apparent that this improvement was short-lived. Two days after the last session, they had the most dramatic and alarming fight of their marriage.

Several more sessions of structured communication did not seem to alter what was becoming a basic pattern in which conflict was defused during sessions but escalated between sessions. Bill decided to shift the focus of the sessions toward an exploration of Mary's family history. It did not take much exploring to see the connection between her current feelings and her parents' divorce when she was seven years old. Mary wept as she spoke of her sense of abandonment, rejection and loss when her father left. Bill tried to get John to support Mary in planning letters and visits to her father. Again, however, Mary's uncontrollable jealousy and rage at home interfered with their compliance on these tasks, and they teetered precariously on the brink of divorce. Through their focus on her family, Mary also came to realize that her mother had driven her father out of their home by behavior similar to her own, and that realization made her feel even more frightened and ashamed of herself.

Bill referred Mary to another therapist, Sue, for what he recommended to be long-term individual treatment, but Sue decided to use the Internal Family Systems Model and continue to work with the couple. In the first session, after some discussion of the model and the idea of "parts," Sue asked John what he said to himself when Mary became so jealous:

JOHN: I feel trapped, like I have to get away, and angry that I have to put up with this when I didn't do anything wrong.

SUE: So part of you says, "Get out of here," and another part says, "Don't take that from her, stand up for yourself." Is that right?

JOHN: Yeah, something like that.

SUE: Do you hear anything else? For example, do you ever get down on yourself about it?

JOHN: Sometimes I tell myself that I should work less and I feel a little guilty, but then she explodes and I think, "Why should I try?"

SUE: So there's another part that is critical of you and still another that feels guilty, but then that angry part returns. Of the parts we have begun to identify so far, which one would you like to get to know better or change your relationship with first?

JOHN: Maybe that trapped guy because I feel that way all the time.

SUE: Okay, try to focus on that part exclusively for a second, however you experience it, whether it's a voice or a thought pattern or a feeling, and as you focus on it see if an image of it as something alive comes to you.

John saw a Little Boy cowering in a corner of a room, for whom he felt sympathy. Sue had John focus on this image and ask the Little Boy what he wanted from John. The boy answered that he wanted to feel safe and protected. Eventually the boy admitted that he made John feel so boxed in because he felt at risk from Mary's frontal assaults and wanted John to get him away from her. The boy also said that he was afraid of John's angry part because when it took over, it made Mary even more enraged and dangerous.

Sue had John imagine putting his arm around the boy and asking him if he would feel less at risk if John spent time with him and comforted him when he was scared. The boy replied that that might help, but he was not totally prepared to trust John to do this. Sue then had John focus on and image his angry part, a tough-looking teenage kid who said that it had to protect John and the boy from Mary, even though it knew that its intervention made things worse between John and Mary. John asked this Angry Guy whether he would allow John, as his Self, to handle conflict with Mary if John was able to take better care of the scared boy. The Angry Guy thought so, but shared the boy's skepticism regarding John's commitment to the boy, largely because John tended to listen to another part that was highly critical of him and could make that boy feel extremely guilty and depressed. John agreed that he would have to find a way to deactivate that critical part before he could fully care for the boy.

After this work, John said that he was surprised to discover that the trapped feeling was related to being scared of Mary and agreed to try to help that boy by "meeting" with him every day. Mary said she was glad to see that she was not the only one who had work to do and wanted to know how she could help John in his struggle with his internal family. Sue replied that, for a little while, it might be best for each of them to focus on helping themselves and not to change each other or to get closer.

Along those lines, Sue asked Mary to image the scared part of her, and not surprisingly, it appeared as a 7- or 8-year-old girl who told her to do anything to keep from losing John. Sue had Mary negotiate with the various members of her internal family that protected this vulnerable part of her so that some new, more effective ways of taking care of this child-self could emerge. In this process Mary encountered a Guardian who told her not to trust or get close to anybody, as well as the Warrior that attacked John so viciously.

John felt more hopeful after watching Mary's work. The inner selves that Mary revealed were no strangers to him. He said he knew that scared Little Girl and always felt overwhelmed by her neediness yet guilty because he could not satisfy her. John was relieved to see that the Little Girl and the Warrior were just parts of Mary and that Mary could begin to relate differently to them. He also said that he could see how his parts activated Mary's and agreed to work on maintaining Self leadership no matter how Mary behaved.

Over the next several sessions, John and Mary each did more of this kind of internal work, while also negotiating issues they had between them, such as John's long hours or Mary's complaining about John to her mother. During these discussions both spouses struggled to keep their parts in advisory positions and keep their Selves in the lead. When partial selves took over either of them, Sue stopped the action and asked that they calm down the inner turmoil and return to Self-leadership. Gradually both John and Mary became skilled at quickly sensing when partial selves had arrogated control and at getting them to step back.

During this initial period with Sue, the couple continued to fight at home, but those episodes did not seem to have the same destructive effect. John reported that when Mary screamed at him, instead of thinking, "How do I get away from this maniac?" he now said to himself, "There goes her Warrior again. How can I deactivate it and get back to Mary?" Similarly, when John withdrew or became impatient with her, Mary immediately reassured her Little Girl that it was just part of him pulling away and that his Self would return soon.

These changes created an atmosphere in which John's Self and Mary's Self could work together to keep the extreme parts of each of them from interfering in their relationship. They talked frequently about how they could avoid triggering each other in destructive ways and how they could support the inner work that each of them was doing. After six months, they agreed with Sue that they were able to take care of both their individual internal families and their blended family, so they ended therapy.

ONE KEY INTERVENTION IN DOING THIS KIND OF work is helping both partners to accept responsibility for taking care of the vulnerable/intimacy parts in themselves. Doing this helps them both to feel more centered and personally resourceful as well as more able to tolerate intimacy. However, each spouse's network of polarized internal protectors, critics and warriors must be considered and deactivated or their attempts to nurture their intimacy-seeking selves will be, at best, only temporarily successful and will lead, at worst, to more polarization. This is one reason why a systemic appreciation of a person's internal ecology is so important, just as it is for their external ecology. With such an appreciation, a therapist knows which inner selves to deal with first and can predict and prepare for reactions to any intervention. Ignoring this inner world will lead the therapist to keep shooting in the dark, generating interventions without any clear idea of whether they will "take hold."

Another key principle to bear in mind while doing this work is that one person tends to relate to another in much the same way that he or she relates to the parts within him or her that resemble the other person. This is a somewhat different view of what has been called projection or transference. Thus, whenever Mary acted scared or upset, John treated her the way he treated his scared little boy— he withdrew from or became impatient with her. As he changed the way he related to the boy he could also relate differently to Mary when she was upset.

If asked directly, a person's various partial selves will often be able to describe in detail what needs to change and how to do it. Thus, instead of having to use such murky, monolithic and pejorative terms as "resistant," "controlling," "codependent," etc., to describe clients or their relationships, we can trust our clients to describe which of their many selves are bothering them and help them see how they themselves can bring about change. This creates a less hierarchical client-therapist relationship because the therapist's job is to create a safe context in which clients can describe and work on themselves, rather than using the therapeutic relationship as the primary fulcrum of change.

SOME OF MY PARTIAL SELVES ARE UNCOMFORTable now that I have so brazenly extolled the virtues of this approach. My Evaluator thinks I should be more humble and is sure that most people find all this business about "parts" and "partial selves" hokey and simplistic. My Worrier warns that, in sharing my excitement with this form of therapy without sufficient guidelines, I have painted a dangerously incomplete picture. My Evaluator is now complaining that I have not only insulted the competence of the readership but also failed to acknowledge all the people and theories and philosophies that have influenced the development of this model[2]. I tell them that when I have more space I will try to make amends.

My Striver, however, who constantly insists I undersell this approach, thinks I should summarize the valuable aspects of this model for treating couples. First, I find marital therapy far more enjoyable and fascinating now than when I worked entirely at the "external" interactional level. With a map that now goes beyond vague and pathological characterizations, I now have a much greater sense that I know what I am doing and where I should be going. This appreciation of each partner's internal make-up does not replace, confuse or distract from my understanding of their marital interaction. I still view the two levels of system with the same systemic lens. But now my attention is increasingly drawn to understanding the connections between the intrapsychic and the interpersonal levels, and I can shift frequently and fluidly between them.

I also have to do far less work. I'm finding that once I expose a couple to a few techniques and assumptions, I can trust them to make their own discoveries and to change their own internal and external relationships. I no longer have to come up with a spectacularly clever reframe or ingenious ritual, nor do I need to hector people about communicating better. Instead, my focus is on having my Self in the lead so that I can help them achieve Self-leadership. Thus, their therapy is my therapy, and when all three Selves are in the lead, the process is a pleasure. It is a privilege to work with clients as they discover the relief and empowerment that come with finding that they can change aspects of their inner lives that previously dictated their relationships. ■

RICHARD SCHWARTZ, PH.D. *is the coordinator of training and research, Family Systems Program, Institute for Juvenile Research, Chicago, IL.*

1. One of the distinguishing characteristics of people diagnosed with multiple personality disorder is that the degree of this isolation and polarization among their subpersonalities is so extreme that they lack any sense of integration, of an "I-ness" connecting the elements of their experience.

I want to keep interested readers abreast of similar models I have encountered. Since the first paper (Schwartz, 1987), I have been alerted to the fact that many of my ideas are similar to Jung's view of archetypes, and, in this aspect, James Hillman's (1975) *Archetypal Psychology* is particularly relevant. I also have recently encountered two models from the field of hypnothera- py that hold similar assumptions: John and Helen Watkins's (1978) *Ego State Therapy* and David Quigley's (1984) *Alchemical Hypnotherapy*.

See references, page 564.

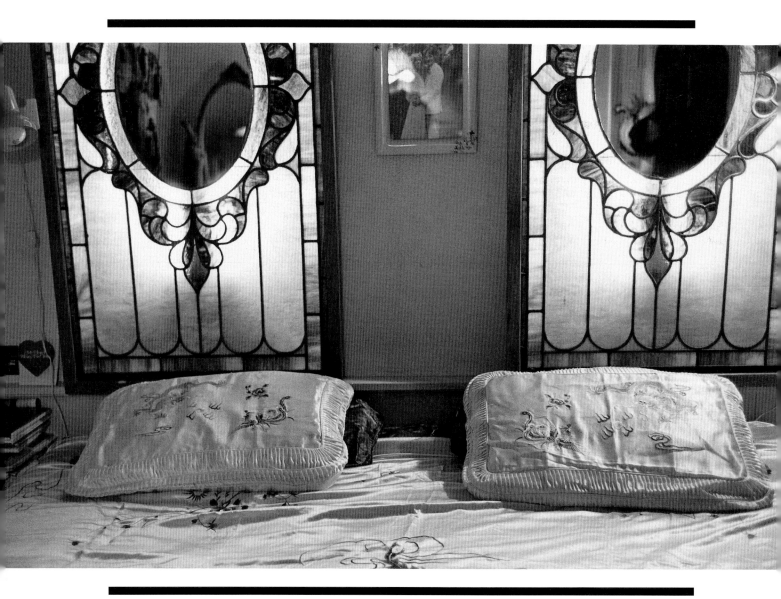

PHOTOGRAPH BY MARLA HIRSCH

MARRIAGE AT THE TURNING POINT

THE AFFAIR AS CRISIS AND OPPORTUNITY

By Don-David Lusterman

BACK IN THE 1950S, DEBBIE REYNOLDS AND EDDIE Fisher, Hollywood's perfect young couple, shocked their fan-magazine public by divorcing after Fisher's scandalous affair with Elizabeth Taylor. In those innocent times lots of people, myself included, took this spectacle very seriously. Newly married, not yet a therapist, I could barely conceive of divorce, let alone infidelity. Affairs happened in movies but almost never involved "real people," even "real" movie stars. Furthermore, I could not believe Reynolds's claims of ignorance about what was going on right under her nose. Didn't she notice that Eddie was always coming home late from the studio? Or that his tie was askew? Or that he didn't croon love songs to her anymore? Didn't she notice that their marriage was failing?

Today, after thousands of hours spent with couples struggling through their own infidelity crises, I know that both victim and unfaithful spouse often believe that their marriage was just fine until the affair struck from nowhere, like a perverse tornado. My goal is not merely to help these couples weather the crisis and patch things up but to help them understand how both spouses created the marital context that made an affair possible and how the crisis itself can be the springboard to a healthier, more satisfying relationship.

By infidelity, I do not mean occasional one-night stands, compulsive philandering, or a mutual "understanding" between spouses that theirs is a non-monogamous marriage. Rather, I refer to the consistent violation of trust by one spouse, who carries on one or more long-term affairs while his or her mate still assumes a relationship founded on mutual trust and fidelity. Generally, among couples I have seen, the infidel is a man, the victim a woman, though I have treated male victims whose reactions were very like those of women. Perhaps because of the stigma attached to being cuckolded, fewer men seem willing to expose themselves in therapy, and many prefer to move quickly toward divorce.

WHEN DORA CALLED, SHE HAD JUST DISCOVered her husband's infidelity. She told me he had admitted to the affair but said it was over and that he did not want to hear any more about it. She felt very angry and couldn't believe even now that he was telling her the truth. When I saw Tom and Dora, she was tearful and red-eyed as she described a fight they'd had in the car. Tom sat silent and stone-faced, only speaking to insist that the affair was finished and he saw no reason for bringing it up. I explained that it was necessary because Dora felt that she had been a victim of Tom's dishonesty and was overflowing with anger against him and the woman. "Right now she feels she'd be a fool to trust you ever again," I told him. "It's important to *both* of you to begin talking about this loss of trust and its consequences."

"Right!" Dora snapped. "How can you ever again trust a liar?"

I was glad to hear Dora's outburst because until the issue of trust is explored and dealt with, there can be no progress in therapy. Furthermore, both spouses must leave this critical first session with the sense that I understand their dilemma, that the crisis ends a long chain of events that must be explored, and that I have a plan for treatment.

Contrary to common belief, the victim's rage doesn't focus on the extramarital sex. Even if he has convinced her that there was no sex, she is still furious—shocked and angered by both his secrecy and her own gullibility. She is deeply grieved by her husband's intimacy with someone else—intimacy that she believed was hers alone. The infidel is by turns silent, apologetic, defensive, protective of the other woman and ambivalent about the marriage. He finds his wife's anger threatening and repellent. Her rage can indeed take on majestic proportions, but until she feels it rightfully acknowledged by both husband and therapist, no other marital issues can be productively explored. Even as other problems are raised in future sessions, I remain alert to the resurfacing of distrust, ready to return as often as necessary until the issue is resolved.

Toward the end of the meeting, I tell the couple that the purpose of therapy will be to work toward a better marriage or a better divorce. When Tom asks, "What's a better divorce?" I answer that a non-adversarial divorce protects children from being caught in angry crossfire and helps the couple mourn the death of their marriage, rather than spending years in endless and exhausting disputes. In a "good marriage," I explain, people talk to each other freely and honestly about what bothers them, so that they can work together to solve problems that might otherwise fracture the relationship. In my waiting room is a framed reproduction of a Chinese word meaning crisis, which is composed of two characters, one meaning danger, the other, opportunity. I ask Tom and Dora if they can look at their own crisis as an opportunity for personal growth, a thought they seem to find appealing.

IN ALMOST EVERY CASE I HAVE TREATED, DORA'S question, "How can you ever again trust a liar?" is critical and must never be shunted aside. Barbara and Leo came to therapy when she discovered that he had been involved in an affair for several years. She was particularly pained because he had had an affair about 10 years earlier. They consulted then with a therapist, who told Barbara that she found her constant expressions of anger "boring" and pressed her to overcome her "jealousy and possessiveness problem." At the time, Barbara meekly agreed, but now she realized her anger had never been resolved, only suppressed. "I felt so betrayed," she said, "by him, his girlfriend, my own stupidity, and by Dr. X, too. She and Leo ganged up on me and shut me up. So how am I supposed to feel now?"

I explained to both of them that anger is a normal and healthy reaction to feeling betrayed. "You'd better be prepared," I told Leo, "for plenty more. She is angry about what happened. She's afraid you're still doing it. And she's checking back constantly over all the lies you told to cover the affair." Leo listened intently as I told him that she needed from him not only an honest admission of the affair but a sense that he was truly remorseful for the years of deceit.

Bill and Claire's situation was different. Bill stubbornly denied that he had had an affair, insisted that he wanted to remain married, but couldn't stand Claire's irrational outbursts. Yet, I felt that an affair was indeed going on, and in an individual session, Bill told me that he was deeply involved with a woman at work. He did not consider this an "affair," since they had not had intercourse. Instead, they spent many hours together talking very tenderly about work, their personal lives and their feelings for each another. I said that keeping secret a deep involvement with someone else, whether sexual or not, made marital therapy based on honest and mutual self-disclosure an impossibility. Bill refused even to consider telling Claire about his "platonic" friendship, but finally, reluctantly agreed temporarily not to see the woman while he worked on his own marriage.

Claire was still convinced that Bill was having an affair and lying about it. Nonetheless, because he was not seeing the woman for the time being, we resumed conjoint meetings. After a few sessions, he admitted that he had been attracted to a coworker and that Claire's suspicions were not crazy, even though "nothing had happened." Once Bill validated her suspicions and became more willing to talk to her, they could begin honestly to discuss what each saw missing in the marriage.

In another case, after an initial meeting with Tony and Lisa, I met with Tony alone. He admitted to an affair of more than three years, including vacations together that were disguised as "business trips." He refused to give up the affair but did not want to terminate the marriage, either. I told him that I could not see him and his wife together under these circumstances. "I'd be backing you up in a lie and keeping Lisa in denial." Admitting that he was confused and ambivalent, he agreed to see me alone for a while to think about his own situation, while I saw

Lisa individually as well. He feared that his secret would come out during my sessions with Lisa. I assured him that I would not break his confidence. If she expressed suspicion of an affair, however, I would encourage her to check out the feelings, as I would any other patient.

Eventually he agreed to cease his extramarital relationship, but he claimed that, as a lawyer, he knew that any admissions could be used against him, and so he refused to admit to the affair. Lisa said that she was all but positive that Tony had been unfaithful but realized that she, too, had done many things through the years to alienate him. In their first meeting together, she said, "Tony, I assume that you were having an affair but are too damned stubborn to admit it. I think you've stopped, because you're around home a lot more now. I'm willing to work on what's wrong with our marriage now if you are." Tony sat impassively, neither denying nor confirming what she had said.

The remaining sessions dealt with a long history of very poor communication between two people who loved each another but didn't know how to show it. Some time after this, Tony came in alone and told me how pleased he was with the change in their marriage. Toward the end of the session, I couldn't resist asking about the other woman. "Oh, her," he said. "I haven't seen her in months. We agreed on a moratorium, but I'm not going back. I couldn't get over how well Lisa handled that confrontation with me." He added that he had been deeply moved by her courage and her commitment to the marriage.

WHEN THE AFFAIR HAS JUST BEEN DISCOVERED, the victim feels infuriated and betrayed. By simply admitting the affair, the infidel rarely satisfies the victim's need for some kind of emotional catharsis. The infidel may say, in effect, "Yes, I did this, but now it's over and let's get on with our lives." But the victim wants much more; she wants clear and repeated statements of remorse and needs to know that he is aware of the pain and feelings of craziness that his dishonesty and unfaithfulness have caused her. She experiences wildly ambivalent emotions about the unfaithful partner, venting intense rage at one moment, experiencing a deep sense of closeness at another, often including passionate sexual longing. The victim may want to spend a great deal of time with the infidel, usually much more than has ever been the couple's normal habit. This period of wild emotional swings can be frightening and disorienting for the infidel, who had never imagined that the affair could generate such *sturm und drang*, as if it had existed in a bubble, somehow completely separate from the marriage.

Furthermore, the victim is often obsessively driven to know every detail of the affair, and afterward the infidel will be pressed relentlessly for assurances that the affair has stopped and contrition is deep. One woman, after her husband had admitted an old five-year-long affair, spent frenzied nights searching through his checkbooks, personal diaries, stacks of office papers and office calendars, to be sure she knew *everything* and could never again be fooled.

In another case, long after Roger's wife had admitted and ended her affair, Roger still called her as often as 10 times a day from his office to be sure that she was at home when she said she would be. He insisted that she write out a daily schedule of her whereabouts so that he could check on her. Frequently he left his office in the middle of the day and drove nearly an hour to drop in on her at work, or at the beauty parlor, or at a PTA meeting. At night he woke her to review her day minute by minute, or to remind her of still another lie he had recently uncovered from the time of the infidelity. Far from finding Roger's hounding unbearable, his wife admitted it was "kind of a turn-on," and both agreed that they felt an intensified sexual passion for each other.

Such behavior is to be expected and may persist for a long time, even alternating with periods of increased closeness. The victim is angry that the affair ever happened and even more afraid that it is still continuing. Sometimes the betrayed spouse uncovers old information that simply opens the wound: "You bought her a *what*!!??" She may mistake such newly discovered evidence of the past infidelity as proof that the affair is continuing. The therapist can expect to receive panicky phone calls and may have to schedule emergency meetings during these times. In truth, these feverish searches rest on the profound hope of the victim, who also feels distaste for this process, *not* to find the very evidence being sought. The victim needs the support and patience of the spouse because each such episode that ends reassuringly is a step toward reconciliation.

Restoring trust also involves the victim's recognition that the infidel needs her support as well. After breaking off an affair, he may feel depression, grief, shame, and the fear that, no matter what he does—stay or leave—he is going to hurt someone. When the victim can accept these emotions and really listen to the infidel, progress is more rapid. And it is very touching to see two people in so much pain reach out to comfort each other.

Arthur and Jean came in following a six-month separation after Jean had discovered Arthur's infidelity. About a year earlier, she had been in intensive individual therapy for severe agoraphobia. During that time, she said, she had been a "real pain," and Arthur had been very patient with her clinging and whining. In an early session, she was outraged to learn that he had had another "fling," as he called it, after they had gotten back together. She told him that she did not consider this a "fling," but a final betrayal.

At this point, Arthur seemed to collapse. He had always appeared at sessions dapper, cheerful, charming. Now he arrived unkempt, sometimes unshaven, red-eyed, and filled with remorse. He had broken with the other woman for good but felt both guilt about his treatment of Jean and sadness about giving up the other relationship. He found himself calling the other woman and hanging up, following her car, wondering what she was doing and with whom, but resisting the urge to contact her again. He told Jean how he felt, how he hated what he had done to her, but how he still desperately craved the excitement of the affair. He associated the other woman with his frenetically glamorous "high life" as an arbitrageur—lots of fast money, easy coke and "foxy ladies."

Jean commiserated with him, saying that they had both had a hard time. Living with her agoraphobia, she pointed out, had been tough on him, too. Now she encouraged him as he poured out his confusion about work and relationships—his fear that he could never be good for anyone, his mistress, his kids, his parents. "Maybe I'm just a selfish bastard," he said, unable to hold back his tears. Months of anguished soul-searching followed, with gradual transformations in his work and home life. For the first time, Arthur and Jean found themselves talking to each other as trusted friends, and five years after therapy they agree their marriage is now better than when they were first wed.

During therapy I often encourage the couple to take risks in speaking honestly with each other. They may eventually discover together that their marriage can never work. A couple came in because their bright and usually academically successful children had begun to do very poor work in school. During early sessions with the family, the tension between the parents was so obvious that I scheduled a period to speak with them alone. The husband knew of his wife's current affair but tolerated it because he had done the same thing in the past. These affairs, both agreed, distracted them from their sense of being trapped in their own bleak relationship. They no longer loved each other but could not bear the thought of breaking up their family and injuring their children. They finally agreed to a trial

separation, to which the children seemed to adjust surprisingly well. After about six months of therapy, the parents decided to divorce. By this time, the children were doing well in school.

ONCE TRUST IS ON THE WAY TO BEING RESTORED, the second phase of therapy begins—an examination of what led to the infidelity. We discuss first their courtship and early marriage. How did they deal with serious differences of opinion? Were there differences in values? Were they discussed and resolved satisfactorily or left unspoken? Generally, reviewing the early days of courtship and marriage tends to bring the couple closer, as they laugh and sometimes cry together, remembering the mutual love and trust they once felt for each other. These reminiscences may even begin a rebonding process. One couple came into therapy with a long history of sexual problems culminating in his affair. As we talked about their courtship, they recalled the hours they spent in his car talking, holding hands, watching the sunset, hugging and kissing. Both came from divorced homes and had promised each other they would build a secure home for their own children. Now they realized they had poured all their energies into parenting and neglected their own sexual relationship, which had all but died. They later reported that this session helped them begin talking about what they still shared and the value their marriage still held for both of them.

Another couple remembered being forced to marry by their parents because she was pregnant. She felt betrayed, he felt ashamed, both felt imprisoned. His first affair began with a woman he met the day his wife gave birth. Eventually this couple decided to divorce, but without acrimony. Mourning their failed marriage, they nonetheless could agree they had done a good job raising their daughter and would continue doing so. They agreed to mediation and arranged liberal visitation rights.

I also explore the model of marriage that each

115

experienced growing up. Did either know of or sus-pect infidelity in their parents' marriage? In one case, a male infidel denied that his father ever had an affair. But his wife remembered that, during their own courtship, his mother had told her about his father's philandering and warned her not to marry the son. The couple had been married for 15 years, but this was the first time he had heard the story. As they talked, they began to see parallels between the two marriages. "Your mother controlled every-thing," the wife said, "the way she raised you kids, how money was spent, and what friends they had. I think I do a lot of that, too." They began talking about their own relationship, rather than fighting over his affair.

We then discuss crisis points in the marriage, like the death of a child, responsibility for aging parents, or radical shifts in work. Healthy couples can weath-er such crises by freely and openly telling each other how they feel. When couples can't talk to each other, however, each crisis seems to drive emotions further underground. Almost invariably, the inabili-ty to talk honestly about their distress increases the likelihood of infidelity.

IN THE FINAL PHASE OF THERAPY, WE BUILD ON A couple's newly discovered ability to acknowledge and support each other. At this point, I often ask, "What is better in your marriage?" One wife recent-ly answered, "I don't feel like a victim anymore. Now I can see how we both contributed to this mess, so I'm not so damned angry all the time. Last week he was late coming home, and I didn't even call the Long Island Railroad to check on his story!"

Sometimes couples are stuck. After a number of sessions, a husband was asked, "What's better?" He replied, "Basically, nothing." She confirmed this with a discouraged look. I suggested that we explore the possibility of separation or divorce, and we dis-cussed different methods (adversarial or mediated), how to explain it to the children, and the spouses'

own fantasies about what their lives would be like independent of each other. In this case, the couple began talking seriously about separating. Some-times, though, merely talking about the grim spe-cifics of divorce can drive couples back to thoughts of how they might improve their marriage.

Even in this final phase, issues of trust and old grievances continue to surface. In one case, a hus-band had long withheld information from his wife about serious business problems. For years he had assumed the macho position of protector, while she had played the protected little woman. Both ac-knowledged that this collusion prevented mutual honesty or empathy. Over time he was able to see that his secretiveness about business was as much a source of distrust for her as his affair had been. He also realized the connection between his frequent headaches and long-denied anxieties. Now he felt greatly relieved to share his fears and burdens, while his wife felt happier to be a more important part of his life.

During this phase, I like to discuss everyday mari-tal conduct and courtesy. When couples cannot face each other comfortably at night, they tend to sup-press painful issues, which then pile up, increasing feelings of distance and suppressed anger. I encour-age couples to review unresolved problems before they end the day. This can be an exhausting process, however, as one couple learned when it took them the entire night to thrash out an issue before they fell into a well-earned sleep.

Few couples I see are good at praising or thank-ing each other or even making requests rather than giving orders. Many show affection only as a pre-lude to sex and need to learn the importance of ten-derness for its own sake. Such couples discover that arguments about withholding or initiating sex are really about the absence of affection.

At the same time, once couples have learned to trust each other, they can more easily respect each other's privacy.

Near the very end of therapy, I urge couples to practice their newfound skills. Small successes make a big difference in their everyday lives. They may not always agree, but they learn to view differences as a natural part of life and find their marriage is enriched. If their differences are irreconcilable, they will know that they are heading for divorce, but they can handle it sensibly, with a minimum of rancor. When they do elect to stay together, however, their marriages are no longer tense charades, clouded by suspicion and anxiety. "In a sense, I'm almost grateful for discovering the affair," one woman said. "We might never have come to know each other." She smiled, "You know what? We're a happily married couple!" ■

DON-DAVID LUSTERMAN, PH.D., *is in private practice in Baldwin, NY.*

ILLUSTRATION BY KEVIN HAWKES

AFTER THE BREAKUP

WHO SAYS EX-SPOUSES HAVE TO BE ENEMIES FOR LIFE?

By Constance Ahrons

WHEN MY OLDER DAUGHTER GRADUATED FROM law school this year, we celebrated the weekend events in the traditional ways. We had a rather large family group in attendance—my ex-husband (her father), his mother (her grandmother), his wife (her stepmother), their two children (her half-siblings) and our younger daughter (her sister). It was a family constellation not unlike many other families in Washington that weekend. We haven't always celebrated our children's accomplishments amicably together, but over the years, with practice, we learned to tolerate our differences in order to reap some of the rewards of our parenting.

It has been almost 25 years since my children's father and I separated. Divorces weren't common then—at that time, I didn't know even one person who was divorced. My mother reacted with shame and outrage: "No one in our family has ever gotten divorced! Even Aunt Sylvia and Uncle Sam didn't get divorced." The fact that Aunt Sylvia and Uncle Sam had lived together in angry silence for at least 10 years only attested to their moral responsibility and familial respect.

I was not only a disgrace to my family but something of a pariah in other social systems. It was 1965, and I was beginning my graduate studies in social work at a large midwestern university. During the previous year, when my husband, two daughters and I were still living together, he was a student, making us eligible for university-subsidized housing. When we separated, I was told I could no longer live in university housing, which was reserved for married graduate students with families. The separation had left me penniless except for a fellowship and small, irregular child support. Penney's and Sears had closed my charge accounts, as was the custom in those days, and the communal support of student housing with its built-in child care was my only hope of remaining in graduate school. Only after an arduous fight did I convince the housing director that even after the divorce, my two daughters and I were *still* a family and that I was *still* a full-time graduate student and therefore entitled to live in graduate-student housing.

Things are a lot different today. Back then joint custody didn't exist. For a father to get sole custody of his children—a rare situation—he had to prove the mother incompetent. My children's father tried to do just that, and it made for a long, terrifying and bitter divorce.

The option of a blameless divorce for "irreconcilable differences," wasn't yet available. So, after waiting almost two years, I finally stood before a judge and stretched and molded the truth to claim that my husband had treated me in "cruel and inhumane" ways. It was a mortifying experience. Because my husband had moved back to the East Coast and chose not to return for the court hearing, our divorce was uncontested, with assignment of custody but no jurisdiction to order child support. I walked out of the courtroom feeling ashamed and alone, wondering how I would pay my legal fees. The next day, upon my lawyer's advice, I went to the district attorney's office to file an interstate order for child support. In the DA's office, I felt like a criminal, vulnerable and stigmatized, while he explained the procedures but offered little hope for enforcement. I wondered, as I left his office that day, how, after having spent seven years as an upper-middle-class housewife, I could have ended up poor, disgraced and isolated.

A DECADE AFTER MY OWN DIVORCE, I WAS ENcountering more and more divorcing couples in my clinical work and finding that many standard clinical assumptions didn't match the reality I was seeing. For example, a client named Sheila had been divorced for several years when she was referred to me by a colleague. According to his notes, she hadn't made a satisfactory "adjustment" to her divorce after an 18-year marriage, hadn't completed the "letting go" process and was still "hanging on" to her ex-husband. Neither Sheila nor I understood what he meant. She said she enjoyed the hour or so on Saturdays that she spent with her ex-husband when he came to pick up their sons. They usually had breakfast, exchanged news of relatives and

mutual friends, and talked about their children. She couldn't understand why everyone thought this was some kind of "failure." After all, she said, "he feels like kin." That stirred around in me for a while, and I realized that although my feelings for my ex weren't entirely friendly, he, too, felt like kin. Not beloved, but kin nevertheless.

In 1974, when I began a thorough review of the literature on divorce, I was angered by the total emphasis on pathology. Psychologists wrote of divorce as both the cause and effect of emotional disturbance and instability. Sociologists defined divorce as social deviance, marking the demise of the traditional American family and responsible for a host of social ills. The therapy literature reflected a consensus that divorce indicated not only a failure of the marriage but the therapist's failure to save the marriage.

Back in the early '70s, divorce law was still based on the belief that divorce was immoral and threatened the institution the family. In most states, adultery was the only grounds for divorce. Although the drive for no-fault divorce began in California in 1964, not until the late 1970s did no-fault legislation become part of legal reforms in virtually every state. But it has taken us much longer to really accept the idea that marriages can end without one party or the other bearing the burden of guilt. According to prevailing stereotype, ex-spouses must be antagonists—otherwise, why would they divorce? We're still surprised, even mildly embarrassed, when we encounter ex-spouses who seem to be friends. Yet all of us know at least someone who maintains a friendship with an ex-lover. Some may think it's weird, or pathological, but most just accept it as a caring relationship that used to be sexually intimate.

The inadequacy of language to describe the present relationship of divorced spouses except in terms of a severed bond, e.g., "ex", or "former," is another indication of how shadowy and vaguely unacceptable these relationships still seem to us.

AFTER THE BREAKUP

Margaret Mead once explained why we're so uncomfortable about a continuing relationship between former spouses in this way: ". . . Any contact between divorced people somehow smacks of incest; once divorced, they have been declared by law to be sexually inaccessible to each other, and the aura of past sexual relations makes further relationship incriminating." In fact, spouses can't really be totally done with each other; divorce doesn't end relationships but rather changes the structure and meaning of them.

BECAUSE THE TERM "NUCLEAR FAMILY" ALMOST universally means *the family*, all other family structures are considered "alternatives" and therefore less than ideal. To help legitimize the increasingly common two-household structure of divorced families and make them equivalent to married families, some years ago I coined the term "binuclear family." Unfortunately, the term as it is frequently used in the current literature often refers only to joint-custody families or to families in which the relationship between ex-spouses is friendly. However, I meant only to indicate a different familial structure, without implying anything about the nature of the relationship of the ex-spouses.

My own life has provided many of the questions guiding my research on the binuclear family. By the time I was deeply into my research, I had remarried a divorced man, the noncustodial father of two children. Although my relationship with my ex was improving, my new husband and his ex-wife were still carrying on a pitched battle. We spent our first few years of marriage trying to blend our families, while negotiating painful transitions in the relationships with our children's other parent.

When I began my longitudinal study of divorced families in 1978, I had been remarried about 10 years. Our binuclear family was less chaotic than it had been in the early years, and my husband and I had more or less come to terms with our ex-spouses.

Even though he lived a thousand miles away, my children saw their father regularly, and we made parental decisions amicably together. He had remarried, and fathered two more children, and his wife and I got along quite well. At the other extreme, my husband's relationship with his ex-wife had deteriorated into a sullen, nonspeaking standoff, and although we lived in the same city, his children rarely spent time with us. This breach remained a painful void in our lives.

In my study, I wanted to understand the complexities of ex-spouse relationships; to chart how some managed to "uncouple" without "unfamilying," while others could not; why some continued a relationship with each other and their past, while others completely cut off the other and their joint history; and how new intimate relationships were affected by these past marriages and how these new partnerships affected the old ones. I also wanted to approach the study from a nonpathological point of view.

With the support of the University of Wisconsin and the National Institute of Mental Health (NIMH), I began interviewing 98 divorced couples and their new partners over a five-year period of their lives, first, one year after their legal divorce, then three years, and once again five years post-divorce. Our interviews were fairly intense, using both standardized measures as well as the divorced couples' personal stories. Genograms were used to map the complex relationships and establish a clinical rapport with each individual.

Drawing together massive amounts of information, we identified general relationship typologies to differentiate one group from another. In reality, each of the 98 divorced couples was unique, and all formed an unbroken continuum of relationship styles from very angry and hostile to surprisingly friendly, with the majority falling somewhere in between. A couple of years ago, while telling my daughters about the four groups of ex-spouses I had

121

identified, they flinched at my multisyllabic jargon and coined four catchy nicknames that seemed to sum up the quality of these relationship types.

STARTING AT ONE END OF THE CONTINUUM, there are the "perfect pals," a small group of divorced spouses whose failed marriages have not overshadowed long-standing friendships. They share decision-making and childrearing, with many stating they are even better parents after the divorce than they were in the marriage. They spend holidays together and keep relationships with each other's extended families. Generally, these couples shared mutually in the decision to divorce. They may not have made the decision simultaneously, but neither partner feels abandoned by the other, while both respect each other as people and responsible parents. Though they were angry at times during the separation, and still occasionally have conflicts, there is a genuine fondness between them, and they try to accommodate each other. Although they were unwilling to compromise themselves to stay in an unsatisfying marriage, they *were* willing to compromise during the divorce.

Sarah and Tom were such a couple. They had been married for 12 years, had been childhood sweethearts and described their marriage as a deep friendship. Married at 19, they had two children within three years of their marriage and had continued to live in the same town as their families of origin. Sarah first mentioned divorce on her 29th birthday. Although she cared deeply for Tom and they shared similar values in parenting, she felt he had become more like a brother than a husband. Sex was rare, they spent more social time with others than together, and Sarah felt that "life was passing [her] by." Tom was hurt and sad when she told him her feelings, but after six months of counseling, they decided to separate. Although angry when the counseling started, Tom eventually began to look forward to being on his own for the first time in his life.

Tom and Sarah adopted an unusual binuclear family arrangement, the "birds' nest," as it is called in divorce circles. The children stayed in the family home, and Tom and Sarah each lived there half the time, at first changing weekly, then biweekly. On Sunday nights, both parents joined the children in a family dinner together. This pattern seemed to work very well for them for about three years, until Tom wanted to live with a woman with whom he had become intimate. Sarah was not upset, and even liked his new partner, but felt uncomfortable about sharing a home with her. On their own, they devised a new, more traditional joint-custody arrangement, in which both had their own places and the children spent equal time with each. At our five-year interview with Sarah, Tom and his new wife Tamara, they were all amicable. Tom and Sarah still had Sunday dinners together, though now only twice a month, and still liked each other, although they were less close than they had been earlier. Sarah was in therapy at the time of the last interview, had a woman lover, and was struggling with her sexual identity.

When I speak before nonprofessional groups about Sarah and Tom, some people respond with heavy moral censure, saying, "these people had no right to get divorced," "their relationship is weird," "they're ruining their kids, living in such strange ways." I think these responses come from people threatened by a divorce in which neither partner is abusive, alcoholic, addicted, or adulterous. Indeed, many people who have left marriages that were not intolerable in the eyes of others feel guilty about their decision.

I remember my own years of inner struggle before divorcing a man who didn't physically abuse me or the kids, didn't gamble, didn't drink, provided well for his family, etc. It took me years to give up the guilt for "inflicting my selfishness on my family." Sometimes couples create a crisis—have an affair, provoke a physical altercation—to establish a focus for blame and anger as well as provide a *(continued on page 126)*

Gullible's Travails: A Modern Marital Misadventure

IN 1965 I MARRIED A MAN FOR TWO GOOD REASONS: HE WAS TALLER THAN I WAS, AND I HAD NO really definite plans after college. Marriage, even to someone unfamiliar, was a familiar state, a culturally approved goal. After all, the only magazine my sorority actually subscribed to was *Modern Bride,* and three of my closest girlfriends were already in the final throes of china selection. For me and for most of my contemporaries, genuine adult life was an ark, accessible only to people in pairs.

While my husband also subscribed to the ark theory of adulthood, he married me primarily because he was going into the Marines and he didn't want to go alone. Also, his hormones were raging, and in the early '60s, the coming sexual revolution was still only a border skirmish. If two people slept with each other on a regular basis, they married—at least some of them did.

We did. And then for almost two decades we created our version of "happily ever after." In retrospect, we acted out the middle-class script. After the Marines, there was graduate school, then suburbia, charge cards, two children, PTA, club memberships, expanding waistlines, receding hair-lines, gas grills, station wagons, the building of a business and—after 17 years—the divorce.

To me, the divorce sprouted overnight like a toadstool on the front lawn. One night we were sprawled on our sofa watching Dan Rather, and the next night we were looking in the Yellow Pages under the heading Attorneys (domestic). Like a Greek chorus, family, friends and children echoed their disbelief, but the ship of connubial bliss, once aground, began to break up rapidly. Checking accounts were raided. Credit cards were canceled and the clean laundry pushed off the hide-a-bed.

So what happened?

According to my husband, it was the C word—communication, a lack thereof. Evidently, he had been unhappy for some years, but he had not realized the depth of his distress until a buxom blond neighbor had engaged him in some active listening. Sessions with her were so therapeutic that he realized our marriage was no longer satisfying. He was shocked by that realization, but there was nothing he could do. Soap opera comes to suburbia.

Because I lost three dress sizes in three weeks and took to sobbing in the Cheerios, my hus-band agreed to see a marriage counselor. Basically, the counseling was outplacement for me. The master plan was that the therapist would assess my state of mental health, and when survival status was attained, my mate would cruise to the courthouse and finalize the decree.

Needless to say, working diligently to achieve a goal I abhorred didn't prove much of a mental health incentive. But in spite of that mind-set, therapy opened new doors for me. From my first therapist, I learned the basics of rational thinking: don't SHOULD on oneself; don't awfulize; emo-tions are filtered through beliefs. Strangely enough, the most important realization I had was that it was possible to be seriously hugged by an adult male other than my husband. No, there were no sweaty liaisons on the Naugahyde, the touching was aboveboard and above the waist, platonic in the extreme—but it was necessary. To a woman who had never once removed her wedding ring, transitional touching was essential.

The next stop was a divorce support group sponsored by a local university and led by a grand-motherly therapist. This group provided another important transitional element: I reentered the world of unattached women. My circa 1965 memory of such women consisted entirely of breathless bevies of toothy Tri-Delts competing relentlessly for fraternity men. Sure, there had been a modicum of feminine support and cooperation, but only outside the dating arena; inside that perfumed amphitheater it was strictly womano-a-womano.

In the divorce support group there was real cooperation and real help. There were those members who provided perspective through their bizarre breakup stories. After all, my story was the standard saga: husband turns 40, husband meets neighbor, husband dumps wife. That tale compared very tamely with coach husband impregnates varsity cheerleader, or gynecologist hubby builds cocaine lab in basement, or budget-conscious hubby moves girlfriend into guestroom. Strange tales, but true!

There were also those group members who provided support through simple listening. Their phone numbers were freely given, and they could be counted on not to use their answering machines unless they really weren't home and, even then, never to leave canned hello messages by jocular Elvis imitators. In the early stages of my breakup, these phone friends kept me afloat by reminding me I was basically a good person whose grim view of herself needed to be examined. At one point, the telling of my divorce story ran almost 90 minutes without commercial interruption and not once did my best phone friend ask me to fast forward to the juicy parts.

In addition, there were those group members who were making their second trip to the courthouse. These combat-hardened veterans marched the rest of us, the raw recruits, through legal tactical maneuvers: ask for a dollar to keep the window of alimony opportunity open, use Lawyer X because Y has lecherous tendencies, request Judge Z, who has a soft spot for displaced homemakers. Be able to pronounce and define the following words: separation agreement, deposition, alimony, joint custody. Know that whether you are the leaver or leavee, the first time you see the official papers with "versus" between your names your stomach will knot up. Such helpful info!

Gradually, the group beefed up my anorexic self-concept and, most important, gave me a replacement network for the one I had been in during my marriage. As I soon learned, the worlds of marriage and divorce are parallel universes. They exist side by side, but they do not really connect. After a decorous interval, most of my married friends faded back into the world of couples, a strange world in which the ritual chant is "We'll have to get together—sometime." Two other tools—a pair of Nikes and a spiral notebook—also helped me revive after the marital meltdown. Because I dreaded being alone in the bungalow at the time when my ex used to return home from work, I began to jog with two other suddenly single women. For a former sofa spud whose major activity had been reaching for the onion dip, jogging was strange behavior indeed. Nevertheless, the exercise reduced the general feeling of defeat and almost turned off the tear torrents—two miles, four days a week, cut my Kleenex consumption in half.

In the spiral notebook, I began to write conversations, some real, some imagined. I also wrote poetry and "rage pages." Every time I would meet my ex at the DMZ for a nocturnal child exchange, I would cover numerous pages with colorful comments, some of them referring creatively to gonads and surgical procedures sans anesthetic. Hell hath no fury like a brunette replaced by a blond.

That sentence was the final one in my 1985 spiral notebook, the last notebook that I devoted almost entirely to divorce issues. In subsequent notebooks, I did write about the event, but it did not consume my energy or cause me to break as many pencil points. Yes, three years after the divorce, the strangely therapeutic brew composed of counseling, running and writing had proven restorative. Some old wounds had healed.

Entries in the most recent series of notebooks refer to new interests, new understandings and, yes—new men. Of course, my standards for male companionship are now much more mature. I mean, the man I'm currently seeing is almost two inches SHORTER than I am. Ah, wisdom. □

—*Victoria Register*
NOVEMBER 1989

VICTORIA REGISTER, M.A.E., *is an English teacher and high school dean in Jacksonville, FL.*

(continued from page 122) plausible excuse for divorce.

HE "COOPERATIVE COLLEAGUES" ARE A CONSID-
erably larger, more typical group. Though not
good friends, they work very well together on
issues concerning their children. They can also talk
amicably about other family members—mothers,
brothers, or old friends. They do have conflict, but
manage it well, and can separate their conflicts as
spouses from their responsibilities as parents.
Nevertheless, for many of these couples, learning to
accept the divorce without punishing the spouse
through the children was not easy. They *did* fight
about parenting. There *were* ups and downs in arrangements, but they could manage to put their children's welfare first. They clearly accept their joint
responsibility as adults and parents and maintain a
united front as far as their children are concerned.
Foremost in their minds is a desire to minimize the
trauma for the children living in a divorced family.

Beth and Stephen did not have the kind of marriage or initial separation that would hold much
promise for a cooperative binuclear family arrangement. Very different in temperament and interests,
they fought through much of their eight years
together. Stephen worked long hours, spending little
time with his children; he bragged that he had never
changed a diaper. Beth worked part-time during
most of the marriage and resented Stephen's lack of
parenting responsibility. At Beth's initiation, they
had separated and then reconciled twice before finally divorcing. Beth told us that Stephen had "alcohol
problems" (which Stephen did not mention in our
initial interview), and Stephen described Beth as a
"cold, demanding bitch" but a good mother. Beth
had custody at the time of our first interview, with
Stephen seeing the children every other weekend
and one night a week, typical for mother-custody
families. Although they parted in anger and continued the battle through adversarial lawyers, they felt
much less angry one year after their divorce.

Beth expressed surprise that Stephen was so
responsible about seeing the kids, and Stephen told
us that he was a better parent now than he was
when married. They spoke with each other on the
phone once a week about the children but almost
never talked about anything else. By the third interview, two years later, Stephen had been in a good
relationship for a year and was spending more time
with his children. Beth had gone back to graduate
school, was teaching full-time, and had a satisfying
relationship in her life. She felt she had not received
an equitable financial settlement, and although she
didn't particularly like Stephen, she still said, "I have
to give him credit for being a good father."

Joan and Saul were cooperative colleagues with a
somewhat different style. After 13 years in a marriage of low conflict but much denied anger, Saul fell
in love with another woman. When Joan found out
about the relationship about a year later, she was at
first outraged, then depressed. Saul felt guilty, found
a therapist for Joan and bolted. Out of guilt, he paid
generous child support and agreed quickly to the
property settlement requested by her lawyer. At our
first interview, he had married Susan, the "other
woman," and was still feeling guilty. Joan was still in
therapy and somewhat depressed but feeling better
than at the time of separation. Joan and Saul had
considerable contact; he fixed her washing machine
when it was broken, advised her on money management, and responded to her every wish connected
with child care. Three years after the divorce, Saul
was angrier than he had been at the earlier interview, complaining that Joan was still dependent on
him, causing a strain in his new marriage.

At our five-year interview, Saul had separated
from Susan and was seeing another woman. He was
more involved with his son than his daughter and
felt relieved that Joan had met someone new. Joan
now said she was happier than she had ever been
and felt sorry that Saul was having a difficult time.
During the two years since our last interview, their

daughter had suffered a serious illness, and both parents had been very involved with her.

JILL AND MIKE COPED WITH THEIR DIVORCE QUITE differently than Joan and Saul, behaving more like "angry associates" than cooperative colleagues. They had been married, quietly, if not happily, for nine years when Jill found out that Mike and his secretary had been having an affair for more than two years. When Jill, who was self-employed and quite successful, discovered the affair, she told us that "all hell broke loose" and she threw Mike out of the house. Both sought lawyers, and a long adversarial battle followed. Even a year after the divorce, Jill's anger was easily tapped. She had custody and closely controlled Mike's access to his children, often canceling visits on the slightest provocation. She permitted him to discuss things with her only through the mail or through her attorney. Three years after the divorce, Jill had remarried but remained angry with Mike.

Mike, at one year postdivorce, felt the legal system had treated him unfairly, and found visiting his children only fueled his anger because of Jill's control. He had ended the affair with his secretary, and after a series of other relationships, felt very embittered about women. Five years after the divorce, this couple had mellowed some, and could communicate like distant, aloof, but not embittered colleagues.

THE FOURTH GROUP I ENCOUNTERED IN MY RE-search, "fiery foes," feel nothing but fury for their ex-spouses. These couples have virtually no capacity whatsoever for cooperating. Their divorces tend to be highly litigious, with legal fights continuing many years after the decree is signed. They are either "leavers" or "lefts," "good guys" or "bad guys," and can remember no good times in the marriage, clinging only to their sense of outrage. Even many years after the divorce, they cannot accept each other's parenting rights; for these spouses, the other parent is the enemy. Like couples in conflict-habituated marriages, they are still very much attached to each other, although they would deny it. For most of these couples, the power struggle pervades the entire family. The children are caught in the middle, often taking sides with one parent or the other. One of the parents, usually the father, may see the children less and less frequently over the years, and both parents blame the other for the declining contact.

Melvin and Sybil were typical of this type. Married 18 years, Melvin told us he initiated the divorce because Sybil was crazy. He said he had put up with her abusive behavior for 18 years because of the children, but he just couldn't take it any longer. Sybil told us that Melvin was crazy, that he didn't speak to her for weeks on end, then abused her emotionally and left the house for two or three weeks at a time. She felt she had initiated the divorce. When we interviewed them the first time—one year postdivorce—they were still suing each other; Sybil had gone through three lawyers, and Melvin was refusing to pay her the stipulated amount. The children were teenagers, and Melvin said his daughter wouldn't talk with him, and his son saw him on the sly.

At three years postdivorce, Melvin was living with a 30-year-old woman, and Sybil had moved to another state. We interviewed her by telephone, and she said she was thankful never to have to see Melvin again. When we asked about how she was going to manage that at the upcoming wedding of their daughter, she stated flatly that Melvin was not invited. At five years postdivorce, not much had changed. The couple had had no contact over the past two years, although Sybil had obtained a court order to get Melvin to pay something toward the education of their youngest child, whom Melvin had not seen during this time.

A fifth group, the "dissolved duos," are divorced

spouses who, after the separation and/or divorce, discontinue any contact with each other. In these cases, one of the partners usually leaves the geographical area where the custodial parent and children live. For some people, the only way they can cope with the stresses of a failing marriage is by totally withdrawing, leaving the remaining spouse to handle the situation. This total withdrawal of one partner provides the one true "single-parent family," a family in which the former spouse is completely absent, except in memories and fantasies.

THE "SUCCESSFUL" DIVORCE IS STILL REGARDED AS an oxymoron by many. According to current research examining the effects of divorce on children, the psychic injury to children can be minimized if supportive and cooperative relationships between both parents can be maintained. So, although the arrangements made by "perfect pals" and "cooperative colleagues" may seem complex, even bizarre, to outsiders, these adaptations are most likely to meet the needs of both parents and children for emotional continuity and stability. A functional divorce allows spouses to split up the nuclear family and then create a different kind of family organization without leaving children, extended kin and friends devastated and caught up in a continuing conflict. In general, constructively divorced spouses seem able to accept their past failures as spouses and move on to create a workable binuclear family.

Although there is little research about the complex factors contributing to the reorganization of divorced families, undoubtedly individual personality and coping styles play a role. Some people have a history of dissolving relationships rather than openly quarreling or facing their own feelings of ambivalence. Thus, someone who habitually deals with conflict by withdrawing and cutting off relationships is likely to react to a divorced spouse in the same manner. The way a person handled a conflictual relationship with a sibling or parent might predict future interaction with a former spouse.

A clinician working with divorced families can bring to clients a knowledge of what works (or does not) to create and nurture a healthier, continuing family. If divorcing clients have been in therapy with me before separating, I encourage them to continue working with me to plan for their divorce and deal with their anger directly rather than hiding behind lawyers. Most divorcing couples are frightened, unaware of their options, and often vulnerable to the well-meaning but inappropriate advice of family and friends. More and more clients now come in for divorce counseling to find ways to uncouple without destroying their family. They know there are good ways and bad ways to divorce but not how to get from where they are to where they want to be—the same dilemma nondivorcing couples and families bring to therapy.

In my work with professionals, I find that almost everyone has had some personal experience with divorce—if not their own, that of their parents or siblings, children or close friends. Much of this experience is negative. Nothing promises more heated discussion, for example, than whether alternate weeks in each parent's home is good for the children. Although this arrangement sounds as if it wouldn't provide enough security and stability for children, sometimes it is the best option. I remember, years ago, seeing a newly remarried family with children from both prior unions. Father's children were nine and 10 years old and had been alternating between their parents' homes for seven years. I had not encountered this situation before and sympathetically told the children, "how difficult that must be for you two." They quickly corrected me, saying it had always been that way, and the only ones sometimes confused were their friends. They had a little store of anecdotes about library books misplaced in one house or the other, lost socks and toys, which they told me cheerfully and without distress. Children can live in very complex arrangements quite contentedly when divorced parents are competent and sensitive to the children's needs.

Not all divorcing families will ever reorganize as healthy, well-functioning binuclear families. But just as we have models and paradigms for healthy nuclear families, we need models for healthy, well-functioning binuclear families.

Characteristically, in healthy binuclear families, the boundaries between spousal (or nonparental) and parental roles are clear. Most divorced people will never resolve all their marital issues; rather, they learn to live with the ambiguity and ambivalence that accompany a failed marriage.

So far, research suggests that about half of divorced couples recombine in successful binuclear families. Even Judith Wallerstein, in her negative portrayal of the 10-year follow-up of her landmark Children of Divorce Project, reports that 46 percent of the children are doing well. When it comes to creating secure, loving environments for children, how much better have nuclear families done? ∎

CONSTANCE AHRONS, PH.D., *is associate director of the Marriage and Family Therapy Program and professor of sociology at the University of Southern California.*

*H*IS AND HER DIVORCES

DIVORCING MEN AND WOMEN LIVE IN SEPARATE WORLDS

By E. Mavis Hetherington and Adeline S. Tryon

JESSE BERNARD (1972) OBSERVED THAT THE EX-periences of men and women in marriage and their perceptions of their relationships are so divergent that we should talk of "his and her" marriages. Research findings suggest that just as there are "his and her" marriages, there may be "his and her" divorces. This is to some extent due to the different life experiences that males and females encounter during and after divorce and to some extent due to their different styles in coping with conflict, family transitions and stress.

THE DECISION TO DIVORCE: EVEN BEFORE THE divorce and during the process of making the decision to divorce, men and women perceive their relationships differently. In one longitudinal study of 72 divorced husbands and wives (Hetherington, Cox & Cox, 1981), divorced women reported having been dissatisfied longer in their marriages and having considered separation for a longer period of time than did men. In contrast, about one-quarter of the husbands said they were surprised when their wives wanted to divorce and

were not sure about the reasons for this "sudden" degeneration in their marriages. Women usually reported that the main thing that locked them into an unsatisfying marriage was too little independent income to support themselves when they left. Unhappily married men were more likely to fear the loss of their children.

Although men and women often voiced similar complaints about their marriages, the salience of these concerns differed. About half of the women said that lack of communication and affection were the main problems in their marriages, concerns far less important to the men. About a third of the women also reported a lack of shared interests with their husbands, who seemed to prefer "nights out with the boys" to spending time with them. In addition, one-quarter of the wives cited their husbands' alcoholism, physical abuse, or extramarital sex as contributors to the breakup. While about 15 percent of the men also complained about their wives' alcoholism and infidelity, the most common grievance voiced by men was their wives' nagging, whining and faultfinding, followed closely by their immaturity and irresponsibility. About one-third of divorced men and women also complained about their sexual relationship, but from different perspectives—men were unhappy about the quantity of sex, women about the quality.

PATTERNS OF CONFLICT: THE HIGH FREQUENCY of complaints from women about lack of communication and responsiveness and the high frequency of complaints by men about their wives' arguing, criticizing and nagging suggest a common fight pattern in unhappily married couples. This pattern has been frequently reported in the clinical literature and most recently in the research literature by such investigators as Gottman and Levenson (1986) and by Andrew Christensen and his colleagues (1988). Whether describing this pattern as a pursuing-distancing pattern, a conflict-confronting/conflict-avoiding pattern, or a demanding-withdrawing pattern, many investigators have noted sex-role differences. Women are more likely than men to confront their spouses with concerns and disagreements and to express their feelings about these problems, whereas husbands respond with factual or conciliatory explanations or defensiveness, avoidance and withdrawal. Gottman and Levenson (1986) have suggested that women may manage the level of intimacy and emotion in relationships by stimulating their husbands to confront problem areas and vent anger. In distressed marriages, when wives try this strategy of persistent prodding, it may result in defensive patterns of withdrawal or stonewalling on the part of husbands and eventual contempt and disengagement on the part of the wives.

Gottman and Levenson (1986) discovered a physiological basis for this pattern where men rapidly become autonomically aroused when confronting conflict, whereas women experience relatively low levels of arousal over sustained conflict, which permits them to tolerate longer, escalating bouts of conflict. Men, therefore, need to shut off or diminish

their arousal or they may be overwhelmed and lose control. Hence, stonewalling is a kind of protective safety valve allowing men to dampen their own levels of arousal. These findings help to explain the nature of the frequent plea of women to their husbands of "why won't you talk to me," as their husbands withdraw behind newspapers, turn on the television, stare into their beer, or play with the family pet.

Researchers do not know how early these sex-differentiated patterns of dealing with conflict emerge. However, even preschool boys seem to be more vulnerable to the adverse consequences of conflict than are girls. It has been suggested that this is in part because parents fight more in front of boys than in front of girls, that boys are offered less support in times of stress, and that as boys grow older they utilize available supports less than do girls (Hetherington & Camara, 1989). Sex differences in self-disclosure to friends and families about personal problems increase between the ages of 4 and 10 (Hetherington, Cox & Cox, 1981). It is interesting to speculate that there also may be an autonomic basis for these early sex differences that is then augmented over time by the increasing social pressure toward the development of expressiveness in the feminine role and emotional constraint in males.

PREDICTING MARITAL DISSATISFACTION, DIVORCE and Separation: The Hetherington laboratory has been involved in a series of longitudinal studies that have included comparison groups of divorced and nondivorced families (e.g., Hetherington, Cox & Cox, 1981; Hetherington & Clingempeel, 1988). During the course of these studies, some divorced adults remarried, and some couples who were in nondivorced comparison groups divorced, sometimes several times. This provided an opportunity to examine prospectively factors that contribute to the survival or dissolution of marriages. A high level of conflict, while clearly related to concurrent marital unhappiness, did not in itself predict future separation and divorce. Two specific patterns, however, did predict the disintegration of a marriage. The first was the existence of a pursuing-distancing pattern in the relationship, in which one person indicates a complaint, to which the other responds by whining, denying the charges, or withdrawing. Wives were more likely to be the pursuers and husbands to be the defender/distancer.

The second pattern predicting divorce was unexpected, occurring in marriages with little overt conflict but significant differences between spouses in their expectations and perceptions about family life, marriage and their children. Although these couples agreed about almost nothing, they actively avoided conflict, frequently leading parallel, but disengaged, social lives. Nortorious and Vanzetti (1983) have proposed that such couples never develop a sense of "relational efficacy"—the confidence that they can weather conflict together. As Gottman and Levenson (1986) and Camara (1984) have suggested, it is not conflict itself, but maladaptive patterns of dealing with it, that has long-term adverse effects on marriage.

PATTERNS OF DISCOMFORT: ALTHOUGH ALL FAMIly members experience separation and divorce as stressful, the patterns of peaks of psychological distress differ for men and women. Women find the time before deciding to end the marriage and the actual separation and divorce most difficult; it is then they are most likely to suffer the most serious psychological and physical symptoms. Kiecolt-Glaser and her associates (1987) suggest that changes in the immune system making divorced women vulnerable to infection and disease peak at separation and gradually diminish in the months thereafter. For men, psychological symptoms often increase following divorce. Men frequently value their marriage and their relationship with their wives and children more after they have lost it. Unrealistic

fantasies of reconciliation are more frequent and sustained in men than in women. Once women have decided to divorce, they are more likely than men to face realistically the challenges of beginning a new, single life. Both men and women, however, experience an increase in psychological distress at about one year following divorce when their hopes for a better new life are being tempered by recognition of the challenges and problems to be confronted in attaining it (Hetherington, Cox & Cox, 1981).

ADJUSTMENT TO DIVORCE: ALTHOUGH DIVORCE IS stressful, most men and women adapt to their new lives reasonably well within two to three years if they are not confronted with continued or additional stressors. Some of the stressors, changes and challenges encountered by divorcing spouses are related to pragmatic issues such as economic support and the management of the household, some are associated with emotional and personality changes, and still others are related to changes in social relationships between the divorced spouses—with children, with friends and kin and in new intimate relationships.

PRAGMATIC ISSUES: IN 90 PERCENT OF DIVORCED families, children reside with their mothers. The economic fallout from divorce is routinely a lowered living standard for women; custodial mothers generally live in economic circumstances far more precarious than do custodial fathers. One year after divorce, there is approximately a 22 percent decrement in the resources available to divorced mothers, and over a five-year period this amount increases to at least 31 percent, compared to their predivorce living standards (Emery, 1988). Forty-three percent of divorced custodial mothers have annual incomes of less than $10,000 (Hernandez, 1988). Child support hardly makes up for the income gap. In roughly 25 percent of mother-custody cases, fathers pay less than the court-ordered support and pay it erratically. Another one-quarter of divorced noncustodial fathers pay nothing at all (Haskins, Schwarz, Akin, & Dobelstein, 1985). Furthermore, court-ordered awards average about $2,000 per child, less than the estimated requirement for raising children at the poverty level. Even in an era of women's rights and affirmative action, the main route to economic security for divorced custodial women is remarriage.

Divorced parents must also establish new household routines. In the immediate aftermath of divorce, both men and women, particularly custodial parents, often lead disorganized and demanding lives. It is very difficult for one parent to perform the duties that two parents usually share. Unfortunately, when divorced parents must work outside, maintain households and raise families, they often drop the "nonessential" but pleasurable, playful activities of parenting—a relaxed talk about the day's activities over dinner, reading to the children at bedtime, playing games, or taking day trips together.

Custodial fathers typically have more resources available to help them deal with practical tasks than do mothers. According to one estimate, custodial fathers pay someone to look after their children for about 24 hours per week, compared to about 11 hours for mothers (Gasser & Taylor, 1976). Fathers also get more help from other people, some of it unsolicited. A father in one of our studies described some of his helpers as "casserole ladies"—women who appear around dinnertime with a covered dish, because they cannot believe that a single father is capable of looking after children. No mothers in our samples, however, have reported casserole ladies or gentlemen who turn up on their doorsteps.

Custodial fathers may also have an easier time managing a household because they are more willing than mothers to assign responsibility for household duties to their children. Middle-class mothers are reluctant to assign tasks to their children that they

view as their own responsibility, unlike lower-class divorced mothers, who generally distribute household chores democratically among the children (Gasser & Taylor, 1976).

EMOTIONAL AND SOCIAL CHANGE: SOME EMOtional responses to divorce are equally common for men and women. In the first year, divorced mothers and fathers are more emotionally labile and feel more anxious, depressed, angry, rejected and incompetent than still-married parents. Divorced parents report feeling they have failed as parents and spouses, and doubting their ability to have a successful relationship in the future. These parents also report functioning less well in social situations and heterosexual relationships during the first year after their divorce (Hetherington, Cox & Cox, 1981). Although the spouse who initiated the divorce does not initially experience the same degree of emotional adversity as the spouse left behind, the emotional adjustment of both spouses is similar after two years.

Other feelings seem to be more related to gender and custody arrangements. For instance, fathers who leave their home and their children undergo greater initial changes in self-concept than do mothers, although the effects on mothers appear to last longer. Divorced mothers complain of feeling physically unattractive, having lost the identity and status associated with being a married woman, and of a general feeling of helplessness. Noncustodial fathers, on the other hand, say they no longer know who they are; they feel rootless and have no structure in their lives, no "home" of their own. A pervasive concern for many noncustodial fathers is the sense of loss of their children.

Loneliness is a common complaint of both divorced men and women, although divorced fathers often get involved in a frenzied schedule of social activities after divorce. Divorced people, especially women, complain that social activities are organized around couples and that following divorce it is necessary to establish a new social network, often involving other divorced individuals. While social life and support systems are invaluable for encouraging positive adjustment to divorce, the most important factor enhancing self-esteem and personal well-being in divorced people is establishing a new, intimate and satisfying personal relationship.

CHANGES IN PARENTING PRACTICES: AFTER DIvorce, mothers most often have custody of the children. Fathers gain sole custody only about 10 percent of the time and usually when their children are older, are boys, or have been found to be unmanageable by their mothers. Even with joint custody, children are more likely to actually live in their mother's household (Maccoby and Mnookin, 1986). Noncustodial mothers also maintain greater contact with their children than do noncustodial fathers. Thirty-one percent of noncustodial mothers, in contrast to 13 percent of noncustodial fathers, see their children at least once a week (Furstenburg, 1988). Thus, for most children, divorce results in loss of intermittent contact with the father.

Divorce alters not only the quantity but the quality of the parent-child relationship. In the first year after divorce, parents' management of their children deteriorates markedly, as evidenced by poor control, less communication, less attention and nurturance, and inconsistent discipline. Although these parenting problems decrease over time, even six years after divorce many divorced custodial mothers are less competent than nondivorced mothers and have more trouble controlling their children than do nondivorced mothers or custodial fathers; however, fathers are less adept than mothers at monitoring their children's activities and peer associations (Hetherington, 1989). Custodial mothers and sons frequently engage in escalating cycles of coercion continuing long after the divorce. Although divorced mothers and preadolescent daughters are often close and mutually supportive, they too often begin experiencing conflict as the daughters reach adolescence and become more independent and sexually active.

Children in divorced families are often described as growing up faster than children in nondivorced families (Weiss, 1979). The former play a more active role in family decision making, share more responsibilities, and are less closely supervised and more independent than the latter. There is some evidence that preadolescent children adapt better in the custody of a same-sex parent (Camara & Resnick, 1988; Santrock & Warshak, 1986; Zill, 1988). However, a recent study suggests that both female and male adolescents in the custody of their fathers may exhibit more delinquent behaviors than those living with their mothers. This may be attributable to the increasingly salient role parental monitoring plays in inhibiting antisocial behaviors as children move into adolescence (Hetherington & Clingempeel, 1988; Patterson & Banks, in press), and to fathers' relative ineptitude in monitoring their children's behavior.

RESILIENCY AND ENHANCEMENT IN THE LONGTerm Adjustment to Divorce: According to our data, a substantial subgroup of daughters and nonremarried mothers but few sons and nonremarried fathers are coping exceptionally well six years after divorce (Hetherington, 1989). Some divorced women seem to be enhanced by having gone through the experience of coping with divorce and appear to enjoy living in a one-parent household. Such divorced women, upon confronting the challenges of raising children alone, develop into "superwomen," excelling in the workplace and in the home. They exhibit remarkable competence as parents, as workers and as responsible social beings, manifesting a level of competence greater than that found in most nondivorced women. While some of these women were capable, nontraditional women before the divorce, others had not exhibited exceptional competencies before the divorce. Many were traditional wives and mothers who had based their identity on the status and achievements of their husbands and children. While they found the separation and divorce traumatic, the demands of surviving as a single parent led to the development of new skills and resourcefulness and to a level of individuation and life satisfaction that was not anticipated, and probably would not have been attained, had they remained in their marriage.

In contrast, a group of nonremarried men who showed marked personal growth or development was not found. Most divorced men achieve more, are physically and psychologically healthier, and report greater satisfaction when they have the security of marriage than when they remain single.

IN CONCLUSION, IT IS IMPORTANT TO NOTE THAT life in a single state following divorce is usually temporary, a way station, not a destination. Although the remarriage rate is declining, 80 percent of men and 75 percent of women eventually remarry, more than half of them within three years of divorce. The formation of new intimate relationships and remarriage play a major role in postdivorce adjustment. Although much research has focused on the negative consequences of divorce, in the long term most individuals prefer being single to living in a conflict-ridden or lifeless marriage.

Although this paper has focused on differences between the responses of men and women to divorce, it must be underscored that there is great diversity within the response of men and women to divorce. Divorce confronts both men and women with stresses and anxiety-provoking change. It also provides both men and women with the opportunity to confront and cope with new challenges, the freedom for personal growth, and the chance to build new, more fulfilling relationships. ∎

E. MAVIS HETHERINGTON, PH.D., *is the James Page Professor of Psychology at the University of Virginia, Gilmer Hall, Charlottesville, VA.*
ADELINE S. TRYON, PH.D., *is a senior scientist in the Department of Psychology at the University of Virginia, Charlottesville, VA.*

See references, page 564.

ILLUSTRATION BY DAVE SHANNON

THE TIES THAT BIND

BOTH ALCOHOLICS AND THEIR FAMILIES ARE BOUND TO THE BOTTLE

By David Treadway

THE MOTHER LOOKS HAGGARD AND TENSE. HER two kids watch as the therapist asks why the father couldn't make the session. They giggle nervously, waiting to see what she's going to say. "He had to work late," she murmurs with averted eyes. . . .

They fight all the time. He says that she is cold and controlling. She says that he is always angry. They acknowledge that the fighting is worse in the evening, but neither of them mentions that they normally have three double martinis and split a bottle of wine every night. . . .

The father is giving the kid a lecture about the evils of drugs. The kid is slumped down in his chair with his arms folded tightly across his chest and a hard, cold set to his face. He stares at his father, who, unknown to the therapist, has been an alcoholic for 20 years. . . .

In each of these cases, alcoholism lurks in the background even though it isn't offered as the problem for treatment. In these families, as in so many we see, talking about a member's alcohol abuse would violate a cardinal rule, as if acknowledging the

drinking issues would threaten the family's very existence. And, in fact, that is often the case. Once the pattern of alcohol abuse is identified, the battle lines must be clearly drawn and positions taken. With its secret problem finally delineated so openly, the family as a whole would have a very hard time returning to the status quo. It is not surprising that many of the families of alcohol abusers come into treatment presenting an acting-out kid, some behavioral symptom, or a marital conflict, rather than talking about drinking.

Many family therapists profess to be relatively inexperienced about treating chemical dependency, and yet in almost half of our cases, substance abuse, in some form, plays a central role in organizing family relationships. Often, however, we don't ask the questions that will help us establish the role of drinking in a family.

Having overlooked the impact of alcoholism, we may find ourselves feeling that something about the family eludes us. Down the road we may learn that the father who always has to work has a severe drinking problem. Or we may uncover the covert family agreement that drinking cannot be brought up as an issue in therapy—or else. And often, of course, these crucial details never come out, and families "mysteriously" drop out of treatment or lurch from one crisis to another without noticeable improvement.

Sometimes families don't talk about a member's alcoholism because they have grown so used to the way that drinking organizes life at home that they no longer even identify it as a problem. For them, the patterns of behavior that evolve from alcohol have become so ingrained they are as taken for granted as the arrangement of the living room furniture.

How is it that so many therapists fail to explore the role that drinking plays in their clients' lives? In most clinical training there is an insufficient emphasis on treating alcoholism. I have seen many alcoholics who, despite years of psychoanalysis, never discussed their drinking problem with their analysts. Family therapists are often just as likely to overlook clients' alcoholism, especially if they assume that the presenting problem a family puts forth is the only one that needs to be worked on. Many therapists tend to adhere to cultural stereotypes about what constitutes a problem drinker. They may be looking for the slobbering drunk who can't hold a job and fail to recognize the insidious pattern of the successful executive who anesthetizes himself with alcohol after work every night while his family goes on about the business of life without him.

What does the substance-abusing family look like? What are some of the central issues that have to be addressed in treatment? What is the potential impact of the therapist's own personal history in relationship to alcohol? These are the key questions that I will address in this article.

I REMEMBER JUST BEING IN A HAZE. EVERYBODY was always mad at me, and all I wanted to do was get away from the house. I knew that my drinking was out of control, but I always had an excuse. Whenever my wife started to bitch at me, I knew that would be my ticket out of there. . . .

The thing I hated the most was when my mother got all sentimental and weepy. She would take me in her lap and sing to me and tell me she was sorry and how much she loved me. Her breath stank. . . .

I could always tell what kind of night it was going to be by how my father came in the door. I would listen for how he put the key in the lock. If he fumbled around and didn't get the key in, I would know it was going to be the kind of night that I would just make myself scarce. I could always tell. . . .

These are the voices of people in the alcoholic family. Each feels trapped and out of control, hanging on for dear life. The question of whether the family will be okay or blow up into a crisis is always in the air. Some families live in a state of perpetual turmoil and conflict, while others simply harbor a pervasive sense of dread, feeling that something is definitely wrong, but never quite sure what.

The more the parent drinks, the more he becomes an outsider in the family. Eventually he ends up as a problem that the family is managing rather than a family member. Increasingly, the drinker feels isolated, and this further reinforces even more withdrawal into alcohol use.

As this happens, the other parent usually takes over the primary executive role in the family. In many instances, the caretaker spouse is the wife, who becomes more and more a single parent whose competence and overresponsibility enable the alcoholic to be increasingly peripheral. She balances the checkbook, coaches the soccer, brings in the money, and covers up for his unexplained absences from work while sacrificing her own needs and even her sense of self. When the drinker is the wife, it is very common for the man to abandon her and the family. Thus many female alcoholics are single women struggling to bring up children while also being unable to control their drinking. The men who end up staying with female drinkers more often than not have a significant chemical or emotional dependency of their own.

To grow up in an alcoholic family is to be shaped by an environment in which the people upon whom you are most dependent behave in a very inconsistent and unpredictable fashion. How does a 4-year-old understand the confusing message of being dressed up in party clothes in order to spend Saturday mornings in a bar with Daddy and his friends? How does a 6-year-old understand when Mom forgets to come to the school play, accuses him of never having told her about it in the first place, and punishes him for lying when he reminds her that she promised to come? How does a child integrate the experience of watching his parents have a fistfight only to be told the following morning that nothing happened and that all parents have disagreements from time to time? Clearly, these kinds of experiences instill in children a profound difficulty in trusting people or even being able to trust their own experience of reality. "Did I tell Mom about the school play? I thought I did. Maybe I didn't."

Children survive growing up in alcoholic systems by learning to distrust others and by becoming self-sufficient, by blocking out their feelings, and by becoming rigidly attached to roles that give them a sense of their place and identity within the family. When these children grow up, their early survival strategies can become major stumbling blocks in adult relationships. Often they develop rituals and patterned responses that allow them some measure of personal control in the face of what they experience as a chaotic maelstrom. Is it any wonder that a girl who at the age of seven was pinned to the wall by her ordinarily distant father and berated about where she had hidden his bottle might grow up to be a single woman who owns two cars just in case one breaks down?

One of the most successful survival skills for children from such families is to learn how to ignore what is going on at home or to repress any feelings

about it. The child is trapped in a scary situation he can neither understand, control nor leave. Typically, children in alcoholic families learn how to get along on very little in the way of parental constancy and support. Like the poor kid standing outside the toy store window who walks away from the window saying to himself, "I didn't want that dumb old toy anyway," these children generally give up their expectations about either parent. They feel betrayed by both the inconsistent alcoholic and the codependent parent who, although providing love and nurturance, fails to protect the family from the alcoholic.

The strategy of repressing needs and feelings often leads these children to be unaware of how much they expect their later relationships with spouse, children and coworkers to make up for their early deprivation. Thus, even while the adult children of alcoholics (ACOAs) often appear to be extremely independent and self-sufficient, they communicate an underlying emotional dependency that can sabotage relationships. Spouses, for example, often experience ACOAs as very difficult to ever fully satisfy and frequently become frustrated and distant because they feel that they can never do enough. This response only confirms for the ACOA their basic fear that other people will never really be there for them anyway. Children who grew up in alcoholic homes are looking for signs of dishonesty, inconsistency and rejection in their adult relationships. If you're looking hard, you'll always find it.

Those who have brought the Adult Children of Alcoholics phenomenon to popular attention, people like Sharon Wegsheider-Cruse, Claudia Black, Robert Ackerman and Janet Woittitz, have all discussed how such children tend to develop rigid roles to help them cope. The most common of these family roles are:

The Hero: This is usually the oldest child, who ends up in the position of the assistant parent. This child takes on a large measure of responsibility for the younger siblings as well as serving as a parent's confidant and helpmate. The child's sense of identity and self-esteem often becomes quite dependent on being a competent caretaker whose sense of intimacy and relatedness is derived from an ability to give to others. As an adult, this child stands a reasonably good chance of marrying a dysfunctional spouse, becoming a caretaker or a workaholic.

The Scapegoat: This child serves as a lightning rod for all the family tension and conflict. By routing family tension through this child, the family is able to avoid a confrontation around the drinking issue that might threaten the family status quo. The acting-out kid protects Dad from being confronted, protects Mom from having to challenge Dad, protects his siblings from getting the heat, and ultimately protects himself from the anxiety of being passive and waiting for the next crisis. Since scapegoats act out, they are frequently brought in for treatment and therefore are usually the first family member to get help. If they are not helped, the likelihood that they will become alcoholic or drug dependent is quite high.

The Lost Child: This child develops the skill of being unobtrusive and uninvolved. Usually one of the younger children, this child intuitively recognizes that the best method of staying out of harm's way is to make oneself scarce at all times. These children will frequently avoid being home as much as possible and will turn to other adults and families for surrogate support and closeness. As adults, these children are often unable to develop close relationships and tend to remain peripheral and detached.

NEEDLESS TO SAY, THE SCARRING OF CHILDREN IS not unique to the alcoholic family. All the tendencies described above also emerge in families in which there is a chronically ill or insane parent, an early death of a parent, incest or physical abuse, or a particularly difficult divorce. The point is that growing up in an alcoholic family can be equally traumatic as these other scenarios, and the defenses

learned are likely to be just as strongly ingrained. Imagine the dilemma for these kids as adults when those who are closest to them say naively, "Relax, you can trust me."

Bob speaks softly with a thick Southern accent. His reddened eyes look like a road map. Susie sits hunched over, knees pressed tightly together. She is sitting on her hands. Her eyes flit back and forth as she watches her husband, her therapist and me. This is a demonstration interview and I am nervous. I am showing the audience how to work with a family in which the alcoholism has not been clearly acknowledged as part of the presenting problem. Susie wants to talk about Bob's daughter, who lives with them. Bob wants to talk about Susie's sex problem. They both lost their fathers at a very young age. They both had very destructive first marriages. They both acknowledge that Bob's drinking has been an issue. They describe their relationship as the best that they have ever had. No one wants to talk about Bob's drinking. Neither do I. I have been in the room with them for five minutes, and already I can feel their anxiety and their unspoken wish not to be pushed into an issue that they can't handle.

Should I work with the presenting problems and deal with the drinking indirectly, or do I need to push the alcohol issue at the risk of losing them? Is the drinking the "real" problem or another manifestation of a dysfunctional system? Does he have to quit drinking altogether, or can he learn to drink appropriately? What will happen to the relative balance in their relationship if he does stop drinking?

I begin each case with a fairly high level of vigilance regarding alcohol-related issues. Regardless of the presenting problem, I will look for signs and ask questions about patterns of alcohol use in both the nuclear family and the family of origin. It is important to do this in an offhand and nonjudgmental way in order to avoid eliciting family defensiveness. If I suspect alcohol abuse, then I look to see how the presenting problem may allow the family to elicit help while at the same time it protects them from dealing with the drinking.

The pivotal issue as a therapist treating a family with unacknowledged alcoholism is getting the family to confront one another about a member's drinking rather than usurping this responsibility and confronting the drinking myself. I want the emerging struggle around this issue to be among family members rather than between the family and me. If I push the alcohol issue, it usually unites the family in resistance toward me.

I will say to the alcoholic whose son is the presenting problem, "So your wife seems to feel that your drinking affects your ability to really help the kids. Can you talk it over with her and find out what's going on?" Conversely, I might say to a wife, "It seems that you're saying that you really don't depend on your husband very much because he drinks a lot. Could you go ahead and talk frankly with him about your concerns? See if he is willing to listen to your worries without getting mad at you for having them." I always remind myself that the main job of therapy is not to report that the light bulb has gone on in my head but to create the circumstances in which it goes on for the family.

The major problem with keeping the problem among the family members is that the shift to the alcohol issue generates tremendous anxiety and often results in an intensification of the presenting problem. It is important for the therapist to anticipate this escalation and discuss with the family whether or not they can handle talking about the dad's drinking. I might say to the kids right in front of Dad, "Do you think Dad really wants to know how the family feels about his drinking, or is he going to be super mad when you all get out in the car after this meeting?" Or I might say to one of the parents, "Do you think this talking about drinking is so uncomfortable for Johnny that he might get even worse this coming week so that in the next session this stuff doesn't even get brought up?"

DR. T.: I mean, what's your idea of an acceptable maximum that would allow you to say to Susie, "If I don't drink any more than this amount, then as far as I am concerned, I don't have any real problem with booze."

BOB: A maximum, huh? I've tried that, but I have always set something up that was way too low.

DR. T.: Well, that's what people usually do. But what I want you to come up with is a maximum that you would really take a stand on. I remember I had one guy who said he would drink no more than two double scotches a day plus only one case of beer.

BOB (laughing): I think I know that guy.

DR. T. (to himself): I better make sure Susie doesn't think I'm giving this guy carte blanche.

DR. T. (to the family): Susie is looking at me like I'm crazy, but this is very important for you to figure out. What amount of alcohol is really alright for you, and what might indicate that this whole thing is way out of control? You might decide that you can stick with a very high amount of alcohol, and then Susie will have to decide what's right for her to try and live with.

Once the alcoholic's drinking is out in the open, I work to help the family disengage from either protecting him or confronting him all the time. My basic message to the family is that it is *his* problem and that he will either be responsible for demonstrating that his drinking is under control, or he will discover that he has a serious drinking problem and perhaps needs to give up drinking entirely. In order to do this, I typically set up a controlled drinking contract with the problem drinker. I ask the drinker to set a maximum daily limit on his alcohol intake. As with Bob, this intervention is designed to push the drinker to set his own standards and live within them. The high limit allows me to push for the agreement that if the drinker exceeds this limit even once, then he agrees that he should get treatment of some kind for his drinking. Clearly, the implicit assumption is that the drinker will tend not to be able to keep any limit very easily. Thus the therapist should be able to confront the drinking issue not by siding with the wife against the husband but by genuinely expecting the man to live up to his own commitment.

Watching me negotiate a liberal standard for alcohol use will often make the family upset because they think that as the doctor I am giving the drinker permission to drink excessively. It is important to reassure the family that I know that the drinking contract may not be acceptable to them. I will frequently say that the limit set is neither safe nor appropriate by my standards either. I make clear that the contract is a way for the drinker to resolve his own confusion about his relationship to alcohol and also bring into focus the issue of drinking without simply replicating the mutual recriminations from the past.

Sometimes people are really able to use the controlled-drinking contract to discover that they need to stop drinking. However, there are a variety of other typical responses the therapist needs to be prepared for. If the drinker stays within his limit successfully, then I help the family decide whether or not the pattern of alcohol use is acceptable to them. They have the option of going to Al Anon, doing an intervention à la the Johnson Institute, breaking up the family through separation or divorce, or just accepting the status quo.

The controlled-drinking contract has a tremendous impact on the family because their willingness to deny the problem and be protective of the alcoholic tends to dissipate after the whole issue is brought out in the open and negotiated straightforwardly. If the drinker does not stay within his limit and refuses to accept the negotiated consequences, then usually the family is truly prepared to confront the drinker.

Finally, either the original presenting problem may intensify severely in order to rescue the family from the crisis around the drinking, or the family may drop out of treatment. In either case, it is important for me to let the family go graciously rather than struggle with them to stay focused on the drinking. In one case, I thought treatment was proceeding right on schedule. Dad had cooperated by coming drunk to the interview and forcing the family to confront his drinking problem. What happened before the next interview? The suicidal daughter tried to kill herself again. I had to move back to focusing on her, while acknowledging the family's need to sidestep the drinking problem for now.

Using this approach, I am able to assess whether the drinker's problem can be treated simply within the context of family therapy or needs to be labeled an illness in its own right and treated as a disease using abstinence and AA. Throughout, I openly discuss the possibility that the alcohol use may be a problem that cannot be controlled with willpower and limit setting but, in fact, may need to be treated like a disease. I don't push this metaphor, but when it becomes apparent that the drinker cannot control his behavior, I provide the benign reframe that the alcoholic has not failed but has simply been using the wrong approach. My message is, "You can't heal a broken leg by exercise, and you can't cure drinking by willpower."

DR. T.: This might surprise you, but I think you might quit drinking at some point, and what I'm worried about is that Susie is going to expect that she can suddenly turn on her feelings for you if you get sober. If it doesn't work that way, and it usually doesn't, she's going to be awfully disappointed in herself, and then if she can't be with you, it's going to make you go back to drinking. You know she can't turn her body on like throwing a light switch. Help her not to be too hard on herself.

BOB: Well, you know you might be right. She gets down on herself pretty easy. But it's going to be hard for me too.

DR. T: That's right. It's going to be hard for both of you. It's one of the reasons why I would want you to use AA and for her to use Al Anon.

BOB: I'm not much for meetings.

DR. T. (thinking to himself): Hold on. He doesn't have to get sober today. *(continued on page 149)*

"If He Keeps This Up He'll Die Soon"

Denial is the staple of the alcoholic. Recognizing this, the therapeutic technique known as "the intervention" attempts to confront that denial in a caring but decisive manner. The following is a description of one such confrontation. Though the names are fictitious to protect the privacy of the participants, the description is an otherwise factual account.

H E KNEW. JUST ONE LOOK AT THE SHOCK ON HIS FACE AND YOU COULD TELL," RECALLS DANIEL Weisman, a 40-year-old Philadelphia accountant. As if it were yesterday, Daniel remembers the way his older brother Alex stood slumped as he entered the room that was filled with family, friends and business associates. "There was an awkward quietness. We had met in secret for so many weeks, planning that moment. But when he entered the room, we just looked at each other. It was suddenly embarrassing. We could tell instantly that he knew."

Sitting down obediently in the chair offered him, Alex demonstrated none of his old command—the biting repartee, the combative look. Although not a large man, the 43-year-old Alex was often imposing, aggressive, even intimidating—especially when he was drunk. And he'd been drunk nearly every night for the last 10 years. Alex was now consuming a quart of liquor a day and one—maybe two—six-packs each night. "He was killing himself," reflects Daniel.

Curiously, the person who had set this meeting in motion was neither a family member nor a longtime friend but one of Alex's clients. Businessman Martin Ferber had watched Alex become increasingly volatile and erratic over the span of their acquaintanceship. He had repeatedly seen him get drunk at business luncheons, and it finally registered with him—"This man is in trouble. If he keeps this up, he's going to die . . . soon."

Nevertheless, Alex somehow managed to keep his highly successful career as a trial lawyer going. His practice continued to grow and his income increase at the same time that his drinking and paranoia were escalating. His wife, Sara, and two daughters had learned to avoid the subject of his drinking. Each had come unwittingly to play her role in the family drama, puppets to Alex's compulsion.

"Alex just refused to talk with anyone about his drinking," relates Daniel. "I had tried every kind of one-on-one encounter, but my attempts to reason with him went nowhere. He would always tell me he could handle it, or that I was exaggerating, and it wasn't really that bad. If I pressed him, he'd tell me to mind my own business. Finally I just said 'fuck it.' "

THEN ONE DAY, FERBER, A MAN DANIEL HAD NEVER MET, CALLED TO TALK ABOUT ALEX'S ALCO-holism. On his own initiative, Ferber had contacted a local therapist and told him about Alex's situation. Together they had decided to see if they could organize an intervention, a special approach to reaching the alcoholic unwilling to seek help on his own. In this approach, family, friends, colleagues, employer—everyone and anyone who cares for the alcoholic—meets with him to express their concern and their determination that he receive *immediate* attention. To ensure the success of the intervention, participants first meet secretly to educate and prepare themselves and to make all arrangements for the alcoholic to receive professional treatment.

Weisman quickly agreed to be part of the group, even though he would have to commute more than 100 miles to attend the half-dozen meetings preceding the actual intervention. Other family members approached the prospect of participating with more wariness. Sara, Alex's wife, was scared. More than anyone, she stood to lose the most from meeting secretly behind Alex's back. He depended on her for support and understanding, and she feared she was betraying his trust. But, finally, Sara decided that 20 years of support and understanding had only made Alex's drinking worse. And then there were the kids.

Jeri, the oldest daughter, was furious—embarrassed with her father and unable to understand why her mother would submit to such hypocrisy. Andrea, on the other hand, was remarkably identified with her father—sort of his alter ego. Typical of many children of alcoholics, she was withdrawn and uncommunicative, a silent sufferer, so bottled up with emotion that she seemed in a constant state of panicked vigilance lest she might express some unacceptable feeling.

SARA, THE CHILDREN, DANIEL AND MARTIN FERBER BEGAN MEETING WITH JOHN LACY, A SOCIAL worker attached to family services court who had conducted dozens of interventions. Later they were joined by Alex's business associates and even his secretary. For the first time, they began to acknowledge openly the toll Alex's drinking had taken on them all. Lacy, part facilitator, part teacher, explained how everyone around Alex had become caught up in the denial that surrounded his drinking. To sort out their entanglements, each participant was encouraged to exchange stories about Alex's behavior and to share feelings of guilt, anger, resentment, frustration, fear and despair.

Phil Tabor, a partner in Alex's law firm, recalled a luncheon with a judge in which some details about a particularly crucial case were being discussed. "I couldn't believe it. I knew that Alex occasionally had a few too many for lunch, but I didn't think he'd jeopardize such an important conference. After the fourth martini he actually forgot our client's name. He laughed it off but then insisted on remembering it himself. When I reminded him, he froze me with that look he gets and never said a word the rest of the meal. I could have killed him."

"You should see him when *we* go out to eat," shot back Jeri. "If the waitress doesn't bring everything instantly, he makes a federal case out of it. And when she does bring the food, he's had so much to drink he doesn't eat it. It's like he's a king or something, and we're supposed to sit around and laugh at his corny jokes."

"There was a time when I tried to keep up with him," offered Daniel. "I thought maybe if I drank with him I could get through that shell—God knows we were superficial enough when he was sober. But it's like something out of Edgar Allan Poe—always wondering when the walls are going to close in. Besides, he would always outdrink me, and I could never drink enough to keep from feeling rotten."

"I remember when my father had a stroke," recalled Sara. "I wanted to take the next flight and go be with my mother. I asked Alex if he could handle things around the house for a couple of days. He said 'Sure'—but it was like he didn't even hear me. He just had that dead look in his eyes. I didn't dare go."

The night before "The Day," the group met to rehearse their speeches one last time and to share their fears and anxieties. "What will he think of us meeting behind his back like this?"

"What if he's hung over, or drunk?"

"I'm afraid he'll make a scene."

"I'm afraid he might kill himself!"

"He could just walk out. He's done that every time I've tried to bring the subject up to him."

"He just gets angry with me and starts yelling."

"Really? He always gives me the silent treatment."

"All we can do is try. Let's just remember that we're here because we love him and want him to get the help he needs."

NOW THEY ALL SAT, FIDGETING UNCOMFORTABLY, IN THE LIVING ROOM OF MARTIN FERBER'S HOME. Alex had been lured there under the pretense of a business meeting, but when he saw them all assembled, he knew the agenda had changed.

Daniel, the designated spokesman, broke the ice. "Alex . . . uh, we're here. . . ." His voice began to get husky. He fought the tears. "We're here because we love you . . . and, uh, well . . . well, we need you, and we need to tell you what your behavior and drinking are doing to us.

"Do you remember the time . . . ?"

And so, gathering courage, Daniel began. He shared his memories, his pain, his anger and his hope. And the story passed around the quiet room—the same story in the varied forms that each person had experienced it—the story of living with alcoholism. It was interrupted only by Andrea's sobs.

When everyone had finished, Daniel took over, a new conviction in his voice. "Alex, we want you to go to the clinic. We've arranged everything, and we want you to go with us right now."

In silence, they looked at Alex fearfully, expectantly.

"Let's go," Alex whispered.

"What?" responded Daniel, not sure he had heard correctly.

"Okay, let's go to the clinic."

Daniel walked over to his brother, embraced him, and kissed him gently. "Thank you," Daniel said hoarsely.

An excited, stunned and disbelieving cortege left the house and headed for the clinic where John Lacy had made a reservation on the hope, on the chance, that Alex would agree to accept treatment.

Daniel recalls, "I was scared. I was afraid he'd jump out of the car, and we'd have to shoot him like an escaped fugitive! We were all scared he would change his mind."

As they drove to the clinic, Alex began to worry about his professional obligations in the coming weeks.

"But what about the Johnson case?" Alex remembered. "I've got to be in court tomorrow!"

"We asked Judge Steiner for a postponement, and he granted a 30-day extension."

"Oh God! You mean Steiner knows about this?"

"Don't worry. He said everything was fine, and just for you to get well."

"Jesus! But what about my conference presentation on the fifth?"

"They've agreed to have Phil read it."

"My reservations to Salt Lake?"

"They've been refunded."

Every possible snag Alex could contemplate had been looked after in advance.

"You mean I can just forget it and do this. . . ." Alex's voice trailed off.

WE ARRIVED AT THE CLINIC, DROPPED HIM OFF, WATCHED HIM REGISTER, AND SAID OUR GOOD-BYES,"
recalls Daniel Weisman. "Sara, John and I drove to a nearby restaurant."

There they shared their excitement and amazement.

"God, I was so scared."

"I couldn't believe it when he said 'Let's go.' I mean, Jesus, do you realize it only took 11 minutes? And I've been trying to get him to do this for 11 goddamn years!"

And so they repeated over and over how scared they had been, how they thought he might
get angry, or sulk, or accuse them of conspiring against him, or kill himself, or. . . .

And what of Alex today? After sobering up for 30 days in the clinic, he returned to his family
and his work. Daniel says he became something of a workaholic instead of an alcoholic, but that
he's "a little softer" now than he used to be. Some months later, Martin Ferber, the client who had
initiated the intervention, and Alex had a falling-out. The friendship was severed. Daniel and Sara
braced themselves.

Alex took just one drink. But Sara would have none of it. "I'll do anything for you. I'll stand
by you whatever the situation. I'll be there for you because I love you. But I won't go through this
again. Not ever. I'll leave you first."

Alex hasn't taken a drink since that day. □

—Dick Anderson
JULY 1987

DICK ANDERSON, M.A., *is the creative consultant to* The Family Therapy Networker.

(continued from page 144) Patience, patience.

It took me a long time to fully appreciate how traumatic it is for a family to have an alcoholic member go sober. This event completely throws out of balance the family's familiar pattern of behavior. It is like trying to run a car engine without lubricating oil. No one knows what his role is or how he should behave, and everyone is worried that if he does the wrong thing, Dad will start drinking again.

Every family member has tremendous anxiety, hurt and rage bottled up after years of dealing with the drinking, and yet the situation calls for them to all plaster smiles on their faces and act as if they are thoroughly thrilled with their newly recovering member. On the other hand, the alcoholic has to discover that the family really has learned to get along without him and that he is truly an outsider in his own home. Furthermore, as he becomes aware of the destructiveness of his past behavior, he realizes there is absolutely no way of making up for it. His level of shame and need for forgiveness are extremely high at the same time that the family's ability to genuinely forgive and accept is extremely low. This period of adjustment is so traumatic for families that many of them break up. Others develop a symptom bearer whose behavior allows the family to maintain their old crisis-oriented structure.

What sets these families up for a return to drinking behavior is the effort to change family relationships at a time of peak vulnerability. Therefore, it is very important at this stage of treatment for the therapist to initiate a restraint from change intervention that essentially says to the family, "Don't try and change the old structure and pattern of behavior. Don't try and make up for the past by attempting to improve family relationships precipitously."

The following are some samples of how I talk with family members about this point in recovery.

To the recovering alcoholic: "Don't try and make up for the past. It won't work. Your family is trying hard to let you in, but in reality they have so much buried resentment against you that they really can't let you in. If you try to move in too quickly, you will just be putting pressure on them to resolve their feelings before they are ready to. Give them time, and when you are feeling those periods of being a stranger inside your family, use AA."

To the spouse: "I know you think you're supposed to be able to welcome this guy back with open arms. However, I think that your trying too hard is very hurtful to him and his recovery. He'll be able to sense the part of you that is locked away that can't trust and can't forgive and that maybe doesn't even want to recommit to this relationship. You can't will away the scars of the last few years. Also, I want you to appreciate that you not only took over control of the family in order to help everyone survive, but engaging in the day-to-day effort of getting by is how you survived. The minute you try to let him into the family and begin to share some control, your rage and bitterness will become overwhelming. Don't force it. Let him work his program, you work yours. Use Al Anon. They will help you appreciate that you need time for healing also."

To the kids: "You know your dad would desperately like to make up for the time he lost with you. He's missed a lot of your growing-up years. But I don't want him to try and come on like Super Dad because that will only put tremendous pressure on you. Don't be afraid of your resentment and mistrust. If you didn't have these feelings somewhere inside you, you wouldn't be normal. Lots of kids are so afraid of their dad's going back to drinking that they don't know what to do with the feelings of anger that well up inside. It takes a long time for the fear to go."

After setting up the therapy so that expectations are reduced and family members' feelings are normalized, I start working on the presenting problem. If it is one of the kids who is having trouble, then I reframe the behavior as an inadvertent test to see if the newly sober member is going to be able to sustain his recovery.

I combine these benign reframes with interventions that are basically symptom-focused and use the old structure to work on the problem. For example, in a case in which a teenage boy is acting out and there is a newly sober dad, I will ask Mom to stay in charge. Dad's role will be, by and large, defined as sticking with his recovery program as a means of giving leadership to his son. In such cases, the rather standard family therapy move of empowering the father would have disastrous consequences because the father has invariably lost his credibility and authority during his drinking years. It is an insult to every family member's experience to try and re-establish him as an effective coparent prematurely.

Obviously, generic moves that restrain families from change in early recovery have to be tailored to fit the needs of each individual case. The fundamental steps of restraint from change, reducing family expectations, normalizing underlying negative feelings, focusing family members on their own individual recoveries using self-help programs, all need to be introduced into each unique family situation in a way that matches the family's own sense of its needs.

When I teach about alcoholism and family therapy, I always ask my audience about the extent of their personal connection to alcoholism. Invariably, 80 percent of the audience have either been married to alcoholics, grown up with alcoholic parents, or are recovered alcoholics themselves.

For most of us who have a personal connection to alcoholism, it is truly a mixed blessing. On the one hand, growing up in an alcoholic family is a form of on-the-job training for future clinicians. The survival skills one learns, e.g, the ability to manage crises, take care of others, and work hard with little recognition, are often highly useful attributes for thera-

pists to have. On the other hand, we have to be always aware of our own intense reactivity. In our work, we tend to easily become overresponsible and controlling. Either we end up in the classical position of trying to rescue the family in spite of itself, or we are too distant and punitive. I am prone to vacillating between both positions. One week I'm trying to rescue, and the next week, since no one has gotten better, I move toward confrontation. If that doesn't work, I might feel guilty and move back toward the rescuing position. At this point, I need someone to say, "David, take two Al Anons and call me in the morning."

Alcoholism is an odd and deadly game. If one is going to work with alcoholics and their families, one has to be willing to care deeply but not too much, to tolerate being afraid without becoming immobilized, and to exercise therapeutic leadership while having no control. Every time I think I've got it down pat, a new family will make me feel like a beginner again. Occasionally I experience despair, but I am rarely bored.

I don't know yet about Bob and Susie. I met with them for only an hour, but it felt like a good session. Not much changed, and I don't know if or when he'll give up drinking. It was a turning-up-the-soil type of session. I try to be patient, but I'm not, really. I frequently tell my inpatient clients that they shouldn't rush into the garden the day after they planted the seeds, looking for flowers. All they are going to see is dirt. And yet, when it comes to me, I find myself spending a lot of time looking eagerly for the first tender shoots of green. ∎

DAVID TREADWAY, PH.D., *is in private practice in the Boston area.*

PHOTOGRAPH BY STEPHEN SHAMES/MATRIX

Us AND THEM

THE PASSIONATE DEBATE ABOUT DOMESTIC VIOLENCE

By Maggie Scarf

L AST MAY I ATTENDED A SYMPOSIUM ON DOMESTIC violence in the '80s—attended, hell, I was the keynote speaker for the event. Although intimate violence had not been the central focus of my concern while doing research for *Intimate Partners,* my book on marriage, I had, as I explained to the conference official (Ms. Jodi Gossage) who called to invite me, certainly run across instances of it in the process of talking with couples. What I'd encountered, I added, was not violence on an MGM-spectacular scale; there had been no Joel Steinbergs or Hedda Nussbaums among the people whom I interviewed.

But there *had* been mates who got physically rough with their partners—who acknowledged having kicked, slapped or punched each another. There had also been cases in which I considered a couple at risk for physical violence to occur. One wife, for example, was busily setting the stage in her own life for a replication of the abusive dramas she'd witnessed as a child. The urge to replay in the present the charged scenarios of the past can exert a powerful, almost tidal force on the psyche.

Certain families seem to have their theme songs—such as depression, problems in separation, alcoholism, physical violence—which are sung at different times, by different members, from different perches on the family tree. What I had seen, I told my caller, were a number of instances in which intimate partners seemed to be replicating—in their own marriages and family lives—the same fraught images and concerns with which they'd been presented in the helpless years of their childhood. It was as if one or both mates were reenacting an old script and searching for a different ending this time—a real resolution. But the danger was that the ugly parts of the original script would be repeated in their entirety.

Ms. Gossage listened, but did not respond immediately to my remarks. After a puzzling silence, she said at last, "Good, sounds like a really interesting talk, and that approach will give the symposium some . . . some balance. Another point of view." But I could hear the underlying worry in her voice.

After another long hesitation, she added, "There is, you should know, a very militant element among this group." Militant in what way, I asked her.

153

A number of the people (mostly women) attending the conference were, said Ms. Gossage, professionals and volunteer personnel who worked in the trenches; they dealt directly with the victims of domestic abuse. A vocal segment among them disapproved of the mental health establishment and of family-oriented approaches to the understanding of intimate violence. In these workers' opinion, seeing wife battering as a systemic, family-wide problem was a way of blaming the victim—of suggesting that the beaten woman had brought the violence down upon herself, somehow.

Their point, an understandable one, was that such a notion appeared to mitigate and diminish the responsibility of the battering male—who was, after all, engaging in criminal, assaultive behavior. Ms. Gossage and I agreed, nevertheless, that since domestic violence *does* tend to be a repetitive problem within certain families—one that is reenacted from generation to generation—the family viewpoint should be included in the intellectual smorgasbord offered at the symposium.

T HE DOMESTIC VIOLENCE CONFERENCE WAS HELD in the Holiday Inn in Columbus, Ohio. It was a three-day meeting, during which more than 50 workshops were offered (on topics ranging from "The Role of Churches in Perpetuating Anti-Female Imagery" to "Working with Survivors of Incest" to "New Research Findings on Batterers' Characteristics"). My speech was scheduled to be given just after dinner on the second day of the symposium.

On that evening, the dining room was filled with round tables, each of which held eight to 10 people. At the front table near the dais where I was placed, a spirited conversation began; it was a discussion of a recent article about Hedda Nussbaum. This article, titled "Madly in Love," had been included in the conference folders mailed to us in advance. It was by Susan Brownmiller and had just appeared in the April issue of *Ms.* magazine.

I'd read the article on my way to the conference and thought it was wonderful: lucidly reasoned, beautifully written. But when a woman across the table said furiously, "How do you like the way Susan Brownmiller *trashed* Hedda Nussbaum?" everyone around me voiced agreement.

How could Brownmiller have condemned Hedda Nussbaum in that way, someone else demanded, adding: "As if *she* could understand what happens to a woman like Hedda, a woman in a battering situation! How devoid of self-esteem and the capacity to act on her own behalf she becomes! How isolated she is in her shame. . . ." Everybody at the table nodded, looking equally outraged and indignant.

What Susan Brownmiller had actually written, as I recalled, was that feminist analysis of the case should not exclude Ms. Nussbaum's moral responsibility for the death of her 6-year old adoptive child. That is, even though Hedda Nussbaum *had* been a battered woman, her complicity in Lisa's death must be acknowledged. The movement to aid battered women, observed Brownmiller, did the cause of feminism a disservice when it excused every beaten woman's behavior, no matter what criminal acts she might engage in. The battered-woman's movement, she suggested, should drop its simplistic attitudes. The idea that every abused woman is the victim of a patriarchal system that has rendered her a passive robot—unable to act on her own behalf or on behalf of her helpless children—appeared to absolve women of all personal, adult responsibility for their acts.

I was in agreement with Brownmiller's position; the notion that every battered female is not responsible for what she does is, in my opinion, sexist. But the pro-Hedda Nussbaum feeling ran high among my companions. It gave me a peculiar feeling, as if, like Alice in Wonderland, I'd fallen into a world whose rules I didn't grasp or understand. And, to compound my confusion, a victim of domestic violence, a pretty young woman named Peggy Simpson, paralyzed and confined to a wheelchair, sat directly across from me at the table. Ms. Simpson had, I knew, been shot and crippled by her ex-husband. She had offered a workshop session titled "One Survivor's Story" earlier in the day's proceedings.

The woman seated next to me soon claimed my attention; she began describing a workshop on incest that she'd attended. As far as she was concerned, it had been the best session of the entire conference. For the leader of the incest workshop had expanded the definition of what was meant by the term itself: it wasn't just penetration but also inappropriate touching of the girl's genitalia.

I nodded my agreement; this I knew. Leaning closer to me, my companion continued: "In this newer definition—the one the workshop teacher offered—incest is also anything that the dad does that makes the adolescent daughter feel—well— *uncomfortable*." I stared at her. Uh-oh, I thought, better build some new prisons fast. For, having seen three daughters through puberty, I knew that what could make an adolescent girl uncomfortable was not much more than her father's walking into the same room!

Nevertheless, looking around the buzzing dining room, I reflected that the people here were spending their lives working with the mostly female victims of male violence. If these people are outraged, I thought, it's easy to understand. They are living in a sexual war zone, and in war zones passions run high and the distinctions between Aggressor and Victim tend to hold sway with a cartoonlike clarity.

Human complexity doesn't fare well under this kind of stress. Life on the front lines generates polarities, a stark Us (the all-good female victims) and Them (the all-bad, all-brutal male attackers) mentality.

My speech that evening ran almost 15 minutes overtime—a crime I commit very rarely. But on this occasion I had much ground to cover, not only information about marriages in general, but about the particularities of physically abusive relationships.

WHAT I HAD TO SAY ABOUT MARRIAGE WAS THE following: It is in our intimate relationships that, "for better or for worse," the present and the past converge. It is in the context of close emotional attachments that what is most secret and defended against, most vulnerable and irrational, forever threatens to make itself palpable and real.

At one level, when we marry, irrational hopes—of giving and receiving perfect gratification—run high. At another level, the urge to resurrect old patterns and conflicts that existed in each of the mate's own families arouses unconscious fears that "something new" will turn out to be "something old," something very much the same. The loved partner who was to help one to improve upon the past turns out, so frequently, to be the individual who *aids in recreating* the familiar family system, and the ghosts of old struggles rise again.

Claudie Benedette, for instance, had grown up in a violent family. She had seen her father beat her mother frequently—to punish her mother's presumed infidelities. "She *was* cheating on him," Claudie told me, in a conjoint interview with her husband, Carl, "but he was cheating on her, too. I mean, they both had affairs."

She had spent most of her childhood, she said, with her head under the pillow, thoroughly terrified by all of the yelling and the screaming. Her early memories were, however, sparse and few. "I don't want to remember things," Claudie told me, "but the sadness and the fear wash over me. I just try to blank out my mind, to not think about it." She did, however, retain a vivid image of waking up one morning and finding her mother's face a bloody pulp: "My father—oh God!—had put my mom's whole head through the glass window!"

Claudie and Carl Benedette had, at the time of our conversations, been married for 17 years. While their marriage was troubled, there had never been physical violence; Carl simply withdrew when he was feeling negative or angry. But what became clear to me was that a marital storm was gathering. For, in a one-on-one interview with Claudie, she told me that she was feeling frightened by the anger she was showing toward her children and also that she was "completely obsessed" at the moment by another man. The pair of them were drifting toward an affair.

What did she think Carl would do if he were to learn the true facts of her life, I asked her.

"I think," said Claudie slowly, "that he would be crushed. I think it would do such a thing to his manhood to know that his wife, who hasn't gone to bed with him in recent history, was able to get turned on by another man. And I think he would become abusive, physically abusive, which he's never done before." She paused, then added, "I think he'd beat me to a pulp." Her use of that particular phrase reminded me of what, long ago in another family world, had happened to Claudie's mother's face.

IN MY TALK, I USED THIS PARTICULAR COUPLE'S story to illustrate several points. The first and most striking one was that the transgenerational transmission of emotionally loaded issues was involved; that is, history was being helped to repeat itself. Claudie Benedette was at risk for becoming a victim of marital violence (as her mother had been) in the context of an extramarital affair.

Another point worth noting was that while Carl Benedette had never been a battering husband, he was now being recruited to become one. He might, however, since he himself did not come from a violent family, resist colluding in the recreation of Claudie's fearful family scenario. Despite his wife's certainty that he would "beat her to a pulp," Carl might respond to revelations about Claudie by becoming furious—even by leaving her—and yet never harm her physically in any way.

Finally, Claudie's basic loyalty to her original family's patterns for being in close relationships was another matter that I addressed. In Claudie's family,

people had not resolved hurt and conflict verbally and by negotiation; instead, they'd come out swinging, with screams, violence and betrayals on the grand scale. Children growing up in families like this learn, as Richard J. Gelles and Murray A. Straus have observed (in their excellent book *Intimate Violence*), that "those you love are also those who hit you, and those you love are people who can hit." What their lives teach them is that love and violence are intertwined and interconnected.

It is the major lesson that children from violent families must *unlearn* before the same instruction is passed on to a new generation.

AFTER TALKING FOR A WHILE ABOUT THE BENEdettes—in whose relationship domestic violence was a serious threat but not a present reality—I went on to discuss my interviews with another couple, Bob and Julie Heller. In the Hellers' long-term (24 years) marriage, spouse abuse *had* erupted and been extinguished immediately.

The attack had occurred one summer evening, as the Hellers described it, when the pair of them had gotten involved in a long-running, furious argument. Bob, at the peak of the battle, had hauled off and hit his wife in the face. "I walked out immediately," Julie said. "I don't *take* that, because I'm not your abused-woman type. I told Bob if he ever did that again, it would cost him the family jewels, because there was no way that I was going to stand for it!"

Julie refused to respond to the profuse apologies that followed. Instead, she made her own position very clear: physical violence was unacceptable, and she had to be protected against its happening again in the future. Her condition for returning to the marriage was that her husband go into therapy—a condition to which Bob (most reluctantly) agreed.

The psychiatrist whom he then contacted placed Bob Heller in a group therapy setting; there were, he told me, four women and three other men in attendance. When he was asked, as a newcomer to the group, to say why he was there, he described his argument with his wife and its culmination in a violent incident. The effect upon the women in the group had been electric—one even burst into tears.

Another woman, sitting next to the one who'd gotten so upset, stared at Bob with a horrified expression on her face. "Do you know what your menacing your wife in that way actually *felt* like to her?" she asked him. "Can you imagine yourself being attacked by a guy who's maybe 6 feet 8 inches tall and who weighs about 40 to 50 pounds more than you do? That's the difference, you know, between a lot of women and a lot of men."

His response to this, Bob told me, had been to *experience* the fear that he himself would feel in such a situation. "I thought—'Oh God, what have I done?' And I came home and said to Julie, 'I'm really, really sorry,' and I've never touched her or threatened her again."

"Yes, you did—once," Julie amended at that moment, with a grin. "You grabbed my arm, but I slapped you—remember?" The events they were reporting had occurred 15 years prior to our interviews, and there had been no violence since.

In this instance, neither member of the couple had grown up in a family in which spouse abuse had occurred. Physical violence was, therefore, not part of anyone's expectations of what would happen in an intimate relationship. Also, the so-called cycle of violence (from tension buildup to the battering incident itself to promises of reform) had never been allowed to get under way. Battering, once introduced into a relationship, tends to increase and become more violent over time; but Bob's first blows were *not* rewarded by feelings of mastering and of having taken control. On the contrary, his behavior was punished; there were immediate consequences for what he had done. Most important, what had been a hidden act—striking his wife in the privacy of their home—became a publicly shameful act in the group therapy setting.

Moving the battering event from a private to a public arena had an enormous effect upon Bob Heller's future behavior—and this, I felt, was a point well worthy of stressing. There should be consequences for physically abusive acts, ranging all the way from social exposure to arrest. But the difficulty is, as Geller and Straus point out, that "the nuclear structure of the modern family, and the fact that it is the accepted norm that family relations are private relations, reduces the likelihood that someone will be available to prevent the escalation of family conflict to intimate violence." It is the norm of privacy that tends to shield the male perpetrator of domestic violence and to silence his cowed, embarrassed mate.

It is also the norm of privacy—of not wanting to intrude on personal turf—that permits dangerously, even lethally, misguided policemen, lawyers and judges to urge beaten wives to kiss their battering husbands and make up. Marital violence is treated differently from other forms of interpersonal assault. All too often, as Geller and Straus observe, the marriage license is a "license for hitting"—a license to commit violent acts that go unpunished.

AFTER MY TALK, THERE WAS NO TIME FOR TAKING questions; I merely apologized for having run overtime. But no sooner had I left the stage and reclaimed my seat at the table then a young woman rushed to the empty stage and seized the microphone. I cannot now recall details of her appearance; all that I can remember clearly are her eyes, which were blazing. The pupils seemed in some strange way to have disappeared entirely, so that her eyes looked like illuminated sockets.

She wanted, she said, her voice cracking with emotion, to correct some "erroneous impressions" that my talk might have created in people's minds. "The first is that the man Ms. Scarf described could have been cured in one session. There is *no* male batterer," she stated flatly, "who could ever possibly be cured in one session. And the fact is, the man *did* batter his wife again, that time he grabbed her by the arm!"

She paused momentarily, inhaled deeply, then continued. Another important thing that people in the audience should understand, she said angrily, had to do with the woman who'd come from a violent family background. "To say—or even to *imply*—that that woman is unconsciously soliciting the beatings she got is a classic case of blaming the victim!" She leaned closer to the microphone. "It's the woman's fault, *always,*" she added in a bitter tone of voice. Then she stalked away from the podium.

I was taken aback. The impromptu speaker seemed to think that Claudie Benedette was *already* a victim of marital violence, when what I'd been discussing was the real danger that she might become one. And in the case of the Hellers, the important messages had been: (1) the need to respond decisively to a first incident of spouse abuse, (2) the effectiveness of moving the battering from a secluded to an open form, and also (3) making sure there were *consequences* for any violent behavior.

But what had the speaker herself been saying? That once a batterer, a man is a batterer forever, and he should thenceforth wear the scarlet letter B upon his forehead? Bob Heller had grabbed his wife's arm once in the 15 years that had elapsed since an incident about which he'd expressed great remorse, yet in this woman's eyes he remained (apparently) an unregenerate brutalizer.

In the hush that followed, the organizer of the symposium ascended to the platform and made some remarks meant to conciliate the disparate factions of the conference audience. I, too, spoke again briefly. I reiterated a statement that I'd made at the outset of my talk, which was that my observations had more to do with couples engaged in lower levels of violence—the degree of marital violence I'd encountered in the interviews for my study—than with the lethal kinds of violence that made headlines.

But in any event, I went on, we women do our-

selves no favor when we attempt to deal simplistically with issues that are inherently complex. Certainly, I said, there is a clear way to deal with any incident of spouse abuse—*it must be stopped*. Not only must it be stopped, it must be met with the consequences that the abusive act merits. But to think in terms of caricatures—of females as the ever-faultless victimized human beings and males as brutal, animalistic members of an alien species—is reductionistic and a way of spuriously solving problems by refusing to think about them.

MUCH LATER, LEAVING THE DINING HALL, I walked alongside Peggy Simpson's wheelchair and talked with her about the conference. She was, she said, feeling exhilarated by the concern and attention she'd received but nevertheless ambivalent about some things that had happened at her own talk earlier in the day.

She'd been disturbed by efforts to get her to make a definitive statement regarding the famous case of the burning bed—the woman who'd doused her abusive husband's bedclothes with gasoline while he slept, then lit the match that burned him to death. "Some of the people at the workshop wanted me to say that any woman who's being violently abused by her husband has a right to commit homicide to defend herself," Peggy told me. "And I just couldn't make that statement, because that's *murder* we're talking about. And that's not me: I can't go that far; I can't give that advice."

Peggy then related the details of her own story to me. She had left her battering husband and had been living with her parents when her husband came after her and shot her. He had shot her with several bullets, "including the bullet," she said straightforwardly, "which left me paralyzed on my right side."

Her life as a normal, healthy young woman and mother had ended there. And what had her husband's punishment been? "Actually, he hasn't gotten any," Peggy said. "He was put in a psychiatric ward for 45 days, then released. The judge's reasoning was that if he went to jail, he couldn't get a job and support me and my children!" Her voice was indignant, but tears were welling up in her eyes. "His only supposed 'punishment' is that he cannot enter the state where I reside for five years. And if he does decide to do so—if another fit of 'temporary insanity' comes over him—what's to prevent him from jumping in his car and coming after me to finish the job and then, perhaps, committing suicide? Everyone, including that judge, can then weep crocodile tears for me!"

But why, she asked plaintively, was he being given this opportunity to come after her again? "He hasn't *threatened* to commit a crime; he's already become a perpetrator." I shook my head, but said nothing.

What had happened was so outrageous that I could think of no words of solace to offer her.

A story like hers could make you crazy, I thought. It could turn you into a cynical man hater; it could make you feel thoroughly alienated from a criminal justice system that seems to stack the cards in favor of males.

Earlier, at the dinner meeting, I'd had a feeling of having gone behind the looking glass and into a world where men were the universal enemy and persecutors. But now, on the other side of the mirror, where the lawful agents of justice, fairness and rationality presumably operated, the world seemed equally distorted. ■

MAGGIE SCARF *is a writer who lives in New Haven, CT.*

ILLUSTRATION BY BRIAN AJHAR

BRIEF THERAPY ON THE COUCH

ANALYZING DRS. ERICKSON AND FREUD

By Mary Sykes Wylie

BRIEF THERAPY CASE STUDIES OFTEN HAVE THE quality of little miracle plays. A homeless alcoholic and multiple drug abuser, whose first "session" occurs in a breadline, comes in for several more sessions some time later, and as a result quits drinking and doing drugs, and gets a full-time job. An alcoholic schizophrenic, who has driven her psychiatrist to despair by regularly holding her breath until he is forced to call in paramedics to resuscitate her, stops drinking, cleans herself up, and behaves herself after seeing a problem-focused brief therapist. A family of bed-wetters is cured, and the unemployed parents find jobs after a single session of solution-oriented therapy.

That success stories like these fill the brief therapy literature is in itself not surprising. Long-term therapists do not parade their therapeutic failures in print either. What is striking about the cases, however, is the therapists' speed and virtuosity at resolving the problems. School refusers, depressives, alcoholics, violent couples, abusive families, incest victims and obsessive compulsives all trot briskly through therapy without undue strain. Whether they dutifully do

their homework tasks or not—it doesn't seem to matter—their presenting complaint, redefined and simplified in the first session, has frequently all but evaporated by the second or third or fourth.

Reading about the rapid dispatch of so many apparently intractable human dilemmas produces a kind of vertigo and an uneasy sense of philosophical incongruity. If terrible problems can be swept away with such efficiency and cost-effectiveness, are they such terrible problems? More to the point, if brief psychotherapy resolves these issues so quickly and cheaply, why would anyone spend thousands of dollars and years of effort trudging through the tedious wastes of long-term therapy? What is brief therapy, and what do brief therapists do that gives them such an edge?

WHAT SIGMUND FREUD WAS TO LONG-TERM psychotherapy, Milton Erickson has been to the development of brief therapy. Freud was the quintessential European scholar and scientist, whose goal for his patients was not emotional happiness but self-knowledge, not "mental health" as much as truth. The archetypal analytic therapist is like a patient archaeologist, meticulously sifting through layers of defense and resistance, helping patients understand their own unconscious motivation.

If Freud was a philosopher-priest from Vienna, Erickson was a samurai warrior from Wisconsin, whose stories accumulate like legends around a fabled knight-errant. Optimistic, active, aggressive, Erickson did not wait for the slow dawning of insight in the fullness of time. "If you do not, I will do," he said to his patients; if they were unable to move or change themselves, he pursued, cajoled, manipulated or bullied them out of their dilemmas. On occasion he told them what to eat, how to dress, what to do and say, where to go. But much of his therapeutic activity was in the form of indirect suggestion—stories, metaphors, riddles—delivered while the patient was in trance. Erickson was not particularly interested in helping his patients consciously understand their predicaments; he thought insight and interpretation were largely useless. The goal of therapy was change, which occurred when patients learned what they already unconsciously knew, though they might never know *why* they had changed.

Brief therapists fall more or less on either side of the line separating the Freudian from Ericksonian worldviews. The term "brief therapy" often obscures more than it reveals, conflating a variety of approaches, techniques and philosophies. Though all brief therapists are necessarily actively directive in therapy, those at the psychodynamic end of the spectrum are more clearly influenced by classic psychoanalytic ideas. Peter Sifneos, a short-term psychoanalytic therapist, regards clients' problems from a Freudian perspective (having roots in oedipal conflict, for example) but, unlike traditional analysts, immediately addresses their specific presenting complaints, actively provokes their anxiety, and conducts therapy as a fast-paced collaboration between thera-

pist and client. More mainstream is the psychodynamic model of Simon Budman and Alan Gurman, who focus treatment on the presenting complaint, but ask why the client is seeking therapy *now*, and connect the present crisis to deeper issues in the client's life, like unresolved grief, repressed trauma, unsettled interpersonal relationships or unrecognized developmental impasses.

Brief therapists who trace their lineage to Erickson are themselves hardly a monolithic group. Ericksonian hypnotherapists often rely on the use of trance to bypass limiting conscious belief, prejudice, negative certainty, self-criticism and fear—all the obstacles that they believe blockade the inner process of change. They sometimes engage in what might be called a therapy of befuddlement, using metaphor, drama, ambiguous task assignments, confusion techniques and paradox to create a serendipitous revolution in the unconscious mind. Stephen Lankton, author of several books on Ericksonian hypnotherapy, including *The Answer Within*, describes therapy as a kind of "enchantment," arousing a sense of pleasant mental excitement and expectation, producing a curious, intensely felt experience outside the boundaries of ordinary conscious life.

Other brief therapy approaches reflect the more strategic, pragmatic and directive side of Erickson. Jay Haley, codirector of the Haley-Madanes Institute in Washington, D.C., was one of the first to introduce Ericksonian methods to the psychotherapeutic community, bringing Erickson's use of paradox, suggestion and personal power to family therapy. Haley made the skills of power brokers and military strategists respectable therapeutic techniques. Comparing the therapist's craft to the martial arts, he remarked, "It is not helpful to say that therapists should not be interested in power, when skill in achieving power over others is often necessary in helping people."

A more minimalist, problem-oriented approach,

also based on Erickson's work, distinguishes the Mental Research Institute (MRI) in Palo Alto and the even more spare solution-focused interventions of the Brief Family Therapy Center (BFTC) in Milwaukee. The MRI method, developed by a group of collaborators that includes Paul Watzlawick, John Weakland and Richard Fisch, focuses solely on the client's complaint and failed attempts to resolve it. Steve de Shazer, Insoo Kim Berg and their team at BFTC elicit from clients solutions to problems they have begun to implement even before coming to therapy, or that they can imagine for the immediate future. Unlike Budman and Gurman, for whom history, background and internal motivation are essential, neither MRI nor BFTC is interested in origins of the problem, personal history, insight, catharsis, family dynamics, or much beyond the unembellished behavior that constitutes the problem and its attempted or successful solution. Nonetheless, about *changing* behavioral sequences they are adamant.

An even briefer therapy, Neurolinguistic Programming, originated with two young, iconoclastic Californians, Richard Bandler and John Grinder, who analyzed and formalized the language patterns and hypnotic methods in Erickson's largely intuitive work. Bandler and Grinder created laserlike techniques that they claimed could solve many presenting complaints in a single session. By precisely tracking and altering the microprocesses of thought and fantasy that create and maintain problems, NLP practitioners say they can cure a wide range of conditions, including phobias, allergies, depression, anxiety and obsessions, with staggering speed.

If NLP is the most condensed version of brief therapy, the Milan method of Mara Selvini Palazzoli and her colleagues may be the most protracted. In *Paradox and Counterparadox*, Palazzoli and her colleagues Luigi Boscolo, Gianfranco Cecchin and Guiliana Prata described a method of "long brief" therapy with families of schizophrenics or anorexics,

seeing everybody in the family once a month for three months up to a year and a half. The team issued paradoxical directives, prescribing a family's roles and rules in ways that blocked their usual interactions. Most recently, Palazzoli has developed a new form of longer brief therapy based on a single intervention—an invariant series of prescriptions, one of which is telling the parents to leave the psychotic child at home while they go out for the evening, or even for a few days, not explaining, but leaving a note that they have left. The intervention itself is "brief" and "minimal," but it may take months to convince the parents to do the task, and months more to study its effects on the family.

IF THE NATURE OF THERAPY IN BRIEF THERAPY IS hard to categorize, the word "brief" isn't very enlightening either. Budman and Gurman point out in their book *Theory and Practice of Brief Therapy* that the median length of most psychotherapy is only about five or six sessions, which is fewer than many self-defined brief therapists allot for treatment. In fact, patients commonly expect to be in therapy for less than three months, according to Budman and Gurman, and the vast majority of research studies on therapy outcome are based on data from 7 to 17 sessions. Research has also shown that positive results from family and couples therapy, even when not specifically intended to be "brief," generally occurs in fewer than 20 sessions.

So when does brief therapy end and long-term therapy begin? Brief therapists are reluctant to define their practice only in relation to time. "'Brief therapy' is an unfortunate term," says Weakland, associate director of the Brief Therapy Center at MRI. He prefers to call his work "efficient therapy," as does de Shazer, codirector of BFTC. "Therapy should be as efficient and effective as possible, and brief therapy is built around ways of knowing when therapy is finished," says de Shazer. "In part, brief therapy is a state of mind of the therapist and of the patient," write Budman and Gurman. "Brevity is a metaphor for clarity about what needs to be changed, an attitude of being task-oriented," explains Gurman.

Indeed, brief therapists of whatever stripe hold in common the belief that therapy must be specifically goal-directed, problem-focused, well defined and, first and foremost, aimed at relieving the client's presenting complaint. In some settings therapy is rationed by design to last a predetermined number of sessions. MRI's research program limits therapy to 10 sessions, while three to seven sessions is the mean at BFTC.

What brief therapists also share is a view of therapists, therapy and what people need and want from treatment, which often departs radically from traditional psychodynamic or even family systems models. In the popular culture, the magisterial and cultivated demeanor of the psychoanalyst has long since become a caricature, but there still clings to the psychiatrist an aura of arcane wisdom, mind-reading talent and shamanistic power. Most brief therapists, on the other hand, regard themselves more prosaically, like lawyers, family physicians, accountants or consultants. The brief therapists at MRI and BFTC even express a spirit of *épater les bourgeois* in their blue-collar descriptions of what they do, comparing their services to those of television repairmen and auto mechanics. Practitioners of both models refer to serious clients as "customers" and the uncommitted as "window shoppers," as if therapists are just more or less successful salespeople.

IF MOST BRIEF THERAPISTS DEMOCRATIZE THEIR calling, suggesting they're all just folks, they also hold a populist view of emotional problems. They abhor clinical metaphors picturing symptoms as "tips of the iceberg" or problems as having "deeply buried roots." Working with family problems, brief therapists generally find irrelevant the notion that the "identified patient" may be the family's

"symptom carrier." They do not believe that the whole family must participate in lengthy treatment aimed at overhauling the entire system. Brief strategic and solution-oriented clinicians base therapy on straightforward empiricism: what you hear from the client is all you can know; what you see is what you get. "We do not presume what clients need, beyond what they tell us," says MRI's Fisch.

Brief therapists suspect long-term individual or family therapy of extending, broadening and complicating the problems it was meant to eliminate. Too often therapists set themselves the utopian task of reconstructing the patient's psychic structure from the ground up, according to Paul Watzlawick, research associate at MRI. As a result, psychotherapy becomes an indeterminate search for the ineffable. If solving the patient's presenting problem—marital unhappiness, drug abuse, depression, overweight—is made contingent upon a complete character transformation, "a goal that is so distant as to border infinity," Watzlawick argues, therapy itself becomes an endlessly self-renewing justification for more therapy.

The brief therapist has both less and more responsibility than the long-term psychodynamic therapist. Clients do not undertake soul-searching voyages in brief therapy, they come to get something fixed. Accordingly, brief therapists insist that they have neither the obligation nor the right to rebuild fractured psyches or rehabilitate jerry-built families. "The first obligation of a therapist," writes Haley, "is to change the presenting problem offered. If that is not accomplished, the therapy is a failure."

Nonetheless, the idea that engineering change, *any* change, in behavior is the goal of therapy does not preclude the belief that even a minor difference can have far-reaching and dramatic effects in clients' lives. Many brief therapists subscribe to what they call the Archimedean lever theory, the rolling snowball theory or the butterfly effect theory of therapy. On this principle, a single, well-targeted intervention causing a small change in behavior or attitude can shift the client's entire intrapsychic and interpersonal system. At the very least, the therapist pays attention to what the *client* says and addresses what the *client* thinks is the problem.

Indeed, brief therapists use the client's complaint as the lever for prying the system out of its rut. Compared with the murky *longueurs* that can sink extended family or individual therapy, brief therapy sessions are sparse, crisp, cleancut. In a recent videotape from BFTC, Steve de Shazer elicits in about 10 minutes an abbreviated account of marital difficulty (the husband gets angry when his wife isn't available to him, but won't admit he's angry and retreats to sulk; she pursues him, tries to "communicate," ends up furiously yelling). During the next two sessions, first de Shazer, then codirector Insoo Kim Berg reiterate variations of the same few questions about "exceptions" to the problem, which are the hallmarks of their work. "When was the last time things were okay or better than okay between you?" "What were you doing differently during those times?" "How can you make that happen again?" "What do you need to do to keep things going this way?" There is an almost hypnotic quality to the droning repetition of the same question ("What else did you do to make things different?" "What else did you do?" "What else?") that would seem to induce coma, except that the one-note refrain evokes a gradual flowering and transformation in the couple. Two people, folded in their cocoons of tension and anger, begin to emerge, growing by turns interested, hopeful, eager, enthusiastic, confident, giggly and affectionate. It is hard to doubt that they will think about each other differently and be nicer to each another than before they came into therapy.

In practice, brief therapists believe that even complex and intractable problems can be negotiated—redefined or reduced to more workable components. Some brief therapists reframe the concept of "problem" right out of existence. William O'Hanlon and Michele Weiner-Davis write in *In Search of Solutions* that they "do not believe there is such a thing as 'the real problem' underlying the complaint." In *Tactics of Change*, Fisch, Weakland and Lynn Segal suggest that people create their own problems either willfully or out of ignorance—hardly an original idea in the world of common sense and ordinary morality, but at odds with psychodynamic theory that personal "impasses, deadlocks, knots, etc." originate in early experiences beyond conscious control or that family problems are embedded in a deep context of intergenerational dysfunction. Weakland suggests that human beings fabricate problems by misinterpreting ordinary life difficulties—ascribing to them an exaggerated weightiness, complexity and malignity. The problem is not in people—their psychological makeup—or in the world they inhabit as much as in their attitude. To illustrate his point, Weakland points to sub-Saharan Africa, where syphilis is so common that it is considered an ordinary, not particularly problematic part of everyday life. If endemic syphilis is not a "problem," then what is?

Even when they exaggerate (Is endemic cholera a "problem"? Is starvation? racism? anything?), brief therapists make a telling critique of the modern tendency to pathologize virtually any life difficulty or personality quirk. According to the popular media, we are all narcissistic, depressive, obsessive, compulsive, addicted, codependent adult children of terribly disturbed people. Brief therapists work at getting clients to relinquish the self-defeating view of themselves as sick, dysfunctional and helpless. Weiner-Davis describes the case of a woman depressed for a year, whose marriage was failing and whose business was on the brink of collapse. As Weiner-Davis tells it, she said to the woman, "I am surprised that you are doing as well as you are, considering what you have been through." The client sat up in her chair, looked vastly relieved, and said, "I'm so glad to hear you say that; I thought there was something wrong with *me*." Weiner-Davis explains that she had both accepted the woman's reality and depathologized it at the same time, so the problem—an inherent condition called "depression"—disappeared.

SUCCESSFUL BRIEF THERAPY CASES LIKE THESE are inspiring and fun to read— everyone likes a happy ending—but how serious are the problems with which they concern themselves? What of follow-up studies? Do the clients remain free of the difficulty that brought them into therapy? Critics suggest that strategic and solution-focused therapists do not, by and large, see very troubled people, and they doubt that clients who are can be helped much in such short periods of time.

"Most therapists engage in a kind of 'double bookkeeping,'" says Ronald Taffel, director of family and couples treatment services of the Institute for Contemporary Psychotherapy. On the one hand, there is "the public storytelling that makes new ideas clear and easy to follow, sells books, and fills conference rooms." On the other hand, "there is the matter of everyday clinical practice—symptoms that won't quit, 20-year habits and substance dependencies, biologically driven conditions, realities of gender, generation and race." What about multiproblem families, in which alcoholism, spousal violence and perhaps the decompensation of a psychotic sibling or two are the presenting problems? Can brief therapists really make lingering massive depression vanish by eliciting "exceptions" to the symptoms? Can cocaine addicts stop their habit after five or six sessions? Can adult survivors of severe child abuse achieve a sense of security and equilibrium in a month?

The answer to all these questions is probably, "Yes, in some cases, sometimes." But critics of brief therapy say that believing chronic problems will almost always disappear in a few sessions, however skillful the technique, is itself a utopian fantasy, and

there are enough brief therapy failures around to prove it. Taffel has seen a host of such characters. One woman, he remembers, had suffered for 15 or 20 years from psychosomatic disorders and depression, during which she had tried, among other modalities, Ericksonian therapy, Neurolinguistic Programming, nutritional analysis, Reichian work, Gestalt therapy and psychoanalysis. "Each method made her feel better each time," says Taffel, "and if the therapist of the moment had written her case up, we would have half a dozen success stories." But she also relapsed after every "solution." Since then she has been in family-of-origin therapy, taking antidepressant medication, and has been less depressed for several years now, as she slowly puts together her life.

Taffel, who has supervised family therapists for 10 years, is particularly sensitive to the promise of certainty inherent in much of the training. He has experienced the illusion of quick success himself. Years ago he saw a couple who had tried various forms of psychotherapy. The husband had been in analysis for seven years, to which he arrived late about 60 percent of the time. Taffel decided to take on the man's chronic lateness and in one session reframed it as an "addiction," telling him it would be impossible for him to change unless this "addiction" was understood.

The next week the man came in, shaken, and revealed something he had not yet admitted openly. He *was* addicted—to cocaine—and he had been smoking crack every day for a year and a half; his entire life was falling apart. Within four to six weeks the man was off crack and seemingly much better. "At this point," says Taffel, "if I had written the case up, it would have looked like a spectacular success for brief therapy. Unfortunately, a little later, he relapsed." After that, according to Taffel, the therapy "*really*" began." The man was persuaded to go to a rehabilitation hospital; once released, he relapsed again. This time Taffel got him and his wife to stay with AA and Al Anon. Work proceeded slowly, and some time afterward the couple began to see an addictions specialist.

Four years later, Taffel asked the man, who had been drug- and alcohol-free for two years, "what made him confess his addiction to me, fondly remembering my 'brilliant' reframe of his lateness. What he remembered, in fact, was that I was the first person who talked straight to him, at a time when he was finally ready to change. This may ultimately be the answer to our 'quick successes.' We help only those people who give us permission to do so."

Therapy concentrating solely on problem behavior may be less efficient than long-term therapy, according to Gurman, if it never addresses the function or purpose behind the behavior. "Doing no more than interrupting the sequence of behaviors in marital conflict may solve the problem," says Gurman, "but not if one spouse begins fights in order to maintain distance because of a lifelong fear of intimacy."

Critics complain that brief therapists often ignore the system that maintains a problem, the hard-wired family network of codependency and collusion. A woman may present with the simple goal of losing 50 pounds, which she may do with great dispatch following three brief therapy sessions. Success. Until her husband and her mother, who both have their own reasons for wanting her fat, begin a subtle campaign of sabotage so that two years later she is fatter than ever. Or what happens to an alcoholic who successfully quits drinking after a session or two if his habit has been masking chronic, deep depression? Was therapy a "success" if he commits suicide a year later? Brief therapy's critics argue that it is not hard to produce dramatic change in a few weeks, but they wonder whether such changes last and what they mean in the life of the whole person.

To brief therapists, these criticisms are beside the point. In the first place, relapse and failure are not unknown in long-term therapy either. Besides, brief therapists do not pretend that solving one problem will "cure" the client for all time; it would be as foolish for a therapist to aim for such a goal as it would be for a physician to expect that treating patients for the flu will inoculate them for life from all other ailments or even a reoccurrence of the flu. Brief therapists, in fact, often compare themselves to family practitioners and expect to see clients for what therapist Nicholas Cummings calls "brief, intermittent psychotherapy throughout the life cycle."

Therapy generally works much better, brief therapists insist, if it addresses the problem, not the person. Spending months or years trying to understand the function or purpose of the complaint can delay indefinitely focusing on the problem behavior and the solution. The goal at MRI, for example, is to "interrupt" the sequence that maintains the problem as it happens *now*, and let the future take care of itself. Presumably, for example, the overweight woman whose family wanted her fat would learn to change her behavior in ways that would shift the entire family context. "From doing something different comes different thinking and feeling," says John Weakland. And brief therapists are determined that clients *will* do something different. In the spirit of Erickson's legendary bulldog tenacity, Haley once wrote, "A therapist must be willing to go to the mat with a client and struggle with the problem until it is solved or the participants are dead."

MANY THERAPISTS BELIEVE THAT, OCCASIONAL exceptions aside, there are certain problems for which brief therapy is simply inadequate. Alcoholism and drug addiction are special sticking points between minimalists and other therapists. Solution-oriented practitioners at BFTC treat heroin or cocaine addicts and alcoholics no differently than any other clients. "In almost all cases of drug or alcohol abuse, there are exceptions, when the clients weren't abusing; we ask them how they did that, how they can keep on doing that," says de Shazer. MRI encourages alcoholics neither to lecture themselves, nor solemnly swear to stop drinking, nor make pledges to control it by waiting until 5 p.m. before taking a drink (tactics most alcohol counselors agree are futile). Instead, one alcoholic at MRI was assigned the task of rigidly drinking on schedule, one drink every hour on the hour whether he wanted it or not. After two days, he came into therapy and said he just didn't feel like drinking anymore, at which point the therapist asked him, "How are you going to get over your drinking problem, if you don't drink?"

Many therapists find this approach incomprehensible. Gurman, who frequently recommends Alcoholics Anonymous (which many brief therapists disparage because it "pathologizes" heavy drinkers by assuming they have a lifelong, essentially incurable condition), believes that clients can make no therapeutic gains on any front if alcohol and drug abuse are not addressed first. Says Gurman, "Anybody who can make a claim like that, who can regularly and substantially reduce an alcoholic's intake in six sessions or so, and have the client maintain that change over two years, deserves the Nobel Prize."

Perhaps the most serious charge leveled against brief therapists is that they avoid or deny serious problems that are not part of the package of overt complaints the client presents in the first session. Minimalists will not even address alcoholism, or spouse and child abuse, or remembered childhood abuse, or anything at all, unless the client presents it as a complaint. They hold what Fisch calls a "non-normative model" of therapy, based on the constructivist idea that there are no objective values, therefore no real external standards, by which to judge normal, abnormal, sick, healthy, good or bad behavior. If there is no complaint, there is no problem.

But what if a couple comes in, and the wife seems afraid to speak without looking at her husband for implicit permission? What if the therapist suspects

she is being beaten? Fisch says he cannot recall such a case at MRI, but says therapists would ask about issues only if they were at least alluded to in the interview. Similarly, child abuse would become part of therapy only if a verbal complaint were made, most likely by a child agency outside the family. Any suspicions on the part of the therapist would be mere "presumptions," not admissable as therapeutic evidence for focus of treatment.

What of adult survivors of incest or abuse? How useful can brief therapy be for the frequently profound disturbances these clients experience? Again, the answer cannot be arbitrary. Seattle therapist David Calof, who treats adult survivors of child abuse, says "readiness is all" and that "*sometimes* people have taken an issue as far as they can go by themselves and are on the cusp of change, so that a transformative experience can occur in a very short time." Or such clients come in, work briefly on related issues, and then leave when they have gone as far as they can manage at that time.

Most strategic and solution-oriented therapists, however, insist that there is a healthy, well-functioning person just below the surface of the presenting complaint in even the most abused of survivors. When asked about the severe, long-term problems that therapists specializing in such cases describe, John Weakland says, "I wouldn't be quick to say that this [abuse] has enduring effects . . . If you focus on the presenting problem, things can change very rapidly."

With adult survivors of abuse, brief therapists are so adamant about respecting the client's stated wishes that critics suggest they may make questionable clinical decisions. In one case, a brief hypnotherapist acceded, during the first session, to the wishes of an incest and abuse survivor who said she "would just as soon forget all about it." The therapist told her, during hypnotic trance, that she could say good-bye to that abused child, "experience an emotional detachment from her," and "get on with her life."

But therapists who regularly treat adult incest survivors suggest that what looks like respect for the client's wishes not to delve into the messy past may simply reflect the therapist's own anxiety about confronting such painful material. Furthermore, says Calof, the therapist's evasion often dovetails with the client's own well-honed skills at dissociation and denial. "People from traumatic backgrounds are experts at splitting off memories they don't want to remember," says Calof, "and have learned very well to give back to people, including therapists, what they want to hear." As for some brief therapists' allergy to history and background, Calof suggests that they "often imply that we are unnecessarily 'dredging' up past miseries, as if the past weren't already omnipresent. It isn't as if we are 'ruining' things by foolishly opening up Pandora's box. People come into therapy because the past is only too much with them."

Furthermore, if the relief felt by abuse survivors is only temporary, Calof believes they are "likely to think they 'failed' brief therapy, and that it's their fault, which just reinforces the usual feelings survivors have that the original abuse was somehow their fault as well." Calof wonders if all these feelings may not go underground again, repressed for years, even pushed onto the next generation, when abuse victims act out the same patterns of abuse on their own children.

Even with less dramatic cases, brief therapists may rush people into solutions before they are psychologically ready. Their relentless insistence on fast change reflects what Calof describes as "the Western notion that if you don't like where the river flows, change the course of the river." But some rivers cannot be rechanneled at will, regardless of high-tech manipulations. People seeking therapy are not necessarily ready to leap immediately into a bright future, says Jay Efran, professor of psychology at Temple University. Clients may have uncompleted business from the past, the meaning of which they must first integrate into their lives. Efran describes a depressed client whose therapist relentlessly assigned her tasks of a "jolly" nature associated with "exceptions" to her depression, for which she would earn a specified number of "points." Finally, the woman grew weary of her therapist's attempts to engineer a change in her mood and told him bluntly, "I'm just not ready yet to cheer up."

PROFESSIONAL PRIDE, PERSONAL FERVOR AND anecdotal case histories aside, is there statistical evidence that one sort of therapy is demonstrably better than another? Probably not. Budman and Gurman report that virtually all studies of individual, marital and family therapy, taken together, show positive results for two-thirds to three-quarters of treated patients, compared to untreated subjects. On the other hand, while improvement continues to rise with number of sessions, the rate of improvement increases more slowly after the eighth. The major positive impact, in other words, for most people, occurs during the first six to eight sessions.

Until recently, little research had been done on the results of planned brief therapy. But in 1988, BFTC conducted what is probably the most ambitious, comprehensive and long-term follow-up study ever done of therapy designed to be brief. Family therapist David J. Kiser tracked the progress of 164 BFTC clients for 6, 12 and 18 months after therapy, using a questionnaire similar to one employed in an MRI study of 97 cases done in 1974. The earlier study had reported that 40 percent of the clients had achieved "complete relief" of the complaint, and 32 percent, "clear and considerable, but not complete" relief. Kiser's study showed even better results. Of 69 cases receiving 4 to 10 sessions, 64 clients, or nearly 93 percent, felt they had met, or made progress toward, their treatment goal (about 77 percent of the 64 met the goal, and more than 14 percent made progress). At the 18-month follow-up, of all 164 clients (94 percent of whom had 10 or fewer sessions), about 51 percent reported the presenting problem was still resolved, while about 34 percent said it was not as bad as when they had initiated therapy. In other words, about 85 percent of the clients reported full or partial success.

BFTC is the first therapy center to subject itself to such painstaking scrutiny, measuring outcome results across a broad range of clients of different ages, ethnic backgrounds, economic circumstances and presenting problems. Other therapists, however, are dubious about the reported success rates of 80 to 90 percent. Gurman, himself an expert on statistical measures of therapy effectiveness, is the most outspoken. "No method gets that kind of result," Gurman says, "except maybe for certain kinds of phobias. Those numbers are unparalleled, incredible, unbelievable." William M. Pinsof, of the Family Institute of Chicago, also an authority on statistics, says that "every research group that does its own research gets 80 to 90 percent success rates, but nobody who tries to replicate those studies gets anything like the same figures." He suggested that factors weighting toward success include clients knowing what sort of treatment they will be receiving, and identifying follow-up interviewers with the institution where the therapy was done. Other critics cite the lack of control groups, failure to take into account "chance" improvement, and the subjective nature of the responses.

Kiser agrees with the methodological criticisms, which are hard to avoid in most therapeutic outcome studies. He adds that when you separate the percentage of clients who fully attained their goals from those who partially met them, the former come close to the standard success rates for all psychotherapy. Furthermore, those who stayed in therapy longer (4 to 10 sessions) did better than those who were seen only three times or fewer, which may, Kiser suggests, reflect higher motivation in the client and more satisfaction with the therapist. "One factor influencing high attainment rates is the good job

BFTC does of defining and making explicit client goals," says Kiser.

In spite of these caveats, however, the study would seem to demonstrate, at the very least, that brief therapy is as successful overall as long-term therapy. Indeed, as Budman and Gurman point out in Theory and Practice of Brief Therapy, there has never been any good evidence that extended therapy has a better outcome than short-term therapy, regardless of type and severity of the problem or how long it has been going on. De Shazer says that he and his colleagues at BFTC have found "no correlation between treatment success or failure and diagnosis, severity or chronicity" and that, in his opinion, "God does play with dice—you cannot absolutely predict with any accuracy whether therapy will be successful or not." Or, as addiction expert Michael Elkin says, "Even bad brief therapy can't be as bad as bad long-term therapy. It lasts a shorter time and costs less money."

PERHAPS THERAPY, EVEN WHEN BASED ON EXplicitly defined goals, is too ambiguous a relationship ever to be successfully quantified. And it is a relationship; even the briefest of therapists are not computers, and if they were, it is unlikely that clients would get much out of the therapy unless, possibly, the computer could convince them that it, too, truly believed in its powers to heal. Lankton compares therapy to a kind of romance. In a sense, this is true: client and therapist often come together in the mutual hope and expectation that remarkable things will happen, which frequently do if the match is right.

But the right therapist-client match is probably as much a matter of economic realities and social definitions as of personal inclination. In today's mental health marketplace, brief therapists have the advantage because, in an economy that no longer provides third-party payments for seven-year excursions into the unconscious, their methods are cost-effective.

Increasingly, long-term therapy is a luxury available to fewer and fewer people.

The argument made by brief therapists of "more for less" is attractive not only to HMOs setting strict limits on therapy sessions for members but to a society that admires the traditional American entrepreneurial traits of the efficiency, pragmatism, action and optimism. Michael Kerr, director of training at Georgetown University Family Center, says, "Schools of therapy are like religions; most therapy is 98 percent heart, 2 percent science." He suggests that therapies follow fashions in consumer demand, and in a society that is "reactive, driven by anxiety and demanding answers," brief therapy is appealing. As Gurman points out, most people in psychotherapy are not interested in major personality reorganization, nor do they need it. Nonetheless, they come to the therapist because they are caught in a dilemma, deadlocked. Something is not working in their lives, and they hope the therapist can make the problem disappear, do something fast, even perform a bit of magic. "I want everybody I see to expect a miracle," says Michael Elkin. While brief therapists do not believe in "cure," they do believe in the little miracles that can transform everyday life. ∎

MARY SYKES WYLIE, PH.D., *is the assistant editor of* The Family Therapy Networker.

See references, page 565.

*I*N PRAISE OF SOLUTIONS

FOCUSING ON WHAT WORKS IN CLIENTS' LIVES

By Michele Weiner-Davis

BRIEF SOLUTION-ORIENTED THERAPY IS SECOND nature to me now, but that wasn't always the case. Growing up in New York, I inherited psychoanalytic genes. The hardest part of my training in brief therapy was letting go of the deeply ingrained idea that therapy is about exploring problems. I had to learn that instead of tuning into what was wrong with clients, the therapist's job is to help them find the resources they need to move toward solutions. The key element in this process is defining the ambiguous concerns clients bring to therapy in manageable ways that elicit people's natural competence. When this is done with skill and sensitivity, the process of change can be breathtakingly sudden. One therapist's prospective long-term client can be transformed into another's satisfied ex-client within a few sessions.

Well dressed and attractive, 36-year-old Gail was a highly successful businesswoman. The consulting firm she had founded already had more business than she could manage single-handedly, she told me in our first interview, obviously enthusiastic about her career. I was so intrigued by her knowledge of the business world and her ability to make things happen that I wanted to find out more about her work. But it was her session, not mine, so I asked the question I always put to new clients: "What do you want to change?" Although people don't always provide me with answers to *that* question, opening the session this way gives clients the message that I assume there *is* something they want to change and that making that change will be the focus of our work together.

"I don't know what I want to change," Gail responded, "but I know what I want to do that I'm not doing now."

"Okay," I said, "what do you want to do?"

"I want to be in a committed relationship," Gail said. "I'm tired of being single. But I don't know how to meet anyone, and I'm not very good at being in relationships. I just don't know what I need to change. Maybe I'm afraid of intimacy, but I don't know what I'm doing wrong."

Immediately several warning flares went up in my mind. I recognized the temptation to take the pathology route and pick up on that classic bugaboo "fear of intimacy" or to analyze extensively whatever Gail might be doing "wrong." But knowing what to ignore can be a therapist's most critical skill. Gail had given me a negative image of herself that I could reinforce by discussing it further, or I could look beyond her pessimism and find a way to work with her based on her obvious strengths.

As I continued to listen, the depressing statistics about the chances for marriage for women her age echoed in my mind. Quickly dismissing this temporary distraction, I thought instead of R. D. Laing's *Knots* and his expression of a self-fulfilling litany: "I want to be in a relationship, but I don't know how to meet people and I am not good at being in relationships." I knew it was time to intervene.

"When did you decide you wanted to be in a committed relationship?" I asked.

"About a year ago," she said, "and then I met a guy . . . actually, two."

GAIL'S FEW WORDS PROVIDED ME WITH ENOUGH material to alter her doom-and-gloom view of herself as socially inept. I emphatically responded, "Oh, so you decided only about a year ago that this is something you want, and since then you have had *two* relationships! That certainly changes things." Gail looked puzzled. "After all," I reassured her, "a year is a short period of time, and during that year you somehow managed to meet and engage in relationships with not one, but two men."

I carefully watched for her response. Was she a client who would feel supported and encouraged by this kind of feedback, or would she let me know in some way that I was missing the boat? Quiet for a moment, she nodded and added, "Actually, in my heart of hearts, I have really only been serious about wanting to be married for the last few months." I was relieved and encouraged by how readily Gail saw herself in a new light. We were already chiseling away at her hopeless view of her situation. A few moments before, she had seen herself as a person who had *always* wanted a relationship but was *never* able to meet people. Now, she saw herself as someone who had simply decided a few months ago on a new goal that hadn't completely materialized yet. Although this rapid shift within a few minutes to seeing problems as more manageable happens with great regularity in my practice, it still feels like magic to me, as it did that day with Gail.

Later in the session, Gail told me how awkward she often felt socially. As she spoke, her countenance changed completely, and she seemed more like a shy, gawky 16-year-old than a successful, self-assured businesswoman. "I just fall apart," she said dejectedly. "In my work, I make lots of eye contact, but in social situations, when I am trying to meet someone, I find myself looking anywhere but at other people. If guys talk to me, I get weird and uncomfortable."

Much to Gail's surprise, I was not interested in how those feelings developed. When clients talk of their inabilities, inadequacies and incompetence, I search for ways to change their perceptions. Reinforcing what I call "solution talk" is one way. When clients describe what they are good at, what they can do, and how they are already moving, even uncertainly, toward their own goals, I show intense interest—no psychoanalytic blank stare for me.

I had an idea about Gail. She could not have established a thriving business, particularly one requiring her to consult with many business executives, without considerable social skills. Knowing that she might well have denied the connection between her professional and social abilities, I nevertheless asked, "If one of your clients came to you saying, 'I want to be in a relationship,' what would you tell him or her?" Gail looked at the floor and was silent for several moments. I was afraid that she would reject outright any suggestion that she possesses her own clues to resolving her dilemma. Instead, she sheepishly admitted that she had given this considerable thought and had come up with a plan. Although embarrassed to admit that she had approached her goal of being in a relationship like a business objective, with my reassurance she revealed the details of her strategy.

"Well, in order to be more marketable, you need to increase your visibility," Gail said. "When I started my business, I got myself in front of groups constantly. So, if I want to meet someone, I realized that I needed to join more groups, and I have already started doing that." She went on to recite a long, thoughtful list of efforts she had recently made to meet people. Gail's response reminded me of some research I did several years ago. I found that between the initial call for an appointment and the first session, at least two-thirds of clients beginning therapy have already taken specific steps to improve the quality of their lives. So Gail's actions did not surprise me.

As Gail described her "marketing strategy" for meeting men, her self-consciousness all but disappeared. She looked self-confident and determined. My reinforcing the link between her competence in business and her ability to seek a satisfying relationship was probably the turning point in therapy.

At the end of the first session, I gave her lots of positive feedback, suggested that she look for signs that she was continuing on the right track, and set an appointment for two weeks later. I felt that since she had a specific plan, all she needed was the time to implement it. But when, a few days later, she called, asking if we could meet several days before our scheduled appointment, I became apprehensive, wondering whether I had misjudged the situation.

When she came to the session, I was prepared for the worst. Although I felt like asking, "So what went wrong this week?" I bit my tongue and opened the session on a positive note. "So what other things have you been doing to implement your plan?" I asked. Her gigantic grin surprised me. "I've had a great week," she said. "I even met some guys. The reason I called you is that I didn't want to screw things up, and I wanted to bounce some ideas off

you." I was delighted, and thankful that I relied on the basic principle of solution-oriented therapy: always demonstrate your expectation that change is inevitable.

I was particularly interested in her description of how she had handled herself socially that week. She said, "You know, it was really odd. On Friday night, I went out with a friend for a drink, and when we walked into the bar, for some reason I just *felt* like I was hot stuff—none of the old insecurity. In fact, come to think of it, I felt more the way I usually do with my colleagues, really self-assured. I couldn't believe it!" The dramatic shift in her self-perception impressed me. And, because she was not self-conscious, she noticed that lots of men were attracted to her, and she liked it. In the weeks that followed, her new self-confidence did not waver. In fact, six months after initially contacting me, she met the man of her dreams.

WHEN I REFLECT BACK ON MY DAYS DOING long-term therapy and how strenuously I worked to help people reach the same point Gail had reached in two sessions, I find it hard to believe, like many of my trainees, that doing successful therapy can be so easy. Gail and I never discussed why she felt inadequate or how those feelings developed. I knew little about her family background or the details of her failed relationships. All I knew was that Gail had a goal that she believed, for some reason, she was unable to accomplish. My seeing her as capable and resourceful brought out her innate capability and resourcefulness. For me, the primary challenge of therapy is using all my skills to help clients see that they are the experts on their lives. They have the solutions. Therapists only ask the right questions.

Students often comment on how quickly I shift the focus from problems to solutions. They imagine that they would lose rapport with their clients if they were to follow my lead. "Don't clients feel that you are not really listening to them?" or "Isn't it necessary for the client to ventilate a bit?" they ask. Clearly, not everyone is ready to focus on positives as quickly as Gail. Some people need to feel that I understand their problems before moving on. I am convinced that the most important skill therapists can develop is the ability to carefully observe their clients and abide by the basic principle "If it works, don't fix it; if not, do something different." I reassure trainees that, although it doesn't happen often, if I were to sense that someone really needed to describe the details of their unhappiness, I would respect that. If we are open to what they tell us, clients teach us how to work with them.

OF COURSE, NOT ALL BRIEF THERAPY CLIENTS move as smoothly as Gail into a solution orientation. Susan and Jack needed to give me a clear picture of what was troubling them. Throughout our first session, Jack sat tensely on the edge of his chair, and Susan nervously wrung her hands as they told me about their daughter, 8-year-old Iris.

After only the first week of school, Iris's teacher had told them, "I've never met a more insecure little girl," and suggested counseling. I asked why the referral occurred so early in the school year, and Susan told me that Iris's teacher last year had spoken with this year's teacher, and both wanted to nip the problem in the bud. Susan spoke softly and quickly as she explained to me, "Iris is a perfectionist. She is a gifted little girl, but terribly afraid of making mistakes. In school it takes her an excruciatingly long time to write her letters, and if she makes an error, she cries and quits. In fact, anytime she is challenged, she quits. In her class she raises her hand constantly and asks directions over and over again. She freaks out if she doesn't get perfect scores on her papers. Socially, she is doing terribly and seems to have no friends." Susan told me that her teacher didn't discipline Iris because she didn't want to further damage her already minimal self-esteem.

The teacher even allowed Iris to check all her papers and tests over before they were graded, so she could change incorrect answers. No other child had this privilege.

Jack now seemed anxious to speak. "And that's not all," he said. "She has developed this cough, which increased to a croup. In fact, sometimes she coughs so much she throws up. Her voice has grown fainter and fainter, and we thought that perhaps she was developing a polyp on her throat. We have taken her to lots of physicians, who think the cough and voice problems are psychological. We also visited a urologist because of her frequent urination and bladder irritation. He treated her with antibiotics, but since Iris acted even weirder on the medication, we discontinued it. Most of the doctors have told us that her physical symptoms are stress-related, and so we decided to make an appointment with you."

Trying to redirect the attention of Iris's parents to more positive aspects of their child's behavior was fruitless; both seemed annoyed by my attempts to focus on what was working. When I asked, for example, what was different about the times when Iris appeared relaxed and was doing well, they were quiet for a long time, then offered vague answers. They continually reverted back to discussing Iris's problematic behavior. When asked, "If things continue as they have or even get worse, what do you think will happen?" they both emphatically agreed that "Iris will have a nervous breakdown."

Shocked by their idea that a "breakdown" was a real possibility, I asked them what they meant by this. They both said that Iris would "lose touch with reality." Although there was no history of psychiatric hospitalization in their families, they felt that their daughter was "spooky." Jack even showed me photographs so I could see how "weird" her eyes appeared. "When you look at her eyes, they're not always looking back, they're cloudy," he said. "The teacher told us that one day when the bell rang to signal the end of recess, Iris just sat under the tree staring into space. She hadn't realized the rest of the kids had gone back to the school building."

At this point, I thought that if these folks went to family services, the girl would probably receive a psychiatric evaluation and be hospitalized. The physical symptoms, the extreme anxiety of her parents, and the concern of two teachers made me wonder just how big a challenge this case would be. Although I reminded myself of the brief therapy mantra "Change is inevitable," even the eternal optimist in me wondered what could be done in a situation so filled with expectations of disaster.

D URING THE SESSION, HOWEVER, THE SEEDS OF change were planted. Susan had told me of her daily ritual with Iris. Whenever Iris would put herself down, Susan would offer praise, trying to get Iris to see herself more positively. Not surprisingly, this never worked; Iris would only intensify her self-criticism, leading her mother to try even harder to convince her of her worthiness. "It could be about anything," Susan told me. "She could say 'I'm ugly' or 'I'm stupid' or 'My clothes are dumb,' and I will just tell her, 'No, you are beautiful' or 'You look pretty.' Today when she came home from school, I asked her, 'How was school today?' and she replied, 'It was terrible. I'm stupid. I got two wrong on my math test.'"

I asked, "What happens when she comes home from school and you don't ask her how her day was?"

"She tells me anyway," Susan replied.

"What happens when you simply ignore her response?"

"I've tried that, too, and she keeps going and then withdraws."

Finally, I asked, "What happens when you almost jokingly agree with her that she is stupid, and she should have done better on her test?"

Perplexed, Susan said, "I have never done that;

are you suggesting that I should?"

"No," I answered, "I'm not suggesting anything yet."

Jack vehemently insisted that he could never do that because it would only reinforce Iris's low self-image. I said nothing further.

The parents gave me more evidence of Iris's problems. "Homework struggles are unbelievable," they told me. "It takes her forever to do something, and then she starts crying and wants to quit."

"What do you do then?" I asked.

Susan and Jack described a lengthy interaction that typically ended when they gave up struggling with Iris and sent her to bed. "What else can we do?" they asked. "We don't want her to feel worse."

I began seeing an image of a spoiled little girl without limits at home or in school. This clearly did not match the way Susan and Jack saw their daughter, but I wanted to suggest, indirectly, this alternative view without alienating them. I asked, "So am I correct in thinking that she has learned that when she throws one of her fits or has a temper tantrum, you eventually give in?" Both parents answered "Yes," though I was not sure whether they fully absorbed my implicit description of Iris's behavior.

At the end of the session, I praised their dedication as parents and love for Iris and asked them during the next week to notice the times Iris seemed relaxed and observe what was different about those times. I hoped that this task would redirect their energy and attention to what was healthy about Iris.

The day before the second session with this family, I contacted Iris's teacher, who told me that Iris's school behavior had much improved. I was puzzled when the teacher attributed the change to "the suggestion you made to her parents." Besides the homework assignment at the end of the session, I recalled no specific suggestion.

When Susan and Jack arrived for their second session, they presented a long list of what they had noticed about Iris when she was calm and peaceful.

177

A happier Iris coughed less, concentrated better on schoolwork, appeared cheerful, and played with friends. Her parents also described some differences in the way they had handled her that week: Dad insisted she finish her spelling list, whether she liked it or not, and they paid less attention to her when she coughed. Finally, Susan said, "We did what you suggested; we agreed with her when she put herself down. It was fun!"

When Iris complained, "Oh, Mom, I'm really ugly," Susan had replied, "Yes, you really are." When Iris said, "I don't like my hair, it's stupid," Susan had agreed, saying, "Yes, it really is awful." "Well," Susan said to me, "it stopped her completely. I thought I saw tears in her eyes, and she said, 'Mom, do you really believe that?' and all I did was shrug my shoulders and say, 'I don't know.' I was really neutral. Then Iris smiled and I smiled. She laughed and I laughed. I've never been able to get her to stop before. This was the first time, ever! Even Jack was having fun with it." "I don't know what else to do," Jack conceded. "It stops her. It's not the answer, but it does help."

JACK WAS RIGHT. AGREEING WITH IRIS DIDN'T solve the whole problem, but it did interrupt her pattern of making self-denigrating remarks and created an opportunity for her parents to view her differently and reconsider the way they treated her. They had used *un*common sense, taking a light-hearted approach to a "serious" problem, and it led to a change in Iris's behavior. This success gave them confidence that they could do other things that would yield additional results. The problem no longer seemed to reside "inside" Iris; maybe she wasn't really "sick" after all.

If she wasn't sick, what *was* wrong? Sensing her parents' readiness to hear new information, I explained that perhaps all the special treatment she received from them and from her teacher had back-fired and inadvertently given her the message that

she wasn't like other kids and couldn't really handle things. If she were more capable, then she wouldn't need so much coddling. "All kids are different," I said. "Hyperactive kids calm down on Ritalin, even though it is technically a stimulant. Similarly, pampering Iris has had the reverse effect of what was intended. Rather than giving her self-confidence, it made her afraid she is unequal to life."

I asked Susan and Jack, "If you were to treat her more like other kids, what would you do differently?" They came up with an extensive list, demonstrating the extent to which they treated her as incapable and incompetent. At the end of the session, I complimented them on their creativity and open-mindedness and suggested they treat Iris more like other children.

Two weeks later, we met for session three. Jack said, "Before we begin, I have a question. How do we know when to stop coming?" (Clients ask useful questions, too.) There was no more coughing, no frequent urination, and more cheerfulness in Iris. Jack said, "We have our little girl back." We all agreed that since they had asked the question about ending therapy, they probably knew the answer. We terminated with the understanding that they could call again if they wished. When I contacted them several months later, everything was going well. Unexpectedly, I recently saw Susan in a local restaurant, a year after our last meeting. She couldn't wait to tell me how well Iris is doing. Her face lit up with pride as she listed Iris's accomplishments.

DOING SOLUTION-ORIENTED THERAPY HAS changed me. I now have a deeper respect for people's inherent abilities to resolve their difficulties. The more I observe people making significant changes easily, the more I believe it is possible, even with difficult cases. The more I believe people can change their lives, the more this belief is reflected in my behavior toward clients. Sometimes I think that the Pygmalion Effect—we think, therefore they are—is the overriding dynamic in therapy.

Not all of my clients live happily ever after. Needless to say, I have my share of failures. However, as a brief therapist, my reactions to times when I feel stuck or lost is quite different from times past. Earlier in my career, when things did not go smoothly, I alternated between blaming myself and my "resistant" clients.

Today when I get stuck, I usually feel challenged, even stimulated. I ask myself, "What haven't I tried?" and always discover there is some avenue left unexplored. When I have creative dry spells, I consult with colleagues and feel fortunate that there is always more to learn. I have realized that, for the therapist as well as the client, thinking about solutions is more energizing than thinking about problems.

Learning to be a brief therapist has stretched my thinking. I have come to realize that what I once believed to be impossible is really quite possible. I now regularly see people quickly make enduring changes in their lives, changes that remind me of a statement by David Ben-Gurion, Israel's first prime minister: "Anyone who doesn't believe in miracles is not a realist." ∎

MICHELE WEINER-DAVIS, M.S.W., *is in private practice in Woodstock, IL.*

PHOTOGRAPH BY JOAN LIFTIN/ACTUALITY

EMPOWERING THE ELDERLY

THERAPEUTIC STRATEGIES FOR A GENERATION SUSPICIOUS OF THERAPY

By Marilyn Bonjean and Richard Spector

THE IDEA THAT COPING WITH LIFE'S DIFFICULTIES involves an occasional stop at a therapist's office is of very recent vintage. It is only during the past couple of decades that psychotherapy has achieved anything like widespread acceptance. The attitudes of today's elderly population, however, were shaped in an earlier time. For many of them, the kind of emotional expression and soul-baring associated with traditional therapy seems at best frivolous and at worst a stigmatizing sign of deep pathology.

In recent years, many clinicians have discovered that strategic, problem-oriented approaches are far more compatible with the outlook of elderly clients than more traditional clinical approaches. For one thing, the hallmark of strategic therapy is the achievement of change by utilizing each client's unique way of organizing experience. Converting people to the belief that exploring intimate personal feelings is the secret to mental health is unnecessary. For another, many elderly clients, often in situations of physical deterioration or impending death, find it more hopeful to participate in a form of treatment

that is short term and in which goals are defined in specific and realistic terms. Finally, strategic approaches can be used effectively with people who consider themselves so self-reliant that they would never define themselves as therapy "patients."

What follow are four case vignettes describing strategic interventions with elderly clients. Each demonstrates how the principles of strategic therapy provide a useful problem-solving framework for practitioners working with the elderly.

MRS. BROWN RESTED AGAINST HER PILLOW, TINY and frail, her arm purple from the intravenous needles that had been withdrawn from her body only a few days before. She had just returned to the nursing home following a hospitalization in which she had undergone a number of invasive tests and an amputation. An urgent call from the nursing supervisor—"Mrs. Brown is not eating"—had brought a therapist to visit Mrs. Brown in order to do an assessment.

The nurse had already lectured Mrs. Brown about the importance of eating and tried to coerce

THE EVOLVING THERAPIST

her into taking food, but that had only intensified the power struggle between patient and staff. Actually, Mrs. Brown had refused meals for only one day and sent a nursing aide to the cafeteria for a doughnut that morning. The large glazed doughnut rested near the water pitcher on her bed table. Mrs. Brown's eyes glared as she nodded her permission for the therapist to sit down.

"I suppose they called you because I sent the tray back," said Mrs. Brown.

"Yes, you know how excited they get when something different happens," replied the therapist.

Mrs. Brown sniffed loudly and shifted her position, carefully covering her stump.

"Well, I'm not eating that food," Mrs. Brown announced defiantly. "They can't make me. Doesn't taste right—probably something wrong with it."

"Well, I'm not surprised," said the therapist knowingly.

"What—about what?" asked Mrs. Brown, still hoping for a fight.

"You've been very sick lately—probably makes everything taste like cardboard."

"Yes, and my stomach hurts whenever I eat that stuff."

"Probably."

"Well, I won't and that's it," said Mrs. Brown with a flourish, trying to dismiss the therapist.

"You aren't planning on eating all *that,* are you?" asked the therapist, pointing to the doughnut.

"Yes. Why not?"

"Well, I hope not all of it. With what you've been through, you must be very careful about how much and what you eat."

Taking the doughnut, the therapist broke it into two pieces, put the smaller piece near Mrs. Brown, and said, "There, I think that might be okay, but certainly not all of it."

"And why not all of it?" demanded Mrs. Brown angrily. "I know how much to eat. Give me the rest."

"No—you'll make your stomach hurt."

"Well, I have to eat something! I have to keep up my strength. The nurses said so."

"*They* probably did," replied the therapist in a tone of disapproval. "But I'll talk to them. They need to realize how sick you've been, and besides, you don't use up that many calories. I'll tell them to give you very little on your tray tonight."

"Now, I know how much to take—you don't need to interfere with this."

"Yes, I do. You were planning to eat that whole doughnut, which would be a mistake. Tonight I'll have them give you very small portions."

Mrs. Brown angrily raised herself in her bed and told the therapist, "It is my tray. Tell them to give me potatoes and carrots—I like that."

"We'll see," said the therapist, leaving the room.

The therapist then went to talk with the nursing staff taking care of Mrs. Brown. She complimented them on how well they were preventing Mrs. Brown from getting depressed by allowing her to express her anger and tolerating her unpleasant and uncooperative behavior. The therapist agreed with them that nutrition was important to healing but added that a fighting spirit was also important. The nursing staff agreed to try an experiment with Mrs. Brown for two days and to carefully chart her reactions.

They were to take in a full food tray with a smaller plate on the side. While grumbling about the instructions not to give her much food, they were to place very small portions on Mrs. Brown's plate. In this way, they would mirror her ambivalence about eating. They were to argue with her in favor of small portions but let her convince them to give her a little more. They were to increase the portions at each meal but ask her to promise not to tell the therapist or they would get in trouble. Each day the therapist would go to Mrs. Brown's room to urge her not to go too fast in resuming eating. After several days, Mrs. Brown was again eating full portions, and the intervention was discontinued.

182

The key to the intervention with Mrs. Brown was recognizing the positive objective of her refusal to eat as an attempt to exert some influence over her situation. By asserting a sense of mastery over the nursing staff, she was fighting back in her own way against the assaults to self-esteem and independence she had experienced. The intervention was designed to support Mrs. Brown's attempt to salvage her autonomy without resorting to a life-threatening symptom. It was also important to join with Mrs. Brown's nurses, accepting their concerns but offering an alternative way of resolving what might have turned into a life-or-death struggle about food.

CARING FOR A FRAIL SPOUSE CAN DOMINATE THE entire existence of the caretaker and introduce extraordinary tensions in even the best of marital relationships. A spouse's illness dashes hopes for the future and can embroil the caretaker in a bewildering tangle of feelings of loneliness, anger and guilt. Some elderly spouses become so involved in their caretaker role that it becomes the basis of their identity and self-worth. Therapists who wish to relieve the "burden" of such clients must proceed carefully. For them, complaining about their situation can become a badge of honor. Therapists who assume that reducing these complaints is a measure of the success of therapy may find themselves in an unwinnable battle.

George and Marion Klaus were referred to a family therapist by their physician because of the fights he witnessed during George's medical checkups. They had married, both for the second time, in their late sixties, and now, after seven years of marriage, George had been diagnosed with Alzheimer's disease. Both George and Marion understood that this was a progressive brain disease that affected his memory and judgment and would eventually render him in need of complete care.

George had been an architect and was a precise and demanding man. As the memory impairment progressed, he became increasingly critical of his wife, who would, in turn, indignantly defend herself. Their fighting had gotten so frequent and bitter that they were beginning to lose their friends, who no longer wished to be around them.

"We'll be riding in the car and I will make a remark like, 'I think we'll make it through the traffic light,'" Marion told the therapist in the first session. "Then I'll say, 'See, we made it.' But he will tell me, 'We did not, the light was amber.' He will ask me who folded his undershirts into thirds instead of in half. When he forgets something, he insists that I've written it down wrong or that I'm deliberately tricking him. He used to be a sweet, considerate man, but he certainly isn't anymore."

George was in the middle stages of Alzheimer's disease and required a good deal of redirection and supervision from his wife. She compensated for him very well, filled in sentences when he reached for words, and patted the chair next to her when he became restless. In therapy sessions, George made notes of the conversation on a pad of paper using a ruler to make sure his writing was straight. He constantly corrected his wife

In the first session in a private meeting with the therapist, Marion agreed that arguments with her husband certainly seemed intolerable. The therapist coached Marion on what to do when an argument seemed imminent, instructing her to change the subject, leave the room, do anything to keep from engaging her husband. For the next week, Marion was asked to keep a notebook recording how her husband tried to provoke her and how she managed to avoid getting into a battle.

In the second session, Marion described the variety of things she had done and admitted that their fights were much fewer. She then spent much of the session detailing how difficult her circumstances were and how impossible George was. When the therapist asked if the reduced fighting had made things better, Marion emphatically informed her that they were as bad as they had ever been.

The therapist complimented the wife on how much she was doing to care for her husband and on her willingness to continue therapy, even though things were not better. Since Marion had described some difference in George's behavior due to her using a variety of argument-avoidance techniques, the therapist asked her to continue using this method and to keep track of what happened.

In the next session, Marion again reported that arguments had continued to decrease. But she still insisted that things weren't any better. When asked what she did for herself, she replied, "Nothing. When would I have the time? When George goes to play golf, it's such a relief to have him gone I just sit there and catch my breath. I used to go to an exercise class but got out of the habit when everything got so tense."

"Anyone who works as hard as you do needs to let off steam so they can keep going," replied the therapist. "I know it will be hard, but will you try going back to exercise class? Because you are right, your situation probably will continue to be bad, since I have not been very successful at getting improvements."

By the fourth session, Marion had resumed exercise class. Arguments had almost stopped, and friends had begun to socialize with George and Marion again. It was obvious to friends that George was as critical as ever, but now Marion was seen as long-suffering and tolerant rather than as her husband's antagonist. As she told me, "One of my friends said to me the other day, 'How do you stand it? He's so critical of you, but you just don't fight with him. How do you do it?'" Marion began to get more sympathy and invitations from her women friends. Nevertheless, Marion was again emphatic that nothing had really changed.

At this time, George's two children came for a visit and were very upset at what they found. They insisted on meeting with the therapist. "We were really not against Dad's remarrying after Mother died, but you should see the way Marion treats him now," George's son told her. "I know Dad has an illness, but he isn't a child. Marion supervises everything. The way she is taking over, I'll bet she will have him changing his will next."

Often those who do not provide daily care for an Alzheimer's patient do not realize how much supervision is needed or how much compensation for lost skills is provided by the caregiver. The relative looks normal and may function well in superficial social conversation.

The therapist asked Marion to cooperate in an experiment. She was told that George's children needed to really get to know the changes in their father. To do so would require their spending at least a full day with him without Marion's being there to compensate for him. The therapist knew this would be difficult for Marion, because to let her husband show his true level of disability might reflect poorly on the job she was doing in caring for him. Nevertheless, George's children needed to learn what caretaking was really like by giving them a real taste of it. Marion agreed that they needed to know what she was dealing with.

At the next meeting with George's children, they told the therapist, "He didn't know how to read the menu at the restaurant and kept putting salt on everything. When we asked him questions, he often didn't know the answers. He tried to go to the men's room and ended up in the kitchen. He's really confused. He just didn't seem like Dad. If Marion is willing to take care of him, I don't mind if she takes all the money. I know I couldn't do it."

By the eighth session, Marion reported that the arguments with her husband had all but ceased. She now went regularly to exercise class and often went out with her friends. George continued to play golf and began to attend an adult day-care center twice a week, allowing Marion some respite. Marion, however, insisted that this was an opportunity for social stimulation for George, since she did not believe she needed respite.

As in previous sessions, she spent much of the time telling the therapist how difficult everything was and that, although some things were different, nothing had really improved. The therapist apologized to her for not being able to help make things better but admitted that perhaps just a little difference was all one could hope for under her circumstances. In this case, the therapist needed to look to other measures of change beyond Marion's self-report, respecting the central role that complaining had come to occupy in her life.

Complaining against the injustices of life may be a very valid response for older adults who must cope with the unfairness of illness or the betrayals of an aging body. Complaining educates others about one's circumstances and may be a natural response to a younger therapist viewed as probably unable to understand the insults of an aging process not yet experienced. For the client in this case, to admit improvement would imply a need for help and undermine her self-image as an independent, self-sufficient caretaker. But looked at from another angle, Marion was simply being accurate, her situation was different but not really better in the way she defined "better." A long career of caregiving lies ahead for Marion, with many new challenges.

JANET WHITE, 68, HAD ALWAYS BEEN CONSIDERED a go-getter, the kind of woman who enjoyed the challenge of hiking six hours up and down her favorite mountain four times each year. Still working full-time, she lived with her daughter Loraine and son-in-law Rob and her two grandchildren. It was Janet's paycheck that enabled the family to rent a house with a backyard and separate bedrooms for each child.

Two years ago, Janet developed clogged arteries and needed a heart-bypass operation. Less than a day after the operation, she suffered a mild stroke,

which affected her ability to walk. When Janet returned home after discharge, she found the stairs to her basement apartment were impossible to maneuver in her wheelchair, and she was now forced to sleep in the living room. The family did its best to adjust to the change in circumstances, while Loraine, who had once depended on Janet, now struggled to take care of both her children and her mother.

Janet was not the type of person to let her disability control her. She worked hard in physical therapy and eventually returned to work on a part-time basis in an electric wheelchair. A county bus for the handicapped picked her up at 6 a.m. and got her and six other wheelchair-bound people to a suburban subway stop by 8 a.m. She then maneuvered her electric wheelchair through the subway system at rush hour, even transferring trains in the busiest station. She would make it to work by 10 a.m. At 3:30 p.m. she'd leave for the long trek home in reverse, arriving exhausted by 7:30 p.m. In exchange for contributing her paycheck and disability income to the household, Janet expected that Loraine would feed her dinner and tend to her needs in the evening.

Loraine tried her best to adjust to her new role. After all, Janet had brought her up all by herself, and Loraine had always been the apple of her mother's eye. The two had been unusually close when Loraine was a child, going on long camping trips, always doing things together. But Loraine was in a tough spot now. Her children, getting less attention than they were used to, were a bit out of control in the evening. And Rob, increasingly resentful of his disabled mother-in-law's presence, had become sulky and distant. Loraine felt caught between her husband and mother. Her attempts to discuss the matter with Rob led nowhere.

Janet began to feel that not only was she ruining her daughter's marriage but that she was only wanted for the paycheck she brought in. Increasingly depressed, she spent long hours staring at the TV set trying not to bother anyone, yet seething inside. When Janet tried to discuss her sense of being a burden, Loraine would dismiss her concerns, saying, "Don't be silly, Mother. We all love you and want you here with us."

By December of the second year after the stroke, Janet became extremely depressed, took an overdose of pills, and was hospitalized on a psychiatric ward. Upon discharge, family therapy was recommended, but Rob refused to participate. When in the room together for their first session, both Janet and Loraine put the best possible face on their situation, minimizing the difficulties they confronted, insisting that everyone was doing their best to pitch in. However, when interviewed separately, each woman told a very different story.

Bitter at her disability and depressed at the burden she felt she was placing on her family, Janet said she was no longer interested in her physical therapy, didn't think it would help much anyway, and was resigned to life in a wheelchair. In private, Loraine also opened up. She felt her mother had given up trying to make things work and grieved for the happy days when Janet was a second mother to her children. She had always relied on Janet and counted on her leadership; now she expressed concern that she didn't think she *could* be a decent mother to her children all by herself. Although she knew it didn't make sense, she felt as if her mother had abandoned her—even though she realized it was not Janet's fault.

When I asked Loraine what kinds of things she'd like her mother to do, she talked about Janet helping her cook, clean and watch the children. Loraine believed that the wheelchair was just Janet's way to justify not being part of the family. She didn't think her mother really needed the wheelchair to get around the house. It seemed she was choosing to remain anchored to it out of spite.

When mother and daughter met back together after their separate interviews, they once again became close-mouthed and protective of each other, unwilling to discuss any of the issues they had shared privately. While the therapist had never promised confidentiality in the individual interviews, he felt that confronting them with what each had said privately would just lead to more denial and perhaps their departure from therapy. Instead, the therapist decided to take another tack.

Janet was again interviewed alone. The therapist asked Janet at length about her previous life-style of exercise and physical challenge. They discussed the tension-reducing benefits of exercise. Finally, the therapist asked whether it was at all possible for Janet to get up and push her own wheelchair even briefly. With some effort, she was able to do it.

Loraine was then brought into the room and asked whether she would be surprised if, as part of an in-home physical activity program, her mother would stand up and push her own wheelchair around a bit. Loraine smiled and said, "Well, my mother can be full of surprises." Having already demonstrated to the therapist that she could push the chair, Janet could hardly deny her ability when asked to show Loraine. The two women giggled as Janet pushed the wheelchair around for about four minutes. Looking at Loraine and commenting on how tired she looked, the therapist asked Janet if she was willing to give her daughter a little treat. Would it be possible for her to push Loraine in the wheelchair for 30 seconds? Again the two women giggled spontaneously like schoolgirls at the playground. Loraine seemed thrilled by the idea.

Janet got up slowly and with determination pushed Loraine around in the wheelchair for a good 45 seconds. Loraine gave a regal little wave as she exclaimed, "I feel like Miss America in a parade." The task had given the mother and daughter the chance to interact in the playful way they had when Loraine was a little girl. And for 45 seconds the old mother-daughter bond that had been so important to them was brought back to life, and the somber standoff of the past two years was briefly forgotten.

The two of them were asked to spend a few moments each night doing this form of exercise. Janet was to begin on the first night by pushing Loraine around in the wheelchair for 45 seconds. Each night thereafter Janet was to challenge herself just a bit by extending the time five more seconds. They laughed and agreed. The smile on Loraine's face suggested a new hope that things might get better.

The two returned a week later, reporting that things had gone very well. Janet had been able to wheel Loraine around the living room for four minutes by the end of the week. Not only that, but Loraine, who had previously refused to ask her mother to help her cook brunch because it was more of a nuisance than it was worth, had enthusiastically asked Janet to help her cook a Southern-style brunch on Sunday morning. Janet had heartily pitched in, standing at the kitchen counter for 30 minutes.

Mother and daughter were asked to continue as they had for another two weeks. Janet was to shoot for an additional five seconds of exercise a day; more if she could handle it. She was to stop immediately if she felt any signs of pushing herself too hard. After two weeks, the women returned, saying that Janet was pushing Loraine for a five-minute ride around the downstairs each night. What was more, Janet had begun giving up the use of the wheelchair around the house. She walked independently, however slowly, and used a walker when necessary, although she still needed to use the wheelchair for getting to work. In addition, the two women had agreed to regularly prepare Sunday brunch together.

The therapist spoke to Janet alone and congratulated her on her incredible progress. Janet was enthusiastic about her increased mobility and tickled by the idea that Loraine received such a thrill from the wheelchair ride. It was suggested that Janet organize a surprise celebration for the family. She was to meet with the grandchildren and arrange for

them to place a crown on Loraine's head, throw confetti, and present her with flowers on next Sunday evening's wheelchair ride. Janet chuckled and agreed. They were to return in 10 days.

Monday morning, the therapist received a call from Loraine. She was overjoyed by the party the children had thrown for her. Nevertheless, she was glad that the session for that week was still scheduled. She felt that though Janet and she were now friends again, there were still major problems that needed to be solved. The same Loraine who seemed so emotionally immobilized in her mother's presence just a few weeks before now wanted very much to come in for a frank discussion of the problems in the family.

In our next session, Loraine brought up all the concerns that she had been avoiding in the previous months, including the question of long-term living arrangements, how best to deal with Rob, the new household division of labor, the planning of vacations, television and phone schedules. Together, the two women tackled these difficult problems, eventually agreeing on some more workable arrangements.

When, through the illness or disability of an elderly family member, the normal hierarchy is upset, ordinary communication can become more difficult. Out of protective motives, family members may avoid unpleasant topics. Unfortunately, the more difficult issues are circumvented, the more resentments may build. An atmosphere of gloom and fatalism can grow in a family. Older members may feel rejected.

In this case, the playful ritual of the wheelchair ride worked on a number of levels to make it possible for Loraine and Janet to talk directly about the problems they were facing. In a symbolic way, the ritual restored some of Janet's status, establishing her once again in Loraine's eyes as someone who, though disabled, could still "take care" of her in an important way. It was not only a joyful reminder of a very happy time, it also gave Loraine an opportunity to relax and enjoy herself in the present. The ritual established a different pattern of interaction between mother and daughter, one that empowered them to work together to make the best of a difficult situation.

ACCORDING TO THE STAFF, GERTA FLEET WAS THE nicest of all the nursing home residents. Deeply religious, she always greeted the other residents in the sitting room with a blessing, and when anyone assisted her, she thanked them profusely. Through prayer and rigorous determination, she had regained control of her bladder and bowels after a series of three strokes had left her left side completely paralyzed. She was the perfect model of a cooperative nursing home resident. Gerta, however, saw it differently. She thought the other residents were suspicious of her German accent and suspected that she had been a Nazi during the war. The staff, she felt, was whispering behind her back about her being a pest for needing so much assistance in using the bathroom at night.

When Gerta described to staff members how other residents at the lunch table had accused her of being selfish and stuck-up, the nurses became concerned. That same day, Gerta's daughter Margo received a call from her mother quite late. Gerta begged Margo to pray for her—she was convinced that the nursing home staff and residents would be voting the next day to ask her to leave. Margo reassured her mother that she had nothing to fear, that Gerta had done many nice things for both staff and residents and that they liked having her there.

The residents were awakened as usual at 5 a.m., so that everyone would be in place for breakfast when the day shift arrived at 6:30. Gerta, as usual, greeted the aides with a morning prayer and blessed some of the shyer residents who sat in a corner by the window. She sat down for breakfast at 6:30, but by 6:45 she had scratched both her wrists with a butter knife and was weeping for forgiveness. The aides

were bandaging her wrists and wheeling her to an emergency area by the time Margo arrived at 7 a.m.

Margo ran to her mother's side, hoarsely gasping, "Oh, my God. Oh, my God." Crying, she bent down to Gerta's wheelchair, embracing her mother's bony shoulders and squeezing the fragile flesh. For a long time the two women wept together, their tears mingling on each other's cheeks. When she was finally able to speak, Gerta explained that she just couldn't take it any longer at the nursing home. That morning, she was sure she had heard 88-year-old Mrs. Pomerance, a moderately demented double amputee, call her "a power-hungry German who could not even speak English right." The aides who had been present assured Margo that Mrs. Pomerance had made some groans and uttered a few confused words—nothing hostile, and not directed at anyone in particular. Gerta insisted that Mrs. Pomerance had indeed made accusations toward her and that the staff members were politely hiding their intentions to kick her out of the nursing home.

As always, Margo attempted to reassure her mother that there was nothing to worry about. She again reminded her mother of all the good deeds she had done for others in the home and of how appreciated she was. Gerta once again collected herself and begged her daughter to forgive her for creating such a stir and making Margo late for work.

The next day, Margo and her mother went for a consultation at a nearby family therapy clinic that specialized in work with the elderly. The therapist spent some time interviewing both Gerta and Margo separately. In that session, Gerta, who was born a year after World War I ended, described her youth in an impoverished German farming village. As a young child, Gerta frequently went to bed so hungry that she could not sleep. Scarcity was so extensive that there was nothing for anyone to share and no way, really, for anyone to help another materially. In such an atmosphere, other forms of help were also difficult to give. Though the aftermath of the war had made things worse than they had been before, the villagers had lived in this manner for centuries. Over the centuries, a belief system had developed in the community that explained suffering as the cost of original sin. Believers learned the necessity of rigorous self-reliance and the importance of accepting God's will.

When Gerta was nine, her parents sent her to live with her maternal grandparents on the other side of the village. As the second-oldest girl, Gerta was selected because her older sister was needed to raise the younger siblings. She had badly wanted to stay with her parents and siblings, and the separation was difficult. She ran home repeatedly, but the family always insisted she go back to her grandparents, who needed her to cook, clean and care for them in their old age. Overwhelmed by these responsibilities, the little girl kept returning to her parents desperate for help. But her family was too hard-pressed to take her back.

Finally, her parents dealt with Gerta's wish to return by ignoring her. When she would run back home, her siblings would tease her, call her names, and throw rocks at her. Seventy years later, she still vividly remembered one beautiful spring day when she sat in a lush green field, wildflowers in bloom all around her, heartbroken and hoping for comfort from God. Suddenly she heard God speak to her and tell her it was her duty to suffer in this life, but that she would be rewarded in heaven if she devoted herself to helping others.

This was, in fact, what Gerta had done for most of her life, nursing her paralyzed grandfather after her grandmother died and coming to the United States as an indentured servant to take care of two paralyzed invalids after her grandfather died. After she married and had two daughters, Gerta continued to work as a caretaker for the sick, sending whatever money she could to her parents, who still lived in the same small German village. Though her parents had rejected her, she felt it was still her duty

as a daughter and a Christian to support them to any extent she could. She felt it was up to God to judge their having given her away; her responsibility was to find understanding for them in her heart.

When asked about the lack of pleasure and fun in her life, she said God blessed her with children and grandchildren whose lives were filled with fun and pleasure. When asked about suffering, she described the strength God had given her to survive. When asked whether she wished anyone had given her help as a child and adult, she replied that we must rely on ourselves and God. God's help was enough.

Gerta, who had given so much for so long, had now reached an age when she herself needed help. But she rejected the reassurance that she was indeed a person who was worthy of help, because her worldview and life accomplishments were based on the belief that she was essentially an undeserving person. She had been chosen by God to sacrifice for others as her only justification for existing in the world. For Gerta, it would have been extremely arrogant to consider herself worthy of help.

Finding herself now in the nursing home, wheelchair-bound, her left side paralyzed, Gerta was unable to make up for her unworthiness by sacrificing for others to the extent she had before. Her life was no longer justified. What's more, the praise and reassurance of her daughter and the nursing home staff implicitly requested her to reject her notion of herself, and everything she had accomplished in her life, as unworthy. The subtle invalidation inherent in the reassurance made her feel more alone and suicidal.

Was there a way that Margo could help Gerta without invalidating Gerta's lifelong devotion to self-sacrifice? Could she embrace and comfort Gerta without undermining the main premise of her mother's existence? The only way seemed to involve respecting Gerta's religious principles and her belief that she was indeed an unworthy person.

The therapist acknowledged Gerta's bind. If she

allowed herself to accept help without protest, Gerta was committing the sin of feeling arrogant enough to be worthy of help. On the other hand, she knew that her inability to receive her daughter's reassurance and praise was making Margo feel like a failure at being a good daughter. In this sense, Gerta's refusal to receive help, when she knew she objectively needed it, was also a form of arrogance because it denied Margo the opportunity to fulfill her responsibilities as a mature, adult daughter.

Gerta was caught in an impossible dilemma. If she accepted help, she was arrogant because she deemed herself worthy of it. If she did not accept help, she was arrogant because she was denying her daughter the opportunity to perform the way a good daughter should. The therapist told Gerta that he knew of no human solution to such a spiritual dilemma. The answer could come only from God.

The therapist asked Margo if she felt that she had a problem with arrogance. Margo said yes, she had, indeed everyone had a certain amount of arrogance and needed to work on it. He then gently suggested to Margo that it might be considered arrogant to expect a mother to give up her most cherished beliefs in order to be comforted by her daughter. Margo smiled, only a bit embarrassed. The two women were now joined by their common spiritual dilemma. The therapist asked Gerta and Margo if, at the beginning and end of every conversation with each other, they would pray to God to be delivered from arrogance. They agreed.

Gerta and Margo went to therapy every week to discuss the spiritual implications of arrogance and humility. They worked on revising and improving their prayers. Gerta's minister attended a session to participate in the discussions. He empathized with the two women's plight, and he strongly endorsed the idea of their praying together.

In this way, Gerta was being helped by Margo without being asked to change her worldview. Margo was being allowed by Gerta to feel helpful as a daughter, while Gerta felt respected and comforted by her daughter. At the same time, Gerta felt no need to punish herself, since she was no longer being praised and reassured for attempts to be helpful that were not up to her standards. Her helplessness in accepting an appropriate degree of dependence was directed toward God, in the company of her daughter, rather than toward lonely self-destruction.

Over the course of five weeks, the prayer was refined. Whether it was because God answered this prayer or because a behavioral sequence was altered in a way that changed a dysfunctional power relationship, Gerta made no more suicide attempts. ∎

MARILYN BONJEAN, ED.D., *is a research associate at the Brief Family Therapy Center in Milwaukee and director of social services, Marian Catholic Home, Milwaukee, WI.*

RICHARD SPECTOR, M.S.W., *is clinical staff member at the Family Therapy Institute of Washington, D.C., and Coordinator of Services to Older Adults, Their Families and Friends at Woodburn Center for Community Mental Health in Fairfax County, VA.*

JULY/AUGUST 1983

RESEARCH: WHY CLINICIANS SHOULD BOTHER WITH IT

BRIDGING THE GAP BETWEEN THE ART AND SCIENCE OF THERAPY

By Richard Schwartz and Douglas Breunlin

Here is Edward Bear, coming downstairs now, bump, bump, bump, on the back of his head, behind Christopher Robin. It is, as far as he knows, the only way of coming downstairs, but sometimes he feels that there is really another way, if only he could stop bumping for a moment and think of it.

—Winnie the Pooh

THREE DECADES AGO, GROUPS OF SOCIAL SCIENtists all around the country began to stop bumping. For a variety of motives and from a variety of perspectives, they began to think about, study and treat problems like schizophrenia and delinquency in daring new ways. Making fine distinctions between research and practice was apparently not a major preoccupation during family therapy's pioneering era. In a recent paper, Lyman Wynne describes this period as one in which "research and treatment were fundamentally fused" and cites Jay Haley's comment that the 1950s was a time when "it was taken for granted that a therapist and a researcher were of the same species."

There were many reasons for the wedding of research and practice in those days. The early investigations of the family represented mapmaking expeditions into previously unexplored territory, and the researchers-cum-clinicians-cum-theorists who conducted them banded together for guidance. A good example of the marriage of research and treatment was the Bateson research project in Palo Alto, where pure "look but don't touch" researcher-theorists like Gregory Bateson (and, at that point, Haley and John Weakland) and clinicians like Don Jackson strongly influenced each other.

One important way in which research influenced practice in that period was by providing a license for departures from tradition. In those days, there were psychoanalytic taboos against including anyone but the individual patient in therapy. By describing what they were doing as "research," the early investigators were able to find an acceptable way to interview whole families.

Whatever the reasons for it, the early mixture of research and practice in the family therapy movement established an orientation toward creativity and discovery. It is no accident that many of the

---

193

movement's pioneers became and continue to be central figures in the field. Today, however, it is no longer clear that we have sustained that creative drive or have gone much beyond the work of these first explorers.

Some believe that there has been a fundamental shift in the relationship between research and practice in the family therapy field since the 1950s. They see the field today as divided into tribes of researchers and practitioners, each tribe assuming it is different from the other, each having its own distinct rituals and languages. Although he believes that these tribal divisions have begun to break down, Wynne has observed that "during most of the 1960s and 1970s family research and family therapy became different realms."

Among the questions the family therapy field faces today is determining the optimal relationship between research and practice. Are these two endeavors fundamentally different enterprises? In light of the apparent gap between research and practice that characterizes the field today, how can the connection between them be improved? Are we even sure that it should be?

To EXAMINE THESE QUESTIONS, WE INTERVIEWED many people who are involved in research or practice or both. But before describing the comments we heard, let's do a brief assessment of the research/practice marriage where you work. If you see yourself as primarily a clinician, when was the last time you more than skimmed a research article (you know, one with tables and statistics)? To what extent has your practice been influenced by research you have read? Do you really believe researchers have anything to offer you?

Most of the practitioners we spoke to reported that they rarely read research papers because they found most of them to be of little relevance to their work. Generally, the attitudes clinicians voiced about research reflected combinations of intimidation

and contempt, distrust and awe. The picture of research that emerged was of an inaccessible domain of knowledge that might contain something of value, but which usually seemed hopelessly remote from the experience of the clinician.

Certain complaints about research were stated again and again. Many clinicians questioned the researcher's reliance on families' self-descriptions as a major source of information. To clinicians who have logged thousands of hours with families and know how unreliably families can portray themselves, it seemed naive to place much emphasis on this kind of data. Also, clinicians disdained the belief that counting observable responses revealed something about important family processes. Generally, practitioners expressed more interest in the larger patterns of family life, which form the context of events, than in the number of times specific behaviors occur. But perhaps more than anything, clinicians objected to the technical language of research articles, which seem to recite findings drained of all life and interest.

While few practitioners we interviewed seemed to find practical relevance in the research literature, that is not to say they found it completely without value. Michael Berger, associate professor of psychology at Georgia State University, expressed appreciation for another quality that he finds in some research: "I read the research literature like I read novels, because I'm a curious person rather than because it will be helpful to me. If I read only what was helpful, I'd spend most of my time looking at case studies."

Now, for the researchers reading this, consider a few questions before going any further. How often do you observe family therapy sessions? If you are a clinician as well, to what extent have your own research activities influenced your therapeutic approach? If you are not a clinician, what contribution have your clinical colleagues made to your research work?

The views of some of the researchers we contacted are summarized in a distinction Jay Haley once drew: "Today it seems more apparent that the research stance and the posture of the therapist are quite opposite. The researcher must . . . explore and explain all the complex variables of every issue since he is an explorer after truth. The therapist's stance is quite different . . . He must . . . use simple ideas that will accomplish his goals and not be distracted by the explorations into interesting aspects of life and the human mind."

OFTEN THE LACK OF COMMUNICATION BETWEEN researchers and practitioners is explained as resulting from their working in very different settings. But Mert Krause, director of research at the Institute for Juvenile Research (IJR) in Chicago for many years, where at one time as many as 60 researchers and 120 clinicians worked, has had first-hand experience observing what happens when researchers and clinicians have the chance to work together. Krause reports that the researchers at IJR showed little interest in the process of therapy, maintaining that there was little research evidence demonstrating that therapy was effective. But even those researchers interested in therapy had to contend with clinicians who did not want researchers looking over their shoulders and did not want to invest the time or energy in operationalizing what they were doing. From the point of view of other researchers we spoke to who are skilled in meticulous observation and precise measurement, clinicians all too often are seen as impulsive in their actions and undisciplined in their thinking.

There was, however, one point on which the clinicians and researchers we polled agreed. They all viewed research on the outcome of therapy as an essential activity and as the type of research that has had the largest impact on practice. A few outcome studies were mentioned by virtually everyone with whom we spoke. The two projects referred to most

frequently were the research on psychosomatic disorders done by Salvador Minuchin and Bernice Rosman and their colleagues and the recent drug abuse research by Duncan Stanton, Tom Todd et al. Also frequently cited was the psychoeducational work of Carol Anderson and colleagues with the families of schizophrenics at the Western Psychiatric Clinic in Pittsburgh.

These three studies have several qualities that set them apart from many other outcome studies. First, they are easy for clinicians to read and understand, avoiding the arid technicalese of many research reports (probably because they are written by clinicians-cum-researchers). Second, the treatment used is precisely described and spelled out at length. Commenting on how rarely this occurs, Alan Gurman, editor of the *Journal of Marital and Family Therapy,* observes that in the typical research report, "there is usually very little sense for the reader of what actually occurred in treatment. People have to resort to their stereotypic fantasies of what, for example, structural family therapy might have been like in that situation." A final factor contributing to the influence of the studies named above that should not be discounted is that each study offered impressive results with a treatment population that typically frustrates clinicians. Such results command attention.

But do outcome studies—even those of outstanding quality—really change the minds of clinicians? Alan Gurman thinks not: "Clinicians get attracted to a brand of family therapy for reasons that have little to do with empirical evidence . . . The assumption is that if the data says that Therapy A is better than B, the open-minded clinician doing B will start doing A, That assumption is preposterously naive." Supporting Gurman's assertion is Michael Berger's candid observation: "Since I happen to practice structural/strategic therapy, I teach Psychosomatic Families as if what Minuchin et al. said was fact. But if you reported a psychodynamic intervention with the same statistical table of results, I probably wouldn't believe it, and I would point out all its methodological flaws."

Even if outcome studies do not typically lead clinicians to make great theoretical and technical shifts, it would be a mistake to assume that they made no difference. George Saba, director of training at Midwest Family Resources in Chicago, describes the impact of the Minuchin/Rosman research on his work: "When I'm with a family of an anorectic and they start trying to convince me to see it their way, things can get very tense. A lot is at stake—the anorectic could die. So I feel like I have more strength and conviction knowing that the model I use has been proven to be extremely effective."

Good outcome research can also be important in increasing the credibility of family therapy within the psychotherapy community. In our own work with eating disorders, we meet many therapists who have traditional orientations. They invariably are familiar with the work of Minuchin and Rosman and often are more receptive to the point of view of family therapy as a result.

UP TO THIS POINT WE HAVE BEEN SPEAKING AS IF everybody agreed on what the term "research" means. Increasingly within the family therapy field, however, this term has itself become the subject of some debate. Bradford Keeney, director of research at the Ackerman Institute, for example, holds a view of research that few traditionalists would endorse: "I would say that a good clinician is the finest researcher around and has the most to say about research." According to Keeney, understanding some of the differences between those officially designated as "researchers" and clinicians means appreciating the differences in the philosophical assumptions underlying clinical and formal research methodologies. He believes that most family therapy research does not reflect the fundamental intellectual shift away from linear thinking that is embodied in family therapy practice: "When family therapy was born, people took great pride in saying that it represented an alternative paradigm, a different map that directed us to think and act clinically in a radically different fashion. The paradigm underlying most family research, however, has not been similarly questioned."

The differences Keeney is referring to may be at the very heart of what maintains the gap between the worlds of practice and traditional research. It is possible that the very core assumptions guiding family therapy research and those underlying practice are incompatible.

"Hard science" research approaches, based upon the philosophy of logical positivism, contain assumptions that many family therapists have rejected. Underlying traditional research methods is a belief in an *absolute* reality that can be measured objectively, as opposed to the relativistic belief that the version of reality measured will be a function of one's point of reference and of the degree to which the act of measuring affects the phenomenon being measured. The methods of hard science are guided by a faith that breaking a phenomenon down to its most basic elements yields the most thorough understanding, and that it is both possible and useful to distinguish simple causes and effects.

Given these assumptions, traditional researchers have placed an emphasis on carefully quantifying the variables under study, tracking their occurrence, and analyzing large samples of data. These procedures lend themselves to a research focused on verifying observations or theories, not on describing complex phenomena or making new discoveries.

More and more researchers in the social sciences are questioning these traditional scientific practices. As the well-known psychological researcher Donald Keisler recently observed: "As a young and insecure science, we incorrectly began by aping the philosophy of science offered by physics while ignoring models offered by disciplines such as biology and astronomy. . . . All of this pulled our profession away from ecological, naturalistic research approaches and away from intensive study of single cases." Doug Sprenkle, associate professor of child development and family studies at Purdue University, concurs: "Academic snobbery has been such that in the past if someone just sat down and attempted to describe a phenomenon, that was not considered good enough."

Other family therapy researchers we interviewed questioned the relevance for clinicians of specific aspects of traditional methods. Commenting on the studies that compare groups of subjects receiving one form of treatment with groups receiving another form, Alan Gurman says, "for the clinician, group comparisons, both statistically and phenomenologically, don't say anything about the individual case. Even if a study is very well designed, clinicians generally feel hesitant in generalizing results of group averages to individuals."

Bernice Rosman, now director of outpatient service and formerly director of research at the Philadelphia Child Guidance Clinic, questions the relevance of cause-effect experimental designs for our field. "My style of research is typically correlational; but then you're really stuck in terms of cause and effect relationships. If you have a belief in a circular model, however, that's not such a problem . . . I've handed in research grants where I had a correlational design and people said, 'Aha! You're not going to be able to tell what's the cause and what's the effect.' To me, the cause and effect are usually a part of the same process."

Given that much of the research related to family therapy has been governed by these traditional assumptions and practices, it is not surprising that it has not had a great impact on the practice of family therapy. Rosman believes it is time for a change: "The model many family therapy researchers use comes from the hard sciences, but even the hard sciences now cannot stick with those models anymore.

Some of their theories about measurement and its relationship to the object being measured have changed, and we haven't caught up with that."

Certainly, many family therapy researchers are well aware of the drawbacks of strict adherence to traditional hard-science assumptions. The issue for the field has become whether we should throw the baby (rigor and clear methodology) out with the bathwater (outdated assumptions and attitudes about understanding reality) or whether we can develop an approach to research that fits better with the systemic assumptions of family therapy.

In an upcoming paper, Gurman presents convincing evidence to support his stance that "traditional research designs and methods are far more compatible with systemic thinking than some observers have suggested." He argues that most psychological researchers are quite aware that their research cannot be completely objective or value-free and that researchers need not be ashamed of linearity when conducting studies of therapeutic outcome. Defending the value of traditional research, Gurman concedes that although "much of the reductionism inherent in psychotherapy research has led all too often to trivialization," we should not conclude that since "we are not capable of seeing the wholes . . . we should stop looking at the parts."

Gurman believes that research usually involves breaking down a phenomenon under study into its component parts. Others are not so sure that we cannot develop methods for looking at larger problems than those encompassed in traditional research. Bradford Keeney, for example, argues that there is "a smorgasbord of paradigms for doing research" and that our bias toward the reductionistic and quantitative paradigm of logical positivism has relegated other methodologies to second- or third-class status. Says Keeney, "My prediction is that people will more and more become aware of different choices regarding research and that research methodology will become research *methodologies*, and that each methodology will be seen as a recipe for constructing a particular reality." Findings furnished by these alternative methodologies might be compared to movies done on the same subject but with different directors and editors. Each movie can have a totally different look conveying different levels of excitement and appreciation of the subject, and leaving the viewer with different levels of understanding and enthusiasm.

IN LARGE PART, THE FUTURE DIRECTION OF FAMILY therapy research will be based on researchers' assessment of our current state of knowledge. Are we now at the point of verifying a body of well-established observations about families and family therapy? Or are we less far along than we would like to think? John Weakland, one of the pioneers in the family field and research associate at the Mental Research Institute in Palo Alto, takes the latter position. "Most researchers and clinicians today are coming on as if we're a long way down the road of understanding and application," says Weakland. "Once we admit that we aren't, we might be less defensive about the differences in our positions. That would make it more possible for researchers to look at things not in terms of 'we have a methodology, let us apply it,' but in terms of 'how do we approach this territory since we're still so little acquainted with it?'"

Weakland compares his work to the Bateson research project and subsequently to "a sort of natural history exploration of the territory rather than 'we know where things are, so let's pin down the facts.' I may be a voice in the wilderness, but what I'm talking about is sitting down and taking a look at something and seeing what you can make of it rather than defining your methods before you know what your problems are."

Weakland believes we need to return attention to the process within both families and therapy. A number of researchers have been exploring this

area. Recently William Pinsof did a review of the quantitative research on the process of family therapy and concluded that this research "has not produced a clear or consistent body of results." He recommends doing more of the same kind of research, suggesting that "researchers need to follow through with more studies of their own and each other's coding systems." In light of Weakland's comments, however, perhaps the problem is not only the quantity but also the kind of research needed.

NEEDLESS TO SAY, THE COURSE OF FUTURE RE-search in the family therapy field will not be determined entirely by philosophical or methodological preferences. Of obvious importance is the money-granting power structure within the mental health field. As Weakland says, "It's damn hard to make a living doing research in this field. . . . If you apply for a research grant, the emphasis is almost always given to what your methodology is, the preference being for 'hard methodology,' i.e., quantification and tests. . . . If you say, 'I've been doing some work in this thing and need some time to observe things,' you are very unlikely to get money. After we were turned down on a couple of proposals from the Brief Therapy Center, we finally came to the conclusion that it is less work to volunteer time than it is to keep beating your head trying to write a proposal that would be accepted."

If the kind of situation Weakland describes is to change, the family therapy field may have to heed the advice of people like Larry Feldman, director of research at the Family Institute of Chicago, who recommends that family therapists make finding money for research a higher priority. His suggestions include lobbying Congress and NIMH for family research money and having national family therapy organizations like the American Association for Marriage and Family Therapy and the American Family Therapy Association set aside more funds for research grants.

RESEARCH: WHY CLINICIANS SHOULD BOTHER WITH IT

Like funding patterns, the university tenure system is a force outside the family therapy profession that will have much to say about the future of family therapy research. As Doug Sprenkle's earlier comment on academic snobbery implies, many of the assistant professors in our field face great constraints on their ability to stray from the "hard methodology." As Michael Berger says, "The kinds of research you can easily get published usually address questions of a different level than those that clinicians need to answer." We are reminded of the Sufi story of the man who lost his key at one street corner but was looking for it at the other corner because the light there was better.

Today much of the funding of traditional forms of research is left to private training institutes not set up to support such activities or to academicians who either have tenure or are in more flexible departments. One noteworthy exception to this trend is the Philadelphia Child Guidance Clinic, where the marriage between research and practice continues to thrive. There researchers and clinicians work closely together to test and explore a well-developed treatment model. Currently under way at the clinic are several large, federally funded projects that contain both descriptive and experimental aspects.

ANY ATTEMPT TO DRAW SOME CONCLUSIONS about the future relationship of family therapy research and practice should first acknowledge some public secrets. First, there will always be clinicians who are technique-mongers, who found the truth in one model of therapy and who cannot or will not think beyond their 25 clinical hours per week (you, obviously, are not one of these, since you are still reading this article). Likewise, there will always be "researchers" who have never watched a family nor spoken to a clinician nor questioned their own methods, assumptions or language (that's not you either, of course). These groups probably will not and should not get together more often.

Fortunately, there also seems to be a growing number of people who are willing to examine non-defensively how they and the field are doing research and practice. They are typically people who are engaged in both research and practice or are in close communication with those who are. (Incidentally, their numbers may be artificially swelling due to Reaganomics; i.e., "pure" researchers are losing their grants and increasingly turning to practice to make a living, and laid-off clinicians are weathering the economic crisis by entering Ph.D. programs. And we thought Reagan was the enemy!)

Also encouraging is the increasing discussion no matter how polemical, among the proponents and interpreters of the various research methodologies, that is gracing our conferences, journals and this magazine with increasing frequency. We on the sidelines of this debate must rise above the level of rabid hockey fans watching a good melee, goading the player on our team to "kick him in the epistemology!" We should look at the contents of each argument and allow ourselves to be perturbed.

But to understand some of the current turmoil and debate within our field, we need to look beyond our own jargon and professional preoccupations. Our current concerns about epistemology and the relationship between research and practice echo a far older conflict, which has been debated through the centuries. It is this fundamental conflict that Hermann Hesse evokes in *Narcissus and Goldmund,* in which one character tells another: "Natures of your kind with strong, delicate senses, the soul-oriented dreamers, poets, lovers are almost always superior to us creatures of the mind. . . . You are endowed with the ability to feel. Whereas, we creatures of reason, we don't live fully; we live in an arid land, even though we often seem to guide and rule you. . . . You are in danger of drowning in the world of the senses, ours is the danger of suffocating in an airless void."

In many of us, intuition and rationality are relatively alienated. The polarization between right and left brains, between yin and yang, which is manifested at many levels of our culture, is no less apparent in our field and in our ideas about research. We must exercise both hemispheres, or we will continue to operate according to "half-brained" ideas.

Fritjof Capra has examined how this duality of reason and intuition has had an impact on every aspect of Western science. He summarizes the duality this way: "The rational and intuitive are complementary modes of functioning of the human mind. Rational thinking is linear, focused and analytic. It belongs to the realm of the intellect, whose function it is to discriminate, measure and categorize. Thus, rational knowledge tends to be fragmented. Intuitive knowledge, on the other hand, is based on a direct, nonintellectual experience of reality arising in an expanded state of awareness. It tends to be synthesizing, holistic and nonlinear."

Clearly, our traditional research methodology provides plenty of exercise for our rationality. We must find, or elevate to higher status, methodologies that unbridle our intuitive side. Donald Kiesler underscores this point: "Research is a multidimensional enterprise requiring diverse talents and approaches, all of which have heuristic value. . . . But if our profession is to implement multidimensional research, we need to stop denigrating all but nomothetic experimental research as we have done in the past."

Recognition of this need to attain a balance between intuition and rationality, subjectivity and objectivity, is appearing in other fields as well. For example, Theodore B. Schwartz, a veteran of many empirical, quantitative, experimental medical studies, wrote recently: "Is it not possible that the discredited techniques of introspection, reexamined in a modern setting, could be shown to compare favorably with cumbersome, expensive and still less than perfect, controlled clinical trials? Perhaps in time there will emerge sophisticated introspectionists, who, like expert wine tasters, will provide valid guidelines in assessing the efficacy of treatment in studies where subjective responses are being assessed."

Thus examination of our own "subjective" experiences may be a useful and underexplored avenue of research. Bradford Keeney believes that our current interest in theory and assumptions will lead to a form of epistemological research concerned with tracing the patterns of one's own thinking.

To examine experiences, we must first have them, but taking the effort and risks necessary in doing so can be a stumbling block. For example, how many of us are willing to taste the wine of family therapy and go with our own family into treatment for the good of the field? Still, further examinations of our experiences with our own families and with the families we treat may offer an important focus for future research. Instead of looking at other people's families and responses, it may be time to begin looking more closely at our own.

Such research would bring family therapy more in line with other social sciences, such as anthropology, which value methods that include the researcher as a participant in the process being studied. This approach is dramatically illustrated by the controversial research of Carlos Castaneda in his books on the Mexican shaman Don Juan and, perhaps closer to home, the work of such skilled observers as Erving Goffman on psychiatric institutions and Jules Henry on schizophrenic families.

Disciplined observation was also the focus for the work of Richard Bandler and John Grinder, which (according to Keeney) Gregory Bateson considered to be "the finest contribution to clinical research in the past decade." Bandler and Grinder used the linguistic model of transformational grammar to study the extraordinary effectiveness of such master therapists as Virginia Satir, Fritz Perls and Milton Erickson. And yet, because the work of Bandler and Grinder was not methodologically traditional, it is not usually thought of as research.

The procedure Bandler and Grinder used was exhaustively to observe taped therapy sessions of these masters, concentrating on repeated patterns in their interactions with clients and noticing in which contexts these patterns occurred. The model of transformational grammar served as a guide to help Bandler and Grinder know what to look for and to organize what they saw. At the same time, their approach was flexible enough to permit the discovery of unexpected patterns. According to Robert Dilts, who was instrumental in the research of Bandler and Grinder, this "modeling" method has been shown to be an effective technique for identifying essential patterns of competency in a variety of skill areas, from learning to spell to the designing of video games. Through this kind of nontraditional research, the abilities of highly competent people, in any field, can more effectively be passed along to others.

It may be that in the years ahead, various nontraditional research methods will be elevated in status, and more time, energy and money will be devoted to pursuing them. In the meantime, however, it is important for clinicians to realize that they are doing valuable research every time they enter a therapy session, form a hypothesis about a family, or try out an intervention. Don Keisler emphasizes this point: "The very practice, then, of psychotherapy is a scientific event encapsulating the application, whether systematic or not, of scientific methodology to the single case."

But it is also important to remember that our intuitions represent only partial realities and, where possible and appropriate, should be corroborated by quantified tests and studies testing out previous findings. We should heed John Weakland's caveat and try not to skip steps on the path to wisdom by preoccupying ourselves with the complex business of measurement and hypothesis testing before we have discovered what we are looking for. We need to develop and celebrate a variety of research methodologies so that, like a cameraman with a zoom lens, we can move in and out between the forest and the trees.

We agree with Alan Gurman that there is much of value in the systemic adaptations of the reigning research methodology, but disagree with those who believe it is sufficient by itself and inherently superior to any others. In this position we are joined by Fritjof Capra, who argues that "Descartes' method of thought and his view of nature have influenced all branches of modern science and can still be useful today. But they will be useful only if their limitations are recognized . . . Reductionism and holism, analysis and synthesis, are complementary approaches, that, used in proper balance, help us obtain a deeper knowledge of life."

In summary, we believe that the field has reached another turning point in its history where, unlike Edward Bear, it is taking the time to stop bumping. The assumptions that have separated research and practice are being questioned. Although challenging to some traditional beliefs, we predict that this questioning will enhance the family therapy field.

RICHARD SCHWARTZ, PH.D., *is the coordinator of research at the Family Systems Program of the Institute for Juvenile Research in Chicago, IL.*

DOUGLAS BREUNLIN, M.S.S.A., *is on the staff of the Family Institute of Chicago.*

See references, page 566.

It is worth looking at . . . what new metaphors are emerging today from the vast numbers of families inventing new ways of being, for we are increasing our stock of models, as well as changing or abandoning old ones.

MARY CATHERINE BATESON

PHOTOGRAPH BY ELI REED/MAGNUM

PHOTOGRAPH BY J. ROSS BAUGHMAN/VISIONS

PHOTOGRAPH BY POLLY BROWN/ACTUALITY

PHOTOGRAPH BY JENNIFER BISHOP/ACTUALITY

Defining Our Task

PHILOSOPHY AND ETHICS IN PSYCHOTHERAPY

PHOTOGRAPH FROM GEORGETOWN FAMILY CENTER

FAMILY THERAPY'S NEGLECTED PROPHET

A PROFILE OF MURRAY BOWEN

By Mary Sykes Wylie

AT HIS FINAL PUBLIC APPEARANCE TWO DAYS before he died last October, Murray Bowen was obviously very ill. Shrunken and frail, he sat hunched in his chair before an audience of 800 people at the annual conference of the American Association for Marriage and Family Therapy (AAMFT), hardly able to breathe even with an oxygen tube, his voice raspy and faint. Nonetheless, he looked out at the packed room with glittering, almost defiant eyes, as if to say, "However sick, however fragile I appear, I am still very much *here*."

Every person in the room, certainly almost all 5,000 conference attendees and probably every family therapist practicing in America, uses or at least knows about the theory Bowen developed and the terms he invented. The concepts of differentiation of self, family emotional systems, triangles, emotional cutoffs, the family projection process, sibling positions and the multigenerational transmission process have been woven into the fabric of the field. "Bowen was the intellectual beacon for everyone who was first trying to understand the family," says Braulio Montalvo, who together with Salvador

Minuchin helped create structural family therapy in the early 1960s. "Almost every major concept in family therapy can be traced back to him. He taught everybody." Yet Bowen looked out at the crowd honoring him at AAMFT as if he believed that whatever his influence, however many among them called themselves "Bowenians," the vast majority had completely missed the point; they hadn't really understood what he was saying at all.

Bowen had always been something of a loner, never in the mainstream of pragmatic, problem-oriented family therapy practitioners. Since the earliest days of his career, he had considered family therapy a by-product of the vast new theory of human behavior that he believed it was his real mission to develop. Toward the end of his life, he had denounced family therapy for its intellectual vacuity and dismissed it as an "evolutionary misadventure" doomed to extinction.

At this last meeting, he let the audience know that he had not changed his views one whit to suit the Tower of Babel that family therapy had become. "When you know you're right, you're right, and you stand there, and you say so," he said. He still believed that theory—by which he meant a comprehensive set of interlocking principles accounting for the entire range of human behavior and its evolutionary origins—was "more important than anything else" for understanding families and that a way of thinking, rather than a set of techniques, was the legacy he wanted to leave behind. But the "way of thinking"—the theory—was being lost as the field continued moving in the wrong direction.

The story of family therapy, as Bowen saw it in his last years, was not so much about a great cause betrayed as about a golden opportunity carelessly abandoned. The promise of the field's early years had collapsed into a heap of shattered expectations, the chance for a new science of human nature lost in the torrents of marketable new therapy techniques. And Bowen himself resembled a neglected prophet who had offered his vision of truth like a priceless gem, only to see the herd sniff it and stampede off in other directions. It was true that most therapists who borrowed this or that of his concepts had little interest in the whole theory behind them. Yet few could understand his disillusionment with the field that had, after all, raised him to its pantheon of eight or 10 semilegendary "master therapists."

BOWEN'S ALOOFNESS WAS NOT ENTIRELY UNusual for an original thinker. To some extent, each of the master therapists—Nathan Ackerman, Don Jackson, Jay Haley, Salvador Minuchin, Virginia Satir, Carl Whitaker—has stood alone; all innovators and pioneers explore new territory ahead of the pack. But Bowen's preoccupation with discovering a new science of human behavior—an overarching *natural systems* theory—set him apart from the other pathbreakers of the field. He thought that all (except Jackson) were far more interested in therapy than theory. Whatever new theoretical insights they acquired were incidental to their practice; they were all primarily clinicians, healers, not

scientists or researchers, as he thought of himself. They may have been master therapists, but they weren't master thinkers—by his lights, anyway.

For someone considered by many to be the most magisterial presence in the field, Bowen wrote relatively little—50 articles and a 1978 book, *Family Therapy in Clinical Practice*, a collection of previously published papers and articles. Nonetheless, his status as a founding father is secure. Before Bowen, early family thinkers like Ackerman and Whitaker "ingeniously tried to stretch psychoanalytic theory to fit around families," says Robert Aylmer, a Bowen student and director of LifeCycle Learning Center in Newton, Massachusetts. "Bowen was the first to realize you can't translate individual psychoanalytic concepts into the language of families, and the first to see the family as a structure in itself, which had its own wiring." The family, in short, wasn't just a collection of mutually influential but separate psyches living together under the same roof. For Freud, unconscious motivation was the unperceived prime mover of intellectual and emotional life; for Bowen, the submerged ebb and flow of family life, the simultaneous push and pull between family members for both distance and togetherness, was the driving force underlying all human behavior.

While Bowen did not invent systems thinking, he was the first to conceptualize the family as a *natural* system—more like an ant colony or an elephant herd than most people cared to admit—that could only be fully understood in terms of the fluid but predictable process between members. Such a major part of the official family therapy canon have Bowen's ideas about the family system become that it is almost impossible to imagine the field without him. He did more than give intellectual legitimacy to the scruffy, make-do empiricism of family therapy. In large part, he created the field's intellectual scaffolding, gave it the conceptual structure that distinguishes it as a system of thought and a discipline from all other psychotherapies.

Furthermore, Bowen introduced a highly novel form of family therapy based on one family member's researching and coming to terms with his or her own family of origin. Unlike most family or individual therapists, Bowen conceived personal growth and family interaction as part of an indivisible whole, creating a therapy that involved both the self of the individual and the multiple relations in the family.

Finally, Bowen gave family therapists a new way to know themselves. "He transformed the psychoanalytic process of finding yourself into something particularly appropriate for family therapy," says Carl Whitaker. "He showed family therapists a way they could look at themselves and their own lives, analogous to Freud's self-analysis, and bring that awareness into their work." Bowen, alone, made it a critical point that therapists differentiate themselves from their own families before trying to help others do the same.

Bowen's ideas have been used to improve the functioning of businesses, religious congregations and other organizations; applied to ethnic, cultural, economic and gender issues; and synthesized with object-relations and other psychodynamic models. But none of these variations on his orthodoxy gave Bowen any pleasure. "He wasn't very happy with what most of us were doing," says Philip Guerin, a former student of Bowen's and now director of the Center for Family Learning in Rye, New York. "He was an absolutist who saw much of what we did as divergent—going too far from the original, and watering down the core concepts." For Bowen, therapy was of a single cloth with his entire theory; tear out this or that piece and the whole tapestry became a tattered rag. "He was not a religious man," remembers one therapist, "but you are forced to use religious terms when describing his view of theory. It wasn't just a practical, useful aid to therapy; it was critical in itself and had an almost Platonic quality, as if Pure Ideas were the essential reality."

In the rough give-and-take of family therapy, which often resembles a football scrimmage more than it does a Socratic dialogue, Bowen was something of an anachronism. It was as if the intellectual messiness of these new, hybrid therapies reflected a failure to think coherently, a failure of rationality that only reinforced the general state of emotional chaos in the world. According to Bowen, therapists should not encourage people to wallow in emotionalism and muzzy confusion but should teach them to transcend it by setting examples as reasonable, neutral, self-controlled adults. Therapy should be, in fact, just like a Socratic dialogue, with the teacher, or "coach," calmly asking questions until the student learned to think for him- or herself. Defending his own principles, however, Bowen was far from dispassionate; always a steadfast critic of social conformity and orthodoxy, he became a zealous and, some would say, dogmatic defender of his own faith. In his dedication to creating an objective science of human nature, he became something of a visionary pilgrim seeking his own Zion.

BOWEN OFTEN DESCRIBED AN INCIDENT THAT occurred when he was 15 years old. His large extended family had lived in a rural pocket of Tennessee since before the American Revolution, and his maternal grandfather had established, in the town of Waverly, where he was born, a funeral home and ambulance service, which his father and uncle inherited. Bowen remembered working as a helper on the ambulance and, one day, taking an unconscious teenage girl to a university hospital. All afternoon he watched the frenzy in the emergency room while fumbling doctors made frantic attempts to save her. After she died, Bowen later remembered, he decided that medicine must be better than this, and he determined to have a part in making it so.

The memory of those highly trained doctors rushing around in ignorance, fear and helplessness seemed to encapsulate for the adult Bowen a basic human dilemma: the overwhelming power of primal emotion over so-called rational life. Like Freud before him, he thought that human intelligence and reason ran short of human conceit about them. "Far more human activity," he wrote in 1975, "is governed by man's emotional system than he has been willing to admit, and there is far more similarity than dissimilarity between the 'dance of life' in lower forms and the 'dance of life' in human forms."

That terrible scene in the emergency room, playing in his memory, would convince him that if he were to be of use as a doctor, it was not enough to be a sympathetic, detached observer—as he had been then. He must have a plan, a system, a theory, even an entire worldview that would not fail to guide him when he cared for his own patients. But what had begun as a worthwhile, though not unusual, goal for any bright, idealistic young man who wanted to be of use to the world, evolved for Bowen into a far more consuming mission.

During the course of his journey through medicine and psychiatry, Bowen pursued knowledge like a starving hunter after elusive game. He read Freud, Darwin, works on the biological, physical and social sciences, not for pleasure or education or even career but with dogged determination to find some underlying truth, a hidden network of connection that he believed *must* bind the millions of disparate facts of the physical universe into one overarching system. He had believed, he said late in life, that his ideas would eventually "supersede the current ways of thinking" about human nature and that a truly scientific theory would encompass all of life, from the protoplasm constituting each individual cell all the way to the most complicated interactions of human beings. The science he had in mind would "connect living matter with the universe, the sun, the earth, and all living things . . . the seasons, the tides, [all] natural phenomena."

In search of this grail, however, Bowen made many stops along the way, including medical school,

surgical and psychiatric training (the two had more in common during the 1930s and 1940s than they do now), and a stint in the Army during World War II. After the war, Bowen went to the Menninger Clinic in Topeka, Kansas—then famous for its radical psychoanalytic approach to major psychiatric illnesses. Bowen was exhilarated to be part of an intellectual revolution that promised to transform human civilization, and excited to be working with Karl Menninger, the most eminent psychoanalyst in the United States. "If I had a model of a person," said Bowen in his last interview, "it was Karl Menninger." In the heady atmosphere of a new psychiatric world order, Bowen joined the band of devoted, zealous Menningerites and committed himself to furthering the cause of psychoanalysis.

At that time, some of the best and the brightest young psychiatrists were drawn to the intriguing, so-far-insoluble problem of schizophrenia, and Bowen thought he might find clues to the etiology of the disease by studying the family within a psychoanalytic perspective. At that time, about the only psychoanalytic idea relating schizophrenia to the family at all was Frieda Fromm-Reichman's concept of the "schizophrenogenic mother," a needy, insecure woman whose aggressiveness and smothering overprotectiveness made her child ill. In 1951, in order to study *in vitro* the relationship between the schizophrenogenic mother and her child, Bowen set up a cottage at Menninger's where both mother and disturbed offspring could live together, and in 1952 he included a few fathers in his study. Even so, the focus of treatment was the "disease" assumed to exist within the individual patient's mind.

Initially infatuated by psychoanalysis, Bowen was, within a few years, annoyed by the lack of scientific precision in its language—its dependence upon what he called subjective "feeling" concepts like id, ego, superego and Oedipus and Electra complexes that were drawn from literature and mythology, rather than objective physical facts. Besides his dissatisfaction with analytic theory, his growing interest in the family—the dynamics between family members rather than within the individual psyches of each—was putting him at odds with the Menninger establishment. As Bowen remembered it, his first presentation of his family work (much of which he had been doing at night and on the weekends) was greeted politely by the staff, with the tactful suggestion that perhaps his interest in families represented an unresolved oedipal problem in his own life. Perhaps he should work harder on his own analysis. After his second and third presentations, his colleagues made no bones about their displeasure. In effect, Bowen said, "they told me, 'You're sick, you'd better do something about it.'"

No doubt, he was getting some flack for his unorthodox interests, but Arthur Mandelbaum, then director of social work at Menninger's, suggests that there was something overclose and cloying about the atmosphere at the clinic that made Bowen restive as well. "It wasn't so much that his ideas were frowned upon—you could bring in new ideas as long as you didn't flaunt them. But there was a general spirit of intense loyalty to Dr. Karl and the Menninger family itself that made him feel somewhat enmeshed. Bowen had a kind of love-hate relationship with the foundation. He admired its high standards, liked the intellectual challenge, and thought he had learned a lot from working as part of a team—the team concept was very much advocated there. But he felt even then a great need to separate himself, to differentiate himself from the intense personal loyalties of the group. He was a very independent man, with real pioneer spirit, and he needed to spread his wings more than he felt he could there."

In retrospect, what Bowen would call his "eight damn years at Menninger's" contributed to his deep suspicion of groupiness and a work environment that purported to be "just like family." The forces for togetherness that seemed to oppose his individual

exploration were already perhaps too much like a family, too likely to quash the individual spirit in the interests of family unity. "About 1950," he wrote in 1988, "there was a continuing deep feeling within me, which said, 'If I ever come to know precisely what I think about psychiatry, and I have the courage to say it in open forum, I will be kicked out of the profession.'"

At the time, Bowen was both collecting evidence for his embryonic theory of differentiation and creating a personal self, a kind of serene Faust who is free and unafraid to strive for knowledge and mastery because he has risen above what he later called "the emotional togetherness that binds us all." But a person trying to do just that, Bowen decided, inevitably stirs up anxiety and opposition in the group, which wants to maintain a sense of unity and common identity at almost any cost. So Bowen took the differentiating step of following his own inclinations, and began looking around for a workplace that would not stand so much in his way.

He settled in 1954 at the newly organized National Institute of Mental Health (NIMH) in Washington, D.C., at the time a kind of heretic's heaven for bright, young nonconformists. According to family research pioneer Lyman Wynne, who had come to NIMH in 1952, "Murray was only one of a number of mavericks there. Almost everybody was on the outs with the orthodox psychoanalytic establishment of the time, and anybody interested in the family who paid much attention to analysis was considered a kind of enemy. It was all very loose and lively, and you could do whatever you wanted as long as it was interesting."

When Bowen first arrived at NIMH, he continued studying schizophrenia but soon found the original schizophrenogenic mother theory inadequate to describe what he was seeing. For one thing, the intense emotional attachment between mother and child was supposed to be fixed, rigid and essentially unchanging from day to day, month to month, year to year. What Bowen observed was a fluid, mobile relationship, a constant cyclical transfer of anxiety from mother to child and back again, with functioning predictably deteriorating in one as it improved in the other.

Furthermore, Bowen and his colleagues were beginning to suspect that the ghastly duet between mother and child might actually be a trio, or "interdependent triad," of mother, father and schizophrenic offspring. So Bowen began bringing fathers, and then healthy siblings, onto the ward along with mother and sick child. Eventually the NIMH researchers were studying four entire families living in the hospital, as well as several other families living at home.

For Bowen, the next few years would provide one revelation after another, not only about schizophrenic families, but about healthy ones as well. For example, he had noticed that the members of the families he studied all appeared to be constantly in the process of forming and dissolving triangular alliances with one another. In each of the research families this "triangle" comprised a very close, virtually fused relationship between dominating, active mother and her impaired child, while the odd man out was usually the distant, passive husband. At moments of severe stress, however, the father and child might align with each other against the mother, who would then try to triangle in another person to take her side, perhaps the sick child's sibling or a staff member.

In spite of what Bowen called the "flow and counterflow" within the triangles, the members of these families experienced very little sense of freedom and independence. Indeed, there was an almost gluelike quality about these family conglomerates that was, to Bowen, practically a definition of their problem. The less the dysfunctional child was able to separate from her mother—to "differentiate" herself from what he called the "undifferentiated family ego mass"—the less capable she was of independent,

adult behavior and the "crazier" she became. He found this same process true, though less marked, in healthier families as well.

By 1955 Bowen also began investigating the multigenerational origins of schizophrenia, based on the suggestion of a colleague that the disease required three generations to develop. It seemed to Bowen that emotional disturbance was not only a precisely definable relationship pattern (instead of an individual pathology), but it was also very like an evolutionary process, with origins deep in the history of the family. The pattern of emotional development in more "normal" families evolved in exactly the same way; the level of maturity and independence in any one person was the product of many generations.

Within a few years of arriving at NIMH, Bowen had crystallized the main concepts of his theory of family systems. He had defined the family emotional system, fusion and the differentiation of self. He had concluded that the triangle was the "molecule or the basic building block of any emotional system"—including extended family networks, friendships and organizational affiliations. And he had hypothesized that the emotional processes in families extended over many generations. All in all, he had the main building blocks of a new descriptive framework for understanding human psychology, based not on the presumed psychodynamic circuitry within each individual but on the invisible yet living, vibrating, almost palpable web between people. Little wonder that he no longer visualized the family as three or four discrete individual ids, egos and superegos but as "a single organism."

During these years, along with the Bowen theory, the peculiar Bowen persona—part philosopher-scientist, part Zen master and part secret agent—began to emerge. At NIMH, according to colleagues, he didn't talk much about what he was doing, and appeared to cultivate an air of distant superiority. "Murray was always very mysterious, very oblique about what he was doing," says Lyman Wynne, who remembers Bowen as something of a guru figure, appearing both aloof and knowing, as if he had a secret the others weren't ready to hear.

Bowen drew around him a close circle of about five coworkers no more eager than himself to join the vociferous debates about philosophy, theory, technique and the meaning of mental illness that were meat and drink to the other Young Turks at NIMH. "He aroused intense personal loyalty from those on his team," remembers Wynne. "They talked about his work as if it were something very special, very exciting, but never shared much of it with the rest of the staff. I wanted to know him better, because I liked his ideas and wanted to hear more about them. But unless I became a member of his group, I knew I wouldn't hear about them."

In meetings Bowen "had a habit of remaining silent until nearly the end of the period, by which time everybody was waiting breathlessly for his pronouncements," according to Wynne. After a dramatic pause, he would make his brief utterance, and there would be a kind of sigh, "as if the gospel had just been spoken." Wynne believes Bowen may have been trying to differentiate himself from the family ego mass of NIMH, just as he had done at Menninger's, paradoxically by creating what looked like his own little family ego mass. Years later, Salvador Minuchin would agree that Bowen was something of a "puzzle," who "responded to questions with a mysterious smile and seemed satisfied to leave the responsibility of interpreting his smile to the other." On the other hand, says Wynne, "I think he was very shy."

Bowen complained often during his career that his theories were misunderstood or ignored because most therapists were too emotionally bound to the "family of family therapists" and their traditional therapeutic ideologies to hear what he was saying. But part of the problem was his own difficulty bringing his soaring vision down to earth. Not only

did people find the concepts foreign—a systems view of human nature is even now as hard to grasp as psychoanalytic ideas were a century ago—but they found the formal style of his papers and presentations off-putting.

Particularly in his writing, Bowen used words in a hyperrational, idiosyncratic way, combining psychological and biological terms in an odd hybrid language that many found affected and stuffy. His determinedly neutral, "scientific" style, even when writing about personal events in his own life, sometimes produced curious results. For example, his epilogue to *Family Evaluation*, by Michael Kerr, which is about himself and his odyssey, is written entirely in the third person and is, according to one critic, "an autobiographical piece with no person in it, a theory moving through time with no person attached."

By 1957 Bowen's days at NIMH were numbered. As Bowen remembered it, he was seeing at NIMH the kind of shortsighted pragmatism that would dog him most of his life. Bowen believed that he was on the track of an entirely new theory of human behavior. But his superiors wanted something less visionary and more concrete; they wanted a "cure" for the "disease" of schizophrenia. The harder Bowen lobbied for his big theory, the more he experienced delays in funding, restrictions on his space, and not-so-subtle pressures to shift his work away from his vast, evolutionary-psychological schemes to more practical matters.

Ironically, just as Bowen's ship was foundering at NIMH, a family therapy movement was rumbling to life around the country. Bowen at first viewed this movement with cautious gratification. He thought that from this "healthy, unstructured state of chaos," an awareness might emerge of the theoretical breakthroughs made possible by the new family systems viewpoint. To his chagrin, however, the floods of new recruits were generally uninterested in the higher rewards of pure theory, but avid in their pursuit of new, practical therapeutic techniques presented by the score at every meeting.

In 1958 Bowen found a new sanctuary in the Department of Psychiatry of Georgetown University's School of Medicine. At last he had a mandate to "work on a theory that moved toward the sciences, rather than the 'therapies' that were so responsive to the media and popular approval." There he established around himself a dedicated group of trainees who volunteered their time to learning and using Bowen theory in their own work.

While Bowen built his small kingdom at Georgetown, he was also working on the larger empire of himself, struggling to achieve the kind of independent personal and professional identity that he described in his theory. To this point, he had assembled his ideas, but he had not yet been able to integrate them into a seamless whole. It was as if he had written what he knew was an epic poem, but the stanzas were still mixed up, and he did not yet know, from the inside of his own cells, what their final order would be. He *did* know that the way out of the labyrinth would be his idea of the differentiation of self.

T O BOWEN, DIFFERENTIATION OF SELF MEANT THE ability of an individual to separate emotionally from the undifferentiated family ego mass—to achieve independence and maturity without losing the capacity for free emotional connection. He concluded that the emotional problems in families were directly proportional to the sway members' feelings had over their ability to think. The more undifferentiated they were, the more they fell into the category of "no-selfs" or "pseudo-selfs"—people whose insecurity and emotional neediness forced them to give up individuality in exchange for love and acceptance. More differentiated, "thinking-oriented" people, on the other hand, were far more secure about their identity, free to pursue meaningful goals and engage in close relationships (without fear of smoth-

ering), and were usually more successful in every area of life.

The process of achieving greater self-differentiation, however, even for the relatively intact, was very difficult. A person's basic level of differentiation was the product of several generations and could not be altered in a few weeks. For this reason, Bowen took the long view of both theory and therapy. Differentiating oneself from one's family required not only understanding entrenched and complex patterns of family interaction, but acquiring the skill, patience and self-control to talk directly with one's most intimate relatives without blowing up, giving in, going crazy or running away.

Bowen had seen his ideas work with client families. He had made progress differentiating himself within his profession. He had even had some small success clarifying his relationship with his parents. But he had never really tackled the entrenched triangles of his whole family, a process that would require him not only to enter the lion's den but also to throw rocks from close range at an entire pride of sleeping lions. The opportunity for this daring adventure came in late 1966, when a distant relative of Bowen's died, and Bowen began making plans to return home in February 1967.

Bowen had spent years tracing the genealogy of emotional patterns in families, including his own, in an effort to help himself and others extricate themselves from the emotional quicksands of family life. But if it is impossible for anyone to emerge completely from the family ooze, Bowen's own family presented a particularly formidable obstacle to differentiation. Not only was Bowen's family large, but he claimed that his father knew all 15,000 souls in the county, by looks if not by name. He once tested his father, he said, by asking him if he knew a strange boy standing at a distance. No, he didn't know the boy's name, Bowen's father said—had never seen him—but he knew whose son he was by the way he walked and the (continued on page 223)

The Man Who Never Explained Himself

And I won't miss his moods / His gloomy solitudes / His brash, abrasive style
But please don't get me wrong / He was the best to come along / In a long, long—while
(Lyrics from the Broadway musical *Pippin*)

BOWEN ENTERED MY LIFE ON A SUMMER DAY IN 1967, AS A GEORGETOWN PROFESSOR WHO LEC-tured to the second-year psychiatry residents during our rotation at the university hospital. As a lecturer, his constant focus on theory created a dryness that left something to be desired, but there were rare times when he would take on the fire of a Southern evangelist passionately spreading the gospel of differentiation in his mesmerizing Tennessee accent. That day his message to the residents was provocative and clear: "You people are among the brighter ones on the planet. Trouble is, you think you have all the answers, when you haven't even found the questions yet." Having challenged our arrogance, he went on to share a portion of his own professional history. He spoke of his days at the Menninger Clinic, his 13 years of personal training analysis, his research on schizophrenia, and how the more he attempted to explain his new theories, the more he was in trouble with his peers and mentors. From that last experience, he developed a philosophy to which he firmly adhered: Operate from your principles, and never explain yourself. In 23 years of Bowen-watching, I never heard him explain himself once. That summer day, his message began a process that would change the course of my professional life.

Two months later, I asked Bowen to supervise me on an individual psychotherapy case that I wanted to convert into a family case. He said he wasn't interested in family therapy anymore but was now trying out some of Ross Speck and Carolyn Attneave's methods of family networking with schizophrenia. If I were interested in that and found a suitable case, he would supervise me a couple of times a month. My response was to convert the case I had mentioned into a family network experiment. The supervision consisted of 13 meetings during a nine-month period, plus attendance at a networking meeting that Bowen himself was doing once a month. During those nine months of supervision, he never once told me what to do in the meetings of my network. Instead, he would listen, pad in lap, playing with his pen, frequently reaching into his coat pocket for another cigarette. When he did speak, he would tell long, involved stories of his work with schizophrenia. The moral of these stories was always the same; it had to do with the intensity and power of the emotional process in schizophrenia and how only a few people could face up to it without "getting caught" by its power and behaving like anxious robots. Bowen believed that schizophrenia was the "great teacher" and that an essential ingredient in becoming a competent psychotherapist was having the experience of wrestling with its power.

By the following spring, I had decided to leave the residency at Georgetown to take a position as chief resident at Albert Einstein College of Medicine in New York. During my first year in New York, I commuted back to Washington once a month in order to continue my contact with Bowen. The first Thursday evening of each month, I would leave New York and head for Washington. By 6:30 Friday morning, I was at Bowen's house, ready to drive him to the Medical College of Virginia in Richmond for a day of watching him work with families.

The rides to Richmond and back were often the most enlightening parts of the day. Having access to his considerable experience and his unique wisdom was the gold, but the rich ore had to be sifted from the dysthymia and the disillusionment of a prophet undervalued in his time. On the return trip, I would pick at theory, especially as it related to my family of origin, and practice detriangulating. Bowen would sleep, smoke, speak of his beloved Redskins and even, at times, get personal. On one return trip, he informed me that there was no rush to get back because his wife was attending a play at the National Theatre that evening. I chided him as to why he wasn't going as well and how he shouldn't be so phobic of togetherness. In typical fashion, he snorted and said that as far as he was concerned, plays were nothing more than "faked emotional systems."

Another highlight of those times was the annual Georgetown Family Symposium. Every fall, alumni of the Family Training Program would converge on Georgetown for the annual homecoming weekend. Instead of a football game against the Baltimore Psychiatric Institute, each graduate would compete to demonstrate the latest and the best twists that had been given to Bowen's theory. A guest lecturer was also invited. The finale would be the most recent wisdom of the master. It was a wonderful refueling ritual.

One year Nathan Ackerman, who was that symposium's featured guest speaker, asked me if I would allow a "poor old man" one question. "Explain to me, if you can," he said, "how a cold fish like Bowen, who is so afraid of his own feelings, attracts such a large cadre of loyal sons?" The astutely observant Ackerman was somehow puzzled by the way his own dominant and emotionally pursuant temperament evoked a response of distance from so many of his professional children, while Bowen's almost mystical aloofness seemed to encourage discipleship.

Bowen's favorite stories about Ackerman always centered on a game they played in which Ackerman, often in front of large audiences, would prod Bowen to express his feelings more freely, especially his anger. Bowen would respond by telling the story of his favorite Menninger patient, a person with a world-class talent for provoking anger in others. Bowen related that on leaving Menninger's, he expressed a wish to take the patient with him so that he (Bowen) could become the best person in the world at not being provoked to anger.

Family therapists have wondered for years about Bowen's lack of expressed emotion. Was it that he didn't believe in the value of expressed emotion and therefore was uncomfortable with it? Or was it that he was uncomfortable with it and therefore made up a principle to minimize its expression in his presence? Bowen's goal was always to get people to speak factually about their feelings without the surrounding capsule of anxiety, which he believed produced reactivity in others.

Whatever his personal allergy to the "stickiness" of expressed emotion, Bowen could stand tall in the midst of the thickest jungle of intense emotion and anxiety, somehow connect with the person or people experiencing it, and by his own calmness, calm them and lead them out into the clearing.

How did he connect? He listened. He respected people, their intelligence and their personal boundaries. His questions, which accounted for more than 90 percent of his communications, at once let people know that they were being heard, while giving them the simultaneous experience of his wisdom and his strength. He believed that pushing people to express feelings did two things: produce distorted or pseudoemotional responses and retard movement toward differentiation and improved functioning. By his fact-focused questions, he hoped to prod people's thinking about important issues and events. If he was successful, anxiety would be lowered and an undistorted flow of expressed emotion would occur. The patient was thereby offered the opportunity of an experience in distinguishing between thinking and feeling systems. The purpose of each of these steps was to produce a flow of movement toward differentiation.

From 1973, when the Center for Family Learning was founded, my contact with Bowen remained consistent. He came once a year to the center as a visiting professor in our postgraduate training program. His teaching time was divided between a formal lecture and a case consultation. His interviews were superb to watch, at least for those who knew his theory and could track what he was doing clinically. The question-and-answer periods that followed his interviews would be filled with his preacher stories of clinical encounters from different times and distant places.

One interview stands out in my mind. The patient was a woman in her early thirties who desperately wanted a baby but was fearful that her parents' concentration-camp experience might produce a genetically defective child. During the consultation Bowen asked the question, "How in the world would you explain that?" more than 20 times. In response to his questions, the woman wove a fascinating tale of intense anxiety permeating the family, cutoffs from the extended family driven by an argument over the distribution of restitution money that the family had received from Germany, distance in her marriage, and her anxious overfunctioning for a younger sister. At one point in describing her relationship with her family of origin, she spoke of "feeling like we were all wrapped in one skin." Bowen smiled, appearing just a little stunned, and told the woman she had "a beautiful problem." It was as if his concept of the "undifferentiated ego mass" had been reborn, live and on videotape.

Near the end of the session, in a grandfatherly way, he placed a hard candy in his mouth, raised the index finger of his right hand, and said, "Let me share a few thoughts." Bowen told her that her anxiety about potential genetically defective offspring was more "psychological than real" and that he thought that if she decided to have a baby, "everything would work itself out okay." He encouraged her not to take her husband's distance so personally and to make a project of getting out of the overresponsible position with her sister by giving responsibility for her sibling back to her parents. Most members of the audience that day were amused by his description of the "beautiful problem." Some thought he was turned on by the very attractive person he was interviewing, but those who knew Bowen realized he was invigorated by her validation of his theory.

The last three years of Bowen's life were often painful for those who loved and respected him. The stress of increasing infirmity amplified his irascibility. Some would have preferred his fading from the scrutiny of public appearances. But Bowen didn't believe in lying down or giving in before the time had come, certainly not in response to someone else's discomfort. Clearly, he had decided that the time had come in early October 1990. At the annual meeting of the American Association for Marriage and Family Therapy, he chose to say good-bye as he had lived, on a stage, preaching his theory with his last available breath.

When I heard of his death, I reflected back to one of his visits in the early 1980s. Bowen had spoken of the family emotional system and cancer. Blanche Kaplan, one of our faculty members, commented after Bowen's presentation, "I finally got the message. If you're differentiated enough, you won't die." On October 9, 1990, however, the master of differentiation proved Blanche to be wrong.

People like Bowen, calm in the absolute assurance of their truth, provide us with an emotional anchor, an object of constancy. When they die, only those parts of them that we have incorporated into ourselves remain. Bowen's ideas, his clinical work, his dedication to values, have made a difference to the many people whose lives were touched by him, directly or indirectly. For those people, for at least a little while, when someone says "Bowen," it will matter. □

—Philip Guerin
MARCH 1991

PHILIP GUERIN, M.D., *is the director of the Center for Family Learning in Rye Brook, NY.*

(continued from page 218) expression on his face.

Most people in his family, Bowen was proud to say, had "left their tracks wherever they went," certainly in Humphreys County, where family businesses included a farm, a store (selling, among other items, furniture and coffins), two funeral homes, a tin shop and other concerns amounting to one whole block of downtown Waverly, Tennessee (pop. 1,000), of which his father—a "go-getter," said Bowen—had also been mayor for 18 years.

Though of old Protestant stock, the Bowen family was no longer particularly religious, and yet they were immersed in an ethic of hard work, personal responsibility and self-motivation of which the Puritans would have approved. In such a family of nonstop overachievers, Bowen, as "an overresponsible oldest son" of a father who was "an only child who has functioned as a responsible oldest" and a mother who was "a responsible oldest daughter" of a "responsible oldest son," must have grown up feeling, well, *responsible* for leaving *his* tracks as well.

Making it even harder to differentiate from such a large, close-knit and overpowering kin network, Bowen's family was remarkably stable and congenial. No alcoholism, divorce, suicide, and not much overt conflict ruffled the waters of a rural family that might have been painted by Norman Rockwell. Why would one even want to differentiate from such an ideal, all-American family?

Bowen never discussed how his family background motivated his personal and professional interests; he would have objected to such a traditional, psychodynamic perspective. "The idea to differentiate came from his theory," says Joan Winter, director of the Family Institute of Virginia in Richmond. Says Winter, who spent many hours interviewing Bowen, "That was the lens through which he viewed everything. He thought all families were pretty much the same—the patterns he was describing were universal, and fusion wasn't just something that happened to 'pathological' families—he figured his own

relatively healthy family would be a good lab for testing his ideas. Besides, he had better access to them."

The death of a kinsman in late 1966 gave him an opportunity to put his theory to practice in his own family. Bowen decided to go back to Tennessee and, applying his new understanding of triangles, engage in a short, intense, all-out campaign for his own differentiation of self. Taking advantage of the shock waves of anxiety the death sent through his family of origin, which he believed made them more vulnerable to positive change, Bowen spent weeks before his trip home planning an emotionally nonviolent confrontation with them that would help him both neutralize their anxiety and achieve his own independence. He worked out a byzantine strategy calibrated to raise as many old emotional issues in the family as possible. In a calculated pose of innocence and helpfulness, he wrote a series of letters and made several phone calls to his parents, two sisters and two brothers, telling some what the others had said about them, warning some of imminent catastrophe in the family, hectoring others about their family duties. It was a masterwork of manipulation worthy of a double agent, and it did exactly what he intended: "stir up a 'tempest in a teapot.'"

As part of his plan, Bowen drew the fire of each family member toward *him*, on the theory that as odd man out he would be less likely to be drawn into any triangles and thereby seduced back into the family mass. In order to remain safely outside, he worked "to keep the entire family in one big emotional clump, and to detriangle any ally who tried to come over to my side." Typically, he told no one about the scenario he had planned, not even his wife, who accompanied him home to the emotional whirlwind he had precipitated.

As Bowen tells it, everything went exactly according to plan. His brother, who had been avoiding him for years, now turned up in a righteous lather, threatening a libel suit and accusing Bowen of being drunk when he wrote the letter. Soon Bowen was at the center of a three-ring family circus, cleverly turning away wrath, pouring oil on troubled waters, and generally conducting the family orchestra like a maestro. At the end of the epochal visit, by remaining detached, good-humored and undefensive, he had calmed his family's anxiety, initiated a higher level of mutual understanding, and differentiated himself once and for all.

"I had actively participated in the most intense family emotion possible and I had stayed completely out of the 'ego mass' of my very own family!" Bowen exulted. "I had gone through the entire visit without being 'triangled' or without being fused into the family emotional system . . . It was the total success of the operation that was surprising, exhilarating, and exhausting . . . It was equivalent to having finally mastered the secret of the [family] system and having gone all the way to the goal line in one try." Even 20 years later, he remembered the occasion with characteristic Bowenian hyperbole. *"My arrival [at home] on February 11, 1967, was a hallmark in the history of the family . . . By the time this new meeting was 30 minutes old, I knew that I was totally successful on the first try . . . I finally knew one way through the impenetrable thicket which is the family emotional system"* [italics in original].

Well. Bowen clearly experienced the event as something between being born again and inventing the wheel. Indeed, his account of the experience is instructive, often amusing, and oddly appealing: we see a man actively gaining independence from his family, and we feel a kind of envy. Would that we could be so self-possessed, so cool-headed, so quietly masterful when surrounded by our families—the people who can still reduce us to pouting childishness, no matter how suavely adult we are away from home.

Yet there is the disturbing sense that this is exactly the vision we are meant to see, that Bowen has prepared for us an allegorical coming-of-age drama—Arthur claiming the sword Excalibur—written, pro-

duced, directed by and starring himself. The story does not reveal someone "selfish and hostile and hurtful," as Bowen said critics called him, but rather a man who believes he has taken ultimate responsibility for himself by literally creating himself. When asked about his life and work at his last interview, Bowen said, "It is not so much my family that produced it as *I* produced it," as if his family—that powerful Tennessee clan—had had almost nothing to do with the making of Murray Bowen.

Having tried to be the wise son to whom nobody much listened, he had finally left his own tracks on the family turf, and he intended to do the same in the profession. He decided to use his successful struggle for independence from his family as the springboard to a similar victory for differentiation from his profession. Months before he made his trip home to Tennessee, Bowen had been scheduled to present a paper about his theory at the Family Research Conference, to be held in Philadelphia in the spring of 1967, before a small, select group of family therapy's leading lights, including Salvador Minuchin, Carl Whitaker, Jay Haley, Paul Watzlawick, James Framo and John Weakland. Instead of presenting the paper he had already prepared (advance copies of which had been sent to all participants), Bowen made his visit home the subject of a surprise paper about his own family. Not unreasonably, the conference, at which he now planned to present his own personal story to the unsuspecting leaders of his field, assumed the importance to him of a heroic ordeal. "I wondered—did I dare do the same thing to the 'family of family therapists' that I had done with my own family? I did dare to do it!"

For all the triumph he felt about his success at home, however, the figure who presented the paper was a rather unusual Bowen—not the highly intellectual, superior and rather arrogant person he could sometimes be, but a quieter, softer man. Whitaker remembers that at the meeting, "He spoke very personally, as if speaking to close friends, or like an analysand, and we were all his analysts listening to him." Others cite his courage in talking about his own family at a time when personal revelations were considered an embarrassing gaffe in professional circles. "Bowen always had the rap of being so intellectual, so cool," says Carolyn Moynihan Bradt, one of the founding faculty members at Georgetown's family therapy training program, now in private practice. "But here he was, the first person to be so self-revealing in presenting his own family at a conference. He was so daring to do it."

Bowen considered the paper not only a major breakthrough for himself, and a smash-hit at the meeting, but a benchmark in the history of family theory and therapy. He had initiated, he later wrote, "a new trend nationally . . . [that] also spread into international areas." As a historical event, the 1967 paper has been compared to Freud's self-analysis; but even Freud had never publicly presented such a straightforward and undisguised case history of his own family. For Bowen, and later his followers, the presentation had the almost legendary quality of Martin Luther's appearance before the Diet of Worms in 1521, when Luther declared his independence from all authority but his own conscience and finished with a resounding, "Here I stand. I cannot do otherwise."

THOUGH BOWEN MAINTAINED THAT DIFFERENtiation was essentially a neutral reference to the degree of a person's emotional separation from family of origin, his discussion of the term seems to ring with approbation of the more, and disparagement of the less, differentiated. There are mutterings among Bowen's critics that his discussion of human differentiation as a giant step up the evolutionary ladder brings him uncomfortably close to suggesting the emergence of a race of *ubermenschen* standing above the rest of the hoi polloi. As one therapist commented, not entirely jokingly, "Differentiation measures the degree to which we have

evolved from the organic web, how far we've come from the primeval slime mold" of instinctual life. Another, who had trained with Bowen, suggested that he had implicitly postulated a form of Social Darwinism (the belief that the wealthy, successful and powerful are more highly evolved beings, biologically superior to the less well endowed) that could sound almost fascistic at times.

Bowenians respond that this is a blatant misrepresentation, though they agree that the term "differentiation" can be "a very elusive concept," says James Framo, distinguished professor in the School of Human Behavior at U.S. International University in San Francisco, because it refers to a degree of inner freedom and independence that can't easily be assessed by an outsider. "Basically, it has to do with having a secure sense of who you are, a strong sense of your own values, standards, and the ability not to become reactive to your closest intimates." Michael Kerr, Bowen's successor as director of the Georgetown University Family Center, says it is very simple: "Differentiation is the ability to think, feel and act for oneself."

Some therapists wonder how new the concept of differentiation really is. "It includes characteristics that are generally highly regarded in mental health circles," says Alan Gurman, professor of psychiatry at the University of Wisconsin Medical School. "Maturation, moral development, the ability to cope with stress, modulate anxiety and assert yourself without stepping on other people's toes; in short, being your own person—psychodynamic therapists have been talking about all that for years."

But Bowen's concept of differentiation has acquired an almost mystical overlay in some circles. One therapist compares it to the enlightened state of the archetypal Zen warrior, and Bowen himself wrote that a person measuring a hypothetical 100 on his early scale of differentiation—if such a being existed—would be "perfect in all levels of emotional, cellular, and physiological functioning." Charles

Paddack, a Bowen-trained family and marital psychiatrist in Kensington, Maryland, describes it as a profound but sometimes mysterious state of total selfhood, saying, "If you don't know whether you're differentiated or not, you aren't. It's like asking how much a yacht costs—if you have to ask, you can't afford it."

INDEED, AS A TEACHER AND A MENTOR, BOWEN LET his students know that differentiation, both personal and professional, would never come cheap. "You have inherited a lifetime of tribulation," he said in his last interview. "Everybody has inherited it. Take it over, make the most of it. And when you have decided you know the right way, do the best you can with it." Within this homiletic piece of advice is a truth that he believed most people, including many family therapists, had forgotten: learning to know oneself is the most compelling and yet the hardest of human tasks, requiring the most courage, determination and faith. The goal, the reason for attempting the task at all, is freedom, an elusive, ambiguous reward that may exact a high price in loss of love, popularity, wealth and the cozy security of togetherness.

Bowen's theory, to which he gave his life, virtually demanded a kind of hardness, an internal discipline that precluded the gregarious congeniality that might lull the anxiety of his trainees wondering how they were doing. Indeed, learning to live with anxiety was part of the training. To be a good, differentiated therapist required the capacity to outgrow the hungry, insecure need for praise and approval from others, especially the most significant other. Said Bowen, "We all have some kind of vulnerability to believe what we are *supposed* to believe, rather than what we ourselves believe." His goal was to transcend this vulnerability as much as was humanly possible and to instill the same goal in his students.

Bowen made it very clear that the seeker along this path could expect a good deal of discomfort, and he often made his students very uncomfortable. His trainees complained that they were expected to take vows of poverty, chastity and obedience while working at the Georgetown University Family Center, which he founded in 1975. The poverty was quite literal; funds for the center were limited, so most of the faculty and students worked as volunteers. Bowen, who never cared much about money anyway, was not always tolerant of those expressing pedestrian needs to make a living.

The demand for loyalty included a requirement for a kind of intellectual chastity. Bowen required complete allegiance to his ideas and allowed little deviation from the true path. He seemed to believe his own theory was still too new, too fragile, to withstand the blooming confusion of the therapy marketplace, and his students too vulnerable to expose themselves to the promiscuous eclecticism of the outside world.

Some students compared the center to a cocoon, but if so, it was hardly a cozy, comfortable one. Bowen was strict, businesslike, and countenanced little frivolity at the office. An implicit code of behavior prevailed, though few of the rules were ever spelled out. People were expected, for example, to dress rather formally, with men in dark suits. "There was a kind of undercover joke," recalls Jack Bradt, a psychiatrist and former Bowen student now in private practice, "that you could tell Bowen people because they all wore G-men suits and looked like FBI agents."

Just as at NIMH, Bowen's mystifying reticence only fed the guru image he allegedly detested. "He didn't often make comments to us and was very cautious about what he said," remembers Bradt. Still, "Everyone always sat on the edge of their seats waiting for what he would say, which was generally very little. He would make a strange remark, like 'Wet birds fly at night,' and we would go off pondering and puzzling what he meant. We spent a lot of time asking each other, 'What did he mean by that?

What was he thinking?' We were always trying to read into him something more than he'd actually said. It seemed to be part of his power that he kept people riveted to him, waiting for a message."

If Bowen could not bring himself to approve of any deviation from his fledgling theory, he tried hard to distinguish between loyalty to the theory and to himself. He may have inadvertently encouraged discipleship, but he did not really want disciples. Framo remembers that he considered Bowen his mentor, but would not have dreamed of telling him so. "He didn't like that kind of relationship," James Framo says. "He thought it was of a piece with being commercial or social," as if the mentor-student relationship smacked too much of mutual dependency, an unhealthy merging of selves, or of an unholy contract between two people who were covertly using each other for their own gain.

Bowen seldom agreed outright with people or complimented anyone. It was as if agreeableness and personal ingratiation were a kind of "lending of self," at odds with the high standards he set for his own and his students' differentiation. But however uncomfortable trainees may have found the Georgetown Family Center, everybody interviewed—regardless of whether they had broken with Bowen or not—had only gratitude for what they learned, and respect verging at times on a grudging kind of love for the man.

In spite of his reputation as a grouch, he could be an inspiring teacher, deeply funny, and for all his presumed elitism, down to earth and rather modest. He was famous for off-the-cuff remarks and queries that were more like psychotherapy koans than formal academic questions. When he thought a student was being too unctuously sympathetic with a client, he said, "Can't you listen to him without licking him?" He set his trainees pondering the question, "Who was more differentiated: Adolf Hitler or Martin Luther King? "

Bowen was "a charismatic character in an unde-finable way," says Philip Guerin. "He drew people to him who would end up sounding like him and imitating him [including his Tennessee accent, by other accounts], and it was sometimes hard knowing who really knew his methods and understood the theory, and who were just going through the motions." Carl Whitaker agrees that Bowen had a good deal of personal power and probably not a little ambivalence about its use. "He said to me he didn't believe in transference," recalls Whitaker, "but I told him that five minutes after I saw him, I was transferred up to my ears myself, and he became my mother or father whether he knew it or liked it or not."

BY THE MID-1970S BOWEN'S INFLUENCE WAS AT its peak. His 1967 paper had been published in 1972 and started a national surge of interest among family therapists in doing their own family-of-origin work. In 1975 the center expanded to new, off-campus quarters, and the yearly Georgetown Family Center Symposium, started in 1965 as a small, informal meeting for people who had worked with Bowen, now attracted up to 1,000 attendees. In 1977 Bowen helped found the American Family Therapy Association (AFTA) in order to restore a serious research effort in family therapy, and became its first president. The next year his book, *Family Therapy in Clinical Practice*, was published. By this time, a number of family therapy institutes emphasizing Bowenian concepts had sprung up around the country.

Still, Bowen looked at this evidence of his success with a good deal of skepticism. The main source of his disappointment was the persistent failure of his theory to be taken seriously as a new science of human behavior, and he questioned the assumption that *science* and *scientific method* were one and the same. "There is no way to chi-square a feeling and make it qualify as a scientific fact," he said, suggesting that the empirical validation and quantification of data were somehow beside the point of his science. Bowen seemed to believe that standard scientific methods were too crude and too cut-and-dried, to measure the vast complexities and subtleties of his systems theory.

The paucity of empirical data on Bowen's ideas remains troublesome to many. "As far as I know, there is no published empirical research whatsoever on the basic principles and concepts of Bowen theory, let alone the outcome of Bowen therapy," says Alan Gurman, an expert on therapy research. "Many of the more prominent Bowenians seem to regard the truths of the theory as so self-evident that empiricism is actually unnecessary. But the lack of empirical research has limited the spread of Bowen's theory."

Bowen's dissent from the scientific world grew along with his alienation from the family therapy mainstream, and late in life he began what some therapists have called his own "cutoff" from the field. Some have suggested that his increasing self-isolation from the field during the '80s reflected less on his personality than on his deteriorating health; he suffered from chronic obstructive lung disease and had undergone surgery twice for aneurysms, during which his vocal chords had been paralyzed. As he grew sicker, he found going to meetings, talking with people, and even writing letters a painful and exhausting effort.

Bowen abandoned AFTA in 1989 because he believed that it was simply collaborating in what he saw as the cheap commercialization of family therapy. He announced that he did not wish to spend the rest of his life working for the glorification of individual practitioners of this or that fashionable therapeutic trick. James Framo remembers Bowen at earlier AFTA meetings, scolding the board, "You are only interested in therapy, not theory. That's not what we're here for." Toward the end of his life, according to Framo, he was "ashamed and embarrassed by family therapy."

THEORY VERSUS THERAPY. THE FORMER POINTED the way to science, which, for Bowen, was "a search for universals," more a metaphysical quest for ultimate truth than a pedestrian method for quantifying data. For his efforts to replace old scientific paradigms with a vast, new *summa scientifica,* some have compared Bowen not only to Freud and Darwin but to Galileo and Kepler as well. Indeed, Bowen's quest for a universalizing truth was reminiscent of the great intellectual systems of the past, in which all the truths of science and philosophy were supposed to be compatible, and creation was imagined as a great, indivisible chain of being.

Bowen believed that the purpose of science was to reveal the undistorted, unsubjective truth about the *real* world, at a time when postmodern intellectual discourse was dissolving in a sea of relativism. Constructivist therapists and deconstructive critics were arguing that there was no single, unifying Truth, only an unlimited number of different "truths," all contingent, contextual, changeable and circumstantial. One therapist regarded Bowen's memorial service as the passing of an era. "It reminds me of the funeral of Queen Victoria," he said, marking the death not only of a man but of a way of thinking perhaps out of sync with the times.

Yet the spirit of the quest is timeless, the desire of human consciousness to embrace the cosmos as old as history, and perhaps just as irreversible. Bowen, like many thinkers before him, had perfection as his goal, however unattainable he himself thought it to be, and at some point on his odyssey the twin struggles to differentiate himself and to create a perfect theory seemed to have merged. "I tried to make it all the way to science," he wrote in a letter near the end of his life. "An impossible goal, but I gave it my best. I could do no other . . . When perfection is the goal, success is mostly an illusion. When perfection is the goal, all of the 'trying too hard' is often a failure toward what might have been. No matter what, the inner me cannot stop trying."

But he hadn't given up the dream of a perfect theory, only put down the torch for a little while. "I am neither a prophet, a fortune teller nor a messiah. I am just a simple human, with a brain that knows a theory, and the theory knows its way into the future." And, whatever the current scientific paradigm, whatever the current view that Truth, or even truth, is an impossibility, his theory may indeed find its way into the future. The most hardened postmodernist can't say that it won't. ∎

MARY SYKES WYLIE, PH.D., *is associate editor of* The Family Therapy Networker.

*D*O FAMILIES REALLY NEED PROBLEMS?

WHY I AM NOT A FUNCTIONALIST

By Jeffrey Bogdan

WHY DO FAMILIES DEVELOP PROBLEMS, AND why are these problems often so hard to resolve? Ask a family therapist this question, and chances are you will get something like the following answer: Troubled families need, at least temporarily, to have a problem, even when they say they want to solve it. If they didn't have *that* problem, they would suffer from something even worse. If the school-phobic child were not staying home, his mother would become anxious about being alone during the day. If the delinquent teenager were not worrying and upsetting his parents, they would fight with each other and end up getting a divorce. In other words, the I.P.'s problem protects, or serves a function for, the family.

I will call this view of the meaning of symptoms *functionalism*. (The words "function" and "functionalism" have other uses in the behavioral sciences, but we will ignore them here.) The writings of many well-known family therapists and theorists—Jay Haley, Lynn Hoffman, Cloë Madanes, Peggy Papp, Mara Selvini Palazzoli and Salvador Minuchin come immediately to mind—are filled with functionalist

language. Why has this way of thinking been so influential among family therapists?

There are several reasons. Functionalism links the symptomatic behavior of the individual to the organization of the family and therefore justifies the practice of working with whole families instead of just with individuals. Functionalism also purports to account for the phenomenon of resistance. Just as a family develops a symptom to mask a worse problem, family members presumably fail to carry out directives or engage in sabotage for the same reason. According to the theory, a family with a school-phobic child would resist attempts to help the child go to school unless something happened so that the phobia was no longer needed.

Many therapists who espouse functionalism are very good at helping people. Quite naturally they assume that the effectiveness of their clinical method validates their theory. Common sense suggests that they wouldn't get such good results with an inadequate theory. However, the relationship between theory and practice is more complicated than common sense allows. Some very good therapists have used simplistic and even ridiculous theories to achieve their results. Consider Franz Mesmer, the father of hypnosis, from whose name we get the term "mesmerism." A spectacularly effective therapist, Mesmer thought he owed his success to his ability to transmit a healing energy he called "animal magnetism" to his patients. Does anyone want to claim that Mesmer's successes prove the theory of animal magnetism?

I believe that functionalism is to the practice of family therapy as the theory of animal magnetism was to the practice of mesmerism. Although many powerful therapy techniques have been inspired by functionalism, the account it offers of symptoms and resistance is deeply flawed. What is more, it has practically nothing to say about how families change. There is an alternative framework—essentially a variation on a theme originally stated by John Weakland, Paul Watzlawick, Richard Fisch and their colleagues at the Mental Research Institute in Palo Alto—that has a number of advantages over a symptoms-serve-functions approach to understanding families. But first let's examine the shortcomings of functionalism.

FUNCTIONALISM IS BASED ON AN IMPLICIT ANALOgy between families and organisms. If you think of a family as something like a multicelled organism, it is natural to compare what goes on in families to the homeostatic processes that, for example, keep your body temperature at 98.6°F. But the closer we look at the idea that symptoms serve functions in families, the more apparent it becomes that there is a difference between the biologist's way of theorizing and that of family therapists. When biologists hypothesize that the heart, for example, serves a particular function, they do not stop there. No biologist would consider a functionalist explanation complete without a detailed account of the *process* by which the function—in this case, pumping blood—is accomplished.

Most versions of functionalism in family therapy, however, fail to specify how families produce the symptoms they supposedly need. The closest thing to such an account is Cloë Madanes's notion that family members can "plan ahead" to produce symptoms. In the first chapter of *Behind the One-Way Mirror*, Madanes describes a child who develops a symptom in order to "help his father pull himself together" by giving him an opportunity to be a competent parent. Because of the child's "planning ahead," his father is no longer afraid of the possibility of losing his job.

It is not entirely clear how committed Madanes is to the idea of planning ahead. She herself notes one of its difficulties: it is very hard to determine whether the symptomatic person plans ahead or if some other family member induces the symptom-bearer to perform the symptom. Another difficulty is that clients usually deny that they produce symptoms to protect each other. So, why not believe them?

Madanes's response is that planning ahead is ordinarily not a conscious process; therefore, the fact that clients are not aware of planning their symptoms does not prove that they don't plan them nevertheless. But why should we suppose that Madanes or any family therapist can discern her clients' unconscious motives? Most family therapists would not allow a psychoanalyst to get away with this claim. The only reason to revert to the practice of guessing at unconscious motives that I can think of is that an explanation like "planning ahead" is needed to make functionalist explanations work.

What about those cases in which family members do admit to planning ahead? Even these do next to nothing to support functionalism. I once worked with a family in which the 13-year-old boy was a chronic truant. His parents had divorced several years before, and his nearly blind father now lived alone in a boarding house. His mother, who had been physically abused by her ex-husband, was still bitter and severely limited father-son contacts. The boy said that he cut school in order to have more opportunities to visit his father.

A functionalist might theorize that something about the way the family was organized required the boy to cut school. If he didn't cut school, the father would be extremely lonely. The boy's behavior could be regarded as serving this function for the family. But the boy's cutting school also had other consequences. His depressed mother felt betrayed by her son. The boy, who was quite intelligent, was throwing away a chance to do well in school, to attend college, and to become a productive, independent adult.

Were the problems associated with the boy's truancy protecting the system against a worse set of problems? Most people would prefer a simpler explanation, that the boy felt sorry for his dad and wanted to visit him. His mother made this hard to arrange, and so he hit on the idea of visiting his father during the only time his mother was not closely monitoring his activities. Only a theoretical commitment to finding deeper meanings in everyday life would lead one to go beyond this common-sense account.

NO ONE DENIES THAT FUNCTIONALIST ASSUMPtions enable us to generate a profusion of interesting hypotheses about families. However, in order to be useful, functionalism should supply criteria for choosing one hypothesis over another. Early on, psychoanalysis was criticized by philosophers of science because the methods it used to test its hypotheses—analytic interpretations—were apparently capable of confirming *any* hypothesis of a certain type. I'm not sure if the situation is any better in the functionalist camp.

Many functionalists believe that their hypotheses are confirmed by the success of their interventions. Even if this criterion were valid, it would not be of much use, since what is needed is a criterion that

will help us choose *beforehand* which hypothesis we should use. But apart from this, some very odd kinds of interventions will work if they happen to fit clients' views of reality. After all, if I come from a culture that believes that depression is caused by devils, and you perform an exorcism rite that relieves my symptoms of depression, this is not a demonstration that I was in fact possessed by devils.

Another criterion that is often used to evaluate functionalist hypotheses is whether or not family members agree when the therapist begins to build his case. Strong agreement, or suspiciously strong disagreement—"Methinks yon father doth protest too much"—is often taken as evidence that the hypothesis has, as the Milan group used to say, "hit the target."

But this will hardly do. For one thing, families are rarely unanimous in these matters. Whose opinions should be given more weight? For another, whether or not I agree with your reframing depends a lot on how well it fits my previous view of the situation and on your powers of persuasion. If we refuse to accept a client's word when he says he is possessed by devils, why should we take his agreement with our hypothesis as evidence that the hypothesis is on target? And what about all the patients in psychoanalytic psychotherapy who assent to *their* therapists' interpretations of the meaning of symptoms?

Other therapists insist that a functionalist hypothesis is on target if the symptom or problem behavior seems obviously linked to consequences that jibe with the hypothesis. For example, if a child's disobedient behavior visibly detours conflict in a therapy session, these therapists conclude that the child's disobedience is *explained* by its role in regulating conflict between his mother and father. However, this conclusion seems to be based on a logical fallacy. When a child acts up, it might happen that his parents' attention gets focused on him, and, therefore, the parents have fewer opportunities to argue between themselves. At issue is not the existence of such patterns, but their appropriate interpretation. Are these consequences accidental or are they, for lack of a better word, meaningful?

The idea that the consequences of behavior are equivalent to their purpose or function can lead to some very wayward forms of reasoning. For example, suppose I win the New Jersey State lottery. As a consequence of my new wealth, I embark on a major transformation of my lifestyle. My wife doesn't like the new me, and she files for divorce. Should we say that the function of my not having previously won the lottery was to protect my marriage? More explicitly, would it make any sense to say that my former state of poverty was *explained* by the fact that it had this consequence? I think that someone who said this would be regarded by most of us as a little crazy. Transparently, the effect of my relative state of poverty on my marriage was accidental. The same faulty logic seems to be involved in jumping from the consequences of a problem to its purpose.

WHEN BIOLOGISTS USE FUNCTIONALIST LAN-guage, they always know what they mean by "the organism" for which a given process is said to serve a function. Until now we have proceed-ed as if the application of the term "family system" were just as clear as that of "organism." But, in fact, it is not clear at all.

Let's assume that a problem serves some function for some system, however defined. It is a common-place of systems theory that systems are subsystems in relation to higher-level supersystems and super-systems in relation to their own parts. The difficulty this raises is that there is no way to tell which level of the system is the relevant one. Is the function of the symptom to stabilize a parental dyad, to permit an older brother to leave home, or to reinforce a moth-er's one-down position vis-à-vis her own mother? Is it some need of a dyad, of the nuclear family, or of the three-generational, family plus Aunt Becky's chi-ropractor that requires the symptom?

The answer will depend on how the boundary of the family is drawn, and this may vary greatly de-pending on a therapist's preference for complex or simple hypotheses. While no one, to my knowledge, has ever suggested that a symptom arose because it served some function for the system made up of all the peoples of the NATO alliance, I see no obvious grounds for ruling out such a hypothesis. Now that family therapists are getting bored with psychother-apy and have started to apply their ideas to large institutions and even international relations, it is not unlikely that just such a hypothesis will one day be vigorously defended at one of our national confer-ences. (Intergalactic therapy, anyone?)

EVEN IF FUNCTIONALISTS COULD RESPOND ADE-quately to all of the criticisms raised here, they would still have one more hurdle to leap. Func-tionalism is a theory of why certain problems arise and why they stick around. Functionalist writers have a lot—and a lot, I want to emphasize, that is useful—to say about how families do change.

The problem is that what they have to say about change has no clear connection to functionalism. In fact, by working backward from certain techniques of change that functionalists typically make use of, you arrive at a conception of why families don't always change that is rather at odds with functional-ism. Perhaps an example can make this more clear.

A family in therapy improves greatly when the behavior of several of its members is reframed from, say, "cruel" to "lovingly stern." Logic suggests that if a long-standing pattern of interaction can be trans-formed by changing the ideas that family members have about what is going on, then the ideas they held prior to the intervention must have had a lot to do with keeping the problem going in the first place. So it looks as if the presence of a problem is very much related to the beliefs and plans of family mem-bers. But what has *that* got to do with whether or not the problem, or even the pattern of which the

234

problem is a part, serves a function for the family as a whole?

Evidently, the family changes when the family members' ideas—sometimes called "the context"—change, not because the problem no longer serves a function or because something else capable of serving the same function has been put in its place. It is utterly mysterious how any of the usual activities of therapists—offering interpretations or reframings, asking questions, assigning tasks or directives or rituals—could be supposed to have the power to transform a system so that something that was once presumably vital to its organization becomes obsolete. And if families change according to principles that have nothing to do with removing functions, there doesn't seem to be much reason for thinking about functions at all.

But where does this leave us? If we give up functionalism, are we condemned to do family therapy by the seat of our pants, without any theoretical framework to guide us? (Despite appearances, I am not advocating the abandonment of family therapy.) Fortunately, things are not so bleak. There are alternatives to functionalism.

IN THE THEORETICAL MODEL USED AT THE BRIEF Therapy Center of the Mental Research Institute (MRI) in Palo Alto, problems are thought of as the unintended side effects of (usually) well-meant efforts to resolve life's ordinary difficulties. Some solutions have the effect of reinforcing, rather than dampening, problem behavior. This occurs because people frequently do not realize the connection between their efforts to help and the evolution and maintenance of the problem.

Typically, in MRI-style brief therapy, only those members of the family who are suffering from the presence of a problem enough to want to do something about it are seen. The main goal of the therapy is to get those persons to change the way they are going about trying to solve the problem, and to this end a variety of ingenious tasks and reframings are employed.

All this is sufficiently familiar to require little elaboration. There is one aspect of the model, however, that has not gotten much attention, and it is this aspect that I particularly want to emphasize. The main idea is that problems evolve not to fulfill an intricate systemic purpose—not "in service of" the marital subsystem, for example—but because ordinary life difficulties are mishandled. And they persist because no one realizes that it is the *mishandling* that perpetuates the problem. The result is that the participants keep doing more of the same, and the problem continues to crop up. Since this point of view is easily distinguished from functionalism, and since it currently lacks its own name, let us call it *accidentalism*.

Accidentalists believe that people mishandle problems not because of anything so mysterious as "the needs of the system," but because of the way they think about their difficulties. The Palo Alto model is sometimes described as behavioristic; however, their view of human behavior is actually very "mentalistic"—though still interactional. The point of view called "mentalism" has been very neatly set forth by philosopher, linguist and cognitive psychologist Jerry Fodor, who argues in the following way: "Suppose I want to talk to the girl next door. Suppose further that, unbeknownst to me, the girl next door no longer lives there but 'languishes in Latvia.' If you want to predict whether or not I will go next door to ring the bell, what information do you need to have? That the girl is in Latvia, or that I *believe* she is right next door? Pretty obviously, the important thing is not reality as such—'what is the case,' in some neutral sense—but the way I represent this reality. Not the world itself, but my ideas about the world, constrain my behavior."

Compare Fodor's point of view to anthropologist Gregory Bateson's: "There are in the mind no objects or events—no pigs, no coconuts, no mothers.

The mind contains only transforms, percepts, etc. . . . It is nonsense to say that a man was frightened by a lion, because a lion is not an idea." Paul Watzlawick calls this perspective "constructivism," a term that emphasizes the constructed or invented aspect of our personal worlds. If the constructivist thesis is granted, it cannot, strictly speaking, be the case that behaviors, problematic or otherwise, are maintained by other behaviors. I have no access to your behavior per se, only to my representation or interpretation of it. Therefore, it must be my *interpretation* of your behavior, not your behavior per se, that maintains my own actions. And my interpretation depends as much on my "habits of punctuation," in Bateson's terminology, or my "readiness," as psychologist Jerome Bruner puts it, to view your behavior in a particular way, as it does on the movements or sounds that you make.

Given this framework, how does an accidentalist explain the phenomenon of resistance? Let's say that I developed the idea that you are a meddlesome person. Then your effort to help me may be interpreted not as an instance of "help" but as an instance of "meddling." My ungrateful response to you may seem bizarre, and this may persuade you that I need even more help than you had supposed. But your increased efforts to help are only likely to persuade me that you are even more of a busybody than I thought. That is, your view of me may lead you to behave in ways that repeatedly confirm my view of you, and vice versa. In this literally haphazard way, all kinds of problems arise and are maintained. The chief claim of the accidentalist is that *that* is all there is to it.

Before going on, let me point out that, in practice, using this way of thinking about families is more difficult than I have made it sound. Three-and-more-person systems are harder to describe, obviously, than couples. Also, there is the fact that many of the ideas we use to guide our actions are ideas about others' ideas, ideas about others' ideas about our

ideas and so forth. However, such Laingian complexities enrich the model without fundamentally changing it.

F AMILIES ARE OFTEN COMPARED BOTH TO ORGANisms and to ecosystems, sometimes within the space of a single article. Each of these analogies, however, implies a very different view of the family. The organismic metaphor implies that it must be difficult if not impossible for the family to change in any fundamental way. If the pattern of interaction that is kept in place by the symptom is necessary to the family in the same way that a body temperature of 98.6° is necessary to my health, this doesn't leave much room for maneuvering.

On the other hand, seeing the family as resembling an ecosystem leads one to expect the family to be really quite delicately balanced in its internal organization, not characterized by a rigid homeostasis. Just as the introduction of a new species or a change in climate can compel an ecosystem to reorganize, so any move on my part or yours to change the pattern between us could, in theory, result in a permanently transformed relationship. In fact, this is what accidentalists say about change, and the reason they believe family therapy can be done with one or two key persons.

However, if change is so easy, why aren't all therapists more successful? The functionalist answer is that the family in some sense needs to have the problem. The accidentalist answer is in two parts. First, people behave according to their personal definitions of the situation, and the perspective of each family member is repeatedly confirmed by the behavior of other members. Therapists, too, often behave in ways that inadvertently reinforce the perspectives of their clients. Second, family members regard their own points of view as just common sense, part of the unverbalized and seemingly self-evident system of presuppositions within which all events are interpreted. As such, they tend to be peculiarly self-confirming.

For example, just because you change your behavior toward me, it doesn't automatically follow that I will perceive you differently. My conception of your character has been acquired through many experiences of interacting with you. The way I think of you is a kind of habit that, for the most part, allows me to make accurate predictions of your behavior. Why give it up just because you seem temporarily to be acting out of character? Perhaps you really haven't stopped meddling at all. Perhaps you've just decided to do it more subtly from now on. Thus "common sense" doth make conservatives of us all.

THE IMAGERY OF FUNCTIONALISM IS OF THE FAMIly as One. Its point of view is of the hypothetical system-as-a-whole. In contrast, the picture of the family drawn by accidentalism is the more familiar one of many minds, each with its own perspective on the world, communicating with and adapting to one another over time. Instead of an organism, the family is viewed as an "ecology of ideas" in which the point of view of each family member is confirmed or reinforced by the behavior of other family members. Accidentalism is a genuine alternative to functionalism in that it offers a very different and, I believe, more plausible account of the phenomena—symptoms and resistance—that functionalism was invented to explain. Furthermore, the account it offers is not vulnerable to the criticisms that have been made of functionalism.

Accidentalism does not rely on the concept of systemic need and, therefore, has no reason to postulate a process as improbable as "planning ahead." Instead of having to base their reframings on a therapist-constructed myth about the function of a symptom, accidentalists can to use any reframing that is likely to be persuasive. Since the family is not thought of as a kind of organism, the fact that its boundary is rather vague has no great theoretical

importance. The system is simply whoever happens to be relevant to resolving the problem. From the standpoint of intellectual economy, it is a further advantage that accidentalism is consistent with the basic assumptions of modern cognitive psychology. In other words, we don't have to think that if accidentalism is right, cognitive psychology must be wrong, or vice versa.

FINALLY, WHILE IN FUNCTIONALISM THE CONcepts used to account for change and those used to account for stability barely make contact, the theory of change in accidentalism is a built-in feature of the theory of stability. Since the ideas of individuals are assumed to be involved in maintaining interactional patterns, it follows that changing those patterns is going to involve changing the ideas of family members. There are, indeed, lots of ways to do this, just as there are lots of ways to cook a meal. This suggests that some of the differences between the various schools of psychotherapy, perhaps many of the differences that have seemed most important to adherents of those schools, are not especially important—perhaps no more than the difference between Chinese and Italian food, from the standpoint of nutrition.

Let's take a look at those interventions—positive connotations, restraint from change and some of Madanes's "pretend techniques"—which, historically, are closely intertwined with functionalist ideas. What do therapists actually use these interventions for? Such interventions can be used to express empathy or concern, to redefine the meaning of someone's behavior, to provoke a crisis by encouraging the temporary escalation of a problem-maintaining solution, or to induce one or more persons to change their behavior in order to prove the therapist has the wrong idea about them. In other words, all of these interventions can be understood purely as forms of rhetoric. (I like the term "rhetoric" more than "persuasion" because the latter carries with it a connotation of *rational* persuasion. And reason, to echo the words of a famous film star, has nothing to do with it.) Lynn Hoffman once wrote that, for the Palo Alto group, psychotherapy is "the art of rhetoric." Perhaps this is true not only of Palo Alto-style brief therapy but of *all* kinds of psychotherapy.

THERE ARE THREE COMMON OBJECTIONS TO accidentalism. The first is the idea, which apparently originated with Don Jackson, that symptom resolution, by itself, leads only to the formation of a substitute symptom in the family. There is a germ of truth in this connection. Transient periods of boredom, disorganization, depression and anxiety do sometimes appear following improvement in a problem. Any change requires the modification of mental as well as behavioral routines and habits, and some of us make these adjustments more easily than others. Also, marriages do sometimes dissolve as a consequence of the changes facilitated by therapy.

But is there any reason to suppose that the transient difficulties just alluded to typically develop into full-blown problems? Or that the dissolution of a marriage that depended on the existence of a problem is a worse problem? Also, what from the functionalist point of view is symptom substitution, is, from the accidentalist point of view, simply a family falling into a brand-new, problem-maintaining cycle. Since there are no research data relevant to this topic (only anecdotes) and since the categories of problems, symptoms and transient difficulties are lumped together, the objection to accidentalism based on the phenomenon of problem substitution is not a very powerful one.

The second objection is best put in the form of a question: Isn't it wildly improbable that the intricate concatenations of mutually self-fulfilling prophecies that I have described could have evolved purely by *accident*? Is accidentalism too reductionistic a theory? Aren't there more things in heaven and earth than

are dreamt of in the accidentalist philosophy? Perhaps, but the other danger, that of putting more things into one's philosophy than there are in heaven and earth, is just as acute.

Darwin tells us that all the examples of mutual "fit" that are found in natural ecosystems—the horse's hoof and the grassy plain, to use one of Bateson's examples—evolved in just this way. Biologists don't say that grassy plains are the way they are because they serve a function for the horse's hoof, or vice versa. Horses are the way they are, and so is the grassy plain, because of the way the process of evolution through natural selection happened to work out. Things had to work out in some way, didn't they? So why not in *that* way?

The third objection to accidentalism goes like this: Isn't all this talk of changes in one individual influencing other individuals just more of the same old linear, unsystemic thinking? To this question there is only one reply, "So much the worse for your concept of 'systemic.'" For if this sort of talk about families and therapy explains more than functionalism and explains it more simply and elegantly, the fact that accidentalism does not fit someone's *a priori* definition of "systemic" is of no account. "System," after all, is just the name of an abstraction. You can't kiss a system. You can't impress "it" with your authority, speak "its" language, or change the way "it" views reality. I conclude, therefore, that you can't do psychotherapy with "it," either.

I WANT TO END BY REEMPHASIZING THE FLEXIBILITY of accidentalism. Although historically connected with the Palo Alto brief therapy style, it can also be used, we have seen, to explain how other styles of treatment achieve their results. Some therapists may feel there is something wrong with a theory that is loose enough to apply to different styles of therapy. But such looseness is characteristic of theoretical frameworks generally, and it is usually seen as an advantage.

DO FAMILIES REALLY NEED PROBLEMS?

Suppose you are a scientist trying to explain what makes different foods smell the way they do. Wouldn't there be something wrong if your theory accounted for the smell of fish but not chicken? A theory like that—and many of the theoretical frameworks used by family therapists are more like that than otherwise—smells pretty fishy to me.

I believe that the ideas of the Palo Alto group, more or less, can serve as a unifying framework for family therapy and, perhaps, for psychotherapy generally. However, I want to underline what is not implied by this statement. I am *not* saying that playing one-down, directing interventions toward individuals or small subgroups rather than doing "full family" sessions, positive relabeling, warning clients to "go slow," and other items from the brief therapy bag of tricks are necessarily superior to the clinical methods of other schools of treatment. Maybe they are, and maybe they aren't. Who beats whom in the Anorexia Nervosa 500 has no bearing on the subject of this article. Even if all of the appropriate experimental comparisons were done and some other school of treatment turned out to work better, or faster, or more reliably than Palo Alto-style brief therapy, a roughly Palo Alto-ish or accidentalist account of this fact would still be the most intellectually satisfying. ■

JEFFREY BOGDAN, M.S.W., *is program supervisor, Catholic Charities, Diocese of Metuchen, Fords, NJ.*

See references, page 566.

*L*ET US SELL NO INTERVENTION BEFORE ITS TIME

DOES FAMILY THERAPY NEED WARNING LABELS?

By Richard Schwartz and Peter Perrotta

SEVERAL YEARS AGO, THE FIRST AUTHOR OF THIS article published his maiden paper. It described a type of paradoxical intervention with which he had experimented. With pride and trepidation, he showed the paper to his father, a physician-researcher who has authored many medical papers. The following conversation ensued:

FATHER: "It's interesting and well written, Dick, but it seems a little manipulative of people."

SON: (*using a line he had heard recently at a workshop*) "Well, all therapy is manipulative, Dad. We are just more honest about it. Besides, it's effective."

FATHER: "Well, that may be so, but something like this would never be accepted by a medical journal. It's based entirely on anecdotal evidence."

SON: (*defensively*) "But it's important to share new ideas and techniques that can build on one another without having to wait for elaborate studies. Besides, there is no money for that."

FATHER: "Maybe so . . . By the way, I looked through some of the rest of the articles in that issue of your journal. You know, there's a lot of bullshit in your field."

The conversation ended at that point, but his father's observation has continued to percolate inside the son's head.

AN UNMISTAKABLE TONE OF IMMODESTY HAS long characterized the family therapy literature. As a field, we have reveled in our creative freedom and our propensity for daring and unusual interventions. Over the past 25 years, we like to think of ourselves as having compiled a record of such overwhelming clinical success that our nonsystemically minded colleagues have been hard pressed to justify their professional existence. But in recent years, increasing numbers of family therapists have begun to see the family field's idealized self-image and its tendency to make great claims for itself in a different light.

As Don Ransom, associate editor of *Family Systems Medicine*, puts it, "Creating a climate of enthusiasm is a stage in the sociology of any new profession. The early claims made by family therapy—that it might be *the* panacea—were important in turning many of us on, getting us involved in the field."

But what about family therapy's early claims? What was their basis? In retrospect, it is now clear that family therapy first attracted adherents not because it offered such convincing research evidence but in large part because of the clinical flair and persuasiveness of its charismatic originators. We have been a field dominated by a group of leaders with enormous crowd appeal and stage presence. Today they continue to shape attitudes within the field and establish the standards against which practitioners judge their own work.

"The prominent purveyors of family therapy often seemed to be making across-the-board assertions about what their methods could accomplish—it is as if they were saying they had the cleanest wash no matter what the dirt was," says Alan Gurman, editor of the *Journal of Marital and Family Therapy*. "Mostly this has been communicated indirectly by rarely reporting failures and not providing clear research data."

Developed largely outside university settings, family therapy has never demonstrated much affinity for the discipline of the academic research tradition. Actually, too much preoccupation with the constraints of scientific proof might have meant stifling the field's remarkable creativity and growth.

If today family therapy is plagued with an inordinate amount of questionable notions and inflated claims, isn't that the price we pay for our creative freedom? Maybe the trick is to be a good sifter, to have a quick nose for trash and a strong instinct for ideas with a solid foundation.

On the other hand, how many half- or even quarter-baked ideas are being thrust at hungry and impressionable therapists desperate for help with their tough cases? How often are techniques that may be effective in certain contexts with certain families at certain stages of treatment sold to eager consumers as cure-alls? How many warning labels are attached to or recalls issued for ineffective or destructive products in family therapy's long-run-

ning battle of the brand names? And how many families are casualties of this battle?

As a field shaped by polemical struggles with other therapeutic approaches hostile to the systems paradigm, we have often tended to rely more on rhetoric than evidence in establishing our legitimacy. As polemicists, we incline toward sweeping generalizations and are sometimes less than eager to temper these with the qualifications, refinements and disconfirmations learned from clinical experience. Family therapy is a wide-open field in which innovation and clinical experimentation are strongly encouraged. But perhaps we are now at a point at which we can look at the price we pay for our creative freedom.

TO BE SURE, FAMILY THERAPY IS NOT THE ONLY new therapeutic approach propelled into prominence by impressive early claims. The field of sex therapy burgeoned in the early 1970s largely as a result of the overwhelming success reported by Masters and Johnson in their book *Human Sexual Inadequacy*. Masters and Johnson maintained that common sexual problems, previously thought to be very difficult to treat, were easily cured in a short time with their simple techniques. They claimed that only 20 percent of the nearly 800 patients they treated failed to improve.

In the wake of the publication of *Human Sexual Inadequacy* and the media attention it attracted, sex therapy suddenly achieved legitimacy. And as couples began seeking this kind of help, therapists around the country rushed to get training from Masters and Johnson or to emulate their techniques without any formal training. Yet, despite all this activity, it took a full decade before Masters and Johnson's research received much critical scrutiny.

In 1980 Bernie Zilbergeld and Michael Evans, after being unable to approach Masters and Johnson's success rate in their own practices, decided to reexamine the original study. They concluded that

LET US SELL NO INTERVENTION BEFORE ITS TIME

"Masters and Johnson's research is so flawed by methodological errors and slipshod reporting that it fails to meet customary standards—even their own—for evaluation research. . . . Because of this, the effectiveness of sex therapy—widely assumed to be high since the advent of Masters and Johnson—is thrown into question."

Even Robert Kolodny, one of Masters and Johnson's colleagues, in defending *Human Sexual Inadequacy* against Zilbergeld and Evans's charges, conceded that the book was incomplete and premature. Kolodny suggested that criticisms of Masters and Johnson's work might have been preempted had they waited until they knew enough about the effects of their techniques to publish an in-depth explication of their methods and research data: "Had this [the in-depth explication] been written earlier, perhaps some misconceptions about our therapy mode would have been avoided." Maybe so, but by publishing only an outline of their techniques accompanied by such impressive outcome claims in *Human Sexual Inadequacy,* Masters and Johnson inspired poorly conceived and mechanical attempts at replication across the country.

It may be argued that premature and overly enthusiastic reporting by Masters and Johnson was needed to generate enough excitement to launch a new field that, without doubt, has helped many desperate people. The flaw in this ends-justify-the-means argument lies in the damage done to those patients whose problems were oversimplified and whose hopes were raised and dashed.

FAMILY THERAPY ALSO HAS RISEN RAPIDLY ON THE wings of big promises. It has been common for new models of family therapy to debut accompanied by the suggestion that they should work with nearly all cases within a vaguely specified population. Typically, the models offer simple instructions for the use of techniques, along with the implication that "anyone can do it." Many practitioners faced with the overwhelming demands of their caseloads are so desperate that even the most anecdotal or vague outcome reporting can become gospel. If an authority says, "Try it—you'll like it," the odds are that many therapists will do just that.

How then are practitioners to orient themselves in a field in which claims are often grandiose and guidelines minimal? The first author of this paper is a case in point of how a fledgling therapist can be influenced by a therapy approach's grand claims in the absence of specified guidelines. Ten years ago, he was an eager but green member of a psychiatric crisis team. That year he discovered the book *Change*, by Paul Watzlawick, John Weakland and Richard Fisch, of Palo Alto's Mental Research Institute, and embraced it as the solution to all his therapeutic muddles. This attitude was not discouraged by the authors of *Change,* who made statements like ". . . second order change through paradox—is undoubtedly the most powerful and elegant form of problem resolution known to us," and "We see our basic views on problem formation and resolution, persistence and change, as usefully and appropriately applicable to human problems generally."

He seized on a small footnote in the book that said a wide range of psychiatric problems were at least significantly improved in 73 percent of nearly 100 cases, and in an average of fewer than 10 sessions. Taking this as compelling proof of the validity of the paradoxical approach, he brazenly prescribed that all kinds of psychiatric morasses he encountered in his crisis work remain the same.

On one occasion, he made a home visit to a chronically depressed older man who had an established pattern of becoming bedridden for weeks, being hospitalized, getting better, returning to work, then getting depressed and returning to bed for weeks. The first author, with barely hidden sarcasm, told the now bedridden man that he should continue in his current helpless state because his wife was a retired nurse and needed to have a patient to care for. Enraged, the man bounded out of bed, grabbed a broomstick, and chased the well-meaning young therapist out of his house.

Did this incident point toward a positive outcome? After all, the man was activated to get out of bed and express his anger directly. But the couple never wanted to see the therapist again and quickly fell back into their old pattern. The point once again is that had the therapist been given more extensive guidelines to temper his enthusiasm, the same intervention, delivered in a different way at a different point in treatment, with more sensitivity to the systemic predicament of both husband and wife, might have been useful.

D ESCRIPTIONS OF CASES IN WHICH PARADOXICAL maneuvers have left clients more confused and resentful than cured have rarely made their way into the professional literature. And while paradox is best understood as an orientation to understanding human problems rather than a technique, this is not the way it has been generally portrayed. Instead, paradoxical methods have often been promoted, with a kind of magical allure, as levers for bringing about miraculous turnarounds in impossibly difficult cases.

What has received less attention are the difficulties that the Milan group, whose book *Paradox and Counterparadox* touched off much of the interest in paradox, experienced in training people in their model. According to Sergio Pirrotta, who has written a paper on the Milan group's training program: "The Center's students began to return with reports of treatment failures and disappointments. . . . In some cases, the students' experiences were near disasters, as attempts to introduce this kind of therapy within their own working contexts in the public mental health centers and psychiatric units in hospitals had resulted in stirring up the wrath of coworkers, the administrators of these places, as well as the clients themselves. Many had faced the ridicule of

colleagues and disciplinary action from their superiors not only for treatment failures, but also for what was seen to be unorthodox and perhaps dangerous conduct in the therapeutic contact with the patients and their families.

It became clear to the [trainers] that they had made a major epistemological error. In their attempt to impart to their students the family therapy technique that had been so successful for the Milan team's work for so many years, they had overlooked the fact that their technique had been developed within a context that was quite different from the [one in] which the students worked."

As a result of their trainees' experiences, the Milan team recognized that they had placed too much emphasis on the teaching of technique. Training methods were changed, and students were discouraged from directly transferring the Milan team's techniques to their own work settings. The training focus changed to helping students find ways of applying systemic thinking to their work instead of just grafting on a set of clinical methods.

Word about these problems and the adaptations they necessitated, however, has reached far fewer therapists around the world than were inspired by *Paradox and Counterparadox,* which contains few guidelines, while promoting paradoxical technique with some impressive anecdotal outcome claims. Indeed, the Italians concede in the introduction to *Paradox and Counterparadox* that they felt pressured into publishing their work "despite the fact that publication is undoubtedly premature."

A MPLE WARNING AGAINST THE INDISCRIMINATE use of paradox is found in Jay Haley's *Leaving Home.* Haley emphasizes the need for restraint in applying "Milanese paradoxes" without careful study: "The average therapist, working in a situation where he must deal with social control agents, colleagues with power over his case, administrators of his clinic or hospital whom the family members can appeal to over his head, a regular therapy schedule, undesirable medication and families only tentatively involved and uncommitted, should approach such paradoxical interventions with caution."

Ironically, however, Haley uses more ink in *Leaving Home* warning about the potential misuse of the Milan model than he does discussing the problems that may arise from his own approach to troubled young adults. The present article was inspired, in part, by our encountering a significant number of casualties of the Leaving Home Model (LHM).

We wish to emphasize that the damage we have observed could usually be accounted for by mistakes of therapists who were ill prepared, poorly supported, or who applied the Leaving Home Model to cases that were inappropriate. We are *not* taking the position that the LHM is itself ineffective or inherently destructive. On the contrary, our experience indicates that when flexibly applied by a well-trained or supervised therapist to an appropriate family, the model can often help families make very significant changes. The problem is that, as with other therapeutic models in the family field, the published literature on the Leaving Home Model paints an oversimplified picture of its implementation without examining what can happen when use of the model goes awry.

In *Leaving Home,* Haley says little about the level of training or supervision required for successful implementation of the model. Nor does he have much to say about the types of families on which it should *not* be tried, the range of dilemmas a therapist might encounter in applying the model and how to get out of them, or details on the cases where it has not worked. Instead, the LHM is presented as an instrument that "causes positive change and has a low risk of doing harm." In addition, Haley suggests that it can be applied to most troubled young adults regardless of diagnosis or symptoms.

His book contains only two qualifications to this carte blanche. Early on, Haley warns that the LHM may be only partially effective in cases where family issues may not be the major cause of difficulty—e.g., retardation, brain tumors, damage from drugs, the debilitating effects of repeated hospitalizations, etc. Later the reader is advised against using the LHM with younger adolescents because they are "trapped at home, so a different approach is needed . . . it is more reasonable to put the parents in charge, but with emphasis on [the adolescent's] rights in terms of decisions and privacy."

With these cautions aside, *Leaving Home* is devoted to making the case that by persistently following an arduous but relatively straightforward and simple approach, therapists at all levels and settings can resolve some of their most difficult clinical problems. Agency caseloads are usually overflowing with mad or "eccentric" young adults, and since other therapy approaches addressed to this population are invariably far more pessimistic, it is not unusual to encounter mental health workers whose reading in family therapy is virtually limited to Haley's book. *Leaving Home* seems to have filled a void in the clinical literature and has had a large impact on the mental health field.

Yet, despite its widespread application, we can find no published discussion of the actual difficulties therapists have encountered in using the Leaving Home Model. In fact, the only reference we have encountered is a comment by Haley himself in a *Networker* interview several years ago: "Well, there are people who, after reading *Leaving Home,* go out and tell families that the problem is that their kids need to 'leave home' and even that the parents should expel them. The fact that I say at least 10 times in the book that a therapist shouldn't say that does not seem to make any difference. Sometimes what you write for therapists spills into the community in unfortunate ways, and then you're sorry you ever wrote it."

Nevertheless, little if anything has been written to correct the "unfortunate" interpretations of *Leaving*

Home, even though we believe the exaggerated displays of parental authority that the model encourages have led to many family struggles with less than optimal results. For example, an overburdened single mother who worked full time was challenged by her therapist to take charge of her 22-year-old son, whose life had been a series of failures. Caught between the persistent prodding of the therapist and her fear of her son, she vacillated between extremes of outraged restrictiveness and despondent apathy. The struggle between mother and son eventually escalated into physical fighting, at which point they left therapy.

In this case, as with others we have seen, the therapist did not accurately assess whether this single parent had the resources needed to impose the degree of authority that is so central to the Leaving Home approach. But beyond a particular therapist's faulty assessment is the larger question of the applicability of the Leaving Home Model to various kinds of nontraditional families, of which single parents are only one example. In their rush to apply the Leaving Home approach, therapists have often failed to question whether the model's basic tenets fit all family configurations. So, in stepfamilies, therapists who see a child's misbehavior as an attempt to help maintain a parent's marriage, instead of as a reaction to the intrusion of a stepparent, may orchestrate an elaborate intervention that misses the family's developmental issue. Even in traditional family structures, there is the question of the implicit cultural assumptions of the LHM. The value systems of some ethnic families are at odds with the idea that young adults should establish American-style independence. Therapists who ignore such factors are inviting "resistance," premature terminations and, sometimes, worse.

Even when the family seems to be appropriate for the LHM, the approach can be so demanding to implement effectively that many therapists burn out. As Jay Haley points out, "As change is threatened,

the therapist will find his or her character tested by the intensity of the involvement." Our experience has been that even the best-trained or most-experienced therapists have trouble passing this test of character if they are practicing in isolation without a supportive team or supervisor. And the fact of the matter is that most therapists, trained or untrained, practice in isolation.

IN ITS FOCUS ON DESCRIBING A RANGE OF CLINICAL methods, the written literature of family therapy has tended to ignore the difficulties practitioners encounter with techniques that "should" work. In this piece we have devoted so much attention to the Leaving Home Model because it so clearly demonstrates that the very potency that can make a method an effective clinical tool also creates the potential for its misuse. We believe that presentations of clinical methods such as Haley's, which rely so heavily on the therapist coping with the intensity of a therapeutic crisis, need to consider what happens to these methods in the hands of fledgling therapists, as well as the masters.

It is one thing to see videotapes of a master family therapist like Salvador Minuchin using extreme tactics to get the parents of an anorectic to eat. It is quite another for therapists without great skill and long experience to attempt those same tactics. Unfortunately, this distinction is too often ignored. As Carol Anderson, coauthor of *Mastering Resistance*, puts it, "We haven't really regulated training in any thoroughgoing way. A lot of people get all their training in workshops—which means they develop their concept of what family therapy is by looking at highlight films."

This highlight-film approach to training has created the idea that when *really* practiced skillfully, family therapy inexorably leads to profound change. "The idea has circulated that if you were good enough, you would never have a failure," says Monica McGoldrick, coeditor of *The Family Life*

Cycle and *Ethnicity and Family Therapy.* "It's as if the major proponents of the different schools have been giving the message that their model is so powerful that the therapist only gets in the way."

The result of this kind of attitude is to discourage a careful examination of the limitations of the various family therapy models. We have all come to accept a curious lack of self-corrective feedback in the family therapy literature. All kinds of theories and clinical methods are offered to the community of practitioners, but their collective experiences of frustration and difficulty in applying these models are not regularly fed back into the professional literature. In the absence of such feedback within the professional literature, a distorted picture of clinical practice has come to dominate the field.

"I've been practicing for almost 20 years, and I know I haven't been able to create the kinds of changes that the leaders in the field talk about," says Susan Stewart, Anderson's coauthor of *Mastering Resistance.*

"I think someone has to shake us awake," says Anderson. "There has been a tendency for people to stretch their work to make it seem more impressive. That may be because of the competition within the field or the belief that just to be heard, you have to make hyper-claims."

Developing a more realistic picture of practice has also been complicated by other factors. Sometimes the focus on abstract or theoretical issues obscures the more basic issues of practice. "Among some of Murray Bowen's students, it's considered somehow lower class to talk about how you engage with a family," observes McGoldrick. "Somehow that's not 'pure' systems thinking. But the fantastic thing about Bowen is how he uses his humor and personal warmth in therapy. Nevertheless, it's gotten established that you don't talk about joining with people. And if you don't talk about that, then Bowen's approach gets taught as if you just apply it to the family. It's as if the therapy is so powerful that it's supposed to work by itself."

McGoldrick thinks that the lack of attention to the differences between the personal characteristics and working context of a model's developers and that of those who apply it in practice is by no means confined to one family therapy model. "The main teachers haven't addressed such contextual issues as the age and sex of the therapist," she points out. "While most workshop performers are older males, most trainees are young and female. The question is how to prepare *them* to comfortably and effectively use these methods. And, despite Haley's great essay 'Why Mental Health Centers Should Avoid Family Therapy,' we still haven't given enough attention to the institutional contexts in which the various therapeutic models get practiced."

WHY HAVE MODELS OF FAMILY THERAPY BEEN sold as wonder drugs with unlimited applications and few side effects? Certainly, the field's battle of the brand names tends to discourage discussion of limitations or warnings. But there is also another factor at work. The theorists behind the various models of family therapy appear to have believed that, while their map was not the territory, it was the one that led to the buried treasure. That is, they believed that they had captured the essential pattern that needed to be transformed—whether that meant prescribing people's typical behavior, regulating proximity and distance among family members or breaking up transgenerational triangles. As they developed techniques that accomplished these goals, these theorists must have felt a growing urgency to convince an unenlightened professional public to try their new discovery.

What is often missed in the process of promoting a theory are the qualifications. The general applicability of a model is emphasized without clear specifications about the contexts in which it is effective. Less attention is given to determining whether the model works only with certain families or therapists, or in conjunction with other models or techniques. In other words, these essentialists have broken what might be called the Paul Masson Rule— they sell their model before its time.

We believe that usually the originators of a model move beyond this essentialistic stage as they continue to get feedback on their model's limitations. Unfortunately, it is rare for theorists to publicly qualify their original fervor even after they recognize that it is unwarranted. Says family therapy researcher Nathan Epstein, of Brown University Medical School, "In any new field, a lot of ideas get enshrined early on, even if later evidence disproves them. I have a lot of therapist friends who take as gospel everything Freud said in 1890."

Have we reached a point where we can forgo some of the messianic fervor in which the field started and be clearer about questions like—what kinds of people do we do best with? With what kinds of problems are we effective? Where is our record not so great? How can we begin to create an atmosphere where discussion of the failures or limitations of our models is not taboo?

There are a number of positive signs that the field is emerging from this essentialist stage. Says Anderson, "Early on I think we had a need for people to be our gurus and inspire us with their absolute conviction. Today I see much less focus on the field's superstars and more interest in a serious integration of ideas on the conference circuit." According to Alan Gurman, "When Bergin and Garfield were first organizing their *Handbook of Personality and Behavior Change* in 1968, there wasn't enough quality family therapy research to merit a chapter. Things have progressed extraordinarily since then. In a recent note to me, in fact, Bergin wrote that after reading our most recent review of the family therapy research, he's finally become a believer."

Some influential theorists are finding that they can no longer describe families or therapy in simplistic, unidimensional language or recommend all-pur-

pose techniques. As Salvador Minuchin observed recently, "When I first began to teach family therapy, I did so with a deceptive simplicity. Today I talk a lot more about complexities."

The family therapy literature is beginning to tackle some of the thornier issues of clinical practice. Michael Berger and Greg Jurkovic recently compiled a book titled *Practicing Family Therapy in Diverse Settings*, which is the first work to systematically examine the issues in applying family therapy across a range of such different institutional contexts as the child-welfare system, the schools and the court system. David Campbell and Rosalind Draper have put together a book in which a number of practitioners discuss how they adapted the Milan approach to their particular work setting. Sandra Coleman has just edited *Failures in Family Therapy*, in which some of the most prominent senior people in the field—Paul Watzlawick, Carl Whitaker, Lyman Wynne, W. Robert Beavers—open themselves to an in-depth exploration of some cases that went awry.

We are at a point where we can seriously examine the strengths and limitations of our current methods. Perhaps we are ready to confront the fact that, whatever the considerable merits of the various family therapy models, they contain far less magic than we once dreamed they did. "We have to learn how to lower our sights and realize what we can accomplish," says Braulio Montalvo, a senior trainer at the Philadelphia Child Guidance Clinic. "I think our effort now needs to be highlighting the various areas in which we have some honest knowledge, and away from clinical mythmaking."

S O IF WRITING ABOUT TECHNIQUE IS DANGEROUS because of the potential for misuse, what is the alternative? Should we retreat to a Batesonian prohibition against intervening or writing about our interventions? The Sufis offer an example worth considering. According to Robert Ornstein, manuals for Sufi practices are notoriously difficult to come by because "the Sufis hold that technique must be administered with time, place, and the state of the student taken into account, and the publication of their practices may lead to faulty application of the exercise. They say, for instance, that a technique such as meditation is useful at a specific stage of development, and persistence in any technique after the appropriate period would be a waste of time or might even be harmful." Rather than risk the misuse of their techniques, the Sufis keep them a mystery to all but those deemed ready.

The secrecy of the master-apprentice model of disseminating wisdom is clearly inefficient for training more than a select handful; however, we could benefit by adopting some of the Sufis' rigor and responsibility toward training, and perhaps counteract our Western tendency toward the hard sell.

Fortunately, the field of family therapy has achieved enough status that it no longer needs an immodest voice to attract attention. In light of this situation, we have the following recommendations for those who would write about family therapy interventions:

1. Do not rush to publish. If a formal outcome study is not possible, conduct an informal one in which both the immediate and longer-term effects of the intervention(s) can be observed and the intervention(s) tested in a variety of contexts with a variety of family constellations, problems and therapists. Study the failures as closely as the successes.

2. Warn the reader. Devote as much ink to guidelines for anticipating and avoiding problems in the use of the intervention as is given to guidelines for implementing it. Discuss the kind of training, experience, time, or support therapists will need before they use it. Be clear, and give examples of situations in which it is not effective.

3. Do not overpromise. The proponents of most new models or interventions seem to go through an essentialistic stage during which they believe they have found the essence of the problem as well as its

solution. This stage is characterized by grand claims and simplistic explanations. To avoid overpromising, one may have to wait until the essentialistic stage is over or waning before writing about the interventions.

4. Follow up your work. Consider the consequences of publication. Before making a final decision to publish, ask yourself two questions: (1) Even if I do not overpromise and I provide plenty of warnings, what is the potential that the model will be misused? (2) If the model *is* misused, how much harm might accrue? Certainly, some models or techniques are more difficult to understand or apply than others. And some involve more provocative steps, and more potential harm, than others.

We are calling for a kind of risk-benefit estimate. Where the risk ratio is high, we recommend deferring publication or at least considering ways to reduce the ratio.

5. Do not hesitate to qualify or correct previous claims. It is too much to expect that the four recommendations listed above will be followed faithfully, and when they are, inevitably mistakes will be made. This is a major problem only if the mistakes of influential models remain uncorrected. Just as a responsible carmaker will recall defective models, it is our responsibility to make public the defects in our previous work. Unfortunately, many theorists either find such admissions distasteful, or remain in an essentialistic stage throughout their careers, or move on to other projects before they become aware of the defects of previous models.

To the consumers of models of family therapists, those wandering the marketplace struggling to find an approach that "feels right," our basic message is *caveat emptor*. In addition, we recommend that as a consumer, you heed the following:

1. Learn the basic principles of outcome research, after which you will find you have become skeptical of even the most elaborate studies in our field.

2. Thoroughly immerse yourself in a particular

model, but stay close to a colleague with a different viewpoint who can temper your zealotry.

3. Avoid experimenting with new techniques you learn from a book or workshop unless you have good supervision and support, or a solid systemic conceptual base with which the technique is a good fit. This is particularly true where the technique is sold with big promises and few warnings.

4. Consider following the example of Charles Fishman, former director of training at the Philadelphia Child Guidance Clinic, who, in preparing an upcoming book, has been conducting a series of two-year follow-up interviews with families he treated over the past five years. "Doing these follow-ups, I've come to appreciate better what a family does with initial interventions and how change takes place in stages," says Fishman. "Talking with people several years after treatment, you learn what changes and what doesn't. You see better the links between what happens with individuals and the changes in their families. You also see how focusing more on an individual family member earlier on might have made a big difference in their later functioning."

5. Note that the baseball adage, "You are never as good as you think you are when you are winning or as bad as you think you are when you are losing," also applies to therapists and models of therapy.

In the process of selling family therapy to a skeptical mental health field over the past two decades, we have created a facade of perfection and omnipotence that has kept us from letting our guard down or admitting that we cannot cure everyone. In this atmosphere, the average family therapist can wind up feeling like a fledging superstar when his or her techniques work, or like a total incompetent when they do not.

FINALLY, WE, THE AUTHORS, KNOW THAT WE ARE holier-than-no-one. Our house contains as much glass as those we criticize. We have made all the mistakes we cite here in our teaching, writing and practice. Indeed, the whole field has had the freedom to be reckless and, overall, has benefited from this freedom. But the point is that we are developing potent medicines and there is no Federal Drug Administration for psychotherapy. Unless we devote more attention to the consequences of our efforts, we do not merit our luxurious freedom, and one day it may be taken from us. ■

RICHARD SCHWARTZ, PH. D., *is the coordinator of training and research, Family Systems Program, Institute for Juvenile Research, in Chicago, IL.*
PETER PERROTTA, PH.D., *is in the Department of Pediatrics, Christ Hospital, Oak Lawn, IL.*

See references, page 567.

ILLUSTRATION BY DAVE SHANNON

LOOKING FOR THE FENCE POSTS

EVERYDAY PRACTICE PROVIDES A BLIZZARD OF ETHICAL QUESTIONS

By Mary Sykes Wylie

IN HIS MOST RECENT BOOK, *AGAINST THERAPY*, Jeffrey Moussaieff Masson argues not that there are "bad" or "unethical" or "incompetent" psychotherapists, but that "abuse of one form or another is built into the very fabric of psychotherapy," whether it be psychoanalysis, individual psychotherapy, family therapy, gestalt, humanistic psychology, or any of the 250 or so variants now practiced. For Masson, honesty, integrity and mutual trust in the so-called therapeutic relationship are poisoned by the imbalance of power between therapist and client, the cash nexus around which therapy revolves, specious claims by therapists of "scientific" expertise, and the implicit social indoctrination in what purports to be a politically neutral "curative" process. Masson writes, "In the world of therapy, it is therapy itself that is at the core of the corruption," and no individual therapist, however noble his intentions or theory, however humane, can resist the taint of "a profession that depends for its existence on other people's misery."

However distorted, shrill and wrongheaded, Masson's book strikes a raw nerve, particularly in a public climate of growing disillusionment about the integrity and competence of many in positions of public trust. Witness the spectacle of lawyers, lobbyists, politicians, stockbrokers, bankers and medical researchers jailed, fired, or otherwise disgraced for malfeasance.

Therapists themselves have been uneasy with the language of ethics, which they have associated with atavistic notions of moral absolutism—prohibitions, obligations, guilt and sin—all incompatible with professional values of tolerance, flexibility, relativity, freedom and choice. And if therapists, on the whole, have not believed in moralizing to clients, they have also been excessively touchy about external professional regulation and complaisant about their own rectitude. The threat of imminent lawsuit, however, like impending execution, concentrates the mind wonderfully. Recently, litigation against psychotherapists has become something of a growth industry. In the last two years, lawsuits against therapists have doubled, making clinicians willing to think more deeply about their ethical responsibilities.

Legal liability and ethical behavior are not the

same, of course, though fear of litigation can lead therapists to conflate the two. Jay Efran, professor of psychology at Temple University, worries that many regard ethics simply as technical maneuvers for avoiding lawsuits. According to Efran, the field of psychotherapy is becoming more like medicine, in which "physicians give every test in the world simply in order not to be sued. This is not good medicine, but it is legally clever."

Ethical behavior requires something more than goodwill, the ability to follow rules, and an inclination to stay out of court. Formal moral codes have limited utility; they are neat generalizations in a world of messy particularities. In classical Greece, writes philosopher Alisdair MacIntyre, the virtuous person was distinguished by "the capacity to judge and do the right thing at the right time in the right place." According to Aristotle, good moral judgment rested upon the ability to balance reason, feeling and desire, but most of all, it demanded intelligence—one could not be both good and stupid at the same time.

Moral intelligence, the mark of a fully realized human being in Aristotelian terms, was taught and learned within a social context; the characteristic virtues were expressed socially as justice, friendship, self-sacrifice, loyalty, truthfulness, courage. The virtuous person was, in other words, a profoundly "good and wise friend." Two ethical rules revered by the Greeks, and particularly relevant for psychotherapists today, were accountability—being answerable for expectations that accompany a particular role—and self-restraint, a virtue associated with aristocrats who had power and authority but chose not to abuse them.

Ethical codes are not moral rules themselves; for the latter, consult the *Bible*, the *Koran,* the *Dharma Shastras,* or the *Analects of Confucius.* The word "ethics" refers to the *study* of what constitutes moral conduct, not the conduct itself. One commentator has observed that a therapist is "probably" ethically responsible if he or she acts with personal and professional honesty in the best interest of the client, eschews malice or personal gain, and can justify his or her actions on the best current judgment of the profession. Such ethical rules of thumb must look to a therapist floundering in an ethical quandary like barely visible fence posts in a blizzard—one only hopes they'll lead home.

MOST ETHICAL FORMULAS HARDLY BEGIN TO cover the subtle and complex ethical dilemmas daily confronting the practitioner. In a world of multiple, often incompatible, methods for treating every variety of psychic pain, responsible therapists are familiar with self-doubt. David Treadway, a family therapist from Massachusetts, says, "We can all give a good speech about what we're doing, but many of us struggle with the question of whether this is an ethical way of life at all."

A major source of ethical difficulty for psychotherapists is the ambiguous nature of therapy itself. Unlike physicians, lawyers, accountants, or teachers, therapists can provide little empirical evidence for the value of their services—no broken bones set, legal documents drafted, tax forms completed, reading or writing skills taught. The "welfare of the client" is paramount in every code of ethics. But what does that mean in therapy? Is therapy supposed to make the client happy? Freud thought the goal of analysis was merely to exchange the patient's neurosis for the ordinary unhappiness of human life. On the other hand, some New Age therapists believe they can totally transform their clients. What works and what doesn't work? And what does it even mean to say something "works"? Some therapists consider the eradication of symptoms—whether agoraphobia, bulimia, childhood misbehavior, marital strife, or fear of flying—a "cure," while others view every symptom as the tip of the iceberg and the client family as the *Titanic*. Often therapists must determine who the client actually *is*—the whole family conceived as a unit? Each and every individual in his or her own separateness? Just one "identified patient"?

Fairly standard procedures exist for setting a broken leg, regardless of the personality hobbling around on it, but far less consensus exists about treating the troubled psyche. Clinicians variously advise, lecture, exhort, question, mystify, cajole and browbeat their clients. They listen quietly to a solitary soul haltingly tell a story, or they magisterially direct a huge cast in a family extravaganza. Well-established psychotherapeutic interventions that work superbly in one case may fail miserably in another case that looks exactly the same.

In some sense, the most perplexing aspect of therapy is that the relationship itself between therapist and client *is* the "service" delivered. This service will be delivered by therapist and client together, according to some idiosyncratic, and largely unpredictable, logic. The exact quality of the therapeutic relationship, regardless of the therapist's determination to be no more than a "consultant" or a "good and wise friend," will still most likely be obscure, changeable and ambiguous.

The most scrupulously ethical therapist may not be the most effective one. "To be successful," Massachusetts psychotherapist Mark Karpel argues, "the therapist must be both trustworthy *and* influential—the nicest guy in the world can't make a dent if he has no influence." Because they *are* granted so much influence and authority, therapists have the same ethical responsibility as the ancient Greek aristocrats: not to abuse their power.

BECAUSE THERAPISTS HAVE A HARD TIME DEFINing exactly what they do, other than claiming to "help" people, many are tempted to regard themselves too literally as "healers," drawing models for their profession from the practice of medicine. Indeed, because mental health providers now often work within a medical setting, as part of HMOs or as adjuncts to hospital services, they are more likely than ever to apply the medical model wholesale to their clients. Using a medical model becomes ethically suspect when therapists claim the same kind of empirical validation and predictability for their own methods as physicians and research scientists do for theirs. Biomedical science and psychotherapy are not interchangeable disciplines. The therapist who takes too seriously the metaphors of "sickness" is claiming an undeserved scientific expertise, piggybacking on the implied authority of science to diagnose, prescribe for and predict the outcome of complex conditions that are not easily defined, let alone "cured."

On the other hand, a group of mental health professionals calling themselves biopsychiatrists cite the recent advances in brain chemistry studies as evidence for the efficacy of pharmacological intervention in a wide range of major and minor psychological problems. These practitioners quite openly, even proudly, "pathologize" mental and emotional conditions. Psychiatrist Mark S. Gold, an expert on drug abuse, writes in favor of "medical psychiatry" because "it returns psychiatry to the medical model, incorporating all the latest advances in scientific research, and, for the first time in history, providing a systematic method of diagnosis, treatment, cure and even prevention of mental suffering."

These words freeze the blood of many family therapists, who believe their colleagues often overpathologize clients and misapply medical diagnoses to families whose values they personally find repugnant. In fact, family therapy developed partly in response to what was felt to be the repressive and nontherapeutic use of drugs, shock therapy and psychosurgery for social control of people considered rebels, troublemakers, or just nuisances. That the major antipsychotic drugs commonly have severe, sometimes irreversible, side effects, the worst being tardive dyskinesia, still makes their use highly controversial.

Nonetheless, drugs are now routinely prescribed for, and frequently alleviate, the symptoms of schizophrenia, depression, manic depression, anxiety, even bulimia, agoraphobia and addiction. Evidence exists for genetic and neurophysiological factors in most of these conditions. Many practitioners of "talk therapy," even family therapists, use medication in conjunction with other interventions. Carol Anderson, professor of psychiatry at the University of Pittsburgh and president of the American Family Therapy Association, insists that family therapists have an ethical obligation to be knowledgeable about neurobiological approaches, about which clients themselves have a right to know. For example, lithium is considered highly effective in treating manic depression. Anderson argues that a therapist has an ethical responsibility to inform clients of this option.

Anderson has harsh words about the narrowness and dogmatism of some family therapy training. She charges that many therapists "think their theoretical belief systems are facts. They don't read, they don't keep up to date, they don't know about other materials." She believes that the ignorance of many therapists about areas beyond their immediate field, especially medicine, leaves them vulnerable to practicing beyond their competence—unethically negligent behavior, even if unintended. She related one case of a woman seeing a family therapist for marital problems who suffered headaches that the therapist called "psychosomatic." Though the headaches did not abate over an extended course of treatment, the therapist never referred her to a physician, and eventually the woman died of a brain tumor.

FAMILY THERAPISTS ARE NOT THE ONLY PSYchotherapists inclined to dogmatism, of course. Although psychoanalysis may have pioneered this failing, family therapy, having grown into respectable middle age, has inherited the same tendency to speak in tongues, or in what psychiatrist

Thomas Szasz has called "private languages" and "mysterious theories." Some family therapists seem to regard terms like "enmeshment," "boundaries" and "individuation" more like laws of physics than useful references to socially determined styles of relationship.

Ethical problems arise when the jargon-ridden language of psychotherapy assumes a life of its own, somehow divorced from the everyday reality of its clients. Family therapists can be so fascinated by theoretical abstractions that they are oblivious to quite glaring hardships faced by the families they treat. Judith Grunebaum, one of the coordinators of the Ethics Interest Group of the American Family Therapy Association, remembers a team discussion about a case of a previously hospitalized adult man living with his two elderly parents. The man, depressed, paranoid and considered potentially dangerous by the evaluating therapist, announced that he had a loaded gun at home. A family therapist on the team, trained in structural and strategic methods, insisted that the parents be told to take the gun away from their son, on the premise that since the son was not acting like an adult, the parents should reassert their parental authority and be "put back in charge" of their family. The other team members, however, were appalled by the thought of a potentially lethal confrontation between two old people and their very unstable son over the disposition of his loaded gun. They overruled the structural therapist in favor of treating the man individually as an adult, straightforwardly asking him to bring in the gun and telling him of the possible legal consequences if he did not. The structural therapist, recalls Grunebaum, still "could not see beyond the context of his own terms—what he called the 'hierarchical incongruities of the structure'—to the real dangers posed for real human beings. He finally said, 'This is the only way I know how to do this.'"

Less dramatically, blind allegiance to a particular therapeutic model becomes an ethical failing when the therapist consistently gives more weight to the model than to what clients say they want and need. Therapy trainer Bill O'Hanlon, coauthor of the recently published *In Search of Solutions,* describes the case of a woman who came into treatment for help with her bulimia. The therapist decided that first the woman's entire family must be restructured. The family changed radically, but the woman herself did not. She left the therapy, says O'Hanlon, "still stuffing herself and vomiting her guts out."

The ethical concern here is not the therapist's sincerity, commitment, or technical expertise, or even the decision to "reframe" the bulimia as a family problem. Rather, the therapist needed to exercise some rudimentary ethical judgment about the "success" of an intervention that seemed so totally to disregard the immediate needs of the person seeking help, a woman whose life was possibly threatened by her bulimia. He might have consulted with specialists on bulimia; he might have considered using other approaches in conjunction with family therapy—individually oriented interventions or group therapy for the bulimic herself. Instead, his rigid overinvestment in one theoretical approach suggests that the individuals of the family were less important to him than the system, that he regarded his therapy as an artist does his painting—what came first was *his* masterwork, *his* creation, and the needs of the client who did not fit the "big picture" were overlooked.

Individual family members can be sacrificed to the "good of the whole" in family therapy, but there are also times when seeing only one member of a family threatens the well-being of both the family and the individual. Many therapists regard proceeding with individual psychotherapy unethical under these circumstances. Mark Karpel once saw a young woman who was very depressed and anxious. She had dropped out of college four times, could not get a job, and did not get along with her parents. Karpel invited her parents to come in, and witnessed the terrible relationships between the three—he remembers that all were unremittingly horrible to each other. In the course of the session, he discovered that the father himself was a deeply depressed man, who, in his youth, had suffered a devastating career failure, followed by a nervous breakdown and several suicide attempts. He was currently working at a low-level position with the post office. At one point, the father contemptuously said about his daughter, "She doesn't even have a job," suggesting to Karpel that the "failure" of his daughter probably was all that stood between him and complete fragmentation of his self-esteem. Possibly his daughter's demonstration that she was even *more* inadequate than he was kept him from attempting suicide again. Karpel's dilemma was that if he treated only the daughter in therapy, her growth and "success" might indirectly cause the father's death and devastating guilt in the daughter. Karpel believes the ethics of this situation virtually demanded a family systems approach.

THE SEVEREST CRITICISM OF FAMILY THERAPY IN recent years has come from feminists, who do not question the value of family therapy but rather the patriarchal and sexist values implicit in much of the field's theory, language and current practice. Feminist therapist Deborah Luepnitz, author of *The Family Interpreted: Feminist Theory in Clinical Practice,* has argued that family therapists mask social ideology and political realities in a fog of pseudoscientific mumbo jumbo. In such an environment, women suffer disproportionately. Luepnitz and other feminists argue that family therapy has blatantly devalued women and ignored the social and historical realities of their oppression. Feminists have particularly excoriated systemic models for obscuring the realities of power in theoretical formulations such as the presumed "equivalence" between abusive husbands and their wives—as if the two were equal partners in a marital "complementary dance." Feminists also argue that family therapy is guilty of provoking a kind of double bind in mothers by blaming them for being "overinvolved" with their children while sidestepping the fact that society expects them to be just that. According to family therapist Thelma Jean Goodrich, coauthor of *Feminist Family Therapy: A Casebook,* "For years, the standard family therapy prescription was, 'Get Mother to take a powder, and bring in father to straighten things out.'"

Goodrich believes that feminist and patriarchal ideas of ethics may differ, but that male-biased family therapy has been unethically disrespectful of women and negligent in disregarding the relationship of power to personal accountability. Abusive men have more raw power, however defined, than their abused wives and ought to be held to proportionate standards of accountability.

Several therapists have extended the feminist critique to encompass the moral poverty of systems thinking as a whole. Family therapists often fail to acknowledge the social and economic history of their clients—the generations of racism, oppression, crime and deprivation in the background of one family. Critics insist that this blindness to social issues outside the immediately present "family system" is unethical, a form of negligent disregard for the nonclinical realities contributing to the "pathological" situation. It is as if a pediatrician were to prescribe aspirin for a very sick child, blame the patient's mother for the child's illness, and completely ignore a raging epidemic of poliomyelitis in the community.

SOME CRITICS VIGOROUSLY COMPLAIN THAT MANY therapists confuse their own values with clinical wisdom when they try to impose on clients naive and idealized myths of what they believe family life should be. Jaime Inclan, director of the Roberto Clemente Family Guidance Center in a prominently Hispanic neighborhood in New York City, is particularly concerned about this tendency in young, unmarried, middle-class clinicians seeing older, poorer families from a different social class and culture. Young therapists, Inclan says, "have an absolutely idealized view of the way families and couples should be, and have the illusion that there are unidimensional universals to family life." Inclan describes the case of a 60-year-old Ecuadoran wife whose 63-year-old husband was having an affair with a 33-year-old woman. The wife knew of the affair (not the man's first), to which she was resigned, but was galled that the woman was somebody she knew personally.

The young social worker, holding strong convictions about both marital fidelity and women's rights, insisted that the woman must be "denying" her "real" emotions of grief and anger at her husband's betrayal. This clinician refused to believe that the wife might be operating within a traditional cultural world view in which male infidelity was acceptable as long as certain protocols were obeyed. Inclan felt that the social worker was on the verge of catapulting the wife and husband into a therapeutic maelstrom—suggesting divorce, for example—for reasons that had more to do with her own needs and values than with those of her clients. Inclan suggests that young therapists may emerge from training with ironclad theoretical systems and personal values but little tolerance for human cultural diversity.

NIGHTMARISH ETHICAL DILEMMAS CAN RESULT when therapists treat abused children and their families. On the basis of limited information, the therapist may have to choose between the danger of letting a child stay at home in order to salvage the family and the psychic damage that may result from placing the child in the physical safety of an institution or foster care. Michael Nichols, professor of psychiatry at New York's Albany Medical College, says the cases that raise the most troubling ethical issues are not those involving severe, intolerable and unremitting abuse, but the less dramatic examples that require Solomon-like wisdom to pre-vent tragedy. Reporting abuse to social service agen-cies, says Nichols, activates the "stern, retributive voice of authority," which, in practice, seems more inclined to punish than to help the offending family.

At the same time, feminists and others have often denounced family therapists for not doing enough to protect vulnerable family members by immediate-ly reporting known or suspected cases of child abuse and incest. But even when such reports are required by law, therapists may find themselves wrestling with questions of whose interests will be served by such action. A therapist was seeing a family that included several children in late adolescence. During one session, the oldest daughter and the father revealed an incestuous encounter that had occurred between them years before and had not recurred. The therapist was required by law to report the incest to the authorities, which she did, after telling the family of her legal obligation to do so. The fami-ly was furious, left therapy, and initiated legal action against the therapist.

On the other hand, not every reportable case gets reported. In one clinic, the staff argued vehemently over a case involving a young, single mother begin-ning therapy who admitted that she periodically lost control of her temper and hit her 2-year-old child. The state in which this happened requires that any *suspicion* of abuse be reported, and the staff was divided between those who adamantly insisted that this child abuse be reported and others who wanted to give the mother more time. The therapist who took over treatment said he found "a young, single mother, hardworking, the sole supporter of the household, cut off from all social ties, whose only source of love was her child. She didn't know how to discipline the little girl, and couldn't stand the dis-tance between the two of them that any effort at dis-cipline involved." As a result, the child's misbehav-ior and the tension of the mother's life had created serious problems, but did not constitute what this therapist considered true child abuse. So he began working with her to alleviate the stress in her life and to help her develop a better relationship with her child.

Bill Doherty, professor in the Family Social Sci-ence Department at the University of Minnesota, describes another case that he thinks falls into the "gray zone" between legality and ethics. A father and 16-year-old daughter came to a family therapy ses-sion, both sporting black eyes. During an argument, the daughter had hit her father with a lamp (his black eye), he had socked her in retaliation (hers). The family showed no history of violence, and the father had never shown himself to be a violent man; indeed, the family was in treatment partly to help the father assert some authority over his rebellious daughter's life. Doherty did not turn this family in, either. He is aware, however, of the large area of dis-cretionary power he assumes in deciding how much and what kind of physical abuse are ever to be "hid-den" by the therapist from the law.

THERAPISTS ARE NOT POWERFUL, BUT THERAPY is," says family therapist David Treadway. "People use it to make major decisions about their lives." However true Treadway's statement, no one who has ever been a client believes the therapist is not powerful. Much traditional psychotherapeutic theory is devoted to the idea that the client's belief in the therapist's "power" is a critical part of the transference necessary to improvement. In any case, power, or the ascription of it to a therapist, is not a neutral commodity and is particularly susceptible to ethical abuse.

A troublesome, but quite typical, ethical dilemma is the puzzling difficulty of how therapists most effectively use their power without consciously vio-lating their own sense of ethics or unconsciously imposing their own needs on the client. Any skilled therapist has a good many manipulative skills at his or her command and an often vulnerable and willing client expecting something. What might "work" that he or she chooses not to do for ethical reasons? Besides the controversies around paradoxical interventions and therapeutic deception are the more prosaic ethical issues of how much truth to tell a client, and how to determine the line between giving clients what they want and what the therapist perceives they need. Observes Jay Efran, "I think you can never give a person precisely what they ask for. This would simply be to replicate the situation they bring into therapy. If they could truly ask for what they needed, they probably wouldn't require treatment in the first place. The job of the therapist involves shifting the way questions are posed."

Yet, giving clients what they need—telling them the truth in their own "best interests" from a sense of personal and professional integrity—raises ethical problems in the area of free choice and informed consent. Treadway believes that therapists often fail to consider the full ramifications of therapy and the possibility that the therapeutic process can sometimes make their clients' current situations completely untenable. Clients who come into therapy with specific, limited goals may find their lives overturned. "Someone may come in with a particular problem in mind," says Treadway, "like a weed he wants pulled from his garden, while you may think that the entire garden needs to be uprooted and replanted. But enhanced consciousness can make some people's lives unbearable."

Even highly specific, problem-oriented therapy can be unpredictable. Treadway recalls the case of a woman whose life radically deteriorated after her successful treatment for mild agoraphobia. "Since her recovery," says Treadway, "she is in terrible pain, because she is no longer in denial about some God-awful stuff in her life—child abuse, the death of a brother for which she was held responsible." Treadway says that she has spent the last seven years receiving a variety of psychotherapeutic treatment, which has not helped much. As Treadway puts it,

"Her whole craziness had been distilled into one little black hole of phobia." In many ways, she was perhaps "happier," though far less "conscious," before she was "cured."

Many therapists apparently avoid these dilemmas by assuming a straightforward contractual relationship between equals, in which the client brings to therapy specifically articulated problems, which the therapist addresses as an expert problem-solving consultant. Says Insoo Kim Berg, director of the Brief Family Therapy Center in Milwaukee, "We want to know what they want to change. They spell it out, and if we have the technology and knowledge to help them, and we come to a mutual agreement about how this should be done, we are obligated to follow through." Berg believes it is unethical—an implied breach of contract—not to use the technology at her command to relieve the pain of her clients.

Fundamental to Berg's ethical stance, however, is her belief in her clients' basic rationality and good intentions—they know better than she what they need. Berg believes in the importance of therapeutic neutrality and suggests that many family therapists share "a very widespread illusion that we know exactly what is right for people. I don't have any clear idea of how they should behave or live their lives, but want to help them determine what is relatively right for them."

How much freedom should therapists allow themselves in departing from accepted therapeutic conventions? What separates a leap of brilliant innovation from a lapse into unethical eccentricity? Lothar Salin, a California psychotherapist in private practice, believes that any experienced therapist at least once in a while will do something unorthodox. He cites the case of a classical psychoanalyst who began his work with a new patient, a sickly and malnourished woman, by taking her to the supermarket and helping her shop for groceries. The analyst reasoned that he could not help her until she fed herself better. Jay Efran was once called by an old client in the midst of a crisis for an emergency session. The client lived in a different city, and Efran arranged to meet him at a motel on the turnpike halfway between the two cities. Efran, however, prudently took a graduate student along as a "witness," and the three men engaged in an all night "marathon" therapy session that got the client through his crisis. Salin himself once held a therapy session in his car when, because of scheduling conflicts, there were no offices available. But, says Salin, "there is a dividing line between willingness to do something unorthodox for a specific purpose, knowing the risks, and making a habit of it." And nobody could argue that the examples cited here entailed *great* risk.

Sometimes treatment that strikes some therapists as inspired and inventive strikes others as ethically appalling. As a result, bitter personal and legal disputes can arise, particularly between enthusiastic, young practitioners and older, more conservative supervisors. In one case, now under litigation, two therapists, John Comley and Laurel O'Meara, and a case manager, all employed by the Personal and Family Counseling Services of Tuscarawas Valley in Ohio, worked as a therapeutic team with a young, thrice-married mother and her family. The mother, an incest victim as a child, had been hospitalized several times and was taking an impressive variety of psychotropic drugs. Her marriage was failing, her children were having severe behavioral problems in school, and child services authorities were prepared to declare her an unfit parent.

In 1987, after a year of what Comley and O'Meara thought was limited progress, the two therapists and the case manager began, with the support of the social service agencies, a short-term blitzkrieg of therapeutic interventions, including home-based individual psychotherapy and marital counseling, family therapy, trance work, therapeutic rituals, relaxation techniques, guided imagery, training in

parenting skills and crisis management. One, two, or all three of the team saw the woman and her family every day, sometimes two or three times a day. Some sessions, held at home, in the car, while walking in the park, at the agency, could last from one to three hours. The relationship between the woman and the two therapists became particularly close. Comley, the team leader, said he became "like a brother" to the family.

When the team therapy ended in early 1988, the woman, by her own account, was feeling happier and more in control of her life; she was down to one tranquilizer. Her marriage had improved and she had begun a small business of her own. She now refers to the therapy as "the most magnificent thing that ever happened to me."

Representatives of the Tuscarawas Valley counseling service refused to comment on the case, claiming they were protecting client confidentiality. But Comley and O'Meara's supervisors apparently did not share the client's enthusiasm—as a result of this case, Comley says, he was fired, and O'Meara quit in protest amid accusations of inappropriate and dangerous therapy, negligence in completing paperwork, insubordination and sexual impropriety. According to the two therapists, their superiors said that trance work was potentially dangerous for "borderline personalities," which they believed the woman to be. The supervisors thought the therapy was too ambiguous, too emotionally intense, too negative and too unstructured to buttress the client's inadequate sense of emotional control. They objected to the amount of time expended on the case, and what they thought were the therapists' cavalier attitudes about submitting reports and financial records. They believed the therapists' professional credentials (an M.A. in counseling and an A.C.S.W.) were not up to the complexity of the case.

Most damaging, however, were accusations of "countertransference," exhibited in "sexually provocative," "seductive" and "flirtatious" behavior with the client. The therapists had made a videotape of one of the trance sessions they conducted with the woman. During this session, the supervisors maintained, the therapists made "inappropriate" sexual innuendoes to each other and to the client, which, the supervisors felt, created an untherapeutic atmosphere for a woman with a history of being sexually abused. At issue, too, was the fact that Comley had, on various occasions, hugged or touched other clients on the shoulder, which, according to Comley and O'Meara, one supervisor said was always in error, especially with adult survivors of sexual abuse.

Comley is currently suing the agency, but in such cases nobody wins. Clearly, the question of inappropriate erotic behavior in a therapeutic setting does not only arise in dramatic, highly publicized trials of therapists charged with flagrant sexual abuse. The matter of physical touch itself can be the subject of intense ethical debate. A handshake, a pat, a stroke on the shoulder, a helpful boost up or, on the other hand, a shrinking away, a withholding of a hand, an insistence upon physical distance, all can convey powerful emotional messages. In the highly charged therapeutic relationship, a seemingly insignificant touch can carry disproportionate emotional weight; it can symbolize human acceptance, love, benediction, or it can seem like an intrusion, an aggression, a kind of ownership. As Virginia Satir, one of family therapy's pioneers, knew well, physical contact could convey affirmation and reassurance. Inappropriate touch, however, can do great harm, and a therapist insensitive to this issue is at the very least ethically obtuse.

Touch is one measure of the way a therapist establishes boundaries in his or her practice. David Calof, a Seattle therapist who specializes in treating adult survivors of abuse, takes a generally conservative view about touching clients. "I believe, theoretically, in 'no touching,'" he says, "because you can assume that the abused person will misconstrue the touch; you can assume they are misinterpreting it as

seduction, and will take it as a cue that the therapist will not be able to sit still." On the other hand, when Calof has developed a bond of trust with clients, he engages occasionally in "child touch—like the locking of little fingers" or a consoling touch on the shoulder of a weeping client. He is nonetheless reluctant to grant client requests for physical contact—hugs, for example—because he is so aware of the entrenched dynamics of seduction in the client's family of origin.

Abuse cases bring into high relief the professional and ethical struggles that all therapists face in learning to distinguish between their own needs and those of clients—the bugaboo of countertransference. "To what extent," asks David Treadway, "are we allowed to meet our own needs in therapy?" Treadway suggests that it is irresponsible for therapists to pretend they can "be always there 100 percent" for clients, because personal needs will simply go underground, while exerting an unconscious, unrecognized and unacknowledged influence on the therapeutic system. David Calof remembers that in his early years of treating survivors of childhood abuse, he would "take on" their anger for them. "They would tell me outrageous stories, I would rage in horror, while they just sat and watched," in effect "protected" from working through their own anger and grief

Therapists who do not know their own minds are unable to recognize or accept responsibility for their own feelings. They cannot separate their own emotional reactions from those of their clients and are therefore poorly equipped to fulfill the ethical mandate to exercise good clinical judgment in their practice. But a therapist's own *recognized* needs can provide a sense of empathy, an intuitive understanding of the client. Treadway reports that about 80 percent of the therapists he trains for work with alcoholics are themselves children of alcoholics. Is this good or bad? Observes Treadway, "Too much detachment doesn't engage people; too much caring won't work either."

LOOKING FOR THE FENCE POSTS

Psychotherapy is something of an ethical balancing act. Daily problems in its practice regularly overflow the narrow definitions of its official codes and standards, and yet no field seems so utterly dependent upon the ethical strength of its practitioners. The issue is not so much the ethics of *therapy* as the ethics of the *therapist.* Is he or she honest, trustworthy, sensitive, knowledgeable, courageous, open-minded, modest and rigorously self-reflective? The last seems particularly important. Several family therapists admitted that one of the undeniable strengths of the old enemy, psychoanalysis, is the requirement of a "training analysis" before professional certification. Because, if the very first rule for all the healing professions is "Primum non nocere"— First, do no harm—only in psychotherapy is this injunction so inextricably bound up with the exhortation to "Know thyself." The line between self and other, my needs and your needs, is perhaps in no other profession so difficult to distinguish and so critical an ethical requirement. ■

MARY SYKES WYLIE, PH.D.*, is the assistant editor of* The Family Therapy Networker.

See references, page 567.

CONSTRUCTIVISM: WHAT'S IN IT FOR YOU?

KNOWING WHEN A TABLE IS NOT A SOFA

By Jay S. Efran, Robert J. Lukens & Michael D. Lukens

EVERYWHERE THAT FAMILY THERAPISTS TURN these days they run into constructivism. With his *The Invented Reality*, Paul Watzlawick gave us a widely cited book about it. Lynn Hoffman (1988) recently called constructivism the most significant shift in clinical thinking since family therapy began. Various other well-known workers in the field—Karl Tomm, Tom Andersen, Harry Goolishian, Peggy Penn, Luigi Boscolo and Gianfranco Cecchin—have filled family therapy's journals and workshop platforms with presentations of therapeutic methods that are presumably based on constructivist insights. Actually, it could be argued that due to the influence of Gregory Bateson, constructivist thinking has been woven into the fabric of family therapy since its inception and that this influence has only been amplified by the more recent writings of thinkers like Chilean biologists Humberto Maturana and Francisco Varela.

Still, a family therapist who is faced with the day-to-day travails of clients in crisis, and unused to the esoteric philosophical speculation, may be forgiven for asking, "What's in it for me?" In fact, such a family therapist may, without realizing it, already be influenced by the basic insights of constructivism. For instance, techniques such as reframing and positive connotation, which constitute the lifeblood of many family therapy practices, have a decidedly constructivist flavor. Moreover, the many family therapists already accustomed to thinking pragmatically in choosing clinical strategies may, unwittingly, be revealing their constructivist bias. Unlike traditional Freudian analysts, who torture themselves over the *accuracy* of a given interpretation, such therapists are more apt to worry about whether a particular formulation will "sell well" to the family. "Utility," as opposed to "Truth," is high on the good constructivist's list of priorities.

An objectivist enterprise such as psychoanalysis is built almost entirely on the belief that objective truth is discoverable, and, when properly revealed, leads to improved psychological health. By contrast, family therapy is just as often based on the constructivist belief that a good intervention generates its *own* truths. Objectivist therapists want to know what *really* happened in the past; constructivist therapists are more interested in "history" as a key to the unfolding family narrative that gives contemporary events their meaning. Objectivists are convinced that they can, and should, discover the "facts" about how families really are; constructivists believe that whatever "facts" they assemble tell as much about the nature of their conversation with families as about the families themselves.

Given that versions of constructivist tenets—some accurate, some highly distorted—have seeped into the thinking of family therapists, it is perhaps time to describe the essence of this epistemological stance a bit more formally and explicitly.

AT ROOT, CONSTRUCTIVISM SIMPLY REPRESENTS a preference for the Kantian model of knowledge over the Lockean. The 18th-century philosopher Immanuel Kant, one of the pillars of the Western intellectual tradition, regarded knowledge as the invention of an active organism interacting with an environment. In contrast, John Locke, founder of British Empiricism, saw knowledge as the result of the outside world's etching a copy of itself onto our initially blank, "tabula rasa" minds (Rychlak, 1981). Thus, the card-carrying Lockean regards mental images as basically "representations" of something *outside* the organism, while the Kantian assumes that mental images are wholly creations *of* the organism, produced as a by-product of its navigation through life. Thus, the images of the objectivist can be thought of as "discoveries" about the outside world, and the images of the constructivist are more like "inventions" about what is out there.

Psychologist George Kelly, who introduced personal construct theory and is considered by many the first person to formally bring a constructivist perspective to the fields of personality theory and mental health, insists that we not confuse our inventions with discoveries. For example, in describing the creation of his own theory, he explained: "I must make this clear at the outset. I did not find this theory lurking among the data of an experiment, nor was it disclosed to me on a mountaintop, nor in a laboratory. I have, in my own clumsy way, been making it up." (Kelly, 1969)

Watzlawick (1984) emphasizes a similar distinction when he suggests that the shift from objectivism to constructivism involves a "growing awareness that any so-called reality is—in the most immediate and concrete sense—the *construction* of those who believe they have discovered and investigated it." In other words, objectivists are inventors who think they are discoverers—they do not recognize their own inventions when they come across them. Good constructivists, on the other hand, acknowledge the active role they play in creating a view of the world and interpreting observations in terms of it.

In physics, Isaac Newton would be considered a Lockean, who, in the spirit of his times, went about discovering the objective laws of the outside universe. By contrast, contemporary theoretical physicist John Wheeler, inventor of the black hole, would be a good example of a Kantian. Wheeler has explicitly stated that without people, neither black holes nor any of the prevailing laws of physics would exist. Many of us have trouble grasping the import of such a radical pronouncement because we have been brought up to be thoroughly objectivist in our outlook. We are convinced that the principles of physics, including Wheeler's black holes, are really out there. After all, we have seen a black hole—in the Disney movie of the same name!

To make the shift to the constructivist perspective, it might help to imagine some other species—let's say, Martians—starting off on a completely different line of inquiry and, consequently, developing an entirely different body of observations and conceptualizations concerning the "natural universe." Martian physics might end up bearing little resemblance to our own, but unless physicists from these two different traditions happened to bump into one another at a convention, each group might continue along happily in the belief that its view was a direct revelation about how things actually are.

The heart of constructivism is the recognition that our hypotheses about the world are not directly provable. To the constructivist, scientific hypotheses persist mainly for two reasons, neither one having much to do with objective truth: first, because we find them useful in our work (utility); second, because no one has yet been able either to disprove them or to come up with a better alternative. Hypotheses that persist are, at best, part of a temporarily acceptable working framework. As George Kelly (1969) put it, "None of today's constructions—which are, of course, our only means of portraying reality—[are] perfect and, as the history of human thought repeatedly suggests, none is final."

ANOTHER CRITICAL CHARACTERISTIC OF CONstructivist thinking, which fits reasonably well with what many of us do, is the emphasis on context and meaning. For the constructivist, "everything said is said from a tradition" (Varela, 1979) and has meaning only within that tradition. Take something out of context, and it becomes meaningless. Put it in a new context, and it means something else. Problems—mental or otherwise—are not circumstances or actions taken in isolation. They are ascriptions of meaning that arise within a particular tradition.

For example, retirement, by definition, is a circumstance in which a person is no longer expected to work. In and of itself, it is neither a curse nor a blessing. However, in a person's life, situated as it is in a particular familial and cultural context, retirement may prove to be either. Moreover, when a retiree spirals into a depression, dragging the spirits of those around him or her down as well, the constructivist therapist is apt to seek an explanation in the rearrangement of meanings that occurs. For example, the retiree's definition of self as a productive worker may

not have been replaced by a framework of equivalent importance and clarity. Therefore, in terms of meanings, the retiree may have become more or less "lost in space."

With some hesitation, we mention another, more controversial, example of this phenomenon—rape. We are tempted to put the term in quotes to emphasize that, for the constructivist, "rape" is not an objective event that carries with it predetermined meanings and predictable sequelae. Rather, it is an interpretation rendered within a tradition—a tradition that shapes and molds the reactions that both the person experiencing rape and others will have. The language community determines by consensus (and, sometimes, by concession) what role-options are available to the person who has been raped, and which entitlements, good and bad, he or she can anticipate receiving. In other words, to the constructivist, rape is not just an action or an event—it is a framework of activity and interpretation, made possible by the shared language system in which we all operate.

Note that we are not condoning nor lightly dismissing the potential consequences of rape. Nevertheless, as constructivists, we must insist that the "trauma" of rape takes place in language, as part of a socially sanctioned narrative. Rape isn't just a fact established by a medical examiner, even though—obviously—it has physical sequelae.

Perhaps our reader is wondering if the physical aspects of rape, such as pain, are also part of the "socially sanctioned narrative." We believe that even experiences that people consider purely physical are, in fact, language-dependent. Pain, for instance, is not simply the firing of nerve endings—it is a "package" of interpretations surrounding sensations. Pain, therefore, is part sensation, part fearful ideation.

In anticipating receiving an injection, a person's reaction may incorporate thoughts of bodily invasion, danger, loss of control and so on. The resulting experience is much more than nerve stimulation by a needle. Similarly, proponents of natural childbirth, while they cannot entirely eliminate the sensations of giving birth, can help recontextualize the experience by dispelling fear-arousing myths and giving parents-to-be a useful framework for managing the event. As part of their tutoring, they speak of "contractions" rather than "labor pains," recognizing that our vocabulary colors our experiences.

As we have noted, many of the core elements of constructivist thinking are apt to have a familiar ring to many family therapists. Actually, constructivist epistemology sets much of what family therapists do into a broader and more easily understood context. In turn, it grants some measure of intellectual respectability to those practices. However, respectability never comes cheap. To be properly sheltered by the constructivist umbrella, a family therapist may have to give up certain beliefs and attitudes. For example, constructivist psychotherapists are not "allowed" to consider psychotherapy an objective, value-free enterprise that simply aims to "improve psychological well-being." Such rhetoric is incompatible with the emphasis in constructivism on the value-laden nature of all human undertakings.

Even the scientific establishment itself has found its traditional claims of "neutrality" eroding under the onslaught of constructivist arguments. The discovery of objective truths—the original *raison d'etre* of science—has increasingly been revealed to be a chimera. It now appears that—even in theory—the interests and activities of the scientific *observer* cannot be fully disentangled from the *observations* he or she produces. In other words, with the shift toward constructivism, even the "hard sciences" have had to become softer. As some have suspected all along, science turns out to be a political "club" of sorts, with its own specialized canons of operation and stringent rules of membership. Although the club of science still justifiably has many avid supporters, its

major product—scientific knowledge—can no longer be sold as the absolute and universally acceptable commodity we were once led to believe it was.

Also, family therapists who want the constructivist badge of approval will have to loosen their tight grip on the concept of "the family." The family therapy movement, which encouraged a shift away from the then prevalent focus on the individual, was liberating. However, each liberation signaled the beginning of a new rigidification. Thus, in some circles, "the family" has been objectified and is now being worshipped as the new intervention unit.

The theoretical sword of constructivism cuts in all directions. It teaches that hard-and-fast boundaries cannot be objectively drawn around *any* particular unit, family or otherwise. Even in "hard" biology, it isn't necessarily clear whether a given organism is a plant or animal, an individual or a colony. Units are definitions in language, and they invariably have an arbitrary quality—they can be created, selected, rearranged and dissolved.

If we are forced to acknowledge that not only black holes, but the very laws of physics, are "invented," then we must also admit that families exist as units only in the mind of the construer and that there are as many different "families" as there are construers. Moreover, the same person may construct different families for different purposes or occasions. To take a perhaps sad, but not trivial, example: People in need of borrowing money may suddenly discover in themselves a genuine and renewed feeling of family kinship where none previously existed. Similarly, at a family funeral, people's sense of who their family consists of may undergo a rapid, if temporary, expansion.

Actually, a number of benefits would result from more family therapists' getting into the constructivist spirit and taking the concept of the "family" more lightly. Any unit of analysis selected for attention, no matter how arbitrarily chosen, has an impact on the direction our thinking takes and the problem-solving pathways that appear to open before us. New units suggest new possibilities. A student who is trying to improve his or her grade on the next test will adopt different strategies from one who has decided that a change of major is needed. The issues of retirement we mentioned above, examined from the point of view of the individual retiree, look different from the retirement issues considered on a much larger scale by a politician in Washington.

It is useful to have the freedom to change lenses from time to time, first considering one level of analysis and then shifting to a larger, smaller or different unit of study. Each analysis opens up new possibilities for intervention. The individual, the couple, the family, the extended family, the community or, perhaps, as Goolishian and Anderson (1987) have suggested, the "problem-determined system"—that is, all those who "language" an issue in similar terms—can all be considered fair game for the constructivists. Moreover, given that a construed system is a kind of interlocking jigsaw puzzle of arrangements among the defined parts, the constructivist maintains an interest in the intersections of the units that have been separately defined.

To HELP GRASP THE SITUATION, THE READER might picture a number of playwrights who have been invited to present little playlets, simultaneously and on overlapping stages. Furthermore, each playwright, since he or she was going to be present anyway, has been given a part in every other playwright's productions.

Constructivism leads us to anticipate that we will all be enacting our own unique "constructed" playlets in roughly the same performance space, using each other as members of the cast. Under these seemingly bizarre conditions—what we typically refer to as "living"—is it any wonder that there are a number of bumps and bruises, accusations and con-

fusions? Moreover, constructivism alerts us to the fact that it will be hard to find a neutral judge with access to the conflicting scripts and the authority to sort out the mess. In this sense, constructivism is broadening. It moves us beyond a preoccupation with individual or even interactional dynamics into an appreciation of the ways life plans fit together, each one inadvertently reinforcing and forcing accommodations in many others. Even when the proverbial robber with a gun asks for your money, your next reply, whatever it is, will inevitably affect the outcome of Act II of his planned thriller. For that reason alone, your response takes on considerable importance to both of you.

We have been suggesting a constructivist metaphor for the coordinations of action that develop in a human community, and which constitute the essence of that community. The most elaborate and advanced coordinations are made possible by language and take place primarily in that medium. Baseball, for example, may look as if it takes place on a field—and, in one sense, it does. But although you can play forms of baseball without the usual field, you cannot play it without symbolization—language.

Language is the one essential that such complex coordinations of action in a social community cannot do without, and that is why constructivists insist on talking about human lives as basically being "conversations." Constructivist therapy, then, is figuratively and literally a specialized form of conversation.

Because constructivists regard the language community as all-important, therapists who are working from this point of view must get used to the idea that they are engaged in an essentially political endeavor. Like other human pursuits, therapy fosters the establishment, exchange and maintenance of particular traditions and language formulations. Issues of personal responsibility and ethics can neither be ducked nor masked by objective-sounding terms like "treatment," "mental health," "the normal family," "family loyalties" and so on. The ethical concerns of constructivist therapists go well beyond the usual issues of professional misconduct, such as having sex with clients. For constructivists, the *entire therapeutic venture* is fundamentally an exercise in ethics—it involves the inventing, shaping and reformulating of codes for living together. In other words, from this point of view, therapy is a dialogue about the interlocking wants, desires and expectations of all the participants, including the therapist.

As one of the first to go on record as a constructivist therapist, George Kelly found it useful to characterize his role in such a dialogue as that of "research consultant." Kelly was not interested in fixing problems—he was interested in coinvestigating testable hypotheses about productive ways to live. In our opinion, that idea still has a great deal of merit.

As early as 1950, in the service of these therapy "research projects," Kelly did what many family therapists are still doing today: he told parables, acted out scenarios, arranged demonstrations, made direct suggestions, gave odd homework assignments and issued provocative challenges. Of course, because this was prior to the advent of "family therapy," he was as likely to do this work with individuals as with family groupings. However, the most distinguishing feature of his conception of therapy had little to do with the unit he chose to focus on—it was the "twist" he placed on the role of behavior and symptoms. For Kelly, behavior per se was never the problem. It was a means to an end—the human instrument for posing questions. In other words, when an adolescent really wanted to find out the penalty for staying out all night, he or she stayed out all night. Behavior is what behavior asks!

Kelly saw symptoms as nothing more or less than human questions, behaviorally expressed, that had lost their moorings. The connective threads, which

might have led the person to either a satisfactory answer or a better question, were missing. This left him or her stranded in midair, somewhat like the depressed retiree we described earlier. He wanted to help such individuals reformulate their questions so that inquiry could begin to move forward again.

KELLY WOULD HAVE BEEN COMFORTABLE WITH the circular questioning techniques that are now becoming popular among family therapists. However, he would never have been willing to limit himself to any particular investigative formula. In his view, good "research" demanded much more flexibility and creativity than that.

Kelly's abiding constructivist belief was that no matter how disturbed people might appear to be, and no matter how long they had been rattling back and forth in the same old conceptual tracks, they had the ability to notice the kinds of "templates" they had created and that they typically used to make sense of the world. He also believed they had a largely untapped capacity to invent and make use of alternate conceptual "glasses" that would bring new perspectives into view. His philosophical credo was: "There is nothing so obvious that its appearance is not altered when it is seen in a different light. . . . *Whatever exists can be reconstrued.*" (Kelly, 1969).

In this fashion, Kelly, a constructivist par excellence, helped launch clients on a voyage of exploration. In training therapists and working with clients, he continually made a distinction between explorers who played it safe and stuck to "academic" questions versus those who were willing to venture into riskier waters. The adolescent who only sat around and wondered about the consequences of missing a curfew—but did nothing about it—was, in Kelly's estimation, an "academic." In his view, responsible living involves taking calculated risks. It is when a question calls for action that the questioner learns whether he or she has the courage of his or her convictions. *(continued on page 273)*

What's All the Fuss?

FAMILY THERAPY IS FOREVER BUZZING WITH ONE FASHIONABLE WORD OR ANOTHER. THE LATEST, "constructivism," tells us that the world we perceive is, in some sense, invented or constructed by us rather than merely found or discovered. I regard myself as a constructivist of sorts. Nevertheless, I often wonder what all the buzzing is about.

Humberto Maturana and Francisco Varela are two biologists from whom constructivists in family therapy have lately derived a great deal of inspiration. In their most recent book, *The Tree of Knowledge: The Biological Roots of Understanding*, Maturana and Varela claim that normal, unsophisticated folks "live in a world of certainty, of undoubted, rock-ribbed perceptions." Believing this, Maturana and Varela are understandably convinced that constructivism amounts to a radical shift in the way we understand ourselves and our relation to the world. However, in my experience, absolutely naive realists, people who think, in the words of Maturana and Varela, that "things are the way we see them and there is no alternative to what we hold as true" are rare past the age of three.

Most people will acknowledge under questioning that there could be a difference between what they think and what is, or that points of view other than their own could possibly have something useful to offer. The distinctions between "what seems" and "what is," and "what one believes" and "what is true" are, as far as I know, built into the structure of every language spoken on the planet. Add to this that it is scarcely possible to grow up in a family without bumping into the fact that people often view the same situation in very different ways, and the leap from common sense to constructivism may not be very big at all.

Many Western intellectuals have tried to make a case for our ability to arrive at the absolute truth. Hindu and Buddhist philosophers, however, have for millennia regarded our everyday images of reality as mental constructions. Even in the West there were always those who doubted that absolute truth was attainable. And the explicitly constructivist solution to the problems of epistemology, i.e., how we know what we know, has been around since Immanuel Kant. A great many modern scientists and philosophers have shared the conviction that both our everyday and our more scientific formulations of reality are constructions, among them Edmund Husserl, Karl Popper, Jean Piaget, Nelson Goodman, George Kelly and Gregory Bateson. Even Freud's concept of transference is a type of constructivism: the notion of transference is that ideas built up in early stages of development are later used to construct our experience of reality in the here and now. All this suggests that the so-called radical constructivism of Maturana and Varela is not so discontinuous with the tradition of Western epistemology as it has been portrayed.

Neither, it seems, is radical constructivism markedly at variance with ideas that have always informed the strategic family therapies. In Jay Haley's work and in that of the Palo Alto brief therapists, the central place of reframing presupposes that people construct both the definitions of the situation and the personal historical narratives that guide their behavior. Paul Watzlawick, of course, has written extensively on the topic of constructivism and has edited a book of essays by prominent constructivist thinkers (See *How Real Is Real?* and *The Invented Reality*). However, I think it is fair to say that his ideas about how to do therapy have not changed very much as a result of his involvement with constructivist epistemology. And this, I would suggest, is because the writings of the radical constructivists do not add all that much to the ideas about frames and reframing already developed within the traditions of strategic family therapy.

This is not to say that there is nothing new in the writings of the radical constructivists. One aspect of their influence, in fact, may have a profound and, to some, a surprising effect on the future of family therapy. Family therapists have in general tended to shy away from biology and medicine. When family therapists say that reality is constructed, they typically mean *socially* constructed, through language and learning and expectations and other psychological and interpersonal processes. However, for Maturana and Varela in particular, constructivism follows directly from an appreciation of modern biology and evolutionary theory. In their version of constructivism, it is the whole organism, including the genetically hard-wired parts of the brain and the nervous system, that does the work of constructing a reality. Now that family therapists are permitted to use the language of neurobiology and still maintain their position in the systemic avant-garde, we can perhaps look forward to the day when family systems and medical-biological approaches to helping people are no longer looked upon as diametrical opposites.

One last thought: Granted that how we perceive and understand reality is a construction, it is nevertheless absurd to suppose that there is nothing real out there to perceive and understand. Sticks and stones, if thrown with sufficient force and in the right trajectory, *will* break your bones, I'll wager, no matter how, or even whether, you perceive them. And I'll wager, too, that if you constructed a theory that enabled you to avoid them, you'd prefer it to all others.

This suggests that although every view of reality is a construction, some views are better than others for certain purposes. From the evidence of their book, for example, Maturana and Varela appear to be strong advocates of a particular way of constructing a scientific "reality." The methods of the sciences have often been misinterpreted as ways to discover the pure, unvarnished, indubitable truth. Nowadays all that scientists—the community as a whole, not just Maturana and Varela—expect to come up with is a formulation, a construction that is a little more coherent and a little more powerfully predictive than the last.

Of course, it's never wise to get into arguments with your clients over which of your views is the most scientific or accurate. The aims of therapy are different from the aims of science. But lately some family therapists have been tempted to equate constructivism with relativism, the idea that every view of reality is just as good as, and no worse than, any other. Let's try resisting this temptation, shall we? □

—*Jeffrey Bogdan*
SEPTEMBER 1988

JEFFREY BODGAN, M.S.W., *is program supervisor, Catholic Charities, Diocese of Metuchen, Fords, NJ.*

CONSTRUCTIVISM: WHAT'S IN IT FOR YOU?

(continued from page 270) (Fortunately for the history of aviation, the Wright brothers had that courage. Not every psychotherapy client does.)

THIS IS WHY COMMITMENT BECOMES SUCH AN essential ingredient in psychotherapy. Without it, therapy is an empty exercise—a trivial pursuit. To keep it from becoming trivial, a clear therapeutic contract—one that spells out everyone's obligations in no uncertain terms—is needed. The contract is what helps put the teeth into therapeutic work. It serves as the vehicle for monitoring progress, for establishing the criteria of success and failure, and for keeping everyone honest. It is the contract, not objective authority, that grounds the work of the constructivist therapist. Inattention to contractual details virtually guarantees a therapy that meanders everywhere and gets nowhere.

Constructivism is, of course, a theory of knowledge—not a collection of therapeutic directives or techniques. However, the constructivist viewpoint, if adopted, places certain restrictions on how therapy is to be construed. As we have already suggested, it makes the political nature of the venture apparent. Simultaneously, it clarifies how important it is for both therapists and clients to accept full responsibility for the consequences of their association with one another, even though those consequences are not entirely predictable at the outset. Although you can voluntarily sign aboard a voyage of exploration based on the allure of the printed itinerary, in the final analysis neither you nor the captain of the vessel can guarantee smooth sailing or a safe passage. No one knows for sure what adventures—for passengers and crew alike—lie beyond the bend in the river.

One of the hazards of all "conversation," including therapy, is that you never know exactly where it will end, and it is not altogether clear who is at the helm. It is a little like when two or more individuals have their hands on the pointer of a Ouija board; the coproduced motions that result are interesting,

but they are not necessarily what any of the individual participants originally had in mind or would have predicted. The very nature of the setup precludes being clear about who did what to whom.

That is why conversations in the consulting room never consist of simply "transmitting" intact chunks of knowledge from one person to another or stuffing information into a waiting, receptive (Lockean) mind. The process is (and must be) 100 percent participatory—a play with continuous and often noisy audience participation. In that sense, constructivist psychotherapy is not something therapists "do" to a family, nor, for that matter, that families do to therapists. Like a theatrical presentation, it is a thoroughly collaborative enterprise.

IN OUR VIEW, A PROPERLY INTERPRETED CONstructivism clarifies rather than complicates theorizing about therapy. However, as might be expected, the "break-in" period for this new perspective has been rocky—accompanied by a flurry of false starts, hollow claims and misleading interpretations. One of the most widespread and mischievous misinterpretations of constructivist thinking is the notion that since reality is "invented" anyway, "anything goes." This interpretation misses the fact that we do not live alone and that our shared language distinctions quickly become our realities.

In the social domain, the way an event is construed becomes inseparable from how it is experienced. Constructivism should therefore not be interpreted as a recommendation to trifle with established words and meanings. For example, it would be inadvisable for the reader to suddenly decide that he or she was now a plastic surgeon. There is the matter of going to medical school, completing a residency, taking board exams and the like. These requirements are built into the community's definition of the term. Such definitional components constitute the very fabric of social reality, and they cannot be modified by just a wave of the hand.

273

An invented social reality—once it has been invented—is as real and solid as any other. Try turning your kitchen table into something else—let's say, a living room sofa—through simple word magic. No matter how hard you try to "language" your table differently, it remains a table. It has, so to speak, earned the right to be a table through years of being languaged and experienced that way. Even within the most liberal interpretations of constructivism, it is considered necessary and useful to distinguish between pretense and heartfelt belief and to take note of the criteria a community uses to distinguish between "reality" and "fantasy."

IN THIS CONNECTION, WE SHOULD SAY SOMETHING about some popular family therapy techniques, such as "reframing," that have become associated with the constructivist ideology, and that have been taken by some as permission to play fast and loose with words and facts. "Reframes" sometimes work, and make sense, because they evoke alternative, viable and socially acceptable frameworks of interpretation. However, some "reframes" are little more than cheap carnival tricks. For example, telling a teenager that cutting school was really his or her way of keeping the family together, or of distracting attention from an extramarital affair, strikes us as disingenuous and foolhardy—unless, of course, one truly believes such a thing. As we have attempted to make clear, constructivism is not a license to fabricate indiscriminately for immediate effect. If it is true that those who live by the sword, die by the sword, then those who make their living being experts on the implications of language ought to think twice before taking too many liberties with it.

As constructivists, we are interested in simplifying and demystifying life's problems, not in adding additional layers of counterintuitive, half-believed, poorly substantiated mumbo jumbo. Quirky and facile yarns may yield momentary therapeutic leverage, but we fear that the long-term costs in terms of

increased suspiciousness and loss of credibility are too high a price to pay. We do not want constructivists to become known as the hucksters and con artists of the mental health profession. Unfortunately, there are professionals in the mental health field who are already reluctant to consult a family therapist about their own personal or family problems. They have no intention of being "positively connoted" or "reframed," even if it might be "for their own good." They prefer a therapy relationship they can trust—where they can count on receiving straightforward advice and honest feedback.

Notice that there is a subtle but critical difference between taking liberties with established definitions and proposing fresh problem-solving frameworks. As constructivists, we can endorse the latter but not the former. Suggesting that a teenager's absence from school was virtuous seems to us to be potentially shortsighted; suggesting that the family agree to consider its teenager's school career entirely his or her own business might be more helpful. The first is a pronouncement of dubious validity; the second is a research proposal of potential merit. One offers a ready-made rationalization for evading moral culpability; the other invites increased personal responsibility.

The leverage inherent in constructivism—the hopefulness of the approach—lies in the possibilities generated by the exploration of fresh terrain. Malleability is gradually and inevitably lost as new inventions become established traditions. For that reason, it would be unwise for a Monopoly player to try to turn Park Place into Happy Acres. If the person is intent on choosing new property names, let him or her devise a brand-new board game and then sell that to Parker Brothers.

A couple that has been trying to win approval from their in-laws ought to consider giving up on that tired and largely predictable game. It perpetuates interactions that circle round and round the same dreary track, ultimately pleasing no one. There are any number of alternative arrangements worth putting to the test: For example, it can be useful to call upon grandparents to create for their grandchildren experiences that only they are equipped to provide. This invites a different and more rewarding interaction pattern. One family was quite surprised to discover how readily the grandmother accepted an invitation to share memories of her own childhood spent growing up in a Russian *shtetl*. This was a pattern of relating that pleased everyone.

W E HAVE ALREADY IMPLIED THAT HUMAN behavior can never be fully predicted or unilaterally controlled. This constructivist insight, taken to extremes in some family therapy circles, has led some therapists to abandon all attempts to plan, predict or strategize. In our opinion, there is nothing in constructivism to support such a decision. It stems from an amalgam of several conceptual confusions.

First, the recognition that humans *sometimes* do surprising things does not mean that *all* attempts at predicting human behavior must be abandoned as worthless. Similarly, the fact that neither minds nor systems are directly controllable does not mean that individuals and families operate in a social vacuum, totally impervious to changes in the environment. Humans do what they do *in connection with* what goes on around them, not as social isolates. After all, language represents a coordination of actions among people. So, of course, human conversation permits a modicum of predictability about the behavior of others and promotes the development of reciprocal influence patterns. Thus, it continues to make good sense to arrange definite appointments with people because—more often than not—they will show up at the agreed-upon time. Moreover, it is still a good idea to try therapy strategies that have worked well in the past when a similar situation presents itself because those strategies may very well work again. Yes, it is all an experiment—but human behavior is

not chaotic, and past experience counts.

To avoid any and all planning, predicting and strategizing just because living systems are not absolutely predictable or directly controllable is not constructivism—it is nonsense. Such a position, if taken seriously, would bring responsible human action to a halt—and arrest therapeutic "dialogue" in its tracks. It would paint every therapist—not to mention every physician, dentist and lawyer—into a hopeless corner of passivity, "neutrality" and indecision.

Therefore, constructivist therapists hereby have our permission to engage in full frontal action. We, at least, will not bring those who are active, direct and forthright up before the Constructivist Court of Theoretical Violations on misdemeanor charges. The constructivist therapist is entitled to have opinions and to be articulate about his or her values, goals and methods. It is even alright for constructivist therapists to admit to being experts in what they do. Just as Wheeler can legitimately claim to be an authority on the black hole—something that does not objectively "exist"—constructivist therapists can properly claim professional expertise in their preferred ways of working with families. The only thing they are *not* entitled to claim is that they are "fixing" objective problems that have an existence independent of the human language community. Whereas objectivists are used to retreating into the position that the world at large justifies their actions, constructivists do not have that luxury. They are obliged to acknowledge that the only justifications for their actions are personal attitudes, beliefs and opinions, however arrived at.

H UMBERTO MATURANA, CLARIFYING SIMILAR issues at a recent therapy conference in Horsham, Pennsylvania, used the example of a cockroach walking across his kitchen floor. He pointed out that it might very well find itself quickly dispatched to cockroach heaven. "Good-bye, beautiful little cockroach, I am going to kill you," was how he put it. Families aren't cockroaches, of course, but we do suggest that Maturana's expressed willingness to take explicit, vigorous action might serve as a useful corrective to some of the passive models of operation that have been purported to be derivatives of the constructivist philosophy.

Note that constructivist philosopher Maturana is not shy about having desires, acting on them and accepting full responsibility for the consequences of his actions. His methods are direct—not mysterious, ambiguous, or obscure. As a constructivist, he appreciates the invented nature of reality, the centrality of language, the time-bound nature of human judgments and evaluations, the continuous fluctuation of motives with changes in structure and environment and the unpredictability of life paths. Nevertheless, he has no trouble acting unashamedly in accordance with the current dictates of his conscience.

Incidentally, to the poor cockroach it matters not a whit whether it finds itself under a constructivist or an objectivist foot. Kantian and Lockean feet can be equally lethal when it comes to exterminating cockroaches.

A THERAPIST WHO HAS SHUCKED THE ILLUSION that he or she is employing objective methods to fix deranged systems is left with a sobering but simultaneously freeing realization—namely, that the buck stops here. That is different from thinking one is just patching up a few errant behaviors, rehearsing clients in "healthier" cognitions, selling family members a few snazzy "reframes" or searching for that mysterious, hidden lever that might trigger a major systemic reorganization.

Engaging in constructivist therapy is more like offering clients a college course—especially one with demanding fieldwork. Sometimes a student signs up for such a course only to satisfy a program requirement or to keep a boyfriend or girlfriend company. However, the potential of good education is that before he or she realizes what is happening, sweeping changes in life plans may have been hatched. By signing up, clients indicate a willingness to be changed through their participation in a dialogue with a definite starting point and some specifiable procedures, but a less than definite endpoint. Possibilities and prospects pop up that were not previously envisioned or anticipated. Now that they are here, they demand consideration.

Good education and good constructivist psychotherapy have much in common. They put one at risk. Both are designed to support inquiry, and both work best when conceptualized as hands-on adventure rather than as purely academic pursuit. ∎

JAY S. EFRAN, PH.D., *is a professor in the Department of Psychology, Temple University, Philadelphia, PA.*
ROBERT J. LUKENS, M.S.S., *is a social worker and former addictions counselor.*
MICHAEL D. LUKENS, PH.D., *is a psychologist at The Atlantic Mental Health Center, Inc., McKee City, NJ.*

See references, page 568.

Letters to the Editor

ANYBODY WHO BELIEVES THAT "THE 'TRAUMA' of rape takes place in language" ("Constructivism: What's in It for You?") is somebody who has never been raped. Survival as a human being requires the maintenance of both psychosocial and biological integrity, or autonomy. Rape is an act of violence in which one individual negates the autonomy of another and reduces her from a person to a thing. In constructivist terminology, rape, like murder, interrupts autopoiesis and nullifies the interpersonal context, or co-ontogenic structural coupling, upon which language depends.

Llewlee L. Sawyer
Raleigh, NC

THE AUTHORS OF "CONSTRUCTIVISM: WHAT'S in It for You?" insist that the 'trauma' of rape takes place in language." We disagree. The trauma of rape takes place in a woman's body, as do its possible consequences: lacerations, AIDS, VD, pregnancy. Of all the examples available to illustrate how open to interpretation human behavior is, why did these authors choose rape?

Whatever their motives (and we cannot think of any good ones), the authors seem to offer yet another instance of men interpreting women's experience for them, trying to talk women out of what they know. This epistemological effort is distinctly not new.

We wonder what the authors would say to the bruised and shocked survivor of rape after they remind her that her rape was "a framework of activity . . . made possible by the shared language system in which we all operate." What is the next sentence in their therapy chat?

Barbara Ellman, Thelma Jean Goodrich,
Kris Halstead, Cheryl Rampage

I AM DELIGHTED THAT THE *NETWORKER* DEvoted an issue to exploring some of the implications for our field. But I am appalled at one of those implications, the answer to, "Constructivism: What's in It for You?" if you happen to be a rape victim. According to the authors, what's in it for you is more of the bitter heritage Deborah Luepnitz describes so well elsewhere in the issue.

If only Efran, Lukens and Lukens were empiricists! We could ask them to test out their hypothesis about rape. Certainly there are prisons that could serve as laboratories—and the authors could be the subjects.

Carlla R. Shaw
Akron, OH

AUTHORS' RESPONSE:

Our aim was not to trivialize the pain of rape, but to highlight the contribution of language to the creation of powerful events in people's lives. We were interested in bucking the "sticks and stones can break my bones but words can never hurt me" tradition that has such sway in our culture. We wanted it to be clear that language is consequential—it hurts and maims as well as helps and rescues.

Rape is not simply a physical act—it is an attempt to alter meaning. A rape is the rapist's statement about women, men/manhood, sex, power, revenge, rejection, hostility, and other such issues. If rape did not have that potential to alter meanings for both the rapist and the person raped, it would have no appeal for the rapist.

Events such as rape are not simple acts with objective, predictable outcomes—they are arenas of profuse shifting and idiosyncratic meanings that vary with the histories of the individuals involved.

Jay S. Efran, Robert J. Lukens, Michael D. Lukens
NOVEMBER 1988

SPIRITUALITY RECONSIDERED

FACING THE LIMITS OF PSYCHOTHERAPY

By Katy Butler

ONE COLD JULY EVENING TWO YEARS AGO, I stood on the steps of Most Holy Redeemer Church, two blocks from Castro Street in San Francisco, surrounded by men and women holding white helium balloons in their hands. It was windy, and the balloons—symbolizing people from the neighborhood who had died that year, mostly of AIDS—kept bumping against one another. Church bells tolled. A young woman with black, spiky hair read out the names of more than 200 dead. The parish priest shook holy water over the balloons—it landed with a thwack—and then we released them into the foggy air.

I am not a Catholic, and except for an occasional wedding, I hadn't been inside a church in 25 years. In fact, I thought of the Catholic Church as the home of authoritarianism and emotional repression. I was on the steps of the church that night not as a congregant, but as a reporter covering Most Holy Redeemer's annual Forty Hours of Devotion, a medieval ritual of incessant prayer first used in times of plague and Turkish invasion and now invoked as a plea for an end to the AIDS epidemic.

Six years ago, the priest of Most Holy Redeemer—then a dwindling, working-class parish—had formed a Gay and Lesbian Outreach Committee and welcomed 600 new members. The former convent across the street had been converted into an AIDS hospice, subsidized by bingo in the church basement. Each week older women—whose own sons had long since moved away—prayed to Mary, visited the sick, drank from the communion cup, and made friends with gay men over bingo cards.

At Mass that evening, I watched a Polish American widow in her seventies hold a black man, emaciated by AIDS, up by the belt to take communion. Later a white-haired, Italian American woman in thick, black orthopedic shoes hobbled up the aisle, saying "Peace be with you" to gay men wearing T-shirts, leather jackets and business suits. For the next two nights, I watched relays of parishioners pray quietly before the communion bread that was for them the living body of Christ.

Just before dawn on Sunday morning, I sat in a back pew, almost alone. Votive candles, sputtering and clicking like tiny castanets, went out one by one.

On the altar, a windowed, silver vessel, called a monstrance, held the white communion wafers. Struggling to translate this ancient Catholic symbol of Presence into language I could understand, I tried simply to be fully present with the Host, seeing "Christ's body" as a window into *here and now.*

I stared at the monstrance, shining in the candlelight. Silver rays shot out from its sides, like the sun embossed on a New Mexico license plate. I could not connect. I felt unacceptable. I realized for the first time the depth of my feelings of separation and shame. I cried quietly; my throat hurt.

What happened next was not dramatic. God did not speak to me, as he spoke to Paul on the road to Damascus. No Buddhist enlightenment descended, nor did I see my separate self and my suffering as a fiction. The room did not blaze with light, as it did for Bill Wilson, the founder of Alcoholics Anonymous, when he prayed for deliverance from alcohol while drying out in a hospital room. No great wind blew through me, nor were things quite as prosaic as what William James called, in *Varieties of Religious Experience,* a sense of "a proper connection with the higher powers."

But sitting in that human church, whose parishioners had adopted society's outcasts, I had a small, spiritually healing experience—one of a handful that have punctuated my life, all impossible to fully describe. I was aware of a presence emanating from the monstrance. In trying to describe its steady delicacy, I think of a line from an e. e. cummings poem: *"nobody, not even the rain, has such small hands."* For years I had felt so damaged that I thought I should hide myself. But the God I sensed glimmering from the monstrance included everything, even me. How could I hide from the universe when I was part of it? Connection was possible, even though I could only barely sense it. I did not need to hide anymore; there was nowhere to hide, and nothing to hide. My shame was a delusion; it came from inside, not outside.

Late that Sunday, I walked out of the church into

the sun. On Wednesday I took my experience into that modern confessional, my therapist's office. Like many educated, upper-middle-class, urban and suburban people, I had nowhere else to go. I had no priest. My grandparents were dead, my friends didn't think much of Catholicism, and my parents were thousands of miles away. For better or worse, my therapist had inherited the ancient robe of the priest or shaman who drew no distinction between spiritual and emotional healing. She looked at me and said very little. She did not reduce my experience to psychological terms. She told me she thought what had happened was powerful and important, that it had meaning and that such experiences had been excluded from the therapeutic universe for too long.

Then our psychological work began. The perception inside Most Holy Redeemer had radically shifted my view of myself. I no longer felt like a cripple fashioning a better set of crutches. I knew things could be different, and I also knew I would have to face my memories if I wished to deepen that fleeting vision into something I could live each day. The lid of shame was off. No human being, no therapist, no friend, no 12-Step group, no self-help author, no Zen master had ever been able to convey this to me before. But the parishioners of Most Holy Redeemer had made Christ, in whom I did not believe, visible.

SPIRITUAL EXPERIENCES LIKE MINE—FRAMED IN archaic language, and challenging commonly held paradigms of psychological change—make many therapists squirm.

"If a client mentions a religious interest, most psychologists will pass it over, or there'll be a quiet lift of the eyebrow, with the assumption that the client is immature or neurotic, and that religion is a symptom of something wrong," says John Tisdale, a former pastoral counselor and secretary of the American Psychological Association's small division for psychologists interested in religion.

Not all of this queasiness is mere prejudice from the narrow-minded. "Spirituality is often misused," says James Bugental, one of the founders and leading theorists of the existentialist humanist psychology movement, and no stranger to deeper questions of human meaning. "It can be a cop-out, a way of not taking responsibility for one's life, for not confronting that we die, that what we do hurts those we don't want to hurt, that we don't live up to our own potential and our own values."

Ever since modern psychotherapy first challenged religion's ancient monopoly on methods for human transformation, each realm has looked upon the other with some suspicion. In the late 1970s, a bioenergetics therapist bluntly told me that meditation "ungrounded" me. When I seriously considered spending six months in a Buddhist monastery, he blew up like a man discovering a secret rival. "Then what are we doing here?" he asked, and after that, I left an important part of myself outside his office door.

At the same time, the Buddhist meditation teachers I met were equally arrogant. Psychotherapy, they thought, increased preoccupation with a "self" that they believed was a fiction. I remember a popular Tibetan Buddhist teacher—who later died of alcoholism—saying that psychotherapy taught you to unpack your knapsack item by item, while Buddhism let you drop the whole thing.

Like children shouting garbled messages across a lake at twilight, the whole conversation seemed to be at cross-purposes. Each vocation seemed so sure of its superior ability to engineer human development and change, and at the same time was unwilling to admit to any common ground. The result was an underground rivalry. "Psychotherapy and religion are in direct ideological competition," says longtime critic of psychiatry Thomas Szasz. "Psychotherapy is not different in any way from religion. Psychotherapy deals with how one should live, with family life, sexual behavior and the purpose of life—and that's what religion is about. Freud was a rabbi in disguise. For some, psychotherapy is a god that failed, and for others, it's a god that still works."

Given this climate of mutual antipathy, it's hardly surprising that religious questions have long been taboo in most therapists' offices. But recently some therapists—reflecting an inchoate, barely understood, national, spiritual renaissance—are exploring the once-hostile borderline between the spiritual and the psychological.

"Something's cooking," says professor Allan Bergin of Brigham Young University, who has studied the spiritual interests of psychologists for a decade. "Therapists are coming out of the closet with their religiosity. Some are religious people who never used to say anything about it, and others have changed their minds about religion. There is apparently a blend of humanistic philosophy and spirituality out there among therapists that has not been well articulated."

In a 1986 survey of 425 mental health professionals across the country, Bergin and fellow BYU psychologist Jay P. Jensen found that even though some therapists remain actively hostile to organized religion, a sizable majority are deeply interested in a vaguely defined noninstitutional spirituality. Sixty-eight percent of the family therapists, clinical psychologists, social workers and psychiatrists surveyed said they sought "a spiritual understanding of the universe and one's place in it," even though only 40 percent—about the same proportion as the rest of the population—regularly attended church services.

A key factor in therapists' new spiritual openness is the enormous growth, not of old-fashioned religion, but of the informal spirituality promulgated by Alcoholics Anonymous, Adult Children of Alcoholics, and other 12-Step programs. In the late 1980s, in a grass-roots explosion that took both psychologists and theologians by surprise, hundreds of thousands of ACOAs entered the self-help groups as atheists and stayed to follow the "12 Steps"—a deceptively simple recipe for psychological and spiritual transformation involving surrender to a loosely defined "higher power." When many ACOAs also entered therapy, they took the common-sense language of 12-Step programs with them and helped bridge the two worlds.

"The ACOA movement has made spirituality user-friendly for therapists," says family therapist and addiction specialist Jo-Ann Krestan, coauthor of *Too Good for Her Own Good* and other books linking family systems theory with the insights of 12-Step programs. "Therapists who used to dismiss the spiritual can't anymore. They have investigated the ACOA movement out of the economic necessity of appealing to prospective clients and have come to recognize the profound significance of the spiritual. One finds, in the 12-Step groups, an experience of community that can be the first step along the road of recognizing that one is part of a larger system."

In another expression of the national hunger for a bridging of the psychological and spiritual realms, more than three million people have bought psychiatrist M. Scott Peck's *The Road Less Travelled: A New Psychology of Love, Traditional Values, and Spiritual Growth* and kept it on the best-seller list for a record-breaking six years. The surprise best-seller, which probably would have gone nowhere if it been written by a minister, rehabilitates once out-of-date subjects like discipline, love and sin by recasting them in psychological terms. The book sold well even though Peck made none of the facile promises found in most psychological self-help books. Its first sentence—"Life is difficult"—challenges the American myth that anything is possible and that unhappiness is always remediable. The book seeks instead to give human pain and sacrifice a broader meaning.

And in 1988, in a further display of spiritual yearning expressed in psychological terms, hundreds of thousands of families, each alone in its house, turned public television into a flickering electronic

shaman's cave presided over by anthropologist Joseph Campbell. The unexpectedly popular six-part interview with Bill Moyers touched a nerve, and the shows were expanded and repeatedly rebroadcast. Campbell, a scholar with impeccable establishment credentials, lifted the world's mythic traditions out of the hands of museum curators. He popularized Jung's theories of pancultural archetypes and supported Jung's view that the psychotherapeutic journey was a version of humankind's "one great story" of spiritual quest and awakening. By implication, Campbell gave respectability to the spiritual-psychological quest itself, even in modern times. But he could not restore to such quests the sense of community, ritual and ethics that keeps them from degenerating into empty consumer commodities.

AS THE INTERVIEWS WITH CAMPBELL ILLUStrated, a clear division between the spiritual and psychological is a relatively new phenomenon. For millennia, shamans and witch doctors, the therapists of indigenous and preindustrial cultures, made no distinction between physical, emotional and spiritual healing. To them, all symptoms were signs of something awry in the individual's relationship with a larger universe of spirits and animal powers. Using drums, dances and hallucinogens, they reached trance states, made diagnoses that reframed people's complaints and enacted rituals to reconnect them to the tribe, to nature and to the cosmos. In nonshamanic traditions, the same blurring applied. For centuries Buddha was called "The King of Doctors," and Jesus earned a reputation as a faith healer.

Then came the divorce. Western Europe industrialized; feudal villages emptied and city slums filled; extended families, communities and religious supports frayed. Europe burned its witches, deified its doctors, lost faith in exorcism and confession and fell in love with scientific materialism.

Sigmund Freud, a neurologist by training, believed religion was primitive, outmoded by his scientific "talking cure." Insight and catharsis, he thought, would lead, if not to happiness, at least to self-knowledge. He saw spiritual searching as consolatory and regressive, not evolutionary, a powerless infant's longing for the oceanic feeling of the mother's womb. Perhaps because of his eagerness to have psychoanalysis accepted by—and as—hard science, Freud deliberately distanced himself from the mystical. An atheist, he wanted to model the psychoanalyst on the white-coated scientist, not on the beaded shaman or the black-robed minister.

With the exception of C. G. Jung, Roberto Assagioli and a few other mavericks, most therapists in the first half of the 20th century followed Freud's views on religion or kept their differing opinions quiet. To most practitioners of the "new science," religion was guilt, superstition and repression; it was psychology's eccentric great-uncle, dressed in dark, old-fashioned clothes, mumbling phrases in a half-forgotten language on the fringes of the wedding feast.

It was Jung who first challenged Freud's pathologizing of the spiritual. Jung popularized the Chinese Taoist text the *I Ching* in the 1920s, and strongly believed in the authority and the healing power of the nonrational, the mythic and the dreamlike. In fact, he characterized psychotherapy as a ministerial occupation.

Jung's was only the first of many challenges—including family, behavioral, cognitive, hypnotic and brief therapy—to the perceived limitations of the effectiveness of insight, catharsis and the medical treatment model of solving human problems.

In the 1950s, during the first "Zen boom" among American intellectuals, psychoanalysts Karen Horney and Erich Fromm studied at Columbia University with Japanese Zen teacher D. T. Suzuki, and parallels were drawn between Buddhism and psychotherapy. Both systematized ways to alleviate human suffering through a transformation in consciousness.

Halfway across the country, hypnotherapist Milton Erickson showed no interest in Buddhism or any other religion, but his work proved that intuition, paradox and trance states—all traditional tools of the religious trade—could be effective where science and rationalism failed.

Also in the '50s, anthropologist Gregory Bateson introduced therapists to systems thinking, emphasizing epistemology and patterns of communication rather than fixed notions of "self" and "disease." While Bateson was popular among family therapists for his scientific analysis of small systems of interaction, such as those within the Balinese culture, or between a mother and her schizophrenic son, few followed Bateson into his explorations of the much larger systems that contained them. Bateson ultimately came to see a world consisting of relationships rather than objects—an epistemology that challenged the Western notion of a self-contained "self" extending no further than the boundary of the outer skin. This approach had affinities to Buddhist thought, which also teaches—although in vastly different language—that notions of a fixed "self" amount to a convenient fiction. Bateson was a scientist, but he admired both Buddhism and Alcoholics Anonymous. AA's reliance on a "power greater than oneself" reflected what he thought was a more correct epistemology: that there are limits to human will and that human beings are part of systems far larger than they can conceive or imagine.

In the 1960s, the intellectual rehabilitation of the spiritual got a different sort of boost from psychologist and theorist Abraham Maslow, who, as one of the leaders of the humanistic psychology movement, challenged behaviorism and psychoanalysis. In contrast to Freud's pathologizing of the spiritual, Maslow considered spiritual longings to be legitimate in their own right, and not a reflection of unresolved emotional conflicts. He posited a "hierarchy of needs" that placed longings for transcendent experiences and moral values at the top of the ladder, saying that all people would seek them after more basic needs—for food, love and self-respect—were met. In his final years, Maslow helped found the Association for Transpersonal Psychology to further explore mystical questions within the language of psychology. But he opposed the tendency of some transpersonal psychologists to seek the spiritual in exotic chemical substances like LSD, or in foreign monasteries. He wrote, "The great lesson from the true mystics [is that] the sacred is in the ordinary, that it is to be found in one's daily life; in one's neighbors, friends and family, in one's backyard."

THESE EXPANSIONS OF THE DOMAIN OF PSYCHOLogy hardly filtered down to the Boston suburbs of my childhood. There, in the '50s, Psychology and Spirituality weren't speaking, because Psychology was doing all the talking. My parents, both formerly devout Anglicans, were immigrants from rural South Africa, where the church steeple was the tallest building in town. They left that all behind, lost their faith, and abandoned the distant, authoritarian God of their childhood and His impossible rules. They stopped using the language of sin and redemption. They spoke less of good and evil, and more of healthy and unhealthy choices. They joined a prosperous, postwar American generation for whom therapists became a secular priesthood.

My family moved 14 times before I turned 18. We never joined a church. We had no grandparents or aunts or uncles to turn to in difficult times. We subscribed to *Time* magazine and got the issue asking whether God was dead. At our house it was more like He went to the corner for cigarettes one day and never returned. My parents' guidance came not from priests or neighbors but from new icons: the psychoanalytically influenced Dr. Spock and the books of Freud and Betty Friedan. When that didn't work, my parents turned to therapists, who

were increasingly burdened by the breakdown of communities and extended families outside their office doors.

During the next two decades, at least in the comfortable suburbs and city neighborhoods where many of my friends lived, psychotherapy thoroughly usurped the role religion had long filled. The professional office, with its book-lined walls and oriental rugs, replaced the confessional, the sanctuary and the parish hall. The therapists who set up shop were as deeply motivated to relieve human suffering as any priest. But few had training that equipped them with a language to address deeper questions of human meaning that many of us inevitably brought.

It is to therapists that my friends often turn with a wide range of soluble and insoluble problems—an alcoholic mother, a vague sense of loneliness or purposelessness, an unhappy child or a stalled career. The consumers of therapy expect its practitioners to be not only teachers of communication skills and problem-solvers, but spiritual guides, mothers, fathers and even paid friends.

In a simpler time, people filled most of those roles for one another, for free, in church and at village festivals, or during long summer afternoons on the front porch with cousins and grandchildren. Now we try to pour all our questions of meaning into one expensive, weekly therapeutic hour—and into a language that can barely contain them.

Some of the problems clients bring have roots in a system far larger than family communication patterns. What shows up in a therapist's office as loneliness or purposelessness originates in a culture where people spend so much time commuting, working or watching television that they have little left to develop what sociologist Robert Bellah calls "habits of the heart" with one another. Therapists cannot replace what organized religion, for all its drawbacks, provided: a sense of community, connection to something beyond ourselves, of help freely given and a broad view of human *(continued on page 288)*

Fields-of-Flowers Therapy

AS A CHARTER MEMBER OF THE FALLEN CATHOLIC, ZEN BUDDHIST, NONSECTARIAN CHURCH, I often find myself worrying about the effects of my semi-apostate condition on my children. My own childhood world was filled with the strange, dark drama of Catholicism—the quiet, dim churches, the anxious isolation of the confessional, the threatening priests dressed all in black save for a single square of perfect white at their throats, the long ecclesiastical history of suffering, martyrdom, corruption and rare ecstasy. The god I learned about as a child was a vengeful god, a punishing god, a god who kicked ass and took names, a god who was everywhere, knew everything and could do anything. Now, as I tighten my tie in readiness for work in the morning, I hear my 6-year-old and 4-year-old sons playing video games upstairs; the elder gets Elevator-Action Man to jump some abyss.

"God gave you that power, you know," I overhear his younger brother say.

"No!" I yell up the stairs, almost against my will, "God didn't give him that power. It's just a video game!"

THERE SEEMS TO BE A SPACE IN FAMILIES THAT CALLS OUT TO BE FILLED WITH AWE AT THE REMARK-ableness of things, with an awareness of just how improbable it is that we should be here, right here, right now. The other day, as I was pulling on my socks, my 6-year-old son approached me with one of those overwhelming questions kids ask:

"Dad, how did people first get here?"

Wanting to be a good liberal, I gave him some blather about evolution, which he dismissed out of hand.

"But how did they get here?" he asked again, impatiently.

I tried theology. "Some people believe that God created people, that he made them and then breathed life into them."

"But how did God get here? Where did God come from?"

"God is everywhere," I responded, like a good pantheist. My son furrowed his brow. We both knew this answer was not satisfactory, proving yet again that dad is not God.

"But where did God come from?" he asked, his voice filled with exasperation.

I thought for a moment, then gave my best answer.

"What kind of cereal do you want for breakfast?"

HIPPIES WHO ONCE FERVENTLY BELIEVED IN UNITY, PEACE AND TRANSCENDENCE GREW UP AND became family therapists. Is it that, having fallen away from our religion of origin, we needed to fill the space with something that seems as mysterious and uncanny as religion once did? So now we sit in rooms with families, struggling and strategizing, until finally, now and again, a moment of magic occurs when patterns change, people change.

I am in a session with parents and their three teenage children, doing what I call "gossip thera-py"—better known as circular questioning—asking different family members what they think other members feel about one another. Around and around we go, until finally I become aware that Dad is eyeing me intently. His gaze is soft, exposed, vulnerable. I ask him to look with the same atten-tiveness and receptivity at the other members of his family. Slowly, one by one, they begin to *notice* one another. Containing my own anxiety, I let the silence be; Dad becomes tearful, and the family joins. Maybe it's water, maybe it's love, but it will do for now; I know my job is simply to witness what is there.

During a recent family walk in the hills of southern Vermont, we came upon a field of wildflowers and berries. My son, who has not had an iota of religious training, spontaneously said, "These are God's flowers. God put them here." What seemed to fascinate him was the fact that the flowers were *already there*, that we had not planted them or cultivated them, but they had appeared by themselves, they had emerged mysteriously and there they were, shining in the sun, until that moment unwitnessed.

We have all experienced those moments in therapy when, as if from nowhere, a family develops right before our eyes, when we share with the family the discovery of something that seemed to be already there, like the berries and the fields of flowers. But is the wonder we feel at these small epiphanies just a retrograde projection, a way we mythologize what we do not expect or understand? Are we witnesses, midwives to the birthing of the essential humanity of the family, or are we technicians, reprogramming malfunctioning patterns of interaction?

It was just the other day that my 4-year-old son ran into the kitchen on a Saturday morning. "Do you know what makes Wonder Woman so great?" he asked excitedly.

"No," I responded from the sink, "I don't know what makes Wonder Woman so great."

"Cuz she wonders about a lot of things!" he said, and dashed back into the living room.

THE PHILOSOPHER IMMANUEL KANT BRILLIANTLY DEMOLISHED THE VARIOUS PROOFS OF THE EXISTENCE OF GOD—the cosmological proof, the ontological proof, etc. In the end he said that we should believe, not because we are certain, but because it does us good to do so. Perhaps, as family therapists, we should believe in the innate wisdom of the system not because we have empirical proof, but because it does both clients and therapists good to do so. This means that we must choose to be effective witnesses, listeners and watchers, participant-observers, of the treasure of meaning that is latent in all families.

Some believe that being a therapist means creating realities. Others believe the therapist is primarily a witness whose job is to revere—from the Latin revereri, to fear and honor again—what is already there, that maybe reverence holds the key to clarifying our confusion about whether we are primary interveners—reality makers—or reality seers. Of course, just witnessing the predicaments that present themselves to us every day is a frightening prospect. Witnessing the abuse, the victimization, the turmoil and pain, calls forth our need to control, to take responsibility, to *do* something. But we cannot in the same moment be both actor and audience, doer and observer, change agent and seer. Each moment we must choose, and sometimes holding back from assuming a position of power is the most difficult task we face. For us therapists, all too often to revere, to love, seems not enough. We lack faith in the curative power of simply seeing.

MAYBE WE NEED FAITH THAT THE PAIN AND THE JOY, THE FRUSTRATION AND THE SATISFACTION, THE sorrow and the laughter of life will balance out in the long run. Back in the hippie days we used to say, "It will all come out in the wash"—meaning, if you give without worrying too much about how much you'll get back, you probably won't end up being ripped off. It wasn't easy to do then, and now, with a lot more responsibilities, it still isn't easy to do. But sometimes, when we least expect it, we do find, deep in the forest, surrounded by brambles and weeds, a field of flowers. □

—Michael J. Murphy
SEPTEMBER 1990

MICHAEL J. MURPHY, ED.D., *is a psychotherapist at Northern Berkshire Counseling Center, North Adams, MA.*

(continued from page 284) suffering as inevitable, part of a historical context thousands of years old.

Unrealistic expectations of therapy are shared by both clients and therapists. Caught between sacred and profane metaphors for their work, sensing in their hearts their clients' pain, yet trying to apply technique with their minds, the secular priesthood is supposed to have all the answers, but doesn't.

No wonder some therapists are tongue-tied when clients hint at deeper questions of meaning. "Once you relieve the immediate distress in therapy, questions of meaning or values often arise," says psychologist Bergin, adding that the 1986 survey showed that only five percent of today's therapists received any training in dealing with religious issues in therapy. "For example—is there a higher reason to endure the pain in a relationship, or does one just withdraw? Many therapists are so caught up in techniques that they shy away from these bigger issues."

Like a doctor attempting microsurgery with a lug wrench, some therapists sensed early in their careers that the principles of psychotherapy are insufficient to provide them with guidance for a more profound level of self-exploration, much less for addressing such issues in their clients' lives. Perhaps this is what leaves so many therapists frustrated, at midlife, with their impossible profession.

"Many therapists enter this work with a sense of what might be in themselves and those they work with," says James Bugental, who sees an outpouring of spiritual searching among therapists he trains. "For many, the work is frustrating. Their hopes for themselves are not realized. They sense that there's more to life than their training has told them about. And that's when this turning to the spiritual makes sense."

Phillip Friedman, a family therapist in Philadelphia, for example, had "done all the things you're supposed to do to be happy" by the early 1970s. He had a house in the suburbs, a Ph.D. and a job at a respected family therapy center. But he was full of

emotional distress, and his job was a hornet's nest of backbiting, professional jealousy and competition. He wondered why people who were supposedly experts in human behavior were so nasty and unhappy. Then he went to a yoga workshop with the Hindu teacher Swami Satchitananda, who "radiated a peace I had never seen in my professional colleagues." He sampled other spiritual paths, including EST training, *A Course in Miracles* and meditation with the charismatic teacher Swami Muktananda. "At first I tried to keep doing therapy in the regular way and hold those experiences in another part of my life," says Friedman. "But now I integrate them. I meditate every morning, focusing first within myself and then on the people I'm going to see that day. To clients who are open to it, I sometimes talk about invoking a creative intelligence for help."

WHEN A THERAPIST BECOMES INVOLVED IN A spiritual practice, his or her outward techniques with clients may remain the same, while his or her inner conception of the therapist's role may subtly but decisively shift. Sometimes the change is no greater than a willingness to try a little guided imagery with a client, or to take out the earplugs when a client hints at religious beliefs that might be helpful. For instance, Mark Kolkto, a clinical psychologist in New Jersey, used a Mormon woman's belief that she was a "child of God" to counteract feelings of shame arising from childhood sexual abuse.

Sometimes, however, baffling and intriguing therapeutic miracles do occur. In California, for instance, psychiatrist Seymour Boorstein once prescribed Carlos Castaneda's *Journey to Ixtlan* and other spiritual books to Jack, a man so suspicious and hostile and so overcome by weeping and murderous rage that he had left his job on permanent disability.

Each week the two discussed the perspectives

provided by the spiritual readings and how they applied to Jack's hanging on to old grudges, especially his rage toward a former supervisor who had slept with his ex-wife and harassed him on the job.

Boorstein also taught Jack a traditional Buddhist "mindfulness" meditation technique that helped him develop an "observing ego" capable of witnessing feelings of hate and jealousy and then letting them pass away. Jack turned out to be adept at it—far more successful than Boorstein himself. Jack's weeping and murderous thoughts diminished. After 14 months of this unconventional therapy, Jack returned to his former job, under his former supervisor, and was later named Employee of the Year.

Such miracles are as rare and unexplainable as they are in conventional therapy. More common is a therapist relinquishing a view of him or herself as a clever magician, battling resistance with an armamentarium of flashy techniques, hypnotic suggestions and ingenious reframings. Instead, these spiritually minded therapists see themselves as the servants of a larger system—a role at once humbler and less lonely.

Michael Elkin, a Massachusetts hypnotherapist and family therapist, was a strategic therapist long before he began studying the Christian mystical book *A Course in Miracles* five years ago. Not long afterward, an enraged and terrified woman came to him.

"None of the tricks I'd used with high-resistance, high-denial people worked," says Elkin. "Any time I tried to explain her experience, she'd respond with a level of rage that could peel the paint off walls."

Elkin was frustrated. He forgot an appointment. He took long walks with his dog, cursing his difficult client. He did not abandon techniques, but he also began praying for 15 minutes before the woman's session. "I would pray for the ability to keep my ego out of it, not to feel threatened, to see her as undamaged, and just to be loving to her," he says. "I stopped trying to *do* anything. She became

much more relaxed and pleasant. Since then, it's been a steady, uphill climb.

"I pray for help before every session now. I keep in mind that I am not the one doing the work—God does it, through the agency of the Holy Spirit. I don't always remember that, but I know that I have to learn to if I'm ever going to have any peace."

Tom Chancellor, a family therapist in Texas with a behaviorist background, attended a Buddhist meditation retreat for psychotherapists in Boulder, Colorado, last summer. There, he learned 2,500 year-old techniques for generating pleasant states of mind through meditation and awareness of the breath. What Chancellor discovered was that the greater his ability to feel good no matter how unhappy his clients were, the greater his empathy and compassion for them. "When I came back, I focused more on my breathing and on being at peace with myself, rather than pulling my hair out," Chancellor says. "In the past I struggled more with coming up with solutions so that clients' problems would go away," he says. "Now I'm more comfortable realizing the problem isn't the problem, it's the reaction to it. And now I might say, 'It's real incredible you've been able to live through that,' when in the past I might have said similar words—'Well, obviously you're a strong person because you've been able to live through so much'—but I would have been more mechanistic, not so involved, with less of an empathic connection."

THE GREATEST DANGER OF RELYING ON SPIRITUAL approaches is the sentimental hope that a sense of connection to a larger system will take away the pain of being a human being, or substitute for work that must be done on a psychological level. Although the spiritual and the psychological realms may overlap, they are not identical, and both are important, says Jack Kornfield, a meditation teacher and a clinical psychologist in Woodacre, California. Kornfield is the author of *Living Buddhist Masters* and other books, and was one of the founding teachers of the Insight Meditation Society, which pioneered the practice of Vipassana Buddhism in the United States in the early 1970s. When he was 21 he journeyed to Thailand shortly after graduating from Dartmouth College. He lived in a little hut in a forest monastery, took vows of celibacy, was ordained as a Buddhist monk, owned only a single robe and took alms in the traditional way in neighboring villages for his food. At the same time, he followed classical Vipassana Buddhist meditation practices. He meditated in charnel grounds, watching corpses burn, and spent most of his time alone.

"I learned a lot about facing death and about not being able to possess things," says Kornfield. "I had some stunning spiritual experiences. Then I came back to the United States, started driving a taxi and going to graduate school, and it took me six months or a year to come down from a great sense of equanimity, detachment and calm. When I did, I found I had many of the same fears I'd had when I left."

What followed, Kornfield says, was a series of disastrous relationships with women, all of whom left him because he was needy, jealous and insecure. During the same period, his father was in a serious accident. Kornfield meditated calmly outside the Intensive Care Unit. When his father recovered and asked how Kornfield would have felt had he died, Kornfield replied calmly, "I didn't want you to die, but we all are born and we all die," which upset his father enormously.

"In retrospect, I was pathologically detached," Kornfield told me. "I wasn't feeling what it would mean to have my father die in front of me."

Kornfield entered therapy and later became a therapist himself. "Meditation taught me many things, but it didn't acquaint me with my feelings," Kornfield says. "I didn't know if I was angry, sad, or happy unless it was very obvious. I spent the next 10 years using therapy, along with meditation, to reclaim my capacity to feel."

The spiritual yearning for a state of enlightenment in which there are "no boundaries" and "no self" can tempt people to think they can escape from the hard work of managing the give-and-take of everyday human struggles. When Michael Reeds, a recent graduate of Naropa Institute's contemplative psychology program, first began working in a halfway house, he found that his Buddhist training had taught him to remain calm in the face of obvious turmoil. But it did not train him to be a therapist.

The first day he walked into the halfway house kitchen, a resident told him he could raise dead bodies. Reeds nodded and listened, internally congratulating himself for what he thought was an enlightened tolerance. "Five minutes later," says Reeds, "I was fighting to survive. I felt dizzy, I was sweating, and I felt horrible. I lied to him and said I had to go to a meeting and went to the office and chilled out. Later I sneaked out hoping he wouldn't corner me again."

Reeds now believes that an idealistic Buddhist emphasis on generosity and unselfishness had not prepared him for the mundane task of setting limits and telling the truth about his own feelings and limitations. "Now I'm learning, and it's painful and awkward," he says. "Caregiving was my style, and it was mistaken by some within the Buddhist community as a spiritually evolved state."

ONE NIGHT LAST SUMMER, A YEAR AFTER MY small epiphany at Most Holy Redeemer, I found myself at a retreat center in Santa Barbara with a Vietnamese Buddhist monk named Nhat Hanh, a handful of other Vietnamese, and 20 American veterans of the Vietnam War. I was there as a reporter once again. The air smelled of orange blossoms, and crickets were chirping.

On the first night of the five-day retreat, Nhat Hanh sat in full lotus position at the front of a meeting room, a microphone clipped to his brown, polyester robe. "When it comes to healing, Western psychotherapy has been very helpful," he told the veterans softly. "But Buddhist meditation—and meditation just means to look deeply—is also a way of healing. It's very easy, very pleasant."

The veterans, sitting cross-legged on the carpet with me, were strong, muscular men, but not cocky—it was as though they'd had the corners knocked off. Many were social workers for the Veterans Administration, and most had been in therapy and sharing groups. All had suffered what one called "inner bruises" from the war—bruises simultaneously political, psychological and spiritual. One had burned a village on a routine mission; another had coordinated bombing raids. A third had shot two Vietnamese to death on Nui Ba Dinh, the Black Virgin Mountain, when he was a young soldier. Later he found family photographs on their bodies.

We were silent for most of the first three days. Every morning we meditated, ate a silent breakfast and took a slow walk, staying aware of our breath, past orange groves and beds of purple statice. In short daily lectures, Nhat Hanh recommended against calling up emotions intentionally. "Sometimes we think we have to express our feelings in order to feel better," he said, challenging the Western psychological tradition of emotional release. "But sometimes you don't have to touch your suffering a lot. You should have a reserve of refreshing images to counterbalance the suffering within you."

On the third morning, I sat in the meditation hall next to a slim, fine-featured man named Michael Stevens, a social worker from Portland, Oregon, who counsels homeless veterans at the VA hospital there. He had gone to Vietnam at 22, straight from what he described as "a world of limited choices" in the foothills of the Appalachians. "At first I liked the Vietnamese and managed to feel neutral about both sides even though I was coordinating bombing raids," he had told me the previous evening. "Then

one night a friend of mine was ambushed, and he radioed our command post for protective fire. This was when Nixon was winding down the war. My commanding officer told me we had used up our ammunition quota for the night, and we couldn't protect him. That's when I wanted to bomb; that's when I began to hate."

Sitting in meditation that morning, I could hear him sucking in small breaths, trying unsuccessfully to hold back tears. "There was a block inside me," he told me later, "something that still hated the Vietnamese. In meditation, I watched my breath and felt my stomach get tight and my breathing get shorter. I saw Vietnam again—the jungle, the smell of diesel oil and dung—and I said to myself, 'forgiveness.' I moved my consciousness down my throat, thinking 'forgiveness' until I got down to my stomach. Then I shook with happiness, with sadness. I was obsessed with saying I'm sorry. I thought, 'How am I going to say this? Where am I going to say this?' And tears came down my face."

That afternoon we met together—vets, nonvets and Vietnamese—in small, Western-style sharing groups focused on self-expression, apology and forgiveness. In one group, Stevens apologized to a Vietnamese nun named Cao Ngoc Phuong. "I needed to say, 'Please forgive me for the suffering I helped cause,'" he told me later. Sister Phuong said fiercely, "That was then. This is now."

In my group, an acupuncturist named Daniel Bruce, who had burned a village as a young Marine, turned to a refugee Vietnamese monk named Chan Ly. "I want to apologize for being a part of destroying your country," Bruce said, somewhat formally. "And to all the people you probably helped after I made them homeless."

Chan Ly put his palms together and bowed until his knees and forehead touched the carpet. "I have been a monk for many years, and I thought I could control my emotions, but today I can't," he said. "I was born in 1948, in a tent, because the French troops were bombarding my father's house, and I have wandered ever since. During the war I used to give funeral services, but my heart was hard, like ice, like steel, because the suffering was too much. Then I got a telegram saying my own brother had been killed, and I knew true suffering." Chan Ly turned to the veterans. "Today the voice of Jesus Christ speaks through you."

As I looked around the room at us all—Vietnamese and veterans, warriors and victims—I could not tell whether the healing we gave one another was spiritual or psychological. ■

KATY BUTLER *is a free-lance writer living in Mill Valley, CA.*

ILLUSTRATION BY KEVIN HAWKES

THERAPY FOR A DYING PLANET

WE ARE THE CAUSE, WE ARE THE CURE

By Terrance O'Connor

THERE IS A STORY, PERHAPS APOCRYPHAL, ABOUT an incident that occurred in Frieda Fromm-Reichmann's practice shortly before she left Germany for the United States. A young woman with numerous irrational fears went to Fromm-Reichmann for help. During the course of the psychoanalysis, the patient gradually overcame her fears, and after three years the therapy was successfully ended. A few weeks later the young woman, who was Jewish, was picked up by the Gestapo and sent to a concentration camp.

By helping people adjust to a destructive society, are we doing more harm than good? Today, as desert sands advance across Africa like conquering armies, and life is on the retreat in every continent, it occurs to me that the sad tale of Frieda Fromm-Reichmann's client is more relevant than ever.

We sit in our offices helping parents raise children, divorcées get their bearings, couples find ways to deepen their relationships, while outside the air gets fouler and the oceans rise. In a year's time, if we are successful, the parents and children are doing well, the divorcée is enjoying her independence, the

couple has developed a more satisfying relationship. Meanwhile the air is fouler, the oceans higher, and hundreds, perhaps thousands, of species have vanished forever from this earth. Each hour five square miles of rain forest are destroyed. By the end of a year, this area of destruction is the size of Pennsylvania.

We are facing an unparalleled global crisis, a disaster much greater than Hitler or Stalin or the Khmer Rouge could ever create. What is the meaning of therapy, and what is the responsibility of the therapist in such a world?

A FEW YEARS AGO, I GAVE A TALK ON "THE MATURE and Healthy Intimate Relationship" to a group of divorced people. Midway through the talk, a woman asked, "Last week we had a speaker who said that some people are satisfied with very limited relationships. So why should we want this mature relationship? Why should we bother?" The question caught me off guard. "I don't know," I admitted. "I would think that the benefits would speak for themselves. But obviously everyone has a choice."

I went on with my presentation, but her question kept nagging me until eventually I lost all concentration and came to a halt. "I need to stop here and go back to the question I was just asked," I finally said. "Let me say something about the status quo. Status quo is that the hole in the ozone layer is as big as the United States. Status quo is that some scientists are predicting that by the middle of the next century, global warming will result in most of the coastal cities in the U.S. being below sea level and will make the grain belt a wasteland. Status quo is that acid rain, besides destroying the lakes and forests, is now considered to be the leading cause of lung cancer after cigarette smoke. Status quo is that 35,000 people die of starvation every day. Also, every day two or more species become extinct, not due to natural selection but due to deforestation and pollution. By the year 2000—that's only *11* years from now—this is expected to accelerate to 100 species a day. In other words, mass extinction. What does this say to you? To me it says that the status quo is that the planet is dying! The planet is dying because we are satisfied with our limited relationships, in which control, denial and abuse are tolerated. The status quo is that we have these petty relationships with one another, between nations, with ourselves and the natural world. Why should we bother? Because healthy relationships are not an esoteric goal. It is a matter of our very survival and the survival of most of the life upon this earth."

After this outburst, I stood silently facing an apparently stunned audience staring back at me. I was trying to remember where I had been in my presentation when a man in the back stood up and began talking about the destruction of the rain forests. The whole feeling in the room had shifted. The greater part of the audience had come in concerned with their own loneliness. As we began to look at all of our personal concerns from a global perspective, we could see that the patterns of control, denial and projection that sabotage intimate relationships are the very patterns that endanger the world. To change these patterns is to change not just our social lives but our relationship to the planet.

In *The Unheard Cry for Meaning,* Viktor Frankl says that in finding meaning, we are "perceiving a possibility embedded in reality" and that "unless we use the opportunity to fulfill the meaning inherent and dormant in a situation, it will pass and be gone forever." Citing his own experience as an inmate in Auschwitz and Dachau, and his work with POWs, he asserts that the will to meaning has survival value, that those most likely to survive were those who were oriented toward something outside themselves, a meaning to be fulfilled: "In a word, existence was dependent on 'self-transcendence.'" And so it is today. A transcendence of sorts is necessary if we are to meet the challenge of the global crisis, a transcendence of who we are in relationship to the human community and to the planet. Another way of saying this is that it is time for a shift in context. As Watzlawick et al. say in *Pragmatics of Human Communication,* "A phenomenon remains unexplainable as long as the range of observation is not wide enough to include the context in which the phenomenon occurs."

WE TOOK A POWERFUL LEAP WHEN WE widened our view of the individual's problems to include the family system in which they occurred. Perhaps it is time for another leap. It is time to begin to go beyond our individual families to attend to the Family of Man.

Of the 35,000 people who die of starvation each day, the large majority are children. Whose children are these? If we are the Family of Man, these are our children. Pure and simple. Tens of thousands of our children starve to death each day, not because there is not enough food to feed each and every one of them, but because we are a dysfunctional family. Look at us! We are at once overcontrolling and dreadfully neglectful. And, like the alcoholic family, we ignore the bodies piling up in our living room—and we ignore them at our growing peril.

As the problems become more evident, I am getting a more receptive response when I talk or write about the global crisis. Still, avoidance reactions are common. Most boil down to, "I don't want to hear about it," or "It's not my responsibility." Some people convince themselves that "It's not happening" and "It's not my planet." Some even mask their despair in a quasi-spiritual facade of nonattachment: "What the hell, it's only one planet. There are billions." More common are those who will admit to feeling a bit guilty about not doing anything. The equation here is, doing nothing plus feeling guilty about it equals doing something.

Action is called for, but action motivated by guilt may only compound the problem. We are in disharmony with the world because we are in disharmony with ourselves. Guilt is an indication of this. Guilt is a warning that there is an incongruity in our value system, a schism in our sense of self that needs to be investigated. If we act without introspection, we simply throw our weight to one side of the inner conflict, increasing the disharmony. Our actions will be incomplete and fragmented. We will make some token move and fall back into denial and minimization. To heal is to make whole.

A FEW YEARS AGO, I SPENT SOME TIME ALONE IN an isolated cabin far from a road, without water or electricity. I hiked in with a stack of books. For a week, I sat on the porch of that cabin and watched the black snake lying in the rafters, the chipmunks scurrying between rocks, and listened to the song of the wind through the trees. I read about the state of the world. I cried. It was like reading the minute details of one's mother's cancer. When I had enough of reading and crying, I went for long hikes. I followed a magnificent stream. The woods were lovely. I saw deer and grouse and wild turkey and once, I think, a coyote. I went back to the porch and read some more, and sometimes I cried, and sometimes I raged, and sometimes I looked up at the ancient stones and beautiful trees and the abundance of life around me and I loved it so fiercely I thought my heart would burst.

If this is not my planet, whose is it? If this is not my family, whose is it? If not my responsibility, whose? I am both the victim and the victimizer. I am the cause, and I am the cure. When I act out of this realization, I act not out of guilt but out of self-love, a love that includes my family, a self that includes my planet. When I look, I see. When I educate myself, I break through my denial and see that mankind is facing an absolutely unprecedented crisis. When I act from this knowledge, I act not out of obligation or idealism, but because I live in a straw house and I smell smoke. I realize the truth that, in Krishnamurti's words, "You are the world, and the world is on fire."

An awareness is dawning, and a shift is occurring. In the face of the darkening clouds, there has been some very positive movement around the globe. The lessening of tensions between East and West is the absolutely necessary beginning to saving the world. We all know that if Mom and Dad can get together, the rest becomes workable. If the U.S.S.R and the U.S. can continue to build trust, we can liberate enormous energies in the forms of money, natural resources, technology, intelligence and manpower to meet the common threat. And in our own backyards, a revolution is taking place, a powerful grass-roots movement. I am referring to the astounding proliferation of 12-Step groups in the past few years.

While there are many healing aspects to the 12-Step groups, two interest me here. The first is the philosophy of giving up the attempt to control that over which one has no control. Ultimately, this seems to me to be blowing the whistle on our hubris, our worship of that will that has allowed us to gain dominion over the world. This is the will with which spouses try to dominate each other, and with which our clients struggle to get control over, rather than find harmony with, themselves and the world. This will is a useful tool, but it is a jealous and petty god. The second quality of these programs that gives me hope is their emphasis on responsibility for oneself and to each other. There is a recognition that we are all in this together.

AS THERAPISTS, WE HAVE LEARNED SOME UNFORgettable lessons about our limits, but we have also witnessed the wondrous unfolding of human potential. We know better than most that reality is dependent upon our perception of it and that a simple change in our point of view can yield a host of new possibilities. So how does an awareness of the global crisis translate to specific behaviors in our offices? In my waiting room, I have a shelf stacked with literature from environmental organizations. Above the shelf is a photograph of the Earth taken from space. Above the photograph is a sign that reads, "Mother Earth Needs You." Beside the photograph is a brief synopsis of the dangers and opportunities of the global crisis. Some of my clients are suffering from personal crises of such intensity that they are unable to focus on anything else. For them, my "Opportunity Corner" has little interest. But overshadowing many of my clients' genuine issues is the general malaise that President Carter was so impolitic to refer to a decade ago in a speech to a nation yearning to escape to the good old days. To these clients I mention the global crisis as I might tell an Ericksonian story or an incident from my own life: I bring it in intentionally when it is relevant and therapeutic.

Clients struggling with the purpose and meaning of their lives are often doing so in obsessive isolation from the movement of life around them. They are attempting to achieve a goal such as marriage with-

out first being in relationship with themselves and the human community. Coming to grips with the global crisis offers both a deeper understanding of the human condition and a motivation to break down the psychological barriers that allow us to tolerate our starving children and rising oceans. I have even, upon occasion, interrupted a client's obsessive, self-absorbed soliloquy with, "Are you aware that the planet is dying?" I might interrupt a professional debate on the best therapeutic modality with the same question.

I am not suggesting that we drop our therapeutic tools, but that we use them with awareness of a rapidly and profoundly changing planet. Perhaps Frieda Fromm-Reichmann should have simply advised her patient to flee. We do not have that option. When I speak of global consciousness, I am taking a perspective in which the difference between client and therapist is only a difference of role. We are equally responsible for the state of the planet and equally affected by it. I must say that I do not see my colleagues being much more free of the malaise and denial than are my clients. Isn't it strange that we supposed experts and healers of human relations give but passing notice to our extraordinarily unhealthy relationship to the planet as a whole, a relationship that will ultimately undermine our work completely? We must become more aware and contribute that awareness, rather than our denial, to the stream of human consciousness. An active membership in just one environmental group puts one in the pipeline to receive all the information and direction one needs. We must become part of the solution rather than part of the problem. What is the responsibility of a therapist on a dying planet? Physician, heal thyself. ■

TERRANCE O'CONNOR, M.S.W., *is in private practice in Silver Spring, MD.*

P*ain—and fear of pain —is probably the substance abuser's only source of motivation for change.*

ROBERT FORMAN

PHOTOGRAPH BY CHARLES GATEWOOD/MAGNUM

PHOTOGRAPH BY GILLES PERESS/MAGNUM

PHOTOGRAPH BY POLLY BROWN/ACTUALITY

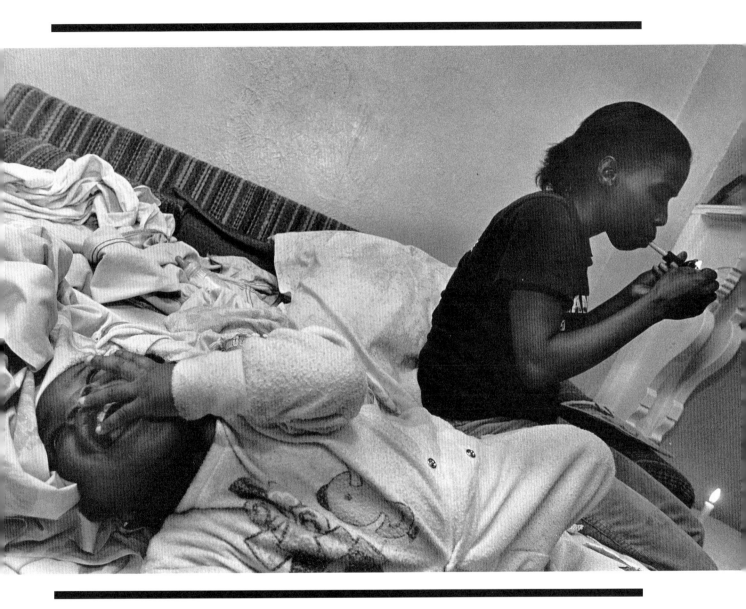

PHOTOGRAPH BY EUGENE RICHARDS/MAGNUM

Gender Riddles

New Answers To Old Questions?

PHOTOGRAPH BY CHARLES HARBUTT/ACTUALITY

WARNING: FAMILY THERAPY MAY BE HAZARDOUS TO YOUR HEALTH

PUTTING FEMINISM INTO PRACTICE

By Virginia Goldner

I'VE SOMETIMES WONDERED THIS YEAR WHETHER feminism has become our newest fashion, replacing epistemology as a high-status subject for competitive family therapists to claim as their own. I'm pleased, as any outsider wanting to "get in" would be, since epistemology, with only a few exceptions, has been a turf owned by men. But now that everyone is declaring themselves a feminist, I can't help being concerned that the critical edge that is feminism's essential attribute has been blunted by quick success.

This would not be an unusual outcome. Taming a dangerous idea by claiming it as one's own is a time-honored political strategy, and I do believe that feminism is dangerous to family therapy. One of the most effective tactics I've seen for disarming this subversive point of view is a simple one—transforming feminist commentary from a threatening critique into a banal who-could-disagree piece of liberal cant.

In the interests of protecting feminists from success on these terms, and in the hopes of reducing our swelling ranks, I would like to present the feminist case in terms that will probably be incompatible with the core beliefs of many committed family therapists. Since I count myself within these ranks, I can only report that subscribing to mutually exclusive visions of truth is a long-standing habit of my mind. It is unnerving, but I want to point out that we often prescribe just such an approach for families stuck in their ways.

THE INFLUENCE OF FEMINISM HAS BEGUN TO BE heard in the everyday rhetoric of family therapy. Instead of talking about families exclusively in abstract terms—our familiar language of "boundaries," "hierarchies" and "triangles"—we have begun to acknowledge that the "elements" within social systems are men and women. As a result, a new set of terms has entered our standard vocabulary, and phrases like "gender issues" and "gender roles" have become commonplace. Some may argue that this represents an advance in the awareness of the social and political context of our work. But I believe that framing these enormously important issues in terms of constructs like "gender roles" has served to trivialize the feminist critique of society and the family.

Like any cliché, referring to "gender roles" presumes that what is being named is self-evident. Moreover, the term functions as a cliché within a cliché, with the connotation that sex-role stereotyping is a dehumanizing burden for both men and women that we must all try to "get past." In other words, the idea is that gender is something that can be transcended, a "role" one can "play" or not. A related notion is that men and women share a common enemy, "sex roles," and that we have suffered equally, unnecessarily and arbitrarily. This is the kind of seductively bland, even-handed truism we could all agree on—precisely because it is false.

Seeing domestic strife between men and women as a problem of arbitrarily rigid gender roles allows us to fit the potentially subversive critique of feminism into our old categories. It enables us to reduce the problems of men and women in families to merely a dysfunctional division of labor, no more or less problematic than any other family dilemma. Our job as therapists becomes a matter of getting the partners to change positions—tricky, perhaps, but nothing that forces us to rethink our premises. Larger questions about power and inequality disappear as we assign the family its therapeutic tasks— put Dan in charge of the social calendar and Dana in charge of the car. It's a good, conservative solution.

The problem with proceeding in this way is that it conveys a message of "separate but equal," even without an explicit assertion to that effect. This obscures the difference in power between men and women, implicitly reducing a political and social problem to a technical operation. Of course our job as clinicians is to help families solve their particular dilemmas and not to make speeches about social injustice. But, as we know better than most, no therapeutic intervention is apolitical, and what I shall argue is that by denying the reality of patriarchy in our clinical work, we are inevitably colluding in its perpetuation.

One element in this denial system is the very use of the term "gender roles." No one, for example, writes of "class roles" or "race roles." This is because it is somehow self-evident that class and race are not inherently individual or interpersonal phenomena, no matter how profound their psychological consequences. Rather, they are understood as macrosystems, which hierarchically organize society as a whole.

By regarding gender as a role that a clever therapist can rectify through some technique like "role reversal," we confine gender to the realm of the individual, even though it is an overarching organizational principle of all social relations. Indeed, in most cultures, gender is a basic metaphysical category by which the whole universe is organized.

Most languages, for example, are elaborately gendered, with gender-differentiated modes of address, verb and noun forms, and so on. Moreover, all the significant elements of the social, natural and spiritual world are linguistically differentiated by gender, and the mythologies of most cultures rely heavily on gender symbols. This is true not only of primitive societies. In a fascinating study of the origins of modern science, sociologist Evelyn Fox Keller argues that our image of science as an abstract body of theory that is emotionally and sexually neutral is itself a cultural myth. She demonstrates that from the days of Francis Bacon and the birth of the scientific method down to the present, science has been consistently depicted as a masculine force mastering a female Nature.

Working along similar lines, psychologist Carol Gilligan has investigated the cognitive styles of men and women with regard to their approach to moral reasoning. Her work is a convincing demonstration that abstract thinking is not necessarily gender-neutral. Rather, Gilligan has observed that men and women conceptualize moral dilemmas very differently, with men emphasizing hierarchy, rights and autonomy and women emphasizing context, caring and attachment.

The examples cited here are a means to argue the point that gender differentiation is not primarily a psychological state or a social role, but a universal principle of social and cultural life, manifesting itself in the individual psyche, the metaphysical framework and the ideologies of a society. And, as feminists must tirelessly point out, this cultural fact of gender differentiation then provides the legitimization for the social fact of male domination in the material and political structures of a society. Indeed, many feminist scholars now take as a point of departure the axiom that human history can best be understood in terms of three semiautonomous systems of human domination: class, race/ethnic, and sex/gender.

I F THOUGHT IS GENDERED AND AFFECTS ARE gendered and the world is gendered, then in the deepest possible sense, so human identity itself must be gendered. Indeed, the developmental literature, now also informed by feminism, has demonstrated that gender identity gets established between 18 and 36 months, much earlier than had previously been thought. It now appears that the process of gender formation occurs during a crucial developmental phase, the period in which the most fundamental aspects of existential identity, myself-as-a-person, get established. The late psychiatrist Margaret Mahler and her colleagues have imaginatively named this period of identity development "the psychological birth of the human infant" (the title of their 1975 book). Sociologist Nancy Chodorow has shown how this birth of the self and the acquisition of gender become fatefully intertwined. In other words, personhood and gender identity develop together, coevolving and codetermining each other. As a result, one could no more become "de-gendered" than "de-selfed."

The social origins of this psychological process are located by Chodorow in one key phenomenon: the fact that parenting is asymmetrical. This means that both boys and girls develop in relation to a primary parent, the one who "mothers" them. And in most societies mothering is done by women. (The exceptions are so rare and idiosyncratic as to prove the universality of the rule.) This social arrangement, argues Chodorow, has decisive consequences for the creation of gendered personalities, since children of both sexes must begin the project of becoming a person by separating and differentiating from a single, psychologically gendered woman.

Both mother and child's strategies for coping with this difficult task will vary as a function of the child's sex. Chodorow argues that mothers are less able to separate from girl babies, and tend to enhance the similarities between themselves and their daughters. This promotes the development of an emotionally fused relationship that in turn diminishes the daughter's capacity to individuate. For better or worse, daughters do maintain a continuous emotional involvement with their mothers throughout their development in a way that boys do not. By contrast, male children, who can have an equally intense relationship with their mothers, are nonetheless better able to separate merely because they are of the opposite sex. Mothers experience them as different from themselves, as more of an "other." Moreover, boys can use this "difference" (and its reciprocal, their likeness to their fathers) as a psychological vehicle for separating and disidentifying with their mother.

Thus, while the girl's psychic structure develops in the context of a continuous, proximate relationship with someone "just like her," the boy constructs his identity via an experience of difference, and at a greater psychic distance from the mothering person. Each of these distinctive developmental contexts provides a unique set of opportunities and constraints that, Chodorow argues, can account for many of the standard personality differences between men and women.

In brief, growing up under these gendered social

arrangements produces women with relatively permeable psychological boundaries, who fashion their identities in terms of other people, have a greater capacity for empathy, and are at greater risk of losing themselves. Men, on the other hand, emerge with relatively rigid psychological boundaries, disown their dependency needs and fear being engulfed, have relatively greater difficulty empathizing with others, and are better able to think for themselves. In other words, men and women emerge as psychological reciprocals, and both are psychologically hobbled.

IN CHODOROW'S VIEW, THE SOCIAL CREATION OF these two dichotomized personality structures has consequences that extend far beyond the psychological. According to Chodorow, by reproducing gender-differentiated people with particular desires, capacities and limitations, families are ultimately reproducing the oppressive social order itself.

If class society and patriarchy are to prevail as social systems, they require the participation of individuals psychologically suited to their unique demands. Such individuals are produced and reproduced in the contemporary family. More specifically family systems, as they are currently constituted, produce women with a talent for relationships, nurturance and submission to male authority. This makes them well suited for managing intimate relations in the domestic sphere and poorly adapted to the demands of the public realm. Similarly, the contemporary family can be seen as producing men with a subjective conviction of male superiority, with the abstract, instrumentally oriented personality that prepares them for a marginal position in family life and dominance in the capitalist world of work.

ONCE WE ACCEPT THE CULTURAL, SYMBOLIC, linguistic, psychological and political preeminence of gender as an organizing principle of human history and society, it becomes simply impossible to reduce the feminist critique of family therapy to a matter of sex roles and consciousness-raising. Moreover, if gender is to be understood critically and systemically, feminists argue, it cannot be understood apart from the continuing reality of patriarchal domination. Moreover, they will maintain that the family is the major vehicle for reproducing the patriarchal order of the wider society. Granting these premises means that no serious discussion of gender can occur apart from a substantive critique of the family as a social institution.

Such an approach, however, is fundamentally discontinuous with the dominant modes of discourse in family therapy. As an increasing number of (still friendly) critics have argued, standard theorizing in family therapy lifts the family out of history and society altogether. The use of what is primarily an organizational model reduces the family to merely "a special case of a system . . . [so that] a theory of the family [gets] collapsed into a theory of structural organization."

Outside of history, severed from political economy, the family appears as a given, as if it were natural, universal, unproblematic. To argue that the family as an institution is deeply implicated in women's oppression is simply to stand outside the terms of the discourse. More specifically, both the cybernetic and functionalist models of the family, which dominate our theoretical traditions, presume an ultimate "consensus of interests" between family members, who are conceived of as "parts of a whole." This vision of harmonious interdependency and equity cannot (unproblematically) coexist with the picture of inherent domestic inequality that feminists maintain.

Moreover, feminists reject the idea of the family as some kind of freestanding entity organized on its own terms. Rather they offer us a view of men and women as members of two distinctive social groups who, because of the sexual division of labor in all societies, have very different relationships to both the public and private spheres and therefore have very different experiences of "The Family." Given their different contexts, men and women enter relationships on such different terms that intimacy between the sexes is presumed to be *inherently* problematic and disturbed.

This deeply pessimistic view of the possibilities of heterosexual love, which emphasizes the structural constraints against domestic happiness, challenges the vision we all still maintain of the family as a "haven in a heartless world." It is one thing to see the public world of work as hierarchical and unfair. It is quite another to entertain the idea that love and family, the historical antidotes to the harshness of the marketplace, are themselves vehicles of human domination.

MANAGING THE CONTRADICTORY IMAGES OF the family that the organizational and the feminist paradigms evoke is essential to creating a politically principled and informed model of family treatment.

Given the enormousness of the enterprise, it begs the question to appeal to an androgynous ideal "beyond gender roles," or to cite people from one's personal life or clinical experience who have transcended their "sex-role stereotype." We all know men who are nurturing and women who are not. Such an approach distracts us from the task at hand, which is to proceed from the fact of a gendered world, and then to use our special expertise as family therapists to document how this fact of life unfolds in intimate relationships—to describe it, capture its ironies, paradoxes, ambiguities and dilemmas, and then to use our observations to assist those who come to us for help.

This, I believe, is the challenge and opportunity feminism offers us, but it is not necessarily the direction in which things will go. Capturing this kind of interpersonal detail requires accepting gender as an irreducible category of clinical observation and theo-

rizing. This cannot be done without calling into question the whole body of theory on which our practice rests, and as philosopher of science Thomas Kuhn has documented, within any scientific community resistance to facts and formulations that threaten the reigning paradigm is inevi-table. Such resistance protects members of the group from seeing what they already see and from knowing what they are reluctant to know.

Otherwise, how are we to explain the complacent brand of moral relativism that allows family therapists, even now, to pervert the concept of circularity by confusing an elegant truth, that master and slave are psychologically interdependent, with the morally repugnant and absurd notion that the two are therefore equals? I do not wish to suggest that relations between men and women are inherently master/slave affairs, but I do believe that when we make the wife responsible for her husband's drinking, or for her broken nose, we are not so much reframing a complex reality as we are protecting the man and blaming his wife, and that way, at least in the short run, we keep the case. In other words, by choosing to highlight the power of weakness instead of the abuse of power, we are utilizing and exploiting our knowledge of the real power differentials between the sexes, while simultaneously keeping this knowledge out of critical awareness and therefore out of our theory.

Looking at relationships in this way serves a double function. It allows us to feel we are clinically effective: The couple comes back, and, hardly a trivial matter, maybe the husband actually reforms. But at the same time, this way of working protects us from having to confront any troublesome questions beyond technique, questions about moral responsibility in family life or about the ultimate sources of interpersonal power. By clinging to a theoretical perspective in which power and inequality are discredited as clinical concepts because they are deemed products of "linear thinking," we can always restrict our definition of an interpersonal problem to one dysfunctional sequence or another, and never have to ask any questions beyond the particular.

In this way we are spared an encounter with the most troublesome question of all—whether there might not be something fundamentally wrong with the social institution of the family itself as it is currently constituted. If we accept this possibility, the issue would no longer be a matter of interdicting that nasty sequence that maintains the husband's drinking, but of facing up to certain social realities: If things got bad enough, would the wife have the money, and therefore the option, to leave her husband (if not, she doesn't have many bargaining chips)? If the husband is violent when he drinks—or doesn't drink—does the fear of his violence keep the wife from a real confrontation with his drinking? If the wife has no life outside the home, will she be too emotionally dependent on her husband to ask anything from him and, as a result, will she collude in minimizing the problem? Finally, merely because she is a psychologically gendered female, will she reflexively protect her husband and their relationship, at the expense of protecting herself?

Generating this list of contingencies does not require advanced training in feminist theory, while sidestepping it would appear to be a sign of advanced training in family therapy. Most of the elements in this everyday calculus are common sense, and while they clearly inform our clinical experience, they are not at the center of our therapy. It is as if we were afraid to name the obvious for fear of getting stuck with it.

This fear, which therapists too often keep outside of their critical awareness, is usually some variant of the thought: "This is an impossible marriage. Even though I don't think any real change can occur, I don't think either one of them would necessarily be better off alone. I don't know what would be better for the children. They cannot let themselves know how bad things really are, and I would only do harm by telling them."

One way to protect everyone from the consequences of that grim view is to frame the family's problem in such a way that the wife takes responsibility for more of the changing. (Since she has more at stake, and more to lose, she is likely to be willing.) By keeping her busily engaged in improving things, both wife and therapist can feel purposeful, deny their helplessness, and keep the family together.

Now this may be the best alternative under the circumstances. The question is whether such an approach represents an informed clinical choice or is merely a means of avoiding making conscious the interior monologue sketched above. In other words, we must ask ourselves what happens when we sacrifice simple thoughts for elegant, clinical constructions, and assess who gains and loses in the process.

If we were to risk the thought—which is now a virtual sociological given—that marriage and family life do not benefit men and women equally, we might be less inclined to blame ourselves or the family for relationships that are just "wrong." As a result, we might even be in a position to reconsider the axiom that individual well-being is usually best served by keeping families together.

Systematizing this kind of critical thinking could put some of our favorite ideas at risk. Here are some examples: the Batesonian notion that power is an illusion, which in its current fashionable form becomes the radical constructivist stance that nothing is real beyond point of view, and, therefore, that inequality is entirely a matter of perspective; the systemic (if not moral) idealization of the family as some kind of poetic, transcendent unity; the belief that gender can be comfortably subsumed into our preexisting categories and ways of doing business, and if not, the assumption that it is therefore an extraneous political category. Let me briefly elaborate. While no sophisticated family therapist would choose to be identified with a "save the family at all costs" brand of treatment, our training and what it was designed to counteract (the overfocus on the individual) encourages us to think of families virtually as if they were living, biological organisms and to believe, as a moral, political and philosophical truth, that to be for the family *is* to be for the individual. This, I believe, makes us inclined to minimize evidence to the contrary, whether clinical or sociological, and to unwittingly collude with women's willingness to betray themselves in order to hold family relationships together.

Indeed, for all the talk of a paradigm shift, our metaphors often transform the family back into a kind of "self" with its own needs, thinking processes and ultimate, albeit paradoxical, wisdom. Ironically, by making the family into a person, we may be compromising the personhood of the "components" who compose it—most especially the women.

Having worked so diligently, and against such cultural odds, to demonstrate that individuals are not islands unto themselves, family therapists are understandably reluctant to lose any hard-won ground by entertaining the idea that families might actually be damaging to women. Nonetheless, it seems to me that we do families and women a disservice by rhapsodizing about the systemic cohesion of the family organism, either as an epistemological stance or as a moral good. The fact is, families are *not* organisms, they are social arrangements, and their dissolution should not be poetically associated with death, which is what the organism metaphor evokes. Indeed, if psychiatric social worker Judith Wallerstein's recent findings are to be believed, unhappy as former spouses may be with the lives they put together, 10 years after the breakup, very, very few of them regret their divorce or believe they made a mistake.

ANY REAL ENCOUNTER WITH THE ISSUES RAISED by feminism will necessitate rethinking our attachment to many of our fundamental axioms and metaphors. Moreover, any integration of family systems with feminist theory will require

that we introduce new categories of analysis and maybe even revive ideas long since abandoned, seemingly transcended, or simply discredited.

For example, we would have to broaden our field of vision with regard to what the relevant social dimensions of family therapy ought to be. This would mean integrating a theory of the material and social bases of interpersonal power with a psychological theory of families. It would also necessitate devising clinical strategies that would bring this wider context into the consulting room—not as ideological harangue, but as change-inducing clinical interventions. This means finding ways to talk about gender issues in treatment, and that means talking about money, power, access to power, fairness, the ability to leave and so on.

I also believe that if we take feminism seriously, we will have to make a place in our thinking for some theory of the individual. The work on gender from developmentalists, psychoanalysts and sociologists has made it impossible to be satisfied with a context-is-all theory of mind. If gender identity is, as it appears to be, so deep-seated as to be virtually impossible to unlearn, we might even have to reconsider some supremely unfashionable and heretical notions like the enduring significance of early experience and of unconscious fantasies. At the least, we can no longer complacently leave a blank where formulations about individual psychic reality must be confronted.

And finally, with regard to gender as an extraneous political issue, let us remember that the metaphors we family therapists like best about our work derive from political imagery—most pertinently, the notion that domestic relations involve the inevitable pursuit of power between people bound by love. Indeed, our training has made us exquisitely sensitized to what feminists call "the politics of personal life." Given this unsentimental vision of the problems of love, it is striking that we have maintained our commitment to a sentimentalized, neo-Confucian vision of the family, in which parts and wholes are harmoniously balanced and the weak are ultimately as powerful as the strong.

If patriarchy begins at home, we will need to consider, as a field, the extent to which this vision of truth has served the interests of some more than others, and whether, like the Confucian ideology of feudal China, it has functioned to reward the powerful and silence the weak. ■

VIRGINIA GOLDNER, PH.D., *is on the faculty of the Ackerman Institute in New York, NY.*

See references, page 568.

PHOTOGRAPH BY ABIGAIL HEYMAN

*T*HE MOTHER KNOT

CAN FAMILY THERAPISTS UNTIE IT?

By Mary Sykes Wylie

A DOZEN YEARS AGO, WHILE RESEARCHING AN article on attitudes toward motherhood, Rachel Hare-Mustin, professor of counseling and human relations at Villanova University, was disturbed by a pattern she saw repeatedly in the taped therapy sessions she watched. "I became very aware that the mother was often considered the most unattractive, most inadequate person in the room," she says. According to Hare-Mustin, mothers typically came into therapy feeling "terribly responsible for whatever went wrong, and the therapist seemed to assume that they needed to be taught better 'mothering skills.'"

Hare-Mustin's article was the first feminist analysis of family therapy. Citing studies demonstrating that loss of power or chronic powerlessness are often precursors of psychological disturbance, she wrote, "The inequality in the traditional family is rarely recognized by individual or family therapists . . . power aspects of sex roles are largely disregarded or denied. . . . The formulation of dominant mother/ineffectual father as the cause of practically every serious psychological difficulty is made with-out regard for the underlying inequality that leads to such a situation."

Hare-Mustin was the first to uncover what many now think was family therapy's dirty little secret. Family therapists didn't like mothers any better than had psychoanalysts. Beneath the sanitized terminology about dysfunctional executive systems, enmeshment and detriangulation, family therapists still talked about mother as enemy—a querulous, dependent, overcontrolling woman who emasculated her husband and emotionally stunted her children.

For some years, Hare-Mustin's article remained a lonely sentinel on a barren plane. Since the mid-'80s, however, there has been a small blizzard of books, articles, conferences and workshops describing women in families and redefining the assumptions, theory, methodology—in short, the discourse—of family therapy. Whether this flurry will result in a renovated family therapy, in which gender counts as much as generation, remains to be seen.

Publicly and officially, the movement has become impossible to ignore, while openly dismissing or deriding it is no longer quite respectable. (In fact, critics of a feminist orientation to therapy were generally unwilling to be interviewed for this article, worried that they would be lumped among the disreputable partisans of male chauvinism.) Nonetheless, much of the apparent palatability of feminist ideas may reflect diplomatic politesse more than it does a genuine transformation in the way therapists regard mothers.

In a survey of the four leading family therapy journals (*Family Process, Journal of Marriage and Family Therapy, Contemporary Family Therapy* and *American Journal of Family Therapy*) for the years 1978 and 1987, Judy Myers Avis, associate professor of family therapy at the University of Guelph in Ontario, and family therapist Cathryn Haig found that mother blaming had not declined during the intervening nine years, and may actually have increased. According to Avis and Haig, family problems were attributed to mothers twice as often as they were to fathers, and the behavior of mothers was described in much more pejorative and judgmental terms. "Mothers just could not get it right," says Avis about the approximately one hundred cases they studied. "They were either 'overinvolved'—that is, 'nagging,' 'too permissive,' 'intrusive,' 'domineering,' 'crushingly overprotective,' or they were not involved enough—'distancing,' 'stony-faced,' 'cold,' 'cerebral' or 'overcontrolled.'" Fathers, Avis and Haig report, were regularly brought in to instruct, supervise and correct their wives in such "masculine" talents as paying bills, balancing a checkbook, or disciplining the children, while mothers were *never* asked to share their particular expertise.

MOTHERS, IT SEEMS, ARE STILL EXPECTED TO live up to what Rachel Hare-Mustin has called "the myth of motherhood," a contradictory hotchpotch of ideals and expectations that no human being, female or male, could possibly meet. According to this logic, mothers can only be all good or all bad; those who are not perfectly lov-

ing, wise, selfless and benignly powerful are rejecting, incompetent, self-centered and malignly controlling.

Beneath this ideology lies the unconscious double-bind premise that mother is at fault precisely because she does what mothers are expected to do in our culture—shoulder the full burden of her family's day-to-day emotional and physical care. Critics of family therapy believe that too many family problems are still forced into the classic procrustean diagnosis of "enmeshed" and "controlling" mother, "distant," "peripheral" father and symptomatic child. This unholy triad, the so-called perverse triangle, is the source primeval for family therapists, literally the "mother lode" of clinical material from which much of the field's theory and practice evolved.

Any reader of the literature is thoroughly familiar with the stock characters in this archetypal drama. A son or a daughter is generally the "identified patient," suffering from a disabling physical or emotional problem—anorexia, for example, or diabetes, asthma, drug or alcohol abuse, phobias, psychogenic vomiting, obsessive *fear* of vomiting, academic failure, sexual promiscuity, disobedience, aggression, nightmares and, of course, schizophrenia. The father is described as passive, withdrawn, depressed, apathetic, physically aloof from his children, uninvolved in their care or discipline. He "never" or "rarely" expresses anger; except, perhaps, when galvanized by his wife to "do something" about a refractory child, he acts out a clumsy show of parental despotism, for which he is then ridiculed by both child and spouse. The mother is cast as the controlling power of the family, regardless of what she actually does. She may be seen as excessively nurturant or coldly withdrawn; she pretends to support her children, while showing only condescension and uninterest; she nags at her husband for more help in disciplining the children, while cunningly building coalitions with them to undermine his authority. She demands that her children behave in ways that will please her, while implicitly telling them that they never will. When family-of-origin work is done, not surprisingly, the therapist finds that the mother's mother, as well as her husband's mother, were just as bad.

In a typical case, the mother of an obsessive 9-year-old boy, who constantly and ritualistically washed his hands and checked behind doors, was "talkative and animated" during the first session. She engaged in continual eye contact with her son and played "footsie" with him, while her husband was described as "quiet and impassive." The therapist called this "a fairly standard sequence of interactions: Mother focuses intensely on the child; father withdraws; child exhibits symptomatic behavior; mother worries, urges father to take action; father says it's not so serious and that mother is overreacting; mother assumes father doesn't understand, becomes anxious, and focuses on the child; father withdraws; child exhibits symptomatic behavior, and so on."

The therapist's prescription was also fairly standard: "Because the boy's compulsiveness was assumed to mirror his mother's obsessive concerns about him, functional mothering behaviors were to be encouraged, whereas obsessive concerns were not." The therapist's goal was, she wrote, to create a "gradual decrease in the mother's intrusiveness and gentle increase in the father's involvement." She told the father that "he was needed by his son in a unique way, as a male with expertise" on homework, baseball, girls and men's clothing, and advised the mother not to help her son in the morning, but to "take time to prepare the family a nice breakfast and to relax with a cup of coffee."

In another case, with darker overtones, an adopted daughter suffered from chronic anxiety and depression because she had never really been accepted by her "somewhat sullen, silent and withholding family." The father was "a hard-driving, successful businessman, superbly reasonable and cool"

and often "dispassionately critical" to his children. But, according to the therapist, the mother was "clearly acknowledged by others as the family leader" and presided over a family presenting a facade of complete unity and agreement about every issue. Emerging only after several sessions was the secret, unknown to the four children, including the adopted one, that the mother was slowly dying of a progressively debilitating disease. The therapist determined that the family's "unidentifiable but deadening malaise" originated with the dying mother's "central role in the family's organization. The family. . . reflected many of her issues, including her repeated complaints of too little energy and too much responsibility. This suggested interventions to make her, in effect, less central in the family. She was given permission not to attend sessions."

Once the therapist had maneuvered the dying but "dominating" mother out of the picture, he worked on promoting "open, authentic, egalitarian communication" among the rest. The family made limited improvement, though the mother was "absent from the final session, signaling her dissatisfaction," and the therapists anticipated future problems between her and her oldest daughter, who identified with and protected her.

In both of these case studies the mother clearly calls the shots, whether she is the silly, footsie-playing coquette of the first or the angel of death in the second. The mother may be "central" to the family scene, alright, but much the way a virus is central to the flu: the family needs to be inoculated against her. As Hare-Mustin observed, mothers don't seem very attractive in the therapy room.

FEELING GUILTY AND INADEQUATE, MOTHERS themselves are often the first to agree that they are not any good at what they do. Traditionally, mothers have been excellent candidates for therapy, dutifully or desperately presenting themselves before a therapist in order to be "cured" or at least to be taught how not to botch the job so badly. And training "good mothers" has been a kind of crusade for family therapists from the beginning, a task the field's originators often approached with the zeal of missionaries converting the heathen. Peggy Papp, senior supervisor at the Ackerman Institute and one of the cofounders of the Women's Project in Family Therapy, remembers one case supervised by family therapy pioneer Nathan Ackerman that sharply outlined the attitude toward mothers held by some of family therapy's founding fathers.

The husband in this case had had a series of affairs over the course of his marriage and indicated he had no plans to stop. His wife had had one affair. Ackerman attacked the mother, virtually shouting that it was *different* for her to have an affair because she was a *mother* and responsible for her children. "We women therapists observing the interview were disturbed by this kind of thinking," Papp remembers. "It was very insidious. But in those days we didn't feel enough mutual support from one another to challenge it. To question it meant you had a problem with your own 'feminine' identity."

Often, first-generation family therapists who were mothers shared with the mothers they saw as clients the same chronic sense of guilt, unmet obligation, conflict between work and family, and again guilt. Their own conviction of overriding motherly obligation—reinforced by the sheer magnetic power of the Master Therapists—kept them quiet in the face of attacks on the inadequacy of other mothers. Olga Silverstein, another cofounder of the Women's Project in Family Therapy, was already the mother of four grown children when she began training. She remembers the soothing, patronizing advice commonly given to mothers: "'You need a little rest. Why don't you take a vacation, and let your husband take over,' which really meant, 'You're lousing up the kids, so get off the scene.' Many of us were always uncomfortable with the tendency to blame mothers for everything," Silverstein continues, "but

women and mothers were used to blame and too intimidated to challenge these powerful authorities. After all, they were not only *men*, they were *doctors*, and we were just social workers. We saw a lot we didn't like but thought we couldn't be right. As usual, we questioned ourselves before we questioned others."

Feminists in family therapy's first generation were themselves too swept up in the new field's revolutionary promise of therapy for, by and of the people to be much interested in "mothers," even when they were mothers themselves. Many rejected their own mothers as remnants of a reactionary past, double agents enforcing the patriarchal law of female dependency, self-denial, invisibility and silence. Mothers were nannies, governesses, housemaids; they went on no adventures, dreamed no dreams, had no glamor, no sex appeal.

At least since 1955, when Philip Wylie wrote *A Generation of Vipers,* about the voracious moms who were destroying the masculine fiber of America's young men, the institution of motherhood has been under a cloud of suspicion. Even feminist women during the '60s distanced themselves psychologically from the concept of Mother, which even the political left did not redeem from contradictory stereotypes. The New Left tended to visualize Mother either as a guerrilla madonna (baby on one arm, M16 slung over the other shoulder) or the monstrous Big Nurse of Ken Kesey's *One Flew Over the Cuckoo's Nest*, neither of which was much of a role model. In the spirit of the times, early family therapists were mesmerized by their own Big Nurse—the "schizophrenogenic mother"—a powerful witch who destroys her children's freedom before driving them mad.

Ironically, while Mother was the family nemesis, her presence was critical to the feasibility of the entire therapeutic enterprise. As Virginia Goldner, faculty member at the Ackerman Institute, wrote in her pivotal 1985 essay, "Feminism and Family Therapy," mothers not only brought their families into therapy, but were the family "gatekeepers" as well, "regulating the interaction between the family and the outside world, and . . . communication patterns within the family." The therapist, writes Goldner, needed the mother "first, to gain entry into the private sphere of family life and then to carry. . . his message of reform to the rest of the domestic circle." Indeed, fathers were notoriously silent, withdrawn and helpless in therapy, while children were often angry and resistant. Therapists frequently had to elbow their way into tightly defended family enclaves, anyway; without the urgent involvement of mothers, family therapy probably would have sunk like a stone.

Nonetheless, however important the mother's position in therapy, she could not have inspired much envy in women therapists. "As the lynchpin of the family," says Goldner, "a mother was the most dependable member, the least likely to bolt, the most easily ignored. She was the facilitator who carried the family. We would be using her throughout the therapy, but we didn't have to seduce her; compliance was her middle name." Like the furniture in the family living room, mothers were indispensable for livability, but who ever worried about hurting the feelings of a sofa?

Yet sometimes, during the course of their work, many family therapists remember experiencing a kind of cognitive dissonance, a sense that family therapy techniques often resembled confidence tricks: within a framework of neutrality and equal respect for all, mothers were being had. Goldner describes how she became aware of the massive fault line between the lived experience of mothers and the practice of family therapy while writing the first draft of "Feminism and Family Therapy." In 1982, she recalls, she was asked to speak on "How Family Therapy Looks at Women." Pregnant at the time, her baby was born early, the meeting was postponed, and she took time off to write the paper while caring for her son at home. Never before particularly aware of contradictions between feminism and family therapy, she now "saw," as if in one piece, the field's entire pattern of sexist assumptions and practices. Something about the daily routine of mothering made her aware of the profound contradictions in women's lives that were replicated in family therapy. Goldner says, "I saw that women had all this centrality in the family but no authority to back it up, and family therapy did not see the incongruity between their 'power' at home and social debasement outside."

Ronald Taffel, director of family and couples treatment services at the Institute for Contemporary Psychotherapy in New York City, once watched a family session in which the husband kept dozing off, and every time he woke up, the therapist "reframed" his short periods of consciousness by fulsomely complimenting him for taking part in therapy at all. Taffel says that the therapy "never did get to why it was so hard for this family to change," related, possibly, to the father's tendency to nod off psychologically rather than accept any responsibility for family relationships.

Some therapists began to wonder whether the field hadn't become infatuated by clever interventions, innovative uses of metaphor and imaginative conceptualizations of family dynamics, which had blinded them to the world that mothers inhabit. Deborah Luepnitz, a psychoanalytically oriented therapist at the Philadelphia Child Guidance Clinic and author of *The Family Interpreted: Feminist Theory in Clinical Practice*, remembers witnessing this bland unawareness in therapists who were, she says, often deeply insensitive and disrespectful to women. Parents of misbehaving children, for example, were told they had let the children "throw their weight around." To "unbalance" the system, Luepnitz recalls, therapists at PCGC aggressively demanded to know how much each member of the family weighed, the idea being to metaphorically equate weight with authority as a way of reinstituting the executive function in the family. Housewives coming to the clinic were often depressed, overweight and deeply ashamed of being fat. According to Luepnitz, the woman would squirm and turn red while the therapist relentlessly dragged out of her the shameful figure—190 pounds, 220—and wrote it on a blackboard. While not intending to humiliate and debase the mother, says Luepnitz, this line of therapy showed no sensitivity to the self-loathing that overweight women already feel in our culture, nor did it show any understanding of the common relationship between depression and overeating among American housewives and mothers.

WITHIN THE LAST DECADE OR SO, LARGELY IN response to the late-blooming feminist critique of family therapy, therapists have begun to view the classic definition of the "unholy triad"—enmeshed mother, peripheral father, symptomatic child—as an inherently flawed conception, a house without windows, closed and airless. Thus, they tirelessly emphasize the social context that has created the family. Marianne Walters, cofounder of the Woman's Project in Family Therapy and director of the Family Therapy Practice Center in Washington, D.C., maintains that a family is not an isolated mass, its members not just parts attached to a system operating within its own internal laws. "Family relations are socially constructed," Walters says. "Men and women enter marriage and parenthood already acculturated to the rules and expectations of a gendered world." But therapy can open up richer possibilities for each, validate *his* capacity to be involved with the children, *her* capacity to be competent and independent. "I tell parents," says Walters, "you both have inherited a belief system that says she owns the skills of mothering and you don't. This is not true."

Indeed, the classic treatment paradigm—use the mother for access and leverage into the family, then join with the father to loosen the mother's stranglehold on the child—strikes many feminist therapists as therapeutically irrelevant. Rather than shift family members around like chess pieces, they are more likely to encourage each to question so-called normal arrangements of family life. These therapists will be particularly aware of the conflict a mother experiences between the power she is presumed to wield at home and her lack of power in the "outside" world, even to define what "mothering" means. Teachers, doctors, politicians, police, psychotherapists, neighbors and her own husband are all experts on what she is doing wrong—why her child gets poor grades, won't eat, takes drugs, beats up other kids, or joins a neo-Nazi cult. Underlying this barrage of advice and criticism is a common assumption that mother may be "central" to the family, but as servant, not master. Like any loyal, compliant, but somewhat dim old family retainer, she needs to be constantly retrained, and almost anybody knows more about her job than she does.

Rather than join this chorus, therapists may now resist neat hypotheses inexorably implicating the mother in her child's difficulties. A clinician casting a net beyond the immediate family, for example, may find that a child is failing in school for reasons that have nothing to do with mother. Perhaps he is so terrified of school bullies that he can't concentrate; maybe she is constantly fighting with a rigid, overbearing teacher. Maybe the child simply doesn't like school; perhaps he lives to play the trombone and ignores all his other subjects except band; or, possibly, she is a talented athlete and natural leader who spends too much time at swimming meets with her friends to do her homework. By thus "depathologizing" mothers, therapists can help them see that their children are not necessarily "disturbed" offspring of "dysfunctional" families, but kids with their own personalities who resist being pounded into the system.

While much of the impetus for reconsidering

mothers has come from feminist therapists, there is no single specifically feminist clinical methodology or technique, no separate "cookbook" of skills with which to concoct a better, less patriarchal family. Some feminist therapists use strategic and structural interventions, others Bowenian family-of-origin techniques, while still others view families through the lens of constructivism or analytic object-relations theory. What they do share is a determination to bring gender into the very core of family systems thinking, and to make explicit in therapy how the outside world of economics and ideology shapes behavior and relationships within families. Therapists sensitive to gender issues, like other family therapists, want to improve relationships between family members but not, as Houston family therapist Morris Taggart says, by "taking the family's health out of the mother's hide."

What these new-wave therapists do to or for mothers is less important than the worldview that informs their therapy, one based on a new sensitivity to the extraordinary complexity, difficulty and contradictions inherent in the lifelong work of mothering. Such a therapist will hear the self-doubt and worry, the inner struggle, of a mother who, without prior training, is expected to transform a helpless, inchoate little consciousness into a mature, civilized, reasonably happy human being.

FEMINIST FAMILY THERAPISTS PARTICULARLY WANT to validate a mother's instincts by freeing her of socially generated fears about her own mothering. Olga Silverstein remembers a divorced mother with a 9-year-old son of whom she was terrified. He was loud, aggressive and badly behaved, but she could not bear to discipline him for fear he would become a "sissy." She had been told by her husband that she was "controlling," and she was willing to put up with the child's awful behavior because she was afraid that by "dominating" him, she would squelch his masculinity. Silverstein wondered aloud why a

grown woman could not and should not control her own child, and encouraged her to provide the necessary discipline. "Suppose he does grow up with some 'feminine' traits?" Silverstein asked the mother. "Would it be so terrible if he became a kind, generous, gentle, decent human being who knows how to control his behavior?"

Nonetheless, feminist family therapists empathize with the mother's overblown sense of responsibility and guilt, even as they challenge it. Marianne Walters says she jokes with mothers that they're *supposed* to feel guilty, that *all* mothers feel guilty, because they can *never* get it right, in this way both clarifying and ridiculing the social origins of the myth of motherly perfection.

Many family therapists have learned just how painful the social guilt trip can be, particularly for mothers who don't play by the traditional rules. Michelle Bograd, a family therapist in Watertown, Massachusetts, is seeing a woman in her early fifties, who separated from her husband of 30 years and left him in their suburban home with the younger of two nearly adult sons. One day the woman went into therapy very upset by a compliment from a co-worker, who had said, "I never knew you had two grown sons! You look too young, and you're too much fun!" The client, says Bograd, "heard in that statement, 'What kind of mother are you? You never talk about your children. Mothers are not playful. Mothers should look their age. And why did you leave your child, anyway?' "

Bograd says that before becoming aware of mother blaming, "I, too, might have wondered 'why *did* she leave her son?' or I might have asked her why she couldn't take a compliment, not aware of its sharp edges, or I would have supported the client's courage without comprehending her own real fear that she was failing as a mother. I would have oversimplified the complexity, the real social and emotional costs of being a 'different' kind of mother." Instead, Bograd and the client talked about the omnipresence of the maternal ideal in our society, and how vulnerable the woman was—even though a highly responsible, "good" mother—to the merest hint that she might not be good *enough*.

Mother-sensitive therapists now ask questions they might not have asked before. Most interviewed here, for example, favored bringing the question of money into therapy because mothers, of all women, are most likely to be economically dependent on their husbands and therefore without real power, even in their own families.

Thelma Jean Goodrich, faculty member at the Family Institute of Westchester in New York and senior author of *Feminist Family Therapy: A Casebook*, points out that men may be deeply shaken by the threatened loss of wife and family through divorce, but if the woman has children she does not want to lose and no economic resources of her own, "he knows she's not going anywhere." Goodrich and other therapists sometimes break an old rule of therapy, not to bring up money matters, by making explicit the economic inequity between husband and wife. Goodrich then may suggest that the couple see a mediator or attorney to discover how the joint property would be divided after a divorce. This suggestion lets both know that the wife may indeed have an alternative to remaining in the marriage, and the panic felt by the husband at the possibility, says Goodrich, "might make him more attentive in the relationship."

Yet fathers can also be liberated when therapists tear apart the web of the "enmeshed family" paradigm to free the mother stuck in the center. Therapists challenging the traditional family pattern can help men express and fulfill their own buried yearnings for what might be called a more "motherly" relationship with their children. Virginia Simons, a family therapist teaching at the Institute for Juvenile Research in Chicago, has worked with divorced fathers who have lost custody of their children. She found them feeling "traumatized, scared, not know-

ing if they had a place in their families anymore. . . . These men were lost and had no way to process their grief." One man she remembers, a blue-collar worker, said, "'I weep over my children, and I want my family. So I go to a bar, where the guys slap me on the back and tell me to forget it.'"

Morris Taggart believes that men must talk more to each other about what really matters to them if they are ever to dismantle the conceptual wall that keeps them locked out of their families and women locked in. He leads men's groups in which participants talk about what it means to be a father, what they missed in their own childhoods. In a recent group session, Taggart says, one man wept as he recalled himself as a boy, proudly bringing home a newly won Eagle Scout badge to show his father, who brusquely said, "That's great," and immediately began telling the boy what further awards he should win. Now, the man said, he was putting the same pressure on his own son. "We hear a lot about the insatiable needs of mothers," Taggart says, "but very little about the insatiable demands made by fathers."

Dorothy Wheeler, director of the family intervention team of North Shore Children's Hospital in Lowell, Massachusetts, is troubled by the extent to which women in families and family therapists protect men from change, reinforcing their inaccessibility to their families and increasing the burden on mothers. Nowhere is this more striking than in families with sexually abusive fathers, in which the mother is castigated for not protecting the child, while the father often receives a kind of back-handed sympathy for having been "driven" to molest his child by a cold or inadequate wife.

The source of this odd inversion of blame, according to Wheeler, is in the socially endemic disrespect for mothers, intensified in abusive families. Abusive fathers tell their children that what they are doing is "alright with mother" and that "your mother doesn't like you," thereby shifting blame from their own behavior to the mother. Wheeler counters this in the later stages of therapy by asking the sex offender in front of his wife and children what he did to hide the abuse from his wife, how he kept her from knowing, how he frightened her into silence, what he would have done if she had tried to stop it. In these questions, she not only confronts the abuser's denial but helps the children see their mother as less villain than victim.

But mothers as victims do not make good role models for their children, either. Judy Myers Avis says she often hears from mothers that they can't afford to take care of themselves because they've got their children to think of, which sends a message to their own children that they do not value themselves. "I sometimes challenge these women," says Avis, "by asking them if they want to model a life of personal servitude for their daughters."

A rather poignant example is described by Thelma Jean Goodrich, who saw a family in which the husband and wife ran a small business with one employee. The couple also had four children, and every morning while her family ate breakfast, the mother made boxed lunches for them and the employee.

In traditional family therapy, questioning this arrangement would be breaking the sacrosanct law of therapeutic "neutrality." But Goodrich decided that her professional and ethical responsibility required her to draw out the unspoken rules governing the family's marital and domestic arrangements, and openly encouraged the clearly overburdened woman to fight for some autonomy.

As it turned out, the wife never could bring herself to demand full equality (and presumably the "right" to eat breakfast with everyone else), but Goodrich did coach her to take small steps on her own behalf, such as telling her husband that sandwich making would go faster if he helped her. "Unfortunately," says Goodrich, "she had to ask him every day for his 'help' with 'her' work and often preferred doing it herself to going through this tiresome routine."

CASES LIKE THIS REVEAL THE SUBTLE BUT PERVAsive origins of contempt for mothers in our society. Context creates personality, so the argument goes. If the context is a society that demands the impossible and expects the worst of mothers, then little wonder that they "fail." Their children, including therapists, carry into adult life the bitter sense of disappointed entitlement that they did not get the mothering they rightfully deserved. Mothers, needless to say, can hardly flourish in such an environment.

During the mid-1970s, a famous study done by the Timberlawn Research Foundation defined the characteristics of "adequate," and "optimal" upper-middle-class families, "all producing healthy children." Mothers in the "adequate" or "normal" families were found to be "generally unhappy, needy, lonely, feeling isolated from husbands and overwhelmed by children, tending to obesity, depression and fatigue." Their interests outside the home were found to be "limited." Their husbands, meanwhile, were "successful, aggressively work oriented, more satisfied with [their] lives than wives—distant and providing material but not emotional support."

This is the "normal" family that family therapy implicitly endorses, from which the field draws its famous triad and its theories about the need to "individuate" and "separate" from mother. Indeed, if family life makes mothers fat, depressed, needy, lonely, self-denying whines, why wouldn't their children look to their fathers as role models rather than these pathetic creatures, whom even therapists don't much like?

Deborah Luepnitz describes how this process actually happens in a family when a father subtly degrades the mother in her daughter's eyes. In such a case a father ignores or demeans his wife, while forming close bonds with his daughter, who is his real companion and soulmate. In what Luepnitz considers a kind of emotional incest, the father encourages his daughter to become a "star"—to go to graduate school, enter a professional career, become successful in the "outside" world, while dull Mom remains a household drudge, unimportant, unrespected, her own goals or expectations without interest to anyone. As a result, the daughter grows up identifying with her father but deeply divided between loyalty and contempt for her mother—a housewife, a nag, a nobody—and feeling disdain for the female, the "mother part," of herself.

Indeed, mother hating by daughters is a familiar theme to family therapists. As one wag put it, "If you want to get an adolescent girl to change, tell her she is just like her mother." Marianne Walters turns this formulation on its ear, by helping mothers and daughters restructure their relationship so that their similarities become sources of individual strength and mutual connection. The daughter then can recognize in her attachment to her mother an opportunity rather than a burden; the mother can see in her daughter's growing independence a tribute to her own mothering.

During a consultation, Walters saw a mother and her 15-year-old daughter, who had been truant from school more or less constantly for three years, causing considerable conflict with her mother and consternation among school authorities. Rather than responding to the conflict, Walters framed the truancy as the daughter's wish to please her mother and make her feel safe. The mother, a veteran of the hippie generation, was covertly proud of her mildly "punk" daughter's unconventionality and felt better knowing the girl was hanging out in the park with her friends rather than having her individuality and freedom flattened by the school system. Walters told them that, far from being at odds with each other, the two had sacrificed other aspects of their lives to perfect their respective tasks of mothering and daughtering.

Instead of pulling the two apart by reestablishing "executive functioning" and "appropriate hierarchy," and "setting boundaries" between the mother and

daughter, Walters celebrated their attachment. "Most therapists," she says, "would definitely have considered this a pathological situation—a flaky, unemployed mother, a suspicious character who didn't know how to 'manage' her 'parentified child.' What I did was to validate her authenticity, her inspiration in offering her daughter a different way of understanding herself. I also emphasized how much the daughter cared about her. At the same time," Walters continues, "I let them both know that there was a risk involved in dancing to a different drummer and that both would have to weigh the costs in living this way." As it turned out, the girl, in a nice balance of loyalty to her mother, recognition of her own needs and defiance of the "system," scrupulously stayed away from school for several more months, only to begin attending again the day she turned 16.

THESE CASE STUDIES AND CONVERSATIONS WITH therapists about mothers suggest that many clinicians are growing tired of invoking managerial and mechanistic incantations that no longer seem to explain how families really work. But if the comfortable old theory about the dysfunctional family trinity is wearing out like a threadbare suit, what is to take its place? Challenging one of the field's most venerated hypotheses hardly makes therapy easier.

When many family therapists began practicing, the techniques and goals seemed clear and straightforward: a therapist applied ready-made interventions like poultices to the wounds of family life, intending to bring about healing as quickly and efficiently as possible. Today, says Michele Bograd, the situation has changed. "Now I look at the knots and complexities of situations, and I'm more likely to bring my own perplexity into therapy, to ask more questions of clients about how they feel and what they want. I don't feel as powerful, because I use much less technology, and it isn't as clear where therapy is going."

For some this new attitude represents a kind of fertile confusion, the matrix from which a new paradigm is emerging. If a new system *is* forming, however, it cannot be expressed in a neat graph, theorem, equation or arc sequence; it is more like a shift in perspective, a view from higher up on the mountain. Virginia Goldner now tells her students not to "gloss over" mothers but to spend time finding out who they are and what they do. "We want to create an environment," she says, "in which mothers are more interesting than theories."

Mothers over theories. It sounds nice, but some therapists still wonder uneasily if family therapy does not inevitably perpetuate mother blaming by shoring up the families in which it originates. Others respond that they are in a unique position to break the grip of the mythology that both sanctifies and demonizes mothers. Working with individual families, family therapists can help men, women and children to respect the qualities associated with "mothering"—empathy, protection, connection—and the human being, male or female, who expresses them. "Mothers are always with us," says Rachel Hare-Mustin. "Everybody had one, and so everybody is an expert." Perhaps *everybody*, therapists included, should try to become a little bit more expert at mothering, and not leave the entire job to mothers.

MARY SYKES WYLIE, PH.D., *is the associate editor of* The Family Therapy Networker.

See references, page 569.

THE CODEPENDENT CINDERELLA WHO LOVES TOO MUCH . . . FIGHTS BACK

ARE WE ADDICTED TO CODEPENDENCY?

By Marianne Walters

ACCORDING TO THE REAMS OF SELF-HELP LITERA-ture on bookstore shelves and in the women's mass-circulation magazines, the American woman is fighting an uphill battle against lifelong dysfunction, addiction and neurotic dependency. While sampling some of this outpouring, I discovered not only that are there "Women Who Love Too Much" but that these very same women are really "Smart Women Who Make Foolish Choices"; that they "Fear Success" and have a "Cinderella Complex" that could be described as a rescue fantasy. Moreover, although some of them are not "Beyond [their] CoDependency," they have had mothers who ". . . Love Men Who Hate Women" and "Toxic Parents" who suffered from an addiction to each other. This very same woman, trying to be "The Perfect Woman" and reject the "Doormat Syndrome" that had plagued her own mother, found that unfortunately she had become "Too Smart for Her Own Good!" Perhaps she was one of those "Daughters Who Love Their Mothers but Don't Love Themselves." Or maybe, although she had worked through the "My Mother/Myself" syndrome

and had been successful in "Reclaiming Her Inner Child," she was finding herself "Falling Off the Fast Track." Tired of trying to be a "Super-Mom" and "Have It All," she was searching for a "Mommy Track" where she could begin to cope with "The Drama of the Gifted Child" and provide the empathy, space and approving attention that her emotionally starved family needed. Yet, as a woman, she would need to remember that for mothers and daughters, "Loving and Letting Go" was what it was all about, and that in the end, it was damn hard to have "A Life of One's Own."

Well, now, let's get serious.

There are several levels on which I think we need to take a critical look at the recovery/codependency movement. For, indeed, it has become a movement that has its roots deep within the social fabric of the last decade. The rapid development and popularity of the codependency/recovery movement and the concurrent proliferation of books and articles directed at women and their problematic relationships is no accident. The Reagan decade, with its glorification of the individual, of me, mine, the self and the celebration of being good to oneself, encouraged a counterreaction to the changes in families and intimate relationships that had been engendered by the women's movement. It was also a decade in which community had become less and less available to people; a decade marked by a sort of social alienation, when being involved in social causes seemed naive. Taking care of your own needs became the hallmark of personal power and of the truly well-adjusted individual.

Consciousness-raising gave way to networking; potlucks were replaced by power lunches. And psychological buzzwords helped define this culture of the self—separation, boundaries, individuation, hierarchy, self-esteem, space. Mental health was not measured in terms of interdependency, affiliation, connection, involvement, or taking care of others. Unsuccessful separation from one's family could lead to the most dire of behavioral disorders. There was no room for the concept of family as an ongoing process of negotiating and renegotiating affiliation—where the operative word is *affiliation* rather than separation. The pull, both economically and conceptually, was now the ideology of the self. And as money to alleviate poverty and to provide services to the disadvantaged disappeared, and the haves and have-nots grew farther apart, the haves found themselves without a cause—except themselves. At the same time, the expectations of women in the world were undergoing a dramatic transformation, and the traditional rules governing marriage, work, divorce, career and family life were in flux.

And it didn't hurt that the decade produced, for at least a sizable portion of the population, a considerable amount of disposable income—income that could support psychology as yet another "Me" commodity. So the decade of the '80s was indeed ripe soil for the proliferation of any commodity that made people feel better, or that laid blame for any stress or distress on anything other than the body politic. The dysfunctional family had come of age

and converged with the codependency movement and the literature of problematic women.

Of course, it is clear that many people have been helped by their involvement in the deprofessionalized, grass-roots groups of the codependency movement. For some, this involvement has, quite literally, been a lifesaving experience. Millions of people have found release there: recognition and validation of their pain; community with others who have had similar experiences; new freedom from anger, blame, mistrust; and safety—many for the first time in their lives. Nonetheless, I have some reservations.

FIRST, I BELIEVE THAT THE CODEPENDENCY MODEL blurs the power differential between the doer and the one who allows or enables the doing. Codependency in action reads "coculpability," or equally liable. She who helps he who does is as responsible for the doing as the doer. This is not explicit in the model (although some proponents suggest that there is no addict, no abuser, without a codependent), but it is as much there, in inference, as those old axioms about the provocative girl who gets raped or the overbearing wife who gets beaten up. Unfortunately, some systems thinking similarly blurs the distinction between the actor and the audience, an audience that, however indulgent of the performance, is, in fact, *not* doing the performing. Despite whatever reciprocal, complementary loops activate each, they are simply *not* the same order of business. What began as a way of helping people to understand how they get pulled into a set of behaviors and become part of a destructive system has been translated into a model in which the codependent is as instrumental in a set of dysfunctional interactions as the one with the behavioral problem.

In a book about families with an alcoholic member, there is a description of the dysfunctional pattern of an "alcoholic couple." An *alcoholic couple*—the label itself is disconcerting, since in this instance only the husband drinks. Why do we call a whole family, or a couple, "alcoholic" when only one member drinks? Doesn't it reflect a way of thinking, that everyone is metaphorically alcoholic, so that the distinction between the one who abuses and the ones who are engaged in the abuse is blurred? Now whatever goes on in that family becomes filtered through that label. No longer are they a family where someone plays tennis and others watch "L.A. Law"—or where one member gets angry about one thing and another gets jealous about something else—no, they are a family in which individual identity is submerged in the configuration of the addiction.

The writer of this book describes the couple's dysfunctional pattern as: drink, nag, drink, nag, drink. But, the author points out, the couple disagrees about the punctuation of that sequence: the wife punctuates the sequence *drink*, nag, *drink*, nag, whereas the husband's view is *nag,* drink, *nag,* drink. The author prescribes a therapy that validates both punctuations, intending to give an active role to both husband and wife. It follows that either way you cut it, the sequence is okay—the nagging may precipitate the drinking or vice versa. The inference is that these are acts of equal significance, equal power in the relationship of the couple, equally productive of dysfunctional interaction.

Moreover, consider the message the author is conveying to this couple when you set them down in the real world of gender differences, when you attach a "he" and "she" to their roles with each other and in families. Codependents fit the archetypes usually drawn to describe themselves—overinvolved, depending upon others for approval, not taking care of themselves, having poor boundaries, intoxicated with relationships, too willing to assume blame, putting the needs of others before their own. Publishers report that 85 percent of the readership of codependent materials are women. So women are offered equal power in the creation of these dysfunctional patterns in families even as they are seeking power of another sort in the world. I'm not sure

that this is such a good bargain.

The self-help books for women are basically about the ways that women bring about their own destruction, usually leaving out any discussion of the way this self-destruction is socially sanctioned. How often do we encounter an "ACOA" who is as angry or angrier with the mother who didn't protect her as she is with the person who abused her? And how often does the movement, and even our own therapy, encourage full expression of this anger, while encouraging forgiveness of the abuser?

I suggest that the codependent movement and the self-help literature, while clearly intended to empower, in fact pathologize behaviors and personal characteristics that are associated with the feminine. These characteristics presumably cause women to become addicted to men who hate them, to abusive relationships, to repeated affairs with irresponsible partners, or to overeating, compulsive shopping, premenstrual syndrome, or loving too much. And the literature offers us step-by-step solutions to healthier, more adult—autonomous, independent—behaviors, so we can establish appropriate boundaries, set our own agendas, take better care of ourselves, and attend to our own needs. Mature behaviors are conceptualized as taking care of oneself, putting one's needs fist, loving oneself. Whatever happened to the poor reputation of narcissism?

WHILE THE MODEL FOR THE CODEPENDENCY self-help groups was the consciousness-raising groups of the women's movement, there is a marked difference between the ideology of these two movements. Both the codependent/ACOA/recovery movement and the women's movement offer community in a society where this has become a rare commodity. Both provide a safe place for people who feel lost, lonely, subordinate, damaged or shamed, enabling them to come together and share their grief and to find a path toward growth. But one movement encourages individuals to surrender to a spiritual higher power, while the other encourages people to join together to challenge and restructure power arrangements in the larger society. In one movement, community is used to empower the individual; in the other, community is used to empower the group as well. Their very names suggest the profound difference between these two movements—"codependency" and "adult child," on the one hand; "consciousness-raising," on the other. One is based on a deficit model of human personality; the other, on a model of competency. One focuses on the personal roots of individuals' problems; the other, on the social origins of problems that transcend the experience of the individual.

I am concerned about the codependency movement's promulgation of the disease model to explain a vast array of human behaviors; the use of what is essentially a medical term—addiction—to describe activities as disparate as substance abuse, loving, gambling, shopping, sex, incest, lateness, intimacy, affairs, relationships, eating, worrying, work and more. Codependency, which originally referred to some of the problematic behaviors of people married to alcoholics or drug addicts, now refers to an amorphous disease configuration that has become a national epidemic and that, apparently, can include almost any behavior. In fact, the literature suggests that people in the helping professions are notorious codependents with an addiction to rescuing.

So pervasive is the "illness" of codependency that if you are not in recovery, are not a survivor, then you must still be in the throes of the disease, or in denial. The term "adult children of alcoholics" originally referred to those whose adult lives were scarred by the substance abuse of one or both parents. But the typologies of ACOA began to appeal to a much wider audience and to include people who had grown up in any family that could be loosely described as dysfunctional—a vast cross-section of families whose characteristics could even include mothers who choose to work because they enjoy it!

One of the more disturbing aspects of the disease model is that it trivializes those truly addictive behaviors associated with substance abuse by likening them to so many ordinary human behaviors whose excesses are labeled addictive. And it comes dangerously close to equating the feelings of deprivation generated by having been insufficiently nurtured as a child, to the utterly decompensating experience of having been sexually or physically abused by a family member.

It is very important for us to be able to distinguish an order of significance between things, if only to be able to set priorities, both socially and personally. In our professional work it is even more compelling. The understanding of alcoholism and drug addiction as illness has been enormously useful for diagnosis and in the development of treatment modalities. And I know of no treatment for substance abuse that is as effective as the 12-Step model of AA and NA, a model that eschews blame and holds people responsible for their own recovery. But it is a disease model holding that one is never cured and that abstinence is necessary for the continued process of recovery. Imagine abstinence from loving or worrying or shopping or working! And the disease model conjures up the medical model, which gives rise to a culture of prescriptions, subordination to a higher authority, and conformity to treatment protocols. The movement books have contributed to the development of a readership that expects prescriptions—10- or 12- or 15-step programs for recovery; recipes, directions, typologies. Each disease must have its delineated program for recovery—most of which resemble each other.

CLEARLY THE WIDESPREAD APPEAL OF THE codependency movement has elevated the authority of psychology as providing the ultimate explanation for all human behavior. Increasingly the realm of psychological explanation has become a closed system, excluding other perspectives on human behavior, narrowing our understanding of the complex cultural and social forces that shape our experience. Our preoccupation with the psychological leads us to enshrine simplistic formulas within the common wisdom, like the idea that achieving mental health merely is a matter of dispelling the demons of an unhappy childhood and "being good" to ourselves. And there is no doubt that psychological knowledge has become a commodity in our ever-expanding marketplace—a fast- growing and lucrative one at that. What is too often missing is the integration of the *social* construction of behavior into our theories of causality, motivation, interpersonal dynamics and individual problems.

Most popular books about problematic women briefly mention that the dysfunctional behaviors and patterns they describe are *learned*, that they have roots in the values, power structures, history, language and institutional practices of a patriarchal, dominantly white, middle-class culture. Yet seldom is this idea reflected in their assumptions and formulations, nor in their proposed solutions.

For instance, Dr. Susan Forward, in *Men Who Hate Women, and Women Who Love Them,* does have several paragraphs on the cultural support of men's aggression toward women and does refer to misogyny as learned behavior. But here is how she describes the source of that learning (italics are mine): "While both parents work together to raise their son, they also have separate jobs. Mother is the nurturer and the boy's primary source of comfort, while father helps him *to pull away* from mother so that he does not become *overly* dependent on her. However, in the family background of misogynists, just the opposite occurs . . . so that the boy has *no other option* than to make mother the center of his universe. *Mother,* instead of meeting her son's needs for comfort and nurturing, is liable to try to get her son to meet her needs . . . whether a *woman* does this through the extremes of overwhelming demands, severe rejection, or smothering control, the

results are the same: the boy becomes too dependent on her." Imagine how this information is experienced by a single mother of boys. "Without realizing it, in adulthood he transfers this dependency, as well as the conflicts and fears that go with it, onto the woman in his life." So much for the source of aggression and anger in men . . . it's women!

In a book about "adult children," the author states, "If someone tried to make love to me when I said I didn't want to, this would be an individual boundary invasion." It still sounds like rape to me! These same writers consider incest the result of "weak intergenerational boundaries," and others go so far as to define it as an inappropriate expression of love. Whatever happened to the notion of the *abuse of power?*

Alice Miller, whose book *The Drama of the Gifted Child* inspired the "inner child" movement, has 27 references under the indexed heading "mother," with a cross-reference to "parent"; "parent" has 16 cross-references to "mother." There is *no* heading for "father." Yet the book is about the damage to the child of early dysfunctional *parenting*.

These are a few examples of closed-system thinking. To be informed by the many interesting realities and systems that shape our way of being in the world and to understand the social construction of behavior can offer an antidote to the deficit constructions of most psychological theories. We badly need a broader landscape on which to locate our clients' problems and to help us see how their individual stories fit within the wider contours of our collective experience.

RECENTLY, IN A CONSULTATION GROUP, A THERApist presented the case of a working-class, first-generation Italian family he had been seeing for almost a year: mother, stepfather and four children—two boys and two girls. The oldest daughter left home when she was 17 because she couldn't get along with her stepfather, and now lives with a maternal aunt. The second daughter, Gina, 16, became pregnant, an event that brought the family in for help. She was also dealing drugs. Both the boys, 12 and 8, have school problems, while the youngest, the only child of this marriage, has muscular dystrophy. When Gina got pregnant, her stepfather threatened to disown her. She left home and is currently living with her boyfriend's parents. Now Gina wants to come home, but her stepfather refuses to allow it, although Gina is back at school, has had an abortion, for which she had her parents' approval, and is no longer dealing. The therapist describes the stepfather as extremely rigid, the mother as the go-between in the family. When her husband is present, she takes his side, but when she is alone with her daughter, she takes the daughter's side. The situation has become intractable, with mother attempting to appease both sides in this warring family, and stepfather and daughter barely able to be in the same room.

How do we begin to think about this family? At first, the consultation group focused on the triangulation of Gina between mother and stepfather, a pattern repeating itself in this family, as witness the angry, premature leaving home of the older daughter. The group considered issues related to marital conflict, family-of-origin, and stepfather's rigidity. But thinking about this family within a social context offered a different perspective, not structured around psychological "deficits." Here was a tough, working-class man, a first-generation American whose culture and ethnic traditions not only created expectations for his behavior as head of household but held him accountable for the protection of the women in his family. Living in the inner city, his fears for the safety of his stepdaughter, given her behaviors, were surely appropriate. How could the stepfather not feel he had failed, within his code of duty and ethics, in light of the events in his family? And what was the mother to do? Her job was surely to be supportive and loving to her daughter, as well

as supportive and subordinate to her husband.

Using culture and social context as behavioral determinants, we viewed this family in terms of the stepfather's fear of failing his duty, not his rigidity; the mother's belief about what the family needed from her, not her triangulating behaviors. We approached our work with stepfather and Gina around ways that he could accomplish his paternal mission without continuing to jeopardize his connection with his stepdaughter, nor compromising his view that people need to face the consequences of their behavior in order to be safe in a risky world. Mother helped by contributing her expertise in creating alliances. And Gina, in understanding her stepfather's anger as concern for her safety, could begin to allow herself to experience his protection.

I RECENTLY SAW A YOUNG BLACK WOMAN WHO IS A chemistry major on scholarship at a local college. Although on graduating high school she had received a National Science Award and is an A student in college, she keeps dropping out of courses, defers credit by taking incompletes, forgets classwork, and makes endless changes in her course schedule, making it difficult to get into courses required for her major. She is frustrated and unhappy and considering dropping out. She's also concerned about two recent failed relationships with men. In previous therapy she had discussed some of the problems in her family: 11 children, never any space for herself, no privacy, little time with her working mother, and a father who, always tired from carrying two jobs, only relates to his children as disciplinarian. She had tried some behavioral prescriptions for coping with those behaviors she understood were self-destructive. She had explored her poor self-image, fear of success and problems around that. In therapy she had located these issues in her conflictual relationship with parents who never showed her approval or acknowledged her accomplishments, thus making more difficult her struggle to separate and be her own person.

Using a wider lens, my take was different. I saw a young woman caught between a rock and a hard place. Her family is struggling financially, seeking upward mobility, and she is the first to go to college. She becomes the hope of her family, the promise, the justification for the hard work of her parents—and yet her success, her fulfillment of that promise, will surely distance her from her family, from a world that feels familiar and safe. She will, in effect, be entering a new world, a world in which, sadly, her parents will be strangers. Her success will be costly; the price: distance from her family, alienation from her cultural roots. Further, as a black woman in a racist society, she probably fears that her relationships with black men will be compromised if she is successful in her own right, and this makes her angry—and her anger, however justifiable, sometimes interferes in these relationships. Within this perspective, the goal would be to help her to find ways to remain affiliated to her culture and connected with her family while embracing success; to reduce the price she will have to pay for being young, black, beautiful . . . and smart.

A T OUR CENTER THIS YEAR WE HAVE BEEN seeing a lesbian mother of three little girls. The mother, Leah, came in about her relationship with her eldest daughter, Betsy—a precocious, intrusive, mouthy kid, who interrupts her mother constantly and is intensely interested in her activities, offers advice on the parenting of the younger children, worries about her mother's welfare, even tries to monitor her telephone conversations. Betsy also gets into difficulty at school and with peers because she is so argumentative. Leah feels this behavior began about the time of her divorce—18 months ago—and when she set up household as a single parent with an open, committed relationship to another woman. The lack of boundaries, the permission to interrupt, mother's deference to her daughter's end-

less questions and comments, her willingness to be distracted, her patient listening to and exploring of her daughter's feelings, was such a compelling, even alarming, scenario that the therapist began early on to work with boundary formation, parental expectations, limits, and Betsy's "parentified" behaviors. It was hard going, with much resistance from both Betsy and her mother. Leah believed that children needed to express themselves and deserved such attention from their parents; she had received very little from her own family.

Considering the social determinants of behaviors in this family offers alternative interventions. First, a lesbian mother, feeling marginalized in a homophobic culture, would want, in every way, to legitimize her own daughter—validate her daughter's feelings and ideas and offer her the careful, respectful attention and emotional access that she herself feels denied. Since it would be difficult not to internalize the social disapproval attached to being a lesbian mother, she probably feels inadequate as a parent, guilty for denying her daughters a "normal" family life and fearful of the consequences of their being separated from their father. One way for Leah to compensate for these perceived deficits would be to give her daughter large doses of support, validation and approval. In a society whose values are so oppressive to this mother, she must want most passionately not to oppress her daughter, not to impose her values, but to encourage her to be expressive, strong and self-directed. And so she avoids setting limits, fearful of being authoritarian and oppressive.

This way of "knowing" Leah moves us beyond our usual psychological concepts and language. It is informed by our understanding of, our sensibility to, and her experience of herself in the world, and offers both therapist and mother a frame of reference that legitimizes mother's behavior even while reckoning with its excesses. The therapist can now use mother's competencies as a parent—her patience, her ability to listen, her connectedness—to modify those excesses caused by her self-doubts in a world that at best reinforces them, at worst *fundamentally creates* them.

WHEN THE NEWLY ELECTED PRESIDENT OF Czechoslovakia, Vaclav Havel, appeared before a joint session of Congress, he said his experience of recent events in his country had given him one great certainty, that "consciousness precedes being, and not the other way around." The way we understand ourselves in relation to our world, the way we know who we are—our consciousness—will surely determine how we will be in that world. In our work as therapists we can't change the larger society, but we *can* help people to feel less oppressed in their lives by knowing that they are not just passively reacting to events but are actors whose performance will be largely shaped by the way they *understand* the drama they are enacting. ∎

MARIANNE WALTERS, M.S.W., *is the director of the Family Therapy Practice Center in Washington, DC.*

Letters to the Editor

I ENJOYED MARIANNE WALTERS'S ARTICLE "The Codependent Cinderella Who Loves Too Much . . . Fights Back" and just wanted to add my observation that these women's self-help books all work with the same basic assumption: that there is a perfect man out there. It seems that authors want women to quit being crazy and find the man who doesn't misuse them.

This is a fatal mistake. There are not perfect men. In fact, with men trying to copy women and get in touch with their feelings as women do, rather than finding their own sensitivity along a masculine vein (the notions of Robert Bly and others), James Garner is the only real man left. The rest of us were trained to feel like Virginia Satir.

Man, am I confused!

Ches C. Edrington
DeKalb, IL

IN GENERAL, I APPLAUD MARIANNE WALTERS's stand against pathologizing women in the self help literature. Nevertheless, I think it is important that professionals understand the difference between the movements and the literature that helps to spawn them, but that also promotes the excessive pathology of its members.

Both Codependents Anonymous (CODA) and Adult Children of Alcoholics (ACOA) are grass-roots, mutual-help movements that borrow their central ideas from Alcoholics Anonymous, including the disease model. In the rhetoric of AA, the disease is not simply physical, but mental and spiritual. The real disease is of the soul, and it is with this condition that members of CODA and ACOA identify. Therefore, while it may seem nonsensical to equate the behaviors addressed by AA, CODA and ACOA, the identification is with the internal condition of despair. If we, as professionals, do not understand the identification and try to talk our clients out of their pathologies or discourage their membership in these movements, we may deny them the help available through the spiritual solution these groups offer. We would be insisting that our solution is better than theirs, that personal and political power is better than a spiritual journey—an arrogant position.

We need to be reminded that the success of AA is largely due to the fact that it eschews social reform.

Susan Stewart
Greensboro, NC

MARIANNE WALTERS'S ARTICLE ON CO-dependency ignores a major influence on the proliferation of woman-centered self-help literature: marketing. While she reports that 85 percent of readers of self-help materials are women, Walters treats this as some type of side-line phenomenon rather than a major reason for the existence of the literature.

Women, as a group, have created an enormous, fast-spending market for identity-seeking products: cosmetics, fashions and pop literature. *Books in Print* lists more than 8,000 volumes under "Women," compared with less than 200 under "Men." A reasonable number of sales is guaranteed to authors and publishers who properly court this huge market.

While the ACOA/Codependency movement is based on significant issues, much of the attendant literature is based on the profit motive. Walters's article missed the conclusion inferred by its own premises: save your snake-oil book money, then spend it on a good therapist.

James A. Kruse
Bettendorf, IA

(continued)

Letters to the Editor

I HAVE RECENTLY HAD MY RATHER HEROIC image of one of my teachers of family therapy shaken. I was surprised and saddened to see a brilliant teacher like Marianne Walters drawing conclusions about the codependency movement based on incorrect information.

She equates codependency with "coculpability," meaning that codependents are blamed for their partners' alcoholism. I do not doubt that some codependents view the teachings of 12-Step programs in this way, but this is a misinterpretation. 12-Step programs (as Walters notes later) teach responsibility for one's own behavior and not for others' behavior.

Walters criticizes the codependency movement for its affirmation of "narcissism." I am reluctant to believe that a complex thinker like Walters has not grasped the paradox that one is most able to give to others when one takes care of oneself first and does not hold oneself responsible for others' feelings or actions.

My reaction to her critique was anger, but the anger soon turned to sadness, a feeling of loss. This master teacher of family systems theory had somehow felt the need to reincorporate notions of power from which I felt systems theory had freed us.

I choose to believe that the concept of power is an illusory god, particularly when it refers to changing someone else. I find this belief to be more humanizing for my therapy and myself.

Dwight McCall
Glen Allen, VA

AUTHOR'S RESPONSE:

*To deny the power differentials between men and women, black and white, worker and owner, etc., is to deny the very humanity Dwight McCall seeks in his work. While it may be comforting to theorize that behaviors and interpersonal interac-*tions are reciprocal or symmetrical, and thus equally productive of problem or solution, it simply ignores differences in the social realities, and relation to power, of the people involved. Thus, constructing a codependent concept in a world of gendered inequality lends itself to the production of an experience of coculpability.

As to "narcissism"—I disagree with McCall's formulation (and certainly don't consider the idea that "one is most able to give to others when one takes care of oneself first" to be a complex paradox!). In fact, I believe it is illusory and simplistic to separate and prioritize "taking care of oneself" and "giving to others." The emotional anarchy that must result from "not holding oneself responsible for the feelings or actions" of others does not appeal to me. Social concern, and a sense of responsibility for the life conditions of others, may prove to be as healing as personal space, setting limits, the health club, or exploring the life of one's inner child.

Finally, while I'm flattered by the heroic stature McCall attributes to me, I am compelled to point out that this idealization of the "master" (sic) teachers in the field is part of the very problem to which I am alluding. For it is about power after all: those who construct the pedestal do ultimately control its location and who rests upon it, and thus help to reproduce hierarchies of power.

Susan Stewart is certainly on target in her appeal that therapists validate the experience of those who identify with the CODA and ACOA movements, and I agree that we need not polarize solutions to the despair of which she speaks. That is exactly why I was moved to critique a philosophy that, as Stewart points out, "eschews social reform," thus limiting the range of alternative solutions available to people.

As for Mr. Kruse, I would note that the profit motive is not the exclusive province of booksellers and that snake oil comes in many containers. I

Letters to the Editor

only hope he understands why women comprise such a ready market for self-help literature.

Finally, I want to join Mr. Edrington in cele-brating the masculinity of James Garner—one of

our shared favorite stars!

Marianne Walters
Washington, DC
—MAY/JUNE 1990

ILLUSTRATION BY KEVIN HAWKES

WOMEN TREATING MEN

CONFRONTING OUR GENDER ASSUMPTIONS

By Michele Bograd

A WOMAN REACHES OUT HER ARMS TO A man—whether to embrace or beseech him is unclear. He responds by folding his arms angrily over his chest, turning his back to her, then crumpling into an unmoving heap. A small drama played out by a couple in marital therapy? Not exactly. It's the most common human sculpture female family therapists enact in workshops I give on gender issues when I ask them, "Think of a time when you got stuck with a male client and, without words, show us the treatment impasse."

What difference does it make whether the therapist or the client is male or female, and what role does gender play in the therapeutic interaction? The binds male and female therapists may find themselves in with opposite-sex clients often have more to do with the way gender roles structure intimate relationships than with individual countertransference or family-of-origin issues. Men and women occupy different places in the social order and are oriented differently to the ideas of authority and power. In our society a powerful man still evokes different reactions than does a powerful woman.

This has bearing on the different ways male and female clinicians choose to take charge as therapists. Female therapists struggle with balancing the power of their professional position with women's more traditional roles of nurturer and caretaker. Nowhere is this balancing act more evident than in their relationships with male clients.

After a difficult session, behind closed doors, female therapists express many of the same complaints about their male clients as these men's wives and lovers—"What can I say about him? He's a typical man." When the therapist feels stuck or ineffective with a male client, she may be inclined to blame the difficulty on his affinity to the male stereotype. When women therapists are asked to generate a quick list of adjectives that describe male clients, they choose manipulative, hostile, intellectualizing, passive, distant, rigid, dominating, childlike and generally uninterested in change.

Women have been taught to take care of men without asking them to face their own vulnerability, presumably out of sensitivity to men's horror at appearing "unmanly." But what about the secret fear

343

that if men are weak, women will have to give up their childhood fantasy of the strong protector who will take care of them?

In live supervision, a trainee found it difficult to probe a husband's role in a marital spat. I directed her to explore his feelings before a typical outburst. After delicately posing the question, she immediately offered an array of responses, filling the airtime, while he sat mostly silent except for a few monosyllabic answers. During the break, I asked if she realized that she was having a conversation with herself. Even with careful supervision, it was tough for her to ask a question and wait for the man's slow, clumsy reply, without rushing to his rescue.

A vivacious, theatrical woman married an emotionally isolated son of a Holocaust survivor. Their female marital therapist patiently tried to enter the husband's inner world, which the husband described as "barren as the lunar landscape." In one session, the husband burst into dry sobs and wailed, "What do you two want from me? I'm trying to feel. I'm doing the best I can!" As his wife hurriedly handed him a tissue, the therapist felt overwhelmed with helplessness. Later, a male colleague asked, "Why did you stop there? I would have said to him, 'You can and must go further, just as your wife does.' You let him get away with too much." The female therapist replied, "It never occurred to me to push him. I guess I accepted that men just can't do more."

THE RELATIONSHIP BETWEEN FEMALE THERAPISTS and male clients can be distorted into an incongruous hierarchy. The therapist may be formally in the superior position but may still feel disempowered because of her gender. Many women have great difficulty asserting authority because it is not "feminine" and because they have learned that the best way to influence men is indirectly. Thus some female therapists have a hard time being assertive, commanding, or challenging with male clients.

Once on his soapbox, the father of an acting-out adolescent was unstoppable, lecturing and berating his child, tirelessly justifying himself. Although the therapist and the wife exchanged glances, neither challenged him. As the therapist later reported, "He's older than I am, and he's an upper-level hospital administrator. I get intimidated. I make suggestions with great hesitation . . . and I hate the sound of my voice when it shakes and trembles."

A more paradoxical dilemma arises when the man wants his female therapist to be powerful, but only in a way that pleases him. As one therapist put it, "As a woman, I'm just not comfortable with some of the ways we're taught to be family therapists. I'm not forceful, directive, challenging, and I don't want to be. I work collaboratively with most of my clients, and take a lot of time to understand their beliefs and ways of being.

"I have a hard time with certain men. I was working with a man who constantly challenged my expertise. Even as he resisted my efforts, he told me he wanted me to help him in a specific way—a way I consider 'male model': he wanted me to give orders, be 'one-up,' and know all the answers. That was the kind of authority he respected and used himself, though it exacted a toll on his family. I couldn't win. Either I handled power the way I wanted, which he demeaned, or I did it his way, which would have violated something fundamental for me."

FAMILY THERAPISTS HAVE TENDED TO IGNORE THE sexual component of therapy, and even in individual therapy with men we often don't find it clinically vital to explore male clients' fantasies and feelings about us. But that doesn't mean they don't exist. Not uncommonly, female therapists report unsettling interactions with male clients: he flirts, compliments her looks, talks explicitly about sexual exploits, reports dreams about her, or openly acknowledges sexual feelings toward her. The client's seduction or attraction can mean different things, since sexuality is a socially approved mechanism by which many men express not only lust, but care, dependency, connection, sadness and anger. Obviously, this is all grist for the therapeutic mill. But many female therapists find it difficult to address and clarify what is going on. They may be ill at ease with their own reactions—feeling flattered, attracted, uncomfortable, angry or anxious. Sometimes they cannot set clear limits with men without being overly concerned about hurting their pride or making them feel "rejected."

Even well-seasoned clinicians may feel caught off guard by the confusing power tactics of seduction. "It took me a while to get it, but then I realized that my client switched to sexual material whenever I was getting close to his grief and sadness," says one therapist. "All of a sudden the focus would be on me or on us. For example, when we'd get to something that made him feel helpless or sad, he'd 'suddenly remember' a dream about us on a beach together. Or he'd ask me to dinner at one of the most expensive restaurants in town. I was flattered and confused. This guy was not a lech or a weirdo. He was a nice, ordinary man. With a lot of supervision, I realized that the moment he sexualized us, I lost control of the session. I was no longer the professional, but simply an object of his desire. In the office I was his superior, but once he sexualized things, it was like walking down the street and having men whistle at me. It reminded me to keep my place."

NOTHING INTIMIDATES MOST FEMALE THERAPISTS more than their male clients' anger. Some men try to control therapy by yelling, storming out of sessions, refusing to speak, or aggressively engaging in intellectual argument. More subtly, but no less powerfully, they clench their fists, flush, or breathe irregularly. Female therapists are sensitive to these cues and can be intimidated by them. Their fear of men's anger has a realistic base; women's physical vulnerability to men is not just a figment of the imagination. Furthermore, a fair number of women

therapists grew up with angry fathers or are survivors of physical and/or sexual abuse. As women, we are all taught to tread gently with men, not to incur their wrath. We are told as children, "Don't disturb your father after work." We may believe that the man's anger is our fault or our responsibility—either we provoked it or it is our job to mop up the mess after the explosion takes place.

"After what I thought was successful therapy, a man left treatment owing me money," a female therapist recalls. "I billed him monthly for a year, during which time I got up my courage to call him. He promised to pay, but never did. Finally I decided to go to small claims court, and I called him one more time. He threatened to countersue and tried to intimidate me. The day of the court date, I had fantasies that he was going to hurt me."

I asked this therapist whether she would have felt the same with a woman client. "No, not at all," she answered. "I talked to some colleagues at my agency. None of the men said they'd ever felt that way, but almost all of the women had a story about feeling afraid of a male client—even when there was no real concrete reason for fear."

In a recent live supervision, a group of therapists watched a man respond to a simple question with an unexpected outburst against his wife. The therapist and wife froze. After a moment the clinician turned to the wife and asked her a question about a different subject. Afterward the group of female trainees observing the session easily empathized with their colleague's reaction. All described having similar responses to men's anger: "I freeze," "I go blank," "I feel nothing except wanting to get out of there," "I feel just like I did when my father yelled at me as a child." Given that many male clients struggle with anger and don't understand why their use of anger to control others is so alienating, female therapists' inability to tolerate and work with male anger can be a serious obstacle to their effectiveness as clinicians.

Male clients don't have to make a lot of noise to

control female therapists; flight or withdrawal is as effective. All family therapists have been taught that men have to be carefully reeled in to therapy and that the hook is rarely secure—one awkward move or lapse of attention, and off he goes. In workshops I've given on women treating men, the most common issue for female therapists is their concern that the male client will flee therapy if the therapist talks too much, too little, is too active, too passive, confronts him, asks "too much of him," etc. In other words, women therapists may find men's threats to walk out of therapy particularly difficult. After all, most of women's training as females is geared to getting men's attention, making them comfortable, keeping them close—and women were taught to take it personally when men are unhappy or annoyed enough to leave. Women are also not practiced at asking men to be accountable for their half of a relationship. Initially, women clinicians look at me blankly when I ask whether they have ever talked to clients about their threats to jump ship. A female clinician can fall victim to the belief that it is her responsibility alone to make therapy work. Some female therapists don't feel comfortable setting basic conditions for treatment—it's as if we have to make the best of a blind date.

GETTING STUCK IN THERAPY WITH MALE CLIENTS doesn't require dramatic scenarios of rage, rejection and abandonment. Sometimes a more dangerous pitfall is therapy that feels *too* good, with the male client satisfied but unchanged. Not only are many women highly skilled at mirroring men and drawing out their thoughts and feelings, they often long to be the one special woman who sets this man free. Our culture bombards us with images of the driven, emotionally cutoff man who flowers into a sensitive soul when the right woman comes along. Women fight other women to be the chosen one; daughters sympathetically reach out to fathers they feel their mothers pushed away. A female therapist

working with a couple may find herself defending the man against the demands or angry accusations of his wife, empathizing with him, irritated by her.

I supervised a trainee who cherished being "daddy's girl." In one case presentation, she pointed out that the wife was insensitive to her husband, careless about housework, and resentful that he made less money than she. The trainee described the husband as sweetly eccentric, a "hurting puppy." Seven sensitive and experienced female therapists listened to this description without question. Eventually we learned that he had suffered a major depression a year ago, during which time his wife had fully supported the family in many ways. In this case, overempathizing with the male client obscured important data. Protecting him, the therapist jeopardized her alliance with the wife and kept the husband from the painful but healing work ahead of him.

The therapist may feel the satisfaction of culturally ingrained female pride as the male client shows her the tears or trusting confidences he withholds from his spouse. Or both women—therapist and wife—may sit patiently as the man holds court, both oozing concern, subtly deferring to him, careful not to push or challenge him "too far." One woman at a therapy workshop revealed, "I've been listening to these other women, and I just haven't related because I love working with men. But I now realize that I rarely challenge them, disagree with them, or even remind them that I'm in the room! I just listen, and I love hearing their stories. It reminds me that as a child I was the one who went into the living room when Daddy came home from work, and he would tell me about his day. I loved being the one he talked to. It was only later I realized he never asked much about me."

SO WHAT'S A WOMAN TO DO? A GOOD WAY FOR women to sensitize themselves to these issues is to think about where they typically get stuck with their male clients. What kind of man pushes their buttons, and why? What were women taught, growing up, about men and how women should take care of them? Does the female therapist feel equally strong and nurturant with male and female clients? Women should compare how they respond to men in their personal lives and in their practices.

Some of the best experts on gender dynamics are male clients. What they choose to learn from female therapists reveals much about their expectations of themselves as men and their hopes for what they want to discover and build with women. The therapist can be an anthropologist and explore whether men's and women's experiences are qualitatively different. Remember, the language of therapy is not a man's native tongue. Women, therapists and spouses alike, often read men's confusion about feelings as evidence of male hostility, withholding, or manipulation.

I've come to believe that many men have never learned to name and experience their feelings. The trick for women then becomes how to invite male clients to experiment with a new language without shaming or outdistancing them. In return, the female therapist's task is to enter his world, to understand it, and to help him value and cherish parts of it. No man changes if he only hates who he has been. At the same time, female therapists must not only understand a male client's world but challenge it, help him recreate himself in ways he needs to grow.

The belief that men are unable to express feelings and incapable of real relationships can be a terrible trap. If the therapist treats the male client as emotionally incompetent, both are likely to believe it. The female clinician must dare to be stronger, learn to confront without being critical, to set limits without being punitive, to push without being impatient. If she starts feeling tentative or adrift in the therapy relationship, she can remind herself that it *is* a relationship. Therapy is a good place for some men to learn that they, too, can nurture and take responsibility for what happens in the relationship. If a man

is unwilling to meet the conditions for therapy, the therapist can let him go. Befuddled by the expectations of women, men feel protected by clear guidelines in therapy and often respond to efforts to strengthen the connection with the therapist.

Most important, female therapists don't have to ignore the obvious fact that they are women. If the client tries to control or intimidate, the therapist can educate him about how that makes her feel as a woman. If he responds with surprise to her self-confidence or frankness, the therapist can explore how he expects a woman to act. If there is an impasse, the therapist can find out what would be different if she were a man. Gender is not the only dimension to therapy, but it can't hurt to ask.

Even as female therapists are inviting their male clients to examine what difference the gender difference makes, they can question their own long-held assumptions about men. Most men who come to therapy are not trying to maintain the status quo, but are reaching for a way to change. When I automatically assumed that my male clients would be threatened or critical of my being stronger or more outspoken than many women, I made myself seem defensive or oppositional. When I was ready to be more open to men's understandings of things and more willing to establish a different kind of therapeutic partnership with them, I learned that they were sometimes unsettled by me, but also intrigued. Besides, if therapists, male and female, can't begin to transcend the cultural prison of rigid gender expectations, how can we hope for anything better in a society still wracked with conflict between men and women? Therapists with any wisdom know they get as much from their clients as they give. If I have enlarged a male client's notions of what women can be, he has deepened my understanding of men. Both of us have gained in the process. ■

MICHELE BOGRAD, PH.D., *is a psychologist in private practice in Arlington, MA.*

PHOTOGRAPH BY MILLICENT HARVEY

THE BIRTH OF A MOVEMENT

EXPLORING THE EMOTIONAL UNDERWORLD OF MEN

By R. Todd Erkel

I STUMBLED INTO MY FIRST GATHERING OF MEN AT age four, not under my own power. My grandfather had to steady me as I maneuvered the one step up to the door of his favorite tavern. I sat dutifully on the high, backless stool enjoying my reward—a bag of potato chips—and took in the strong, new odor of the room. The men sitting around, most of them large, old and black, wrapped me in their smiles. I remember wanting to sit there a long time.

Not long after that my grandfather died. He drank himself to death. It's a memory that many men share: losing a close relative or friend to alcohol. Men, we know, have been watching each other drown for years.

Those memories are part of a shared history that men are only now beginning to acknowledge. For years there has been a conspiracy of silence about what it means to grow up male. Boys who share intimate secrets develop a selective amnesia on their way to becoming men. Conversation begins to dwell on sports, sex, success. Friendships wither. Relationships fade. And men stand idly by, denying that anything might be done to save them.

But a growing number of men have begun to break the silence. In wooded cabins and in dusty classrooms—far removed from the anesthetizing effects of the bottle—men have begun to gather and to rebuild a sense of community. In the process, men have begun asking questions that women have speculated on, rather unsuccessfully, for years. What are men feeling? What do men want?

What emerges in response to these questions is not so much a clear set of answers as a flood of long-suppressed emotion. As suspected, beneath the tough male exterior lies an emotional underworld: a place where men stockpile everything from wild joy to furious rage to deep sadness. While the therapy profession struggled for years to direct men to delve into their inner world, men seemed immobilized by the pull of collective male opinion. Now men may have found an even stronger pull in the words of poet Robert Bly and others, who are calling men to join them in what they describe as "a descent into the soul."

While the call for men to change their lives has been made by many before him, Bly has emerged as a spokesman for an ancient understanding in a time that seems increasingly cut off from the past. The 63-year-old, silver-haired Bly, described as a cross between Garrison Keillor and Zeus, is a spiritual guide of sorts, a mentor who treats his students to the wisdom of centuries-old stories and his own folly, alternating strokes of criticism and concern as he encourages men to change. Bly bristles at emotional pretense, daring men to drop whatever mask they're wearing and come clean. They oblige. He shifts with ease from serious to silly. Bly can be both a parent and a guardian to his children, and the biggest fool in a room full of admitted dolts and dunces. Six-foot-three and barrel-chested, Bly is a burly, sometimes sharp-tongued, bawdy mentor, a writer and teacher who began more than a decade ago urging men to put down their competitive clubs and to find the common ground of feeling.

Born on the Minnesota prairie and schooled at the University of Iowa and Harvard, Bly became an outspoken critic of the Vietnam War and won the National Book Award for poetry in 1968 for *The Light Around the Body*. But in the wake of his own midlife crisis, Bly discovered something missing, from his poetry and his life. Long a student of writer/philosopher Joseph Campbell, Bly began to make connections between the insights found in the ancient stories and mythologies of the world, and the questions erupting out of his own experience. The son of an alcoholic father, Bly says that he was 46 before he wrote his first poem exploring the pain and estrangement of that relationship and the impact it had on his life.

Over the next decade, Bly's interest in mythology, poetry and Jungian psychology began to coalesce into a framework of ideas and language: a road map for consciousness-raising that he felt allowed men to move forward without simply retracing the footsteps of the women's movement. Bly and others began sharing stories and ideas with other men, at poetry readings and, eventually, on weekend and week-long

retreats. Today Bly, along with Jungian psychologist James Hillman, storyteller/philosopher Michael Meade and others in the mythopoetic vanguard, draws sellout audiences around the country. Men's groups, organized around the "mythology of gender" and group drumming, are forming from Austin to Ann Arbor. Bly's call for men to reconnect and to examine how the conditioning they received as boys is sabotaging their lives as men reached a new level of interest last January, when Bill Moyers interviewed Bly in a PBS broadcast called "A Gathering of Men." Some are calling this a "men's movement," but it's not clear yet whether Bly's appeal will inspire anything like a mass movement.

BLY'S ANALYSIS OF THE DEEP CONFUSION AND alienation experienced by modern-day men goes back to the start of the Industrial Revolution. It was then, Bly says, as men moved off the land and into the factories, that fathers began separating—physically and emotionally—from their families. Those most affected, according to Bly, were young boys, who lost not only the emotional security of the father but the participation of other, older men in their lives. The result, he says, was that young males in America no longer experienced a conscious, ritualized initiation into the community of adult men. Where men once felt accepted and secure, Bly maintains, they now feel lost and inadequate.

Over time men lost touch with what Bly calls "the male mode of feeling," an elusive rubric he uses to describe the various tendencies and processes men employ to sort out information and feelings. "When we stand physically close to our father, something is exchanged that can't be described in material terms," he says, "something that gives the son a certain confidence, an awareness, a knowledge of what it is to be male."

Men, during the past century, have responded to this absence of initiation, and the longing they felt for their fathers, by storing away any feelings of grief and anger, says Bly. That denial, or "wound" as he prefers to call it, led men to distrust older men and to ask too much from the women in their lives. Men found it easier to overinvest themselves in their work, and suppress their feelings, rather than face the demands of their relationships, explains Bly. A cycle of emotional detachment was born.

Hope arrived during the political and cultural unrest of the 1960s. A generation of men and women—the baby boomers—began to question the traditional model of masculinity: the man who appeared outwardly strong, steady and not easily moved to emotion. But while the impulse to change was undeniably correct, Bly says that many men, himself included, looked for alternatives in all the wrong places.

In a 1982 interview in *New Age Magazine*, which many within the mythopoetic movement consider an emancipation proclamation of sorts, Bly offered his belief that "the male in the past 20 years has become more thoughtful, more gentle. But by this process, he has not become more free." Bly labeled this group of hybrid men "soft males." He said that while they had discovered a new set of values and a deeper appreciation for their own feminine consciousness, they were, in fact, no more emotionally liberated than the generations of men before them.

"They're lovely, valuable people . . . not interested in harming the earth or starting wars or working for corporations," Bly said. "There is something favorable toward life in their whole general mood and style of living. But something's wrong. Many of these men are unhappy. There's not much energy in them. They are life-preserving, but not life-giving."

In other words, Bly felt that the long-overdue integration of more nurturing, less aggressive behaviors in men had become a panacea. In its wake, men began to assume any display of assertiveness was misguided, equating simple confidence with the defensiveness and misogyny of past generations or with the political institutions and brutality these men had so visibly disavowed. Bly's claim was that while passivity may have served the nation politically—helping to end the war in Vietnam and to foster civil rights—its impact on a more personal level was to encourage further imbalance.

"These men learned to be receptive, but it wasn't enough to carry their marriages," Bly said. "In every relationship, something fierce is needed once in a while; both the man and the woman need to have it. The male was now able to say, 'I can feel your pain, and I consider your life as important as mine, and I will take care of you and comfort you.' But he could not say what *he* wanted, and stick by it—that was a different matter."

Bly feels that men have become so isolated from each other, and from the mythology that guided men for centuries, that a deep feeling of inadequacy has become "the primary experience of being male in America today." That claim may be difficult for some to accept considering that Bly's audience of mostly middle-aged, middle-class, white men remains the most privileged and politically powerful group on the planet. But Bly says no measure of wealth or power can fill the emotional void men feel.

THE MEN DRAWN TO BLY'S WORKSHOPS AND retreats, most of them in their late thirties, are struggling with the transitions of midlife, from failed relationships to stalled careers. Bly suggests that the models of masculinity that served these men in their youth—heroes like "Ike" and John Wayne—were never meant to survive under the weight of adulthood and its real-life demands.

Bly urges men to trade in those prefabricated role models and to return, with the help of stories, poems and myths, to a time when the journey from boyhood to manhood was not such a solitary and haphazard affair. Bly describes this journey from boyhood to adulthood not as a simple swearing-in ceremony, but as a four-stage initiation: a process that boys experience and continually reexperience, moving to deeper and deeper levels of awareness throughout their lives.

Bly outlines the four stages as follows: bonding with and breaking away from the mother; bonding with and breaking away from the father; finding a "male mother" (an older, preferably unrelated male who will "care for the boy's soul"); and finally, passing "beyond the realm of the personal mother and father" to find what Bly somewhat mysteriously refers to as the "Invisible Czarina," or the spiritual mating with the Universe. (This last stage is a bit abstract for one men's group leader, who said, "We know what Robert's feet are made of, and we're not afraid to tell him when he's full of it.")

Most American men seldom pass beyond stage one, according to Bly. Part of the problem, he says, is that not only have we lost the present and active father, we have lost the older male initiators as well. "One of the things older men don't do anymore is bless the younger men," Bly says. "If they did, we all would be better off, men and women. Because if you feel blessed, you will talk about anything."

Bly encourages men to assume that role of male mother and to find a male mother of their own. "Yeats was one of my male mothers," he says. "Your male mother doesn't have to be alive." Bly uses myths and stories to jump start men in the search for those roles and role models. "A man might live his entire existence and never meet a man who you could call spontaneous," Bly says. "But in the stories and myths, they meet them all the time."

One of the most evocative of Bly's tales is a little-known story by the Brothers Grimm called "Iron John." It's this story that introduced one of the most debated symbols of the men's movement, the "Wild Man." In the story, wave after wave of hunters disappear near a pond in the forest. When the pond is drained, the source of everyone's terror and curiosity—a grubby, hair-covered creature known as the Wild Man—is revealed.

The Wild Man is captured and brought in a cage to the courtyard of the king. One day, the golden ball belonging to the young prince rolls into the cage. To get the ball back, the young prince must strike a deal with the Wild Man and set him free. At first, the prince hesitates, not wanting to disappoint the king and queen. But finally he obliges the Wild Man and rides off into the forest on the hairy shoulders of his new friend.

The relationship between the prince and the Wild Man symbolizes for Bly the move from boyhood to adulthood. In order for men to make that move, Bly says, they must go alone into their forest (the unconscious) and then, like the prince, make a deal to set the Wild Man free.

Bly is careful to distinguish the Wild Man from contemporary images of brutality. The Wild Man, says Bly, symbolizes man's search for emotional strength and spontaneity, not a regression into bullying machismo. "There are an awful lot of myths and fairy stories that involve tests," Bly says, "but they're not tests like, 'Go up there and kill 14 men.' They're tests of inner courage."

WHO ARE THE MEN WHO FIND THEMSELVES drawn to Bly's message? "We usually see three distinct groups of men," says Bly. "About a third have tremendous difficulty getting near an understanding of their own grief. For some, the pain and denial are tremendously deep. For example, the extent of sexual abuse by men on men is much higher than I ever believed when I began this work.

"Another third of the men cannot get in touch with the fiery part of their nature. They can't express anger easily. They can't express rage easily. They don't enjoy conflict. In their case, what has been suppressed really is not their pain, but their ability to react spontaneously. Instead of being regarded as a spontaneous animal, they were regarded as a machine and somebody shut them down. "The third group of men are those for whom what has been suppressed is their adulthood. These men are sometimes encouraged by therapy to live through their inner child. James Hillman has been critical of the principles of therapy, because he sees that the inner child is not political. If the therapy profession continues to emphasize the child—the spontaneous child, the wounded child, the victim child, the holy child—it isn't requiring the political awareness one would require from an adult."

BLY AND OTHERS IN THE MEN'S MOVEMENT HAVE taken on a task that has often proved a thankless chore to generations of frustrated psychotherapists, namely, getting men "in touch" with their feelings. Men have established a notorious reputation within the therapy trade for being reluctant participants in treatment, especially in couples and family therapy. The conventional wisdom holds that they have to be brought along slowly, coddled, even subtly seduced in order to keep them unthreatened and engaged. Some believe that part of the problem with involving men in treatment is that psychotherapy is itself a feminized pursuit, whose emphasis on self-disclosure and the expression of intimate feelings goes counter to male socialization and puts men at a disadvantage to women. Others have suggested that part of the problem may be the models that therapists themselves offer male clients. "By the time middle-class males reach middle age, they have developed a range of repression that makes them incredibly resistant to therapists," observes Neil Froemming, one of the organizers of the Men's Council of Greater Washington. "What makes matters more difficult is that many therapists tend to be rather repressed and unemotional themselves."

The men's movement has taken a different tack from therapy to help men rediscover their emotional lives, by returning to what Robert Bly calls "the original therapy"—using myth, poetry, music and dance to awaken men from their emotional slumber.

"Poetry, drumming, stories, all bypass the rational, Western mind," says Froemming. "They are so extraordinarily effective because, in a way, you *can't* resist them. They go straight to your soul."

More than 50,000 men have already participated in male-only retreats conducted by leaders in the mythopoetic movement like Bly, Hillman, Michael Meade and Shepherd Bliss. What most men seem to remember from their first experience at such events is not so much the ideas about the meaning of masculinity or the male mode of feeling, but the immediate, visceral experience of walking into a room filled with men dropping their everyday personas. It is a setting that quickly brings buried feelings to the surface. "I was terrified," recalls Froemming. "I had never felt myself as especially male. I remember walking into my first group and thinking 'Everybody here knows how to do it and I'm just faking it.'"

As likely as not, the first thing a newcomer encounters at a men's meeting is the primitive sound of pounding drums. Drumming is a staple of these meetings, especially at the beginning, giving the new participant the message that this experience is going to come through a channel different from anything he's probably experienced before. "For 4,000 years, different cultures have been using drumming to bond the individual to the group," says Alan Decker, a social worker who has been involved in the men's movement for the past two years. "When you walk into a room and see a hundred guys wailing away on drums, the emotion that it produces is phenomenal. That's what first drew me in."

Being in a male-only group devoted to exploring emotional experience creates a powerful and novel dynamic. Presumably, the world of feeling is women's domain. In most relationships, women are the emoters and the nurturers. "In my twenties, I found myself using women to help me understand my feelings," says John Cammack, a member of the Men's Council of Greater Washington. "It was as if

I was trying to get in touch with myself by parroting the emotional accessibility of women." So what happens when men no longer depend on women to draw them into the realm of intimate feelings? "The surprise for many men is the range of feelings that becomes immediately accessible," says Ed Honnold, a prime organizer of the council. "I think there's less of the shame and embarrassment men might feel in appearing 'weak' in front of women. It's also possible to let go of a lot of the posturing men normally do when women are present. There's a sense of homecoming and familiarity, a breakdown of isolation and loneliness."

Poetry, music and stories—like Bly's tale of "Iron John"—occupy a central position in the male-only weekend retreats and offer men resonant images of the male experience that trigger intense reactions. The appeal to the mythic and the imaginative relieves men of their sense of isolation and shows them how their personal experience connects with an age-old journey they are traveling with all men. "Mythology and story provide men a door to participation in an aspect of their lives that, for the most part, they have ignored," says Joseph Jastrab, a frequent guide on male-only outings in New York State. "Men need both the story and the actual participation in the story."

That participation ranges from the physical—dancing, sweat lodges and various rites of passage—to simple conversation. The experience of sharing one's life story—the weariness of always playing the assertive male, the pain of childhood trauma, old betrayals—proves most powerful. And, inevitably, there is the sound of men grieving for the father they never knew.

The skill of leaders who are handling this caldron of emotion is essential, according to participants. "Leaders like Bly and Meade create a strong emotional container within which men feel safe to express many feelings, from grief to wild, unruly joy," says Honnold. "The message is that pent-up

feelings can be released and no harm will be done."

"Part of the power of the men's groups is seeing leaders deal with strong emotions, including attacks from the group," says Froemming. "They show men a possible way to be that men may not have observed before."

THE MYTHOPOETIC MEN'S MOVEMENT—THE TALK of wild men and the legacy of racism, sexism and generally misguided motives associated with male-only gatherings and old-boy networks—has raised more than a few suspicions. There are those within the movement itself who acknowledge its possible dangers. "We have to watch out for a tendency toward arrogance," says Cammack. "It would be disastrous if the men's movement turned into a kind of fraternity or secret society that separated the initiated from the uninitiated."

Others see even more dangers. Judy Goldsmith, past president of the National Organization for Women, says, "What concerns me about their thesis is that as soon as we maintain an essential—not minor and not physical—but essential difference between the two sexes, there is always the potential for that to be interpreted in language that reads better/worse, higher/lower, superior/inferior. And we see that throughout the history of our culture, and most civilizations, what ends up being devalued is everything labeled as feminine."

Men active in the mythopoetic movement insist there is no tolerance of women bashing. "We are very conscious of the fact that men might come in with unresolved resentment and fear toward women and think that they can get away with that and get our support in dumping on women," says Jim Lovestar, active in the Minneapolis Men's Council. "We make it very clear to them that we have no room as an organization for women hating. We are willing to hear a man's rage and to support him as he heals it," continued Lovestar. "But we have no room for blaming women for our problems. Our commitment is to living with one another in a healthy way, rather than participating in the continuing war between the sexes."

Nevertheless, many worry that the language and symbols of the mythopoetic movement offer an entirely different meaning and attraction to men who might be characterized as less politically and socially progressive. Barbara Ehrenreich, noted feminist author, says that whatever the mythopoetics intend, archetypes like the Wild Man and Warrior embrace long-standing models of the heroic male. "I think these men ought to know what strings they are pulling and what these drumbeats are evoking for some men," she says. "For centuries the ideal, the successful model of masculinity was always the warrior. Whether they mean to or not, I think they are glorifying that essentially blood-thirsting tradition."

The mythopoetic men say that while they can be aware of the misunderstandings men may bring to the movement, ultimately, the only minds they can change are their own: collective male opinion will never be enlightened more than one man at a time. Another very active and vocal network of men's groups, however, vehemently disagrees. Loosely organized as the National Organization of Men Against Sexism, these profeminist men, primarily academics and political activists, feel that Bly's analysis of the family is incomplete.

"Bly tends to present the father as the victim—as the one who is pushed out," says Harry Brod, professor of philosophy and director of gender studies at Kenyon College in Gambier, Ohio. "What is missing from his analysis is any sense that more often the father removes himself from the family to seek power and prestige elsewhere—in the public arena."

Profeminist men say that until men acknowledge this and other privileges built into the status quo, women will continue to bear the burden of everything from housework to poverty. Brod says that while he values many of Bly's ideas, he cautions

against the temptation to "buy the whole mythopoetic package in order to feel you belong."

Other feminists find that the movement addresses an absence in many men's lives. "I am a feminist, but I believe that at some point, usually around puberty, a boy needs a male to model adulthood," says Pauline Boss, a family therapist and researcher at the University of Minnesota. "I don't see that as contradictory. I realized its importance with my own son when I saw him dressed in red plaid, going off with his father and two grandfathers to hunt deer for the first time. I realized that was an initiation rite.

"That's not the only way it can be done. A boy and a man can go bicycling or they can build something together. But I believe that boys have to be initiated into life by older men in a way that is supportive and nurturing and ritualized."

Boss says that while most men learned nurturing qualities and vulnerability from their mothers or from other women, those feelings never fully take until men see them exhibited in an older man. "This is what older males can uniquely do," Boss says, "They empathize with the younger boy and nurture him. The grown man can never fully do that for others—his wife or his children—unless it's been modeled for him. I know that many single mothers — and I count among them those women who have a husband who is never home—have done incredible jobs parenting their sons. But I think we're now realizing this is a second-best way to do it.

"A mother can teach a boy those things, and that boy can become successful and become a better father than his own father ever was to him. But the man still hungers for that example from his father or an older male. I could talk to my son about how to be a nurturing male, but never was that talk as powerful as when his father or an older man actually showed him how."

Molly Layton, a Philadelphia family therapist, says that while men may carry a need for contact with the father, their longing doesn't imply that men should reject the knowledge they already own; that is, the mother's contribution. "What I encounter in this culture at this time are a lot of men who were brought up with women and who are mostly living in a world of women. They have a very workable identification with the women in their lives, but many of them deny that identification and don't experience it very strongly.

"Most men learned how to be a human being from their mother. She was the person with whom he interacted over and over and with whom he fought and whose values he understands and whose feelings he understands and who understands him. The mother outside him and the mother he takes away and has within himself are, in my mind, a wonderful source of energy and power." Layton urges men not only to consider where Bly stands today on the issues of gender but also to follow the path that brought Bly to his current self-awareness. "Before Robert Bly got into all this stuff around men, he did a lot of investigating into the female within himself," she says. "In my mind, Bly has really paid his dues in being able, at this point, to proceed dialectically into this focus on men. That's what separates Bly from a lot of other men running men's groups, who still have enormous misogyny operating within them."

According to family therapist Augustus Napier, author of *The Fragile Bond*, the debate over what stays and what goes from the dust-covered trunk of traditional masculinity has only just begun. "Women have had a fairly clear sense of what they needed to change about their roles," says Napier. "There has not been that clarity for men. I think the challenge for men is to avoid becoming defensive about the changes women have won. That is, neither to retreat into a kind of defensive emphasis on male virility, nor to become ingratiating in attempts to concede to women's needs. We need to find some balance; to respond sympathetically and yet to create a sense of strength and purpose in being male. It's pretty clear

that men are far from achieving that balance."

Boss thinks there is a danger that discussions of gender roles and the meaning of masculinity can become too easily intellectualized. "The whole idea of rediscovering gender in mythology is at once both a complex and a very simple idea," she says. "It's easily misinterpreted as an endorsement for becoming Dirty Harry or Rambo if it is read too simplistically.

"But part of the problem is that men have been socialized to expect everything to make cognitive sense, and in this case, it doesn't always. I tell men I see in therapy to experience what Bly is talking about. Go find that important older man in your life and get to know him. Do something with him and maybe you'll realize that he's not perfect and that will give you permission not to be perfect.

"And lousy as he is, try to find something in him that you like. Then decide what you want to emulate and what you want to do differently. That's all it takes. And in the end, you'll know something more about yourself as a man."

I DOUBT THAT MICK JAGGER HAS EVER BEEN CONsidered a mouthpiece for the new man, but it was his carnal, roguish twang that spoke to me as I drove down a forgotten stretch of country road in eastern Ohio. I was trying to avoid the potholes, which looked to be the work of saturation bombing. Ahead lay a much anticipated weekend in the woods. I rumbled on.

My life in the preceding weeks had become an endless loop of interviews with men around the country who promised to lead me to the epicenter of an elusive men's movement. Having temporarily called off the search, I was looking forward to this time away. Needless to say, dragging my assumptions about men all over the map did little for my disposition. Suddenly, everything—this trip, the road, even Jagger's snarl—had come to symbolize the fear and loathing infesting my masculine soul.

The words to Mick's latest single—"Rock and a

THE BIRTH OF A MOVEMENT

Hard Place"—seemed perfectly timed. The song had been getting heavy airplay for weeks, but only in that moment, the tune's emphatic drumbeat keeping time with the crack of my overmatched shocks, did I realize how succinctly Mick and his band of elders had captured my mood.

I had come away from two months of discussion with the leading figures of various men's groups significantly challenged, and enlightened, but, ultimately, feeling stuck. While I found hope in the ideas of Bly and others—the need for men to honor, trust and reacquaint themselves with other men—the remedies offered seemed as narrowly defined as ever. I could only hope that someday men would find reason to spend time together free of anthropological contrivance or immersed in something more than our own suffering. On the other hand, I had come to see the danger of men looking for some sense of themselves in somebody else's cause. I recognize all too well the tendency of profeminist men, myself among them, to cover our own issues in the name of political purity.

Neither of those two extremes appealed to me as I pulled into the circle of cars outside the cabin. The guests this weekend were all familiar faces. Men and women. Some couples. Others floating unattached.

We passed the time in familiar escapist pursuits—walking, cooking and relaxing in front of the fire. On Saturday we met around the basketball hoop and slowly worked up a game. Mixed teams. Our levels of tenacity and skill crossed gender lines. Tina, who stands five feet in mid leap, kept the tallest man on the court at bay with a gnat attack defense. Nobody asked who won.

Later that evening, we played poker and danced to Beatles songs. It was well past midnight when someone suggested a round of "Feather Lifting," a favorite game from childhood slumber parties.

We hesitated for a minute. "Feather Lifting?" Is this what happens when a story conference for "thirtysomething" runs on too long? But our defenses slowly dropped. One by one, we lay on the cabin floor, feigning death. The others knelt alongside the corpse and placed two fingers under the body. The point was to lift the stiff using only our fingers. As we suspected, it couldn't be done.

But then someone revealed the secret, known only to her and her best childhood friends. She instructed us to stack our hands, one by one, over the still body. We then unstacked our hands and lifted again. Up the body went. No matter the weight class. Higher and higher. It worked. Nobody understood why. Simple concentration? Or could it really be explained?

We laughed into the night and through the next day about the mysterious ritual. I drove home trying to assign masculine and feminine labels to the weekend's events. But they wouldn't stick. Those gender distinctions, with their enormous historical weight, still dictate most aspects of our workaday worlds. More than any other categories, they inform our understanding of who we are.

As I drove away, I recalled an olive branch offered by Barbara Ehrenreich in an interview I had with her a few days before. "The idea of men and women scrounging around, trying to find companionship from one another, is a very recent idea," says Ehrenreich. "I mean, the simple idea of conversation between the sexes as something that extended beyond courtship is a relatively recent one. I think it's a little too soon to say we will never get it together."

A few years earlier, Ehrenreich set a course for where we might meet somewhere in the future. "It's not enough, anymore, to ask that men become more like women," she wrote. "We should ask instead that they become more like what both men and women *might* be." ∎

R. TODD ERKEL *is a senior writer at* Pitt Magazine *in Pittsburgh, PA.*

PHOTOGRAPH BY CHARLES HARBUTT/ACTUALITY

*T*HE POLITICS OF MOOD

THE MASKED DEPRESSION OF
THE "DIFFICULT" MAN

By Ronald Taffel

IN THE MIDDLE OF THE NIGHT, I WOULD FIND HIM there. Alone at the kitchen table, he sat bent over a book or the daily newspaper. "What's the matter, Daddy?" I would ask, already knowing what the answer would be. "Oh, it's nothing, Ronnie. I just have something on my mind, so I couldn't sleep." He'd look up at me, the glasses magnifying some expression in his eyes I wasn't able to name. "Don't worry," he would say. "Go back to bed, and I'll see you in the morning."

The next morning there would be a noticeable pall over the house. There would be a more strident edge to my mother's usual concerns about getting us ready for the day. I could see that she hadn't slept much either.

ACCORDING TO STANDARD DIAGNOSTIC CRITERIA, my parents were a classic pairing of familiar psychological types: obsessive man married to hysterical woman. Lately the feminist movement has rehabilitated the woman of this traditional dyad. Historically described as seductive, overemotional, superficial and morally shallow, her "hysterical"

characteristics now tend to be viewed as survival mechanisms in a gender-biased society, her "emotionality," a sensitivity and capacity for human connection often lacking in her obsessive partner.

Our view of her mate, however, has hardly changed over the years. Still described as precise, dutiful, detail-minded, objective, scrupulously responsible, he is often a stubborn impediment to therapy. His fragile ego almost demands condescension and seduction, if only to keep him from dropping out of therapy. Countless times in my practice I have come up against his imperturbable distance, his sullen resistance, or his bland equanimity in the face of imminent family disaster, and have felt powerfully drawn into collusion with his more responsive wife, thus deepening the man's isolation and therapeutic disengagement.

Yet even when most frustrated by the seeming indifference and immovable composure of such men, I am never too far from the memory of my father, of *that face*. I can never completely forget the unnameable look in his eyes on those nights in the kitchen.

359

THOUGH MY FATHER WAS DEFINITELY ON THE serious side, he didn't stand out all that much from the fathers around me. Alan and Leon's father was thought of as being "very quiet." I can't remember him saying more than a handful of words over the 20 years I regularly saw him. It's not that he seemed unhappy. He just sat there, occasionally smiling, passively taking up space while a swirl of women and children yelled, babbled and made their commotion around him.

Art's father lived a block away. He stood out among the fathers because every Saturday when we played ball he actually came out to watch Art. Week after week, through tens of thousands of innings, he stood there, taking everything in. He never once smiled. He never yelled or cheered. He watched without expression of any sort. Once I asked Art, "What did your father say about that game yesterday?" Art shrugged his shoulders and walked away.

Steve's father was considered a man of "ritual." He followed the same routine every morning, every day and every night. He was so reliable that everyone said you could set your watch by him. Even when his son did the unthinkable by moving to California, marrying and then divorcing; even when his friends around him died, his daily ritual never changed. Only as cancer got the better of him and made leaving bed impossible did he give in and alter his routine in any way. When this happened, it was clear the end was coming.

Peter's father was a "wise guy." Nothing seemed to please him. Nothing was quite right. He had an answer and a complaint about everything. I never saw him without a scowl on his face, pacing back and forth like a man who was waiting for the bus to come.

The father of my best friend, Leo, had a "real head on his shoulders." If asked a question, he could recite point by point an unending stream of facts. He didn't actually converse, he simply churned out information. It was important not to ask him any question unless you were near a door and had to be home soon. I don't remember ever seeing him and his wife in the same room together.

PROBABLY NONE OF THE FATHERS IN MY OLD neighborhood would have fit the DSM-III diagnosis of depression. No one thought it unusual that they were chronically angry or silent and passive, that they had no real friends, few interests besides work and no fun, that they couldn't relate well to their wives and children. After all, they did what men were supposed to do.

They had jobs, they held up their responsibilities, they functioned—they were *men*.

After years of hearing clients describe their fathers' lifelong irritability, bitterness, flatness, explosiveness and disconnection, I began to wonder if therapists might not be overlooking something critically wrong in these men's lives. Perhaps by failing to help men face their underlying depression, therapists were doing men as much a disservice as they had done to their wives by pathologizing women's adaptive behavior. In my practice, I now see a red flag when a woman or child complains of a depressed atmosphere in the house and then describes a husband/father who exhibits certain "typical" masculine behaviors. I explore in detail statements like the following: "He broods about everything: he's a worrier. I always have to show him the bright side." "He keeps his feelings to himself. I never know what's going on inside." "I make all the arrangements; he has no friends of his own. He never does anything with anyone else." "He can't do anything for himself. It's like having another child around." "He zones out for hours in front of the TV. He falls asleep on the couch every night. I feel completely alone." "He lost interest in me sexually long ago."

Along with these possible signs of passive depression are descriptions suggesting agitated depression. "It's like living with a caged animal. Something's always eating at him. I'm nervous all the time." "His energy is endless. He thinks he can take on everything. He never says no to a project. He's a workaholic." "He's always had a temper. I've just learned how to negotiate around it." "He wants all of me. He can't stand sharing me with anybody." "Nothing is good enough for him. He always finds fault with me or the children."

Over the past several years, I have studied 125 men, almost none of whom said they were depressed. Only 14 percent would have received a formal diagnosis of depression according to DSM-III standards. But the partners of 62 percent of them described mood difficulties in the men serious enough to color the atmosphere of the entire household. There is a gloomy undertow in these homes, just below the surface of everyday life. Whether the men passively disappear into the woodwork or shake the foundations of the house with their agitation, they share one characteristic—they cannot regulate their moods or affective states, and they depend on their partners and children to do so for them.

WHEN I WAS 13 YEARS OLD, MY MOTHER WENT overnight with "the girls" from her canasta group to Atlantic City. On the evening they set out for the Claridge Hotel, eight fathers were left for the first time in charge of houses and children. I never thought to ask my friends what it was like in their homes, but 30 years later I remember what it was like for me.

The memory is washed in a kind of beige silence. My father and I seemed to wander from room to room, unable to settle down. At dinnertime his normal competence was reduced to fumbling ineptitude. Even though my mother had left instructions with already prepared foods (wrapped and labeled in tinfoil), I can only remember how the Campbell's baked beans turned out. For two days the beans lay like rocks in my stomach, resisting all attempts at digestion, a visceral reminder of what one night without a mother around could do to a person.

IN OUR CULTURE MEN LEARN TO DEPEND EXCLU-sively on external sources of self-validation. Little importance is placed on men taking care of their own physical needs, let alone developing inner emotional resources. They depend on women and home to provide nurture and solace from the depressing realities and wounding struggles of the outside world. A woman, on the other hand, because of her ingrained empathic skills and economic dependence on men, eventually learns to absorb and even take on the very mood the man finds intolerable in himself. She is his mood regulator, a kind of human, time-released antidepressant medication. And when the burden becomes too heavy, she may develop a host of symptoms, including depression, and come in for therapy. If therapists focused on mood as carefully as we do on self-esteem and power, we would recognize the depressed man at the heart of the family system and the wife or mother who bears his camouflaged pain for him.

If ever a television program captured the undertow of men's affective state on the family and the depressive-caretaker pairing, "The Honeymooners" did. Stomping around and raging about hopes and dreams that never saw fruition, threatening violent abuse, ultimately relying on Alice for emotional stability—Ralph Kramden was the depressed Everyman of the 1950s.

Each week when "The Honeymooners" came on the air, I practically dragged my father into the living room so that we could watch it together. As Ralph raved on about his newest scheme to get rich quick—the uranium mine in Vermont or the Handy Dandy Vegematic—my father would laugh so hard that tears rolled down his face. In this way, for 30 minutes at a time, I could cheer him up and we could "talk" about unfulfilled dreams without ever having to mention his own disappointments in life. My mother wasn't interested in the show. She said there was something that was too depressing and loud about it.

EVEN IF THE THERAPIST RECOGNIZES THAT THE "difficult" man is really depressed and unhappy, neither partner may want to hear it. Most men recoil at the suggestion that they are sick, or in pain or even that something is bothering them. A woman, even if she has initiated treatment, may be threatened by the diagnosis as well, despairing about depending on a mate with so vague and obscurely "unmasculine" a flaw. "Depression? That's what women get." She may feel rage that he has refused for all these years to admit that something is wrong, or she may resist a pathological explanation that gives him one more excuse for retreating behind his shield, even while officially dumping another caretaking responsibility into her lap.

Although many family therapists try not to use clinical terminology, it *is* my intention to pathologize what has been incorrectly normalized in men. If the man does not recognize that part of the problem is within himself, he cannot take responsibility for addressing it, and the woman will be left in the old double bind of taking care of a condition that supposedly doesn't exist. Because it is often so difficult for a couple to accept the diagnosis, I generally ease into the subject of depression by first adopting the same phrases the family uses to describe his behavior—for example, "irritable," "moody," "quiet," "restless"—and progress gradually toward more pathological and clinical terms.

In a recent case, the identified patient was an obese 8-year-old girl who was aggressive, difficult to control and a behavior problem at school. Because Lenore, the mother, was high strung, overprotective, and couldn't set limits for the girl, the family thought the problem was between the two of them. But Lenore described her husband, Fred, as hard to live with, critical and possessive of her time, making her feel torn between his demands and those of the children. With their children, Fred was always on the verge of frustration or open anger. The family agreed that he was "irritable" and that it was "like walking on eggshells around him."

Fred insisted that it was his kids who made him so irritable. But when I asked him and Lenore if his irritability had only begun after his marriage, Lenore said he'd been "irritable" on their first date, and Fred admitted he'd been that way as long as he could remember. The only time he'd ever felt different was one day when he was upset and his mother had given him a Valium. "I was stunned at how calm I felt," he said. "My engine stopped idling so high for a couple of hours. I can't remember a time in my life when I haven't woken up in the morning thinking, 'What is going to go wrong today that will upset me?' It's a feeling that I get in the pit of my stomach. For three hours in my life I didn't feel this."

I gradually shifted from using Fred's word, "irritated," to "agitated," and then pointed out that the "agitation and depressed feeling" he had had in his stomach every morning since adolescence could not possibly be his family's fault. Gradually, Fred learned to identify his ruminative angst. He could then begin to assume responsibility for himself, and Lenore could break the mold set by three generations of caretaking women in her family—all married to depressed men.

Both Fred and Lenore began taking better care of themselves; he lost 40 pounds and went on a couple of fishing trips, while she started hypnotherapy to stop smoking. Seeing her parents more in charge of themselves, the daughter grew significantly calmer, quit obsessively worrying that they might die, and stopped binge eating.

THERE WERE ESSENTIALLY TWO FATHERS WHO could arrive home after work each evening. The one I like to remember was loving and attentive. He helped me with my schoolwork, sculpted circus animals out of clay, worked with me on oil-painting-by-numbers kits, and built models of airplanes and battleships. On Sundays we went to Walt Disney feature cartoons and, when I got a little older, to baseball games. And every night of my life, even in the midst of our wildest struggles, he would be sure to say good night to me.

The other father was the preoccupied one. He said almost nothing and was extremely irritable, always on the edge of exploding. When he did go over the edge, and this was not infrequent, the veins of his temples looked about to burst, filling me with dread that some infraction of mine could kill him on the spot.

A friend of mine commented to me, "Why is your father so serious?" I was only 12, but, from hearing my mother's explanation a hundred times before, I already knew exactly what to say. "Business is slow," I answered. That my father was serious regardless of business conditions did not seem to register with either my friend or me. I believed what I was saying and so did he.

MOST FAMILIES LIKE MY OWN, WHO CANNOT explain a father's mood difficulties except in socially sanctioned terms, will resist any attempts to reframe the mood as depression. When a man cannot or will not discuss masked depression, I focus on his family of origin first. Discovering that his mother, father, or siblings were depressed allows a man to consider his unhappiness with less shame. But an ingrained emotional denseness makes some men incapable of either confronting themselves or looking at their own families with new eyes. Their retreat from self-knowledge is often matched by a relentless pursuit of emotional insight by their wives. The more probing the woman, the more blandly inaccessible the man. In such cases, sometimes straightforward task assignment can help these men become more aware of their moods.

Jim and Chris, a successful couple with two children, had been married 15 years when they came in complaining of explosive fighting. Jim said that Chris was self-righteous, glibly facile in her arguments, and unable to apologize. Chris, in her turn,

said Jim would sink into mysteriously sullen, uncommunicative moods that lasted days. The sharper and more insistent she was about trying to get through to him, the duller and more self-absorbed he became. After several fruitless sessions, I asked Jim to write down the warning signals of a bad mood during a one-week period. Weeks later he finally came in with a list of rather blatant signals, like losing items around the house, forgetting appointments, restlessness and heavier drinking.

After the assignment, Jim began to recognize his mood states at least as quickly as Chris, who stopped monitoring him so much. Jim's mood became steadier, and Chris felt she could talk to him more deeply and intimately. Jim, less agitated, could sit and listen. Chris started talking about her desire to begin another career, switching the focus to herself for the first time.

Often a man's own suffering so threatens his idealized masculine self-identity that he cannot even admit to any pain. When no other tactic seems to get this man to start taking his own mood problems more seriously, I intensify a crisis. Danny, a 44-year-old businessman, adamantly denied that anything was bothering him besides the daily demands of the household. His wife, Julie, was enraged by his unwillingness to help with their two children, while he hated coming home from an impossible work situation to the noise, commotion and demands of a household in constant uproar. A binge eater, Danny was seriously overweight, restless and excitable, and prone to sarcastic tirades at home. The only time he stopped worrying about business was when he was yelling at everyone. He frequently threatened to walk out on his marriage, if only to get some peace.

Danny insisted that his only problems were his child's hyperactivity and his wife's nagging, even after he admitted that he had suffered from mood instability since adolescence. Julie did not take Danny's mood seriously either, saying he was probably just going through a midlife crisis. Finally, in some desperation, I took a calculated risk and came down hard.

"I could drop dead myself anytime, so it makes me a little nervous to say this," I began. "But, of all the men in all the families I work with, I worry about you the most, Danny. You've been depressed on and off since adolescence, but you're such a well-trained man that you don't even notice. You keep putting out and producing, even though you are almost falling apart. You're 50 pounds overweight, you never exercise, you binge on junk food. You haven't been to a doctor in two decades. You don't know how to shut the engine of worry off in your head. You can't admit to any of it because you don't see there's anything wrong—you're simply doing your job.

"However, I think you're at great risk to collapse soon. I find myself actually thinking about you between sessions, wondering if you're okay. So, since I think you're at such risk, I suggest you do what's responsible: one, go out and get a bank life insurance plan, for which you don't need a physical; two, make sure your will is in order; three, I think you and Lenore should see a lawyer and begin to look into estate planning."

Two weeks later Danny arrived, furious about the last session. What had really disturbed him about my remarks? That I had worried about him between meetings. "Am I really that bad off?" he asked angrily. "Am I in the worst shape of all your patients?" I repeated my concern, and he left in a rage.

Though Danny did not return to therapy with me, shortly afterward he began individual therapy with someone else. At the same time, Julie applied for postgraduate training, which she had been planning for three years but had postponed from fear of Danny's reaction. Even though Danny was furious when she told him, she went ahead, saying she had better start "getting on with my own life." Their fighting has dramatically decreased, and their hyperactive daughter has begun to calm down.

WHEN MY FATHER RETIRED, HE SLID DEEPLY into the depression that had always seemed like a temporary mood. Not that I thought anything was wrong even then. He was just "having a hard time adjusting to retirement." It finally struck me how bad things were the day my mother blew up at him. Suddenly, she started screaming, "You only see the dark side. I try my best to cheer you up, and all you do is worry. What kind of life is this to live?"

My father sat motionless. The green upholstered club chair seemed to envelop his collapsing body, and from across the room I could see him quietly crying. Despite my mother's fury, she never said another word, nor did anyone else. By dinnertime some of his favorite dishes were on the table, and my mother was as upbeat as ever. The rage and bitterness that momentarily pierced the family's denial had been muffled by a nice plate of pot roast and mashed potatoes.

The ease with which my family could deny the undertow in our house is not unusual. Yet every time I have been able to address the caretaker-depressive dynamic in couples, the structure of the family begins to shift. Once it is understood that the difficult man may be fighting against various forms of depressive experience—chronic rumination, camouflaged obsessive-compulsive disorders, barely managed phobias, quick-cycling mood changes, muted panic attacks and controlled substance abuse—things begin to happen. Once the couple is jolted out of defining the woman as the caretaker and the man as just another version of the difficult man, the woman need no longer bear the exclusive burden of responsibility for change, and both partners can begin to share it equally.

But the process is not easy. The caretaker-depressive relationship is normalized by economics and social expectations. Changing it is a formidable, sometimes impossible, task. Since so many of us in the helping professions grew up in caretaker-depressive families ourselves, it helps to remember that we can't always turn upside down what has become a natural way of life for so many people.

TWO YEARS AFTER MY FATHER RETIRED, HE DIED suddenly while vacationing in Switzerland. It's been 20 years since then. Whenever I visit the cemetery, I am in the habit of leaning over and kissing the headstone. The rough texture of the stone always reminds me of his tired and unshaven face when he came home in the evening.

There was a long hallway in our apartment. Every night when I was a little boy I would hear the key in the door and run down the corridor as fast as I could, jumping, almost flying, so he could catch me.

My mother stood off to the side a little—to give me room, I used to think.

A marriage, a child and several thousand hours of doing family therapy later, I know better. She was looking him over, going through her own kind of hello. Between the time my feet left the ground and I landed in his arms, she already understood what mood he had come home with and was already beginning to make it her own. ∎

RONALD TAFFEL, PH.D., *is director of Family and Couples Treatment Services, Institute for Contemporary Psychotherapy in New York City.*

Letters to the Editor

IF *UTNE* AWARDS WERE PROVIDED FOR poignancy, Ronald Taffel would certainly be one of this year's recipients. Ralph Kramden, "the depressed Everyman of the 1950s"? Pleeease! I suppose when one is making a case for yet another underdiagnosed disorder, then the plight of the helpless victims has to be cast in the most vivid and attention-getting terms possible. How else can family therapists be persuaded to include another obscure "illness" in their version of the DSM III-R?

Though Taffel's sad account of the baked beans lying "like rocks" in his stomach is truly compelling and appeals to our collective sympathies, I am as much concerned for those individuals who have been subjected to such diagnostic vagaries as weak ego, depressive equivalent, pseudoneurotic schizophrenia, latent psychosis and so on. Heaven knows what treatment they ultimately received for their complaints.

As with any of these rather imprecise notions (remember borderline?), the argument can be offered for including a pantheon of woes, dilemmas, frailties, temperaments and transient feelings under the rubric of a psychiatric disturbance. It appears that in the author's memory, almost every dad in his neighborhood was stricken. Somehow, being reticent, retiring, serious, cantankerous, ritualistic, or exact have all become definitive signs of mental malady.

Nevertheless, I must confess I am impressed by Dr. Taffel's use of TV characters for highlighting psychological ills. Perhaps George Jetson could be considered the embodiment of passive-dependency, and Lucy Ricardo an example of the horrors of unrecog-

nized PMS. Incidentally, I have on good authority that Mister Ed was a multiple personality.

Mark A. Hubble
Kansas City, KS

AUTHOR'S RESPONSE:

Dr. Hubble's letter was so well written and humorous it took me a while to realize that he entirely missed the main point of my piece—how much women and children are affected by, and called upon to regulate, men's mood states. I have no problem with his concerns about pathologizing in our field, but to equate depression with arcane constructs such as "pseudoneurotic schizophrenia" is downright nasty to millions of people who live with depression every day. And relabeling the fathers I described as "caretakers" (kinda cute, right?) misses the fact that they were sometimes abusive (remember that term?); calling them "reticent" ignores the numbing loneliness of living with someone who may not talk for years at a stretch; and "retiring" (has almost a cozy ring) dismisses the exhaustion a woman feels when her husband retires from childcare and housework responsibility.

Does Dr. Hubble really believe that women go crazy and children fall apart because men are a little "serious" or "exacting"? Depression in men is one area, as I tried to point out and as Dr. Hubble demonstrates, that we have not overdiagnosed. Positive connotation is always easiest when we don't have to actually live with the behaviors we're reframing.

Ronald Taffel
New York, NY
—MAY/JUNE 1990

PHOTOGRAPH BY ELLIOTT ERWITT/MAGNUM

*T*HE MASCULINE MYSTIQUE

AN INVISIBLE CHORUS HAUNTS MEN'S LIVES

By Frank Pittman

Men weren't really the enemy—they were fellow victims suffering from an outmoded masculine mystique that made them feel unnecessarily inadequate when there were no bears to kill.

—BETTY FRIEDAN

MASCULINITY HAS BECOME A PROBLEM, NOT JUST for the men who spend their lives in mortal struggle with its demands, but also for those who must share the world with such men. The qualities that were useful in protecting primitive society from saber-toothed tigers have few practical functions these days. Cities full of men stomping around flexing their muscles and growling manly noises at one another have become our modern jungles. Men fight for turf and wrestle for control over people and things, whether through war, armed robbery, or corporate takeovers. They aspire to be Masters of the Universe, as Tom Wolfe terms it, and they rape and pillage and plunder, competing with the other boys.

Heavy doses of masculinity are unquestionably toxic and no longer societally acceptable. But all that is masculine is not bad. Some of us make worthwhile contributions even when we're acting like men. The problem is not masculinity but the masculine mystique: the veneration and exaggeration of all that is masculine. In order to come to grips with toxic levels of masculinity, we need to understand how men become men, how they develop masculinity and how they get carried away with it.

I suppose we would have to define masculinity as all those qualities and activities that men think will make them men, that will distinguish them from women, i.e., "balls." The word "machismo" may derive from the Greek word for "battle" or the Spanish *machete.* Masculinity poet Robert Bly talks of masculine "fierceness," a term he softens and positively connotes as "protectiveness." But the word still means "savage" or "undomesticated." Masculinity, when it is ripe enough to he ballsy, macho, or fierce, struggles to tame the environment, to protect the family, to compete for glory and prestige. Or it may only involve the need to control women, to be "head of the household" and to take care of "the weaker sex." Masculinity on the one hand has connoted strength and activity in protection of the family, but on the other hand it has also connoted escape from domesticity and resistance to the control of women.

We like to think of masculinity as natural, but most of its manifestations are cultural and historical rather than biological, so it varies from time to time and place to place. But it doesn't exist just in the mind of a single guy: it is a view of life shared with the other guys. (As one man explained: "If the first space visitor arrived from Mars and was male, I'd have more in common with him than with any woman on Earth.") Most of all, it is a code of conduct that requires men to maintain masculine postures and attitudes (however they are defined) at all times and in all places.

Masculinity includes the symbols and the uniforms and the chants and the plays that make this the boys' team rather than the girls' team. And as a guy develops and practices his masculinity, he is accompanied and critiqued by an invisible male chorus of all the other guys, who hiss or cheer as he attempts to approximate the masculine ideal, who push him to sacrifice more and more of his humanity for the sake of his masculinity, and who ridicule him when he holds back. The chorus is made up of all the guy's comrades and rivals, all his buddies and bosses, his male ancestors and his male cultural heroes, his models of masculinity—and above all, his father, who may have been a real person in the boy's life or may have existed for him only as the myth of the man who got away.

My male chorus is different from my father's or my son's or my nephews'. My son can hear my voice, as I hear my father's, but there are other voices there, too. Many of our voices come from our culture. I was born the same year as Woody Allen and Elvis Presley. Ted Kennedy is three years older, Bill Cosby three years younger. I grew up in small towns in Alabama and Georgia, coming of age when Harry Truman was in the White House, John Wayne was on the big screen, and my father was somewhere in the Pacific being masculine, fiercely battling the

"Japs." Many of the voices in my chorus are shared with the other boys who came of age in those days. The models of masculinity have changed through the years, but it is the men of my generation who are running the world right now, and you can watch them writhe and wrestle with the masculine mystique of our youth. Few of us can drown out the incessant chant of our macho choir.

I'll tell you what I know about a man's struggle with the masculine mystique, from the experience of my son and nephews, my friends and patients, but especially from my own struggle.

BOYS BEING BOYS

Snips and snails and puppy dogs' tails; That's what little boys are made of.
—ANONYMOUS

WE KNOW FROM THE BEGINNING THAT WE'RE supposed to be boys, but the Y chromosome doesn't show. The only visible sign of our maleness is a useless little peanut we're told to keep hidden. So we have to wear boy clothes and play with boy dolls and try to act like boys act. Although there are times when our invisible male chorus is off duty, when the other boys are with us we practice being cowboys or soldiers or football players or space jockeys. We practice pissing off the porch, rolling in the mud, whatever we can think of that boys do and girls don't. Maybe we'll look like a boy if we're dirty or sloppy or scuffed up, if we keep a snake or a knife (or lately a gun) in our pocket, if we climb taller trees than girls will climb, if we're uglier and nastier than girls would be.

We don't want to be mistaken for girls. We avoid answering the telephone because our voice isn't a man's voice, and callers might think we are our mother when we say "hello." As much as we love our mother, as much as we depend on her, as much as we enjoy her company, we don't want to be seen with her. We don't want anyone to think we like

370

doing the sorts of things girls do, so if anyone is looking, we have to act uncomfortable around Mom. We want to be seen with our father, hanging out with men and doing men things.

We go around pretending to ourselves that we're big, powerful men, but our mothers keep reminding us that we are still little boys. When we are prepared to test our bravery against the forces of darkness in the night, Mother tells us to brush our teeth and go to bed. Mother treats us as if she, not we, owned our bodies and our lives. Mother isn't even fazed by our magic peanut. We're still her baby, and as much as we love that when we're hurting or when we need her service, she can bring us back from the soaring fantasy world of masculinity to the inglorious little life of a child.

We long for our father. We wear his clothes and actually try to fill his shoes. Anything of his is charmed and can endow us with his masculinity. We hang on to him, begging him to teach us how to do whatever is masculine, to throw balls or be in the woods or go see where he works. We spend so much more time with our mother, we begin to fear she will stifle the masculinity we know we must develop in ourselves, that she will civilize us and tame us and destroy us as the wild animals we know we must be. We want our fathers to protect us from coming too completely under the control of our mothers. We'll do anything with a man, but we fear that femaleness might be contagious, and we don't want it to rub off on us.

We practice our masculinity, trying to develop enough of it. We feel a bit foolish with it, like impostors, so we practice it in front of mirrors and around strangers, trying to learn how to swagger, trying to mimic the men we admire. We always overdo it. We aren't big yet, or strong, and we can't make our muscles grow very much, so we substitute recklessness. We take risks, daring one another to do whatever frightens us all most. We practice masculinity by stealing things or jumping off bridges or picking fights or swallowing live frogs. We show off for the older boys. The less we know of real grown men, the more daring we seem to become in our efforts to be masculine enough. If we have a father (or uncle or grandfather) we admire, and we can find him in ourselves, we can imitate him. If we don't, we may have to imitate movie stars or sports heroes. We look to the other boys our own age to tell us when we're overdoing it, and the other boys may be battling just as fiercely and desperately to flex their masculinity at the world. So we bounce our absurdly puffed-up masculinity off one another and think we are preparing ourselves for manhood.

THE DISORIENTATION OF PUBERTY

I wonder why men get serious at all. They have this delicate thing hanging outside their bodies which goes up and down by its own free will. If I were a man I would always be laughing at myself.

—YOKO ONO

A BOY'S PUBERTY IS A STRANGELY UNSETTLING transition, perhaps not quite as dramatic and definitive as menarche (though a boy's first ejaculation can be every bit as frightening as a girl's first menstruation). Before puberty, the bodies of boys and girls are similar enough to be easily interchangeable except for the insignificant little genitals. Much is made of those little genitals from birth, or nowadays even before birth, and they become the determinant of everything in life. But for the first 12 or 14 years, they have little significance except as predictors of future events. Early on, girls begin to menstruate, which is dramatic but not immediately obvious to their playmates. For boys, puberty comes later, sometimes much later, and its delay is humiliating. While the tall, round girls are getting themselves up like grown women, the prepubertal boys, with their featureless, hairless bodies, are just dirty little kids who could almost pass for the children of the grown-up-looking girls.

The genitals are the first part to change. First there is a little pubic hair and then with alarming suddenness the penis blossoms into its full glory, utterly inappropriate to the little-boy body from which it dangles. A boy's penis seems so enormous and hard to hide, far too big yet still too small, always too small. It has a life of its own, responding to all the wrong things at all the wrong times, intrusive and embarrassing, yet utterly honest in its responses. It requires much time and attention, much measuring, exploration and comparison with the other guys, and much concern about how it is going to behave in the presence of girls. The boy has little control over it, and for a few years it is not clear who is in charge of whom. He must masturbate constantly to keep it down. But beat it down, however many times a day, and it will spring back up just when it is least expected. Yet when it is needed, it is nowhere to be found; with any anxiety it will run away and hide. The boy has become one of Siamese twins, with this other independent being attached to his body, a constant, unreliable companion, a source of comfort and entertainment when alone, but a steady embarrassment in public.

While the boy is preoccupied, learning to ride this willful creature, thick hair has started at the ankles and moves relentlessly up the body, as if, like a furry monster, to swallow him. All this happens inside his trousers and remains concealed from the outer world until his voice changes and his pants, one morning, are a foot short. The hair reaches the pimply face, and the body exudes goat-like odors. The muscles bulge—never enough, of course—and he bears no resemblance to who he was a year ago or even yesterday. Parts of his body look like a man's, and impatient girls who reached puberty before him expect him to act like a man, so they can feel like women, but he doesn't feel like a man and his parents don't treat him like one. They have no idea what has happened inside his pants and inside his mind. And he certainly doesn't know how to talk

to them about it. At the beginning he clings to other boys who are experiencing the same exciting, terrifying changes, and they form a separate society, a very intimate one, alternately avoiding and examining the sexuality that obsesses them, and passing on fantasy, fears and lies about sex.

A man's relationship with his penis is rooted in that pubertal experience in which his masculinity hangs between his legs. His penis is the first and, for a time, the only part of him that seems truly masculine, and since he has grown up in awe of the masculinity he is supposed to develop, he worships this first confirming symbol of it. He defers to it. He may even let it think for him. (Joke: "Why don't women have as many brains as men? Because they don't have penises to keep them in.")

From the day this man's organ sprouts from this boy's body, the two are in a struggle over who is in charge, whose needs will prevail, and who exists to serve whom. Boys with models of masculinity can learn to keep their penises under control, but a boy without models may turn control over to his penis, which at this most sensitive stage of life seems so much more masculine than the rest of him, and then spend the rest of his life a slave to an insensitive, noncommunicative, unreliable, utterly self-centered, spineless piece of flesh.

LOSING OUR CHERRY

I was never to see her again. Nor was I ever to learn what became of her. . . . Life is made up of small comings and goings, and, for everything we take with us, there is something we leave behind. In the summer of '42 . . . in a very special way, I lost Hermie—forever.

—HERMAN, REFLECTING ON HIS LOST VIRGINITY,
IN *SUMMER OF '42*

IN THE CLASSIC COMING-OF-AGE JOKE, A TENDER-foot tries to gain acceptance in a rough-and-tumble Alaskan mining village. He is told the other men will accept him if he (1) chug-a-lugs a gallon of

180-proof local rotgut, (2) screws an Eskimo girl and (3) wrestles a bear. He drinks the whiskey and stumbles from the bar to his next ordeal. When he returns, bloody and battered, he announces: "I did the bear. Now where's the girl I'm supposed to wrestle?"

I love this story because I failed the masculinity tests. I didn't play football past eighth grade, which meant I wasn't a real man. I had to gain acceptance by risking my life in various exploits, by getting drunk throughout my teens, and by making obligatory sexual efforts with women I didn't know, didn't like, didn't want. These initiations were not pleasant, but they weren't crippling either, and I'm glad I learned to play the macho game well enough to survive adolescence. I still hate football; I'm glad I'll never again have to make love with someone I don't love.

The scariest step in a boy's quest for manhood is sexual. The twins must make it with girls. They may not want to get close to girls yet, but the point of screwing girls is not to get close to them but to remove the homophobic barrier to closeness with the other boys, to prove heterosexuality so the boys won't have to feel unmasculine in their closeness to one another. This is an ordeal the twins must endure.

So our boy, trying to keep his grip on his throbbingly impatient little twin, exhorted by his male chorus, marches forth to find a female whose magic wand will turn him into a man. The quest is fraught with doubts and dangers, and he must choose her cautiously. To whom shall he entrust his nascent masculinity?

At first we need girls who don't scare us, who don't threaten our budding virility. We feel safest with smaller, weaker girls, perhaps damsels in distress who collapse upon us and make us feel strong and important. Yet our male chorus may propel us toward girls who are "popular" and beautiful, trophies that announce our masculinity to our fellows. A virginal 15-year-old boy's dream-woman might be a beautiful, popular, undersized, slightly mentally

retarded, depressed, 14-year-old anorexic (with big tits) who is running away from an abusive family.

These experiences are at least as traumatic and crucial for the girls as for us, yet we are barely aware of our partners as we go through this physically together and emotionally apart. Back in my day, in the sexual dark ages when virginity was valued (for girls and nerds) and pregnancy feared, there were a few girls who could be had, but since they'd had boys with far more expertise than we had, it took balls to expose our amateurish efforts to their possible ridicule. We certainly had no sense of their desperation, only the power of their comparisons.

But "nice" girls set limits on where they could be touched and on just how far the efforts could go, for example, touching only above the waist or through the panties, sticking it only part-way in. (We curried the girls' compassion with the myth of "blue balls," a painful, potentially fatal condition that would occur if a girl aroused us and then failed to relieve us.)

In those days, a nice girl tried to hold on to us by holding us off. She somehow knew that the audience for these sexual experiments was still the other boys and the invisible male chorus and that all we wanted was to get into her pants, and her primary power lay in frustrating us. How tortured we were, and how grotesquely we overvalued sex as a result. We might even have thought we were in love with whichever girl most maddeningly frustrated us.

What enormous power these children grant one another! The two combatants are sure to have very different agendas.

The sex is bound to be a disappointment if anything beyond survival was expected, and there is no way a horny little boy will respect anyone but himself in the morning.

MATING

Woman is the sun, an extraordinary creature, one that makes the imagination gallop. Woman is also the element of conflict. With whom do you argue? With a woman, of course. Not with a friend, because he accepted all your defects the moment he found you. Besides, woman is mother—have we forgotten?

—MARCELLO MASTROIANNI

WE MEN NEED WOMEN FOR MANY REASONS: TO feed and water us, to bear children for us, to point out reality to us. Once we've passed the hurdle of our own virginity, we don't really need women for sex: we might prefer them, but we can do that for ourselves, and we do. Mostly we need women to affirm our masculinity. They can do so by responding to us sexually. They can do so by reassuring us that we are strong and powerful. They can do so by loving us and nurturing us as our reward for being masculine enough—or as our solace if we're not.

When we choose a mate, a partner for a lifetime, should we choose the woman who makes us feel good or the one who makes us look good to our relentless male chorus? Our male chorus demands that we honor our masculinity before we can consider our comfort, our humanity, our soul. So we must consider what woman will make us seem more masculine, perhaps someone younger, dumber, poorer, more scared—or we can try for status. Or we may protect our masculinity by clutching our balls and escaping each eligible candidate just before the wedding bells. Can we have a real partner, or will that just make us look pussy-whipped? Do we want a girl just like the girl who married dear old Dad or more like the girl he eventually ran off with?

Our ability to fall in love, to go into that most revered of sacred insanities, requires enough comfort with our masculinity to join it with someone's femininity and feel enhanced. In order to do it, we must find a woman who doesn't scare us. If our mother scared us by depending on us too much or because we depended on her too much, if we felt her to be a threat to our freedom to be men, we have to find someone very different from her: less

seductive, or more so, less manipulative, more direct, sexier, quieter, whatever it was that seemed to make our mother a threat. But if our mother made us feel secure and proud in our masculinity, then we want to find that again in our wife. If we are really comfortable with our mother, we can even marry a woman who is a friend rather than an adversary and form a true partnership. The boy still inside us is one of the voices in our chorus and helps influence whether we seek a woman who will take care of us or a woman we can take care of.

What we need most in a mate is someone who can enable us to see and understand all those things to which our masculinity blinds us. Dare we find in a woman the lost part of ourselves, and by marrying become whole? Or are we still just measuring peckers with the other boys?

LIVING WITH A WOMAN

Man must partly give up being a man when he is with women folk.

—ROBERT FROST

MATING WITH A WOMAN IS ONE THING, PARTnering with a woman is quite another. One steady refrain from the men's chorus warns us that our balls will fall off if we come under the control of a woman—the choir keeps singing music from *Samson and Delilah*, warning us that a woman can shear us of our masculine glory and thus rob us of our strength. We approach each woman as if she is our mother come to punish us for our independence by taking away our puberty.

The average man feels fully masculine only if he can attract women, thus granting women terrifying power. And he must not only win her but also satisfy her. A woman can utterly deflate a man by refusing to be aroused or satisfied. ("I am the Earthmother and you are all flops." "I know the game. If you're not a stud, you're a houseboy. Which are you, baby? Houseboy or stud?" So goes Martha's test in *Who's Afraid of Virginia Woolf?*)

For a man to feel secure in his masculinity, he must satisfy a woman in many ways, perhaps in all ways. An angry woman makes us feel insufficiently masculine (unless her anger is based on jealousy, in which case the anger affirms the man's masculinity). A woman's anger terrifies men. It returns us to our childhood with Mom. We have learned from the other boys that women are attracted and pacified by a man's masculinity; thus, any anger from a woman must indicate that we are not masculine enough, so we pump up some more of it. We may even panic and become violent in our efforts to show enough masculinity to stop the woman's anger. Why can't women understand that we are showing as much masculinity as we can?

I don't think it's off-the-wall to speculate that most of the problems between men and women are related to man's panic in the face of woman's anger. A woman who misunderstands the male display of power may assume the man is trying to dominate her because he does not respect her. But a display of female anger, however justified, will only frighten the man into a more garish hormonal display. In men whose male chorus permits it, this might erupt as violence —the failing man's last-ditch effort to show enough masculinity to drown out her anger.

When we do marry, we play a new role, discovering the female perspective and the limitations of being male. Are we able to be partners with someone whose perspective is different from our own and then go through a lifetime with binocular vision? Or do we choose to protect our maleness from her femaleness, playing our male role to her female role, going through life obeying our militant chorus?

Our model of marriage isn't likely to have much to do with our wife's model. Our macho chorus might not let us hear her wishes and desires; when he gives advice on "How to Deal with a Woman," a man rarely tells his friend to ask the woman what she wants. If we are obsessed with our masculinity, we may ask our father, our priest, or all our friends how to deal with marriage but completely refuse to talk with the woman, our ostensible partner. Protecting ourselves from her anger comes before learning how to make her happy. I recall the thousands of years when men believed, as priests and rabbis had taught them, that women had more ribs than men; no one ventured to count a woman's ribs. Masculinity has little to do with being married; to be a husband means more than the art of acting macho. To be a husband means "to take thrifty care of domestic affairs." Much of what we've learned about being male involves escape from female control and the civilizing influence of women so we can join the company of other men out there in the wild.

We all go through masculinity training, and the stages of that training are similar for each man, but our models vary. Some of us, mostly those whose fathers fathered well, can adapt to marriage despite previous conditioning. Others, less fortunately fathered, must be dragged, kicking and screaming, into marriage—and, in due time, into counseling. These guys have devoted their lives to becoming men, despite their lack of domestic models; now they are asked to unlearn a great deal, and they are scared. They have yet to learn that masculinity and marriage are compatible. If they are forced to choose, their macho chorus sounds the retreat.

SERIOUS MASCULINITY

All men are not slimy warthogs. Some men are silly giraffes, some woebegone puppies, some insecure frogs. But if one is not careful, those slimy warthogs can ruin it for all the others.

—CYNTHIA HEIMEL

I'VE BEEN TREATING MEN FOR MORE THAN HALF my life—almost as long as I have been one. Becoming a man was not easy for me, and my adolescent failures of masculinity were hauntingly humiliating. It took me years as a therapist to realize that my experience was the usual one, that learning masculinity is a desperate, often devastating ordeal for men, especially if they think about it. Masculinity is won at such a price that it tends to be overvalued for the duration of a man's life.

Some level of masculinity gives us our character, our code of conduct, and defines what is expected of us. Carol Gilligan has described how boys and girls are raised differently. Parents prepare us boys to go forth from the family and take care of ourselves in the world, follow the rules, compete with the other guys, take control, and find women who will take care of us, We must succeed in these tasks if we are to become men, but if we succeed too well for too long, we develop problems of what I call "mascupathology."

Men treat women differently from the way we treat each other; mascupathic men do it to an extreme. Enchanted by the masculine mystique, mascupaths have trouble getting comfortable with women. They are tense and on duty, and they don't let down their masculine armor. Mascupaths can't relax when women are around, can't fart and scratch or sit in secure silence knowing that nothing is expected and no one will be angry or hurt. (As eight-times-married Alan Jay Lerner wrote for *My Fair Lady*, "Why can't a woman be more like a man? Men are so pleasant, so easy to please. Whenever you're with them, you're always at ease.")

In the film *When Harry Met Sally . . .*, Billy Crystal explains to Meg Ryan that men can't be friends with women because sex always gets in the way. I think men and women can and must be friends, but when men can't seem to do it, I don't think it's sex that interferes, it's gender—the macho need to make gender displays at women, and women's impatience with having to reassure men of their masculinity. This level of gender discomfort varies from man to man and tends to diminish as men mature and as their personal success reduces their dependence on masculinity as the cornerstone of their security. But

men in our society have a struggle on their hands to achieve domestic comfort. Their masculine choir follows them into their own houses and bedrooms, and they don't feel at home at home. A man's life may be a long, hard struggle with the demands of his masculinity, often conducted in loneliness, with only his invisible male chorus to comfort him.

I see these men who take their masculinity too seriously, and their lives are limited, lonely and often painful, but they really don't know they have a choice. They're doing what they believe the world expects of them, doing what will make them men and keep them safe from anyone who would try to rob them of masculinity. Some of them see everything in life as a contest they must win. They can become workaholics or street fighters or sports fans, and busy themselves with the male-to-male games, which seem safer than games women want to play with them.

Others devote themselves to following rules, to keeping life rational and fair. They arc comfortable only when the emotional level is so low that they can't get close to anyone, which may not bother the other guys who can't get close, either, but makes life with a woman threatening and contentious.

Some of the men who take their masculinity too seriously may turn to other women to reinforce it, reassuring themselves by scoring with woman after woman, spending a lifetime in courtships and never risking marriage, or marrying one while seducing others and thus gaining the efficiency of being able to fuck over two women with each sex act.

Any way we look at it, those men who take their masculinity too seriously aren't fit to live with and sometimes aren't fit to share the world with. What went wrong?

MEN WITHOUT MODELS

How sad that men should base an entire civilization on the principle of paternity, upon the legal ownership and presumed responsibility for children, and then never

really get to know their sons and daughters very well.
—PHYLLIS CHESLER

AT THE HEART OF THE PROBLEM OF MASCU-pathology is our society's bizarre attempt to raise sons without fathers or at least someone to serve as grown-up models for growing boys. I'm increasingly convinced, after three decades of working with men who can't live in comfort with women, that the problem is not in the relationship with the woman, or with the man's mother, or with the society, but in the boy's relationship with his father.

Boys know they're supposed to grow up to be like their fathers, and if he's there and the boy is not paying close attention, the boy will become a man just like his father. And if the boy finds something in the father that doesn't appeal to him, he may be able to correct it in himself. But most boys nowadays are growing up with fathers who spend little, if any, time with them. When the boy most needs to practice being a man, his father is off somewhere playing at being a boy.

Theories of human development keep assuming that fathers are there, actually living in the same house with the rest of the family, performing some useful functions, interacting emotionally with a wife and children, playing a role in his son's life, being a model for the boy. Such blissful days, if they ever existed, have now parsed, and fathers wield their influence not by their presence, but by their absence. Instead of real-life fathers, boys grow up with myths of fathers, while mothers, whatever their relative significance out there in the world, reign supreme at home and in the life of the boy.

If fathers have run out on mothers, in any of the many ways men use to escape women, then boys can't imagine that their masculinity is sufficient until they too run away from women and join the world of men. The fathers may have used work, sports, war, other women, alcohol, or drugs, or whatever they could come up with to escape home, and their sons would then equate masculinity with whatever they imagined the fathers to be doing that was more important than being at home with their sons. Boys who don't have fathers they know and love don't know how much masculinity is enough.

Fathers have the authority to let boys relax the requirements of the masculine model: if our fathers accept us, then that declares us masculine enough to join the company of men. In effect, boys then have their diplomas in masculinity and can go on to develop other skills. If the father is dead, the boy can invent whatever mythology suits him and imagine his acceptance, but if the father is alive but gone, then the boy can only feel his lack of acceptance. A boy may spend his life seeking that acceptance, the love and approval of his father, and with it a reprieve from the masculine striving. If boys can't get acceptance from their fathers, then they are dependent on the company of men to overwhelm the fathers' rejecting voices or the echoing sounds of paternal silence.

It is outrageous to blame mothers for not teaching boys how to be men. A woman may be president or pope or God with no trouble, but on her own she can't teach a boy how to be a man. A mother may give her son booming self-esteem, may imbue him with a wonderful sense of his specialness, but she can't have expertise on what he as a man is to do with that masculine specialness. Mothers, no matter how wise and wonderful, can only point boys in certain directions, but boys need fathers to show them how far they should go.

Few girls grow up without mothers, or at least some woman as a mother stand-in, but boys often see very little of their fathers and have no other man in the family who is involved enough to demonstrate masculinity. Most likely the fathers didn't get much fathering either, and the mothers got even less, so no one is alarmed by the fact that boys are being raised by mothers alone and that fathers are not teaching boys how to be men, much less teaching boys how to be men with women.

When I go around saying these things, pointing out my firm belief that a woman alone cannot expect to successfully raise a boy into a man, some of the younger women in the audience are uncomfortable and take me to task. Some hear me saying something sexist, perhaps encouraging women to stay in brutal marriages for the sake of the children, or to forgo childbearing when they can't provide the child with a father. I wouldn't go that far, but I am saying very firmly that removing men from the life of the family is likely to aggravate rather than resolve the problem of mascupathology in sons. Many mothers and many sons find themselves in the position of not having a man around. They are trying to be optimistic about it, and I am not offering them the reassurance they might prefer to hear. The mothers who have gone through the experience of trying to raise a son without a father's presence, and without a grandfather or uncle or stepfather in attendance, know just what I'm talking about, i.e., how lost the boy is in adolescence.

Women who have tried to raise a son alone may appreciate my acknowledgment that fathering is one function a woman cannot perform no matter how hard she tries. They have usually discovered what I'm saying, that if a man with a special relationship with the boy is not already somewhere in the network of the family, then one will have to be brought in to do the job. (There is a wonderful example of this in the movie *Parenthood,* in which the thoroughly competent Dianne Wiest finds herself raising a son alone, and he seems headed for disaster until her daughter brings in a boyfriend who is a mess in most respects but who knows how to get a boy through puberty.) When the crises of adolescence hit, it may be too late. If the boy is already hypermasculine, past his puberty and like toothpaste squeezed too far out of his tube, he will resist a new stepfather (or therapist) who is out to protect his mother from him and is trying to put him back in the child position. Every boy must have a man who is rooting for his masculinity.

It's hard to imagine how we can raise a better generation of sons until we have a better generation of fathers. The miracle in what seems like a hopeless paradox is what can happen to a man when he becomes a father—not just a sperm donor or a landlord but a man who nurtures children over time. If a man, even a fatherless father, will let himself learn from childraising rather than just trying to control or perfect his children, they can carry him through all the stages of human development from the other side and make him aware of how men and women develop, how masculinity and femininity are taught and learned, and how to become a complete human being. But if he is a fatherless father, having grown up without domestic models of men, he may see childraising as "women's work," and he may distance himself from the mysterious job of fathering and the disconcertingly enlightening process of childraising. He may thus miss his last chance while he lurks at the periphery of the family, protecting his precious masculinity from questioning its roots.

TREATING MASCUPATHOLOGY

What Can You Do With a Man?
LORENZ HART AND RICHARD RODGERS,
THE BOYS FROM SYRACUSE

FOR THE LAST 30 YEARS, I'VE BEEN TRYING TO free men, including myself, from the spell of the masculine mystique. My own struggle with it goes back even further. I was not a football-playing brute at a time and place when that was the masculine ideal, and the model my father had given me. I never thought I was masculine enough for him. Back in my twenties and thirties, I was still impressed with men who seemed more masculine than I, who were richer and controlled more things and people, who were freer to set the rules and even to break the rules, and who screwed more women. I particularly admired and envied the smoothly beautiful men who drove women mad with lust for them. I didn't seem to have the effect on women that my friends Bob and Charles and Fred and Barry had. I knew I could find a woman to marry me, but I wasn't sure I could find a woman to go mad over me. Luckily, I found and married a woman who stayed very sane with me. I still felt I wasn't masculine enough, and when we had a son, I was afraid I couldn't be the man he needed as a father. I went into psychoanalysis and complained about my mother's failure to make me feel manly enough. My analyst was a man, a man whose masculinity I respected, and he declared me masculine enough, and I got on with my life.

Wherever I turned in my profession as a therapist, I found men who feared they were not masculine enough, so I did what my analyst had done for me and what my father had failed to do: I assured them that they were indeed real men. But it took a while to realize that the men whose masculinity intimidated me, the macho men who could chew nails, the 14-year-olds who were sleeping with their teachers, the tycoons who could buy and sell me and everyone I was kin to many times over, these heroes of my fantasies also feared that they were not masculine enough, and they too were looking for reassurance, and they didn't get enough of it from chewing horseshoes, knocking up the faculty, and buying and trashing the world. They too needed a father who would tell them that their masculinity was quite splendid enough.

My father—the warrior, the athlete, the boss of the town, the object of my mother's lust—loved me as his boy but had never affirmed me as a man. As he was dying, I talked a lot about manhood with my son, who was 18, a champion athlete and a strong man in the mold his grandfather. My son and I could affirm one another. We laughed and cried over being one another's hero and that gave me the courage to finally talk with my strong, silent father

about how I saw him and how he saw me. Dad had no idea that I venerated him so. He thought he was a disappointment to me just as I thought I was a disappointment to him. All my life he'd felt intimidated by me add my power with words. We realized we just approached our manhood differently; we fought our fierce battles with different weapons. Once I knew he saw me as a man, I could hug him for the first time.

Why had we never discussed these things? One of the things about being men is that we don't discuss how we feel about one another. We do think about it, but we don't often put it into words. We accept one another and feel security in knowing that we love one another, but we don't say it. It's not manly—but it feels so good and it brings such peace from the masculine struggles. I try to remember how old I was before I could hug a male friend, and how sad I was that it took me so long, but even so, I could never hug my father until he was dying.

D. H. Lawrence, in *Women in Love*, wrote about the male need for closeness to other men, for an intimacy as safe and eternal as a man could have with a woman. This book and the movie made from it mean more and more to me as I get deeper into examining masculinity. Lawrence characterizes male intimacy by the silent (and not sexual) nude wrestling between Rupert and Gerald. After his friend Gerald dies, Rupert tries to explain to his wife, Ursula, why he needed Gerald, and Ursula finds it perverse and sees it as a threat to the marriage. Rupert acknowledges that he can't seem to have it, but he still wants it.

It isn't easy for men to get close to one another. We can work and play together, and even sit in silence together and feel great comfort; we might even be able, if we're so inclined, to wrestle nude, but most of us have a hard time letting one another see what's inside. We avoid closeness by talking about sports or politics, or complaining about women—anything that will protect us from revealing our loneliness and our need to share the burden of masculinity. After my uncle had his stroke, I'd take him to his club each week to ride around his golf course and finally just to sit with the other men. He never talked much before his stroke, and he couldn't afterward, but that was his life—being with the boys—and when he couldn't do it anymore, he finally told me that he loved me and then he died.

I like to bring men face to face with their fathers while there is still time, and then I try to connect the fathers with the grandfathers and expose the suicidal absurdity of our masculine models and our relentless male chorus. I can't always do this, of course. The fathers aren't always available, and they can't be joined well *in absentia*, but they can be unmasked and exposed, and that brings some relief from their power of disapproval. I find that what men most want to talk about, when the atmosphere is safe and it isn't too embarrassing to cry, is their failure to get close to their fathers. Just try keeping dry-eyed in an audience of men watching *Field of Dreams,* a film about playing ball with your dead father.

We can, if we're not too threatening, add new voices to our clients' male chorus. When we talk from our own lives as men, it seems to mean something to men. We can also direct men to books and films about the masculine experience. Almost every movie I've thought was worth seeing this year has been about the experience of men struggling with masculinity. I've sent male clients to *Field of Dreams, Born on the Fourth of July, When Harry Met Sally . . ., My Left Foot, Crimes and Misdemeanors* and *sex, lies and videotape,* all of which give them a different message than the one they've been getting from *Rambo* or *Rocky,* or some shoot-'em-up that glorifies men when they die for their masculinity. I'm not trying to give these guys wimp models or heroes of unmasculinity. I'm trying to show them that society is giving them permission to expose and question the

models they already have. All men need a variety of ways to be a man so we can be free to do whatever life requires of us and particularly to do whatever our marriage and our family require of us. Just getting men to question their models is a significant step.

Can female therapists help men with these problems? Of course, just as male therapists can help female patients with gender-related issues. And female therapists can help the wives and daughters of these men understand what is happening and what they can do to help. Therapists of whatever gender have to have enormous respect and sensitivity for the man's masculine strivings, his fear of female anger and female control, and his need for men in his life. Some men are more comfortable with female therapists, expecting more acceptance and less competition and disdain for failures in masculinity. Other men are comfortable only with a man. The client can choose where to start, but eventually a complete human being has got to be able to get close to both men and women, and maybe even be the same person with both.

I've had my fill of listening to men complain about women, and I fear I'm nearing my fill of hearing women complain about men. For a few years, I found the most enlightenment in life from talking with women about gender, about both femininity and masculinity. But lately, I'm spending more and more time talking to men about their masculinity, about the models they learned, about the voices in their male chorus, about our shared and contrasted experiences of being men, and above all about our fathers and our sons and how we all can relax the stranglehold of the masculine mystique. I think it's making me and them both better men and better people. I recommend it. ■

FRANK PITTMAN, M.D., *is in private practice in Atlanta, GA.*

A DAY FOR MEN

WHAT IS A MAN WITHOUT HIS SWORD?

By Terrance O'Connor

I AM THUMPING MY WAY AROUND THE DRUM SEC-
tion of the House of Musical Traditions. The
brochure in my pocket reads, "A Day for Men
with poet Robert Bly and storyteller and drummer
Michael Meade." It encourages the participants to
bring hand drums. Is this ridiculous? I've never
played a drum in my life. Am I really considering
buying one for a one-day conference? Yes. Yes, I
am. I select an inexpensive bongo and allow myself
to feel a little boy's excitement.

For some time I've been feeling that it's time for a
men's movement. Maybe this is it. As a therapist, I
have been concerned about how isolated my male
clients are from other men and how this makes them
too emotionally dependent on women. I see that the
lives of my male friends and colleagues follow a similar pattern. The old gang of fiercely bonded, adolescent, adult male friends slowly broke into isolated
family units. Perhaps we kept some of these friendships, but most faded. We made new friends, but
not as quickly as the old ones moved away or
changed or died. But even those of us fortunate
enough to have a number of close men friends have

lost that wonderful sense of tribe. I have been
keenly aware of these losses. I am ready for a day
for men.

I ride there with a new friend. On the way we talk
about growing up as men and our relationships to
our fathers. Later I see this is what always happens.
When men get together to talk about being men, the
first issue is always fathers. Almost to a man, we
were isolated from our fathers, who were also isolated from other men. It is the common wound, the
emptiness we all carry. My friend and I discover that
we both have alcoholic fathers, and I tell him about
a pivotal incident in my life. I was struggling in my
first year of high school. My father had just given
me holy hell for the scores I had received on a standardized test. I felt terrible. In my room, I went over
the results again and again. These kinds of test
results were new to me. Suddenly a ray of hope. I
realized that the numbers were raw scores. They
needed to be converted. I was astonished. In per-
centiles, my scores were in the nineties. Reprieved!
Vastly relieved, I rushed out to show my father. He
took the paper, looked at it in silence, and handed it

back to me. "Then why in hell don't you get better grades," he yelled. It was a dagger in my heart. When would I ever learn? Never a word of love. Back in my room, teeth and fists clenched, eyes brimming, I said a prayer: "Dear God, never, never, never, let me grow up like that son of a bitch."

WE PARK AND ENTER THE BUILDING. AT THE registration table in the hall we can hear the drums through the closed doors. I have never heard such drumming. It sounds primitive. We walk through the doors and are enveloped by drumming. We are early, but there are well over a hundred men here already, about a third of whom are drumming, Native American drums, bongos, African drums. I am bathed in this energy. Beneath my arm, the skin of my drum vibrates in resonance with its brothers.

Men are milling about by the coffee table. The trickle through the door is becoming a stream, the throbbing drumbeat is overwhelming. I take a seat near the back. I put my drum between my knees and prepare to join the chorus. This is new. I look about shyly. All around me men are glancing about, with shy, mischievous grins. We are little boys who have stumbled upon a wonderful secret. We are men in the first blush of rediscovering the harmony of our hearts in the beat of a drum.

Four hundred men have come. Four hundred men in search of a common thread. It feels like a homecoming. Meade tells a story that ends in a dilemma: kill the king, or kill the father. The crowd is divided into two groups: regicide on the left, patricide on the right. The groups argue with each other. A man on the right stands above the rest on his chair. "Kill the bastard. Off with his head!" he screams. "No! Never kill your father," someone on the left screams in return. Waves of emotion crash back and forth. A man in the middle who has joined neither group shouts out, "I will kill no one. I will break my sword." Bly jumps in with a caution.

"What is a man without his sword?" he asks. Meade challenges those of us who have not chosen; he questions our courage. I am unfazed. I think that the king is my future, and I will not kill that. Yet it is dawning on me that I have killed my father too many times already. He is a ghost. Can't I just let him fade? Bly has a good point about the sword. I will hold on to the sword. I will not fear my own power. I am not sure what all this means, but I am bathing in the tides of male energy.

An announcement is made that a sign-up sheet is available for those who are interested in creating an ongoing men's meeting. A few weeks later about 50 of us gather in the hall of a local church. This is the birth of the Men's Council of Greater Washington. What do we want? We want to drum. We want to dance. We want to talk, to make friends. We cannot agree on any structure or purpose. It is too early. We debate, argue, dance, drum. We begin to make friends. We resolve to evolve.

At this monthly meeting some of us decide to create more intimate support groups. In a few weeks I am sitting on the rocks overlooking the waterfall at Great Falls Park with seven other men, talking about what we want from one another, what we have to give. Above the roaring falls there is an air of quiet excitement. In the smaller group our sense of isolation begins to break down immediately. We are hungry for support. We begin to lay out our fears and our personal dilemmas as if we were laying down armfuls of wood we had carried for too long. As the weeks go on, our cares roll out. Thump, thump, our loads released. Some of us cry, perhaps for the first time in front of other men. The themes repeat: love, work, Dad. It is amazing not to be alone with this. An exhilaration begins to rise with the realization that we are experiencing a trust and understanding that are different from any we have experienced with women. It has something to do with intimacy without fear of dependence, ferocity without fear of destruction.

But it is not smooth or easy. We question whether there is too much hard-edged male energy and not enough gentleness. There is a struggle for direction, leadership. One of the men wants to take us to loftier realms of spiritual enlightenment. This requires his leadership but not his emotional vulnerability. The rest of us see a need to go inward, downward. Finally he leaves the group. Yet there is freedom for fierce confrontation that is quite productive. Ben, who is sitting on my right, is talking about his relationship with women. His tone is haughty. Someone comments on this.

"Yeah," he admits, "I guess I've got my nose up in the air a bit."

"Well," I put in, "that is a gentle way of saying it."

"Why," he asks, "what would you say?"

"That you are an imperious asshole."

He winces. The group roars.

"Takes one to know one," someone yells over the laughter. I smile in agreement. We all nod. It is a moment of truth. As a group, we have acknowledged our arrogance as our primary defense.

THERE IS A WEEK-LONG MEN'S CONFERENCE WITH Robert Bly, Michael Meade, the psychologist James Hillman and tracker John Stokes. I registered a long time ago, and now I regret it. I can't afford it. I am too busy. I really need time to myself rather than being pressed together with 100 men for a week. I call the day before to see if I can get out. Too late. Now I must admit that I am just plain scared. But what am I afraid of? Forced intimacy, competition, being judged and found wanting, being dominated by a group? All of the above. I like to have control of my little world. I know that I will not be in control there. Can I trust a group of strange men?

We are divided into groups of eight who eat, sleep and meet together. Our first instructions are to share our vulnerabilities rather than our accomplishments. Eight strange men sit in a circle in the forest and lay them out: fears of aging, body image, career crisis, marital problems, death of a father. I wonder if this intimacy is too fast, but my fear has been reduced a little.

We have left one world and entered another. Morning to night we are busy in large or small groups: conflict resolution, mask making, animal dancing, drumming, sharing. The eight of us are bunked together in a primitive cabin. I snuggle down in my sleeping bag and stare into the darkness. The pouring rain provides a background for the masculine symphony of belches, snores and farts. Is this genetic, or what? I chuckle, but I miss the sweet, soft femininity of my wife.

As the week unfolds, bright and dull moments are blended into the larger fabric. Animal dancing with John Stokes stands out. I can imagine looking at a videotape of a bunch of men growling like bears or hopping about like kangaroos. Out of context it would look supremely ridiculous, a quarry for those who would throw stones. But when Stokes, who has lived among the aborigines of Australia, takes on the form of an animal, he *becomes* the animal. Men have imitated and taken on the spirit of nature for far longer than they have lived in cities and protected their egos with cynicism. There is an awareness this week that male energy has broken away from its roots in mother earth and is creating devastation on the planet. There is a call to reconnect, to align with nature.

And there is sharing. Sometime during the week nearly every man stands and bares his heart to the group. The pain is breaking through. The burdens of isolation are dropped. Most of the sharing is about fathers and grandfathers, but some is of a more immediate nature. One construction worker, a man in his fifties, stands up and tells us that in all his life he has never let another man get physically close to him. This morning in mask making, his partner had touched his face with gentle fingers, (here he chokes up), "and I liked it." He bursts into tears. He is immediately surrounded by comforting men.

In this group, the older men, the elders, are given special respect. They are given seats in the front row as places of honor and to make them protectors of the younger men. The oldest, a man in his seventies, turns spontaneously to the group one day and tells us, "If I cannot protect you with my body, I will protect you with my spirit." We accept this as a blessing. All ages of men are appreciated. One afternoon, after an intense gathering, the doors to the meeting house burst open and a man in his mid twenties flies out and down the hill, discarding clothes as he goes. He hits the pier naked and running and dives off the end. A group of middle-aged men watch silently as he swims furiously across the cold, October lake. "Well," one says finally, his voice filled with admiration, "there goes the youngest."

By the end of the week, I am deeply struck by the many forms of male beauty: Stokes as a deer, cocking his head to hear a noise in the forest; Hillman tap dancing; Meade's smiling eyes and compelling drumming that invites us deeper into the forests of the mythical world; Bly, his silver locks like solar flares, arguing fiercely with the intense young man with lightning eyes and jet-black beard—warmth through friction. Big roaring bears of men, fierce flying falcons of men, deep diving trout of men. Gentle men, angry men, laughing men, men lounging naked on the pier, shaving at the sinks, peeing in the woods. Men gathering leaves for masks, men gathered in council around the fire, men hugging, men howling, men crying, men dancing, singing, drumming, men sitting alone in the moonlight, men wearing masks, men taking masks off. Men, men, men, men, men. Have I been so competitive that I have missed all this beauty? Is it me, or is it them, or is it us?

IT IS A YEAR AND A HALF SINCE THE FIRST MONTHly meeting of the men's council. Tonight I have brought my son. The council has evolved and grown. At this meeting there are more than 130 men, nearly half of whom are here for the first time. In the time for sharing, most of the men do not speak to the evening's topic, but rather they speak in mourning about their fathers. Given the number of new men, this is no surprise. When I stand up to share, I do relate my comments to one theme of tonight's program: the wasteland. I speak to the role of the men's movement in creating something other than a wasteland on the planet. Then, looking at the faces of the new men all struggling with the same old issues, I sense a unique opportunity. "As I am standing here," I say, "I suddenly realize I have an opportunity that I don't think I will pass up. I came here tonight with my son, Sean." My voice cracks and my eyes tear up. I put my hand to my chest and gulp some air. "This is hard for me," I continue. "Sean has just finished his first semester of college. Two days before the semester began, he broke both of his legs. He spent most of the semester in a cast to his hips, dragging himself around a big campus on crutches. He just got his report card. He got a 4.0. And I want to say, 'Sean, I'm proud of you, and I love you.'" I sit down to loud applause. Someone behind me strokes the back of my head. A few seats down, Sean has tears in his eyes.

A man gets up to say how important it is for elders to acknowledge younger men. A couple of other men take turns speaking, and then, to my surprise, Sean stands up. "I didn't think I would speak here tonight," he started, "but when my dad spoke, well, I had to say something, too. He hasn't always had it easy. He had some tough times growing up. He didn't get much support from his father. He went through a difficult divorce . . . from my mother and he's taken some risks. He's created a good private practice, and he's writing and speaking out on things that really matter to him, and I just want to say" he then turns to me, "I'm proud of you, Dad." If there is a dry eye in the house, it isn't one of mine. After the meeting a number of men come up to congratulate both of us. On his way out the door, Ben, from my support group, stops to thank Sean for his sharing. Then he grabs me and hugs me. "I love him, too," he tells Sean.

I T IS THE LAST HOUR OF THE LAST DAY OF THE week-long conference. My small group has decided to lift each person. We start with the largest. He is a big man, but the seven of us have no trouble lifting him high over our heads. I am the last. I fall backward without hesitation. I am surprised. I had anticipated the jolt of being caught, the force of being lifted. The sensation is not like that at all. The moment I stop supporting my own weight I am swept up, weightless. My descent and ascent are one. I rise gently as a cloud. My arms and head hang down. I am utterly relaxed. I have literally never felt so supported in my life. ∎

TERRANCE O'CONNOR, M.S.W., *is in private practice in Silver Spring, MD.*

Childhood is not only the childhood we really had but also the impressions we formed of it in our adolescence and maturity.

CESARE PAVESE

PHOTOGRAPH BY EUGENE RICHARDS/MAGNUM

PHOTOGRAPH BY POLLY BROWN/ACTUALITY

PHOTOGRAPH BY DONNA FERRATO/BLACK STAR

PHOTOGRAPH BY MARY ELLEN MARK

PHOTOGRAPH BY JOAN LIFTIN/ACTUALITY

The Pulse of the Family

INSIDE THE EXPERIENCE OF CHANGE

PHOTOGRAPH BY MARLA HIRSCH

THE MOTHER JOURNEY

TRAVELING ON AN UNMARKED ROAD

By Molly Layton

WHEN I WAS A DREAMY LITTLE TEXAS GIRL roaming the soft hills beside my home, I never thought "too awful long" of becoming a mother. My friend Puddin and I played fashion design and put on elaborate shows—the Months of the Year was a favorite theme—but we avoided dolls. I was a terrible baby-sitter, well meaning but inept. I preferred reading.

Nonetheless, when I was a 23-year-old graduate student and finishing up notes for an oral report on the *Philosophical Investigations* of Wittgenstein, I went into labor. My husband, Charles, and I dropped the paper off at a friend's house so he could present it in my stead at a philosophy seminar. Then we drove through Austin's balmy November twilight to the local hospital where David, six pounds and so-many ounces, was born early the next morning.

It was the ordinariness of becoming a mother that first struck me with a hot blast of wonder. Women had babies all the time, and yet in the great novels I had read, no one ever talked about the experience of becoming a mother, nor about the sticky details of birthing and nursing. As a person accustomed to research, I found even the most practical information hard to come by. This was in 1966, and I had to send off to France for a book about the new Lamaze method of childbirth. Because of the popularity of bottles, even the informal lore of breastfeeding, handed down from older to younger women, had been lost. It seemed I had landed at the center of human life and, surprisingly, found myself alone, engulfed in an inchoate and banal silence. How bewildering that a process as grand and scary and tedious as becoming a mother should be so *unremarkable,* literally not worthy of remark.

I myself was adrift in immaturity, about as unformed and malleable as my own small baby, who, I was now genuinely startled to discover, needed my intense concentration. Before he was born, the fetal David was a rosy abstraction in a blithely comfortable pregnancy. I glowed, I thrived, I brushed aside the cautionary tales. Not until I saw *Rosemary's Baby* much later did I consciously recognize the dark side there all along—the baby as parasite, the sinister "other" placed within the soul self by strange and alien powers, the invasive fetus vanquishing the helpless mother. This is not merely the baby of horror stories and psychotic nightmares: this is the shadow side of symbiosis.

Truly the infant David overwhelmed me. In his presence, I could neither read nor write. Eventually I abandoned my training in philosophy to study instead this small, willful and physically beautiful person. I had to push away my books and my thoughts so that I could hear his tiny demands. David was the person who made me pay attention to the world outside myself, to boiled eggs and washed sheets and flirty babies.

In remembering the early days of motherhood, I feel again that first shock of my own responsibility for this tiny, fragile person, the clear and compelling demand that I harden into a self, a definite persona, that I come out of the mists of graduate study. Because we stubbornly identify with the helpless infants, we human beings find it hard to accept the frail and tenuous humanity of the mother. We easily and sentimentally resonate to the emotional nurturance that we as infants need from mothers. Our infant selves are masters of longing and masters, too, in imagining the mother's unlimited strength and unlimited supply of love. The mother soon learns what is required to support the life of her child. Then she just does it. Whatever she thinks the child needs, that's what she does.

Specifically, the mother's motivation arises from her discovery of a terrible truth: she must keep and hold someone who is perilously fragile in a world now suddenly filled with danger. This demand—the demand to preserve—is so clear and so penetrating that it forces even the most philosophical among us to abandon our relativism and shuck off our existential blues.

It was the bald inescapability of my new identity that shocked me the most, sometimes making me proud of myself, sometimes guilty and confused, sometimes just exhausted. But of course I had to stay in role: my baby held me as I held him. Until

then I had never been so located in time and space.

The relationship with the baby is startlingly intimate, beginning with the privacy of the nursing relationship and continuing *ad nauseam* into all the untidy details of baby bodies. There is, of course, excrement in an amazing variety of textures, colors and odors, all necessarily subject to the intense scrutiny of the mother, a sort of high priestess of fecal matter. But there is also drool, milky spit, vomit, nose runs, boogers, ear wax, blood, urine—every drop and smear of which someone must wipe away, clean up and wash off. The mother must develop a kind of hardiness to face the flow of human juices, and a forgiveness, too. She learns to say, "It's alright," and comes to accept the body, its impolite realness, its frailty, its pleasures. The sly and secret delight of mothers, if I may speak for all of us, is baby buns—smooth, lusciously curved, actually tauter and tinier than the diaper would have you believe. The baby is such a sensualist that the mother must quickly learn the language of holding and stroking.

By the time Rebecca was born, more than three years later, David had trained me into a fairly sociable, level-headed citizen, less likely to drift airily around our tiny apartment like a balloon losing its helium. Consequently, Rebecca and I recognized each other as soon as the nurse handed her to me. Thanks to David, I knew then how to dampen my anxiety in the face of her howls of indignation, and I knew too the companionate pleasures of rocking idly with a soft baby in the empty spaces of the night.

Sara Ruddick has written of the disorienting experience of caring for a growing baby "whose acts are irregular, unpredictable, often mysterious. . . . In order to understand her child," Ruddick concludes, the mother "must assume the existence of a conscious continuing person whose acts make sense in terms of perceptions and responses to a meaning-filled world." A mother "assumes the priority of personhood over action." The foundation of the special mode of perception that Ruddick calls "maternal thinking" is an unquestioning belief in the continuity of the child-self despite enormous changes and even contradictory phenomena.

The illusion of a constant self is great: one long, loopy afternoon, when David was three years old and Rebecca still growing inside me, I tended my own and my sister's children. Suddenly, I was torn open with grief merely watching my young nephew toddle down the hallway stalking the voices of his older cousins and siblings. He wore David's recently cast-off blue suit, one that I had made, and viewed from the back, with the sailor hat on his head, he was for me the 2-year-old David come again. The surprise was that I had not known that *that* person was gone until he magically reappeared.

So there is a bittersweet paradox at the heart of maternal thinking. The mother aches for her child's growth, but the growth is double-stranded with her joy and grief. In the baby's cup-holding, the mother thrills at his growing skills—at his intelligence, at his demonstration of his capacity to survive without her. At the same time, she must prepare to leave behind the cozy and intimate warmth of the baby at her breast. The mother's rock-bottom interest in fostering the child's growth sets her up for the continual experience of separation.

But the most extraordinary demand that infant David made of me was the demand for a resolute good humor. It somehow went without saying that anything negative about myself would be bad for my child—if I threw dishes or sank inconsolably depressed on the couch or growled and cursed at the vacuum cleaner, not to mention growling and cursing at David himself. I had always been a shy, mild sort of person, but as a mother I experienced for the first time my own capacity to be a difficult, even toxic and possibly destructive force. I managed daily to be of good cheer but did not like the feelings that threatened to surface when I was tired or confused.

The first scary hint I ever had of real rage in myself was one long, hot, exhausting summer afternoon when the toddler David would not go down for a nap. After I had tiptoed out of his room for the fourth or fifth time, he cried awake again, and to my eternal dismay, I found myself struggling with the evil impulse to shake him really hard. To protect David, I did not return at once to his room, and so the two of us cried in frustration, David in his crib and me in the kitchen. Once, years later, I lost my temper with David, and my outrage escalated so rapidly that again I found myself perilously close to harming him and at the last minute kicked the door instead. The door was cracked forever after, and I never repaired it so that I would never forget. If we lived there still, I would repair the door now, as a ritual of the mending between the two of us.

But mostly I found myself cheerily, patiently, doggedly pursuing the tedious details of the day, at my worst like some unctuous master of ceremonies for my tiny and captive audience. "Okay," I would announce to a rapt but 2-month-old David, as we strolled down the supermarket aisle, "let's look for the tomatoes!" At my best, I was sweet and low-keyed and optimistic—the kind of sunny outlook that reflected David's demand for someone to instill in him a fundamental trust and interest in life itself. I felt it my duty to point out things: "There's a cow!" "See Daddy?" and even, "Where's David? There he is!" I would talk seductively or pretend to gobble up his foot or cover my face with his blanket and peek out at him, until to my amazement he slowly organized his responses, first arching his back, later squirming in delight, finally singing back at me.

This is the sort of stuff people love to hear about mothers, their delight in their children, their boundless energy, their unending fascination with the simple details of little bodies and daily routines. I like to hear it, too. But like all simplifications, it has its cost. What is the mother to do with her cynicism, her irony, her urge to throw the dinner plates against the fence posts?

Instead the mother constructs a world that is benign and uncomplicated, as bland and digestible as baby food itself. And as she does, she finds herself tuning into the simple shapes and rhythms of living: coming and going, big and little, time for this and time for that, a space for everything. It's a Richard Scarry world, where the happy baker waves hello to the happy mailman, the postal truck is marked "U.S. Mail," the bakery window announces "Bakery," and flowers bloom in the window box. Everything is labeled. I love this world, its industry, its relentless sunshine, its illusory security. Turning the pages of our book, sometimes I needed to believe its truth as much as the toddler on my lap did, feeling always my own longing for a world in which my child could grow up safely. I was saving the stories about automobile accidents and war and horrible diseases for later.

FOR BOTH THE MOTHER AND THE INFANT, THE tension between growing up and keeping safe is sometimes complementary, sometimes opposing. The toddler comes and goes, tumbling back into the lap of the comforting mother when he has stretched his fears too far. The mother fears as well, sometimes experiencing the child's own curiosity as the enemy to a safe life.

It seemed I sat forever on shady lawns, watching David in the sandbox and Rebecca on the blanket, the first of our line of cats stalking the fence of trumpet vines. The effort to be watchful was at times overwhelming for me, my eyes glazing over, my own stuporous emptiness such a bald experience that it seemed to constitute a kind of neglect. I could become a parody of caretaking, or worse, a sort of ghost-mother, out of whose bones the children arose, like mushrooms on a soft, rotting log. When we at last bought our first television set, I found myself pausing beside David as, legs out, mouth open, he watched the gray screen. Both of us were nodding our heads to Mr. Rogers' comforting balm,

"You are special." How much I needed to hear that myself.

Our family did most of its growing up in a little house on an ivied street right outside Philadelphia, where we shared the peculiarly interlocking lives of four busy people and one lone bathroom. As the children's range now took in front porches and sidewalks, then whole blocks, and at last the corner store and the elementary school a short walk away, we evolved a different kind of symbiosis. I could not hold them or pat bottoms so cavalierly, and they no longer fell asleep on my shoulder during the dark drive home from movies. As they launched themselves out, we learned to keep one another in our hearts, the kids down the block, me crosstown at the university. Sometimes I did not even know what they were eating.

When school days came, it seemed we were always madly preparing for the next day, a fictitious time when we would be "caught up," in contrast to the uncontained hysteria of today. To sit on a lawn now seemed the rarest of luxuries. In its breathless busyness, the family was then like some gangly machine, a relentless contraption with the cycles and epicycles set long ago and now lurching along according to its predetermined plan. In the maw of the machine, I struggled with fears of engulfment and, contrariwise, fears of an unknown name, the anger of someone cast into the role of Prime Mover, without whose energy the universe would grind to a halt. I knew it must all make sense, but who had the space on the kitchen table to sit down and figure it out? Often it seemed to me I risked confusing my kids with their laundry, that I spent most of my "quality" time corralling T-shirts and socks, driving them downstairs toward the laundry room, herding the stock from one machine to another, culling the dried clothes into baskets that sat around until our naked desperation made me sort and fold the contents.

In some ways, it got easier as the kids grew older: we were lucky, there were no big disasters. But it got

402

more complicated, too, because the very helplessness of the infant makes the mother's job clear. But an 8-year-old! Messy hair—who combs it? Mosquitoes—who sprays the Cutters? Since when did I become the nag representing order and civilization? It seemed that without me they would have eaten standing in the kitchen, wandering through the house and, most disastrously, plopped in front of the TV set. When did I become the vigilante for such trivia—grease on the sofa, shoes in the living room, wet towels on the rug? In the school years, the issues about discipline and doing things right mounted and mounted, and what I saw demanded of me was even more strength and indefatigable practicality.

Often I felt dumber than dirt. Could Rebecca spend TWO nights in a row sleeping over at friends'? "Duh, I dunno, gee, I have to think about that, duh." How could a person who wrote about Wittgenstein have a brain that just folded in on itself like that, pummeled by an 8-year-old's torturous pleas? My guts said, keep her home, but why? Isn't this just a tad overinvolved? Why not give in? Indeed, why not just let her drift from house to house on the block, eating white bread, wearing dirty, borrowed clothes, while I . . . I . . . get a massage! Wade in the surf, high-heeled shoes tossed on beach! Not brave or selfish enough to head for the beach, instead, pestered and squinty-eyed, I was forced to think about our rules, think about reasons, make decisions, revise decisions, change my mind, hold fast, explain, insist, give up, clamp down.

Because of this persistent centrality, the mother is the object, the bull's-eye, of her children's feelings, some of which could stun an ox. She is intensely loved, hated, seized, ignored. I was thunderstruck by the blunt distortions my children made of my motives and then at other times struck by their keen accuracy. In writing this, it occurs to me that they might say the same of me.

The children grew like kudzu, changing so fast that I struggled always with mothering by hindsight,

barely sizing up one situation as the child metamorphosed into another. I could not shake the anxiety that my faults were magnified in my children's character. As I watched them grow, it seemed inescapable to me that their own struggles were the fruit of my inadequacies as a human being. At my worst, I found myself growing more anxious as a mother, my heart so helplessly tied to my children's growth that their blooming became what I demanded for my own survival as well. *Be happy or I grieve*. What a strange demand.

Once a teacher spoke to me with disgust curling off her lip about how angry and helpless she felt with David, whose work then did not match his brightness. I was so numb with guilt and hurt that I stumbled away from the school, leaving behind another meeting I was to attend, forgot my car, and walked distractedly home.

I can actually remember the first time I felt my maternal anxiety lift a little and drift to one side, and I took a good breath. Charles had brought us to Rose River in the Shenandoah Valley to backpack for the first time. Unimpressed, I had trudged along on the hike up, had dutifully organized our site, had worried about animals, had risen with Charles in the night's drizzle to string tarps over our bare sleeping bags. The next day I sat by a rocky creek watching David and Rebecca and Charles make great Errol Flynn leaps across the boulders above. I should have been afraid for them, but instead I munched a chocolate bar and admired my children's easy grace, their springy legs, their banter with their father. The rain came again, harder, and we left early, hiking down the mountain in a downpour, only my feet dry in new boots, but the kids chirped along like hearty crickets, and my heart was luminously happy at the vision of the family I had seen.

I learned from this and other moments that my own pleasure in the children was vital, that my capacity to treasure them should not be taken for granted but had to be cultivated and treasured itself.

I later learned a Yiddish word, *naches,* the swelling heart a parent has for a child's accomplishments, an experience we did not label so well in my Anglo-Saxon family. I worried less and made more soup and lived for those moments when we were hanging around the dining room table running through our impressive recall of 101 hamburger jokes. To place a vase of feverfew gathered from the backyard in the center of this table was for me a way to celebrate our own gracious capacity to enjoy each other.

In taking on more celebration, I also put more limits on housework, not always with a clear conscience. The sacrifice of the mother is not only the guilty joke of psychiatry but also the heart of the family system. The siren call of the mother is *Never Enough*: she can never do enough, plan enough, love enough, make enough cookies. Whatever she does, it is not soft enough, not tough enough. When I taught my children to use the washing machine themselves, some observers thought this move was smart, and others, no doubt seeing the wrinkled products, thought it an act of callous neglect. Eventually I had the wondrous privilege of giving up housework altogether. When I took the lady from the cleaning service around the house to show her what had to be done, I noticed on my bedside table an empty glass with a comb and a walnut in it, just one of the little vignettes of inexplicable chaos that I was handing over to her, thankfully and with only a little embarrassment.

MY TRANSFORMATION INTO THE MOTHER OF adolescents was far more dramatic and demanding than I had anticipated: it seemed one day Rebecca was sunny and open and the next day she was dashing through the living room with a face preternaturally bright from rouge and slamming the door on her way out. The tiresome question was whether to let it go, confront her later, or get up to follow her out the door. On these dreary occasions I hated many of the feelings I had: I hated it when someone was not home when they agreed to be home, I hated worrying about accidents and city psychopaths, I hated seeing college applications languishing under piles of phonograph records, I hated the worries about drugs and alcohol. So I learned to follow Rebecca out the door.

My worry for the adolescent David befitted his position as first child and fitted, too, his growing differences from me, his lengthening and hardening into someone tall, utterly hip, mysteriously masculine. If Gary Cooper were a witty 17-year-old and read Walker Percy and delivered pizzas, that would be David then. I had a secret grief about David, a worry about his schoolwork and a worry, too, that we were like two boats caught in a squall. Any fights I had with David came to no good, more moods, more misunderstanding. But I watched in amazement as he and Charles fought: stormy scenes with a fine sun coming out afterward, the two of them closer than before.

My identification with David was so complete that I rejoiced to see him happy with his father and felt only the barest whiff of jealousy that he did not respond that way with me. When the Phillies headed toward the World Series, we all waxed rapturous in our family, but it was clear that the two tickets for the big game should go to David and Charles. It was for me the purest pleasure to stay home that afternoon, imagining the two of them making their way on the subway, swarming in with the happy crowds, sitting in the stands watching larger-than-life baseball.

The intensity in a home with adolescents is startling, and I am speaking here not merely of the jacked-up emotionality of adolescents or their ballyhooed rebellion but of the kind of intensity that the parents themselves must bring to the experience: the capacity to be angry, to confront sexual issues—including one's own—and the capacity to fight for trust and respect. So when Rebecca asked me not to observe in her classroom on Parents' Day, at first I said weakly, "Well, if that's what you want," a little miffed, and then something clicked and I said, "Hell, no. I'm your mother! I'm interested in your classes." Not only was I coming, but when I came in, *I would appreciate a gracious greeting from you*—which on that day she smilingly gave me, and I smiled back, and we had a fine time.

I wanted to be as powerful a mother as possible, stubborn and feisty if necessary, an opinionated debater, a force, a serious woman. In struggling to leave behind the Madonna-mother role. I was motivated not only by my own inner needs but also by a longing that my children see me as a real person and a belief that their development as well as mine depended on it. How else could they trust me with their confusion unless I was strong?

It seemed to me that the person in my family to whom my own development mattered most was the teenage Rebecca. I had always admired Rebecca with a mother's ready admiration for sweet youth itself: her clear peachy skin, her demure smile, her tender sympathies. But when Rebecca became convinced that her body was ugly, I found that it did no good to reassure her sweetly that she was attractive. Instead, I learned to fight with her, sometimes on the soapbox, ranting about Twiggy and Jane Fonda and Kim Chernin, sometimes yelling at her when she complained that a perfectly molded thigh was somehow "too big." Finally, whenever she had doubts, she would come to me, serious and trusting:

"How do I look? Truthfully!"

"You look wonderful. The truth."

She took me in through fighting.

So the shift for me was from the accommodating, observing mother of infants to the kind of lively, interesting, kick-ass parent that adolescents need. My marriage became lively and interesting as well: in helping each child to resolve ambivalence about the other parent, we were also forced to settle our own massive ambivalence. Charles and I never played half-court basketball with our children, but it seems that for both of us it was like that: good tracking,

swift darts and changes, sweat and worry, great jokes, heartbreaking misses, angry discussions about the rules.

Of course, you'd have to imagine that after a while the bleachers started to fill up with observers, people commenting on the players, speculating who was good stuff or not. Teachers, admissions officers, neighbors, owners of businesses, *your own friends*! Tillie Olsen's brilliant and raspy monologue, "I Stand Here Ironing," always touches my sympathy and my anger. It is a mother's sharp reaction to a telephone call to come for a meeting about her schoolchild: "*I stand here ironing and what you asked me moved tormented back and forth with the iron.*" That's the kind of raw emotion a person feels before the world court of opinion, which every mother feels. The worry of the mother is not just that she feels judged, too, although that happens inevitably, nor that she is disappointed in her children. The real worry of the mother is that the world court is so often wrong, so often smug, naming and sizing a child's soul so that the name itself is taken for the thing. Olsen's mother's plea to the schoolteacher is to help her daughter believe she is "*more than this dress on the ironing board, helpless before the iron.*"

I knew I had matured as a mother when I could listen to other people's questioning opinions of my children without crumpling inside with guilt and helplessness. As the kids revealed more and more of who they were deciding to be—making decisions about politics and clothes and friends—it dawned on me that my own children were becoming some of the most interesting people that I knew.

I HAD MY FIRST OUT-OF-BODY EXPERIENCE WHEN 16-year-old Rebecca flew to Cyprus for a month. She was by all appearances a solo traveler, but the physical distance she traveled was so palpable that I leapt the space anyway, staying awake all that night arcing across the black Atlantic, getting a little fuzzy for the London stopover, but reconstituting my presence well enough to make the final leg into Larnaca, my mother's intensity paralyzing any terrorists that might have been on board. When we got the call that she was safely in Nicosia, I was content that I had done my job well and settled down happily to my reading—Durrell's *Bitter Lemons*, histories of the Mediterranean, whatever would help me experience the new worlds of a faraway daughter.

THIS PROCESS HAS NOT BEEN EASY, THIS LAUNCHing of my children into space. In the middle-class family, the infants enter the family as if coming into a room that they then leave years later, by another door. It is this entering and exiting that has most vividly helped me measure the experience of mothering. I entered, too, but do not exit. My fear in watching the last kid leave was that a door would close, and I did not know then, although I do know now, whether our lives would continue to carry such rich meaning for each other.

This last May I flew down to Austin to launch David off to Brazil for three months, as far into exotica as his earnings would take him. We had lunch with his Portuguese professor and wife, a Brazilian couple whose excitement about David's journey made my own anxiety at least tolerable. We ran errands and made his tiny apartment shipshape; inevitably I had to reorganize the furniture. I came across a life-size cardboard figure of Indiana Jones in the grocery store, and the manager let me take it after I explained that my son was leaving for the Amazon. We propped it up amid the rearranged furniture, Indy giving a farewell wave of the whip. We talked a lot. I thought, as I often have, how kind, how funny, how artfully wise David is, how much I love his ironic dash and verve, his Thomas Jefferson poster falling off the wall, his cheap and tasteful cotton shirts. I made him promise to call us often in the beginning, knowing by now that all I need are some reports from the scene, some details of that particular reality, even if it is words about

theft and diseases and political unrest, no matter, its incantation of a real place holds me securely.

SPRING 1988 WAS REBECCA'S LAST TIME AT HOME before she too went off to college. That May, during my daily walks along the Wissahickon Creek, I found myself admiring the dogs accompanying their walkers. How nice it would be, I imagined, to get a dog. Maybe in the next year. The dog and I would exercise together up and back Forbidden Drive to Valley Green. She would bound along enthusiastically the way young dogs do. I would be the conscientious owner, careful to train the dog thoroughly and consistently—a reader of dog books, a builder of dog runs, a groomer of dog coats.

It was with a sad shock that I realized the true source of these fancies. One day while reading a short story, I heard one character tell her fictional lover, "Pets are only child substitutes." At that moment, I understood that my happy-dog fantasy was a cover for the decidedly bittersweet departure of Rebecca at the end of the month.

Part of the fantasy was clearly to do a better job with the dog than I was sometimes able to do with Rebecca, who, as the young daughter of an overworked doctoral student, had too often bounded off to school with hair that needed cutting and socks that needed matching. But the truth is, I had to admit, I could never focus on haircuts and socks for long. They were not all that interesting. I groomed Rebecca in other ways. When she had a headache, I tranquilized her with hypnosis and together we made the pain shrink and disappear. I taught her how to write with good, blunt Anglo-Saxon words instead of long, dopey Latin ones. Driving the long route across the river to her new school, we talked of Carol Gilligan. I fought the dark angel in her that would convince her to hate her own body. And always, I insisted that she take herself seriously.

I walked along Forbidden Drive thinking of all the wise and memorable things I still wanted to teach Rebecca: Travel abroad whenever you can. Learn the names of wildflowers. Watch out for the big trucks and tanks. Talk to your teachers. Did I tell her well enough how afraid I am of nuclear war? My neglect was so vast, it made my teeth ache. But I did not remember to say it all, and we were caught in time's implacable grind. Before us was a slant of light, an open door. *There was no shutting it*. Our life together was measured then in weeks. My physical grief was bound only by the thrill of watching my last child step into the glare of a vast and uneasy world. ■

MOLLY LAYTON, PH.D., *is in private practice in Erdenheim, PA.*

THE FACTS OF LIFE

LEARNING TO CONNECT THE DOTS

By Fred Wistow

FIVE, MAYBE SIX, EXCITED BY HER RETURN, WANTing to share something with her—a bit of news, myself—I burst into her bedroom. The unexpected darkness there told me I had done something wrong. Faint evening light edged the closed venetian blinds. I sensed her presence in a corner. There in the shadowy dark, my mother stood, undressing.

The underneath of her, the body below the protective clothing I had always known her through, was visible as if for the first time. Soft, fleshy parts of her I had felt but never remembered seeing now suddenly appeared, sickeningly alluring and, I somehow knew, to be avoided. Dark bits of underthings, flashes of metal and straps stretched tightly about her body held her in, covered up the rest of her. She seemed so complicated—disparate fragments of translucences and opacities, inviting pools and intimidating depths.

Her front leaned forward slightly. As if tied behind her back, her hands were awkwardly undoing one of the contraptions. She smiled uncomfortably. "You shouldn't be in here," she said in that strange tone I had only overheard from other rooms. We

were confused. I blushed, wanting to look up at her and afraid to. I wanted and feared that fabric and skin in sharp contrast. I could not say anything.

I was stopped. For some reason, I could not run into her arms and be held. The joy I ran into the room with had been replaced by spooky unease. How much I had wanted to kiss her ears, smell her powderiness, feel her fleshy presence and be lost in the infinite softness of her, making her laugh with my attentions.

But now there was some boundary not to be crossed. A unity had been destroyed. A formerly unqualified haven, she had suddenly developed limits the nature of which were still unclear but whose emergence into reality had been thunderous.

IF YOU WANT TO BE A SEX THERAPIST, A CERTIFIED sex therapist, the American Association of Sex Educators, Counselors and Therapists requires you to experience something called a Sexual Attitude Reassessment (SAR). In addition to small group discussions, the SAR workshop, which is also open to couples and singles who wish to enhance their understanding of human sexuality, includes—indeed, is notorious for—the viewing of sexually explicit films.

I am not a therapist (sex or otherwise), nor am I (currently) part of a couple, but the moment I first heard about SARs something in me clicked; I wanted to line up for one instantly. It felt like a challenge. The idea of watching dirty movies with a group of people was scary enough—sex is supposed to be *private,* isn't it? Isn't that the message that I, and almost everybody else I knew, had been given since childhood? But then to go on and *talk* about the dirty movies seemed startling: what would happen if you took an essentially private activity—sex—and made it shamelessly public? What secrets would come out?

The very existence of SARs implied that perhaps sex didn't have to take place—as it had throughout my life—only behind closed doors. My family's attitude about sex had always been clear; it simply didn't exist. Throughout adolescence, I had constantly discussed sex with male friends, but there, too, something felt hidden. Often paradoxically prudish about explicit details, these conversations had a nudge-nudge, wink-wink quality to them, as if life took place only in a locker room, as if to talk about love, anxiety, or shame might leave a dangerous mark against one's masculinity. And female friends generally seemed to prefer to focus almost exclusively on the feelings aroused by sex, as if to discuss its embarrassingly physical aspect might debase what they felt.

Why was all that so? Why was it all so *charged?* Maybe the experienced professionals who designed SARs had something to teach about why talking about sex—what we feel about it, what we do when we engage in it—is so upsetting to people, me included, and why it therefore remains off limits. I wanted the secrecy of sex, the *mystery* of sex, revealed and explained.

And then I also wanted to test myself, to see what

prejudices and fears would pop up after being exposed to what for me was an incredibly wide range of previously unseen sexual activities. What might others find erotic that I would see only as disgusting or repulsive? In other words, I suspected that the SAR might answer the question: what made sex so "unspeakable," in both senses of the word?

THERE WERE ONLY 11 OF US, ALL VERY STRAIGHT, very middle class, not a weirdo or sleaze among us: five couples who were broken up for our discussion groups (by chance, four of the five women were housewives)—a fiftyish salesman and his wife, in matching jogging suits; a sincere young minister and his wife; a black academic couple, both in their fifties; an attractive young lawyer and his attractive young wife; and an energetic, small businessman and his somewhat younger wife; all in therapy, all sent to the SAR in the hopes of improving sexual communication (although only the salesman revealed why he was there)—and me, alien single on this tiny planet of couples. Exceptionally quiet at first, we all managed to affect an air of remarkably false calm.

Our leader, Frank, certified sexologist and former schoolteacher, opened the workshop by reading us an allegedly humorous passage about society's long-standing queasiness about the word "f-u-c-k." Then, our first film, a tame animated short, showed a Smurf-like Adam and Eve experiencing something like the shame and confusion of puberty as they are forced to confront new parts of themselves suddenly popping into view.

The film is so sweet and Frank so earnest that we mistakenly begin to entertain the idea that we know more than we thought we did and that this whole weekend may turn out to be a piece of cake. We smile in recognition as the comic cries of our cartoon forebears—"What are *these* things called, God?" "What are they *for?*"—remind each of us of more innocent days.

IT'S WHEN YOUR DICK GETS HARD." TOMMY WAS defining "boner" for me, a word I'd heard in a joke. We were walking down the steep hill to Arch Street on our way to school, a few blocks away.

"What?" I said. I'd heard him but somehow couldn't understand. It was one of those times when one part of my brain was working so hard it prevented some other part from absorbing what my ears were hearing.

"It's when your dick's hard," he repeated, a little impatiently. Two years older, he was as embarrassed teaching as I was asking. We had dropped our standard comic personas so that real information could be conveyed, but without them the subject matter was too intimate. There was something sticky in the air between us, as thick as the fog in my brain. Things felt improper. The faster I got it and the topic changed, the better for both of us.

He elucidated: "Like when you wake up in the morning, or you see a girl, and your dick's hard."

"Yeah," I said, still confused.

"That's a boner."

"Oh," I finally realized, *"that."* A rush of shame and desire flooded me as I remembered something:

A traveling amusement ride had double-parked on the block, recorded calliope music blaring from its primitive speaker. Garish yellow-and-blue mesh fencing partially obscured the ride, whose name— the "up-down" ride? the swing?—nobody knew. Two sets of fire-engine-red stairs faced each other, like the letter V with setbacks, forming two sets of bleachers. The whole contraption was suspended from a bar and, when pushed and pulled by the ride man, would swing back and forth like a giant cradle.

I had sat huddled on the next-to-the-bottom row, hands gently cupping the safety bar, scared and excited as the arc increased. On the uppermost tier opposite me was Christine, her dungarees tight against her thighs, her precocious breasts stretching her sweater, her long hair fanning out on the downswing, her arms outspread, her half-mocking, half-

real screams, her smile, her legs, her hair, her self filling the air, filling my chest. I could not swallow. I wanted to envelop her, be enveloped by her. The exaltation of her presence and the butterfly excitement of the sight and the motion, the sunlight reflecting off the central suspending bar, had produced in me a powerful resonance, a stiffening focus of excitement in a body filled with excitement.

That has a name, I'd just learned.

"Thanks, man," I said to Tommy.

Incredible how everything has a name.

FRANK STARTS THE SAR'S FIRST REAL FILMS. THE moment is ripe with anticipation. Will the secret of sex become apparent by *watching films?* There are lots: videos, photomontages, 16-millimeter shorts, some put together by sex institutes (whatever a sex institute is), others clearly porn films.

What do we see?

First, a series of stills of. . .vaginas: opened, closed, shaved, natural; then a similar display of penises: limp, erect, ejaculating, detumescing. The room is quiet. Nobody jokes, nobody coughs. Nobody *moves.* Sex is serious.

A film of women masturbating then follows. They stroke only their clitorises, no breasts, no thighs are touched. This single-minded focus on genitality is in stark contrast to the next film, in which a man, after hygienically examining himself for testicular cancer (presumably the results were negative), lies down on a silk-sheeted bed, thoroughly oils his naked body and, in colorful close-up, masturbates while inserting a vibrator into his anus.

At the break, our group is a little stunned by what it has seen and its own reaction. Was he gay?, some of us wonder, as if that would explain something other than our own homophobia. The elaborateness of his premasturbatory ritual seemed to our conventional minds a strong indication of homosexuality. Frank assures us, nonetheless, of the star's heterosexuality.

"I don't even know what I think," I say, confused. "I just watched a movie of some guy jerking off, shoving a dildo up his ass. Is that okay? I mean, do I have to stick a dildo up *my* ass now when *I* jerk off?"

No one has an answer.

"Are we ready for more?" Frank asks, rubbing his hands gleefully, the leer in his voice palpable. His joking manner—that we're there to be titillated, that this is somehow the last place on earth you can see sex films (every video store in the country notwithstanding)—doesn't work. The films unsettle us, but if anybody's turned on by them, they're not saying.

Back to the screening room.

Grainy footage of two smiling lesbians on a playground swing, then naked on a bed, making love. A well-made, late-'70s pre-AIDS documentary on gay life in San Francisco depicting, among other things, two men happily engaged in anal intercourse.

The group is really uneasy at the break. Nobody seems to care about the lesbian film (did we even *see* it?), but for all of us, women included, male homosexuality has touched an uncomfortable nerve.

"Well," says the salesman, shaking his head, having given it a lot of thought, "I can take the two women. But I just—I'm sorry—I just can't accept two guys butt-fucking. I just don't understand that." Tight-lipped, the women gently nod.

We go on to theorize why male homosexuality is more troublesome to us than female homosexuality. We discuss the problems of penetration, the messiness of semen. We analyze penises and asses. We examine the lack of symmetry in our reactions: why aren't the women as uneasy in confronting lesbians as men seem to be about male homosexuals?

Well-meaning, curious, prejudiced, we try, to the best of our analytic abilities, to understand what our limits of tolerance are. But we can't figure out what's at the root of our discomfort, even as we fail to take note that we are discussing matters most of us have never discussed before.

"I didn't even *know* there were homosexuals when I was a kid." It's Frank helping us out. He's speaking in that can-you-believe-this-kiddies?-aren't-you-filled-with-wonder? tone of voice used by hosts of children's cartoon shows. "My *parents* sure never told me anything about sex."

Everyone in the group, from 28 to 58, agrees. We all grew up in families never talking about the one subject that obsessed us most.

"Do you want to know what my sex education was?" he asks. "My friend Bernie told me once that if you want to drive a girl wild, really wild, you just wiggle your tongue in her ear while you wiggle your pinky in her pussy. 'They go cra-a-a-z-y,' he said."

We laugh.

"*That* was my sex education. And every time I ever made out with a girl after that I'd be right in there, wiggling my pinky and wiggling my tongue." Each time he says the word "wiggling," his pinky pantomimes the action. "And as far as communication goes, what do you think I kept doing after I got married?" He holds up his pinky, moving it slightly. He's told this story before.

"After five years of marriage my wife turned to me in bed one night and said, 'Frank, would you *please* stop doing that. It doesn't do a damn thing and it drives me *crazy*.' Only she didn't mean 'crazy' the way Bernie did. So I stopped. . . . My sex education was complete."

Laughter abates our tension. We're relieved to learn that even the expert, deep down, has lived a life as riddled with ignorance and secret fears as is our own. Is this the secret of sex: nobody knows what they're doing?

WHEN I WAS A KID, I'D SOMETIMES CRAWL WITH exquisite furtiveness up to my parents' bedroom door. There on the floor I'd lie, barely breathing, proud of my stealth, and listen, waiting to hear, out of their muffled and throatier tones, a secret. Unmasked, their voices lacked the jovial faces with which I was familiar. From those different tones I expected to learn different facts, startling ones, about me and "the older one," my brother—that we were, for example, adopted or hated. The real facts never came.

The search for the real facts went on in my parents' absence as well. I'd hunt through dresser drawers that always seemed to contain my mother's things rather than my father's—the aroma of perfume, strangely soft garments, spangled pocketbooks and sequined scarves that spoke of a forgotten glamour and excitement.

On one such scavenger hunt through my mother's lingerie drawer one early teenage day, I discovered a gross of Trojans. A gross! Did that reflect a pattern of hyperactive coupling or merely a budget-minded lifetime's supply? I had no way of knowing.

I had discovered masturbation by then and stole one of the remaining 137, wondering, as I did, if my theft would prove as obvious as my pounding heart feared it might. I retrieved my treasure trove of clipped-out photos from the *Daily News* and lay on my parents' bed. (In those days, cheesecake seemed more precious than today and therefore worthy of preservation. In the summer, though, bathing suit season, supply increased dramatically as the paper managed almost every day to print a shot of a beauty caught lounging on the beach at Coney or Orchard above a caption whose heading read something like "W-h-e-e-w!" While an editor somewhere might have argued that such pictures were run solely to fulfill the noble journalistic obligation to report what a scorcher the day before had been, the not-so-subtle leer behind the inevitable pun that described the girl herself as capable of raising temperatures was not lost on my lascivious eyes.)

I examined some of my cherished but overly familiar (oh, how too quickly overly familiar) pictures for a while and when I got hard thinking of touching the soft, unattainable, swimsuited bodies (like Pavlov's dog, I may even have gotten hard on simply *seeing* the container in which my harem was

kept—an empty reel-to-reel magnetic recording tape box), I opened the little metallic foil pack and pulled out the contents. A rubber. It was tightly rolled and, unlike its lubricated descendants, covered with a thin powdery coat.

I unrolled the object down the length of my prick which, reaching for the new, swooningly ached with the novelty of the sensation, straining with delight, and in its straining seeking to increase the delicate, teasing, eye-closing pleasure of being completely covered by a sheath so thin and light and which, most miraculous of all, was not my hand. Soon, too soon, my body began to arch, then pulled tight as I shot myself into what now, as I was returning to earth, had become merely an encapsulating device.

Crash-landed, I lay still for a moment, then checked for damage. Seeing none, I hid all signs of my trespass, certain my parents would eventually discover it. They never did. Or if they did, they said nothing; Raskolnikov went unpunished.

A new era had dawned: a secret of theirs had been replaced by one of mine.

The films go on.

A bisexual narrates his split-screen life: we see him democratically having sex with, first, his girlfriend, and then, his boyfriend. A comic film about a first date—from pickup to dinner to sexual advance and conquest to good nights—in which roles are reversed and the woman acts out what we've traditionally come to expect as male behavior, produces titters from the audience for the first time.

But we're quiet again as a mélange of hard-core slides of group sex flashes before us, while on the soundtrack, Roberta Flack inappropriately and repeatedly sings "The First Time Ever I Saw Your Face." Next, a young black couple make love in an open field.

At the breaks we now talk only briefly about the films which, shocking as they may be, have become mere jumping-off points. Our group discussions are turning more and more into public confessions. We seem compelled to aerate our twin sins of fear and ignorance and thereby, perhaps, dispel our shame forever. As for content, female orgasm, the onset of menstruation, and penis size tend to demand an inordinate amount of our attention.

AS KIDS, WE KEEP REALIZING, NONE OF US GOT guidance about sex from our parents, and this single fact starts to grow in significance. ("Maybe that's why we're here this weekend," someone observes.) In the midst of our families, we each maintained a hidden counterlife of proliferating fantasy and confusion, just as our parents must have done when they were kids. And everybody knew everybody else had secrets, but everybody somehow also knew that to let them out of the bag would be impossible. And so everybody sneaked around a little, trying to uncover something, but basically everybody kept mum. And crazy as it all may be, that silence continues to be the way we approach sex today, as alleged adults. *We* don't know how to talk to anybody, either, let alone to *our* children.

Like Frank, we learned what little we did from the streets, picking up misguided information from slightly older friends who had learned whatever they knew in some similarly offhand way, and this garbled oral tradition wound up as gospel. And, incredibly enough, our kids are doing the same, only, of course, they have TV to help them.

We start to make generalizations, which sound like sexist clichés but which, our dues having now been paid by our film-watching, we somehow have the right to utter: Men view sex as a physical act, women view it as an emotional one. Men see sex as an end; women, as a means. Men are trained by the culture from boyhood on to view women as objects; only lately has the culture been teaching women to view men as anything other than people. We make distinctions, we point out differences, we specify.

The group is on a roll, but to where is unclear. We're like a PTA or Concerned Citizens meeting,

well intentioned, but off the mark. We're not getting anywhere near as graphic as the films we've been watching, and we're not evoking deep feelings either. Unable to find the proper vocabulary to give voice to that hidden counterlife we've acknowledged exists, we *still* seem, as always, to be ignoring it. Our propriety keeps it all sanitized.

TOMMY WAS OUR SEXUAL PATHFINDER. GROWING up with two younger siblings in a one-bedroom apartment, Tommy kept the door firmly closed on the dissatisfaction he felt with his tight living quarters and his father's abusive alcoholism by displaying a boisterous bravado. Slightly older, a lifeguard in the summer, concerned with clothes, strong, tall, funny, most of all loudly funny, he seemed, simply, unafraid. Everybody else had issues, fears. For some it was intelligence or size or parental occupation or their own possibilities in life. For most of us it was our would-be manhood, sex. Tommy, though, seemed to live in a special realm, beyond shame and fear.

While the rest of us on the block felt as comfortable around girls as we might have felt around extraterrestrials, Tommy, to our amazement and awe, began having real-life encounters with them. If an actual member of the opposite sex could be attracted to one of us, how could it be to anyone other than Tommy? His journey down into the church basement with Judy Judge one hot August night was a landmark event in our consciousness, the first genuine sexual experience anyone could verify.

Judy had arrived one day from nowhere—no one knew exactly where she lived—as if in answer to a casting call. She was unkempt, her hair straggly long before that style was to become popular. She spoke with a mild lisp, and to top things off, her lazy left eye would gaze off into the distance whenever her right was brave enough to look at you head on. Defective, but a girl alright. Tommy managed to attract her gazes, and before we knew it they had a "date" for Saturday.

The date had somehow become a public event. A bunch of us waited by the church with Tommy, who had dressed in new, white dungarees for the occasion. At eight or so, Judy answered our question by showing up. Her usual messiness looked neater, as if arranged. Tommy invited her inside the church, and the two of them made their way down into the darkness. Even though his mother was a principal member of the congregation, Tommy, true to form, was utterly unconcerned about any consequences from his sacrilegious trespass.

The rest of us hung out on the stoop, wondering what, if anything, was going on down there. We talked about how Mantle had been doing lately batting righty, when one of us grabbed Howie's wallet out of his back pocket. We tossed it back and forth for a while, outside his reach. "Fuckheads!" he shouted when the contents spilled onto the sidewalk. The old ladies sitting on beach chairs down the block turned at the sudden noise, shook their heads at what they saw, then resumed their obliviousness to us. Howie picked up his stuff as we waited for Tommy to come out.

At last, he did. Orpheus, he emerged, discovering under the bright glare of the streetlight how his fashionable white dungarees were now smeared with black grime. His loud whoops of laughter brought still further attention to himself, while at the same time helping him to transcend the ridiculousness of the moment.

A minute later, Judy appeared, her dishevelment worse than ever. When she and Tommy had descended, she had been the focus of attention, the desired, mysterious, albeit imperfect Female. While not very pretty, she had possessed an earthy allure. Now she was a used-up, discarded, repulsive *thing*. Tommy's grime was a comical badge of honor, Judy's was a defilement. Red-faced, Tommy mocked her with laughter. He had conquered something at her expense and hid whatever doubts he harbored behind his pride.

Tommy went up to change his pants. We waited. Judy stood around confused. It was suddenly and awkwardly apparent that she had expected to be taken out and that she was still waiting for the "date" portion of the evening to begin.

No one spoke to her; no one even knew how. We waited for Tommy to come down, to show us the next step. But when, cleaned and refreshed, he reappeared, Tommy said nothing to her either. As he led us all down the hill to the pizza place, it was as if she were not there.

But she was. Judy followed 10 steps behind the group, still magnetically drawn to Tommy, who was filling our incredulous ears with the story of how this being trailing behind us had gone down on the floor of the church basement amid the boxes of mimeograph materials and Christmas decorations and tried to give him a blow job but, unable to position herself in the darkness, failed and, at his insistence, gave him a hand job instead.

Tommy shouted the comic details of his adventure into the night. We laughed in nervous disbelief, too afraid to turn around to actually look at his costar. In tow to our cruel contemptuousness, Judy followed, waiting to be told what, if anything, would come next.

T HE FINAL FILMS: AN OLDER MAN PICKS UP A young coed and back in his apartment, for a mind-numbing eternity, we see his penis enter her vagina, then leave, then enter, leave, etc., etc., intercut periodically with expressions of mutual ecstasy, e.g., heavy lids and slack jaws. This goes on so long we feel beaten.

With the next film a different note is struck: a Swedish couple in their seventies make love, and then a real-life quadriplegic narrates an extraordinarily touching film. We follow a day in his life from the science lab where he works back home by wheelchair to an afternoon tryst in bed, catheter and all, with his tender and patient girlfriend.

Some of us are disgusted by the aging and inoperative bodies in these films, but most have been inspired by what we've seen.

"I never thought about handicapped people making love," says the minister's wife. "It was beautiful. It really shows you how sex is about bodies but that it's about more than bodies, too."

"And the old people. That they were together all those years and still felt a physical connection. I thought that was great," says the young lawyer.

What secret is coming out now? Everybody needs sex. *Every body.* No matter *what* that body looks like, even if it's not young and beautiful. And the pleasure the old and the physically impaired derive from sex is no less than that taken by the young and the beautiful bodies we've been watching all weekend.

In a way this insight is so contrary to what we generally think about sex that it takes a while for the power of it to sink in. We *all* need this stuff, whether we're fat, old, disabled, or playmate of the year. The more we are obsessed with how we look, in fact, the less chance we may have of connecting in as loving a way as the Swedes or the guy in the wheelchair.

Our spirits continue to rise with the last two films, no longer graphic. Gay senior citizens talk about the pioneer days of their sexual youth. And finally, a prim and pudgy Minnesota schoolteacher points out how prevalent are our cultural restrictions on touching each other and then goes on to preach the necessity and miracle of touch not only for the young but for all of us.

Who can keep track of what it all means? On the most cynical level, none of us could dispute that the less explicit a film was, the more openly we received it; the less intimidating the characters on screen were—the less they made us feel inferior—the more we could admire them.

THIRTY, DIVORCED, I AM DRIVING TO A FAMILY wedding with a girlfriend. We have spent the weekend together at a romantic country inn being romantic. It has been lovingly sexual. In the car we continue to kid around. She playfully lifts her skirt to reveal a flash of thigh, giggling with delight at the power she can exert over me simply by showing me parts of her body, the sight reminding me of past joys, promising future ones. We are in a cozy bubble of our own.

As we pull up to the catering hall, the bubble bursts. I notice how the lightness and playfulness of the past two days are slowly disappearing; my desire to hold and stroke and kiss her is ebbing away. I give her an almost grandfatherly embrace before we go in, a final hug before sentencing. I see my aunt observing us through the window.

By the time we're inside, I am struck by how completely neutered I've become. The weekend's spell is gone, a distant memory. If I were now to display sexuality in any way—even a light kiss—I would probably shock myself as much as my relatives. The same behavior that had gone unnoticed in other public places would, here, under the watchful eyes of my parents and aunts and uncles, be unthinkable. Exhibitions of affection are inappropriate in my family; they are embarrassing and must be hidden. The bubble has been replaced by a straitjacket.

Everybody knows (to the extent they ever think about it—and they have to, don't they?—although they never say anything, it's all implicit) that we're sleeping together, but for some reason that fact cannot be acknowledged; the subject is off limits.

My girlfriend, too, is in an awkward position. She must appear, if not virginal, at least not too sexual. She knows she's being analyzed and compared. She doesn't seem to mind that she's forced to act in a certain way, that she can't look like a "tramp." On the contrary, she seems to be proud of her ability to navigate around all these booby traps. Where did she pick up this skill on top of all the others?

It's not just the two of us who have been stripped of our sexual natures; as the night goes on, it is apparent that the room is filled with others like us. There are exceptions, but not many: a few effervescent women in low-cut dresses, dancing suggestively with escorts who look like Rory Calhoun. The only sanctioned references to sex are the tired double entendres about the wedding night. For the most part, however, it's a party of celibates.

My aunt then has a brainstorm. She must get a picture of her nephew dancing with her sister. Refusal proves to be impossible, and soon the marionettes are stiffly waltzing: I with my mother; my father, diplomatically, with my girlfriend. A few feet away on the dance floor, my girlfriend is at the end of an infinitely long tunnel I cannot traverse.

The four of us make jokes about the schmaltzy music, as my aunt snaps away. Years later the rarity of the configuration gives the photographs a doctored feel.

THERE ARE TWO 'THEOLOGIES' UNDERLYING OUR views about sex," Frank tells us during the SAR wrap-up. We have seen and said things we'd never seen or said before and are now hoping he'll be putting it all together for us.

"Where you stand on issues like promiscuity, abortion, homosexuality, really *any* sexual issue, is dictated by your implicit theology.

" 'Theology A,' " he writes on the flip chart. "The 'A' theology holds that sex is about reproduction. Exclusively. Accordingly, an 'A' person is really saying that sperm is sacred. It's function is solely for procreation. Any sexual act or relationship that does not fulfill that mission—the ejaculation of a male's sperm into a female's vagina free of birth control; in a word, procreation—should be condemned.

" 'B' people feel that, in sex, relationships are of primary importance. They are more tolerant of variations in sexual behavior. Acts that may seem wrong to an 'A' person, like oral intercourse, for example,

are not in themselves evil to a 'B' if, by engaging in the act, the participants are obtaining pleasure and furthering their relationship with each other."

Great. We're mastering our A's and B's, but why did we spend the weekend watching all those dirty movies?

"The purpose of the films was to make you educable. The only way we could do that in an area as anxiety provoking as sex was to *increase* your anxiety through such an overexposure to sex that you became desensitized, bored and therefore receptive."

To what? To be B's? Is that the secret secret?

He's right, though, about at least one thing. The more we were exposed to sex, the more desexualized it became. But exactly what did that prove? We had grown more comfortable with the topic, and yet in remembering the intensity of my own feelings about sex—the excitement and fear, the shame and lust, the mystery and passion—I realized they'd all been missing from the weekend. The wonder that has been inside me since childhood was nowhere to be seen. The comfort we felt, while it was a relief, was also a distortion.

Becoming blasé to the shocking, almost unearthly, experience of watching other people engage in sex had not helped me to better understand the mystery and joy I feel when *I* touch a woman or look into her eyes. In fact (except for the disabled and the elderly), the films tended to make it all seem tedious and a little disgusting. Our discussions as well became too comfortable, too safe, and, as we echoed one another, our fears almost comical.

"It's like we're *still* in the family," the salesman's wife says, implying, as we asexually bear-hug each other good-bye, that we still haven't found a way to talk about sex. After the weekend, we're no longer completely mute—we've been able to open the door and reveal that yes, Virginia, people *do* have sex— but having gone that far, we can go no further. We're still tongue-tied, our unruly counterlives sentenced permanently to secrecy.

THE EVOLVING THERAPIST

I AM BARRELING OUT OF THE CITY, A STRAIGHT line, driving north. A relationship with a woman, yet another, has just ended. I am anxious to get away from that hurricane of self-doubt and pain that marks the end of a love affair, the collapse of a world. Maybe the wind whizzing by will blow it all away. Where am I going, and what's the point? Thirty-five, I am traveling fast and standing still at the same time.

At a rest stop that boasts both a Coke machine and a scenic overlook, I drown my obsessive need to review with a swig of soda and a vista of river valley. But the past—what was, what should have been, what could have been—will not rest. Moments of closeness jostle against flashes of betrayals and rejections. Issues of character and trust seem paramount in understanding why we broke up; sex, surprisingly, is secondary. Yet sex is at the core of the loss: if we had not been physically connected, the pain would not be this acute; if we had been more connected physically, I painfully consider, perhaps we might not have broken up.

The memories of recent and more distant pasts line up for inspection. Certain moments stand out in such bold relief that they seem to be of another order than the rest.

It's then that I realize that I have made love no more than five or six times in my life.

My mind stops. Does the number merit gratitude or more self-pity?

From the vantage point of the rest stop all the other times start to resemble masturbation, except that whatever woman I was with substituted for my genitals, as I did, hers.

During sex, even with someone I love, it seems that in spite of everything I know or want or feel, I too often wind up in a mutual manipulation whose only ultimately understandable aim is orgasm. Touching and being touched, kissing and being kissed, sighs, smells, sights—the intimate murmuring presence of otherness, the excitement of difference—

all of that wonder inevitably seems to boil down to the question, stated or not: "Did you come?" Two people become two objects.

I make her come. She makes me come. Our job is done. I have been macho enough to break through her wall of not coming, to overpower her not-coming state, thereby proving my manhood and the wizardry of my technique. She has reconfirmed her own desirability through my erection and ejaculation. Through coming, our anxieties about *not* coming—of not pleasing and being pleased—ease. Relaxed, we can each feel protective of the other. And protected: some private part of us has not been touched; some hidden part has remained hidden.

I feel like an impostor.

Then, the few havens in the heart of my memory rush forward, the half-dozen times when love and the transcendence of shame overshadowed the orgasms and power trips.

Those few times something broke, something very strong and ever-present, yet so invisible I am never aware of it—or what is behind it—except when it is broken. It is a wall behind which hides a self, adamantine in its refusal to emerge, a private self that seeks protection in remaining unseen. It is primal, needy and desiring, and most of all, ashamed and oh so fearful of the pain it might encounter if, in revealing its need, it should be spurned.

The few times I have been brave enough to peer out from behind the wall, a woman always showed me the way. Through a word or gesture she let a terribly private part of her be seen, and I followed.

On those few occasions when the wall has broken, I have felt myself spill into another person. It is a me I rarely see, the trusting, desiring child-me. The threat, the competition—the ability to hurt—that other people represent ceased needing to be defended against, and I, I who was liquid—semen, sweat, sometimes tears—flowed without restraint. And she at those times became not just a doll to touch and rub in order to make come but a tender, welcoming, resonating bowl who in the course of holding me I held, her own private, trembling self revealed, by me embraced. The magic of discovery, disclosure and acceptance. Mutual acceptance of secret selves. We were separate yet entwined.

Looking back, I realize I should not complain: I shared one such magic experience with my most recent lost love.

We are living a connect-the-dots game. The dots are moments of contact, special intimate moments when we see ourselves and others see us, too. Most of our lives are spent in the passage of time between the dots. But when we recall what's meaningful about our lives, we remember the dots, forget our lines.

Sex, the greatest opportunity for contact, makes for the boldest dots. It can also afford the most complex labyrinths in which to hide. The few times I haven't hidden myself, something magical happened: the boy who entered his mother's bedroom —able once more to bestow and take pleasure, unashamed—regained paradise.

I finish the Coke and walk back to the car. A fever has passed.

I start heading back home. ■

FRED WISTOW *is a free-lance writer and lawyer who lives in New York City.*

PHOTOGRAPH BY TOM WOLFF

YOU CAN GO HOME AGAIN

A DAUGHTER AND FATHER STRUGGLE TO FORGE A NEW UNDERSTANDING

By Laura M. Markowitz

I MISS YOU!" SAYS THE VOICE STRAINING ACROSS several continents. It is Father's Day, and I am standing in a dusty phone booth in the post office in Kandy, Sri Lanka. I have been traveling in Asia for more than a year; this is the second time I've called home.

"I miss you, too!" I shout back, trying to ignore the people waiting in line for stamps who are listening with open interest to my conversation.

"Why don't you write?" he complains. The miles between us do nothing to dull the sharp edge of frustration in his voice.

"I'm waiting to get one from you. You owe me," I remind him. It is true, but I feel guilty anyway, for not writing, for letting him down.

"I'm sorry, honey," and I know he is, but I don't feel better. In the 14 months I've been gone, he has written me one short note.

"I'll send you a letter today," I promise, wanting to make nice, afraid of holding on to anger long distance, in case anything should happen and we never see each other again.

"And call more often!" He is pushing it now. I try to describe how many hours it took to place the call, how, because of the time difference, I had to get up at the crack of dawn and wait in line, how the operator had to go through five other operators to get to one in the United States. Now that I've finally reached him, there is nothing to say.

"Dad, how are you?" I want us to connect before my 10 minutes runs out.

He tells me about aunts and uncles, friends of the family. He doesn't tell me that his best friend died suddenly of a heart attack that week—I learn about it later, in a letter from my sister.

"When are you coming home?" The knot in my stomach tightens.

"Soon. I need to finish my work here." I hesitate, then say, "I heard from Susan. We won't be living together when I get back."

The silence is thick.

"Dad?"

"Yes."

A fight breaks out at the telegram counter, and everyone seems to be shouting at once. I can barely hear myself.

"Look, I'd better go. It's crazy here."

"Okay, dear. It was wonderful that you called. Take care of yourself."

I feel like crying. "I will. You, too."

"I love you."

"I love you, too. Happy Father's Day." I hang up and don't care that tears are spilling down my face. I'm crying for both of us because I know he is as bewildered as I am, and neither of us knows what to say.

I DON'T REMEMBER CONSCIOUSLY DECIDING TO tell my father that I am a lesbian; it just never occurred to me not to. He had raised me himself since my mother died when I was 13, and while we never spoke about the important things—like how much we missed her or how angry we were that she died—there was a tacit understanding that we were alike, that we were a team, that we were honest with each other. So it was never a question of telling him, it was just a matter of waiting for the right moment. I had wanted to tell him about me and Susan from the start, but it was never the right time, people were always around. I had felt uncomfortable that he didn't know, as if I were lying by my silence.

It was in December—a year and a half before the phone call and a few months before my graduation from college. I had just been awarded a research fellowship for the following year, and Dad gave me a big grin when I pulled into the driveway for winter break. On the way north, I had driven Susan to the airport—she was off to Seattle to spend Christmas with her family. Dad and I went into the kitchen. It was just the two of us, fixing breakfast and catching up. He asked about the drive up—if Susan had made her flight—and soon I was talking about her. I put my arms around him, and he put his coffee down so he could hug me back—it was rare that I initiated a hug, my reluctance a carryover from my sullen, adolescent years when I had barely tolerated them from anyone, especially him.

"I have something to tell you."

"Uh, oh," he said, lightheartedly.

"I love Susan."

He didn't let go of me, but I felt him tense under the impact of my words.

"I suspected it," he said, his shoulders sagging. He didn't say anything else for a while. He didn't let go.

"What does it mean?" he asked.

"It means I'm a lesbian," I said, amazed at myself for saying the word. I felt dizzy and was glad he was holding me, but I was afraid to look up at him. He wasn't saying anything. The silence made me anxious.

"It's not a negative thing, Dad; it's good. I really love her. I'm happier with her than I ever was with David or Jason. I'm proud of our relationship." I heard my rush of reassurances. I heard that tone in my voice that said "I'm happy. Isn't that what you always told me you wanted for me?"

"What does Ben think about this?" he finally asked. Ben is my best friend. He, David, Susan and I were living together then. Dad must have assumed we were involved.

"He's happy for me," I said, which was not altogether true. "He knows I will always love him, but not as a lover."

"Is he," Dad paused before he said the word, "gay, too?"

"No, he isn't." I read his thoughts. Were Ben and David lovers? Was everyone I knew gay?

"Who else have you told?" he asked.

"Just Debbie." I had told my sister a month before, and she had not been surprised. She told me she was happy for me and that she couldn't wait to meet Susan. Her support had meant a lot.

"And Steve?" he asked. I told him no. I hadn't told my brother because I wanted to tell my father first.

"What does it mean?" he asked again, and I heard something new in his voice—a hint of anger.

Suddenly, I thought of an answer. "One thing it

means is that I still love you. I'm not sure everything it means, but I want you to understand that it is not a result of anything bad. It's not like I'm tortured about it. I don't hate men. I wasn't raped. I just love Susan." The words were pouring out of me, muffled by his strong hug. He just held on, and we breathed together for a while. What was I thinking of? How could I be saying this? What if I was making a mistake, think of the pain I was causing! But then I thought of the past year, even before Susan, how some missing piece of information about myself had fallen into place. I knew I wasn't wrong.

"Why aren't you saying anything?" I asked, after a few long minutes of silence, listening to his heartbeat.

"Because I don't want to say the wrong thing," he said, and I knew why I had been able to tell him.

I AM SILENT AS WE NEGOTIATE THE NEW YORK AIRport traffic and head into the Bronx. It has been nearly half a year since my call from Sri Lanka, the last time we spoke. I've been traveling for 43 hours, I'm exhausted from endless flights, sleeping in airports, and the conflict I feel about returning to the West, but I don't want to take it out on him. He is holding my hand and telling me how glad he is that I am home. He tries to bring me back by telling me the news—my brother's latest business venture, my sister's success in law school.

He has not yet told my stepfamily or my brother that I am a lesbian. I know this from my sister's letters. I am angry at him for being too ashamed of me to tell my stepmother—to tell anyone. On the other hand, I am glad I won't have to face everyone's reactions when we get home—I am too tired to be understanding or diplomatic.

Even after I have gotten over the jet lag, things at home feel tense. Dad is clearly glad to have me back where he doesn't have to worry about me crossing the path of terrorists, but we are too careful with each other. I entertain the family with stories about

my travels from the past 19 months, but I edit out the parts about the lesbians I have become friends with all over the world, the wonder of finding them everywhere, even in the tiniest Asian countries. And I don't talk about the pain I am in over Susan's decision to reject her love for me and her lesbian identity because she is just barely hanging on to her sanity as it is, and she doesn't think she can afford to be any more marginal in the world.

I haven't spent this much time at home in years and have never really spent much time with my stepfamily, who moved in after I went away to college. They have redecorated, and I feel sad when I see my mother's things packed away, untidily, in an attic storeroom.

Following a survival instinct, I leave and spend a week in bed at my sister's house, having the cry I need, hiding out, and trying to get acclimated to America after so many months in the jungle. He calls on Sunday.

"When are you coming home?" he asks. "When you tell my stepmother about me." It has popped out of my mouth, unplanned.

"Tell her what?" he asks, his tone letting me know he doesn't want to hear it, daring me to violate his denial.

"Look, you may not be happy, but I am not ashamed of who I am, and I don't want to lie to her by my silence," I tell him. I sound braver than I feel. "You've had two years to get used to it. I don't like having to leave part of myself behind when I come home." As usual, I can't stop myself from crying.

He softens, afraid I will go away for good and never come back. "Honey, I want you to be happy. I don't know what to say."

"We need help," I answer, softly.

I MAKE THE APPOINTMENT, CHOOSING A JEWISH agency because I think maybe that connection will be a comfort somehow. The whole way there in the car, I am trying to imagine what it will be like.

I fantasize that my father will tell me he's proud that I am doing this brave thing and following my heart.

In the busy agency waiting room, I am surprised at how protective I feel of him. I am not afraid of therapy—I had seen a therapist for almost three years, after my mother died. But he has never had to reveal himself to a stranger. What have I done? I ask myself. How could I make us go through this? But I also know if we don't learn how to talk about it, there will only be more of this tense distance between us.

The therapist, Sheila, looks about my father's age—early fifties—with gray in her dark hair and wearing no makeup. She walks us to her tiny office. There are children's drawings on the walls. We sit in stiff chairs next to her desk. It's like seeing the doctor, except the desk is not between us but faces the wall. She smiles at both of us and starts with me.

"When you called for the appointment, you said you and your dad were having problems communicating."

I look at him, to see if he minds my going first. He has a bemused, distant smile on his face. "Well, we haven't been communicating for a while," I say, thinking how lame and inadequate that sounds. "I was away for a year and a half and he wrote to me only once." I choke up as I say this.

She turns to him, and he smiles pleasantly. "I'm bad about writing," he admits. "I get so busy." He turns to me, "But it doesn't mean I don't love you, honey."

"I know you love me, Dad, but I think there's something else going on. You weren't too busy to write the last time I spent a year abroad."

"What do you think is going on?" she asks, trying to catch the thread. I am scared to say it, scared that maybe she will agree with him, that they will gang up on me and tell me I am wrong for being a lesbian.

"I think he's angry that I'm a lesbian." Her eyebrows shoot up, giving away her surprise, but that is her only reaction. She turns to him.

"Is that how it feels to you?" she asks. I lean forward.

"I suppose that's part of it," he says.

"What else is there?" she asks. I feel cold.

He settles back in his chair, the confident lawyer, the consultant to the therapist, here to talk about his child's problem. He directs himself to her, talking about me as if I am not in the room. "She hasn't been communicative for a long time. For many years, she never spoke to me, never showed affection, was secretive and, frankly, unpleasant to live with. I don't know, she always seems angry." This hurts. I am crying. I want to defend myself, ask him what did he expect from an adolescent living in a crazy house with everyone fighting all the time, and no one ever admitting the scary fact that my mother was dying. I look for a tissue, and he hands me his handkerchief.

"So you both feel the other one is angry. How is Dad's anger expressed?"

"Silence," I say, "but not really, since it is clear what he is thinking even if he doesn't say it. He'll disapprove silently."

"I've never wanted to impose myself on my children, on my brothers, on anyone," he says, a little bitterly. "But can I help it if I have feelings about my daughter being gay?"

"It's okay to have feelings, Dad, but when you don't talk about it, it's like a ghost. I can't address it if you never bring it up!"

"You are moody and unapproachable when you are home," he says. "I feel like a detective; I have to pry information from you, and you resent my asking."

"And I feel like I have to edit everything I say so that it doesn't mention my lesbianism. You don't really want to know who I am or about my life. You tell me that in every disapproving frown when I say anything about it," I say.

"What would you like your dad to say?" Sheila asks me. I remember my fantasy in the car.

"I'd like him to treat me normally, not to shut

down every time the subject comes up," I say, not clear if I've answered her question, feeling fuzzier and less articulate by the minute.

There is silence as I sniffle into the handkerchief and wonder what I am doing here. I am shaking. There are suddenly so many things I have needed to tell him for a long time, but it is scary to think I might say them. Sheila has asked him for some family background, and I hear him describing Mom's death in his matter-of-fact way, with the slightest hesitation in his voice giving him away, at least to me. He describes my brother and sister briefly and mentions that he lives with a woman and her two children.

"How do you feel about your dad's new family?" she asks me, and I am annoyed that she is bringing it up—after all, aren't we here to talk about my lesbianism?

"I'm glad they're there for him, but I wasn't always glad." I take a deep breath, wondering what I'm going to say. "I used to resent all the time he spent with them. I guess it was hard that I didn't have a choice. They were in my life whether I wanted them or not. I used to act kind of grumpy around them."

Dad is smiling to himself, a little cynically. "Grumpy is a mild word for it," he says. His patronizing tone pisses me off. Sheila turns to him.

"What would you like from Laura?" He gives me the raised-eyebrows look that says, "You know and I know that I'm not going to get it, so why ask?" But Sheila is waiting. He has to say something.

"I want her to be happy, and I want her to keep her options open," he says. "And I'd like her to be sweet and marry a doctor." He adds this jokingly, but there's some truth to it.

"So you are disappointed?" Sheila asks. He sighs and shifts in his chair.

"I guess I never realized I had expectations for my children," he says. "I took for granted they would go to college, have careers, meet someone,"

he looks at me, "of the opposite sex, and get married, have families of their own. This just never occurred to me."

"Why haven't you told your new family about Laura?" Sheila asks. I notice she doesn't say the L-word.

"I suppose I don't know what to think. What if this is a phase? I don't want her to be stuck with a label she might regret later."

"I don't want to be labeled," I admit. Who would? Everyone has the strangest ideas about lesbians, that we secretly want to be men, that we want to castrate men—as if this has anything to do with men! "But I am the same me I was before. And I like who I am, whether you do or not. This isn't up for negotiation. I'm not going to change my mind because you are silently disapproving. I'm just going to stop wanting to come home, where I have to divide up my life for your comfort."

"So you don't want me to have feelings about it," he says.

"Sure. I want you to be supportive and happy for me," I smile, "but the point is, whether I want you to have feelings or not, you do have them. And I feel them. But your silence isn't fair. There's nothing to argue with."

"Does it feel risky to say what you're feeling?" Sheila asks Dad.

"Not risky," he says, shrugging. "It feels futile. Look, I can't control what my children do, and frankly, I don't always approve. But what can I do? They want me to approve unconditionally and I can't."

"You're right," I tell him. "You can't change me, and you can disapprove of what I do, but you can't ask me to pretend to be someone I'm not."

"I don't think your dad wants to do that," Sheila tells me. "I think he cares very deeply for you, and you are just as crazy about him. But I think the issue here is not so much the choices each of you has made—you" she nods at me "to be gay, and Dad" she nods at him "to remarry—but that each of you needs to separate and let the other make those choices. You need to know that your daughter is not you, and you need to know that your dad is not you," she tells us. Dad and I look at each other. His eyes are also filled with tears.

"I just want you to be happy," he tells me.

"I just want *you* to be happy, and you're not!" I am crying.

"But it is Dad's life, and Dad's choice whether he will be happy or not," Sheila tells me. "And it is Laura's choice to love whom she loves," she tells him. "You both need to let go of the other."

"So many things are never said," I tell him. "It makes me crazy."

"Like what?" Sheila asks.

I am crying so hard I can barely speak. "Like, we miss my mother." Dad reaches for my hand, holds on. I am saying it for both of us.

The session ends there, and as we walk out, still holding hands, I feel incredibly drained but also peaceful, as if speaking those last words somehow lifted the fog that always surrounds my feeling of loss. In the car we are silent, but the air is clear between us for the first time in years.

On the long drive back, alone, I let a scary thought surface. I am secretly glad he hasn't told everyone in the family about me. How will I face my uncles and cousins, people who thought they knew me? What if they cut me off? Will my father defend me? I can't imagine him not backing me up—maybe that's why he hasn't told them; maybe he's not ready to face them either.

Another thought edges into focus, about being a teenager, the loneliness I felt even when he was around, and the fear that he would bring his lover into our lives—an intolerable thought. He was still mourning, too. But with my tight-lipped rebellion, I was his excuse to keep distance between her and himself. It suddenly seems to me that Dad and I have always held the world at bay for each other.

A FEW MONTHS LATER I MAKE ANOTHER TRIP home for a follow-up appointment. We have not seen each other since the last appointment, but we have been talking on the phone regularly and our former bond of closeness has returned—at once stronger and more tenuous than before. We smile at each other, like coconspirators, as we take our seats in Sheila's office. She remarks on how happy we look. I tell her I am delighted that Dad has told my stepfamily that I am a lesbian, and that they reacted with love and support. Dad says he is glad I am more communicative, and he says he feels proud of me because of my new job.

"Last time you were here, we talked about separating from each other, accepting the other's choices. How has that been?"

"I feel his willingness to listen," I say, "but I still edit what I'm saying. And I'm not sure if he really wants to know what's going on. He never asks me about my relationships or brings up his feelings about my lesbianism."

"I do the best that I can, honey," he says.

"I feel like, now that I'm not with Susan, you're waiting for me to choose to be with men again," I say.

"Well?" he asks.

"Well, no. It's not an option," I tell him. "Don't hold on to the hope that I'll change."

"It's not a choice?" he asks.

"Does it matter?"

"If you're saying to me this is who you are, then I have to accept it, and I have to get used to it. But if you're saying, like I thought you were, that this was a choice you were making, then I do want you to change your mind. Because I'm your father. I worry about you. The world is not a safe place for gays."

"Then let's say I am not making a choice. Let's say this is who I am. I need that level of acceptance from you. Sure, I could have married Jason, and I probably would have been happy enough, but something would always have been off, and part of

YOU CAN GO HOME AGAIN

me would have known it. It's not just about sex"—this is hard to say; we never say the S-word in our family—"it's deeper than that."

"So you want your father to accept you as you are," says Sheila. "Can you accept that he, as your parent, worries about you? About your being gay in a hostile world?"

"Yes," I say, "but I can handle the world's disapproval. It's yours that scares me."

"If you're happy, I'll try to be happy," he says.

"And if you're not always thrilled that I'm a lesbian, I'll try to understand," I say.

I T IS MY SISTER'S WEDDING, THREE YEARS LATER, and I am sitting with my lover of two years, Mary Kay, at a table with my father, stepmother, brother and sister-in-law. They are all fond of MK, and it is a wonderful moment for me, having my family and my lover together all at once, all comfortable.

"When are you two getting married?" my brother asks us with characteristic enthusiasm, already picturing another party like this one.

"You think we should?" I am smiling at the notion.

"Oh, we'll have a big party," promises my stepmother. I look over at my dad. He is also smiling, and in his eyes is real happiness, no cynicism.

My sister-in-law is pregnant, and the baby is kicking. I reach over and touch her stomach. Dad puts his hand next to mine and there is wonder in both of our eyes as we imagine this child of my brother's coming into the world, into the family.

"What about if I have kids?" I ask, suddenly afraid I won't be allowed, somehow.

"I will love them like crazy!" he answers. Something is healed between us.

A NOTHER WEDDING A YEAR LATER, THIS TIME A cousin. I am supposed to go home for the party, but I become sick to my stomach at the thought of going home. I can't get on the plane. I call Dad and tell him I won't be coming. I am hon-

est—I say I can't do it, and I don't know why.

He flies down to see me the next day and takes me out to dinner.

"Is it your cousin?" he asks.

"I'm happy for him," I say, "but I couldn't handle another wedding. Part of me is angry that I don't have that support. I mean, most of my relatives don't even know I've been in this relationship for years." I have been waiting for him to tell the relatives. So far, that has included one cousin. He hasn't even told any of his friends. I haven't pushed. My friends—even my therapist—tell me that I have it good; my father has accepted me, even welcomed my lover into the family, so I shouldn't complain. But it's not always enough. Anyway, I am beginning to think it is my job to tell them, not his. But the idea makes me nervous.

"Does that mean you're never coming to another family celebration?" he asks. He is worried I will cut myself off from the family, from him.

"I hope not," I answer. I think for a minute, trying to find the words to express this sense of loss.

"I won't have those rituals in my life," I explain, "like engagement parties and a wedding and all that attention and support for my relationship. My relationship with MK is one of the most important things in my life, but when I see my relatives, all they ask about is my job. No one knows about my lover, and no one asks. And," I take a deep breath while the waiter comes and gives us our salads. He is wearing a lapel button of a pink triangle—a symbol that he is gay—and I can tell he's heard what I've just said because he gives me a sympathetic look as he leaves. "And, MK and I had a fight this week. Not a huge one, but I didn't feel safe coming home. You always tell me you accept my lesbianism as long as I'm happy, and I wasn't particularly happy yesterday. I know it sounds silly, but I guess I was scared you'd get mad about me being a lesbian if I wasn't totally happy."

"I want you to be able to be yourself," he says. I

like the sound of that. "I'm sorry about the part about no wedding or rituals. What can I do?" He is asking sincerely, and I give him a look that says he is already doing it, just by understanding.

We eat quietly—an earned silence—and I look over at his hand resting on the table. Our hands look alike. So do our feet, and we have a similar way of walking. No one would have trouble recognizing that I am his child. I am comforted by those similarities tonight; they are a bridge across this canyon between us, where I have turned down a trail he can't follow, that he doesn't understand. All the ways in which I am me and not him never mattered before, were sources of enjoyment for him, like my love of Buddhism. But this one has threatened everything. Is it worth it?, I ask myself. Could I have chosen not to be a lesbian and avoided all this pain? But it isn't a real question—even the pain is worth knowing that I am living true to myself, and the truth is, I feel lucky to be a lesbian. I know he doesn't understand this.

I drive him to the airport, and in the dark car he is holding my hand. For the first time, he is grappling with his feelings about my homosexuality aloud, with me.

"It never occurred to my generation that we had a choice," he says. "It just wasn't done. I didn't even know any."

"I've heard a lot of theories about sexuality—that we're all bisexual and we make a choice at some point to be gay or straight," I say. "But when did you make a choice to be heterosexual? And if that were true, why would people give up all the privileges of being a heterosexual to be gay? I love it, but it's never a benign issue, no matter how good people are about it."

After a moment of silence, he confesses, "I blame myself." I feel it like a knife. "Maybe after your mother died, I should have made sure you had a mother figure in your life." I feel myself getting furious.

"It's not about Mommy dying. I was like this long before. I can trace it back to when I was four years old. I don't think it's helpful to find an excuse, or to see it as somehow *caused* by tragedy or bad experiences. Let's just say I was blessed to be this way. And if you had anything to do with it, thanks! I'm delighted with the way I am." He lets that sink in.

"I'm delighted with the way you are, too," he says. Then, "I never would have guessed what a challenge it would be to be a parent."

We are at the airport, but he sits in the car a little longer, putting off the moment of separation as long as possible. We both hate to say good-bye.

"When are you coming home?" he asks, in a mock-aggressive tone. I roll my eyes at him and smile. Right now I feel like I can go home any time. I feel like all of me is welcome.

"When are you going to come and stay with me and MK?" I counter. He never has before, and I'm curious about what he'll say. But he just laughs a deep, easy laugh and says, "We'll talk about it." I laugh, too. I know we will—I'll make sure of it!

I sit awhile longer in the car after he is gone, waiting to see the dot of light in the sky that carries him north. I am awash in the wonder of being his child, connected to him through the filaments of my very molecules, yet free to become someone beyond both of our imaginations. ■

LAURA M. MARKOWITZ *is assistant editor of* The Family Therapy Networker.

GEMINI

WHEN YOU'RE AN IDENTICAL TWIN, THERE'S ALWAYS A MIRROR SELF SOMEWHERE IN THE UNIVERSE

By Marion Lindblad-Goldberg

THROUGH THE AGES, TWINS HAVE INSPIRED great fascination, awe and sometimes even fear. Among some African tribes, young women are forbidden to listen to tales of them, lest they become susceptible to twin conception. In the Niger delta, quarreling women curse each other by holding up two fingers, a gesture meaning "may you be the mother of twins."

Having never encountered an African tribe in Cuyahoga Falls, Ohio, "shock" more accurately describes my mother's feelings upon completion of the last prenatal checkup. My father was in the front yard, meticulously pruning the roses, when she lumbered up the driveway. "Guess what, Al. Better sit down, dear—the X-ray showed two spines!"

The roses were massacred in one convulsive snip!

In some cultures, twins are highly revered, probably nowhere more than among the Yoruba of Western Nigeria. Yoruba mothers of twins practice weekly devotions honoring their twins by publicly dancing and singing special lullabies. The American version of this rite occurs each year when 1,000 twins gather for the convention of the International Twins Association. The Twin Contest is the grand finale each year, with twins competing in 28 categories. The contest starts with a prize for the "most alike infants in arms" and proceeds with awards to "most alike men" and "most alike ladies." At the 1980 convention, a bellboy was heard to say, "It wouldn't pay to get drunk around here."

Mom's only public acknowledgment of having twins was having us all attend the local "Mothers-of-Twins" meeting. She told my father later, "That's it. My God, it was like being on Noah's Ark. There were two of everything." One week later, she was immersed in a do-it-yourself correspondence course form Yale's Gesell Institute aimed at rearing twins as individuals. From the Gesell bible came such child-rearing commandments as :

1. Thou shalt never call your children "twinny" or even refer to them as "the twins." Be original—create for your identical twins unlike-sounding names. Hence, "Marion" (after my mother) and "Karin" (after my mother's fantasies).

2. Thou shalt use different colors in look-alike clothing.

431

3. Thou shalt be aware that unequal treatment will not bring disaster.

Childrearing advice for twins of the Yoruba tribe included feeding them a special food. One Yoruba mother explained: "In our culture beans can cool a person's temper and oil can eliminate trouble. Therefore, feed twins beans cooked in oil to prevent double trouble." (Of course, the Yoruba didn't have to wash the twins' diapers.)

My mother adored Ben Spock, who devoted 10 full pages of his best-seller to outlining survival techniques for coping with "double trouble" American-style. "Your babies are more important than any housework. When you have tiny twins—tiny, hungry, howling, extra-frequent-feeding twins—you'll find that the dust is going to be there forever. Let it be." Spock helpfully continued, "You need all the help you can get for as long as you can get it. If possible, hire somebody even though you have to go into debt, or—beg your mother to come."

Grandma arrived from Detroit. We had different formulas, one on the left side of the refrigerator and the other on the right side. Efficient Mom marked charts taped to the wall to track who got fed what and when. Grandma's loving but inefficient methods resulted in the following scenario:

ME: Waaaa!

GRANDMA (*with Scottish burr*) to mother: Mar-r-r-ion, the geetle [*girl*] willna stop crying, and she's had her bath and orange juice alr-r-ready. Do you think she's sick—a wee cold perhaps?

MOM (*after inspecting the rotund belly of my dazzlingly clean sister*): No, Mother, I think you've bathed and fed Karin twice.

Grandma soon went back to Detroit.

THIS WAS THE "BDD" ERA—BEFORE DISPOSABLE Diapers. Dad bought Mom a new *wringer* washing machine. . . . With the pediatrician and Spock on her side, Mom presented Dad with a bill for the diaper service. Somehow their marriage

survived. Somehow we survived (and speaking as one who prematurely entered the world at three and a half pounds, that's no understatement).

At seven months Mom propped us up on each side of the couch and left the room. Hearing a sudden, loud, joyous chortling, she raced back and found that we had discovered each other for the first time. Mom later described the feeling that, from that moment on, she was shut out.

We invented some games like "sandwich" as toddlers. My ration-conscious World War II mother quivered as she viewed the kitchen floor. We'd taken all the precious butter, sugar and jam and spread it lovingly across the floor—"Sandwich." We invented language—a kind of closed-circuit communication that excluded others. Sometimes all it took was a shrug and we both understood completely. We avoided competition. Instead, together we competed against others. Her accomplishments were mine and vice versa. We shared moments. As she held the telephone receiver in London during her junior year abroad, did Karin ever question who on the other end was painstakingly depositing the $30 worth of quarters into the pay phone? It was our 21st birthday, and she seemed so terribly far away. When the operator signaled us to talk, I cried the entire three minutes. Years later, seeing my son David for the first time, she said with wonder, "He has *your* face," and we both smiled.

The feeling of being extra-unique is an understandable twin phenomenon. This is enhanced both by our ability to deceive others by "twin switching" as well as our frequent experiences of telepathic bonding. While I delighted in fantasizing that my sister filled in for me at such anxious moments as taking college entrance exams or defending my doctoral dissertation, the reality was that we operated by an unspoken code that forbade twin switching. Only once, as college students returning on the Queen Elizabeth from Europe, did we indulge ourselves by deceiving some rather boorish young men

432

from Princeton. Since I had sailed from Southampton, England, and she embarked from Cherbourg, France, several days later, the amorous young men never did see the two of us together. I must admit the confusion we created was much more exhilarating than swapping travel stories with the retired schoolteachers we'd been seated with in the dining room.

Whether the "telepathic" instances were actually the result of extrasensory perception or merely a similar response to stimuli, I don't know. I do know they occurred. Our fourth grade teacher accused us of cheating, since we'd made identical test mistakes. Mother demanded that the teacher immediately retest us on similar material but in different classrooms. After grading this second set of tests, the teacher was chagrined to learn that this experiment revealed the same phenomenon. We had again missed exactly the same test questions.

A more remarkable experience occurred this past summer. I had spontaneously flown to Philadelphia to visit a friend's newborn baby. While en route from the airport, I impulsively veered off the expressway to drive to a store to buy a baby gift. After this purchase, I was walking past the women's department when a blouse caught my eye. As I carried it to the salesgirl, my sister appeared from the dressing room wearing the very same blouse. Not only was seeing her another amazing coincidence, but she saved me the trouble of trying on the blouse.

Moving out of the family into the world of school and peers, we soon left behind our initial social identity as "the twins" and started to seek our own lives. Heeding parental advice, we attended different classes following the fourth grade "experiment." Throughout junior and senior high school, we maintained different sets of friends. Following a seven-year period when we attended different colleges and graduate schools, we were geographically reunited when I went to Philadelphia to pursue a career in

clinical psychology. My sister's doctoral studies had been in English literature at the University of Pennsylvania where she now taught. Although in the same vicinity, we continued to maintain totally separate social and professional lives. Our worlds never intersected, except, of course, for the occasional cases of mistaken identity by her students and my patients.

Perhaps the most unfortunate occurrence was with a patient I had treated for poor self-esteem. The patient constantly ruminated about her worthlessness and had the repetitive fantasy that if I met her in public, I would ignore her. Of course, it was inevitable that it would be my sister she happened to pass in the street one day.

Having had the opportunity to establish a strong inner sense of "I," it was a special event to become a "we" again, first through my marriage, and then in my pregnancy with my son David. At the time I thought these events, coupled with a move to Cincinnati, were surely evidence of a diminishing twinship. However, four months after the move, we received a rather hilarious phone call from my sister about the wonderful man she'd just met—Myron, a neighbor and professional colleague of my husband Marty's. While Karin's dating had generally been limited to Protestant men, often poets or the like, it was interesting that this man shared a similar background with my husband, in that both were Jewish, chairmen of departments in academic medicine, and previously married. I had met Myron briefly at a neighborhood reception held for Marty and me after we'd married, at which none of my family had been present. Several months after this event, Myron drove into the city to pick up a blind date. The woman got into his car, he looked at her, did a double take, and said to himself, "Oh, my God, I'm out with Marty Goldberg's wife." It took him a few minutes to gather the chutzpah to ask my sister, "What went wrong? You and Marty looked so happy at the wedding reception."

Karin and Myron married and now live near our former Philadelphia home. Through my marriage to a widower with three children and hers to a divorced father of three, Karin and I have shared the experience of stepparenting. After so many similar patterns, it was a relief for me to have a son and her a daughter, although people often mistake them for siblings.

Being an identical twin means never knowing absolute alienation, disapproval, or rejection, because one's twin is always there. Somewhere in the universe the mirror-self radiates this shared acceptance of joy and sorrow. Poet Rainer Maria Rilke talks about a kind of ideal relationship between two people—two spirits that touch and meet. With twins, the touching and meeting is already there. Between Karin and me there is one part that is both of us. We're totally separate beings, yet it does exist, this oneness. People who are not twins may find later in life the sort of relationship that Karin and I experienced at the very beginning. After all, is not the ultimate goal of marriage to blend two distinct personalities into one entity? Don't we all strive for that "perfect understanding" with another? As I develop within my own marriage or do therapeutic work with couples and families, my inner tears of joy are inevitably triggered when that moment of intimacy and understanding comes.

The Yoruba believe that if they provide special care for a twin who has gone away, he or she may be attracted back. Thus, the mother will confer devotional rites on an "ibeji"—a wooden statue that is a surrogate of the missing twin. The offer of two exciting jobs in Philadelphia has meant that Marty and I returned "home" this summer. From the third floor of our house, I can see the rooftop of Karin and Myron's home one block away. ■

MARION LINDBLAD-GOLDBERG, PH.D., *is the director of the Family Therapy Training Center at the Philadelphia Child Guidance Clinic, Philadelphia, PA.*

PHOTOGRAPH BY BARBARA F. GUNDLE

*M*Y MOTHER'S KEEPER

A DAUGHTER FACES AN AGONIZING CHOICE

By Lou L. Hartney

ULY 28, 1987: IT IS TOO LATE TO TURN BACK. I have set in motion events that are tumbling me along like a broken branch in floodtide. I have run out of choices. I look at my 94-year-old mother. Her thin, hunched body is dwarfed amid a welter of crates, cartons of books, piles of possessions to go to the Salvation Army, and other stacks of worthless items too precious to leave behind. Her expression matches the disheveled room. She doesn't know it yet, but by this time next week she will be in a nursing home in Colorado, a thousand miles from here, whatever life remains to her drastically changed. The cost of dying, particularly if one does it slowly, is prohibitive in California.

She is leaving kind neighbors who remember spirited bridge games in which she held her own. She now forgets their names and faces from one day to the next, but I will never stop being grateful to them for coming in to see her often in recent years, telling her over and over who they are, for including her in dinner invitations, even though they know the diapers she now wears don't always do all they are supposed to.

Will we ever find people who will brighten her life like that again?

My God, what am I doing to her?

ULY 30, 1987: ALTHOUGH I FEEL DRAINED AND EX-hausted, sleep evades me for hours these nights. While I am turning endlessly, I find myself wishing she could go peacefully in her sleep before I have to do this. She is almost a stranger now, consumed by fear that I will leave her sight to go even as far as the washer in the garage. She watches anxiously from the doorway when I go to the mailbox. If I have a sitter come in when I shop for groceries, she is anxious and hurt; if I take her with me, I am frantic.

I recall her words a few years back about a life-long friend whose son put her in a nursing home where she eventually died. "I could have told her that daughters are closer to their mothers," she said, as if that were her personal guarantee against such a thing happening to her.

Sleep, when it comes at last, is as filled with foreboding as are my waking hours.

August 4, 1987: NOTHING IS GOING RIGHT. I AM sick with fear. The house is sold. The new owners are moving in tomorrow. I expect to hear the sound of the moving van grinding to a stop in front of the house at any moment.

I try to reconstruct the reasoning that led me into this morass. In retrospect, it doesn't make any sense at all. I look at earlier journal entries: "I don't care about golden streets—what I want out of Heaven is not to have to clean the bathroom a dozen times a day!" and "When will I get time to work at my writing—if that day ever comes, there won't be an original thought left in my head." There are other entries made in anger that I'm ashamed to reread. The most civilized is: "It's not her fault or mine that the 'golden years' are tarnished for us both."

Suddenly, the former 10-hour days in my home office seem to be a haven of safety and security. Work deadlines allowed little time for worry, a blessing that had gone unrecognized until now. True, they also permitted time for only the essentials of care for my mother. I fixed her meals, kept her clean, somehow got my work out on time, had crashing headaches.

Am I ready to trade that for a burden of guilt?

August 6, 1987: IT IS DONE, OR AT LEAST BEGUN. Our flight to Colorado was not as difficult as I had feared. Friends are driving my car from California, so my daughter, Linda, who lives in the Colorado town we are going to, meets us and takes us to a motel. Mom can't negotiate the stairs at Linda's home, and I can't bear to take her to the nursing home at the end of an exhausting day for her. She sleeps soundly. After breakfast this morning, I know the time has come to try to explain what is ahead. I force the words out, that I can no longer take care of her, that she will be living at a place called a "care center," that I will see her every day, that I love her as much as ever. "Can you understand?" I ask. Her answer is a qualified, "I'll try."

I am expecting tears, pleas, perhaps anger, but she is outwardly calm. I wonder if she realizes what I am saying, and by the time my daughter arrives to take us to the nursing home, my face is streaked with tears. Linda puts on a cheerful front, and I wonder how I could get through it without her.

The administrator of the nursing home, Mary, comes out to the car and greets Mom with a cheery, "Hello, Emily!" I had met Mary on an inspection trip months earlier and had been impressed by her obvious understanding and honesty. Some of the other nearby facilities we had investigated had a policy of asking family members to stay away at least three days after the patient's admission. "Let us take all the flak at first," they said. "Then, when you show up, she'll be glad to see you." I felt that three days without a familiar face would be shattering to her, so when Mary assured me I could be with her as much as I wished, I made my choice.

She is put alone in a twin-bedded room. I stay until bedtime and am there early the next morning. I find her sitting on the other bed in her room, a puzzled look on her face. "What day is this?" she asks. I tell her it is Friday. Her next question is, "When are we going home?" I start to explain, but she cuts me off. "You say this is Sunday?"

September 1, 1987: SHE HAS BEEN PUT IN A ROOM with 97-year-old Belle. When I walk in today, my mother points toward her new roommate in her chair by the window and says, "That old woman's as deaf as a post!" As I am trying to find the right words of apology, I realize that Belle is, indeed, extremely hard of hearing and has no notion of what has just been said. I didn't appreciate my mother's sense of tact until it was gone.

September 15, 1987: SHE HAS BEEN IN THE NURSing home five weeks now. I am renting a house in the country, and when I walk to my car alone, I'm often dizzy with a feeling of freedom. She begs me daily to stay all night with her. I try to convince her that two people can't sleep in a single hospital bed and, besides, the people who run the care center wouldn't allow it. She brushes my answer aside with, "They wouldn't even notice!"

She has been given a short and simple haircut. I admit I'm relieved to be freed from home permanents, shampoos and settings, but she looks like a frail elf with a too-small head.

Part of the time she thinks she's in a hotel; other days, she asks me if it's a hospital. Today, she says, "Maybe this is a nut house—maybe you put me here because I'm nuts!" But there's no anger in her voice, no hurt, no hint of feeling betrayed. I think she is simply trying to understand.

NOVEMBER 12, 1987: SHE HAS GOOD DAYS AND BAD days. Her disposition, as always, is sweet. But sometimes she doesn't know her great-grandchildren, and they visit frequently. She often says, "And who are these beautiful children?" Sometimes she says to me, "Is Lou coming out today?" I answer, "Mom, I'm Lou." "Oh, of course," she says.

It is snowing, and tree branches sag under the weight. She says, "Isn't this unusual for California?"

NOVEMBER 27, 1987: TODAY IS HER 95TH BIRTHDAY. Linda, the children and I take fried chicken, rolls and apple pie, all her favorites, and reserve the Activities Room, a glassed-in portion of the dining area used for special occasions. Mom goes to her regular table while we are setting things up. When I go to get her, she holds onto Belle's wheelchair. "I don't want to go unless Belle comes too," she says. That's fine with us; we just hadn't thought of it in advance. The children help her open her gifts, and the occasion comes close to gaiety.

DECEMBER 17, 1987: THE CHRISTMAS FESTIVITIES are getting me down. Various groups are singing and bringing handmade gifts for the residents at the center. I sit with Mom as the beautiful voices fill the dining area. The staff people, too, are even kinder and more cheerful than usual. I am touched by their evident sincerity. But I am on the verge of tears throughout the holiday observances, not for my mother, particularly. I tell myself my grief is for the residents who are alone, without a friend or relative there. I look at the faces around us. Some eyes are empty, like the windows of abandoned houses. Some are sad; all are sober. I can sense the weight of memories in those who comprehend the season.

A suspicion takes shape in my mind. Is this season so hard for me because when I look into the faces near me, I see myself and my future? Can it be that, after all, my deepest fears are for myself?

Why can't we all make a choice, while awareness is still with us, as to whether or not we want to live this sort of sad half-life?

JANUARY 11, 1988: I HAVE HORRIBLE DREAMS ALMOST nightly: my mother dying in agony, a grandchild disappearing, myself buried in sliding sand, unable to cry out for help from people nearby. I wake up drenched in perspiration, shaking, crying. Breakfast is little comfort. Food, with rare exceptions, is tasteless, difficult to swallow. I walk from room to room, but the view from every window is bleak and hostile. The trees are gaunt, naked caricatures of their summer selves. Close to panic, I telephone a close friend in California who is a therapist.

"Genie," I say, "Why am I so miserable? Mom is being taken care of, I have time to myself—too much, it seems. I feel paralyzed. I sit for hours and stare at the most stupid television programs."

"I'm not surprised," she says. "You're suffering from loss of purpose and feeling isolated. You miss your friends and the familiarity of your life here." She is a successful writer and knows I share her interest. After reassuring me that I'm not losing my mind, she gives me an assignment to write one page a day on any subject and send her a copy of my first week's output. "Don't worry about good writing. Just be honest. If it's nothing more than a diatribe against ice and snow, that's okay."

I hang up, feeling a little encouraged.

FEBRUARY 2, 1988: MY MOTHER AND BELLE HELP fold laundry with other residents in the dining area. Staff people compliment them all on the job they do. It isn't bridge, but it's companionship.

Belle tells me she and Mom have been friends since they were young girls. I don't correct her.

Sometimes I eat a meal with them, but today I leave for a dental appointment just as they are sitting down to wait for their lunch trays. I glance back as I reach the door of the dining hall. My mother has put her head down on the table on her folded arms. Weariness? Sadness? I wish I knew.

MAY 8, 1988: IT'S MOTHER'S DAY, AND ONE OF Belle's daughters and I plan to make a two-family party of it in the Activity Room. Several of Belle's seven living children are there. She is near the head of the table; Mom and I are at the other end. One of the daughters has brought fresh yeast rolls, homemade peach preserves and real butter; the kitchen has prepared a feast of turkey and trimmings.

Belle is confused by all the visitors. Like Mom, she is rarely sure who's who. Also, her sight is not much better than her hearing. She strains to see the far end of the table. "Who's that?" she asks over and over, pointing toward my mother. "That's Emily, your roommate," Belle's daughter, Jane, tells her each time. By the time Belle asks again, we are all in high spirits, and Jane answers, "Oh, that's just another one of your kids, Mom." I am amazed when my mother answers, "Yes, I'm the youngest one!" It nearly breaks up the party. I never think of asking for a miracle, but this is one. My mother has not been intentionally humorous in years.

MAY 28, 1988: MOM AND BELLE HAVE BECOME inseparable. They share everything they have, even Belle's wheelchair. The only time Belle uses it is to go to the dining room. Aides used to push it to and from meals, but my mother has taken over the job. She is, in fact, rather high-handed about it and doesn't welcome help. It evidently fulfills her need to minister to someone, and holding the chair handles makes it easier for her to hobble down the hall. Between meals, Belle prefers her armchair by the window. At these times, Mom appropriates the wheelchair, sometimes moving it near Belle for a visit, but mostly rolling a foot or so forward, then backward, a motion that seems to be vastly comforting to her. At first, I try to persuade her not to use it so much, but Belle and her visiting daughters urge me to let her continue. I tease Belle and advise her to charge Mom rent on it. She assures me with twinkling eyes that one of these days she will present her bill.

JULY 21, 1988: I HAVE COME TO A DECISION THAT surprises me: I think my mother is actually happier here than she was at home with me. There she lay on the sofa most of the day while I sat at my word processor, my earphones making even casual conversation impossible. Now she is never bored. There are aides in and out of the room all day. Her excursions down the hall to be lifted into and out of her bath by a hydraulic contraption are small adventures. There are exercise classes in which residents sit in a circle and move whatever still answers the command, mostly arms, of course. Various clergymen rotate Sunday services. All holidays are observed with decorations and activities. There is even one called "Harvest Day," with prize-winning vegetables displayed on bales of hay out in front and a hayride in a horse-drawn wagon for those able to manage it. With so many companions of similar age, she is free of the "last leaf on the tree" syndrome.

There is also a weekly class on Colorado history,

that I attend with her one day and find fascinating. Mom pays little attention, but she smiles at me a lot and pats my hand constantly. And twice a week, a mental health professional gathers certain residents, Mom and Belle among them, in the Activity Room. I don't feel that I should ask to listen in, but I understand that the purpose is to help maintain stability for those who are in the greatest danger of slipping away from reality. I wait at the door today for them to come out. On the way back to the room, I say, "What do you talk about in your meeting?" "I'm not sure," she answers and leans down over the chair she is pushing to shout to Belle, "What did we talk about today?" "Oh, not much of anything," is Belle's answer. Still, I sense a feeling of importance in both of them at having been singled out for such special attention.

AUGUST 2, 1988: ON MY WAY TO SEE HER TODAY, I feel strangely lighthearted. I have cut my visits back to every other day, talking to her several times on the telephone on alternate days. I'm living life on a level new to me, walking down country roads as the day comes to life, writing, swimming and trying to capture on film sky and clouds seen through an old barbed wire fence. Best of all, I'm no longer feeling guilty. What I considered a "last resort" a year ago, I now regard as the best decision that I could have made. I don't mean that it's nirvana, but both of us are several steps closer than we were before.

When I walk into the room today, she is glad to see me. She asks me several times if it's Sunday. I say, "No, Mom, it's Tuesday." She rolls Belle's wheelchair up close to where I am sitting. I read letters from relatives to her, and she seems to listen attentively. I am not prepared for her comment out of the blue while I am putting the letters back into their envelopes. "I like my life," she says. I sit, stunned, wondering if mental telepathy is operating between us. I start to tell her how happy her words make me, but the moment is gone. She pats my hand and asks again, "You say this is Sunday?" ∎

LOU L. HARTNEY *is a free-lance writer in Montrose, CO.*

GOOD-BYE …

WHEN SOMEONE WE LOVE DIES, A VOICE INSIDE TELLS US OUR LIVES ARE FOREVER ALTERED

By Fred Wistow

Nobody is interested in hearing about deaths, unless they can be made pleasing or amusing.
—EDMUND WILSON

WHEN MY MOTHER SCREAMED INTO THE phone for me to get over there, "Daddy's dead," a long waiting period ended. My father's failing health over the past several years had left him almost helpless; he had demanded and received from my mother as much care and supervision as an infant.

At their apartment lay my father—the inert body of my father—on the carpet, which he had, in his first posthumous act, soiled. A few hours earlier, sitting listlessly in front of the television set on a late Sunday afternoon, he had stirred into half-marveled consciousness as an instant replay showed Jack Nicklaus sinking an impossible putt. Later, after eating a snack, as my mother cleaned the dishes, he fell off his chair and died. Hearing the thud, she ran in from the kitchen to discover his body on the floor.

Now, before me, he was no longer an animate object. Motionless, LIFE-LESS, he, it, lay there, an unwanted piece of furniture soon to be carted away by special movers.

We waited for my brother and his family. The police and funeral parlor people arrived. They performed their jobs with a mechanical concern that was more irritating than indifference. We wanted more, we wanted to have something explained, transformed, restored. But they did not give us more. They couldn't.

My father was dead, and for me that meant, on the most profound level, that his ability to speak, to smile, even to blink, all those magical talents were gone. No matter how rigid and stiff, how *dead* I'd thought his personality had come to be, all that was purely metaphorical. *This* being rolled out the door on a stretcher was dead, this unmoving, never-to-move-again former human being, my father.

Not wanting to confront the removal of his body and his companionship, my mother scrubbed the stain he had left.

THE EVOLVING THERAPIST

*I don't want to achieve immortality through my work,
I want to achieve it through not dying.*

—WOODY ALLEN

LAUREN BACALL, PHYLLIS NEWMAN AND OTHER show business people are recognizable in the audience at the Shubert Theatre. Onstage, 10 other celebrities await their turn to eulogize. Family members sit in the front orchestra. The public, too, has been invited, privileged to be part of this select group celebrating the memory of the recently deceased lyric writer Alan Jay Lerner.

The event consists of musical selections and gentle reminiscences that poke respectful fun. The audience learns that Alan was an urbane and witty gentleman genius; that he was a loving father who, married eight times, had a passion for women; that his death left a vacancy in the hearts of those who knew him; and that when everyone in the theater is dust, his lyrics will live on for millions yet unborn. An old film clip of Rex Harrison singing "I've Grown Accustomed to Her Face" reveals how sophisticated and beautiful those lyrics could be.

But the remembrances are curiously unmoving. However deeply Leonard Bernstein, Kitty Carlisle Hart and the others may be feeling Lerner's loss, their grief is not apparent. The impression they give is more like "I hope someone does this for me when I go" than "I miss this guy." Perhaps cynicism is unfair. A public ceremony like this has its own rituals; wearing one's heart on one's sleeve may not be one of them.

Paradoxically, it is the usually very proper, very English Julie Andrews who triggers the strongest emotions. She remembers being a young actress not fully aware of the immense gift Alan bestowed on her some 30 years ago when he helped train her for the part of Eliza Doolittle in "My Fair Lady." She wishes she had let him know how much she appreciated what he had given her.

Amid the clubby sense of professionalism, here is

the clearest hint of a human being lurking beneath the glittering facade of celebrity.

Aside from Julie Andrews, though, the celebration is disappointingly flat, lacking that special mixture of joy and sorrow—of life—that the circumstances had promised. There is a staleness in the air. Nothing is capturing the fact that Alan himself is now DEAD.

But is he?

Everything seems to say otherwise. Because the art he produced and bequeathed is eternal, it is as if he has not died after all. He has left his mark upon the world, and in that mark he lives.

There is something comforting about this immortality: a life has not been obliterated. In a way that is impossible for the billions who live and die unknown, remembered only by a few, death has been defeated.

Then something extraordinary happens. Someone announces that one of Alan's surviving children, Susan, "is not here today. She died a little while ago." A gasp runs through the audience.

Death is not supposed to behave this way, is it? Striking again, so soon, so close? A blunt reminder has been delivered. Our hope of a refuge—of death contained, death transcended—is a fiction.

Having set loose our insecurities one more time, death moves away. Then, slowly, the soothing balm of reminiscence spreads itself out again. The celebration closes with Alan Jay Lerner himself singing "Camelot" on the video monitor. Order has been restored.

*No people who turn their backs on death can be alive.
The presence of the dead among the living will be a daily
fact in any society which encourages its people to live.
Huge cemeteries on the outskirts of cities, or in places no
one ever visits, impersonal funeral rites, taboos which
hide the fact of death from children, all conspire to keep
the fact of death away from us, the living. . . .*

—CHRISTOPHER ALEXANDER

GOOD-BYE ...

ARLY ON THE MORNING AFTER MY FATHER DIED, the day he would be buried, my mother angrily emptied the drawers and closets and threw his clothes and artifacts on the living room floor. From the pile, she withdrew a few items—the dark brown, plaid flannel shirt she now wears to bed on very cold nights was one—and instructed my sister-in-law and me to get rid of the rest.

We packed the objects filled with my father into trash bags, loaded them into the car and deposited them at a Goodwill collection point that, for some odd reason, I had remembered passing. We searched awhile for a place to unload his walker and the combination toilet-wheelchair contraption he had used in his last months and finally found a giant dumpster in an industrial area nearby.

On the way back, we stopped at the funeral parlor. There, guided by the mortician through the crowded cellar showroom, I chose, from among a startling array of options of varying price and quality, my father's casket.

Back at the apartment, my two teenage nieces waited in silence for my mother's next outburst of tears and self-recriminations. Meanwhile, in the bedroom, my brother was sleeping off last night's long drive from New England and his hangover. My brother and I were continuing our lifelong roles: one the good boy, well-behaved, helpful, the other a slackabout, letting others do whatever needed to be done.

And, even without my father being present, the family continued to act as it generally did, silently watching my mother display emotion for all of us.

The funeral party consisted of my mother, my brother and his wife, their two kids, my father's corpse and me. No relatives were invited; all contact with them had long since died away. My parents had no friends to call either. It was as if my father had gone and done something shameful by dying, or maybe even by living, and it was our duty to hide that disgraceful act from view as quickly and quietly as possible. We did our job. The service was brief.

The coffin was lowered into a freshly dug hole beside a scrawny young tree. We were in a section of the cemetery now only beginning to be occupied. Years earlier my mother had purchased four adjacent plots at the site. This was the first to be used.

As we drove away, I saw my father pointing weakly to a patch of gray stubble in the creases below his chin, a patch I always seemed to miss while shaving him. I smelled once more, beneath the superficial fragrances of after-shave and talcum, that sickly-sweet stink of age and illness and impending death that both touched and repulsed me.

I asked the driver to stop. I got out to walk back to the grave. I wanted to help the gravediggers bury my father. It was something a friend had done at his father's funeral, something that had sounded melodramatic when I heard about it, but now felt exactly right. So sudden and inexplicable a reaction was unusual for me; I was the one family member who did not act impulsively. Then I heard the impatient cries of "Get back in the car" and "What are you doing?" and felt I was holding everybody up from doing something important. I got back in.

An hour after returning to my mother's apartment, my brother drove off, taking his family with him. My mother, afraid to reveal a need that might not be met, supported his decision to get back to work.

She vehemently objected to my decision to take the week off and stay with her; I was going to leave her alone in a week anyway, so why not get on with it now? I didn't really want to stay. I wanted to flee as much as my brother did, but I couldn't. I could not bear the *image* of my being the one to leave her totally alone in that apartment.

Later she confessed how grateful she was for my refusal to leave. I was glad, too. I needed to be away from people. I needed time to face what now looked like the absurd pointlessness of my father's life and my own.

That night I said yes to everything my mother wanted to cook for me. As we ate, she would suddenly break into tears and hit the table as if the whole thing could have been averted, as if the death had been her fault, as if this or that event had done it to him. Her shrieks penetrated to my bones. I felt helpless to comfort her and angry that I had to try.

"Ma," I'd argue stupidly, as if the content of what I said were relevant, "he was 82. He didn't just die. He was an old man, a very old man. He lived a long life. You're *supposed* to die at that age. It's nobody's fault. He was lucky he lived as long as he did."

"No," she rushed on, not hearing me, angering me still further, going on as if he should have lived forever. It was that fall he took three weeks ago, or those lousy hoodlums who mugged him 10 years ago, or how he worked his guts out for his sons. "If you only knew how much he loved you two guys."

"I know, Ma, but it's not like this was a surprise."

Failure is much commoner than success, though it has seldom been accorded even a small corner in the work of historians; it is also more endearing, and much more human. No death can ever be dismissed as banal, even if it cannot aspire to the proud luxury of a tombstone—a bold claim on the future.

—RICHARD COBB

IT WAS TWO A.M. A FLASH OF RED LIGHT SPLASHED across the familiar cracks in the sidewalk that were guiding me home. I looked up to see a police car, and a few feet behind it, a dead body. The superintendent's son was lying in the middle of the street. Someone had removed his Mets windbreaker and thrown it over his head.

"What happened?" I asked a cop. "He got into a fight, and somebody hit him over the head with a baseball bat." I cringed, feeling the dull thwack that smashed the life out of him, marking the moment that separated living consciousness from inert mass.

What, I thought, trying to bring a historical perspective to that moment, was today's date? July 9, 1971. No, it was already July 10th.

A chill accompanied my realization that earlier that very day, when it was still July 9th and no one knew what was going to happen in the early morning of the 10th, I had argued with him and his father about fixing the broken refrigerator in my apartment. The superintendent's son had stood in the doorway to his basement apartment wearing a T-shirt, holding a newspaper open to the racing page, explaining with excuses that were clearly lies why he could not do the job. How angry his arrogance had made me.

Now, only a dozen hours later, he was dead. Somebody else had confronted that arrogance head-on. Blood covered his T-shirt. The racing page he'd held would be the last he'd ever see. He'd never see the July 10th edition of the *Daily News,* nor the next day's paper nor the next.

Would the story of his own death make the paper?, I wondered. I pictured the giant presses of the *News* somewhere in Manhattan, churning out their product. It was probably too late for this story to appear. Would it make tomorrow's late editions? Or the six o'clock news? The 19-year-old son of an anonymous Puerto Rican superintendent: would the smashing in of his skull merit attention? Would the rest of the world slow down long enough to notice his death? And if it did, so what? Whether the item appeared as headline or filler, or not at all, he wouldn't be around to witness it.

As I turned to go upstairs, I noticed the silent crowd, unusually large for this hour of the morning, staring aimlessly at his body. Another 20 or so people surveyed the scene from windows overhead. Tomorrow our own lives, our own problems, would regain center stage, and we could once again forget the lesson of mortality that this motionless body was now teaching us. For now, a respectful quiet hung over the block. *(continued on page 450)*

To Die At Home

I T IS 1:30 IN THE AFTERNOON, AND MY 94-YEAR-OLD MOTHER IS DYING. SHE HAS HAD ARRHYTHMIA and related heart problems since she was 80, and although early on there were no outward symptoms, now, after 14 years, she has come to this point. She has not eaten much these last few days and has not had much water, either.

Her attending physician, a boyhood friend of mine, made a house call about two weeks ago and noted the initial symptom of failing kidneys: the characteristic red blush on her cheeks. I find it hard to accept that this chronic, systemic disease has finally brought my mother down.

My mother had always said that she wanted to die quietly and painlessly in her own bed at home after saying good-bye to me and my sister. It seems as if her own prewritten script is now being played out. Although I had feared that she might die before my sister, a psychologist in Florida, arrived home, my mother has somehow clung to life—barely. She did not recognize my sister when she got here late at night three days ago, though she did the next day. Each morning she seems better, more alert, only to tire and become almost unresponsive as the day wears on. It is this telling cycle that finally warns me that her death is imminent.

During the last week, she has become completely bedridden, and we have replaced her own bed with a hospital bed so that we can change, feed and bathe her more easily. She seemed somewhat disturbed by this change, but she has tolerated it.

When she developed a small bed sore on her left hip, I consulted with my sister-in-law in Boston, an oncology nurse familiar with the problems of the terminally ill. She advised me to get an adhesive that acts like a second skin, and my oldest son, a third-year resident in pediatrics, got some from the Children's Hospital.

I carry her now, a small, frail bundle. She seems stiff and resistant, scared, but when she is in my arms, she snuggles into me, letting me succor her—she, who has always been a tower of strength.

Now she does not move, and I recognize a stillness that foreshadows her death. I go downstairs to get my wife, who is working on the computer, and my sister, who is reading a book in the living room. Quietly we approach my mother's bedside and study her small, inert figure. She seems enveloped in stillness. Not wishing to disturb her sleeplike withdrawal, we leave her bedside. My sister says she thought she saw my mother's chest move as if she were still breathing. I note that the color is draining from her face. We withdraw to the living room to be with one another and to discuss the next steps we must take. The three of us seem so alone.

EARLIER I HAD BECOME CONCERNED WHEN MY MOTHER STOPPED TAKING LIQUIDS. ON TELEVISION I had been watching Chinese students being hospitalized, near death from their fast in Tiananmen Square. My mother had taken almost no nourishment for sometime. I had called a minister friend whose wife works in a hospice. When I described my mother's deteriorating condition and lack of liquid intake, she suggested that I get a gel-like paste for her lips and cautioned me that physicians are not very familiar with or responsive to the care and comfort of the terminally ill. I called the hospice center, but the nurse was reluctant to advise me without a referral from our attending physician.

I called our physician, who in turn cautioned me about involving the hospice nurse, who he thought would recommend hospitalization and a feeding tube. He said that this procedure is very invasive and uncomfortable and might counter my mother's wishes and our own concern for her. He suggested that we get an ordinary eyedropper from the drugstore and try giving her water this way. We did this, and when my mother responded, we gratefully suckled her. She soon tired, however, and we knew we were not getting enough fluids into her. Still, we kept up this regimen, even though we saw how very little water she was taking.

Weeks earlier, when the physician had made his last house call, I had asked what I needed to do if my mother should die. He had instructed me to call the police and ambulance service and had said they would know how to handle things. Now that the moment is here, I want to make one last attempt to obviate the coldness of the morgue and the brutality of an autopsy that follows an unattended death. So I call him again. I am hoping that since the day is getting late, and knowing that my mother is close to death, the doctor will come by the house on his way home.

"Can you stop by?" I ask.

But instead of answering directly, he instructs me again about calling the proper authorities. Then, after a pause, he adds, "You realize that we cannot be involved in murder." That word, spoken at this time by a person who is my friend, chills me. It is very clear that I have come to the limits of his ability to help, and we are now truly alone.

THE EVENING SUN IS SETTING ACROSS THE WAIANAE RANGE, AND I REALIZE THAT MY SON WILL soon be able to leave his work at Children's Hospital. We decide to wait for his help. When my other son returns home from his job at the university, I tell him about his grandmother's condition, and we both walk to her bedside. Her small, still figure looms large before us.

I recall my sister-in-law telling me how to determine when death has occurred—it would be obvious, she said—by pressing my ear to my mother's chest, listening for a heartbeat. I go back to her bedside and listen carefully. All that I can hear is a stillness that seems to fill the room. Then my sister listens. She is not sure what she hears.

I call Children's Hospital and ask my son if he can come home immediately. He arrives a short time later, still dressed in his scrub greens. He starts his procedure: he listens with his stethoscope on her chest and gently searches with his hands, but I stop him just when he is about to check my mother's pupillary reflex. I do not feel it is right to open her eyes; she seems so deeply asleep. Her mouth, which had slackened into an open drool, is now closed, and my sister notes this change with alarm. It is almost as if our mother has closed her lips to make herself presentable in death. Her vigilant, socially proper self has returned.

But my son calmly explains that it is a normal muscular reaction to rigor mortis, which is now beginning to be apparent. Although she is still quite warm to my touch, I realize she is gradually settling into a permanent stillness.

It is time to give her a final bath and to change her clothes. Now it is we who are concerned about the public presentation of our mother.

I call her friend, a Buddhist priest, who comes to join us in chanting the pillow sutra prayer. There is a moment of distractive panic when we realize that we ourselves are not dressed for public presentation. The rituals of death have begun. The priest pauses at her bedside and is struck by her peaceful countenance. His presence bears witness to an event that is becoming more and more real.

GOOD-BYE ...

IT IS TIME FOR THE AUTHORITIES TO BE NOTIFIED. I DIAL 911 AND GET THE OPERATOR TO SEND A policeman. I explain that even though I am reporting my mother's unattended death, it was not unexpected—her physician had been monitoring her condition, and she was 94 years old. I tell them that I would appreciate sensitivity on the part of the officer when he arrives.

About five minutes after I hang up, while waiting for the arrival of the officer, the phone rings. The same operator I have just spoken to asks if this is 988-1773. An odd thought floats through my mind. Is this a confirmation call like the one we get when we order pizza?

The policeman arrives. He is sensitive and unobtrusive. While he questions me, the ambulance crew arrives—two women in white with instruments and face masks. As they disappear brusquely down the hall, I send my son after them to talk them out of obtrusive measures. Soon they reappear, and now they too seem calm and appropriately subdued.

They ask to speak to the attending physician. I phone him, and after a minimal discussion, they tell me that they will leave my mother's body at home and the certificate of death with the physician. I am very grateful. Saying that the physician wants to speak to me, they pass back the phone.

"Well, I think things are going to work out," he says. "You can call the ambulance."

I am confused, because he has just been speaking with the ambulance crew chief. Disoriented by his absentminded comment and the lack of any words of comfort from him, I hang up the phone. The police and ambulance crew leave. I walk to her bedside. My mother could be quietly sleeping.

It is almost dark when the undertaker and his assistant arrive, and I'm glad they have come in a plain station wagon. Climbing up to my mother's room, the attendant says that the stairs are too narrow and steep for the gurney, so they will wrap and carry my mother down. But I wrap her— tenderly, possessively—and they allow me to. I pick her up to carry her in my arms. She has stiffened in death, and I hardly know what I am doing. When I reach the gurney, I hesitate, noticing that the hold-down strap will cross my mother's chest. The undertaker immediately understands my hesitation and moves the strap down to her waist.

I cannot stand to see them push her into the station wagon. I feel like taking her back and driving her to the mortuary in our family car. I become aware of the nervous shuffling of my family as they stand behind, watching me. While crazy thoughts race in my brain, all anyone looking at me can see is my awkward tapping on the roof of the station wagon.

I SIT WITH A GLASS OF WINE IN HAND. WE HAVE KEPT THE TIDE OF OUTSIDE INTRUSION FROM ENgulfing us because of our resources: a physician who went along with our decision, a son who is also a physician at our side, a close-knit family, our own professional experience in intimate human situations, a relatively simple and benign disease process, a strong mother who, even in death, demanded and got her way. And still, with all that, the event has utterly drained me.

I now sit. My mother is dead. I am overwhelmed by the realization. My *kachan* is dead.

Later that night, I wake up cradled in my wife's arms, wracked by tears. Again and again. □

—*George Y. Fujita*
MARCH 1990

GEORGE Y. FUJITA *is a counseling psychologist at the University of Hawaii and a therapist in private practice in Honolulu, HI.*

(continued from page 446)

> As the days go by,
> I keep thinking,
> "When does it end?
> Where's the day, I'll have
>   started forgetting?"
> But I just go on
> Thinking and sweating
> And cursing and crying
> And turning and reaching
> And waking and dying
> And no,
> Not a day goes by,
> Not a blessed day
> But you're still somehow
> a part of my life.
> And you won't go away.

—STEPHEN SONDHEIM

THE DEATH OF MY FATHER INTERFERED WITH THE realization of a family fantasy. My brother had converted the basement of his New England home into a place for my parents to live. Without my father to join her, my mother at first refused to move. Some weeks later, however, she consented to a weekend trial run, but just for one night. The morning after that first night she announced that she was never going back to the apartment where my father died. And she never did. She moved into the basement. Between her and the rest of the household she erected a Chinese wall on a foundation of shame and gratitude.

She consigned herself to the physical care and supervision of my brother and his wife, and I, at long distance, became responsible for her emotional well being. Her children were taking over for her husband. And was it ever different? Perhaps I just gave up fighting it, and my brother stopped running from it. Several of the physical ailments she had left untreated during my father's last years finally got taken care of. And to me, living 200 miles away, she could express the loneliness she hid from the people with whom she now shared a house.

We began a semiannual pilgrimage.

My mother would come to New York, and I would take her to my father's grave. There, as if on cue, hysteria would reign. She'd cry and wail, "Why did you have to go? Why didn't you take me with you?" I felt pushed further into the role of parent and resented having to watch out for her, having to let her emotional outbursts and needs predominate. She'd forget I was there, then remember, then balance her statements, editing as she went "Why did you leave me? I'm all alone. I have nothing to live for. . . . I mean, of course, I have the boys, but you promised you'd never leave me."

A few feet away, I would squirm, self-righteously enduring this outrageous display. I wondered if I missed the man at all. What ever had he given me? Did he leave a void or just some burden? I couldn't tell, the experience was so totally devoted to my mother's needs. Here she was, specially dressed in old clothes for the occasion, lying on the ground beside the grave and, to my embarrassed eyes, playing a scene, badly.

I felt preempted. It seemed only a husband was lost, never a father. I realized that in the years since his death, and aside from my mother's histrionics, my family had honored my father with silence. We rarely mentioned him and never expressed what, if anything, we felt, either about his life or the fact that he was gone. Our family's muteness had swallowed him whole. With friends I had discussed him at length and often bitterly, but never with my mother or my brother.

To offset the agony of our cemetery visits, I insisted on committing the sin of taking my mother to a restaurant. She would attack me and my idea viciously, railing on about the waste of money, the dishonor to my father of introducing pleasure into the procedure, and even admitting embarrassment at how she looked. In time I added a Broadway show to the ritual. "We're not dead," I'd argue halfheartedly. In time she came to look forward to what she had once fought.

As the years passed, slowly but unmistakably, it became clear that my mother's seemingly endless tears and fits were subsiding. The positive aspect of my father's death was having its effect. His constant complaining was gone. So, too, was the thankless caretaking she had managed to perform under crisis conditions, expecting death at any moment. She started acting and looking younger. My nerves became less raw. I reacted to her less out of anger and self-righteousness, more with patience and reassurance. Gradually her panic lessened.

Changes were taking place, but always individually, never family-style. In addition to her move from the city, my mother started taking sewing classes at the Y. My brother wound up in an alcohol rehabilitation clinic, where he kicked his 20-year-old drinking problem. And my incessant depression brought me to a shrink. We were treating our addictions.

ON THE FOURTH ANNIVERSARY OF NICKLAUS'S putt, we went to visit my father yet again. This time my brother joined us. Our corner of the cemetery was becoming more populated; the tombstones of new neighbors blocked our view as we approached.

My father's absence had by now become less a trauma and more a soft ache. My mother's old theatricality had nearly vanished. She tenderly hugged his headstone and sobbed. Then, murmuring gently, she rested her head on the hard stone slab as if it were a pillow. My brother stood off to the side in the shade of the tree and cried. I loved them at that moment as they let their feelings take hold of them without their customary need for hysteria or flight.

I saw these three people anew. Yes, for there, too, a few feet below us, confused and touched by this outpouring, was my father. Separate and awkwardly solitary they were, heavenly bodies destined to orbit in isolation yet exerting on each other and on me a silent gravitational pull of enormous intensity. The forces and the bonds had weakened substantially since his death, but they remained far more powerful than any others I had known.

This constellation was more than my family, it was my identity, it was me. We were each less addicted now—to alcohol, to hysteria, to sadness and to suffering—but we still could not comfort each other. We sought our solace alone, in silence, as if there were something wrong in seeking comfort. We hid openly, in the shade of a tree, with the support of a stone, in the shelter of a coffin and the safety of detachment. Receding from them, I watched, as always, from outside that mysterious triangle of pain and loss and love, while somehow being trapped in it, too.

From beneath the headstone silently whispering our family name, my father waved good-bye. His burial was almost done.

There is . . . no death. There is only . . . me . . . me . . . who is going to die . . . .
—ANDRE MALRAUX

IN A BOX IN A CORNER, A VERY DARK CORNER OF the mind of each of us, is a voice. The voice says, "I am going to die. One day I am going to die."

We tend not to venture near that corner. We rarely listen to that voice. Sometimes it speaks to us so clearly and emphatically that we have to listen. When we're sick, when we narrowly escape harm, when someone we know dies, we hear it speaking to us. We hear it more frequently as we age, as our bodies fail, as our cumulative experience of death increases. Sometimes the voice emits a powerful, powerful scream that shakes us mercilessly. When someone we love dies, the voice tells us that our life is forever altered, that there is no going back.

The voice reminds us that we are, like everyone else who ever lived, mortal, expendable. How we

THE EVOLVING THERAPIST

react to this voice, how we try to block it out, determines how we live our lives.

I T IS LATE AFTERNOON ON A CRISP, CLEAR SPRING day in New York City. Down the hall, through the 25th-floor office windows, are visible hundreds of buildings—the breathtaking skyscape of New York. But the sight is tempered by a telephone call I've just received. A fellow worker is in the hospital, seriously ill. The shock of the news leaves me uneasy. I'll visit him tomorrow.

My energies turn to a minor problem. Unexpectedly, I have an extra ticket to a play this evening; a friend has canceled at the last minute. I don't want the money to go to waste, so I start calling people to see if anyone's available. One by one they politely reject the offer; other plans and desires stand in their way. The fact that the play is *Hamlet* does not ease my task.

Each time I hang up the phone, I feel a mounting sense of isolation. Everybody's readiness to do other things, to keep going their own way, in spite of my dilemma, is having a surprisingly intense effect on me. Each rejection seems terminal. I feel helpless, almost nonexistent. I can see how I'm overdramatizing things, but I can't seem to help it. I'm gone.

After the fifth call, I must stop. Exactly how I got there I don't know, but I'm feeling the frightening sensation of what the world would be like if I were dead: how it would simply go on, impervious to my absence, just as it already seemed to be going on as if I weren't there.

I walk to the end of the hall. The floor is empty, people have gone home for the day. Through a window I can see the spring sunset illuminating the rows of buildings standing guard over the green carpet of Central Park. It is an awesome display. They are the world, a massive lineup of beautiful solidity, majestic indifference, filled with invisible people making love, having fights, watching TV. A dark spot, the shadow of a cloud, passes over the soft

green tufts of trees. Off to the left, I see the hospital I'll be visiting tomorrow. In the distance, the George Washington Bridge connects this hyperactive island to the rest of the planet.

I think of my father and the other people I've known who have died. The world, serenely and implacably, has moved on. The buildings show their blind faces to today's setting sun. Tomorrow the rains will wash them clean for the next day's sun, whose memory will be washed away by the rain of the day thereafter, and history will continue to unfold, unaffected, as if those lives had never happened.

Now, as I look out through the window and see in their fate my own, I am stunned. I am dizzied by the beauty of the scene before me and how it reflects the fragility of my own life. A deep loneliness overcomes me as my body fully absorbs the simple, unavoidable notion that one day this scene will be when I am not.

Then, as unexpectedly as it appeared, my lonely panic transforms itself. I feel calm. The dispensability I share with the rest of humanity is reassuring. The realization of my mortality has somehow strengthened me: there is simply nothing I can do about it. However I die, or when, the world outside this window and the infinite masses of things and people beyond my vision will go on just as they do now, inexorably, indifferently. My father finally settles in his grave.

As the sun sets, I bask in the light of a stark truth: my efforts to place the ticket or, on a grander scale, to leave my mark upon the world, will one day be as comically irrelevant and as fleeting as ghosts on a television screen.

Comforted by that image, shielded by it, I go down to the nighttime streets, off to the play, alone. ∎

FRED WISTOW *is a lawyer and free-lance writer who lives in New York City.*

PHOTOGRAPH BY GIDEON MENDEL/MAGNUM

SEALING OUT THE NIGHT

THE WARTIME DIARY OF AN ISRAELI THERAPIST

By Sheri Oz

MONDAY, JANUARY 14. IN SPITE OF SADDAM'S threats, in spite of the fact that I believe there will be a war in the Gulf, it is inconceivable to me that missiles will be fired on Israel. While the government-issued gas masks—one for myself and two for my two young daughters—are too conspicuous to be ignored, even high up on the top shelf in the living room, I cannot imagine our actually using them.

In the sex-education course I run for schoolteachers at Haifa University, it is impossible to conduct a lesson today. All the class members can talk about is the paralyzing fear about the impending hostilities. I cannot connect emotionally with their conversation. I feel numb.

At home I am inexplicably exhausted. Tonight I do not want to give in to the relentless fatigue that forced me to sleep at 8 p.m. the past few nights. Instead of going to bed, I decide to take the missile threat seriously and finally select a room for sealing, covering the windows with plastic sheeting by following the directories in a government-issued book on defending oneself in case of chemical warfare.

Magically, I feel wide awake, and then I realize that my weariness was a response to fear of which I had been unaware.

TUESDAY, JANUARY 15. THE DAY BEFORE D-DAY; IT IS still the 14th in Washington, D.C. Even though I still don't believe a missile attack will come, I am scared. I listen to the news every hour, momentarily expecting the announcement that will send everybody into our presealed rooms, where families will be as isolated from each other as bubbles at the bottom of the ocean. Last night I dreamed bands of gas-masked delinquents used the unprecedented opportunity to roam the neighborhoods, robbing houses at will.

Today, at a curriculum planning meeting for training social workers, we spent most of the time in rather manic chitchat. Yesterday I didn't understand the panic in the room; today I am beginning to be affected myself.

Since Friday, clients have been canceling appointments, saying they'll reschedule "after the war." I hadn't actually considered the impact of hostilities on my as-yet-fragile economic security. No clients, no pay; for a single mother this is a chilling thought. Then, unexpectedly, a 16-year-old who has "forgotten" to show up for the past two weeks appears at my door for her regular session. One way or another, she is determined to show me how different she is from everybody else.

It's late now, 1:30 a.m., and I'm tired but too wired to go to bed. In Canada I could let the TV lull me to sleep, but here in Israel they shut off that tranquilizer at 1 a.m. I wander around the apartment, thinking about my kids. Keren, my 10-year-old daughter, says she's not frightened, "because we've done everything we've been told to do in order to be safe." My 8-year-old, Tali, on the other hand, feels she is suffocating much of the day. She asks, over and over, will we know when to go into the sealed room, will we remember how to put on the gas masks, will we know if we need to inject ourselves with atropine against nerve gas, will it hurt. The steady stream of instructive films on television about these precautions do not reassure her, they just remind her of the pressure in her chest.

WEDNESDAY, JANUARY 16. AT 7 A.M. MY DAUGHTERS wake and start getting ready for school, while I turn on the TV to find out whether we can expect war to break out at the end of the American ultimatum. The announcer says all schools are closed until Sunday. Usually a late sleeper by choice, I am too jumpy this morning to go back to bed. Instead, I make phone calls. I call L., a relatively new client who came to see me because she was frightened of the rage and fantasies of violence that her 4-year-old daughter triggered in her. L. appreciated the call. She is feeling good, mainly because her teenage sister has come to stay for a few weeks and relieve some of the pressure on her by helping with the children. I hope the dramatic effects of household help on her mood will reinforce my attempts to involve her husband in therapy.

M. did not show up for his appointment. I am not surprised, but I am worried because he didn't call, either. M. is a young Christian Arab, caught between traditional values and a more modern disposition, who is nearing the end of 10 months of therapy for depression and identity confusion. I can guess at the kind of conflicts this situation must be raising for him and wonder when I'll see him again.

Another scratchy anxiety. My parents have not called yet, though I know that, far away in Canada, they must be very worried. Other North American friends have received more than one call by now, often from distraught relatives pressuring them to leave Israel. On the other hand, some families react to a perceived threat by building a defensive wall around themselves in order to avoid pain. Maybe my parents are feeling too anxious to *want* to know what's going on here. So I phone them, but they are not at home, and I leave a rather hollow message on their answering machine.

All day I feel a driving need to be in touch with people, and find myself talking incessantly—with my daughters, on the telephone, visiting neighbors—but this garrulousness does nothing to stem my growing anxiety. By evening I am so shaky I disobey civil defense rules and open the gas mask kits so we can adjust the straps and practice putting them on. I want to make sure we don't fumble when—I say *when* now, not *if*—the real attack comes. The girls have their masks on in seconds, they have practiced so much in school. They help me adjust mine. Well, I think sardonically, we had fire drills when I was in elementary school, now they have chemical warfare drills. What's the difference?

At 2 a.m. I am awakened by my ex-husband, Moti, who calls to tell me that the Americans have started bombing Iraq. War has begun! Now, he says, we are supposed to open our gas masks and listen to the radio from this point on. My first reaction is relief that the Americans have attacked those who threatened to obliterate us, and my first thought is of Iraqi women at this moment living through what I have so far only had to fear. I see them in my mind, terrified, running, holding their children, and I wish nobody had to go through that.

At the same time, I feel an odd, almost shameful sense of excitement and gratification that the Americans are fulfilling their promise. In a surge of energy, I recheck the sealed room, fill a bucket with water in which to soak the towels that will be pressed against the space at the bottom of the door, move the telephone to the room, lay out a carpet and blankets on the floor, and remove heavy articles from the top shelves. Then I get the utility shed in the backyard ready for the dog—sealing the two small windows with packaging tape and plastic sheeting.

All this activity has helped me remain calm, but now, with these chores done, I'm anxious again. Much to my own surprise, I find myself calling up Moti to ask him to come sit with me for a while. Until now the last thing I would have wanted was to be closed in a small, sealed room for hours with my ex-husband. But now, having him there sharing responsibility for the girls seems like another comforting bulwark against the unimaginable. Moti says he'll come by "later, maybe," and at 4 a.m. he shows up, gas mask in hand. We watch TV, drink coffee, and wonder why the Iraqis haven't done anything yet. We laugh about the eerie feeling that the Americans are shooting at a dog that is already dead: maybe the Iraqi military machine has been destroyed; maybe the Iraqis never really had a huge military machine after all, and it was all just propaganda. When Moti leaves, I fall into a deep, dreamless sleep on the couch, with the TV on, documenting a war so far away, yet unnervingly close.

T HURSDAY, JANUARY 17. AT ABOUT 8 A.M. THE GIRLS and I wake up. I tell them the war has started but that Israel isn't involved. They both chorus at once, "Does that mean we have to go to school today?" No, I tell them, school is still closed. Normally I would have been teaching sex education at Shfeya, a boarding school for children from troubled families. Of course, no clients come in the afternoon, either, so I phone friends and we share our relief that nothing has happened here. Outside the sun is shining, the puddles left from the night's rain sparkle, and the air is pure and clear. I take the dog for a walk. Strangely, all the stores are closed, as if it were a peaceful Sabbath morning.

At 10 a.m. Moti calls to ask if he can come over to see the children. They both sit on his lap, competing with the television news reports for his attention. After a while, he busies himself fixing my computer. The atmosphere is calm, pleasantly domestic. Under no other circumstance would I tolerate him in my house, but today I actually enjoy having him here.

While Moti is puttering around, I am delighted to discover that we have only one bag of milk left, and I have an excuse to get out of the house. I walk to the car, my gas mask kit slung jauntily over my shoulder, and drive to the supermarket feeling like a disobedient child as I listen to the radio announcer sternly order everyone to stay indoors. But at the supermarket I notice lots of other people have developed cabin fever as well, a condition that seems assuaged by buying lots of junk food, if the groceries in their baskets are any indication. Since I am already out, I compound my naughtiness by driving around the mostly deserted streets, savoring another few minutes of freedom.

At 10:15 p.m. whatever euphoria I felt earlier is long gone. I am very tired, nervous, cranky. I snap at the girls, though they have been wonderful, playing quietly, watching TV, having long, interesting conversations, benignly immune to my irritability. All day generals and journalists have been warning us that the Iraqis still have missiles left, and Saddam makes it clear he fully intends to hit us with chemical weapons. So I can't get into their holiday mood, but I'm upset with myself for being so preoccupied with my own anxiety that I can't be more playful and relaxed with them. Meanwhile, a Greek-Israeli basketball game, of all irrelevancies, is playing on TV, and I fall asleep in the middle.

FRIDAY, JANUARY 18. AT 2 A.M. I AM AWAKENED BY the rising and falling sounds of a siren—on and on it shrieks—and I don't know if it's for real or if I'm dreaming. Even when I get up and begin pacing back and forth across the room, I cannot quite take it in—real? not real? real? not real?—until I hear a loud boom that jars me into full consciousness, and I go into action. I put the dog in the shed, wake up the girls, and scurry them off into the prepared room. Suddenly, I cannot find the radio, and for an instant I rush frantically around looking for it, finding it in the kitchen, where Keren and I had last been listening to it.

In the sealed room the girls are wide awake and calm; they put on their gas masks efficiently, with little help from me. I seal the door from the inside while they sit on the blankets, watching me intently. As soon as I have put tape all around the door, I begin to remember things I had wanted to take into the room—pillows, a book to read, our shoes just in case we have to leave the house in a hurry. Too late; we'll do without. Tali begins to scratch at a rash. We don't have any calamine lotion, and I tell her she'll have to use some control and not scratch. She does not scratch anymore.

Moti phones to check if we are alright. I can barely hear him through his mask, and I can barely talk, myself. My mouth is dry, my whole body is shaking. We sit, side by side, on a blanket on the floor, covered by another blanket—I forgot to bring in pillows—and the whole scene seems strange and dreamlike. The radio doesn't tell us much, but it is comforting to hear calm, familiar voices in the room with us.

Cowering in our sealed room, I just wish that the Americans or our own air force would blast all Iraqis off the face of the earth. I don't care anymore about the Iraqi women and children. I feel guilty about my failure of empathy, but I really only want everything connected with this fear to be over and done with. I guess the Iraqis feel the same way about us, especially after being fed hatred of Israel all their lives. It happened to me overnight.

After an hour and a half, the announcer tells us we can take off our masks but must stay in the room. I have already urinated into a bucket several times. The girls are disgusted, until they feel the need themselves. But when I have a bowel movement that I cannot hold (so that's what "it scared the shit out of me" means), Keren tells me she wants to put her gas mask back on. We all laugh for the first time. Then we play card games. Some friends call on the phone, and we give each other mutual emotional support. Talking to her grandmother in Jerusalem, Tali says she was shaking with fear but told herself repeatedly that everything would be alright; when the music started playing on the radio, she could relax.

At 4:30 a.m. we are told that residents of Haifa and Tel Aviv are to put their masks on again. Then we are told to take them off. We leave them on until we hear several more times that it is okay to remove them. Tali dozes on and off. We all talk about how we feel. My whole body is weak and my head feels numb, so that I wonder if maybe I haven't been poisoned by some gas; with no other symptoms, however, I finally attribute my reactions to fear.

At 6 a.m. the radio announcer tells us we can leave our sealed rooms, and we straggle out of our cell to watch television in the living room. The girls seem relaxed and in good spirits; they release their tension by affectionately wrestling with each other. After playing with toys for some time, they join me in front of the television but are soon bored by the repetitious reports and film clips, and fall asleep.

The sun comes up, the sky is clear blue. It is warm for this time of year, I think, perfect weather for a walk on the beach. All in all, five missiles—none of them with poison gas—landed in our area.

I call Moti and ask him to come and be with us. Then I send a telegram home to my parents saying we are alright. Moti arrives and helps take shelving units out of the sealed room to make more space for mattresses. I make sure all the things I had forgotten to take in are now there. Last night was a passable dry run, but next time the missiles may have chemical warheads, and we may have to spend hours in the sealed room.

I usually spend Friday mornings doing supervision and seeing clients. Instead, I sit apathetically in front of the TV. We get a call from my mother, which improves my state of mind (though not my nerves), but as noon passes, I begin to feel weak in the stomach. Already I fear the night. Nighttime, which I always liked here for its mild weather and peaceful darkness, is now my enemy. And now I am as sure that Israel will be hit again as I was sure a few days ago that we would not be. It will happen tonight, or the next night, or the next. It will be night.

It is 6:30 p.m., and I feel sick, shaking all over, my mouth dry. I try to keep an even voice and not let it show on my face because I don't want my girls to be affected. Every slight noise or irregular sound makes me feel faint. I never before knew what fear was—all the risks I have ever taken, the times I felt adrenaline flow through my body, were nothing to the maelstrom of fear now pulling me under.

Moti does not seem particularly scared, and I wonder if his being here allows me the luxury of giving in to my fear. Maybe I am being frightened for both of us. I only know that the waiting is driving me crazy, as if I were a sitting duck for the missile with my name on it. And it will search me out in my own home! How do people in Beirut live any kind of life at all?

Moti's girlfriend calls for the sixth or seventh time, very unhappy that he has come to stay here. She is 29, never married, and does not understand parents' need to be with their children in a situation like this. Moti is irritated by the calls. But this time she does not ask for him, she simply gives me a message she says she received from a "reliable source"—we are to brace ourselves for an onslaught of chemical missiles. I turn white and nearly collapse. When I hang up and tell Moti what she has said, he disappears into the next room to make a phone call.

At 8:30 p.m. we hear the alarm that sends us back to the sealed room and our gas masks. I am perversely glad. The interminable waiting for imminent catastrophe has driven me nearly crazy, and I have wondered if I could get through another night. Now I find we all perform the steps we have gotten used to so quickly, and it is easy. My exhaustion magically melts away, leaving me alert and aware, even though I have had almost no sleep in the last two days. The girls play computer games while Moti and I listen to the radio.

When the all-clear sounds within an hour, I feel considerably calmer than before the alert. Moti and I go back to watching TV while the girls go to sleep. I am sleepy, too, but whenever I close my eyes I see missiles on their way to Haifa, so I go into the sealed room, lie on the mattress beside the girls, and with one ear toward the radio, I doze on and off. Our own planes drone continuously overhead, and the sound is both threatening and soothing. At about 3 a.m. I fall into a deep sleep.

SATURDAY, JANUARY 19. AT 5 A.M. MOTI WAKES US all up for a missile alert. Masks again, computer games again, and now I am no longer afraid. By 7 a.m. we are out of the sealed room and back in front of the TV. From the reports that only the center of the country has to remain in sealed rooms, I conclude that missiles have fallen in Tel Aviv. Moti's sister, who works in the air force, calls and confirms this suspicion, telling us that 10 people have been slightly injured.

I feel more confident now. I'm beginning to believe that we really are practiced and well protected, but more than this I suspect that if the Iraqis were going to use chemical missiles, they would have done so already. But then it occurs to me that they may launch chemicals only when they see that they have lost the war and want to cause Israel as much damage as possible.

All day I feel great—confident, unafraid, optimistic. The relatively mild extent of damage done by the missiles, the comparatively mild injuries, dissipate a good deal of my fear. In addition, all the support from other countries (even though I know they are fickle in their affections) inflates my pride in Israel. In an expansive glow, I call friends and clients, clean up the house, do the laundry, play hopscotch with my girls in the adjacent schoolyard, all the while glad for the opportunity to have this "holiday" with my children.

Then comes nightfall, and the familiar terror insinuates itself into my body, bringing a hollow feeling to my stomach, making me jump when the telephone rings or a window rattles. A door slams, and I feel faint. I strain to hear the siren and feel tired again but afraid to close my eyes.

While I have sunk back into fearful lethargy, Moti keeps the girls busy with calisthenics lessons, laughing and using pent-up energy. Now it's Tali's turn to be teacher, and she decides to give a karate class. Both girls take the "lesson" very seriously, while Moti plays the naughty child. Keren is pleased with the game, and herself, and comes over to kiss me on the cheek. Then, inadvertently, she gives Tali too hard a punch in the chest, and rather than cry, Tali kicks her in the knee. The game ends in anger, Keren begins to play a game of solitaire, and Tali curls up beside me on the couch.

At 9 p.m. we have a false alarm. For Tali, the whole business has become a game, and she likes retreating into the sealed room. I think she and Keren like having Moti here. Their crisis will come

when this situation is over and Moti goes home.

At 3:30 a.m. I am still awake and see lights in the neighbors' houses. On the radio, people are calling in to the station to talk about their fears and insomnia. Meanwhile, the television is screening movies all night now, so at least I have a movie to keep me company. Moti is snoring away soundly, the girls are sleeping peacefully. Planes drone overhead. Israel just got Patriot missiles today, so tonight may be Iraq's last chance to do us serious damage.

SUNDAY, JANUARY 20. TODAY IS A BRIGHT, SUNNY day. The whole country is still in a state of alert, with only essential services in operation, so we are once again home, watching TV, or out standing hours in line at the supermarket to stock up, or taking short walks in the neighborhood. Moti drives into Haifa to visit his girlfriend for a couple of hours.

I must miss seeing clients, because when Moti comes back, I begin a "session" with him, asking him about his relationship with his girlfriend, exploring areas of dissatisfaction, suggesting ways he could improve things. I know him well enough to make playful jabs at him, feeling freer and safer doing this now than I did when we were married. This conversation is a respite from the missile alerts and invigorates me. I am swimming in familiar waters and feel more secure and in control.

Through phone conversations with friends and clients, I begin to see an overall pattern in the way married couples deal with being housebound. Generally, the women are more overtly distressed and frightened than the men, who project an image of greater equanimity and composure. When one spouse wants to change the other's outward emotional state—the husband, for example, is impatient with his wife's "hysteria," or the wife thinks her husband is acting like a cold fish—the position of each becomes more polarized and extreme. They get on each other's nerves and feel trapped together in the house. On the other hand, when the woman finds comfort and strength in her husband's seeming fearlessness, or when the man allows his wife her fear, they find the time together pleasurable.

My client C., for example, came to see me initially because her husband had lost all of his confidence, decisiveness and initiative following a car accident two years before. I had wondered if, having handled the reins for two years, she would even allow him any control during the present crisis. But when I call her today, she and her husband are doing very well. Her husband immediately took charge of delegating tasks, and his wife felt deeply relieved. I point out to her that this crisis may trigger a return of his self-confidence that will last beyond the current situation.

In the case of divorced couples with children from the former union, when no common children have been born to the new marriage there appears to be a temporary reversion to the former family unit. The husband leaves his new spouse, and perhaps the children born to her and her previous husband, and goes back to his ex-wife and his children who are in her custody. The ex-spouses know they are together for a short time, for a single purpose — to see that the children are safe, cared for and secure. This common bond neutralizes, for the time being, the volatile incompatibilities that originally split the couple apart.

MONDAY, JANUARY 21. I GO TO SLEEP AT 2 A.M. and wake at 4 a.m. Everything is quiet. There is a boring movie on TV, so I go back to bed in the sealed room, slipping in between Keren and Tali, and sleep soundly until 7 a.m.

Later that morning Keren has a friend over to play, and I go visit a friend of mine. Gradually, people are returning to the regular routines of daily life, going back to work everywhere in the country except for the Haifa and Tel Aviv areas. The news reports are beginning to sound monotonous, and

even the television station seems to agree, announcing that instead of updates every two hours, the next news program after the noon report will be at 9 p.m.

I marvel at the immediate materialization of special all-day TV programs designed to calm both child and adult viewers. We are presented with comic skits making fun of people sitting in sealed rooms and wearing gas masks. Laughing at ourselves provides an outlet for the release of tension. We watch interviews of families made homeless, but who remain optimistic, and of the brave children who had been rescued from under the collapsed walls of their house. On the TV screen, we meet American soldiers who seem as appreciative of the warmth of the Israeli public as we are of their reassuring presence.

At 6:30 p.m. it has already been dark for an hour, and I only just now noticed it. Am I getting used to being threatened with chemical poisoning? Tomorrow the whole country goes back to work, but schools remain closed, and working mothers are expected to remain home with their children.

TUESDAY, JANUARY 22. I WAKE UP AT 7 P.M. LAST night was the first time since before the crisis that I permitted myself to sleep the whole night through. I accomplished this feat by convincing myself that whether I slept or stayed awake quaking with fear, Saddam had made his own calculations about when to try killing us.

At 8:30 p.m. Saddam sends Tel Aviv another missile that causes more injury and property damage than the previous two attacks together. Even so, the same intense fear I felt earlier just does not come back. My heart sinks at the slightest noise, but in moments between I feel relatively steady.

WEDNESDAY, JANUARY 23. I GET A PHONE CALL from a new referral who wants to see me for sex therapy and am amazed that anyone would embark on non-war-related therapy at this point. Next, M., my young Christian Arab client, comes for a session. He is greatly disturbed by an apparently uncontrollable urge for sexual release that makes him fear he will try to seduce his attractive sister-in-law, as well as other older women in his life toward whom he feels affection. In the session, he begins to separate his physical sensations from his emotional reactions and discovers that what felt like raw sexual desire is in fact a symptom of intense fear and powerlessness. While fantasizing about sexual encounters with women who care about him, he becomes aware that what he really wants is closeness.

I also see L., the overwhelmed mother whose teenage sister has come to help out. During this week at home, not having to put in a full day of outside work as well as take care of her family, she realizes she has been and can be a good mother. She also recognizes that her outbursts of rage directed against her child are expressions of frustration at her own inability to be perfect.

For me, at a time like this, it is reassuring to see clients returning to therapy; it means I am still wanted.

At 9:30 p.m. we return to the sealed room once again. We hear a number of booms and cover ourselves with blankets and pillows in case one of the booms lands in our yard. After the all-clear, we learn that the missile Saddam had directed at Haifa exploded in the air upon impact with a Patriot missile. Suddenly, I feel exhilarated that we are no longer passive and helpless; we have the means to protect ourselves. I can sleep easily tonight.

THURSDAY, JANUARY 24. AMAZING HOW FAST THINGS change. Yesterday I felt urgently compelled to write in this journal; today, I have to push myself. Yesterday, I could not stand the thought of sending the girls to school; today, I look forward to my freedom. Yesterday, I wanted Moti to stay with us; today, I am irritated by the thought of him being here. Basically, I am no longer afraid. I know the

danger has not disappeared, but the powerful Israeli-American response to the threat has boosted everyone's morale. We don't feel like helpless victims with our names inscribed on Saddam's missiles.

MONDAY, JANUARY 28. I WAS A BIT TOO OPTImistic last Thursday. We have not gone back to the normal routines of life, nor are we likely to for some time; instead, we have moved into a stage of what some call "the routine state of emergency," which means expecting a routine attack each night. Moti has gone back to his home, and the girls again sleep in their own beds.

High schools reopened yesterday, so I am back at work at Shfeya on Sunday mornings. Yesterday we had a staff briefing on emergency measures and sealing up classrooms. University courses and organized community programs are not to run after 5 p.m., which is hard for me, since much of my income comes from evening teaching associated with these activities. In addition, most of my clients have not yet returned to therapy, so my short-term financial situation looks bleak. And I have too much time on my hands.

I call various organizations and volunteer to conduct free therapy sessions with couples and families whose relationships have suffered from war-related stress. Not only would I be helping in the best way I know how, but I may also begin to build up a postwar referral base. Actually, in spite of the anxieties about my professional and financial future, after getting through the past two weeks with my psyche intact, I feel really alive—during daylight hours, that is.

MONDAY, MARCH 11. THE WAR OFFICIALLY ENDED one and a half weeks ago. "Here it is," the radio announcer exclaimed excitedly. "This is the moment we have been waiting for! We can repack our gas masks and remove the plastic sheeting from doors and windows of our sealed rooms." Within a day, I began to act as if I believed it, though my heart was still unconvinced. Friday night, *after dark*, I actually sent Keren outside to throw away the garbage, and she went fearlessly, as if this were the most normal request in the world. Later that same night, I took the dog for a walk, and there I was, two blocks from home, alone in the dark of night!

But it took me several days to actually dismantle the sealed room. Saturday, for the first time since peace was declared, I went to sleep in my own bed, in pajamas. For six weeks I had slept in a jogging suit just in case my house was destroyed and I had to run out into the winter air. That night I also went to sleep without the radio on at my head, and I managed to sleep the full night through, without waking every hour or so to check that all was quiet.

What was our sealed room has become, once again, my office; the mattresses are off the floor, chairs are in place, and the shelves are up and filled with books. Of my clients, I see that M. has regressed somewhat, perhaps from the impact of the war. L. came to her last session in a mood of hopelessness. She described a difficult week; having returned to work full time, she felt once again over-

whelmed by pressure. But now she seems angrier, perhaps readier to make more demands of her husband for help. C.'s husband has regained some of the confidence he lost after his automobile accident, and now he and his wife are in the middle of a power struggle for control of their marriage. Some couples I was seeing before the war have responded to the forced togetherness during the alerts either by resolving to work harder on their marriages or by splitting up—sometimes in complete contradiction to the direction of therapy before the war.

Now it seems as if the war took place in another dimension of time, a parallel world, or twilight zone. I remember the nightly terror and can describe in minute detail my body's reactions, but I cannot recall the actual *feeling* of the fear. It's like childbirth; I remember that it hurt but not the way it felt. Now and again an ambulance siren in the distance pinches at my heart a little, not allowing me to totally forget. At those times, Keren and Tali and I look at one another wordlessly, sharing the memory of a common moment in a sealed room from another dimension. ∎

SHERI OZ, M.SC., *is in private practice in Israel.*

I learned that my own pleasure in the children was vital, that my capacity to treasure them should not be taken for granted but had to be cultivated and treasured itself.

Molly Layton

PHOTOGRAPH BY JOAN LIFTIN/ACTUALITY

PHOTOGRAPH BY ERNST HAAS/MAGNUM

PHOTOGRAPH BY JENNIFER BISHOP/ACTUALITY

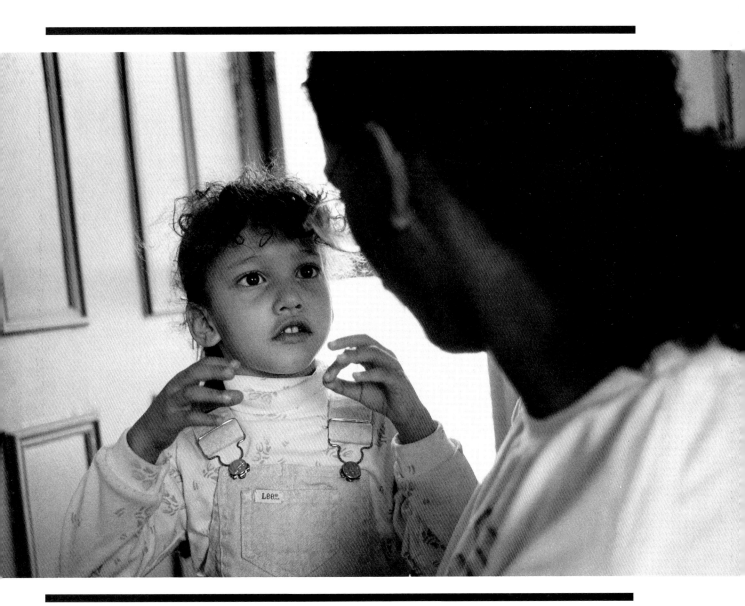

PHOTOGRAPH BY JENNIFER BISHOP/ACTUALITY

Being There

CHARTING THE THERAPIST'S JOURNEY

ILLUSTRATION BY MIKE HODGES

*B*EHIND THE MASK

SEXUALITY IN THE
THERAPEUTIC RELATIONSHIP

By Michele Bograd

THE SEXUAL NUANCES OF HUMAN RELATIONSHIPS have never been a favorite topic of family therapists. In fact, a look through the family therapy literature might lead an observer to conclude that sexuality is almost always a peripheral consideration for the clients who come to us seeking help. But the avoidance of the topic of sexuality extends beyond the way we write about our clients. Family therapists seem to be united in a curious conspiracy of silence regarding the sexual undercurrents in the therapeutic relationship itself. It is as if family therapists were uniquely immune to the attractions and yearnings that seem to afflict the rest of humanity.

Several months ago, a group of family therapist colleagues and I got together in a restaurant to talk about this forbidden topic. Although we had known each other for years, we all felt awkward, almost giggly, trying to talk seriously about sexuality as a dimension of therapy. Despite all the past cases we had discussed together in exquisite detail, it was tough getting started.

"It's hard to begin," said one woman. "How can I talk about this—revealing something so personal about myself and my work? This is different from tales of the latest man I'm tracking or yet another piece of work on my own family. It's too intimate, and I feel exposed."

"I'm worried about how you'll see my work," added a man. "I feel embarrassed talking about having these feelings because *good* therapists don't have these feelings, do they? I feel I should have this all under control. And, by definition, I think I'm doing a poor job if my own needs are getting met in the therapy."

"It's different for me," another man replied. "I don't worry about myself. I worry about my clients. I blame myself if my attraction makes them uncomfortable, and I worry that my own feelings, which I do try to keep track of, can influence or maybe damage the emotional safety of the treatment—even if the client doesn't seem to notice."

More than 20 years ago, psychiatrist Albert E. Scheflen described the therapist/client relationship as a dance of "quasi-courtship." A recent study found that more than 80 percent of almost 600 experienced psychologists reported feelings of sexual attraction toward clients. Though sexual feelings are typically attributed to countertransference or to irrational distortions of the therapist or client, it seems simpler to regard sexuality as a fundamental part of most intimate relationships. And with its intensity and focus on sharing deeply private feelings, therapy must be considered among the most intimate of relationships. As one colleague noted, "I share more, and more often, with my clients than I do with most of my friends."

THE IDEA FOR AN ARTICLE EXPLORING THERApists' sexual feelings toward their clients first began to take shape after a phone conversation I had with a female colleague several months ago. Her voice was uncharacteristically strained as she began. "I'd like to give you a referral," she said, "but there are unusual circumstances. Before I give you the details of the case, you need to know something important." She was quiet for a moment. "I feel incredibly vulnerable telling you."

"What's going on?" I said with concern.

"I've been treating a family with several grown children for the last year or so," she paused. "And I've developed feelings for one of the sons, who's about my age. I think I've fallen in love with him."

Thinking about this conversation afterward, I wondered if her situation really was so unusual or only her courage in examining and confronting feelings that most of us tend to deny. Since that phone conversation, I have had discussions in which family therapists, most of them experienced clinicians, spoke openly about how their own sexual feelings got stirred up in the process of doing therapy. For all of us, these discussions felt risky. Though everyone was eager to talk, relieved at the chance to explore a highly charged and personal aspect of our work that previously seemed off limits, all of us were anxious that our identities be protected.

Several people suggested that family therapists have not addressed the sexual dynamics of thera-

pist/client relationships because we minimize the importance of transference, assume that sexual feelings are diffused when we are working with more than one individual, or fear professional censure, given the concern about therapist/client sexual abuses. But most felt that downplaying the influence of sexuality within the therapeutic relationship just obscures things. It drives uncomfortable feelings underground; it doesn't make them disappear.

"I sometimes see partners individually along with conjoint meetings," said a female colleague. "In one case, I worked with the man for several weeks while his wife was out of town on business. He did intense work on his family. There was a lot of warmth between us. I felt the loss of that special connection when his wife returned."

One male colleague said, "I've been attracted to clients, and not just to women. I notice men, too, even though I'm not sexually interested in them. But I'm aware of myself physically and feel drawn to certain clients more than others."

"Whenever I work with couples, I'm aware that I complete the triangle," an experienced male therapist told me. "I expect certain things to happen. For example, the wife feels a strong attraction to me. After all, for an hour a week she sees me as a caring man, attuned to feelings and relationships. Whether it's conscious or not, I expect her to compare her husband to me, and I expect the man to have feelings about that or about my interest in his wife. Depending on the case, I sometimes bring that out explicitly. But I always keep in mind that I'm in a triangle, hopefully a helpful one, and that it is charged—sometimes lusty, sometimes poignant, sometimes competitive, sometimes playful."

NONE OF US COMES TO TERMS WITH OUR SEXUALity once and for all, so the sexual dynamics in our clinical work are always shifting. Our age, our life stage, and periods of personal vulnerability may influence our awareness of and receptivity to certain feelings toward clients.

"My marriage ended several years ago," reminisced one woman. "Then as I began to think about beginning another relationship, I found myself strongly attracted to several men in my practice. I'd be aware of what I was wearing on the days I was seeing them and sometimes would be distracted in the sessions, acutely aware of how they were sitting. On a vacation, I fantasized about one of them. Though I talked about this in supervision, I focused more on them and what role I was playing for them. But I wondered a lot about how my own loneliness and neediness fueled the attraction."

"I do feel attracted to women in my practice," said a male therapist. "But it is totally safe because I'm happy in my marriage and I know the boundaries are there."

Another male therapist said, "As an older man, raised in the early traditions of psychodrama and gestalt, I feel comfortable touching my clients. But I've made mistakes. I've had women think I was coming on to them and men get anxious with a hug. That doesn't mean I stop doing it. In some distant or constricted families my physical affection is important. But it's also changed now that I am older. Clients seem to see me more like an uncle than a lover."

SEXUAL ATTRACTIONS MAY COME AND GO. THEY may be sweetly entertained as an impossible fantasy or may be disruptive and threatening to the therapist or the therapy itself. But their presence is highlighted when sexual dysfunction is the presenting problem in the couple. And even those of us who have specialized training in sex therapy may be unprepared for our feelings.

"It's almost embarrassing to say this," reported one man. "But I sometimes find myself getting aroused as I get detailed sexual histories. I feel it's purely a professional inquiry. But I sometimes wonder whether my own titillation isn't behind some of my questions. Voyeuristic, you know what I mean? I was taught about objectivity and professional detachment, and my training dealt with the anxiety I might feel. But no one suggested that I might have sexual feelings of my own."

"It was different for me," replied a woman. "I was treating a young, unmarried couple for sexual dysfunction. I dealt with family-of-origin issues for weeks until I realized it was my own discomfort that kept me from exploring the obvious. And then it turned out this couple was into mild bondage and domination, and the woman relished the submissive position. I felt angry with her and more humiliated than she did. It was hard for me to stay neutral about how they made love. So my feelings weren't of attraction or interest but bordered on repulsion and criticism."

THE GENDER OF THE THERAPIST MAY ALSO INfluence how sexual feelings are defined, experienced and acted upon. When I asked male therapists what attracts them to certain clients, they tended to focus on their clients' physical appearance. In contrast, the women spoke about how responding to clients' vulnerabilities or sensitivity sometimes deepened into an emotional and physical attraction. While men generally seemed to feel relatively comfortable with attractions to clients, and vice versa, some of the women felt exposed—as if the attraction or flirtation undermined their professional authority or self-confidence.

One woman described her experience running a group for male sexual offenders. "On the days I lead the group, I dress as if I'm a female eunuch. I wear no makeup, I wear sensible shoes, I tie my hair back. I am sometimes irritated that I feel compelled to make such a choice, but this way I can ensure that I can get some therapy done, rather than dealing with the men in the group flirting with me."

"I was treating a couple about my age, and the husband was quite seductive with me," recalled another woman. "It seemed light and playful. But as a woman, I felt the timing of the teasing was no accident. Usually when I was close to hot material for the couple, he would compliment me or something and I would get flustered or uncomfortable. It wasn't just that it was sexual. [This was how] he regained control when he was feeling uncomfortable because he felt so confident in the sexual arena."

Another woman spoke about doing a role-play interview in a class on gender and marital therapy. "Afterward, one of the men in the class told me he felt I'd been seductive with the role-play husband because of how I was sitting and how I leaned forward and pushed the hair back from my head. I immediately felt ashamed and embarrassed and shifted my entire physical posture. I told him I didn't feel I was being sexual. He disagreed. My male co-teacher then said that, as a man, he didn't see my posture as a come-on. I felt relieved. But then I realized that I was bouncing back and forth between how these two men were defining my sexuality for me! As a woman, that seemed second nature, and realizing that horrified me."

WHO DECIDES WHETHER A PHYSICAL ACTION IS sexual or whether a feeling is appropriate? Therapist, clients and observers may disagree. Although ethical standards prohibit actual sexual contact between therapist and client, there is little to direct us in sorting out how the therapist's sexual feelings should be handled. Whether we acknowledge and utilize our sexuality in therapy depends on personal comfort, our preferred professional stance, and the clinical model we employ. Some family therapists make a strong personal connection with their clients, using their own internal responses as vital catalysts in the therapeutic process. Others employ their sexuality strategically. Still others work from positions of caring and careful distance—neutral and sometimes seemingly neutered.

There are few guidelines for helping us know when it is best to deal with sexual feelings by interpreting them, ignoring them, normalizing them, or using them. What seems important is that we are at least aware of the sexual dimension and make conscious decisions about whether or how we want to employ it clinically. Acting as if it doesn't exist, for us or our clients, means we cannot track and control how it may he operating.

"I remember the early tapes of the master structural family therapists," said one female therapist. "Flirtation and challenge were their strongest suit and damned effective. I've had women friends get riled up about the politics of those moves. I'm not sure how I feel—it works and seems pretty innocent to me. After all, we're all sexual. Why not use it, rather than pretend it's not there?"

"I was working with a young adult incest survivor," a male colleague said. "She was flirtatious with me. Yet she said she felt very unattractive and unloved. It was hard for me to sort it all out. I wanted to let her know that as a man I appreciated and valued her—that I found her attractive.

"I was flattered and kind of gratified by her teasing. But I didn't want to simply recapitulate an unhealthy structure—you know, where she felt she could get my care only through my sexual interest. It was a complicated dance."

One female therapist talked about working with a shy male client about her own age. "I found him attractive but wasn't worried that I would act on it. So I flirted with him, pretty carefully and self-consciously. We even role-played him asking me out because he was paralyzed the moment he got on the phone with a woman. It was fun and playful. But when I told my supervision group about it, the reaction was mixed.

"I felt defensive in a way. The strange thing is that I didn't think about stopping it. I saw nothing wrong with it because I was so careful about the boundaries. But I did think seriously of not telling my group about it again."

BEHIND THE MASK

T IS THIS RETREAT INTO SILENCE THAT IS MOST disturbing. The unnamed remains the invisible. In our everyday practice, most of us lack a supportive forum in which we can acknowledge our humanity as therapists. Consequently, we may struggle with isolation and the erroneous belief that we are the only therapists to have such intense and confusing feelings. And our party line may not reflect the deeply human dilemmas we encounter in our therapeutic relationships.

Breaking through our professional isolation, challenging our conspiracy of silence about the personal side of being a therapist can help each of us view our work in a different light.

Consider what happened to the colleague who fell in love with her client: "This experience was hell for me. I tried to handle it with as much personal and professional integrity as possible. I got a lot of supervision and, with great qualms, talked to some of my friends. Almost all of my colleagues had a story of someone they knew who had dated or even married a former client. It was like this was all going on out there, but I had no idea. At the same time, people gave me incredible support; everyone was worried about me and my professional career. They urged caution about who I spoke to. Since I had decided to discuss what was happening with the family and then to transfer them to other therapists, I had to talk to a number of people. I was anxious, really stricken with self-doubt.

"It has been one of the hardest but one of the most important lessons of my life. No one blamed me, and the family appreciated my care and how hard I worked to deal with them openly and responsibly. I was expecting such censure and blame—at least as much as I censured and blamed myself. But, behind closed doors, I was met with so much understanding and care. More than I could believe at the time, my friends and trusted colleagues accepted that I was going through something very human— that the technical rules of our business can't always address the complexities we face, that the therapeutic relationship carries its risks, and that care can deepen into love." ■

MICHELE BOGRAD, PH.D., *is in private practice in Arlington, MA.*

See references, page 569.

*T*HE CREATIVE LEAP

THE LINKS BETWEEN CLINICAL AND ARTISTIC CREATIVITY

By Peggy Papp

HERE HAS BEEN A DEBATE IN OUR FIELD FOR many years as to whether psychotherapy is an art or a science. The preponderance of opinion is on the side of art, and yet the basic language of family therapy remains that of the sciences. In order to scientifically measure human exchange, family systems so far have been compared to the cybernetic working of machines, the organization of the solar systems, the biological reproduction and division of cells, the interplay of chemical compounds, mathematical equations and the Russellian theory of logical types—to mention but a few. If this trend continues, it will be possible in the year 2001 for a family therapist to come up with the following diagnosis: "The presenting problem in this family is that their metaphysical patterns are low in consensual morphostasis, leading to a dialectic calibration in which the negative and positive feedback loops have ended in negentrophy." And that message will probably come out as a readout on a computer.

The language of science is obviously too abstract and too static to describe human systems. Not only does it eliminate all the political and psychological processes that take place in human exchange, it also eliminates all the individual qualities peculiar to human beings—such as hubris, unpredictability, imagination, creativity and, as my grandfather used to say back on the ranch, "just sheer cussedness."

Imagine, if you will, machines reproducing their families of origin, developing a symptom as a means of communication, or indulging in elaborate manipulations to control one another. These processes are uniquely human and belong to emotional systems, which run according to their own inner logic. They have little to do with scientific measurements and move in mysterious ways, their wonders and devastation to perform. One can approach them only in a spirit of awe and wonder, much the same as one enters the realm of art, philosophy, or religion. One cannot scientifically measure a belief, weigh a myth, or apply an equation to a perception.

What artists have always known is that in order to deal with human dilemmas and ambiguities, one must bypass the rigid corridors of reason, science and logical analysis and concern oneself with imagery, dreams, symbols and metaphors. An artist doesn't explain his work but instead reveals the deepest human truths through universal codes, codes that turn those locks that remain resistant to conceptual thought. As the historian John Keegan says, "Poetic truth explains what happens in life better than most other sorts of truth."

How can one better understand the oedipal complex than by reading Proust's description of a small boy waiting longingly for his mother to come and kiss him good-night while she tarries downstairs with his father? Or how can one better comprehend insanity as a sacrificial act than through watching Blanche Dubois disintegrate in *A Streetcar Named Desire*? Or more quickly recognize the paradox and absurdity of human behavior than through the plays of Shaw and Beckett? Two of the lines I quote most often in my work with families are George Bernard Shaw's "There are two tragedies in life; one is not to get your heart's desire and the other is to get it" and Jules Feiffer's "If only not being alone didn't depend on other people." After you've said that, what else is there to say? Sometimes my whole therapy consists of a variation on those two lines.

In speaking of the difficulties of working with human systems, anthropologist Gregory Bateson says: "In such a world of complex interconnections, the problem of control becomes more akin to art than to science—not merely because we tend to think of the difficult and the unpredictable as contexts for art, but also because the results of error are likely to be ugliness. . . . The rewards of such work are not power, but beauty."

THE BEAUTY THAT INFORMS THE WORK OF BOTH the artist and the therapist is the excitement of discovering connecting patterns, of seeing an analogy never before seen, of suddenly viewing disassociated elements in relation to one another and uniting those elements in a holistic picture through the use of symbols and metaphors. To achieve this requires an artistic process that consists of four

major elements: selectivity, emphasis, dramatization and economy. Artists select a unifying theme and emphasize this theme throughout their work; they choose a dramatic form through which to convey their theme and then execute it with economy.

The trademark of all great art is the seeming effortlessness of the finished product. Paradoxically, this effortlessness comes only from hours and hours of excruciating effort. Again, to quote Shaw: "Genius is 90 percent perspiration and 10 percent inspiration." An artist survives neither by means of inspiration nor by favorable circumstance but by persistence. A large part of creativity is habit, the habit of doing something difficult. An artist in the pursuit of excellence must fail like no other person ever fails— over and over and over again. As we observe the breathtaking movement of a pas de deux, listen to the exquisite counterpoint of Mozart, or are moved by a Chekhovian play, the persistence and failure are concealed, and we see only the illuminating results.

In observing my colleagues over the years, I have become convinced that good therapy encompasses the major elements of artistic endeavor. Some years ago, I saw a tape from the Philadelphia Child Guidance Clinic called "A Modern Little Hans." The therapist, Mariano Berrigan, supervised by Jay Haley, was working with a family in which the 10-year-old son had a dog phobia. His fear of dogs had become so intense it interfered with his going to school or having a social life. There were also other problems in the family, which included a distant and conflictual relationship between the parents resulting in the mother's being overly preoccupied with the son's problem and the father being distant and uninvolved. The therapist discovered that the father was a postman and therefore concluded he must be an authority on dogs, since he met a great variety on his rounds. The therapist selected this aspect of the father's background to design a task. He instructed the father to take his son to a dog kennel, where, together, they were to choose a dog that was afraid of people and teach the dog not to be afraid of people. As I observed the boy happily playing with a puppy in the following session, I said to myself, "This possesses all the elements of art."

From the mass of information and choices confronting the therapists, they had selected a key aspect of the situation and with a masterstroke fashioned a task that changed not only the perception of the problem but the complex web of relationships surrounding it. By helping his son choose a dog and teach it not to be afraid of people, the peripheral father became more involved with his son, mother's intense preoccupation with her son's fear was diluted, and the perception of the problem was changed from the boy needing to be cured of his fear of dogs to the dog needing to be cured of its fear of people. When a relapse was anticipated, the boy was instructed to pretend to be afraid of the puppy in order to help him.

THE MAJOR GOAL OF THERAPY, AS OF ART, IS TO change a basic perception so that one "sees differently." Through the introduction of the novel or the unexpected, a frame of reference is broken and the structure of reality is rearranged.

Writer Arthur Koestler says: "The creative act is not an act of creation in the sense of the Old Testament. It does not create something out of nothing; it uncovers, selects, reshuffles, combines, synthesizes already existing facts, ideas, faculties, and skills." It matters little what theoretical orientation guides the therapist; the process is the same.

New York psychiatrist Ian Alger injects himself personally into the lives of others. He becomes an actor in their drama. In one incident, he used his theatrical flair to virtually create a theater of the absurd around a toxic issue. He was treating a man who was convinced he had profound pathologies and unalterable character deficits. The man felt hopeless about himself and carried on at length about his unworthiness. When Ian asked him how he had arrived at his perception of himself, the man said: "It's in the report." Ian asked, "What report?" and the man reached into his pocket and pulled out a Rorschach report that had been written by a psychologist many years before. The report was filled with devastating clinical judgments, which the man had accepted as true. He had been carrying the report around with him for seven years, right next to his heart, like a bible.

Alger knew the report had to be destroyed—but in a way that was congruent with the special meaning the man had bestowed on it. So he made a pyramid of pillows in the middle of the room and placed the Rorschach in a ceramic dish on top of the pillows. He asked the man to light a match to the report. As it burned, Ian danced around it, making primitive chanting sounds as in a sacred rite. He motioned for the man to join him, and as they went round and round, dancing and hollering, the man began to laugh. Through this symbolic act, the sacredness of the report was exaggerated to such an absurd degree that not only the letter but also its meaning went up in flames. The spell was broken, and he was freed from his bondage—which only proves what we all know: that there is only one step from the ridiculous to the sublime.

THE PRIMARY TOOLS OF BOTH THERAPISTS AND artists in conveying implicit meaning are symbols and metaphors. We continually search for metaphors that are capable of bringing different levels of thought, feeling and behavior together in a unified theme.

In one of his most novel interventions, family therapy pioneer Salvador Minuchin used a pair of shoes as a symbol of differentiation. In a ceremony studded with metaphors, he dramatized a boundary between a symbiotic father and son. So entwined were they that the father bought all the son's clothes, even though the son was 27 years old. The son could never ask for a thing without the father immediately buying it for him in 15 different colors. This prevented the son from asking for anything at all, and he withdrew more and more into himself. Minuchin described their relationship as a jail of love and the son as prisoner because he could not receive. During one of the sessions, Minuchin discovered that the son was actually wearing his father's shoes (their feet, naturally, were the same size). Minuchin asked the son to take off the shoes and give them to him. He wrapped them in a piece of newspaper and handed them to the father. He then instructed the son to walk barefoot to the shoe store and buy himself another pair of shoes. He must buy a different kind of shoe and pay a different price for it. His brother, rather than his father, should accompany him.

In this single symbolic act, the son literally and figuratively leaves his father's footsteps and takes the first step toward establishing a separate identity. At the same time, an alternative closeness between the brothers is substituted for the overly close father/son relationship. The son's walking barefoot beautifully symbolized the nakedness of separation—leaving his father's skin to experience his own.

Psychiatrist Milton Erickson, of course, was the master of the metaphor. His ability to communicate many different levels of meaning, enabling the client to make spontaneous connections, is legend. This ability was particularly apparent in his work with schizophrenics, who lead a metaphoric life. In *Uncommon Therapy*, Jay Haley tells the story of Erickson meeting a patient who called himself "Jesus" on the back ward of a hospital. This man paraded about as the messiah, wore a sheet draped around him, and attempted to impose Christianity on people. Erickson approached him on the hospital grounds and said, "I understand you have had experience as a carpenter." The patient could only reply that he had. Erickson presented him with a piece of wood and asked him to whittle something. He guided

his whittling into more and more elaborate projects, until finally he gave the man a large amount of wood and asked him to make a bookcase. This shifted the man to productive labor. He became an expert carpenter and eventually left the hospital to be gainfully employed.

The metaphor in this case was used as a challenge. The man's identity with Jesus, which was so important to him, was preserved but used to accomplish something new. A different side of Jesus was selected and emphasized.

MILAN FAMILY THERAPIST MARA SELVINI PALAZzoli uses symbols and rituals in a most creative way to demystify family myths. She describes her rituals as "uniting the participants in a powerful collective experience" that "introduces into the system a ritualized prescription of a play whose new norms silently take the place of the old ones."

In one of her most dramatic examples, she describes the treatment of a family that was held tightly together for many generations by the family myth, "One for all and all for one." This precluded any member of the large family clan from saying anything bad about relatives or expressing any anger toward them. The identified patient, who was suffering from anorexia, had a cousin her same age who was jealous of her and constantly taunted her and put her down. However, the family denied this, saying the cousin was like a sister to her, full of love and concern. The team of Milan therapists prescribed a ritual in which, every night after dinner, the family was to lock and bolt the front door. They were to sit around the dining room table, which was to be cleared of all objects except an alarm clock placed at its center. Each member of the family was to listen without making any comment. No one was to contradict or interrupt anyone else, nor continue the discussions outside of these evening meetings.

Without explicitly saying so, this established the right of each member to freely express his or her own perceptions without being contradicted or disqualified. It defined the nuclear family as a unit distinct from the clan, substituting the obligation to speak for the prohibition from speaking. The identified patient's perceptions were soon validated by other family members, as many other buried family truths emerged. This had a remarkable effect on the identified patient. The family came to the next session and reported that the daughter was eating, gaining weight, and losing her depression. The ritual had touched the family's nerve center and changed the family myth that "whoever speaks badly of his relatives is bad."

EXPERIENCED ARTISTS AND THERAPISTS UNDERstand that "truth" should be delivered obliquely, so as not to bruise the recipients. As Emily Dickinson advises us:

Tell all the truth but tell it slant
Success in circuit lies,
Too bright for our infirm delight
The Truth's superb surprise.

As lightning to the children eased
With explanation kind
The truth must dazzle gradually
Or every man be blind.

Tasks, rituals, metaphors and stories are devices that protect people from being blinded by the truth. They allow analogous messages to be communicated and absorbed according to the family's own tolerance level.

A beautiful example of using a story to indirectly convey a painful truth occurred recently during family therapist Olga Silverstein's treatment of a holocaust family.

So fearful was this family of the outside world that they refused to divulge information that was necessary for the continuation of therapy. Every time Silverstein came near an area that the family considered dangerous, Linda, the 22-year-old daughter, repeatedly interrupted with inappropriate and bizarre behavior. After innumerable interruptions, Silverstein leaned back and said, "I want to share with you a story told to my orthodox Jewish grandfather. There once was a tribe of Jews lost in the desert. It was a very small tribe, and so each and every member was especially precious. They were surrounded by danger at all sides—native tribes who tried to seduce or lure members away—wild animals who threatened to carry them away, etc. They tried in many ways to protect themselves against these dangers—they built high walls but never high enough. They built fires around their camp, but the rain would wash them out. Finally they designated one member of the tribe—the one with the sharpest ears—as the drummer. The drummer's task was to remain constantly on the alert and, whenever any danger approached, to drum loudly and warn the tribe of danger. That, Linda, is your task in this family." Silverstein then instructed Linda to drum loudly on the table with her hand whenever the therapist approached dangerous ground.

Through this story of a dangerous world and a protective drummer, fantasy and reality were simultaneously linked. The family, upon hearing Silverstein designate the daughter's symptomatic behavior as protective and the family as needing protection, recognized they were in friendly territory and that they no longer needed to protect themselves from her.

SO FAR, I HAVE LIMITED MY DISCUSSION TO THE similarities between art and therapy. But there is a crucial difference between the two; the artistry of the therapist is not a solitary act but an interpersonal one. Unlike other art, in which the artist's material is usually static, the therapist's material is always alive (at least legally). A therapist's creativity is systemic and can't be separated from the creativity of the client or family. A brilliant intervention becomes brilliant only through the brilliant use made of it by other people. They, and they alone, are the judge of the therapist's artistry. This is not true of most of the other arts, in which the artist's materials are concrete objects with no lives of their own. A musician plays fixed notes on a scale, and his trombone is not capable of talking back to him or stirring up a crisis among the other instruments. A writer's words remain on the printed page as written and cannot rearrange themselves while he is sleeping in order to confuse and mislead him. A painter's yellow chromatic does not develop a transference and turn purple because of a covert agenda to resist the painter's conception.

Therapists, on the other hand, work with ever-changing complexities over which they have little or no control. They never know for certain the limits or possibilities of their material, nor the exact nature of it. Nor do they have any control over the outside forces that constantly impinge on various family members, such as unemployment, accidents, illness, death, or political and social upheavals. Because the therapist's material is always in flux, the end result of the therapeutic endeavor is difficult, if not impossible, to accurately access.

And yet, where in the literature is the family or client ever given credit for the part he or she plays in making the interventions something to write about? In the examples I have cited previously (most of which have appeared in books or journals), no mention was made of the extraordinary resourcefulness, courage, sensitivity and imagination of the recipients who used what therapists gave them to transform their lives. For example, what astonishing resilience and miraculous will power it must have taken for the schizophrenic in the back ward of the hospital to carve out not just a bookcase but a completely new life for himself. And this from a single idea dropped by a perfect stranger. Supposing when Erickson said, "I understand you've had experience as a carpenter," the man had given him a suspicious glance

and replied, "What are you, some kind of nut? I gave that up years ago to serve God." Or suppose he had made the bookcase and it had turned out badly, only confirming his feelings of failure. To this day he could probably be seen staring out of the fifth-floor window in the east wing on visitor's day. That intervention would undoubtedly never have been written up.

THE QUESTION ARISES AT THIS POINT, WHO IS THE artist—the therapist or the client? Certainly, it is a collaborative effort. One of our most basic assumptions in this field is that problems do not exist in people but between them. It follows then that the artistry and magic do not exist in the therapist but between the therapist and the client. And it is impossible to predict the outcome of any particular therapeutic thrust. Sometimes clients turn our most mundane interventions into transcendental experiences (these are the ones we write about), while at other times they remain totally impervious to our strokes of genius (these are the ones we don't write about).

Arthur Koestler says of the creative act, "It is always a leap into the dark, a dive into the deep, and the diver is more likely to come up with a handful of mud than with a coral." He goes on to make the point that the false inspirations that are responsible for bad art were accompanied by the same euphoria, catharsis and experience of beauty as those inspirations that were, post factum, considered to have produced great art. And so it goes with therapy.

The primary material a therapist has to work with is the poetry in people, and we would do well to let it guide us in our work with them. I recall several cases in which I felt my clients were more the artists than I. In one case, a husband was having great difficulty in handling his wife's anger. It frightened him and he habitually withdrew into silence, provoking her to more anger. I offered the suggestion that the next time she became *(continued on page 489)*

484

It Don't Mean A Thing If It Ain't Got That Swing

THE AUDITORIUM IS PACKED. THE MASTER THERAPIST HAS TALKED ABOUT HIS THEORY FOR HALF the morning and is now meeting a family brought to him by a local therapist for a live interview. They sit down and begin the session. Within minutes the audience is spellbound, as the Great One lays open the pulsating heart of the family system. An emotionally reserved father is crying as he talks for the first time about his father's death. The Master even manages to convince the man's wife to replace their oldest daughter as father's comforter. "How does he do it?" I think to myself. "It's magic. I could never do that."

I'm sitting at the bar in Jazz Alley. The band is first rate: Milt Jackson on vibes, Jeff Hamilton on drums, Ray Brown on bass, and Monty Alexander on piano. I keep my eye on Monty because in my spare time I study jazz piano, hoping one day to become a fluent improviser. The group is playing a haunting rendition of "Django" by John Lewis. Jackson's solo has been played, and now Monty gracefully takes up the harmonic line Milt was exploring. Within minutes I'm spellbound.

What the master musician and therapist are doing is essentially the same. They are improvising moment to moment within a specific framework. I realized that my study of jazz was also teaching me a lot about therapy. The processes of learning to improvise in therapy and in music are essentially similar; however, in jazz this learning process is much more defined. Jazz musicians recognize more clearly than do therapists the critical necessity of automatic, unconscious skills intrinsic to the process of free improvisation. In jazz, these skills are the ability to sense and keep to the beat, thorough knowledge of the harmony of the piece being improvised on, mastery of the musical instrument and, most important, the musician's capacity to reproduce on the instrument the personal music he hears. Each of these has its counterpart in the improvisational aspects of conducting therapy sessions.

ALL JAZZ MUSICIANS AGREE ON THE BASIC ELEMENT IN PLAYING AND HEARING MUSIC—THE BEAT, THE pulse, the time. Musicians will say of another player, "He's got good time," which means you can play with him. A musician who plays an occasional wrong note will be tolerated, but if he cannot keep time, he's gone. The beat may be crude, as in some rock music, or subtle, but it underlies everything, as basic to music as the heartbeat is to life. Once the tune is started and the tempo is set, the beat continues, unvarying until the tune ends.

Musicians think of the beat as always there, something they do not cause; it lives apart from them, a constant to which they must relate. They learn to experience it unconsciously, knowing that even if they stray from it temporarily, it is still there, to be found again. The beat is created not by any individual musician but by the ensemble. Unlike improvised melody, which is idiosyncratic to individual players, the beat is a shared experience. In fact, this sharing is vital to ensemble playing. A band sharing precisely the same experience of the underlying beat is "in the groove" and sounds unmistakably different, and better, than a band with "loose" time.

Is there anything as fundamental to family therapy as the beat is to jazz? Is there anything in a session that exists without our putting it there, independent even of our awareness? I believe the emotional pulse of the family system is the equivalent of the musical beat. This pulse is always there, underlying every transaction, sometimes obvious, sometimes subtle. Vital to the therapist's effectiveness is his or her resonance with the family metronome. Are therapist and family "in the groove"? In a single-parent family, for example, in which an adolescent is giving his mother hell, and both mother and son know that the deceased alcoholic father used to give her hell, has the therapist picked up the basic underlying beat of filial loyalty?

The improvising musician is faithful not only to the beat but also to the harmonic sequence spelled out by the composer of the original tune. Even his improvised melody is related to the composer's melody. The original melody and the underlying sequence of the chords must be as familiar to him as his own living room in darkness.

The organization of the family's emotional system, the family's idiosyncratic character, is the counterpart to the harmonic structure of a jazz tune. Who are the key members and how are they arranged vis-à-vis one another? When the therapist can stay attuned to the emotional transactions (the beat) and the systemic organization (the harmony) of the family, he or she can improvise effectively.

Mastering an instrument is grueling work. But all of us have mastered one musical instrument to a high degree. From our first day of life, we began the task of mastering our vocal instrument. From earliest childhood, we were rewarded for our approximations of speech, so we spent hours playing with sounds. This explains why nearly all of us can hear a melody and reproduce it with no strain at all. In ordinary speech we can subtly alter pitch, dynamics, pauses, inflection, to shape the meaning of our words. We do this despite the fact that we are completely unaware of the muscles that must be contracted or relaxed for speech. In musical improvisation, the musician must develop this mastery of an instrument at the same automatic, unthinking level.

All beginning therapists bring to their therapy a personal repertoire in their use of themselves. All of us have a range of behaviors and intensities. Part of the development of a competent therapist is expanding this range. The joiner needs to extend his ability to confront; the high-intensity provocateur must learn how to pull back. The therapist's self is his or her instrument.

THE ESSENTIAL REQUIREMENT FOR IMPROVISING MUSIC, ACCORDING TO JAZZ TEACHERS, IS LEARNING to play what you hear. That's it, and that's all there is. You hear a certain sort of music in your head, and you play it. Consequently, a jazz musician comes to regard his personal music—the kind of music he hears and his capacity to play *that*—as far more important than any formally learned combination of notes. The most dreaded criticism is, "He's not playing what he's hearing," implying that he is playing a preconceived, prearranged, predigested piece of music. He may then be playing music that is "very good, but not really jazz," and he will have to be content only to "sound like" a jazz player.

How do you know that the music you hear in your head is jazz, and what determines if it is jazzy or not? Context is everything. Most jazz musicians come from families in which some kind of music was played at home—their music of origin. Like the rest of us, they also absorbed music from the broader culture—music in church, on the radio, in the supermarket, in TV commercials. We may "know" nothing about music technically, and yet we can recognize that a certain chord leading to another just sounds right.

There is also the music we choose to listen to and how we listen. Jazz musicians listen to a great deal of jazz in a particularly careful way. When they hear something they like, they learn to play it, "take it off the record." The piece then becomes part of their vocabulary and is expressed in their own music, either directly quoted or incorporated into their musical personality.

If the highest praise for a jazz musician's solo is "he plays what he hears," the equivalent in a therapist's improvisation lies in his or her moment-to-moment responsiveness during therapy. Therapists play what they hear in their spontaneous impulses and how they act on them—their gut feeling about what is going on in the family, their instinctive responses to the family's moves.

Doing therapy well requires much thought and knowledge, but the process is only fully realized during the interactional play that occurs among all the participants in the session, including the therapist. If this were not the case, therapy could be done by simply observing families and delivering our interventions in written reports. Our most valuable contribution to therapy is our capacity to partake in the human interaction. Unfortunately, although we pay lip service to respecting a therapist's personal style, we rarely teach trainees to value their own spontaneity. On the contrary, the message they get is to think and behave like Minuchin or Satir or their supervisor.

A competent jazz musician, improvising a solo to "I Got Rhythm," cannot help hearing a melody that is in the tempo and harmony of that song, an inner awareness that has become automatic. The jazzy therapist's impulses and idiosyncratic thoughts correspond to the family's emotional and systemic organization, because he has schooled himself to be automatically in the groove and in tune with their emotional beat and harmony.

When a musician can keep the beat and the harmonic sequence going without conscious analysis, then he can begin listening for the personal music that comes to him within these rhythmic and harmonic constraints. If he has developed sufficient musical mastery, and can reproduce on his instrument the music he hears internally, the result is improvised jazz.

THERAPISTS COULD LEARN A LOT FROM JAZZ MUSICIANS. WE ARE NOT NEARLY AS CLEAR AS OUR MUSIcal counterparts on two fundamental questions: What therapeutic skills should be automatic, i.e., free of conscious, analytic monitoring, to provide a solid base for improvisation? How do we learn to be creative and inventive improvisers?

Were we to "jazz up" the training of therapists, we would first find ways of teaching students how to pick up the beat, the underlying emotional process. I once called a frustrated therapist out of a stilted session in which all transactions were being funneled through her. I asked her what she felt like in there. She responded with a diagnosis of the family structure. I persisted in asking her about her emotional experience, and she finally replied, "I'm feeling intimidated by the father." We talked about who else in the family might be feeling intimidated. Were fear and intimidation the "heartbeat" of this family's emotional process? When she returned to the session, she asked the father who in the family understood best that he felt lonely when people got scared of him. This got the family going and got her out of dead center.

Second, we should increase students' opportunities to watch other therapists at work. The most artful description of Miles Davis's music cannot approach the experience of hearing him play. Similarly, reading books about therapy and observing it are worlds apart.

Third, we should employ many more ways of expanding a student's repertoire for using him or herself. Why not experiment with movement classes, singing lessons, improvisational theater training?

Above all, we should teach students from the start of their training that the most valuable part of their therapeutic work is their personal, idiosyncratic responsiveness, most of which they bring with them from their own life experiences. Training should teach them to organize these personal responses within a systemic context, in tune with the underlying emotional system of the family. Systemic teachers are quick to pounce on what we call "linear thinking" in our students. I've discovered that it helps if teachers follow their own advice. When my class is watching a tape and someone says, "I think that father is a sadistic creep," I no longer reproach them for having abandoned their neutrality. Instead, I might say, "That's a heartfelt response. It might be the most valuable thing you have to bring to the session at this moment. You are hearing the melody of this family. Now, how can you use this in a systemic way?"

Jazzy training teaches therapists not to ignore their emotional response in favor of "systemic thinking" but to act on it. They develop confidence in their spontaneous reactions because they have trained themselves to be in touch with the underlying beat of the family's emotional process. They know the family's unique song, the configurations of the emotional system, and can respond with a broad range of interpersonal moves. They have mastered the basic skills, giving them access to their own most intuitively wise and creative self. □

—Fred Wardenburg
SEPTEMBER 1988

FRED WARDENBURG, M.S.W., *is training director of the Montlake Institute, Seattle, WA.*

(continued from page 484) angry, he was to surprise her by doing something unexpected—it could be anything as long as it wasn't his usual pattern of withdrawing. I made no suggestion as to what that might be, since I sensed the man had an innovative streak. And a good thing that turned out to be.

He went to the library, took out a copy of Shakespeare's *The Taming of the Shrew,* and memorized some of Petruchio's speeches to Katherine (his wife's name also happened to be Katherine). You will remember that Katherine was known throughout the land for being a terrifying shrew. In his encounters with her, Petruchio reframes her anger with speeches praising her eloquence and beauty. So when his wife became angry, the husband quoted appropriate speeches from the text. When she nagged, he told her she sang as sweetly as a nightingale; and when she frowned, that she looked as clear as morning roses newly washed with dew; and when she screamed, that she uttered piercing eloquence. The wife, stunned and confused, stared at her husband in his idiotic pose, with a sheet thrown around him like a cape, and decided he looked too ridiculous to take seriously. She finally burst into uncontrollable laughter, whereupon the husband swept her up in his arms and carried her off into the bedroom—just like Petruchio. Frankly, I could never have thought of anything so splendid.

Another time I was coaching a young woman on how to disentangle herself from the triangle she was in with her mother and sister. Being the eldest daughter, she took upon herself the burden of solving the continual arguments between them. In order to free herself from this position, I suggested that whenever they became embroiled in an argument, she deflect their attention by presenting them with a problem of her own and ask for their help. I made no suggestion as to how she was to do this.

On Thanksgiving day, just as the guests were sitting down to eat, her mother and sister, in characteristic fashion, began a loud argument in the kitchen—

which was the signal for this eldest daughter to jump in. Rather than doing this, she suddenly pretended to faint in the middle of the kitchen floor.

Like a delicate Victorian lady, she simply swooned. Mother and sister, totally forgetting their argument, rushed to her side. She was treated like a queen for the rest of the day. Had my client not had the imagination to follow my suggestion in such an innovative way, I would not be describing this intervention now.

AND THEN THERE ARE TIMES WHEN WHAT WE think creates change is not what has actually created it. In fact, we never know for sure what, out of a great many possibilities, has brought about change. Was it our intervention? Or a chance visit from grandma? A word of praise from the boss? A victory over a competitor? An inspiring movie or play? Or perhaps simply that spring finally came? This is the challenging but maddening part of our art. It forever eludes a final definition.

When I was a neophyte, one of my first cases made me forever humble about what produces change. I was seeing a mother and trying to communicate to her the great insight that had just flashed through my mind. I was under the impression at that time that if one understood why one did what one did, one would stop doing it. In an attempt to help this mother change her behavior toward her family, I said, "You know, Dorothy, you are a very intelligent woman, and I'm sure you can see that you are treating your children and husband in the same way that your mother treated you. She pushed you because she was afraid you wouldn't live up to your potential, just as you are pushing them in the same way." She thought for a moment, then her eyes lit up and she replied, "I have never thought of that before. But, yes, I think you're right. Oh, thank you, Mrs. Papp. This has been very helpful."

Dorothy came to the next session with a glowing face and reported she had had a wonderful week.

The tension in the house had subsided, and she had stopped fighting with her children and husband. I sat secretly congratulating myself on my brilliant intervention until the end of the session when she turned at the door to ask, "By the way, Mrs. Papp, what was that you said last week about my mother and me? All I could remember was, 'Dorothy, you're an intelligent woman.' All week I've been saying to myself, 'Mrs. Papp thinks I'm intelligent,' and it's made me feel wonderful!" So much for my brilliant insight. Here was a woman who used a casual word of praise to turn her life around.

It was out of my desire to tap into the creative side of people that I developed the technique of family choreography in which families describe their relationships metaphorically rather than literally. They are asked to close their eyes and see themselves as symbolic forms that represent their relationships. It has always been my contention that every man/woman is an artist in his/her fantasies and dreams, where the mind distills the essence of relationships into simple and eloquent images. This ability cuts across all barriers of class, economics, religion and education.

A working couple from the Bronx were arguing over who should close the garage door. In order to have them communicate on a metaphorical level, I asked them to have a fantasy about their relationship. The wife described their interaction as follows: "He's King Kong and I'm Fay Wray. He's holding me in the palm of his hand and carrying me to the top of the Empire State Building. If he dies, I go with him because he won't let go of me. But I can't let go, either; there is an invisible force between us that draws me to him like electricity."

The husband, in describing his fantasy, stated: "I also saw myself as an ape, but an impotent ape. The bizarre thing is the ape is helpless. It's a dark street, and I see her on the ground, but when I try to lift her up she fights me. It's a total feeling of frustration in not being able to communicate with her, and then

I turn into the violent ape."

It was the ability of this couple to give poetic expression to their daily, routine experience that enabled me to view the symmetry of their relationship on a different level and to alter it.

AND NOW WE COME TO THE FINAL QUESTION. How does one become creative? Unfortunately, inspiration is not under conscious control and is forever at odds with willpower. When I was a student of family therapy pioneer Nathan Ackerman, he was given to calling me out from behind the one-way mirror and screaming at me:

"Relax! Be creative! Use your imagination!" At which point I froze into a retarded icicle.

Konstantin Sergeyevich Stanislavski, the director of the famed Moscow Art Theater, tells the story of an actor who was straining every muscle in his body in an effort to produce a desired emotion. He was flailing his arms, tearing his hair, and forcing loud sounds, but the results were hollow. Finally, Stanislavski said to him, "If you want to catch a squirrel, you do not chase it. You lie down in the sun with a nut in your outstretched hand and wait."

So it is with creativity. And the nut that you hold in your outstretched hand consists of the techniques that you have spent endless hours learning and practicing. But once they have become consolidated, you release your grasp of them and allow them to lure the unconscious from its hiding place. From then on, one can only trust the gods of serendipity.

Paul Watzlawick, John Weakland, and Richard Fisch, in their book *Change*, describe creativity as "something uncontrollable, even incomprehensible, a quantum jump, a sudden illumination which unpredictably comes at the end of long, often frustrating mental and emotional labor, sometimes in a dream, sometimes almost as an act of grace in the theological sense."

Often inspiration comes only after one has given up and entered what is known as the "Twilight

Zone," where the unconscious is very close to the surface. An example of the collaboration process of letting go occurred to me several years ago, while I was working with a couple. The husband, who had a very strict moral code, was constantly policing his wife in an effort to control her delinquent impulses. The wife felt suffocated, found her husband infinitely boring, and was having an affair with a man who held a strange fascination for her because he was wild and uncouth. However, she knew no permanent relationship was possible between them and kept wanting her husband to save her from descending down the primrose path. Feeling I was getting nowhere seeing them together, I decided to see the husband and wife separately and coach each in changing his position with the other.

On this particular night, I was sitting with the husband listening to him describe, in a self-righteous manner, the way in which he had just defeated my last intervention. I remembered sitting there thinking, "I'm tired, I'm hungry, I want to go home. I have tried everything with this man, nothing worked, I give up." I was planning a graceful exit when it suddenly occurred to me that his situation bore a striking resemblance to that in Ibsen's play *Lady From the Sea*, which had just opened in New York.

This play is an allegory about a romantic young woman named Ellida, who has a mystical relationship with the sea. She is fascinated by its unfathomable mystery and wildness. One day a stranger comes on a ship, and they fall in love with each other. The stranger's eyes are the same color as the sea and change with its moods. In a very dramatic ceremony, they bind two rings together and throw them into the sea, symbolizing their marriage to one another. The stranger then leaves as suddenly as he appeared but promises to return one day and take Ellida away with him. Ten years pass, and in the meantime Ellida marries an older, conservative professor, named Wangel. He takes her to the moun-

tain, where she feels strangled and suffocated by the conventional domestic role of wife and stepmother. She is restless and harbors the feeling that she has sold herself for the sake of security and safety.

Then one day, out of the blue, the stranger suddenly appears and wants to take Ellida away with him. Ellida at first pleads with her husband to save her from herself, but he attempts to do this in a way that only drives her further into the arms of the stranger. He tries to coerce her through physical, moral and spiritual force, taking away her freedom of choice. As Ellida turns to walk down the path with the stranger, the husband suddenly calls out to her, "Ellida, you are free to go. I release you. You may choose of your own free will." Ellida repeats, as though mesmerized, "Of my own free will. I can choose of my own free will." And she turns around and walks back to her husband.

Acting on an intuitive hunch, I suggested to the husband that he go and see the play. He thought the suggestion strange, said he never went to plays, and asked why I would suggest such a thing. I told him I couldn't explain why, that he would only know after he saw it. That intrigued him, and he went. He returned the following session and thanked me for having provided him with a profound experience. He said he finally understood what he must do with his wife, that he must let her go of her own free will. Whereupon, he proceeded to do so.

I experienced this as a truly collaborative enterprise between the husband, myself and Ibsen. Ibsen had the capacity to dramatize a human dilemma in such a way as to convey a universal meaning; the husband had the capacity to perceive the message and integrate it into his own life; and I had the capacity to act on an intuition and bring them together.

Before I close, I wish to address what to me is the most important difference between artists and therapists, and that is the difference in goals. The final goal of the artist is to explore the heights and depths of human experience, to rip off masks and lay bare the dark side of character, to exploit conflict, create crises and embrace tragedy. Artists are not required to put back together the things they have torn asunder. They need not answer questions, only raise them.

Therapists, on the other hand, are expected to put together again what life has broken; to resolve conflicts, shore up weaknesses, shed light on the darkness, heal wounds, reconcile injustices and prevent tragedies. While artists are only required to observe and accurately record life's inevitabilities, therapists are called upon to change those inevitabilities.

Now let us pause for a moment of silence. Did you hear a distant sound? That was the gods laughing at our hubris. ■

PEGGY PAPP, M.S.W., *is on the training faculty at the Ackerman Institute for Family Therapy in New York City.*

CIRCUS MAXIMUS

FEEDING THE TALK-SHOW LION

By Jill Harkaway

THE CROWNING MOMENT OF MY PROFESSIONAL life occurred two years ago. It had nothing to do with getting my doctorate, presenting at national conferences, or even being published in the *Journal of Marriage and Family Therapy*—accomplishments that most of America seemed to take in stride. I was amazed at how quickly the world's indifference vanished when I appeared on "The Oprah Winfrey Show."

Of course I had expected that my parents would be impressed and forgave them in advance for finding my moment on national television more of a mark of professional distinction than my bibliography. And I even anticipated that my clients—and the people who have real control over my life, like my hairdresser and plumber—would feel some degree of awe.

But I never imagined how appearing on Oprah would elevate my status among my professional peers. Now when I mount my soapbox and begin to hold forth about the political implications of fat and women's appearances in this culture, and someone says, "Hey, that's pretty good. You ought to go on

'The Oprah Winfrey Show,' " I smile humbly and pause for a moment until someone who knows the truth says, "She already has." And I see the measure of my stature change before my eyes.

At one time, I believed that there were three types of family therapists: those who never get invited to appear on talk shows, those who get invited and accept, and those who get invited but decline. During the time I belonged to the first group, I always thought that if ever invited, I would join group three, rejecting talk show appearances as a form of professional prostitution.

When the chance to get my allotted 15 minutes of national exposure finally came, however, concerns about professional dignity were not foremost in my mind. Glamour, excitement and novelty were. I got the message from my answering service (already impressed) that the producer of "The Oprah Winfrey Show" had called. I thought about it for a few moments and uttered a silent prayer, "Oh, please, please, please, please. Let them be calling to ask me to be on the show."

They were; they wanted me as the expert on

"Couples and Obesity." I suddenly realized I could do this and still maintain my dignity. I could reach hundreds and thousands of women who would never seek professional help. I saw that my appearance on the show would be an act of supreme humanity. I would become the Dr. Schweitzer of the talk-show circuit. I said yes.

There followed long, exciting phone interviews with Oprah's producer. She listened at length to my views about weight and the balance of power in couples' relationships; obesity as a distance regulator; dysfunctional interactions and attempts to solve the problem as problem-maintaining.

She thought my ideas were brilliant and original. I was impressed by her obvious intelligence.

In the weeks that preceded the broadcast, I had two recurrent fantasies. In one, my appearance on the show would be so powerful that it would make Oprah actually lose weight. With a perfect, Milan-style systemic opinion, I would suddenly and mysteriously liberate her from old patterns and the burden of being overweight. I would become instantly famous as an agent of change for overweight celebrities. Nell Carter would give me tickets to "Ain't Misbehavin'." I would be flown to Hollywood for consultations with overweight stars. *People* magazine and "60 Minutes" would do stories on me.

My second fantasy, deeper, darker and more shameful than the other, was that my "Oprah" appearance would lead to the fulfillment of my secret, lifelong ambition to become an actress. "L.A. Law" would cast me as a psychologist testifying in a case of fat discrimination. I would be so surprisingly good in this—witty, intelligent, sophisticated—that I would be cast in remakes of all the old Myrna Loy movies. I would become the new Myrna Loy. But of course my integrity would force me to give up all the glamour to return to my work as a psychologist. The noble calling of family therapy would prove more important to me than stardom.

REALITY SOON BEGAN TO INTRUDE ON MY FANtasies. I found myself starting to struggle with Oprah's producer. The closer we got to the broadcast, the more this warm and wonderful woman seemed to change. Now she wanted me to furnish clients to appear on the show. I was concerned about how this odd dual relationship would affect any clients I might choose. I didn't want to violate my clients' right to confidentiality by appearing with them on television, nor did I want to spend the next six weeks talking with clients about our TV appearance. I decided a therapeutic lie was in order. I told Oprah's producer I had asked my clients, but to my surprise (and my clients') no one was willing. The producer would have to find her couples elsewhere.

Next she called to ask me to interview a couple on the show. She was clearly exasperated when I explained the dubious ethics of conducting a clinical interview in a nonclinical setting. But after a very prolonged attempt to change my mind, she acquiesced. I guess they didn't have a backup expert.

I was beginning to learn about the enormous differences between my world and the world according to "The Oprah Winfrey Show." Nevertheless, the producer's continuing friendliness soothed me, and I tried to attribute our disagreements to her understandable ignorance of therapeutic ethics. I didn't want to question things too deeply. I just wanted to go on the air.

Recognizing TV's reliance on 30-second sound bytes, I prepared for the show by deciding on three simple points I wanted to make. I practiced translating therapy jargon into lay language. I anticipated tricky questions. I bought a new blouse. I invited a therapist friend who lived in Chicago to join me as an invited audience member so that we could debrief after the show.

I arrived in Chicago, was met by a limousine, and was whisked off to the hotel. There, I encountered a scene beyond anything in my wildest fantasies. A mob of celebrity seekers crowded around the limousine, pushing and shoving to see in and get close to me as the door opened. "Oprah really knows how to make stars," I thought to myself. I emerged from the limousine with great dignity, smiled magnanimously to a confused crowd, and strode into the hotel. Later I learned that Tom Hanks was making a movie in Chicago and was expected to arrive at the hotel within moments.

The next day, only mildly deflated, I was picked up and taken to the studio. In the midst of building construction and malfunctioning elevators, crowds of desperate fans were battling to get tickets to the show. I was escorted through this mayhem to the "green room" backstage, where I was met by my close, personal friend, the producer, who was even more effusive and hyperactive in person than she had been on the phone. She showed me around the theater (surprisingly small in real life) and explained the procedures. Oprah would start by interviewing the three guest couples (who in the end had been recruited in the standard fashion: an advertisement shown locally at the end of the show seeking couples who were having marital problems because of obesity) and then bring me on about halfway through the show to comment on what had been said.

THE PRODUCER INTRODUCED ME TO THE THREE couples, offered us coffee and doughnuts, and bounced out to tie up loose ends. One of the couples was young, good-natured, loving and very insightful. The husband readily acknowledged that he was "being selfish" about his wife's weight and expressed both frustration and guilt that his attempts to help his wife only made things worse. She was unhappy with her weight but felt that if she lost weight now she'd "only be doing it for him" and wanted to be able to do it for herself. I liked them.

The second couple were both of about normal size and involved in a very peculiar conflict about his "massive obesity." I could only guess that they were taking advantage of this opportunity to meet Oprah

and appear on national television.

The third couple, Bonnie and Mike, were a bit more disturbing. They were engaged in a very complicated game of publicly humiliating each other. Obesity was their ammunition. He called her insulting names and told embarrassing stories about how fat she had gotten; she made fun of his weight ("rolls of fat and that disgusting beer gut") and his drinking. With great glee they described the parties and family gatherings at which one of them had "won" by thoroughly mortifying the other. These battles seemed to have provided them with hours of fun. It was not hard to figure out that they had just hit the big time with the "Oprah Show." With an audience of millions, the stakes were now higher than they had ever been. This was an Olympic gold medal contest in the public-humiliation-of-your-mate event. I felt anxious about them, aware that this game could explode under the pressure of their appearance on the air. I was afraid of the consequences for them if this got out of control.

The producer came bouncing back into the room. She told me that Oprah had decided that one of the couples would stay on stage with me and that the discussion would focus on their relationship. That seemed reasonably manageable and benign, but I warned her not to pick the third couple. I explained my concerns about their being too volatile. She came back a few minutes later. Oprah insisted on the third couple. I suddenly realized the enormousness of both my naivete and the difference between the world of therapy and the world of talk shows. As a therapist, I was attempting to protect this couple from their game and its consequences. Oprah was hoping to exploit it for its entertainment value. This outrageous couple would make good theater.

MY WORST FEARS WERE REALIZED. RATHER THAN trying to shed light on how couples get into muddles about weight, Oprah played up the cruel and sensational elements. She introduced the couple by giving examples of the insults they used (elicited in phone interviews), such as, "I would scratch your back if you didn't have two of them," as the audience hissed and booed.

Bonnie and Mike quickly began exchanging insults. His ("She's bigger than the entire Chicago Bears") drew boos. Hers ("I don't [feel sexual] when I look at him") drew cheers. The audience quickly became aligned with the wife against the husband. Long before my entry, the weight issue had become simplified and trivialized into a battle between women and men. Not exactly the kind of clarity and enlightenment I had hoped to introduce on this show.

One woman in the studio got up to tell the horrified, angry audience how her husband forced her to have her jaw wired for six months and then tempted her to eat until she gained it all back.

Another woman told how her husband said cruel things while putting pressure on her to lose weight. Suddenly, she stopped and in exuberant realization said, "I'm getting him back on national TV!" To which Oprah responded, equally exuberantly, "This is good." "Yes," said the woman, with a wide, pleased grin, "this is good. John, look at me, this is Maryann, and I'm getting you back on TV." The audience went wild.

Meanwhile, I sat in the green room and watched on the monitor with growing anxiety and discomfort. The time for my entrance had passed. Oprah was either having too good a time or felt that an expert in obesity was redundant. She was so interested in telling stories about her own weight that she was barely listening to the audience. The makeup man (my sole companion for the last half hour) and I were having a good time anyway, better than I was likely to have on stage. I wanted to go home.

My time came. I walked on stage during the commercial break. I sat down with Bonnie and Mike. This was it. My shot at a national audience. Live.

The cameras came on, and I was introduced as "Jill Harkaway, a couples therapist." (Where was the "Dr." title that all the male doctors get? Why is this woman addressing me as "Jill"?) I took a deep breath. I explained that weight can serve many purposes in relationships and that conflicts about weight frequently mask an underlying problem. Oprah changed the subject. I talked about battles over weight being a struggle over who has power in a relationship. Oprah (who most certainly had the power in this particular relationship) disagreed and said that the issue was really about physical power. I tried to explain. She cut me off. Like a good therapist, I tried to create a balance, to get away from blame and move toward understanding. Evidently, this was boring—Oprah kept bringing things back to "us vs. them." Clearly, I was not good entertainment.

IN A SUDDEN FLASH OF DESPAIR, I GOT IT. OPRAH was the boss, and I was a stage prop. It had been an illusion to think that I would have any control over what I could do or say on *her* show. I struggled to hold on to my position—any position—but felt as if my life-support system was fading away. I am not shy or easily intimidated, but the momentum of the show was too much for me.

Oprah continued to use Bonnie and Mike to provoke the audience. I started trying to dissociate.

One woman called in to describe how her husband had locked her in the basement for a year to make her lose weight. The audience gasped. She said she had gone from weighing 160 to 115 pounds. The audience gasped again. Oprah was appalled ("Amazing Grace!" she proclaimed). When she asked the woman if she was still with her husband, the woman answered, "No." The audience applauded; Oprah raised her arm and cheered.

I was, of course, disturbed by this story (despite my attempts, I had not yet reached a trance state) but even more disturbed by how the story—and the caller—were being used to arouse the audience.

Attention turned back to Mike, who had now come to represent all the bad and cruel husbands in the world. In all fairness, he was doing his part to earn this role.

When Oprah asked him why there was such a double standard—that both he and wife were overweight, but it was only her weight that was a problem—he answered, "That's how men are." Mike had obviously figured out early on what his role was meant to be and was playing it to the hilt. With great vehemence Oprah began to shout, "Kill him! Kill him!"

Oprah then turned to Mike and asked, "Whatever happened to those vows: 'for better or worse, in sickness and in health'?"

MIKE: I still love my wife. I just think if I tease her, she'll have the urge to lose weight.

BONNIE: (smiling) I have the urge to lose it and you go to the store and buy all the junk food.

OPRAH: He does it on purpose? Mike! Why, if she's trying to diet, do you bring her junk food?

MIKE: To test her willpower.

OPRAH: Mike, you dog! You dog!

As Bonnie sat smiling, the audience's anger at Mike reached new heights. Next, a caller asked Mike, "How could anyone who looks so fat and sloppy have anything to say about the way his wife looks? At least she takes pride in her appearance." There was delighted applause from the audience. Oprah smiled, shook her head, "Oh, Mike!"

Mike, finally looking a bit shaken, said, "I had it coming," and tried to smile. Oprah moved in for the kill, grinning a smug, almost dangerous, grin, "Christians one, lions nothing. What do you say to that, Mike? You look like you've put on a pound or two."

MIKE: I have, it's true. I need to lose some weight. We both do. That's why we're here.

OPRAH: Why don't you do it together?

BONNIE: Because he eats his dinner before I do and then goes to bed early.

How does even Oprah respond to that? I wondered.

OPRAH: Well, Jill, what do you have to say to this couple and others who are having problems like this?

I thought I heard someone calling my name. I tried to rouse myself from my stupor. I mumbled something valiant, "If a couple is struggling over weight, they need to look at what the real issue is that they're avoiding." To which Oprah responded, "Well, maybe not," and turned to one of the audience members. Like the dormouse at the Mad Hatter's tea party, I went back to sleep.

BY THE END OF THE SHOW THE WIFE WAS GIDDILY triumphant; her husband, crushed. Oprah wrapped up with one last jubilant jab: "If we can stay with them when they're bald, they can stick with us when we put on a few pounds." The audience cheered. I had ceased caring. It was over.

As soon as the show was off the air, Oprah waved to those of us left on stage and swept out of the room. As far as she and the crew were concerned, the show was done, finished, ancient history, and the survivors were left to fend for themselves. The couples and I drifted back to the green room, a bit shellshocked, not sure what we were supposed to do. No one was available to talk to any of the guests or help them debrief.

The wounded husband disappeared, while his wife held court in the green room, laughing and telling more humiliating stories about her husband. I talked briefly about what happened on the show with my colleague, who had sat through the show. We were worried about Mike. My friend went off to talk with Mike and discovered him hiding in the men's room. We were worried about the wife if the husband's next move in the game was to escalate. Would he go home, get drunk and beat her up? Would he get drunk and wrap his car around a tree? What were we doing meddling in people's lives for entertainment, then abandoning them? (Footnote: I subsequently wrote the producer a letter in which I strategically reframed my clinical concerns as a concern for their legal liability should negative consequences result from a guest's participation on the show. I suggested they provide a professional counselor to help guests debrief after the show and provide follow-up, such as referrals, etc. The producer wrote to thank me. They were going to implement my idea with a show on successful outcomes due to appearances on the show!)

MY GIG ON "OPRAH" TAUGHT ME A LOT ABOUT television and therapist participation in talk shows. Like it or not, Oprah and Phil and Geraldo and Sally Jesse, and whoever, are the major sources of psychological information and education in the country today. Talk shows have developed into the most significant influence in thousands, even millions, of lives and relationships, supplanting extended family, religion and—dare we say it?—professional helpers. An illusion has been created that the talk-show studio is an enormous self-help or support group. Watching in their homes, people come to feel that they know these talk-show hosts intimately, they think of them as close friends and confidants. They are compassionate, understanding and accepting. Oprah has a special place; she "made it" despite the cultural handicaps of gender, race, obesity. She is seen as "one of us." She is trusted, available, a supportive, nurturing group leader/sister/therapist. Do we even have a way to describe this curious 1980s form of media transference?

Although talk shows can provide a useful function in educating, normalizing experience, and in helping individuals break constraining taboos and make a change in their lives, they can also be dangerous. The danger arises when the illusion of familiarity and intimacy entices people into sharing personal information, expressing thoughts and feelings that they never dared to say out loud to anyone before. This is potentially therapeutic. But on national

television? To an audience of millions? An audience that includes one's husband/wife/mother/boss/child/neighbor who have also never heard it before? It is too simple to ascribe this (as I have often heard) to a sudden flowering of "borderlines" in TV audiences. We therapists, of all people, should be aware of the influence context has on behavior.

TV talk shows are contexts in which the normal rules of social behavior seem not to apply. Having been swept away by the emotional intensity in that small, deceptively private room, I have a new respect for and fear of the power of TV. It is easy to be carried away by its illusory intimacy into saying more than is safe, particularly if you are seeking approval and response from Oprah and the group. Once the show is over, Oprah moves on and the "group" disbands. What happens then? Do guests suddenly realize they can't go home anymore? How are family members going to respond? Isn't it a stretch of the imagination to believe that abusive husbands are going to undergo a positive transformation because their stories have been told on national TV?

My experience will not dissuade many people from going on talk shows, nor is it intended to. For one thing, there are many local talk shows that do an admirable job of being both respectful and educational. It is also true that some people have had very positive experiences, even on the "big" shows. And I don't think, in my advanced fantasy state, I could have been dissuaded by someone else's experience. Although I now question the wisdom and ethics of participating in this kind of circus, I do understand the opposing position. There is an argument to be made for keeping family therapists visible in the media. I suppose an argument could also be made that if we, as responsible and competent family therapists, won't do it, the irresponsible and incompetent will take over. The information that we do provide is useful—that is, of course, if anyone can hear it in such a context. And we all have families that will be pleased, or at least amused, by our national appearances. Whatever the position, the growing relationship between our field and talk shows is leading us to the point where we have to at least consider the ethical and moral consequences of our participation in them.

And a follow-up to the story? I have continued to do an occasional local talk show but only when I am familiar with the interviewers and there are no lay guests. Your guess is as good as mine about what happened to the three couples on Oprah's show. And, as just about everyone on the face of the planet must know by now, Oprah has lost 65 pounds. So maybe my appearance did somebody some good after all! ■

JILL HARKAWAY, ED.D., *is the director of the Center for Family Studies at the Northeast Psychiatric Associates in Nashua, NH.*

WHY I LOVE PRIVATE PRACTICE

40,000 Hours And Still Smiling

By Frank Pittman

FAMILY THERAPISTS SPEND THEIR CAREERS IN situations that drive other people nuts. We enter families just as the family members are running and clawing for the exit. We are the experts in facing out-of-control chaos. We bring peace and understanding and sanity to replace violence and warfare and every form of craziness. We're really pretty fierce folks, and it takes a lot to scare us.

But the scariest thing most of us ever do is to go into full-time practice.

Fourteen years ago, I took the risk of offering my services for sale to the public. Since then I have supervised dozens of anxiety-laden therapists going into private practice and found we all share the same fear, even though a look out the window would show that the gutters are not filled with the bones of starving therapists.

The fear of private practice may be largely groundless, but it is there, and I know it well. I went through it again recently when, after raising my fees for the first time in five years, I was overcome by the fear that all my patients would leave me if I charged more. They didn't.

Part of the fear of private practice has to do with family therapists' peculiar attitudes toward money—we're just not sure that it is respectable to ask people to pay us when we are having a good time and they are in pain. My mother taught me that any mention of money was crass. I still shudder when I ask my patients questions about money. My distaste for the subject of money is not unique. Even now, when I mention money at a family therapy workshop, a few people always get so nervous that they walk out angrily or write insulting evaluations.

But I think the fear of private practice goes beyond the subject of money. Sometimes I'm not sure whether therapists are more afraid of a full schedule or an empty one. As the number of one's appointments rises, a new fear develops, the fear of loneliness and isolation, the fear that spending all your time with people in pain will be too depressing or, worse yet, too boring. Fortunately, those of us who have been in private practice for a while know better; we know how to end up seeing only patients we want to see, we know how to make the practice fun, and we know how to make therapeutic relationships therapeutic for us, too. Those who don't learn these things aren't going to be of much help to themselves or to anyone else.

I've logged something over 40,000 patient-hours and have managed to remain reasonably sane and healthy. I've helped most of the people I've seen and have surely hurt a few. After all this time, I still approach the day eagerly and optimistically and don't feel burnt out or bored, at least not for very long. It's still fun. Moreover, it has to be fun, because you can't survive a life in family therapy unless you do make it fun.

As far as I can tell, there are two cardinal rules for family therapists who wish to succeed in private practice.

CARDINAL RULE ONE:
The Therapist Must Believe in Therapy

As a therapist, you must believe that you can do something that will change, or even save, people's lives. You must be optimistic about your abilities to bring about change and your patients' abilities to make and survive those changes. I don't know how any family therapist expects to sell services that he or she doesn't value.

If you don't believe in therapy, don't go into private practice. (And if you're not sure, don't work at an agency either, since the agency's clients and administration have the power to undercut any therapist's belief in therapy.)

Bad therapists—those who accept their patients' sense of helplessness and paralysis under the tyranny of their emotions—can easily become disillusioned and pessimistic by their efforts to change people's emotions without first changing their motions, changing their circumstances without changing their actions.

It is frustrating to try to help people survive if they require the world to be totally just and fair before they'll take the risk of living in it.

CARDINAL RULE TWO:
The Therapist Must Believe in Life

Life is just one damned thing after another. Some of it is nice and some of it isn't, but all of it is fascinating. Therapists who want to stick around for the long haul must never lose their wonder at the vagaries of the human condition. Therapists, for their own sakes and those of others, must love life and bring that love to others, and that means appreciating the full range of human emotions. Life is messy, but anything that doesn't kill you is good for you. We're not in the business of shielding people from life, either its predictable consequences or its fickle fortune. We're in the business of teaching people how to experience life, how to make it work for them, and how to survive it when it doesn't work out quite the way they'd like.

OBVIOUSLY, THE FIRST STEP IN SETTING UP A PRIvate practice is to get some patients. The paradox here is that the most referrals go to the therapist who is seeing the most patients. As we all know, the best patients are those who are referred by other patients. But if you've never had any other patients, there are several things you can do—and some things not to do.

I don't recommend a big ad in the yellow pages. Some of my students have tried this, and the results were disconcerting. The patients who choose their therapists out of the yellow pages want to keep their reasons for seeking help secret. They haven't talked to anyone else about their problems and are so skittish about therapy that they don't want anyone to know they are in therapy.

When individuals come secretly and anonymously, it's likely to be a weird encounter. Yellow-page patients, especially those who call from phone booths, often just don't show up. Sometimes they come under assumed names. One man came to see me three times, only at odd hours, and in disguise. He spent the entire time talking anxiously about

504

how some possible future political career would be harmed by seeing me. He never got up the courage to tell me why he came, and he left with the feeling that therapy was not very helpful.

An introduction through mutual friends or former patients makes the therapy relationship feel more respectable and less threatening. I certainly prefer seeing people who are referred specifically to me and already trust me by reputation. I want people to be proud about seeing me. I learned this from my grandmother who was an undertaker and strived to put on funerals that would make people proud to be dead.

When you get your referrals from other therapists whose schedules are booked, there is another problem. Other therapists only send you the dregs of their practice. There are therapist-eating patients who are shunned by everyone they've seen before. The seasoned therapist can smell them coming and refers them on to the fresh young therapist on the block. This is not all bad. A therapist new to private practice has more time to invest in impossible patients and may be able to provide more help than the busier practitioner can.

When you do get a referral from another therapist, an attitude of distrust is not inappropriate. The other therapist had a reason for getting rid of this patient, and you should know what that reason is. The first referral I got from another psychiatrist was a family of delinquent kids with an unbudgeable mother who sat on my couch making faces for an hour. She was drinking a large cup of coffee. When she left, I realized that she'd poured the coffee all over my beige sofa. I called the referring psychiatrist, who told me she'd done the same thing to his sofa. What's more, the family didn't pay either of us. I don't think she wanted therapy. I didn't see her again, though I thought of her often, until I replaced the ruined sofa with a vinyl one.

I encourage therapists who aren't busy yet to make themselves available to school counselors, nurses, doctors or domestic attorneys—people who don't do therapy but see people with problems and refer them to therapists. You can't afford to be selective with such referrals and should accept whomever and whatever the referrer digs up. If you see the patient and find him or her or them unsuitable for you, no harm is done. You can refer the patient to someone more suitable and thereby do a favor to the patient, the referrer and the referee, all of whom will be grateful and impressed with you and send you more patients.

THE FEW FAMILY THERAPISTS I KNOW WHO FAILED to establish a successful private practice usually made the classic error of setting limits on whom they would see. Family therapists in private practice can't afford to refuse to see individuals (who may bring other family members after the first meeting), or unpleasant cases like child molesters or alcoholics, or difficult cases like maniacs or bulimics, or even people who aren't likely to pay. These cases may work out surprisingly well, and if they don't, you can refer them on to someone whose work you admire and whose friendship you would value (or, if the case is particularly awful, to a colleague who has sent you a loathsome patient). You thus make yourself known in all directions, build your reputation and your network. You should never turn down a referral or tell your referral sources that the cases they are sending you are too difficult or, for that matter, too easy—it may be insulting for you to succeed too painlessly. Your referral source couldn't handle the case, and will be pleased with you if you try and will appreciate your efforts, however they turn out.

When establishing a private practice, it helps to get yourself known in the community. Giving talks to various civic groups may be useful, if you speak well, but it may be most helpful just to appear in public places looking and acting sane. Since everybody knows therapists left over from the '60s who go around making a show of weirdness, as if that is their idea of mental health, the world reacts with grateful surprise to therapists who bathe regularly, wear clothes that fit, and display good manners in public. I've seen patients who came to me after recoiling in horror from a referral to a therapist who was known to do his yard work in a tiny and unflattering red bikini, and a therapist who persisted in wearing flowing robes and conducting her therapy session on the floor. Good public manners are the best advertisement for your mental health—as my great-grandmother so often said, "a lady or gentleman never offends anyone unintentionally."

Even though you shouldn't restrict yourself to it, get yourself a specialty. Become expert at something that drives everyone else nuts. Eating and drinking disorders are maddening to most therapists, violent people are infuriating, and hyperactive kids are disquieting—many established therapists prefer to avoid such people. If you're willing to see them, you'll get them referred to you. If you can do something with them (and you can), you'll build a reputation in no time and can then branch out to easier cases. I had two specialties at the beginning—keeping psychotic patients out of hospitals and hypnotizing dying patients for pain relief. I still get to see such patients—no one else wants them—and I find nothing more gratifying.

Building a reputation requires using whatever contacts and forms of advertising are available to you. If you can get yourself written up in newspapers or interviewed on television, by all means do so. It doesn't bring in the expected deluge of patients, but it may bring in a few. Having a national reputation is indirectly helpful, but only if local people notice that you are well thought of elsewhere. The local reputation is far more important. I've gotten calls from people who saw me quoted in magazines like *McCall's* or *Reader's Digest*, and some of them came cross-country to see me, but I had the feeling they were expecting magic worthy of the trip. I'm a nice guy, but no magician, and some of

them went away disappointed. I have friends who are world famous and can attract huge audiences in obscure places but can't get referrals at home. I'm convinced that more patients come from the clerk at the supermarket than from a paper in *Family Process* or a mention in *Time*.

If you're really desperate about getting your practice going, you can recruit friends and social contacts as patients. There's a simple trick to it—just act painfully serious and sympathetic toward how bad they're feeling, and express deep concern over the underlying problems in the amusing family story you're being told. Of course, there is a catch to all this. You may or may not turn your friend into a patient in this manner, but you will certainly lose a friend either way.

ONCE PATIENTS CALL YOU, YOU THEN MUST MAKE them delighted that they did. Who answers your telephone may determine whether the referred patient comes to you or moves down to the next name on the list. Some people just don't like answering machines and will simply hang up on them. Most people in pain want a real human voice on the telephone. Even though some answering services are no more personal than a machine, I use a service. They are cheap, and I would gladly pay more for a better one. I want a voice on the phone that is personal and involved. One friend of mine had the opposite problem, a service that was too personal. He found that his service was telling frantic patients such things as, "I never know how to reach that guy. He spends a lot of time at the races. You could try there."

I try to be easy to reach. I publish my home number and don't object to people calling me at home. Actually, I can be more readily interrupted at home than at the office. When my wife, Betsy, is in the office, she answers the telephone and does the crucial work of talking skittish people into coming in and usually into *(continued on page 511)*

506

Going Private

I T WAS PROBABLY MORE OF A SHOCK TO ME THAN TO MY COLLEAGUES. AFTER 10 YEARS OF AGENCY work, I simply quit. I was burned out, I had a new baby at home, and I kept having fantasies of writing the definitive satire on psychotherapy that would rock the profession (that should have cued me into my state of mind). Like the adolescent suddenly cramped by familiar faces and old family jokes, I needed to get away and break out on my own. No more surrogate parents telling me to clean up my case records, no more good-son command performances, no more depressed welfare mothers, alcoholic fathers, abused children, no more multiproblem, multigenerational despair and hopelessness. As my agency sibs fought over who would get my room and glowered at me for abandoning ship, I packed up my degrees and was gone. But where?

Private practice, of course. That green pasture of therapeutic self-determination, the land of more than one suit, where men were insightful, women were individuated, and therapists were their own best friends. I could do what I wanted when I wanted—set appointments for 5:18 in the morning, write my case notes on Safeway grocery bags, carpet my office in Astroturf, and never ever clean off my desk. Definitely grown-up stuff.

I quickly learned, however, that like my first apartment in college, all this had a down side. Business records and self-employment tax, lonely Wednesday afternoons, constant hustling ("Hi, I'm Bob Taibbi—Why don't I give you one of my cards?"), and enough anxiety over money to fill the state of Wyoming. I even missed my agency family. My mind sought solace in daydreams of tough, gritty cowboys making their way across vast and hostile prairies with no more than a horse, a bedroll, and a gun named Betsy; gutsy entrepreneurs building vast empires with two dollars in loose change and a lot of hyperactive conviction. In spite of myself, I actually made a little money that first year and spent more time with my kids. (After being told politely by editors that there was a potential market of about 12 for my psychotherapy satire, I ditched the idea.)

But something else kicked in, something that I hadn't expected. Just when I had finally used up my first box of letterhead stationery and had begun to feel more at ease wearing a tie all day, I started to experience a different kind of awkwardness and discomfort. There was some clash that I could not articulate between me, my work and my values. Despite my rationalizations and modified sliding scale, something about "growth issues" and $60 checks in my pocket just didn't feel right. Maybe it was some '60s-style social conscience left over from my college days, maybe my adolescent experiment had run its course, maybe I simply needed to be more creative with my business structure. I didn't know, but after a year and a half, I repacked my degrees and quit private practice.

ONCE I RETURNED TO AGENCY WORK, I FOUND PRIVATE PRACTICE HAD SOFTENED ME UP. NO LONGER emotionally blunted by burnout, or blinded by delicious visions of hanging my own shingle, my hide wasn't so tough. Now the rub of my clients' lives against mine made me aware of just how rough their lives were. In contrast with the suited middle managers who slapped some comp time onto their lunch hour, or just skipped their midafternoon run to make appointments, my agency clients dragged themselves in at 6:30 in the evening with cow dung on their boots, grease still on their hands, or with small armies of kids ready to ransack the waiting room while their parents vacillated between wanting to punch a hole in my office wall and staring numbly at their shoes. Here were people who had so much of life stacked against them that normal developmental crises and psychological traumas were the least of their worries. These clients, I realized, saw therapy as lying somewhere between a last hope and no hope, between a chance to rethink and regroup and one more pain in the ass. I started working differently. I threw out a lot of intellectual fluff; I began to focus more upon problem solving and to believe more in outreach, advocacy and community coordination.

On bad days, what I do now seems to be just another drop in a leaky bucket. But there are good days as well, moments of connection and healing—a hard-nosed father finally steps out of role to talk awkwardly and lovingly to his son about growing into manhood and ceremoniously seals his words by placing his father's hunting rifle in his son's lap; three estranged Japanese sisters alternate between labored chunks of broken English and bursts of Japanese to decide the proper way to honor the memory of their long-dead parents; an angry 6-year-old girl dictates to her mother a letter to her convict father, instructing her mother to leave space at the bottom so she can draw flowers. These moments seem to have less to do with the power of therapy than with the simple power of a family gathered together in one space at one time.

I RECENTLY INTERVIEWED A NEW SOCIAL WORK GRADUATE FOR A JOB POSITION. SO, I ASKED, WHAT are your long-term plans for the future? What would you like to be doing in the mental health field down the road? She answered without skipping a beat. She wanted to work in an agency for a couple of years to gain clinical experience and qualify for licensure; after that she planned on opening a private practice in town. She didn't say "of course," but she didn't need to. Our agency has a difficult time keeping staff more than a couple of years. Like this young woman, most stay just long enough to get supervised for licensure, then move on to the green pastures of private practice. Poor clients wind up getting inexperienced, if not poor, service. We have a waiting list of two months, while the 120 or so private therapists in town scramble to fill their hours.

This pattern is not just typical of my own area. As part of a workshop I conducted last year, I guided the audience of mental health professionals in a fantasy about how their dreams for themselves had changed through the years. Not surprisingly, many of the images focused upon work. What was surprising, however, was the split in the audience. The early idealism of many older participants—to "help humankind"—had evolved into robust empire building, while others maintained a relatively steady commitment to the path they were already following. While the younger professionals certainly pictured themselves helping others, they had little doubt that private practice was the best place to realize their dreams.

I sense a growing gap between myself and my colleagues, particularly my younger colleagues. We have different visions about what we do and whom we serve. Private practice was, for me, an arena for experimentation during an adolescent stage of professional development; for many of my contemporaries it has been a frantic middle-age scramble to becoming one's own man or woman. But for younger therapists, private practice has become a predictable, almost axiomatic, step up the career ladder to success. This bothers me.

What doesn't bother me is people desiring a higher income; how much money one needs to live is a matter of practicalities and values. It would be arrogant of me to say how others should survive financially, especially when many of my therapist colleagues are single parents who are already struggling over money and time. Money problems are a real and present danger, and I don't begrudge anyone striving to get what they need.

What does bother me is not the money to be made in private practice but the motive for going private; not the privacy itself but the implications of privacy. While I know many private practitioners who use their greater freedom in creative service to their communities—through sliding scales, free consultations, research projects, board memberships and the like—in general, private practice seems to offer more privacy to the therapist than to the client. What I hear between the lines of conversations with the young job applicant I interviewed and with many of my colleagues is an unstated but transparent regard for private practice as a refuge, as an exclusive environment that screens out many "less desirable" clients, that is, the therapeutically reluctant, the exhausting, the poor. Through its limited access, private practice brings in "higher grade," or more desirable, clients. Too often our talk of helping others is really about helping *some*.

Private practice not only separates the therapist from the community, it separates the therapist from his or her work as well. In their thought-provoking book *Habits of the Heart*, Robert Bellah and his coauthors discuss the differences between job, career and calling. A job is a way of making a living, making money. The relationship between one's job and one's identity is usually loose and minimal. Career involves a greater investment of the self. It marks the path of advancement, achievement and success within an occupation—and carries with it power, competency and self-esteem. Having a calling cuts even deeper into the self. When one is following a calling, the work has meaning and value in and of itself, not just in the output or profit that results. One's work becomes "morally inseparable from one's life." And more important, a calling links the individual and the community through the notion of common good or service.

Many of my younger colleagues seem to view work as a job or career—or something in between. The differences show up not in work hours—I work fewer hours than most of them—but in attitude, in expectation. I expect my work to carry more of my identity, my values, my sense of overall purpose than they seem to expect theirs to; this creates a distance between us that cannot always be talked about but that I feel.

I'm aware how easily this can veer toward self-righteousness, one generation shaking its head in bafflement and disgust at the foibles of the next one. But the changes I'm describing in our profession are part of a larger shift in societal values about work, priorities and purpose. I sometimes wonder if this new attitude toward work isn't more realistic than that of my peers, who came of age in the '60s.

In a recent letter to the *Networker,* Warren Farrell pointed out that therapy at present is not particularly "user friendly" toward men. I would say this is even more true for the intellectually and economically disadvantaged. After 25 years of trying to establish a comprehensive community mental health movement, maybe we should cut our losses, take satisfaction in therapy as a workable option for the middle class, and recognize that therapy isn't the answer to the overwhelming social and economic obstacles that poor people face. Then we wouldn't have to retreat into private practice as the only escape from chronic burnout; we could choose that path up front, as the best way to make use of our professional skills.

I'm not at all sure that's the way to go. Still, as therapy becomes big business and as "going private" continues to be an alluring choice, we are left with difficult questions. Do we as professionals have a core of immutable values—not only those about client self-determination, or the belief in the capacity for change, but about our responsibility toward the larger society? How do we transmit these values? How do we as a profession integrate and accommodate to the social changes around us?

Private practice certainly has a place in our profession, and I believe it can be an arena for service and calling. But if we are to avoid becoming mired in our own comfort and self-importance, if we are to accept what Eric Erickson defined as the task of generativity, we need to realize that growing up means more than having to clean up your room. □

—Robert Taibbi
JANUARY 1990

ROBERT TAIBBI *is senior social worker, Youth and Family Services, Region Ten Community Service Board in Charlottesville, VA.*

(continued from page 506) bringing in the rest of the family. She has to talk to them about money and arrange for another therapist if these people can't afford me or would do better to see someone else. She may spend up to an hour with them.

When Betsy's not in the office, I take my telephone calls during sessions and may therefore have to settle for merely getting a name and telephone number so she can call them back when she comes in. If a call comes in that promises a problem that might be of some help to the patients in the office, I may deal with the caller at length, in front of the family, and use the call as I would a call from my team behind the screen. Those of us who can't afford to provide our patients with a team and a screen have to settle for whatever happens to come in randomly over the telephone.

One man objected to my answering the phone on his time. He was a large, wealthy, middle-aged man who was telling me about his lifetime passivity. He had slipped to his knees on the floor, imploring me to help him learn to assert himself. The phone rang, and as I reached for it, he shouted, "Don't answer that goddamn phone—I'm not through telling you what a wimp I am." I didn't answer it.

ONCE YOU HAVE BEEN ABLE TO SOMEHOW GET A referral, and that referral has actually reached you, you must then have a place in which to conduct the therapy. I know therapists who do their practice in a spare room at their home, and that's often comfortable for everyone, except perhaps the therapist's family. It is wonderfully personal, and ideal for the part-time therapist. It has disadvantages, though. It does not offer the therapist the visibility that would encourage referrals, and it does not provide a highly professional atmosphere.

Our choice was to rent an office in a doctor's building near our home. We make the office as homey as possible, which is easy since it is a family operation, with Betsy managing the establishment, renting me out by the hour, and handling the money (remember, I was raised to consider money talk crass) and one or more of the kids helping out when they are home from school. We have comfortably elegant furniture, a lovely view and music—usually Haydn piano trios, Mozart string quartets, or the like. Whether or not I improve my patients' mental health, I know I can improve their taste in music. The waiting room is full of good, fresh magazines. I rarely run on time, but people come early just to read the magazines and listen to the music.

We also give people Cokes and popcorn. Popcorn makes the atmosphere festive and keeps people busy. It soothes restless kids and strips away their parents' dignity (no one can look authoritative while eating popcorn). The popcorn also reduces the level of emotional intensity. No one dares scream with a mouth full of popcorn. With hands filled with popcorn, people can't gesture wildly (it would crush the popcorn). And no one can cry, as that would make their popcorn soggy.

I realize that, on stage, therapists like to get everybody in the family to carry on wildly. Such dramas always get a good audience response, but in a busy private practice it is far nicer to keep the emotional level relatively low, and it probably works better anyway. I haven't tried taping a family eating popcorn during therapy, but I fear it would be noisy. (A word of advice: if you have a leather sofa, don't use buttered popcorn. It stains.)

I think the setting of family therapy should be addictively comfortable and agreeable, a place to which people like to come. You need a room large enough for siblings, of whatever age, to wrestle on the floor, yet small enough to hear a depressive's whimpers. It also helps to have an extra room for people to run to when things get too intense, or when one part of the family won't speak to another part of the family. The extra space can prevent runaways and family fistfights in your lobby—which are just not good advertising for your practice.

SO YOU HAVE A PATIENT AND A PLACE TO SEE THE patient and someone to attend to the details. What do you do then? Doing therapy in private practice is different from practice in an institution. In an agency, you are a representative of authority, and the people you see may well be objects of your charity. You are constantly setting limits on what patients can expect from you and the agency you represent. When I worked in an agency, I often thought my day would be better if patients weren't taking up the valuable time I could have been spending doing paperwork, or going to meetings, or having coffee with my fellow therapists. A not uncommon experience in an agency is being more concerned with how your therapy is coming across to your colleagues than with your relationships to your patients.

When I was on a crisis team in Denver, doing therapy in front of a one-way mirror with various colleagues or students or visiting firemen watching, I would try to do brilliant, often outrageous things. I realize now that my primary relationship back then was not with the patients but with my teammates. The important thing was not the family, but the team's discussion of the family. The big, dramatic change upon entering private practice was the discovery that the people to whom I was closest were my patients. I was no longer the agent of an institution—I was my patient's servant. I was no longer in a position to dismiss patients because they weren't "motivated" to make the changes I wanted them to make in order to impress my students or teachers. My alliance was with my patients.

The wondrous thing about private practice is how the exchange of money equalizes the relationship between therapist and patient. Private patients have as much power over you as you have over them, a power that agency patients don't have. (I know that's wrong, but the world just isn't fair.) The relationship, now equal and reciprocal, becomes a friendship. You feel a closeness and intimacy that

may be even deeper than your feeling toward close friends. I would rather spend an hour or two with almost any of my patients than go to a cocktail party. I miss them if they don't come. I mourn a bit when they terminate. Yet I don't socialize with my patients—partially for the selfish reason that a social relationship would be less intense and would bore me. I have no objection to socializing with patients who were social friends before the therapy, and those can be far more intimate and satisfying relationships subsequently. I have no objections whatever to seeing friends or professional colleagues or even distant relatives as patients, and I charge them. I myself would prefer to see a therapist who knew me previously, and I think there are only advantages to the prior acquaintance.

I EXPECT MY PATIENTS TO NOTICE ME THE PERSON, and I expect them to care about me and whatever I'm going through. I'm not satisfied with people who just come and pay money. I want them to have a human encounter, and I want one too. No amount of money would be enough for me to treat people who were unaware of me—unless of course I had no other patients to work with. Yet therapy is not really an act of love, and there is a danger in being too friendly and loving. At times therapy comes closer to being an act of aggression, in which the therapist joins forces with whatever sanity there is in the patient or the family and then beats up on the pathology. I love my patients, in the same way that Michelangelo loved marble—if I keep chipping away, I can free what I see inside.

I have also learned to flounder for the first half of the session, sometimes longer. If you seem confused and don't understand what the family is telling you, they may work hard to explain themselves and structure you. However, if you perform your brilliant intervention early in the session, the family can spend the rest of the time consolidating their resistance to it. I spend half my time as a supervisor trying to stop young therapists from shooting their wad too early in the session, from letting their brilliance peak too soon. In everyday private practice, unlike the show-business style of family therapy, you're not trying to send people away dazzled. You're trying to keep them in therapy through the process of change, which may be brief or may take a long time—the patient, who controls the length of therapy, will determine the pace of change. One of the nicest things about private practice is that the decisions about the duration of therapy are made by you and the patients rather than by an agency administrator.

F AMILY THERAPY, LIKE LIFE, IS FULL OF CONFU-sion and misplaced emotion and misunder-standing and games and things taken far too seriously, and therefore is comic and should be fun. Since part of the family's reason for coming to you is that they are not having a very good time, it's up to you to make the encounter entertaining. Your baf-flement and bewilderment with the problems they bring you can be weirdly reassuring to them—as if you are saying to them, "See, it really is awful to live this way." Part of the therapy is in the therapist's move from the acknowledged awfulness of the situa-tion, through the humor and absurdity of the awful-ness, to the hope and excitement that change can bring. I keep saying things like, "This is awful. I wouldn't want to live like this," and, "If I looked at it the way you do, I'd feel the way you do, and I sure wouldn't want that."

You can't laugh at people at first, but you can permit them to laugh at you as you experience what they live with. Then, when you join with them in teasing out their awareness of the absurdity of their situation, you can all laugh together. As a therapist or a patient, you cry at the beginning and laugh at the end. But you as the therapist know as you begin that you'll laugh at the end, and they don't know that yet.

You know that the therapy is working when it

becomes fun for you and the family, and you all look forward to the hour. Unfortunately, when the thera-py reaches that point, it soon must end. It does not help your practice to keep patients in therapy too long. Each successfully treated patient is a walking advertisement for you and is likely to refer several friends to you. If people stay in therapy for an inor-dinate period, friends and relatives may get suspi-cious that the therapy isn't going right, and they won't come to you. If a patient has arranged for you to adopt him or her or them and has settled in for a lifetime, the patient may become too possessive of you to refer anyone else. Your practice is best served by a turnover of patients with successful outcomes. Let people go as soon as they can. They'll be back if they need you.

Successful therapy and successful private practice require social skills. Therapists must be quite charm-ing to get by with saying the insulting and shattering things therapy must say to people. If the therapist is warm, friendly and delighted with life and with the therapeutic encounter, he or she can convey all of that nonverbally and be free to verbalize the harsh truths that must be put into words. The most suc-cessful therapists tend to be warm people, but not necessarily brilliant. If the therapist doesn't delight in life and therapy and change, those things can't be faked.

There are toxic personalities in the world, sour and bitter people who make others feel bad from the encounter—the sort of people you'd delight in blackballing from your fraternity or sorority. (I've often quoted one such toxic man. When I urged him to be loving to his son, he said, "How can you expect me to love anybody when nobody has ever loved me? The only people who ever tried to love me either gave up or pissed me off.") Some are vic-tims, others may be excessively mechanistic or com-petitive or cautious, or just joyless, but they make poor therapists for the same reason that they make poor friends or relatives. They love pain, their own and other people's. They can see neither the tragedy in comedy nor the comedy in tragedy, so they can't help people see their own absurdity, and they can't help people see the delight in life going on. They just aren't therapeutic—to themselves or others. Such people should not be therapists.

For others, I recommend private practice. You aren't just accepting professional isolation in exchange for money. The isolation from other professional colleagues will not be the loss you may be anticipating. What you get in exchange is people who are choosing to come to you, out of all the therapists in the world, to risk their lives and families on

your sanity and good humor. You're providing an atmosphere to which people come willingly and eagerly for an aura of festivity and a relationship of equality and respect. It's like having friends come over to play. It's like they are coming to your home, and you feel the honor and the gratitude. The give and take of equal relationships makes you feel invigorated rather than drained at the end of the day—if you are doing it right.

I love private practice. ■

FRANK PITTMAN, M.D., *is in private practice in Atlanta, GA.*

COMING OF AGE AS A CLINICIAN

IS DOING THERAPY AN HONORABLE WAY TO MAKE A LIVING?

By Carol Anderson

THREE MONTHS AGO, MY MOTHER, WELL INTO her eighties and already suffering from Alzheimer's disease, was discovered to have cancer. Until this latest crisis, she lived alone, fiercely clinging to her independence. But she was deteriorating rapidly. She almost seemed to be drying up, just withering away. Already there had been several middle-of-the-night scares about gas stoves left burning, falls, possible broken hips, other crises that sent family members scurrying to try to help.

Diagnosing her physical troubles was complicated by the fact that X-rays were almost useless—severe osteoporosis had left her bones so porous they were transparent. I found it deeply disturbing to realize that this once powerful woman had come to weigh 76 pounds and have *transparent* bones. She had long since lost her interest in everything current: news, reading, even grandchildren. The only TV program she watched in recent months was "Mr. Rogers," whom she was convinced was talking only to her when he said, "You are someone special." She had, at least, one kind and gentle delusion.

As a family, we all debated about the surgery. It

was major, and she might not survive it. Even if she did, they predicted she would be disoriented for weeks or months. Wouldn't it be better to let time run out, to let the illness follow its natural course? What kind of life was she living anyway? We worried about finding a way to present the choices to her that would allow her genuine input into the decision. It didn't seem possible.

Eventually, severe pain made the decision for us—surgery became inevitable. After surgery, in intensive care, she was completely controlled by tubes: tubes in her nose, her neck, her arms. She was in restraints, since she would otherwise pull at them, tearing them from her body. She looked like a bird, a wisp of a being. Certainly not like someone who once ruled a family with an iron will. She was delirious and mostly incoherent. We all felt incredibly guilty. She hardly knew us. Should we have allowed an operation? Did we make the right decision? It seemed cruel and inhuman that she should have to go through this pain, this indignity.

Hour after hour she kept repeating "Okay, good-bye," like a parrot, over and over. Was this her

Scandinavian way of dying? It would be typical, no emotion—"Let's just get on with it," she would probably say, if she only could.

Tragedy intermingled with comedy. In the middle of her incoherent ramblings, she suddenly fixed a gaze on me and my sister and said, "Don't say a word to anyone, and get out of here right away."

"But why?" my sister asked.

"They want to do this to you, too," she said in a conspiratorial tone. "Get away."

We weren't sure whether this was total craziness or a mother who, even at her most desperate, was trying to protect her children from harm.

Did the pain, the tubes, the procedures, matter to her? The nurses repeatedly reassured us that she would remember nothing when she came out of it, that it was harder on us than on her. It was impossible to believe them. How could anyone go through these experiences and not have them embedded permanently somewhere in their consciousness?

As the days passed, we stayed with her. Words seemed to mean little to her, but like an infant, she seemed to take some comfort in being stroked, sung to, having her hair combed. Probably the nurses were right. Probably it didn't do as much for her as it did for us—feeling we could still give, still be in contact. She helped us be a little more human, a little more caring, not just to her. We are what we do.

AS WE GET OLDER, EVERYONE HAS THESE BRUSHES with aging, dying, that affect us and our work with families. They add a dimension to what we do, to our view of life and its meaning, that helps us to live and helps us to help others. They also give us an increased awareness of the passage of time. We become acutely aware that life is too short, too short for some of the petty things that too easily become a focus of our time and energy. They also give us an increased sense of our personal vulnerability. When we are young, we feel we can do anything, that we can never be mortally wounded. With age, we recognize the ease with which we can be hurt, impaired, even snuffed out altogether.

These brushes with death help us to develop an increased awareness of how little we really control. As Lily Tomlin says, "Life is what happens to you while you are making other plans." And life goes on making its own plans, producing its own troubles and joys. It isn't fair; it just is. This awareness of how little we control, and the shortness of time, isn't all negative, it also gives us an increased freedom. We become less tyrannized by worry about what other people think, by a need to be liked, and less tyrannized by death itself.

Recently I saw the movie *Moonstruck,* which, aside from being entertaining, contains one of the most memorable lines I've heard a wife address to an aging, unfaithful husband. In trying to understand why her husband is fooling around, the wife (played by Michael Dukakis's cousin, Olympia) asks everyone she knows, "Why do men chase women?" Someone persuades her that the reason is that they fear death. So that night, when her husband comes home, she says, "Cosmo, you can sleep with as many women as you want, but you're going to die anyway, just like the rest of us."

Many things have an impact on us as aging therapists but one of the most profound is the realization that, like Cosmo, whatever we do, we're going to die anyway. We can do therapy, we can come up with clever interventions, but we're going to die anyway, just like everyone else. We can do speeches, write books, give dramatic workshops, but we're going to die anyway, just like everyone else.

So what's new about that?

Earlier in our careers, we didn't really think we'd live forever, that is, if we thought about it at all. Mostly we didn't think about it. When we did, death seemed distant and somehow impersonal. But gradually—or suddenly—as we age, more people around us die. In part this is because we know more people, but more than that, it's because we are older, as are our friends and our relatives. Death becomes relevant, personal, close. Lives once unshakable are shaken by death or by losses: the loss of dreams, the loss of friends, the loss of relationships, the loss of health or an ability to function.

If all of these losses are inevitable, if we're all going to die anyway, why bother? Why isn't everything irrelevant? Why does therapy, or anything else, matter? Isn't this all pretty depressing?

Well, I'm not depressed and neither should you be. The message of my story, the message to Cosmo that he'll die anyway, is not a depressing or hopeless one. It's a challenge, an invitation to come back to something more meaningful than an impossible attempt to recapture youth. Accepting the inevitability and reality of death makes it possible to really live, to get our priorities straight.

The wife in *Moonstruck* redirects her husband from a futile search to something real and in the present. Just as we, as therapists, have the privilege of redirecting families to what is more central, more genuine, and more rewarding in their relationships.

P ART OF COMING OF AGE AS A THERAPIST IS acknowledging how our choices narrow over time and how they change. Over the years, what we do with our time and energies opens some doors and closes others. Our choices, both professional and personal, become more clearly irreversible. We choose a career, a partner, a friend, a life-style. If we are comfortable with the choices we've made, there may never be a sense of real crisis. But even when there is no crisis, as we age, a reevaluation of our commitments seems inevitable.

I am very aware that the choices I've made in my life have shaped who I am. I may have regrets, but I recognize the major life decisions I've made. At the same time, like most people, there are all sorts of choices I didn't know I'd made until I made them—and maybe not even then. Recently a chance interaction brought me face to face with some choices I

usually work hard to ignore.

A little over a year ago, I assumed an administrative position in our institute that made me responsible for supporting the clinical aspects of 11 inpatient units, several large outpatient clinics, and an overall budget of more than $90 million. It is big business, in a way, with all the manipulations, power games and competition for resources that you would expect at IBM or AT&T.

One afternoon, not too long after I took over this job, I found myself fighting for something I believed in, something I thought we shouldn't do, making my points as assertively as I could. Finally, in exasperation, one of my superiors looked at me and said, "Boy, you're tough. I can see why you're not married. A man couldn't get into bed with you."

He went on to say that we were in a crisis, and that in a crisis, theories of management power suggest that what is needed, as he put it, is "extreme concentration at the strategic apex." A few visions of exactly where the strategic apex was crossed my mind. But at the same time, being single-minded and slow-witted, I ignored the remark. I said, "Say what you want, I think that plan is wrong."

After I left his office, I considered what he said and decided it was his problem. His remark, I mused, was made out of weakness. He couldn't counter my points rationally, so he mounted a personal attack, one that was meant to hurt. (One might expect a single woman in her forties to be a little sensitive about this issue.) I told myself that I was right and he knew it, but he couldn't afford to admit it. All's fair in megapower battles, so he tried to shut me down any way he could. Now this was an interesting, if somewhat lopsided, analysis, that even had some truth as far as it went—which wasn't very far.

My next reaction, which occurred about a day later, was to get angry and think of all the things I should have said. A man couldn't get into bed with me? "Did you think for one minute you were in the running?" or "A man could, but you couldn't" or

"How would you like to take a trip and get off at Neptune?" The kinds of things you never think of saying at the time, and it's a good thing because they would cost you your job if you did.

A S I SETTLED DOWN, MY FOURTH REACTION WAS to consider the truth in his remark, however inappropriate it may have been. Was I harder to get into bed with these days? As I have taken on more power, I worry about what has become of my softer side. How has my position shaped who I am? What it takes to succeed as an administrator is not what it takes to succeed as a woman. A woman who flirts, who gets emotional, who is yielding, pays a price. For a woman to succeed as a power figure in an organization, she must be less than what the culture calls feminine. Even then, she is always in a bind—if she takes charge, acts like a man, she is viewed as pathological. If she is soft, she is viewed as ineffective and irrelevant.

It seems, in fact, that the basic struggles of men and women therapists differ as we come of age. We all struggle to reevaluate our lives and our practices, to come to some sort of new balance in our priorities and our skills. As they develop professionally, women, however, seem to become more aware of the issue of power, the fact that they don't have it or don't use it well. They find that the balancing of career and family over time has left them with some very important dissatisfactions and some pretty serious compromises. Those who try to have both a career and a family often pay the price of guilt—and exhaustion—feeling they can never quite do enough in either sphere. For women therapists, the increased emphasis on power, career and achievement that often occurs at midlife can also tend to result in some pretty significant losses: loss of time, loss of the ability to be silly, loss of the chance to be taken care of, loss of a softer side. Most women are acutely aware of the price they have paid in this way.

Men, on the other hand, often make their choices

without ever being aware of what they have lost, or at least not until the clock has run out. They work long hours, and their days are dominated by competition, performing, power games. What becomes of *their* ability to be silly, intimate? What becomes of their softer side? What becomes of their relationship with their families? Many hardly know their offspring or even their wives. It's not surprising, therefore, that when men look at what's missing in their lives at this stage, they are more likely to focus on the personal side, on love, not on power. Power is a given; a sense of connectedness is what they have lost. Unfortunately, by the time they are ready to attend to their personal lives, many find it is too late.

I F MEN WERE MORE COMFORTABLE WITH THE LOVE that is inherent in our work, and women were more comfortable with power, perhaps the misunderstandings that occur in battles such as the one I have described with my colleague would be less likely to occur. He wanted to make the hierarchy clear and to make sure no one got away with anything. He felt that limits and boundaries were vital to the organization's effective functioning. He did not see himself as facilitating, caretaking, while I did not see myself as primarily an agent of control. I was more interested in supporting people, in maintaining morale. We each felt the other "*couldn't get there from here*." We both claimed to have a systems orientation, to be interested in solving the problems of the moment. The way we behaved was not so different from the behavior of men and women, fathers and mothers, in troubled families.

One of the wonderful things about being an experienced family therapist is that it becomes possible to muddy the waters about these issues of power and love. For women, the role of family therapist makes it socially acceptable to have and use power, while, at the same time, feeling and showing love. As therapists, women can use control indirectly, by defining appropriate topics and challenging assumptions. They can appear nurturant without ever having to admit they want and enjoy control and competence. Men, on the other hand, can nurture without having to risk too much or admit to their enjoyment of what many would call the feminine side of themselves. There aren't many other professions that allow you to become more whole through experimenting in these ways.

ONE OF THE REWARDS OF STAYING IN THE THERApy business long enough is getting a more solid grasp of knowledge, theories (such as they are) and skills. It becomes easier to see patterns and sequences, to relate these patterns to themes and dysfunctions in families, and to intervene effectively. We get good at what we do. When we are good, when we are comfortable with our skills, we begin to leave technique behind. It's there, of course, like background music, but it no longer requires our attention.

Nevertheless, the rewards of leaving technique behind are often more meager than we expected—especially when the time between beginning to feel sure of yourself and the need to reevaluate what you're doing seems like a nanosecond. It's at this point that experienced clinicians may begin having some unwelcome second thoughts about their work.

Just as clear writing can expose a poverty of ideas, getting good technically as a clinician—getting good at joining, setting goals, using yourself, handling problems—makes it almost impossible to avoid seeing the weaknesses of the methods, the theories, the whole profession. Most of us, at least occasionally, begin to question the point of it all, to wonder: Is this an honorable way to spend a life? It's a crisis but not a bad one, because there are so many good things that come along with getting to this stage of our lives and work.

First, once we really know the rules, we also know when it's okay to break them. We can be more real and human in the therapy we do. We can put more

of who we are in our work because we are less in danger of losing control of ourselves, our reactions, or our sessions. We can show our own vulnerability, letting things happen without having to overcontrol, without having to have all the bases covered. This brings a greater depth to our relationships with the families we see; whether we choose to actually focus on the existential issues or not, we know about them, and this knowledge makes us more tolerant. We are less likely to assume or imply that the problems people have are simple or that the changes they must make are easy. We have a perspective mellowed by having lived through struggles—we don't need the same life experiences as our patients to help them, but it is helpful to have had and survived *some* life experiences, the more the better.

As we age in our profession, we also acquire an increased appreciation of the amount of stress our families, our students, and even we can tolerate and use to grow. Early on, our fear of hurting people often causes us to try to "help" by avoiding confrontation or encouraging dependency. In time, we learn that people are resilient. When we begin to respect their strengths, we can deal with them much more directly, and we can be much more helpful.

One of the pleasures of maturing as a clinician is learning to mentor younger colleagues. In part, it becomes easier to be nurturing because we are more secure. We know our own strengths and limitations and can use or avoid them in the best interests of our clients or our students. We mellow, find ourselves less convinced there is one right way. We are more forgiving of everyone's faults, including—if we're lucky—our own.

AT MIDCAREER, WE ARE FORCED TO COME TO grips with the impossibility of our dreams of clinical omnipotence. We must grudgingly admit that lots of things can't be fixed, made easy, no matter what we do, no matter how skillful we are. If something can only be made better, not fixed, we must decide if just making something better, not fixing it, is a substantial enough goal to justify our effort and commitment. It isn't always so easy to feel good about a limited role. Some therapists find that anything less than a universal cure is too depressing to live with. They either have to do very short-term work to preserve their denial or go into another business. Those that stay must deal with a loss of simplicity, of black-and-white views of the world that don't work anymore.

Cures are not the answer for most of the situations we see. Instead, we're asked to find ways to help the family of a single parent without money or a good job, who must spend more time away from her children than is good for them or for her. We're confronted with the family of a schizophrenic patient who is increasingly unable to function, who refuses help, whose parents do not have the financial or emotional supports to manage the 24-hour supervision of a suicidal child. We have to think of ways to help parents who are so overloaded that they are furious at their kids for needing the things kids need.

We need ways to help the nurturer whom nobody nurtures—not even us. We need to find ways to help our students see how hard it is for people to be in therapy and how hard it is for some people to even get to the sessions.

Recently one of our students was assigned a client that he described as a "classic resister." Before he had even seen the case he concluded, "This mother doesn't follow through with treatment. She doesn't really want help." A second look by an older supervisor revealed that the woman was a working single mother of five with no child support, who also attended school two nights a week, and who somehow managed to get all five kids to the clinic for an evaluation. Viewing her as a "classic resister" reflected an attitude that wouldn't engage her and wouldn't get her back. But what will, will take a lot more thought and energy.

As clinicians defining ourselves through the years, we are what we do.

SO WHAT DO WE DO? HOW DOES IT CHANGE over the years? How would it look if we were able to step back and really see how we put together our professional and personal lives. Here are three vignettes, one of a novice and two of more experienced therapists, that try to bring into focus the perils and possibilities of coming of age as a clinician.

THE NOVICE: The novice therapist thinks about his/her clients before breakfast and is eager to get to the office to help people. He/she has read a book, attended a workshop, and is driven by the desire to try out a new intervention with a family that has been one step ahead of him/her in every session. His/her enthusiasm is tempered only by his/her fear that the session will get out of control, that someone will tell him/her that he/she is full of it.

He/she is sometimes fighting for his/her life with clients. Today he/she has four scheduled sessions, two of which don't show. He/she is made momentarily uncomfortable by the thought that he/she might be responsible for these unorthodox and precipitous cancellations. Was it something he/she said or did in the last session? He/she concludes that these families were very resistant anyway.

He/she spends 20 minutes setting up the chairs for his/her next session. The session goes well, but he/she doesn't know why. He/she feels brilliant, "I'm finally getting the hang of it," he/she tells him/herself. The next session is a bust and again he/she doesn't know why. He/she feels like a failure, "I'll never be a great family therapist." It's extremely upsetting that everyone reminds him/her of his/her own mother. His/her supervisor tells him/her this too will pass, but he/she doesn't believe it. "It's easy for you to say . . ." he/she moans "you write articles," but he/she bounces back with enthusiasm after watching an inspiring (if closely edited) videotape of a master who cures a family in 45 minutes.

"That's who I want to be when I grow up," he/she tells him/herself.

THE GODSEND: The experienced therapist is always eager, enthusiastic and committed to his/her patients. He/she is involved but not too involved. He/she is differentiated. He/she is never irrational, never imposes his/her issues on patients. He/she is also never wrong. He/she has an appropriate intervention for every occasion, never, of course, becoming too pat. He/she has no ethical dilemmas. He/she knows right from wrong.

His/her patients never cancel, always pay their bills and send thank-you notes full of gratitude and devotion. He/she can see six families in a row without running out of energy or running over the hour. Each workshop he/she does is original, and he/she never tells the same jokes. Videotapes of his/her sessions can be used for teaching without being edited.

To his/her patients, he/she is a godsend; to his/her students, a respected role model; to his/her colleagues, a trusted and admired friend. He/she has a wonderful home and family.

His/her work and professional life are well balanced, neither one ever intrudes upon the other. At the end of the day he/she is never cranky but goes home to cheerfully meet the needs of his/her spouse and children. He/she cooks elaborate Japanese dinners for the family. All of their time together is quality time. They communicate in clear, direct and unambiguous language without incongruent messages. He/she wishes his/her clients could see him/her at home, since it would be such an inspiration to them.

THE PLUGGER: The really experienced therapist gets up in the morning and needs a second cup of coffee before he/she can think about the office. He/she remembers this is one of his/her late nights seeing families and thinks it might have been smarter to be an individual therapist, maybe even a banker.

He/she gets to the office and has another cup of coffee before trying to return phone calls. He/she tries to remember who he/she is seeing today, but he/she only knows there are four appointments. "Just my luck, they'll all show up," he/she thinks. They do.

The first case is moving along. He/she gets moderately enthusiastic. Like a horse that knows the trail back to the barn, he/she plugs along—competently, slowly, not making much of a fuss, but getting there. He/she is satisfied, if a bit bored as they leave. The next case is new, they challenge his/her credentials, and the adrenaline flows for a while. Then he/she hooks them and reels them in like a seasoned trout fisherperson—they are committed to treatment before they know what hit them.

His/her spouse calls before the next session; they have a fight about who is doing what for the kids this weekend. During the next session, his/her mind wanders from the case, thinking about the unreasonable stance his/her spouse took and what he/she should have said. The family discussion escalates into a fight, probably to get his/her attention back to the room. It works. He/she is involved.

As experienced therapists, we don't necessarily have it all together, our personal lives overflow into our therapy and vice versa. Our irrational side is not something we outgrow but something we learn to live with, integrate. We don't have to be perfect to be helpful, to gradually make our careers and our lives have substance, meaning and relevance. Maybe we never achieve our initial goals, but what we do achieve is special. At times our work can become draining emotionally, perhaps even physically, but it is satisfying because it feels real.

We are what we do . . . and we'll die anyway, but that's alright. ∎

CAROL ANDERSON, PH.D., *is an associate professor of psychiatry, School of Medicine, University of Pittsburgh, and administrator of Western Psychiatric Institute and Clinic in Pittsburgh, PA.*

A family's most inti-mate sense of itself grows out of years and years of doing the same things over and over again. A family lives by its daily rituals, even if many of them are so taken for granted that, over time, they become invisible.

RICHARD SIMON

PHOTOGRAPH BY ELLIOTT ERWITT/MAGNUM

PHOTOGRAPH BY CHARLES HARBUTT/ACTUALITY

PHOTOGRAPH BY JOAN LIFTIN/ACTUALITY

PHOTOGRAPH BY POLLY BROWN/ACTUALITY

PHOTOGRAPH BY POLLY BROWN/ACTUALITY

PHOTOGRAPH BY POLLY BROWN/ACTUALITY

The Screening Room

FAMILY THERAPY AT
THE MOVIES

PHOTOGRAPH BY JOAN LIFTIN/ACTUALITY

TERMS OF ENMESHMENT

CELEBRATING THE JOYS OF OVERINVOLVEMENT

By Frank Pittman

LAST NOVEMBER, IN A COLUMN REVIEWING THIS past summer's movies, I wrote about their preoccupation with escape from family and responsibility, time and place. Now a couple of recent movies have come along to remind us that as much as we might be tempted to escape, someone still has to raise the children. Adulthood may be a dirty job, but someone has to do it.

For audiences and critics alike, the American movie of the year is *Terms of Endearment,* and it's about mothering. Shirley MacLaine and Debra Winger portray mother and daughter over 32 years, from birth to death. The audience gets to laugh for the first half of the movie, as Aurora Greenway (MacLaine) dedicates herself to controlling every detail of life, keeping a spotless house, a weedless garden and a sexless bed. Rich, glamorous Aurora has only two passions—orderliness and her daughter Emma (Winger).

The film opens with Aurora ignoring her sexually inclined husband to crawl into the baby bed with Emma, waking her up to be sure she's breathing. When her husband dies, Aurora seems relieved that he will no longer distract her from Emma. The years pass, but Aurora still hovers. She fusses with Emma's petticoats and tightens her bra straps as if they were diapers. She respects no boundaries between herself and her daughter. Naturally, Emma chooses a life devoted to disorder and overcoming all that her mother fears. To ensure that disorder, Emma marries floppy, goofy, sexy college teacher Flap Horton, who later realizes that his job in life is to always let Emma down.

The key to the movie's great appeal is that the villain of the piece is not Aurora, as we first suspect (we've grown to identify movie villains as those who are rich and value order more than personal freedom) but Flap, a representative of a generation of men too weak to love responsibly. Flap seems to want sex and love but not involvement—sharing his life just seems too threatening. Overwhelmed by the messy, honest intimacy Emma offers him, Flap hides with other women. So while Flap has affairs and lets her down, Emma centers her life on her three children and her long-distance phone calls with her mother. Aurora storms, threatens and warns, as

Emma soothes and reassures and prevails.

Eventually, Emma takes a lover—sweet, solid, sexually deprived, married banker Sam Burns. She simultaneously supervises Aurora's seduction of the debauched lecher next door, ex-astronaut Garrett Breedlove (hilariously portrayed by a potbellied Jack Nicholson). Nicholson's Breedlove embodies the wrong stuff for an earthbound life, the bad little boy unafraid of going to the stars but terrified of the altar. He backs off from the affair with Aurora when he begins to feel "obligated."

The comedy is over when Emma gets cancer and demonstrates that not even death will get her down. As Flap pouts pitifully, the aging, postglamorous Aurora takes charge. In a great demonstration of heroic hysteria, a determined Aurora assaults the nurse's station to make sure that her daughter gets her painkiller not one minute after it is due. In another beautifully realized scene, Emma props herself up and says good-bye to her children, reassuring them that they love her. Emma dies softly, Flap goes off with his mistress, and Aurora takes the children. As the movie ends, she's finally able to bring forth from the terminally adolescent Breedlove a feeling for something other than his own self-indulgence. He can't be fatherly, but for starters he can be older-brotherly to Emma's son—he seems to have learned something about love from Aurora. And we are left knowing what Emma knew, that what has gone on between her and her mother is love without limits or bounds but also without danger or insecurity.

The film is an emotional workout, brazenly commercial (*Terms*'s director, James Brooks, used to do the "Mary Tyler Moore Show"), gloriously funny, and irresistibly tear-jerking. Shirley MacLaine's Aurora is the juiciest performance I can recall, and Debra Winger's Emma is the most lovable. Emma is the protagonist, but Aurora is the heroine. The ferocity of her enmeshing love is redeemed, even ennobled in the film. When she tells Emma not to marry Flap because "you're not special enough to

survive a bad marriage," it's a challenge as much as a warning, one that strengthens rather than weakens Emma. When old Aurora chases, catches and pummels her grandson for not loving his mother enough, when she throws herself without vanity at Breedlove, when she takes on the entire hospital staff to win comfort for Emma, we all forgive our mothers (as Emma does) for loving us too fiercely, for sacrificing too much peace and not enough order.

Film history contains few notable mother-daughter movies. In the best previous one, *Mildred Pierce,* Joan Crawford slaves and sacrifices to spoil Ann Blyth rotten. Today such maternal nobility would be considered saccharine. In the Old Hollywood, mothers were supposed to be like Ma Joad in *The Grapes of Wrath* or Marmee in *Little Women,* inexhaustibly patient and loving, whatever the adversity. Little girls in the sentimental musical days of the '40s and '50s usually had mothers, often Marmees, with no thought but to unrelentingly "mother" everyone in the cast. They never raised their voices. It was against the rules for mothers to lose control over themselves or seek it over their kids.

In the '60s, movie mothers became monstrous. Shelley Winters in *Patch of Blue,* Ellen Burstyn in *The Last Picture Show,* and Anne Bancroft in *The Graduate* were either distracted, adulterous, or promiscuous and dedicated to destroying their daughters' romances. They bore no resemblance to Marmee—they were more concerned with their own lives than with their children. In the '70s, mothers became irrelevant, along with anything else that dared to remind us of the adult world. In the bizarre cult favorite *Harold and Maude,* Bud Cort's mother kept walking blithely through rooms in which he was staging elaborate suicide attempts.

After nearly 40 years, the classic effort to show both sides of the mother-daughter relationship is still *The Glass Menagerie,* recently revived on Broadway. In it, faded Southern belle Amanda lives in her fantasies of lost comfort and elegance, while waiting for the gentleman caller who will come to rescue her shy, crippled daughter Laura from their impoverished gentility. Here, too, the men run out on them, and mother and daughter are left with dreams but no hope. Tennessee Williams became famous by creating female characters too fragile to lead their own lives yet too powerful to let anyone around them lead theirs. As much as anyone before Philip Roth, Williams helped establish the popular image of mothers as Freudian monsters who make their children miserable by wanting too much from them.

Unlike Tennessee Williams, whose screwed-up private life was as embarrassing to his mother as he could make it, Larry McMurtry, the author of *Terms*, has obviously been loved. His novels of modern Texas gives us tough, loving women, weak, selfish young men and strong, gentle old ones. McMurtry is largely unknown, although he has written novels that became three of the best films of recent decades, *Hud* and *The Last Picture Show* being the other two. Patricia Neal, Melvyn Douglas, Ben Johnson and Cloris Leachman have won Oscars portraying McMurtry's characters, Paul Newman and Ellen Burstyn should have, and Shirley MacLaine and Jack Nicholson surely will.

McMurtry is on to something about life. His characters hurt one another as much as those in Tennessee Williams's land, but they don't blame their lives on one another or try to escape. They share the experience of living together with clear attachments and unclear boundaries.

Aurora's overwhelming mothering differs from Amanda's (or Mildred Pierce's or Gypsy Rose Lee's mother's in *Gypsy*). Those mothers raised their daughters to live the life they themselves missed. But Emma is loved because Aurora loves to love; involvement is the only goal. The love is uncritical, although the interaction isn't. Emma is not weakened by all that enmeshment but is first secured, then challenged. All save the feckless Flap are strengthened by Aurora's obnoxious love. The problem with Flap is that he is so pitifully narcissistic that he can only sense and fear Aurora's intrusion and can't see the love in people's intense involvement in one another's lives. He can only pretend love in secret affairs, with their built-in protection from intimacy. For Flap, the highest form of love is acceptance, a kind of holiday from criticism, disapproval and advice—something like a parody of bad therapy.

The mother-daughter relationship in *Terms* is wonderful because it is reciprocal. It shifts. Emma faces the sexuality, sloppiness and insecurity Aurora hid from, and then helps Aurora face them. Like all successful parents, Aurora has raised a child who knows her parents fears and prejudices and inhibitions and who goes forth to test and overcome those limitations. With Aurora and Emma, as with all successful parent-child relationships, once the child is comfortable with the world, she can return to raise the parents, to help them through the changes she has learned to negotiate. It is a lifelong reciprocity, unequal only at the beginning and the end.

Yet Aurora and Emma are "enmeshed," a state anathema to family therapists, many of whom seem to distrust anything that goes on between mothers and children past the age of 12. But in the real world, mothers and children live a lifelong struggle to overcome each other's fears and hopes. The more successful of them learn to accept each other well enough to provide comfort and security through the evolving generations. Contrary to our theories and warnings, most parents and children remain comfortably enmeshed—and happy with it—for a lifetime.

The flip side of the triumph of mothering and enmeshment celebrated in *Terms of Endearment* is *Tender Mercies*, whose subject is the isolation and secret pain of peripheral fathers. It is such a quiet, gentle film that it found favor only with critics and grown-ups. (Kids haven't liked it. The only car crash was off camera.) Although it vanished in many cities soon after its release, it'll be back. Its star, Robert Duvall, is front-runner for the Oscar.

Tender Mercies is set in the driest, flattest, dullest part of Texas, at a rundown motel and filling station to which alcoholic, has-been country singer Mac Sledge (Duvall) drifts to sober up. He's dry, flat, dull, rundown, honest and above all, inarticulate. He's lost a career, a fortune, a wife or two and, most painfully, a daughter, now 18. The motel owner, Rosalie, a stoic war widow with a 9-year-old son named Sonny, takes him in. Rosalie is as plainspoken as Mac. After he works and sobers up and settles in, with a humble, taciturn dignity, he awkwardly proposes ("It's no secret how I feel about you. A blind man could see that"). Rosalie marries him. He can't talk to her, but he writes her a song, "If You'll Hold the Ladder, I'll Climb to the Top."

As Rosalie gently steadies him, Duvall feels stronger and tries to repair the mess he's made of his life. His ex-wife Dixie, a country superstar, comes to town. He goes to her show and tries unsuccessfully to see his 18-year-old daughter, Sue Anne. Dixie, still raging over his irresponsible failures, carries on and throws him out and forbids Sue Anne from seeing him. The headstrong daughter defies her mother and visits her father at the motel. They haven't seen each other for years. They don't touch. He can't speak her name. She asks if he remembers the song he used to sing for her, "On the Wings of a Snow White Dove." He says no. She leaves. He stands at the window and sings it. By the time he's finished, everyone in the audience has left to buy another box of Kleenex and to call their long-lost children. Fortunately, I stayed (I had my children with me and clutched them).

Sue Anne defies her mother again and marries a man from her mother's band, an irresponsible alcoholic much like her father had been. Dixie fires him and disowns her. The new groom drives drunkenly; there is a car accident; Sue Anne is killed. Dixie,

enthroned in her bed of grief, carries on theatrically as Duvall stands holding his hat in dignified silence, and we know his pain is no less than hers for its silence.

Meanwhile, Sonny, Rosalie's son, has spent the movie sizing up his stepfather, while asking his mother questions about his real father, whom she's rarely mentioned ("just a boy, a good boy," she tells him). Finally, when a friend asks him if he likes his stepfather, Sonny echoes Duvall with the simple, committed, unadorned "Yes, I do." After his daughter's funeral, Duvall finally notices his young stepson. The movie ends when the boy chooses a father by tossing a football to Duvall. The scene is as nearly wordless as the rest of the move—love means never having to say anything prettified. The scene is touching, but it is disturbing to realize that in our irresponsible world, the children may have to choose and appoint the fathers and then give them on-the-job training.

Neither the world nor the movies have required much from fathers. Failed fathers, from Abraham and Lear and Midas through Henry Fonda in *On Golden Pond,* have been a dramatic staple. We are programmed to cheer when Bambi's father or uncle Ebenezer Scrooge finally does a good deed after a lifetime of neglect or abuse. We don't expect much more parenting from men than Sue Anne or Sonny gets from Duvall—a tossed football, at best a song. A hug would bring cheers. Gregory Peck in *To Kill A Mockingbird,* Dustin Hoffman in *Kramer vs. Kramer,* were rare exceptions—and, significantly, their children were motherless. More typical is the neglect of debauched Alfred P. Doolittle in *My Fair Lady* or the stern disapproval of Andy's father, Judge Hardy.

In contrast, tradition holds that mothers must be totally loving and self-sacrificing but never intrusive, disapproving or neglectful. Minor defects in maternal love can turn Marmees into Medeas. Mary Tyler Moore, detestably distant and unfeeling as a mother in *Ordinary People,* would have been a tolerable father. It's not fair to either gender for the world to expect so little parenting from men, so much from women.

Fathers who love too little bring tears to our eyes, mothers who love too much strike terror in our hearts. Mothers, like herpes, baldness and the poor, are with us always, afflictions for which we've found no cure. Once anyone has been a mother, she retains the power to love her child of any age into a mewling, puking infant. Maternal sacrifice is the undertow against which people paddle into adulthood, unless the child feels childlike enough to deserve it or adult enough to return it. *Terms of Endearment* has made enmeshment seem secure, reciprocal and liberating. It makes it respectable not to totally leave home. McMurtry and MacLaine may even have enabled us to forgive our fathers for loving too little. ■

CATCHING FALLING ELEPHANTS

WHAT'S THE DIFFERENCE BETWEEN CARETAKERS AND THERAPISTS?

By Frank Pittman

PLAYWRIGHTS HAVE EXPLORED, CHARTED AND perhaps even fathomed the many mysteries of sexual and family and friend relationships. But our dramatists and screenwriters can't seem to understand the therapist-patient relationship, either what is therapeutic about it, or what's in it for the therapist. Still, we shouldn't be too hard on them. Hell, even *we* can't decide what is therapeutic about therapy, and we don't often talk about what our personal payoffs are.

The best explanation I know of why some relationships are therapeutic (for patient and therapist), and some are not, comes not from the family therapy literature but from a Vietnamese proverb: "While it is noble to assist a stricken elephant in rising, it is foolhardy to catch one that is falling down."

Obviously, those therapists whose patients arise successfully have a totally different experience from those caretakers who are crushed by their patients' unending dependency. We've all experienced both and know that therapy doesn't work for us unless it works for our patients.

In 1983 two of the most critically acclaimed films

each dissected a complex relationship that was much like that between a therapist and a patient. Both relationships were convoluted enough to be very real (and therefore very funny). They are well worth the attention of family therapists, patients and anyone unafraid of human interaction. Between them, they point up the dichotomy between the Caretaker Relationship (in which the patient fails to change, the therapist keeps struggling, is drained by the effort, and becomes part of the problem) and the Therapeutic Relationship (in which the therapist is successful in promoting change, is no longer needed yet receives something subtle and magical in return).

The Dresser is about a caretaker. In *The Dresser,* Sir (Albert Finney) is an exhausted Shakespearean actor in his dotage who has become a bloated, bellowing bully. He can still function onstage, but backstage he collapses like a brain-damaged elephant on Norman, his dresser-nanny. Norman (Tom Courtenay) is a glossary of twitches and neuroses. He's Mary Poppins with a cupful of vinegar rather than a spoonful of sugar. He's alcoholic, homosexual, anxious, bitchy and uninterested in getting along with anyone but Sir. When Norman must go onstage to make an announcement, he babbles incoherently and then begs for reassurance. He's as pitifully inept onstage as Sir is offstage, but only he can dress, make up and orient Sir for his remembered turn as Lear or Othello or Macbeth.

Norman acts beaten down by the ridiculous needs of Sir, who seems to relish his servant's magnificent dependency. Yet Norman guards his power jealously, with a mixture of anger, loathing, exhaustion, pride and triumph. When Sir dies, Norman is devastated—Sir was his raison d'être. Norman tries to serve a noble function, yet he is among the most unappealing characters ever to hit the screen. He, like many bad therapists, has no talent for life, with its joy and absurdity and adventure. He has nothing to give except the imposition of structure on the perennially collapsing hulk of Sir.

The caretaker, or change preventer, is the flip side of the therapist, or change producer. The caretaker can't provoke health and must be content with protecting the shell of life. Caretakers are rarely seen as noble, and often as villainous, like parents who hang on too long. But I think they are unjustly maligned. They usually started out hoping to be therapeutic and temporary but fell into the trap of believing that providing more perfect love or more complete caring would eventually work. They never learned when to give up and let gravity prevail and how to, sometimes, catch people when they bounce. No one ever taught them that no patient was ever cured by crushing the therapist.

The character of Norman recalls the cynical, burnt-out psychiatrist Richard Burton played in *Equus*. Burton treats a young man (Peter Firth) so torn with sexual guilt and shame that he has blinded the horses who observed his sexual humiliation in a stable. The boy is shown as worshipping horses. The psychiatrist has some monologues about how his life has been changed by being exposed to the boy's extraordinary passion for something. It's all rather farfetched and silly, as only the deadly serious can be, and not helped much by the boy's going through the play naked. Nevertheless, this presumptuous play inadvertently hits an important truth about how therapists without the talent for living look at their patients' inspiration about living. In *Equus*, Burton worships his patient's craziness and mourns the loss of it, since he has no sanity to give in its place.

In contrast with *The Dresser* and *Equus, Educating Rita* shows us a true therapeutic relationship. It concerns a burnt-out college English professor (Michael Caine) and a Cockney hairdresser (Julie Walters) who hires him to give her the benefits of education. Rita has to hold her bored, surly, usually drunk and near suicidal tutor together so he can enlighten her about the meaning given to life by great writers. Despite her tackiness, Caine is delighted by the directness and simplicity with which she gets to the most basic meaning of things. As she begins to read and write and think and feel, Rita starts resisting her doltish young husband, her depressed mother, and her Cro-Magnon father, all of whom see her as merely the bearer of children. When she secretly takes birth control pills, her husband burns her books, correctly seeing education as liberation from tradition. Eventually, she divorces him and begins to change her life. The transformation is gradual and believable, and the stricken elephant that arises, quite lovable.

Caine changes, too. He gives up his unfaithful mistress, curbs his drinking, and resumes interest in his career and his own writing. He is renewed by seeing that his knowledge can make a difference to someone. Rita bestows dignity on the life Caine though he'd wasted, but as it becomes apparent she no longer needs him, he relapses somewhat. She knows what he has done for her, but she never quite realizes what she's done for him. Nothing sexual happens between the two of them. However, the film irritatingly titillates the audience with that expectation. I was relieved when at the end the ex-hairdresser thanks her ex-tutor with a haircut, rather than the expected blow-dry.

The plot is familiar. Bernard Shaw wrote it as *Pygmalion.* Later it was musicalized as *My Fair Lady.* Speech teacher Henry Higgins turns flower girl Eliza Doolittle from a "squashed cabbage leaf" into a princess by teaching her to speak, and in the process they fall in love, though any family therapist would have turned strategic somersaults to prevent such a marriage. *Born Yesterday* also has a similar plot; Billie Dawn, Garson Kanin's greatest creation and Judy Holliday's greatest role, is the junk tycoon's mistress, until her ignorance embarrasses him and he gets her a tutor who makes her respectable enough to want respect. As soon as she can insult the junkman in cultured tones, she waltzes off with the tutor.

In *Educating Rita,* the Billie Dawn character does not fall in love with her Henry Higgins—it is nothing that banal. Rather than attaching themselves to one another, the two characters part, appreciating what they have given and received, and recognizing that their lives have been changed by the experience. The therapy is complete.

The therapist-patient relationship is so much more personal than the usual doctor-patient relationship that Hollywood has usually seen it in sexual terms, a possibility as insulting and alarming as it is potentially exhausting for the busy therapist. Ingrid Bergman treating Gregory Peck in *Spellbound,* Montgomery Clift treating Liz Taylor in *Suddenly Last Summer,* Mia Farrow treating Woody Allen in *Zelig,* and Montgomery Clift again as *Freud* treating Susannah York, all seemed so involved with their romance, I wondered how they kept it up through the day's schedule. Scott Fitzgerald's *Tender Is the Night* showed the result of such a romance. In the 1961 movie, psychiatrist Jason Robards, as Fitzgerald's stand-in, treats, cures, marries and is destroyed by the film's veiled version of Zelda, Jennifer Jones.

The spouse of a schizophrenic or alcoholic may also function as a therapist, but movies typically show the converse, the therapist functioning as a spouse. For most nontherapists, patients and even screenwriters, the only relationship of comparable intimacy is a marriage, but the therapists are doing well to keep one marriage going, much less a caseload of them. Patients, enamored of the marriage metaphor, may see our stock in trade as perfect love. We know whose life we're saving from loneliness. What of love? Norman certainly loved Sir's dependency, and Burton loved the stable boy's crazy passion, and maybe Fitzgerald loved both in Zelda. But Michael Caine as the successful therapist rather disliked Rita's ignorant tackiness until he helped her develop in herself something that could make him love her, himself and life. I think we do better therapy when we find things in our patients to dislike as well as to like.

Occasionally, the therapist-patient relationship is seen as a parent-child one, and this may be a more apt metaphor than the romantic one. Some of the best cinematic efforts at depicting therapists and patients (*Ordinary People, Now Voyager, I Never Promised You a Rose Garden*) have shown the therapist overly involved in raising a poorly parented patient. We do raise our patients, but the differences between parenting and treating are crucial. Maybe we all need both parents and therapists, but we should know which is which.

Therapists can parent their patients far more vigorously and safely than they can parent their children and with less resentment on either side. As therapists, we can be more intrusive and more intimate and reveal more of ourselves; our expectations are more modest and realistic, and more joyous when achieved. But with our children, our narcissism, our future and our grandchildren are at stake. Our patients can and must fire us in time, but our children can't. And patients don't have to take care of us in our old age. It is their health, not their caring, that gives us life. We know we (and they) have succeeded when, instead of returning, they send us more stricken elephants.

I believe it is the safe, temporary intimacy of therapy that we find so addicting, an exposure of souls more incautious than in any other relationship in life. It is like an affair without sex, guilt, jealousy, or the threat of permanence. Of course, we seek the secrets of life through other people's risks rather than through our own. We are voyeurs, we live vicariously, and we like our power. And sure, we make our livings as therapists, and these are often very good livings, but we could make more money in professions that are less personal and more respectable—like proctology or prostitution.

The filmed play that comes closest to understanding what therapists get in exchange for what they give is *The Miracle Worker.* It concerns the relationship between the deaf and blind child Helen Keller (Patty Duke in the play and the 1962 film) and her almost blind teacher, Annie Sullivan (Anne Bancroft). Helen is hardly human, held hostage not only by her infirmities but by her caretaking family, who value their ability to tolerate her intolerable behavior and resist any effort to change it. Sullivan is just a child

herself, handicapped, deprived, alone, but determined to make contact with Helen. And she will give Helen the power to contact others even if she must beat her into the dust.

So they fight. Helen smears Sullivan with food; Sullivan steps on Helen and pulls her curls. The audience (therapists fed up with trying to love their patients into health, I presume) cheers for Sullivan. She finally does teach Helen the word "water," and the play ends with everyone in tears as Helen learns the word "teacher." Part of the therapists' reward is in passing on to others what he or she has learned, to make contact with someone else and share the secrets of life.

When therapy works, we have our belief in life affirmed. At the end it is not *us* our patients love but themselves, and life. It is a magic moment when our patients understand what we know about the human condition and can share it with us, when the stricken elephant rises rather than collapsing on us, and we both can go forth, separately and imperfectly, to spread appreciation of the wonderfully liberating absurdity of the human comedy. ∎

STANDING BY

THERE'S MORE TO COMING OF AGE THAN HAVING SEX AND WRECKING CARS

By Frank Pittman

OF THE UNIVERSAL TRANSITIONS OF LIFE, NONE IS more dramatic or more often dramatized than "coming of age." Most cultures provide some sort of puberty ritual—the Hollywood culture offers movies about getting laid and wrecking cars. The idea seems to be that people become adults by becoming sexual and running wild. In fact, our society uses sex as an alternative to growing up—witness "adult" movies. Sex is certainly one of the joys of being an adult, but there's a lot more to coming of age than that.

Coming of age also means coming to grips with the nature of the world, and the world is a scary place, not totally fair and not totally safe. There are evils, dangers and death out there. Some people are paralyzed with the discovery that the world is not totally gentle and fair. They either attempt a life without risk, or they give up and assume they have no control over their fate. Some like to wallow in the anxiety and self-loathing of a world that is out to get them. Such people enjoy horror movies, which reassure them that they are helpless against the power of fate and the forces of evil. Horror emphasizes our

helplessness, requiring us to tolerate fear, disgust, and all the spooky things in our closet of anxieties, things over which we cannot expect to gain mastery but must learn to endure. Horror stories are counterphobic therapy and appeal primarily to the young and frightened.

The current master of the horror genre is Stephen King, author of *The Shining* and *Carrie*. King specializes in evoking the most terrifying aspects of the coming-of-age experience. His characters, behind their supernatural powers, are children and early adolescents who are awakening to the cruelty and treachery and evil in the world.

The latest film made from one of King's works is outside the horror tradition—there are no supernatural horrors at all. Instead, it describes ordinary people coming of age in a world filled with ordinary horrors, like death, violence, cruelty and neglect. *Stand By Me* focuses on four 12-year-old boys who go on an adventure in search of the body of another boy their age who has been killed by a train. As filmed by Rob Reiner, the real interest of the film lies in the camaraderie among the boys, the many ways in which they stand by one another as they face the reality of death and the dangers of the quite ordinary, quite terrifying world. This bucolic idyll of preadolescence is a sentimental masterpiece, extremely personal and extremely popular.

The four boys are misfits. Vern is fat, cowardly and dumb. Teddy is explosive and crazy, having been mutilated (his ear was burned off) by the psychotic father he still defends. Chris is a thief, the abused son of an alcoholic, growing up in poverty, brutality and social rejection. Gordie is the smart one, admired by his friends for his storytelling skills but overlooked by parents who idolized his older brother, an athlete who died young. These four boys have no one to care about them except one another. The movie shows them banding together as they face parental rejection and abuse, attack dogs, barreling trains, leeches and sadistic older boys. Reiner leaves out many of King's gorier touches and just lets us see these boys standing together facing life and death. The grown Gordie (Richard Dreyfuss) narrates and reminds us that we will never be as close to anyone again as we were to our buddies at 12. This is a love story.

Gordie and Chris know that Vern and Teddy are destined for failure in life. Vern and Teddy know that, too, and accept it—they never expected it to be otherwise. Vern will complain bitterly over his dinner's being delayed, but won't work up enough energy to run when a train is about to hit him. Teddy will risk his life to defend his crazy father's irreparable honor. But all three see that Gordie can be a winner, if anyone can believe in him. And Gordie sees that Chris could make it, too, though the effort would be enormous. So they give one another the push, the support and even the hugs they don't get at home.

All prepubescent boys are misfits. There are no members of the animal kingdom quite so unlovable as 12-year-old boys are. They have lost the cuddly cuteness of childhood and have not yet attained the sensual beauty of adolescence. Their lives are lived without dignity, without that sense that they and their choices matter to the world or even to themselves. They are gross and delight in their grossness, their preoccupation with bodily functions and fluids, their awkwardness and, indeed, their awareness of their own repulsiveness. They are at an age at which they are of no use to anyone and are unlovable and unloved, too old to be cuddled by their parents, too young to be caressed by girls. They are outcasts, and they aren't at all sure that their condition is temporary. They have no one to understand them, or to love them, but one another.

Stand By Me brilliantly captures the four boys' probing confusion about the world they are expected to inherit. They are at an age when they can no longer believe what the adults have told them. They must raise questions and seek answers, and they can't rely on any authority except one another. Their level of intellectual inquiry is not profound, but it is a start. For instance, they ponder the question, "What manner of creation is Goofy?" They know Donald is a duck and Mickey is a mouse, and Pluto is unmistakably a dog. So how can the anthropomorphic Goofy be a dog, too?

The movies have neglected this age group, preferring their cherubic younger siblings or their sexier older ones. Coming of age, in the world of the movies, has come to mean the coming of sexuality. But we did exist before we discovered sex, and it was as King and Reiner remember it. We really were banded together as closely as the friends in *Stand By Me.*

Therapists don't see these kids with their buddies. We don't pay much attention to what they tell us about their friendships and neither do their parents. And it is these friendships that are central in their lives. Only a few years later this male bonding will seem too close, too much of a homosexual threat, and it will be forsaken, self-consciously and sadly. Instead, boys will risk the closeness to girls that will stabilize and succor them for the rest of their lives. But they will miss the closeness of their fellows, they will yearn for that preadolescent comradeship and its bond of mutual repulsiveness.

King and Reiner emphasize the degree to which these boys are rejected, ignored and brutalized by their fathers. (The mothers were nicer but beside the point—this is all about becoming a man.) But even more directly villainous are the older boys, destructive late adolescents, heroes or losers, and often the boys' brothers, who are their natural enemies. These kids, like most boys then and now, are growing up without real live models in their families. It is scary, and their energies are aimed at holding one another together while they face and overcome their fears, without losing their balls to attack dogs or leeches and without leaving too many "Hershey dumps in their Fruit of the Looms."

King's story tries to say something about writing as an effort to overcome mortality (at the end of the book, he gorily kills off all the now grown boys except the writer, a conceit that Reiner wisely softens for the film). But the film is Reiner's rather than King's, and he elicits amazingly natural performances from the four boys, particularly a young actor named River Phoenix, as Chris, the hypermature son of the alcoholic, who has little hope for his own life but takes care of and encourages his friends. He makes you love 12-year-old boys again for the first time since you were one. And if you were never a 12-year-old boy, this film is basic to your understanding of grown men.

THE AWARENESS OF THE HORRORS OF LIFE CAN come at any age. When grown men, rather than little boys, come to grips with the dangers and evils of the real world, we enter the province of film noir—the black, cynical, pessimistic exploration of human evil. Film noir, the stylishly hyperrealistic examination of the blackness of the human soul, popular in the '30s and '40s, showed us the stark evil of the world yet permitted us to stand apart from it (unlike *The Godfather* or *Prizzi's Honor,* where we see the evil from the inside). In film noir, the innocent man is seduced into an amoral underworld by a mysterious, seductive lady. Film noir went out of style in the cheerful '50s and has not fared well since they foolishly started making movies in color and let Humphrey Bogart die. Film noir shows up from time to time as a tongue-in-cheek French import, such as the glorious *Diva*. The British gave us a fine example in this year's *Mona Lisa,* in which the central character was a prostitute's uncouth ex-convict chauffeur—and finally an admirable, even lovable hero.

In recent years, Hollywood resurrected the genre in two oversexed remakes of classic film noir: Jack Nicholson and Jessica Lange nakedly plotting murder in *The Postman Always Rings Twice* and William Hurt and Kathleen Turner sweating on one another in *Body Heat* (plot courtesy of *Double Indemnity*). However, the point of classic film noir was not illicit sex and the joys of immorality but the convoluted treacheries and betrayals of amorality. The best recent American film noir was the incomparable *Chinatown* whose thesis was that it is dangerous for everyone when anyone tries to know what evil lurks in the hearts of men. In *Chinatown,* John Huston, as Faye Dunaway's incestuous and murderous father, tells the latter-day Bogart, Jack Nicholson, that he doesn't blame himself for the incest because, "You see, Mr. Gittes, most people never have to face the fact that at the right time and the right place they are capable of—anything."

This year's effort at reviving film noir is the repulsive *Blue Velvet*—a film I sincerely regret having seen. I can't seem to talk people out of seeing it—it's like asking the traffic not to slow down to gawk at a gory car wreck on the side of the road. Don't believe the good reviews—professional film critics have seen so many movies that they recoil from the experience by responding to anything that seems offbeat and different. And *Blue Velvet* is different.

Blue Velvet's director, David Lynch, who also gave us *The Elephant Man* and *Eraserhead*, is attracted to the repulsive and obviously considers that attraction humane. In *Blue Velvet*, he melds the optimism of the coming-of-age genre with horror, but he does it with nihilism rather than hope. Lynch seems determined to make us recognize our fascination with evil. He seems to be saying that maturity is accepting that civilization is a sham and that evil is the basic reality.

His hero, a young, handsome boy named Kyle MacLachlan, comes home from college to his sleepy hometown when his father has a stroke while watering his bug-infested lawn. In a nearby field he discovers a human ear, which leads him and his angelic girlfriend, Laura Dern, on a voyeuristic investigation of the sadomasochistic relationship between Isabella Rossellini and Dennis Hopper. All manner of horrifying things are uncovered, observed and slobbered over, especially Isabella Rossellini. I'm glad her mother, Ingrid Bergman, is not alive to see what this film does to her daughter.

The plot makes very little sense (it's even more incoherent than Bogart's *The Big Sleep*). Somehow, Hopper has decided to kidnap Rossellini's husband and child, and then cuts off the husband's ear to scare her into going through his sadistic sexual rituals, which our young hero (a voyeur who has just been caught, stripped and raped by Rossellini) gets to watch while standing naked in her closet. Our hero emerges and, at her request, hits her a few times and likes it. The indignities mount. At one point, Rossellini shows up battered, bloody, stark-raving mad and buck naked at our hero's girlfriend's house. As she clings to the boy, and the girlfriend begins to scream, the girlfriend's mother (Hope Lange) ponders what to do. After an inordinate delay, she goes to the closet and gives the poor woman a raincoat.

I spent the film watching our hero's little gold earring, assuming it too would end up in the field behind Rossellini's apartment building. (I also wondered who had thrown her husband's ear into the field. Loving wives don't ordinarily discard their husband's ears like that, and villains who go to that much trouble to seduce a lady are not likely to discard the item that is the source of power over her.) Ultimately, I gave up on *Blue Velvet's* making sense.

This is the adult world as seen through the eyes of a rather innocent boy who must suddenly grow up. Our hero finally becomes a man by first gawking at and then immersing himself in this cesspool of sexuality and evil. His girlfriend at one point asks him whether he is a detective or a pervert, and I suppose Lynch is telling us that we are all both, at least if we like the movie.

Sexually, the film is a total turnoff. Stylistically, I have to admit the film is fascinating. Lynch shows that small town of Lumberton as bright and cheery and straight out of the '50s. Laura Dern could be Sandra Dee, and the kids' parents could be neighbors to the Cleavers. The town and its interiors are cheaply, cheerily tacky and comfortable—like the furnished rooms of the Sears catalogue. But the underground of Hopper and Rossellini is dark, hideous and menacing—filled with freaks, including Dean Stockwell in menacing semidrag. Rossellini's room is painted purplish brown and has furniture the Salvation Army would reject. Lumberton is a strange town—the aboveground people live in the '50s television, and the underground people live in the '80s in rooms left over from the '40s.

My major irritation with the whole bloody mess was Lynch's apparent belief that the underworld was the real world and the nice world was the unreal one. I've worked in some pretty gruesome places, but people never acted as they do in *Blue Velvet*. We can speculate that Lynch presents these two incompatible worlds in Lumberton as they might have existed in the anxieties of a boy who must grow up too quickly. It must be terrifying to grow up in a world in which sexuality and cruelty are confused and commingled, yet we seem to have such a world. Sex-and-violence is a sandwich made jointly by puritans and pornographers, both of whom profit by keeping sex underground. Coming of age, which should mean embracing sexuality and rejecting evil, in this movie means instead the acceptance of sex-and-violence and thus going underground, since the only sex in Lumberton is underground, violent, dangerous and ear threatening.

The world is scary and unfair and dangerous at times, and children don't achieve the dignity of adulthood until they recognize that the world won't protect them. It's not a safe world, and what little security there is comes from making choices wisely. In *Stand By Me*, the horrors of the world are ordinary horrors that we all have to face but can't really face alone, even if we are past the age of 12. These daily horrors of death and cruelty can pull us together. There is evil in the world and evil inside us, too, and we have to know that. And maybe we do have to realize that we are capable of ". . . anything."

In *Stand By Me*, our fear and revulsion at the world's danger helps bring us together. In *Blue Velvet*, our acceptance of evil in the world and in ourselves forces us to stand alone, since we can trust no one else. I don't want to stand alone. I get scared, and I want people to stand by me, so I prefer to think the world is only a little bit scary, that people are only a little bit evil, and that if everyone will stand together, nobody will lose their ears. ∎

SCARING THE PANTS ON YOU

FATAL ATTRACTION BIDS THE SEXUAL REVOLUTION GOOD-BYE

By Frank Pittman

THE MOVIE OF THE MOMENT, PERHAPS THE FILM of the decade, is the wildly popular *Fatal Attraction*. It has packed the theaters for months, but it does more than sell tickets—it arouses audiences to a homicidal frenzy. The anger is directed toward a trim blond with blue eyes and freckles, played by the ever-nurturing Glenn Close, who heretofore specialized in cinematic earth mothers willing to make any sacrifice for their men.

Close debuted as Garp's celibate mother, the feminist nurse Jenny Fields. She may best be remembered as the beatific pediatrician in *The Big Chill*, who loans her husband as sperm donor to her best friend. She's also been the steadfast farm mother of *The Stone Boy*, Robert Redford's haloed rescuer in *The Natural* and Jeff Bridges's oh-so-honest defense attorney in *The Jagged Edge*. Until now, Close's characters, Ivory Soap plain and safe, glowed with goodwill, bathing us in the radiant glow of uncompromised, unconditional love. And so when, in *Fatal Attraction*, this earth mother betrays us and becomes that fury from hell, a woman scorned, the impact is all the more horrific. The movie confronts the audience with the unwelcome message that the Sexual Revolution is over, that sex with the natural woman, which used to be so pleasant, can now be deadly.

Despite its popularity, *Fatal Attraction* is not an aesthetic triumph. Frankly, it isn't even very good. It was directed by Adrian Lyne, of *Flashdance* fame, and it shows. The movie is a philosophically and politically confused exploitative shocker, but that doesn't blunt its impact. It will scare the pants onto you.

The plot, as everyone knows by now, is about the aftermath of a brief sexual encounter. The encountant, Dan, played by the ever-stolid Michael Douglas, is a successful New York lawyer. He and his lovely wife Beth (Anne Archer, an exceptionally beautiful actress reminiscent of a young Jennifer Jones) have a fine daughter, a fine marriage and a fine life—until the fatal night.

They go to a party where Dan meets Alex (Glenn Close), who, in full war paint and Medusa hairdo, is scarily intense, perched dramatically at the bar, attracting and then rejecting men. She isn't sexy in the bimbo, Marilyn Monroe, too-dumb-to-know-better sense. Her message isn't a broad, Mae West "come up and see me sometime" or even a sultry, Lauren Bacall "pucker up and blow" I'm-accustomed-to-getting-what-I-want-so-you-might-as-well-surrender. From her opening appearance, there is something desperate in Alex's sexual intensity, something hostile and frightening—like Joan Crawford or the Spider Woman. This creature is not out to have fun or to give anyone a good time. She wants something more. At first we don't know what, and neither does Dan. He finds out a few hours too late.

Even at first encounter, any idiot can see this woman is dangerous. (If only Dan had remembered Nelson Algren's classic advice: "Never play cards with a man called Doc. Never eat in a place called Mom's. Never sleep with a woman whose troubles are worse than your own.") But Dan is attracted, even though nothing happens except erotic tension. Later he meets Alex again at work; she's an editor connected with one of his cases. They go to lunch. She throws herself at him. He barely hesitates.

Back at Alex's place, an attic over a meat-packing plant—nice, huh?—they begin a frantic sexual encounter in a sink full of dirty dishes, so carried away they don't even bother to turn off the running water. Dan tries to carry Alex away from the kitchen sink, but his pants are down around his ankles. They continue their mating ritual on a stalled elevator while people walk by and stare. It looks pretty unpleasant. Afterward, Alex plays records of "Madame Butterfly" for him and explains that Butterfly commits suicide when Pinkerton deserts her for his American wife.

When Dan gets up to leave, Alex slashes her wrists. She tries to delay him with guilt, and he manages to pacify her until he is able to escape and return to the warm bosom of his family. Wife Beth returns lovingly after a trip to the country to buy their dream house and visit her parents. Beth—the only sympathetic character—is both the goddess of

monogamy and a remarkable sexual presence. She is the ultimate defender of the family. In an erotic moment that seems especially soft and inviting after Dan's encounter with Alex, the camera caresses Beth's naked belly as Dan watches her sitting at her mirror, touching perfume to her shoulders. Sexuality has come home.

Dan is glad to be through with Alex, but Alex isn't through with him. She begins to call and come by, increasingly insistent that he be involved in her life. She informs him that she is pregnant and is going to have the baby. The harder he tries to detach himself from her, the more relentlessly she pursues him. His first concern is to keep their encounter secret. But as Alex begins to attack in ways that make secrecy impossible, he becomes frightened and finally tells his wife what has happened. She kicks him out. He suffers; she suffers.

I have read that the filmmakers attempted several alternate endings, some a bit less sympathetic to Dan. The ending that pleased preview audiences most was the one most shocking and most skewed toward seeing Dan as an innocent victim instead of a man who is facing a tragedy of his own making. It is as if today's audience wants to be shocked not only by blood and suspense but by the revelation that sex can have unpleasant consequences.

The chosen ending left me totally limp and rather angry. Each scene amplifies our anger toward and fear of Alex. The film presents Douglas's character as an innocently inept weakling terrorized by a crazy woman. Dan, who unleashed these powerful furies, seems too hapless to be responsible for what unfolds. The film clearly paints Alex as the villain. It seems to be saying: "She came on to him, therefore she was responsible. She should have known the rules by which such things are played. She refused to get lost and be forgotten on cue, when he was through with her. She had the audacity to bring her own agenda to the bed (or more accurately, the sink and the elevator)."

The level of anger targeted at Alex from both the screen and audience is terrifying. Is this some sort of misplaced feminist backlash? Are sexually straightforward women so scary that they must be seen as villains? In this film, the affair is all Alex's fault. It is as if she should be responsible for protecting Dan's marriage. What ever happened to men being responsible for protecting their own marriages? Are we returning to a Victorian era in which women must be responsible for keeping the monster of male sexuality unaroused? Sexuality here is the stuff of horror and terror.

Surely there is no more dangerous combination in the universe than the philanderer and the romantic, and while the genders can be reversed (the classic is *Carmen*, in which the romantic Don José cannot hold the philandering gypsy), the more familiar disastrous combination involves a philandering man and a romantic woman, a man to whom sex is a counterphobic affirmation of his power over women and a woman to whom the love of a man is the meaning of life.

The romantic must have and hold, the philanderer must use and discard. The game is desperate on both sides, and dangerous. Anna Karenina, Emma Bovary, Aeneas' Dido, *Don Giovanni's* Donna Elvira: these tragic romantics staked their lives on the fidelity of confirmed philanderers, guys who were sure that sexual adventurism was necessary to keep their balls from falling off.

It's hard to present a philanderer as one of the good guys, and this film tries at least to keep Dan from being a bad guy. Previously, a philandering husband was portrayed sympathetically only if his marriage was grotesquely dreadful and/or he was "in love." Dan certainly never fancies himself in love with Alex, ready to give up everything for her, as she does for him. And we see that Dan and Beth have a fine marriage, one in which this sort of thing would not be expected or accepted. We are directed to regard Dan as an amateur who had not done this sort of thing before and could not have foreseen the dangers. This movie turns the philandering husband into an innocent victim of a sexually desperate, single career woman who didn't create a family in her youth and now has the power and audacity to take someone else's.

Perhaps *Fatal Attraction* is best understood as a reflection of our deepest fears. We now live in an era in which you can't blithely walk away from your sex partners anymore: you may carry a particle or two of them with you. Your sexual past can reach over time and space to ruin your life. Suddenly, a sex act can kill you and your family. Suddenly, sex is no longer a friendly way to greet a stranger. The Sexual Revolution has been crushed. The organism is more powerful than the orgasm. The defeated philanderers must zip up and scurry home. And if they don't, they'd better watch out. Glenn Close is out there threatening to wipe them, and their families, out with a single screw.

Fatal Attraction is a terribly important movie, and we will all have much more to say about it. By all means go see it. But don't bother to take a date. ∎

MOTHER LOVE

CAN WE FORGIVE THEM FOR LOVING US MORE THAN THEY LOVE THEMSELVES?

By Frank Pittman

FOR DECADES, MOTHER BASHING WAS *DE RIGUEUR* in mental health circles. Every therapist knew that we were the exorcists in a holy crusade to free tortured psyches from the mothers who held them hostage and enslaved by guilt. The movies joined this crusade, dramatizing the psychoanalytic myths about monster matriarchs devouring the children they had fiendishly crippled. Between *Psycho* (1960) and *Mommie Dearest* (1981), mothers replaced vampires as the stuff of nightmares.

In 1983 I thought we were emerging from that benighted era. The breakthrough movie was *Terms of Endearment*. It was a delicious comedy about an idle-rich widow (Shirley MacLaine) who centers her life on her daughter (Debra Winger), even crawling into the crib with the child to make sure she is still breathing. As Winger grows older, defiantly marries, and tries to break free, MacLaine does all she can to drive her spunky daughter back into dithering dependency. When the daughter gets cancer and her husband takes up with a graduate student, the moods shifts from comedy to tragedy. And when hope is all but lost, over the horizon gallops Mama

to rescue her daughter and her grandsons. But MacLaine must undergo a purifying ordeal before her love can feel safe to her daughter—she must get a life of her own, personified as an affair with the astronaut next door (Jack Nicholson). Finally, when MacLaine storms the nursing station to get pain relief for her dying daughter, her maternal power has been humanized, and we can cheer for all mothers who loved us too much and tried to shield us from life's pain.

I had assumed that *Terms of Endearment* would be followed immediately by a plethora of loving-mother movies. But in fact, only a few lovable mothers appeared (Geraldine Page in *The Trip to Bountiful*, Peggy Ashcroft in *A Passage to India*, Brenda Fricker in *My Left Foot*), and those had weak or crippled sons and were usually British, to boot. Actually, we've had very few mothers on American screens in the last few years. Nevertheless, those few reveal some extremely interesting things about the attitude toward mothers in our world.

The most startling observation is that strong men in the movies seem to no longer have mothers. As

557

Hollywood becomes enthralled with fathers and sons, the movies cautiously sidestep mothers and sons. Mothers may be marginally acceptable for young children, but when a man has a mother, it is either a social problem or a sign of weakness. People like Woody Allen are allowed to have mothers, but even Woody has risked it only a few times, as in his Oedipal nightmare from *New York Stories*. Mothers, however beleaguered or disenfranchised, are seen as far more powerful than sons of any age. The likes of Danny DeVito and Billy Crystal joined forces to *Throw Momma From the Train*, but she was still too powerful for them. Harrison Ford was found to have Sean Connery as a father, but can you imagine Sean Connery having a mother? Sylvester Stallone, Arnold Schwarzenegger, or even Bruce Willis are never shown working out some mother-son conflicts over the kitchen table.

By contrast, in the last year or so, a few mother-daughter films have aspired to a popular audience. They all struggle with the dangerous issues of maternal sacrifice and filial responsibility. In last year's very popular *Steel Magnolias*, a film about hairdos set in a beauty parlor, Sally Field is a flying buttress holding up her fragile, diabetic daughter Julia Roberts, who defies her mother, gets married, and has a baby against medical advice. Field donates a kidney, but Roberts still dies.

Field's noble motherhood, bossy and disapproving in her frantically protective love of her child, was very popular. Field made sacrifices, but she seemed too busy to need her daughter too much. She had her hands full with a goofy husband, two wild sons, and a career as a family therapist. She didn't compete with her daughter, didn't overwhelm anyone with her emotions or her glamour (her daughter calls her hairdo a "brown football helmet"). Sally Field was safe, so we could suspend our caution and feel a mother's pain as she tries to keep her delicate daughter from growing up and dying.

And then there was *Stella*, the awful and deservedly unpopular remake of 1937's definitive soap opera, *Stella Dallas*, with Bette Midler in the Barbara Stanwyck role of the embarrassingly tasteless woman who sacrifices everything to give a higher social status to her illegitimate daughter. This anachronistic film hits a world in which illegitimacy is in vogue, and the major taboos are social class and maternal sacrifice. Audiences run in panic from the theater: would you sleep well at night knowing that the louder-than-life Bette Midler made sacrifices for you?

Happily, two very funny and ambitious recent movies have been more successful in tackling the subject of mother love, and each detoxifies our darkest fears of the evil mother, one by parodying the witch mother into absurdity, and the other by declawing and detoothing the monster mother into something fragile and lovable.

WILD AT HEART IS NOT FOR EVERYONE, BUT then neither is David Lynch. In his big film, *Blue Velvet*, and his TV spectacular, *Twin Peaks*, I couldn't tell whether he is telling us that the world is treacherously and unfathomably loathsome, or that he is. But he has finally made a film so bad it's good. *Wild at Heart* is a black comedy about very tasteless people. At the center is a pair of losers. Lula (Laura Dern) is a simpleminded princess with a dislocated pelvis and various Marilyn Monroe mannerisms, and Sailor (Nicholas Cage), a goofy ex-con who goes through life impersonating Elvis, sporting a snakeskin jacket and a dragon tattoo on his left shoulder. Laura Dern's mother (on screen and off) is Diane Ladd, the ultimate monster mother. She is the wicked queen who has already arranged the fiery deaths of her husband and his business partner. She is now determined to have her daughter's boyfriend murdered, not only because he knows she had her husband killed but because he is taking her daughter away from her *and* because he turned down her sexual advances.

MOTHER LOVE

The movie follows these stupid and trusting young Marilyn and Elvis plagiarists as they tour the cheap motels of the Southwest, trying to escape the killers Ladd seduces and hires, including the perfectly putrefied Harry Dean Stanton. On their travels, Dern and Cage live out a low-rent *Wizard of Oz* but with people so sordid only David Lynch could have created them.

The most disgusting is sadistic Willem Dafoe, with greasy hair, a Richard Widmark killer giggle and brown pus where his teeth might have been. He tries to seduce and then rape Dern and finally meets one of the most graphically unappealing fates ever shown on the screen. Just for fun, Lynch has a man crawl around in a puddle of blood looking for his blown-off hand—but a hungry dog beats him to it. When the embubbled Good Fairy finally appears to reassure us that there's no place like home, we're too nauseated to care.

Lynch's most lethal venom is reserved for mothers. Diane Ladd is everything we fear in mothers—she needs her child so much she will do anything, even kill her, to hold her close. She alternately seduces and kills much of the cast. She even hires killers to kill her hired killers. All of her emotions are too big for her child. When it looks as if this Wicked Queen is losing the struggle over possession of her Snow White daughter, Ladd paints her entire face with red lipstick and glares demonically into mirrors. This cartoonish apparition loves her daughter, and her homicidal good intentions are terrifying. (I must confess, though, that I kept thinking that no sane mother would want to see her daughter run off with Nicholas Cage.)

NOTHING COULD STAND IN GREATER CONTRAST to *Wild at Heart* than Mike Nichols's perfectly civilized *Postcards From the Edge*. *Postcards* was written by Carrie Fisher and is at least semiautobiographical. Meryl Streep plays the Carrie Fisher part, the drug-addicted, struggling actress who is getting

to the age where she should have found herself already. And Shirley MacLaine plays her mother, whom Fisher insists is not quite exactly Debbie Reynolds, merely an alcoholic song-and-dance legend who has never gotten over her husband's leaving her for another actress.

The film tells the slight story of Fisher/Streep's insecurity and how it grew. The daughter had been intimidated by the mother's success, control and needs—and by her own shame and guilt over a misspent life and a string of often public failures. The plot is negligible and really just strings together episodes of subtle assault on a young woman's fragile ego as she tries to recover from her drug habit and rescue the shambles of her second-rate career and is forced to live with her mother, an arrangement neither woman welcomes.

The scenes of movie making are light and clever. We get to see the unreality of everything and everybody as the imperious directors and the anxiously distrusting producers test Streep's precarious balance. In one scene, Streep hides in a clothes rack and eavesdrops as a producer and a wardrobe lady discuss the defects of her body—her cellulite and breasts that fall under her arms when she lies on her back. Streep walks through all this as an anxious good sport with limp, bleached hair and a look of hopeless terror. Streep has never been so lovable, perhaps because she's never seemed so vulnerable.

MacLaine has the flashier role. She shows no vulnerability at all. She makes a pass at her daughter's boyfriend, but the outcome doesn't matter to her. She dismisses the complaint that at her daughter's 16th birthday party, she twirled around the dance floor without underpants on. She always had to be the center of attention, and she was. She takes center stage for Streep's homecoming party, and after coercing Streep into singing, MacLaine upstages her with a showstopping rendition of Stephen Sondheim's survival ballad, "I'm Still Here," with a stunning show of young dancer's legs. In one marvelous sequence, MacLaine puts fruit and yogurt through the blender for her health-food fix, which she then mixes half and half with vodka.

MacLaine looks great, and in full control of her life and her image, until she wrecks her car and ends up in the hospital, where we and Streep get to see the reality of the old, mottled, plucked bird under her makeup. The Wicked Queen, the Good Fairy and Auntie Em become one. Not only that, we realize how intimidated this old bird is by an even tougher old bird, her mother (Mary Wickes). This is so heartening to Streep that she picks herself up and goes out to face the world for another round. The two women join forces and blame it all on the bossy grandma.

Nichols has brought us Fisher's gentle and witty trifle with a delicate touch and a great good nature. I didn't know such a pleasant film was possible these days. MacLaine is not just repeating her *Terms of Endearment* role. This mother, instead of crawling into the crib to make sure her daughter is breathing, got her daughter hooked on sleeping pills so the child wouldn't wake her up. She's had to be tough and selfish, and she was. She can't afford to soften herself and get little to make her daughter feel safe. She doesn't hurt her daughter deliberately, but carelessly. She's sexy, competitive, intrusive, embarrassing and bossy, like Diane Ladd in *Wild at Heart* and Bette Midler as *Stella.* But she's safe, like Sally Field in *Steel Magnolias,* because she doesn't need her daughter to give her life meaning. She's too busy to be a full-time mother. Therefore she doesn't require human sacrifice. Strange how the very qualities that would have gotten her mothering style condemned a few decades ago now restore her to our affection.

In Hollywood a few basic principles determine which mothers get to be heroines and which are deemed villainous:

1. All mothers in the movies are, by definition, too powerful for their grown children. Just having a mother makes strong men feel mortal and strong women feel inadequate. Mothers are visible proof of weakness.

2. Movie mothers with glamorous aspirations are likely to compete with their daughters and undercut their self-confidence. Sexy, glamorous mothers, like Snow White's wicked stepmother, grow more dangerous as they age and lose their looks. Daughters can try to find safety in dowdiness.

3. If the celluloid mother has little life except her child, she is dangerous, but if the mother is busy with her own life, then it is safe for her kids to get close. Filmmakers seem to believe that the most dangerous force in the universe is mothers who have no one but their children to love.

4. If the cinematic mother makes sacrifices for the child, she may except sacrifices in return. Maternal sacrifice is the debt that can never be paid in full. Children might even be left feeling guilty (which Hollywood has decided is very bad for the mental health of adult children).

In a world without fathers, mothers are very powerful. But the movies seem to have decided that we're most afraid of mothers if they have no life except us. Mothers can be forgiven anything except loving us more than they love themselves. We are willing to enshrine them only if they are too busy with their own lives to come to the ceremony. ∎

FRANK PITTMAN, M.D., *is in private practice in Atlanta, GA.*

References

SECTION I

Lasting Rites

Campbell, J. & Moyers, B. 1988. *The power of myth, part 3*. New York: Journal Graphics.

Cassirer, E. 1946. *The myth of the state*. New Haven: Yale University Press.

Durkheim, E. 1915. *The elementary forms of religious life*. Glencoe: Free Press.

Freud, S. 1962. *Totem and taboo*. Translated by James Strachey. New York: W.W. Norton.

Geertz, C. 1966. "Religion as a cultural system." In M. Banton (Ed.), *Anthropological approaches to the study of religion*. London: Tavistock.

Kertzer, D. 1988. *Rituals, politics, and power*. New Haven: Yale University Press.

Malinowski, B. 1948. *Magic, science, and religion*. Glencoe: Free Press.

Myerhoff, B. 1984. "Rites and signs of ripening: The intertwining of ritual, time, and growing older." In D. Kertzer & J. Keith (Eds.), *Age and anthropological theory*. Ithaca: Cornell University Press.

Radcliffe-Brown, A.R. 1952. *Structure in function in primitive society*. London: Oxford University Press.

Turner, V. 1957. *Schism and continuity in an African society*. Manchester: Manchester University Press.

Homosexuality: Are We Still in the Dark?

Berzon, B. 1988. *Permanent partners: Building gay and lesbian relationships that last*. New York: E. P. Dutton.

Bozett, F. W., Sussmann, M. B., Eds. 1990. *Homosexuality and family relations*. Binghamton: Harrington Park Press.

Carl, D. 1990. *Counseling same-sex couples*. New York: W.W. Norton.

Clunis, D. M., Green, Dorsey G. 1988. *Lesbian couples*. Seattle: Seal Press.

Kus, R. J. 1990. *Assisting your gay and lesbian clients*. Boston: Alyson Publication

Marcus, E. 1988. *The male couple's guide to living together*. New York: Harper and Row.

Song Without Words

Coleman, C. 1986. International family therapy: A view from Kyoto, *Japan Family Process*, 25, 651-664.

Doi, T. 1971. *The anatomy of dependence*. Tokyo: Kodansha International.

Doi, T. 1985. *The anatomy of self*. Tokyo: Kodansha International.

Kawabata, Y. 1970. *The sound of the mountain*. Tokyo: Tuttle.

Lebra, T. S. 1976. *Japanese patterns of behavior*. Honolulu: University of Hawaii Press.

Lebra, T. S. 1984. Japanese women. Honolulu: University of Hawaii Press.

Lebra, T. S. & Lebra, W., Eds. 1986. Japanese culture and behavior. Honolulu University of Hawaii Press.

Yamaquchi, T. and Yamaquchi, A. 1973. Permissiveness and psychotherapy in Japan. *Journal of Nervous and Mental Disorders*, 157, 292-295.

SECTION II

Know Thy Selves

Assagioli, R. 1973. *The Act of Will*. New York: Penguin Books.

Hillman, J. 1975. *Re-visioning psychology*. New York: Harper and Row.

Quigley, D. 1984. *Alchemical hypnotherapy*. Redway, CA: Lost Coast Press.

Schwartz, R. 1987. Our multiple selves. *Family Therapy Networker 11*, (no. 2), 24-31, 80-83.

Stone, H. and Winkelman, S. 1985. *Embracing ourselves*. Marion del Rey, CA: Devorss and Co.

Watkins, J. 1978. *The therapeutic self*. New York: Human Sciences Press.

Watkins, J.G. & Watkins, H. 1982. "Ego-state therapy." In L. Abt & I. Stuart (Eds.) *The new therapies: A sourcebook*. New York: Van Nordstrand Reinhold.

His and Her Divorces

Bernard, J. 1972. *The future of marriage*. New York: Bantam.

Bloom, B.L., and Caldwell, R.A. 1981. Sex differences in adjustment during the process of marital separation. *Journal of Marriage and the Family 43*: 693–701.

Camara, K.A. 1984. "Children of Conflict." Paper presented at the Flowerree Mardi Gras symposium, Tulane University, New Orleans.

Camara, K.A. and Resnick, G. 1988. "Interparental conflict and cooperation: Factors moderating children's post-divorce adjustment." In E.M. Hetherington & J.D. Arasteh (Eds.), *Impact of divorce, single parenting, and stepparenting on children*. (pp. 169–95) Hillsdale, NJ: Erlbaum.

Christensen, A. 1988. "Dysfunctional interaction patterns in couples." In P. Noller & M.A. Fitzpatrick (Eds.), *Perspectives on marital interaction*. Clevedon/Philadelphia: Multilingual Matters Ltd.

Emery, R.E. 1988. *Marriage, divorce, and children's adjustment*. Newbury Park, CA:Sage.

Ferri, E. 1973. Characteristics of motherless families. *British Journal of Social Work 3*: 91–100.

Furstenburg, F.F. 1988. "Child care after divorce and remarriage." In E.M. Hetherington and J.D. Arasteh (Eds.), *Impact of divorce, single parenting, and stepparenting on children*. (pp. 245–62) Hillsdale, NJ: Erlbaum.

Gasser, R.D. & Taylor, C.M. 1976. Role adjustment of single-parent fathers with dependent children. *The Family Coordinator 25*: 397–401.

Gottman, J.M. & Levenson, R.W. 1986. Assessing the role of emotion in marriage. *Behavioral Assessment 8*: 31–48.

Haskins, R., Schwartz, J.B., Akin, J.S., & Dobelstein, A.W. 1985. How much support can absent fathers pay? *Policy Studies Journal 14*: 201–22.

Hernandez, D.J. 1988. "Demographic trends and the living arrangement of children." In E.M. Hetherington & J.D. Arasteh (Eds.), *Impact of divorce, single parenting, and stepparenting* (continued on page 565) *on children* (pp. 3–22). Hillsdale, NJ: Erlbaum.

Hetherington, E.M. 1987. "Family relations six years after divorce." In K. Pasley & M. Ihinger-Tollman (Eds.), *Remarriage and stepparenting today: Current research and theory* (pp. 185–205). New York: Guilford.

Hetherington, E.M. 1989. Coping with family transitions: Winners, losers and survivors. *Child Development* 60: 1–15.

Hetherington, E.M. & Camara, K.A. 1984. "Families in transition: The process of dissolution and reconstruction." In R. Parke (Ed.), *Review of child development research* (Vol. 7, pp. 398–439). Chicago: University of Chicago Press.

Hetherington, E.M. & Clingempeel, W.G. 1988. "Coping with remarriage: The first two years." Symposium presented at the Southeastern Conference on Human Development, Charleston, SC.

Hetherington, E.M., Cox, M. & Cox, R. 1981. "Effects of divorce on parents and children." In M. Lamb (Ed.), *Nontraditional families* (pp. 233–288). Hillsdale, NJ: Erlbaum.

Hetherington, E.M. & Stanley-Hagan, M. 1986. "Divorced fathers: Stress, coping, and adjustment." In M. Lamb (Ed.), *The father's role: Applied perspectives* (pp. 103–134). New York: Wiley.

Kiecolt-Glaser, J.K., Fisher, L.D., Ogrocki, P., Stout, J.C., Speicher, B.S., & Glaser, R. 1987. Marital quality, marital disruption, and immune function. *Psychosomatic Medicine*. 40: 13–44.

Maccoby, E.E. & Mnookin, R. 1981. "Custody settlements in a California sample." Paper presented at the annual meeting of the American Association for Advancement of Science, Philadelphia.

Nortorius, C.I. & Vanzetti, N.A. 1983. "The marital agendas protocol." In E. E. Filsinger (Ed.), *Marital and family assessment*. Beverly Hills, CA: Sage.

Patterson, G.R. & Banks, L. "Some amplifying mechanisms for pathological processes in families." In M. Gunner (Ed.), *Minnesota symposium of child psychology*. Hillsdale, NJ: Erlbaum.

Santrock, J.W. & Warshak, R.A. 1986. "Development of father-custody relationships and legal/clinical considerations in father-custody families." In M.E. Lamb (Ed.), *The father's role: Applied perspectives* (pp. 135–166). New York: Wiley.

Spanier, G.B. & Castro, R.F. 1979. Adjustment to separation and divorce: An analysis of 50 case studies. *Journal of Divorce 2*: 241–54.

Weiss, R.S. 1979. Growing up a little faster: The experience of growing up in a single-parent household. *Journal of Social Issues 35*: 97–111.

Zill, N. 1988. "Behavior, achievement, and health problems among children in step-families: Findings from a national survey of child health." In E.M. Hetherington & J.D. Arasteh (Eds.), *Impact of divorce, single parenting and stepparenting on children* (pp. 352–368). Hillsdale, NJ: Erlbaum.

Brief Therapy on the Couch

Budman, S. H. and Gurman, A. S. 1988. *Theory and practice of brief therapy*. New York: Guilford Press.
De Shazer, S. 1988. *Clues: Investigating solutions in brief therapy*. New York: W. W. Norton.
Fisch, R., Weakland, J., and Segal, L. 1982. *The tactics of change: Doing therapy briefly*. San Francisco: Jossey-Bass.

(continued on page 566)

Haley, J. 1976. *Problem-solving therapy.* New York: Harper & Row.

Kiser, D. J. 1988. A follow-up study conducted at the Brief Family Therapy Center of Milwaukee, Wisconsin. Unpublished master's thesis, University of Wisconsin, Milwaukee.

Lankton, S. R and C. H. 1983. *The answer within: A clinical framework of Ericksonian hypnotherapy.* New York: Brunner/Mazel.

O'Hanlon, W.H. and Weiner-Davis, M. 1989. *In search of solutions: A new direction in psychotherapy.* New York: W. W. Norton.

Research: Why Clinicians Should Bother

Anderson, C. M., Hogarty, G. E. and Reiss, D. J. 1980. Family treatment of adult schizophrenic patient: A psychoeducational approach. *Schizophrenia Bulletin* 6: 490-505.

Bandler, R. and Grinder, J. 1975. *The structure of magic I.* Palo Alto: Science and Behavior Books.

Bandler, R. and Grinder, J. 1976. *The structure of magic II.* Palo Alto: Science Behavior Books.

Capra, F. 1982. *The turning point: Science, society and the rising culture.* New York: Simon and Schuster.

Dilts, R. 1983. *Applications of neurolinguistic programming.* Cupertino, CA: Meta Publications.

Gurman, A. Family therapy research and the "raw epistemology." *Journal of Marital and Family Therapy* 9, no. 3.

Haley, J. 1978. "Ideas which handicap therapists." In M. M. Berger (Ed.) *Beyond the double bind.* New York: Brunner/Mazel.

Keisler, D. J. 1981. Empirical clinical psychology: Myth or reality. *Journal of Consulting and Clinical Psychology* 49: 212-215.

Minuchin, S., Rosman, B. and Baker, L. 1978. *Psychosomatic families.* Cambridge, MA: Harvard University Press.

Pinsof, W. M. 1981. "Family therapy process research." In A. S. Gurman and D. Kniskem (Eds.) *Handbook of Family Therapy.* New York: Brunner/Mazel.

Schwartz, T. B. 1980. Naloxone and weight reduction: An exercise in introspection. *Transactions of American Clinical and Climatological Association* 92: 103-110.

Stanton, D., Todd, T. et al. 1982. *The family therapy of drug abuse and addiction.* New York: Guilford Press.

Wynne, L. 1983. Family research and family therapy: A reunion? *Journal of Marital and Family Therapy* 9: 113-117.

SECTION III

Do Families Really Need Problems?

Bateson, G. 1972. *Steps to an ecology of mind.* New York: Ballentine.

Bruner, J. 1973. *Beyond the information given.* New York: Norton.

Fodor, J. 1983. *Representations, philosophical essays on the foundations of cognitiue science.* Cambridge, MA: MIT Press.

Haley, J. 1980. *Leaving home.* New York: McGraw-Hill.

(continued on page 567)

Hoffman, L. 1981. *Foundations of family therapy*. New York: Basic Books.

Jackson, D. 1957. The question of family homeostasis. *Psychiatric Quarterly Supplement*, 31, 79-90.

Laing, R., Phillipson, H. and Lee, A. 1972. *Interpersonal perception*. New York: Perennial Library.

Madanes, C. 1984. *Behind the one-way mirror*. San Francisco: Jossey-Bass.

Papp, P. 1980. The greek chorus and other techniques of family therapy. *Family Process* 19: 45-58.

Selvini-Palazzoli, M., Boscolo, L., Cecchin, G. and Prata, G. 1978. *Paradox and counterparadox*. New York: Jason Aronson.

Weakland, J., Fisch, R., Watzlawick P. and Bodin, A. 1974. Brief therapy-focused problem resolution. *Family Process* 13: 41-168.

Watzlawick P. 1984. *The invented reality*. New York: W.W. Norton.

Let Us Sell No Intervention Before Its Time

Berger, M. and Jurkovic, G. (Ed.) 1984. *Practicing family therapy in diverse settings.* San Francisco: Jossey-Bass.

Campbell, D. and Draper, R. (Ed.) 1985. *Applications of systemic family therapy: The Milan approach*. Orlando, FL: Grune & Stratton.

Coleman, S. (Ed.). 1985. *Failures in family therapy*. New York: Guilford Press.

Gurman, A.S. and Kniskern, D.P. 1978. "Research on marital and family therapy: Progress perspective and prospect." In S. Garfield and A. Bergin (Eds.) *Handbook of psychotherapy and behavior change,* Second edition. New York: Wiley.

Gurman, A.S. and Kniskern, D.P. 1981. "Family therapy outcome research: Knowns and unknowns." In Gurman, A.S. (Ed.) *The handbook of family therapy*. New York: Guilford Press.

Haley, J. 1980. *Leaving home*. New York: McGraw-Hill.

Kolodny, R.C. 1981. Evaluating sex therapy: Process and outcome at the Masters and Johnson Institute. *Journal of Sex Research* 17: 301-318

Masters, W.H. and Johnson, V.E. 1970. *Human sexual inadequacy*. Boston: Little, Brown.

Ornstein, R.E. 1972. *The Psychology of consciousness*. New York: Viking Press.

Pirrotta, S. "The Milan training program." Unpublished manuscript.

Selvini-Palazzoli, M., Cecchin, G., Prata, C. and Boscolo, L. 1978. *Paradox and counterparadox*. New York: Jason Aronson.

Watzlawick, P., Weakland, J. and Fisch, R. 1974. *Change*. New York: W.W. Norton.

Zilbergeld, B. and Evans, M. 1980. The inadequacy of Masters and Johnson. *Psychology Today* (August) 29-43.

Looking for the Fence Posts

Van Hoose, W.H. and Kottler, J.A. 1985. *Ethical and legal issues in counseling and psychotherapy*, 2nd Ed. San Francisco: Jossey-Bass.

MacIntyre, Alisdair. 1981. *After virtue*. South Bend, IN: University of Notre Dame Press.

Huber, C.H. and Baruth, L.G. 1988. *Ethical, legal and professional issues in the practice of marriage and family therapy*. San Francisco: Jossey-Bass.

Quoted in Jeffrey L. Berlant, Irl Extein, and Larry S. Kirstein. 1988. *Guides to*
 (continued on page 568)

the new medicines of the mind. Washington, D.C.: PIA Press.

Leupnitz, D. 1984. Cybernetic baroque, *The Family Therapy Networker*, 8 (Jul-Aug).

Leupnitz, D. 1988. *The family interpreted: Feminist theory in clinical practice*. New York: Basic Books.

Constructivism: What's in It for You?

Bateson, G. 1979. Mind and nature: A necessary unity. New York: E. P. Dutton.

Goolishian, H. and Anderson, H. 1987. Language systems and therapy: An evolving idea. *Psychotherapy* 24: 529-538.

Hoffman, L. 1988. A constructivist position for family therapy. *The Irish Journal of Psycholog*, 9, (no.l.)

Kelly, G. A. 1969. *Clinical psychology and personality: The selected papers of George Kelly*. Edited by B. Maher. New York: John Wiley & Sons.

Maturana, H. R. and Varela, F. J. 1987. *The tree of knowledge*. Boston: Shambhala.

Rychlak, J. F. 1981. *Introduction to personality and psychotherapy* (2nd ed.). New York: Houghton Mifflin.

Varela, F. J. 1979. *Principles of biological autonomy*. New York: Elsevier-North Holland.

Watzlawick, P. 1984. *The invented reality: How do we know what we believe we know?* New York: W. W. Norton.

SECTION IV

Warning: Family Therapy May Be Hazardous to Your Health

(Note: After I wrote this paper, I came across an excellent article by Kerrie James that makes many of the same points developed here. It is titled "Breaking the Chains of Gender: Family Therapy's Position," *Australian Journal of Family Therapy* 5:4, 241–48).

Chodorow, N. 1978. *The Reproduction of mothering psychoanalysis and the sociology of gender.* Berkeley: University of California Press.

Ferguson, A. 1984. "On conceiving motherhood and sexuality: A feminist materialist approach," in S. Treblicot (Ed.), *Mothering: Essays in feminist theory.* New Jersey: Rowman and Allanheld.

Gilligan, C. 1982. *In a different voice: Psychological theory and women's development.* Cambridge, MA: Harvard University Press.

Goldner, V. 1985. Feminism and family therapy. *Family Process* 24:31–47.

James, K., and D. McIntyre, The reproduction of families: The social role of family therapy. *Journal of Marriage and Family Therapy* 9:119–29.

Keller, C.F. 1985. *Reflections on gender and science.* New Haven: Yale University Press.

Kingston, P. 1979. "The social context of family therapy. In S. Walround-Skinner, (Ed.), *Family and marital psychotherapy: A critical approach.* London: Routledge and Kegan Paul, cited in Libow, J., Gender and sex role issues as family secrets. *Journal of Strategic and Systemic Therapy*, 4, 32–41.

Mahler, M., F. Pine, and A. Bergman, 1975. *The Psychological birth of the human* (continued on page 569)

REFERENCES

infant: Symbiosis and individuation. New York: Basic Books.

Stoller, R. 1979. *Sexual excitement, dynamics of erotic life*. New York: Pantheon.

Thorne, B. 1982. "Feminist Rethinking of the Family: An Overview," In Thome, B. (Ed.), *Rethinking the family: Some feminist questions*. New York and London: Longman.

Wallerstein, J. 1985. "Men and Women: Different Experiences in Marriage, Separation and Divorce," American Orthopsychiatry Association Convention, session, April 1985.

Young, I. 1984. "Is male gender identity the cause of male domination?" In Treblicot, J. (Ed.), *Mothering: Essays in feminist theory*. New Jersey: Rowman and Allanheld.

The Mother Knot

Dalton, P. 1983. Family treatment of an a obsessive-compulsive child: A case report. *Family Process* 22(1): 101-13.

Goldner, V. 1985. Feminism and family therapy. *Family Process* 24(1): 39.

Hare-Mustin, R. 1978. A feminist approach to family therapy. *Family Process* 17(2): 181-94.

Hare-Mustin, R. & Broderick, P.C. 1979. The myth of motherhood: A study of attitudes toward motherhood. *Psychology of Women Quarterly* 4(1): 114-28.

SECTION VI

Behind the Mask

Edelwich, J., with Brodsky, A. 1982. *Sexual dilemmas for the helping professional*. New York: Brunner/Mazel.

Pope, K., Keith-Spiegel, P., and Tabachnick, B. 1986. Sexual attraction to clients: The human therapist and the (sometimes) inhuman training system. *American Psychologist* 41: 147–58.

Scheflen A. 1965. Quasi-courtship behavior in psychotherapy. *Psychiatry* 28: 245–57.

Weeks, G., and Hof, L. 1987. *Integrating sex and marital therapy: A clinical guide*. New York: Brunner/Mazel.

Index

Spalding University Library
853 Library Lane
Louisville, KY 40203

DEMCO

SPALDING UNIVERSITY
LIBRARY